THE BALKANS IN OUR TIME

Revised Edition

Balkans
Major Agricultural Plains
Major Railway
100 Miles
U S S R
BESSARABIA
BUKOVINA
MOLDAVIA
CARPATHIANS
MARAMURES
TRANSYLVANIA
AUTONOMOUS MAGYAR REGION
1940
1952
1940 BOUNDARY
RUMANIA
OLTENIA
MUNTENIA
WALACHIA
DOBRUDJA
BANAT
HUNGARY
VOYVODINA
BARANYA
BACHKA
SREM
CARINTHIA
KARAWANKEN
JULIAN ALPS
ITALY
SLOVENIA
ISTRIA
CROATIA
DALMATIA
DINARIC ALPS
BOSNIA - HERTSEGOVINA
YUGOSLAVIA
SERBIA
MONTENEGRO
KOSSOVO - METOHIYA
MACEDONIA
ALBANIA
GREECE
EPIRUS
BULGARIA
BALKAN MTS.
RILA
RHODOPE MTS.
THRACE
Black Sea
Adriatic Sea
Strait of Otranto
VIENNA
BUDAPEST
Maribor
Villach
Klagenfurt
Lyublyana
Zagreb
VENICE
TRIESTE
Riyeka (Fiume)
Mohacs
Novi Sad
Karlovitz
BELGRADE
Smederovo
Timisoara
Iron Gates
Cluj
Blaj
Sibiu
Brasov
Focsani
Cernauti
Iasi
Chisinau
Galati
Braila
Ploesti
BUCHAREST
Constanta
Danube
Zadar
Split
Sarayevo
Mostar
Dubrovnik
Kotor
Tsetinye
Titograd
L. Scutari
Novipazar
Pech
Nish
Morava
Skoplye
Vardar
Durazzo
TIRANA
L. Ohrid
L. Prespa
Valona
Corfu
Janina
SALONIKI
Mt Athos
Struma
SOFIA
Dragoman Pass
Gabrovo
Tirnovo
Varna
Burgas
Plovdiv
Maritsa
Tundja
Adrianople (Edirne)
ISTANBUL

THE BALKANS IN OUR TIME

By

Robert Lee Wolff

W·W·NORTON & COMPANY·INC·

NEW YORK

Revised edition first published as a Norton paperback 1978 by arrangement with Harvard University Press.

Published simultaneously in Canada by George J. McLeod Limited, Toronto.

Printed in the United States of America.

Maps by R. L. Williams.

This volume was prepared in part under a grant from the Carnegie Corporation of New York. That Corporation is not, however, the author, owner, publisher, or proprietor of this publication and is not to be understood as approving by virtue of its grant any of the statements made or views expressed therein.

Library of Congress Cataloging in Publication Data
Wolff, Robert Lee.
The Balkans in our time.
Bibliography: p.
Includes index.
1. Balkan Peninsula—History. 2. Communism—Balkan Peninsula. I. Title.
DR48.5.W6 1978 949.6 78-17753
ISBN 0-393-09010-8

1 2 3 4 5 6 7 8 9 0

For Mary

CONTENTS

MAPS

AUTHOR'S NOTE: JULY 1973

The first seven chapters — about one third — of this book deal with the four truly Balkan countries (Yugoslavia, Rumania, Bulgaria, Albania) in the period before World War II. Intended to prepare the reader to consider the transformations wrought during the war and its aftermath, they are compact rather than comprehensive. The book pivots on the eighth chapter, which deals in far greater detail with the war years 1939–1945, enabling the reader to proceed to the remaining seven chapters. In these I discuss the immediate postwar decade, 1945–1954, describing and analyzing the processes by which all four countries became Soviet satellites, governed by their own communist parties; and reviewing the historical developments by which Yugoslavia, while remaining communist, defied the Soviet Union and survived. In an effort to show what the advent of communism meant to a predominantly agrarian society, I devote almost as much attention to economics as to politics. The book was completed in late 1954, but was not published until March 1956. The interval gave me the opportunity in the summer of 1955 to write an epilogue, peering cautiously into the future.

Looking at the book now, in the summer of 1973, I see at once that the title is no longer accurate. Seventeen years have passed since 1956, a period one year longer than the war and postwar years of 1939 through 1955, here chronicled in such detail and interpreted in the light of the wisdom of the mid-fifties. Theoretically, at least, it should have been possible to give the book a thorough-going revision, and to bring it down to date. I could have reduced the postwar analyses, eliminating an Albanian cement factory here and there, streamlining the details of the processes of Soviet take-over, deleting biographical comment on politicians who in the end proved less influential than had seemed likely in 1955. Yet I could not convince myself that such an editorial treatment would improve things much. As it stands, the work seems to me a still valid account of a period that has a coherence of its own.

To discuss the events of 1955–1973 on anything like the same scale would have meant increasing the length of the book by fifty per cent. It would be difficult to justify such a treatment of a period which, in spite of its many points of interest, gave rise to few events as momentous as those of the preceding years. Instead, I have undertaken to write a somewhat impressionistic essay viewing some of the more important developments of the past seventeen years in the perspective now available. This is now appended to this edition as "Afterword: The Balkans in 1973." The brave reader who has plowed through the body of the book itself should at least find it easy to understand. It is intended also to be provocative.

Mangerton House, near Bridport
Dorset, England
July 1973

ROBERT LEE WOLFF

PREFACE TO THE 1956 EDITION

The planning and preparation of this book have taken a long time. Many people here and abroad have given indispensable help. Trained as a classicist and mediaeval historian, especially of Byzantium, I learned much from my colleagues in the Balkan Section of the Research and Analysis Branch of the OSS, who wrote and helped me write so many studies on events in the Balkan countries during the years of World War II. A wartime visit took me in the winter of 1944–45 to Rumania and Yugoslavia, where I observed at first hand the early stages of Soviet occupation and communization, and talked with peasants and city-dwellers, professors and politicians, priests and soldiers. A grant from the Humanities Division of the Rockefeller Foundation enabled me in the summer of 1948 to return to Yugoslavia and to visit Bulgaria for the first time. That was the summer when Stalin expelled Tito from the Communist bloc, the summer of the Berlin air-lift, when war seemed very close, and a solitary American was looked upon as a dangerous visitor from outer space. Communization had gone a long way by then. It was no longer safe to approach individual citizens without government approval, for fear of what would happen to them later, when they could be accused of associating with an agent of the imperialist camp. Rumania was already inaccessible. By the summer of 1951, when a President's Fellowship from Brown University made possible a third trip to the Balkans, Bulgaria too was out of bounds, but I returned to Yugoslavia, and witnessed some of the changes that had taken place as Tito and his followers maneuvered themselves out of ideological and economic dependence upon the Soviet bloc. I never managed to get to Albania, but on all three trips I visited Greece; on the second, Hungary; and on the second and third, Turkey. Without this opportunity to travel and to develop a feel for the region, the writing of this book would not have been possible; so my thanks go first to all those who assisted me, including the Research Committee of the University of Wisconsin.

In the United States, my colleague, Donald C. McKay, proved an extraordinarily kind editor, as other duties again and again delayed my preparation of this book so long that its present version is far larger than we originally contemplated. The Russian Research Center at Harvard made me a visiting Research Associate in 1949–50; provided me with expert typing assistance when I eventually did produce a manuscript; and has now issued the resulting book as a volume in its own series. To the successive directors of the Center, Clyde Kluckhohn and William L. Langer, and to my colleagues on its Executive Committee my thanks are due. The Center has also afforded me an opportunity over the years to discuss the problems treated here, and the larger problems of which they are a portion, with colleagues and visiting scholars from other universities. If I single out especially Merle Fainsod, Adam B. Ulam, Franz Borkenau, and Emile Despres, it is because I can remember especially lively interchanges with them. Among my students, R. Gerald Livingston has shared with me his experiences of a year's graduate study in Yugoslavia in 1953–54; Joan M. Afferica has taken meticulous care in correcting the manuscript; Margaret Dalton was one of the three skillful typists. My friend, Professor W. T. Jones of Pomona College, generously read galleys with a keenly critical eye, long after my own judgment had deserted me. Mrs. Marion Hawkes of the Harvard University Press was a kind and careful copy-editor.

To other students of the Balkan area I feel an especially heavy debt. Many of them are mentioned in the footnotes or the appendix as the authors of valuable studies of some aspect of our problem. But the chance to travel through Transylvania in December 1944 with Henry L. Roberts; the sojourns in wartime Belgrade and postwar Athens with Robert G. Miner; conversations with Cyril E. Black, John C. Campbell, Alex Dragnich, Stephen Peters, Michael B. Petrovich, Irwin T. Sanders, and Stavro Skendi have contributed immeasurably — as much as the books and articles written by these men and others — to my education and the slow formation of my opinions. Needless to say, they have no share in the imperfections or mistakes which doubtless still mar the book which follows. With much of it they may indeed disagree, as would perhaps my kind host and companion in Bucharest, Georges Constandaky, now dead, from whom I learned so much about Rumania. Other names of men still alive in Communist countries I forbear to mention here, but my debt to them is none the less real.

Two perennial problems need brief treatment in this place. The first is the question of Balkan statistics, which so often reflect wishful thinking or opinion rather than cold, hard fact. In the past, for example, population figures for areas in dispute between any two countries have been as notoriously unreliable as figures for the grain yields per hectare, for example, are today (when available) in the new Communist world. It is obviously impossible to enter a caveat each time one cites an absolute number. Let it suffice to say here that all figures referring to the Balkan countries are automatically suspect: we use them because they are all we have. The second problem is that of transcription from the Balkan tongues. In the case of Rumanian, I have kept the diacritical mark beneath the *s* and the *t*, which turns them into *sh* and *ts*: thus Iași is pronounced Yash, with the final *i* silent, and Galați is Galats, with the final *i* also silent. I have kept the traditional letter *â* for the dull *u* sound; thus *Scânteia,* rather than adopt the Soviet-sponsored "reform," *Scînteia.* In the case of Serbo-Croatian, I have been reluctant to follow the practice prescribed by Slavists, especially with regard to the letter *c*, which represents the sound of *ts*, and, as *č* or *ć*, different forms of *ch*. Nor have I used *j* for the initial *y* sound: which of my readers, encountering the word Jajce for the first time would pronounce it properly as Yaitse? I have therefore in most cases transcribed as nearly phonetically as possible. When it is a matter, however, of the author of a book, who must be sought in a card-catalogue in a library, I have not, for example, rendered Cvijić by Tsviyich, but left the philologists' spelling. In short, I have been inconsistent in an effort to be helpful. In the case of Bulgarian, I have kept the *u* as a rendering for the letter Ъ. Why write *Valko* or *V'lko* or even *Velko* for the first name of the present Premier, Chervenkov, if one is not also prepared to write Balgaria, B'lgaria, or Belgaria for his country? [1] In the case of Albanian, *xh* is pronounced *j;* and *x* is *dz.* I have not tried to render Hoxha as Hoja or Xoxe as Dzodze, however. Nobody is likely to be happy at my solution of the problem, which I have tried to persuade myself was dictated by common sense.

Grateful acknowledgment is made to Cassell & Company Ltd., London, to Thomas Allen, Limited, Toronto, and to Houghton Mifflin Company, Boston, for permission to publish excerpts from Winston Churchill's *The Second World War;* and to Simon and Schuster for permission to publish excerpts from *Tito,* by Vladimir Dedijer.

Robert Lee Wolff

[1] Yet in the case of the word for the Bulgarian parliament, I have not transcribed it as Subranie, because the form Sobranie has become familiar in English, and not merely to cigarette-smokers. Another inconsistency!

PART I

Before 1939

Chapter I

THE PURPOSE AND SCOPE OF THIS BOOK

THE COUNTRIES WITH WHICH THIS BOOK DEALS—Yugoslavia, Rumania, Bulgaria, Albania—are not major powers; their resources are not of critical importance to the United States. American interests in the Balkan region appear to be minimal. But all of us have seen half a dozen movies in which the idyllic peace and quiet of an early twentieth-century American home are interrupted by the announcement that in the Balkans an Austrian Archduke has been assassinated, an announcement to which nobody pays attention. In the next sequence on the screen the hero is invariably waist-deep in the mud of Flanders, and the shells are whistling overhead. Since 1914 we have slowly and painfully been coming to realize that, baffling as they seem, Balkan politics necessarily involve us.

It was only 1938 when Prime Minister Neville Chamberlain expressed his wonder that Britain should be on the point of war because of the problems of a faraway country of which the British knew nothing. Yet Czechoslovakia, about which he spoke, is closer to Britain than the Balkan countries, and Britain in 1938 was closer to Europe than we are today. Even though we have gone through a second World War, even though we have inherited from the British certain international responsibilities which they can no longer afford to shoulder, it is still difficult for many Americans to understand why they should need to know in intimate detail about the problems of people remote in distance, traditions, and attitudes, especially if they are people without vast economic resources and military potential.

It would of course be possible to take a moral stand, and to declare again that no man is an island, that the bell tolls for us all. This is cogent and also true. But it may be even more effective to appeal to unmoral self-interest, and to argue instead that our very lives depend upon the peaceful solution of international disagreements, that national policy in our republic can be based solidly only upon an informed public opinion, and that therefore we should understand as much as possible about the world in general and the explosive Balkan countries in particular.

In 1955, only a decade separated us from the end of the Second World War. During that brief space of time, British warships were sunk in Albanian mine fields, American transport planes were shot down by Yugoslav fighters, a Bulgarian politician was executed just *because* the western powers tried to protect him, and American diplomatic relations with Bulgaria were severed. For several years, Greek troops, partly trained by American officers and equipped with American arms, battled against Soviet-sponsored Communist guerrillas, who received aid and comfort from Yugoslavia, Bulgaria, and Albania. Before that war was over, Yugoslavia's dramatic expulsion from the Soviet bloc created a new threat of war in the Balkans, which evaporated only after the death of Stalin, and the creation of new links in the western powers' security system for Europe. Despite the fact that none of the Balkan countries by itself was a great power, we found ourselves inextricably tangled in their affairs, far more deeply than in the days of 1914, when the Archduke's assassination precipitated the First World War, from which we could not stand aloof. Our interests in the Balkan countries were perhaps negative rather than positive, but they were none the less compelling.

In these years, American relations with the USSR increasingly provided the focus around which the other aspects of our foreign policy grouped themselves. We wrestled unsuccessfully with the problems of atomic energy control, of disarmament, of making the United Nations an effective instrument, with the problems posed by the activities of international communism and the Soviet maintenance of fifth columns in all non-Communist countries. We faced a world divided ever more sharply into American and Soviet spheres of influence. This the United States had opposed during the war, but not effectively, and in the period since the end of the war the great frontier across the globe — from Stettin to Trieste, along the borders of Greece, Turkey, Iran, Afghanistan, and India, between China and southeast Asia, between northern and southern Korea — loomed larger and larger as the line which divided the world politically and economically. Communist victory in China, and the wars in Korea and Indochina only demonstrated more clearly where the frontier ran. The northern boundary of Greece formed one critical sector in this frontier.

To the United States, the Yalta Declaration of February 1945 symbolized the climax of the American hope, cherished during the war, that peacetime collaboration with the Soviet Union would prove possible. The central provisions of the Yalta Declaration were those announcing policies for eastern and southeastern Europe. American disillusionment with Yalta in particular, and with the hope of collaboration between the United States and the Soviet Union in general, arose in the first instance directly out of Soviet violations of these policies which Yalta had proclaimed. The violations took place first in Rumania and Bulgaria, and began less than a month after Yalta. The Balkan countries served as a kind of weather-breeding area for those in the west interested in estimating Soviet intentions.

Nor was this role a new one. In 1939, when Stalin and Hitler reached the agreement that made possible the German launching of the Second World War, Hitler specifically declared that Germany was not interested in southeast Europe. While the Hitler-Stalin pact lasted, the Russians repeatedly insisted on the supremacy of their role in the Balkans. Not all the grandiose German offers of an enormous future Russian sphere of influence in the Persian Gulf and the

Indian Ocean could deflect Molotov in 1940 from returning again and again in his discussions with Hitler to the question of German troops in Rumania and Bulgaria. When the relations between Stalin and Hitler soured, it was because of the Soviet annexation of Rumanian territory, German and Italian guarantees to Rumania, German efforts to enroll the Balkan countries in the Axis alliance, and the question of the mouths of the Danube. Rivalry in the Balkans was the immediate precipitant of the German attack on the USSR in June 1941. For Hitler, as for the western powers today, the Balkan area formed a most sensitive spot in the complex of his relations with the Soviet Union.

After Yalta, Moscow's policies in the Balkan countries offered the west its best opportunity to study Soviet techniques of imperialist expansion. Varying their tactics and their timing according to the degree of local support they might expect, the Russians and their local agents, the native Communists, seized power in one country after another. The tragedy in the Balkan countries was partly our own fault. From it we learned lessons that brought us painfully to espouse a policy of containment. And, though the Republican Party in the United States replaced the term "containment" by the term "liberation," the content of the policy did not change. The development of the European Recovery Program and the North Atlantic Treaty Organization owed much to our understanding of Soviet strategy and tactics, as demonstrated to us in the Balkan countries. Indeed, the "Truman Doctrine," the forerunner of all these later policies, was specifically designed to meet the Communist threat in the Balkan neighbor, Greece, and the Russian threat to Turkey, and was thus the direct outgrowth of what we had learned by watching Rumania, Bulgaria, Albania, and Yugoslavia.

Moreover, the political, economic, and social behavior of the native Balkan Communist parties taught us a good deal about the workings of communism as a movement. As in the Russia of 1917, the Communists had triumphed in an overwhelmingly agrarian region. Though the presence of Soviet troops and the exercise of varying degrees of Soviet pressure formed an essential part of the Balkan Communist triumph except in Yugoslavia, it none the less seemed true that Communists did better in countries with small proletariats. Alone of the Soviet-dominated eastern European states, Czechoslovakia approached the countries of western Europe in industrialization. It was the last to fall to the Communists and it fell by a *coup d'état*. In the heavily industrialized western European countries, thanks in large part to American economic aid, the strong French and Italian Communist Parties had so far been checked. Study of the Balkan countries might lead to conclusions applicable to other backward agrarian regions, especially in Asia and Africa.

Until June 1948, all four Balkan countries were Soviet satellites, acquired as the result of wartime and immediate postwar strategy and diplomacy. In that month there developed the only major cleavage yet to appear in the apparently solid façade of Soviet influence and power. Stalin's failure to appraise correctly the developments in Yugoslavia precipitated a schism in the

Communist world which proved of major interest and value to the west. Unwilling to permit the penetration of Soviet agents into the apparatus of the Yugoslav state, unwilling to accept political and economic dictation which in the end might cost him his power, Tito defied Moscow successfully, and in the process taught the west much that it had not yet known about Soviet techniques of domination. Though the "Titoist" phenomenon raised interesting questions about possible future developments in other parts of the world, it could be properly appreciated only in terms of Yugoslav history and traditions, economic development, and social patterns.

With all these compelling reasons for studying the Balkan countries, the American reader was none the less hard put to it to find helpful books on the subject. For this there were many reasons, all of which went back perhaps to the fundamental fact that the Balkan region was an extremely complicated one. Forty million people of many races and languages and religions, with widely varying historical experience, and with tenacious memories of the past, lived in the four countries we are considering. Although most of them were peasants, their common economic problems had not given them a sense of unity for political or other purposes. They had never been vouchsafed long periods of peace in which to work out their own destinies. Interference from the outside had encouraged a wide variety of hatreds to flourish and to multiply; unscrupulous political leaders had used the frustrations of their people for their own purposes.

Characteristically, a foreigner who observed the region was baffled by everything he saw and heard. Frequently he believed the propaganda of one interested group or another. A westerner fell in love with the Montenegrins, the Albanians, the Transylvanian Saxons, or the Bosniac Muslims, with the brave Communist guerrillas, the reasonable and solid Agrarians, the picturesque peasants, or the cultivated and westernized city-dwellers. His choice of favorites often was determined only by his itinerary. To a typical westerner almost every individual inhabitant of the Balkan peninsula seemed charming, and he was quite likely to adopt the prejudices of the first group he met.

Of course, previous inclination also determined the outcome. If the visitor were a lover of the primitive, he might be deeply impressed by the mountain balladeer, composing still in the Homeric manner, and singing his heroic song. If he were a sophisticate, he might sit at the feet of some university professor in a capital city, learned, persuasive, and only a generation removed from the peasant village. Whatever determined our author's bias, however, bias it remained. No matter how persuasive or eloquent or poetically written his book on the Balkans might be, no matter what his academic reputation or the length of time his book had remained "standard," it would surely mislead the American reader looking for information.

The journalists' books of recent years were sometimes even worse. Based on scraps of information hastily collected from unreliable sources during brief visits, written without the necessary background in the history, politics, and economics of the area, they were composed as potboilers to take advantage of this or that latest sensational development. Yet because there were so few authoritative works on the subject, these poor substitutes were often read years after they had lost whatever merit they might once have had. This book aims then to introduce the four Balkan countries to the American reader as simply and unpretentiously as possible.

Why should it deal with these four countries and no others? Yugoslavia, Albania, Rumania, and Bulgaria formed only a part of the vast region of Europe lying between the Soviet borders and the countries of the North Atlantic Pact. The entire "middle zone" including, besides our four countries, Finland, Poland, Czechoslovakia, Hungary, Greece, Turkey, and perhaps the once independent Baltic states, as well as divided Austria and Germany, formed a natural unit. Yet a meaningful study of so large an area would become unwieldy.

Moreover, the countries of the zone outside the Balkan countries all fell naturally into different categories. Finland presented a special problem because of its long history as a privileged portion of Tsarist Russia and its close linkage with Scandinavia. The Baltic states were now nominally a portion of the USSR. Germany and Austria belonged to Central Europe. Poland, with its 25,000,000 people and substantial industrial resources, its traditional western outlook, its new postwar territorial formation created by the annexation of large western areas formerly German and by the loss of its former eastern territories to the USSR, deserved a book to itself. Czechoslovakia, a western Slav state, successfully industrialized, with a strong indigenous democratic tradition, entirely Catholic or Protestant since the loss of its easternmost province to the USSR, could not be classed with the Balkan countries, but was far more advanced.

This left our four countries, plus Hungary, Greece, and Turkey. All three of these were geographically adjacent to our four, and historically intimately connected with them. There were traditional territorial disagreements between Hungary on the one hand and Rumania and Yugoslavia on the other, between Greece on the one hand and Albania, Bulgaria, and Yugoslavia on the other. Most of the area of all four of our countries was once part of the Ottoman Empire. Hungary, Greece, and Turkey will of necessity appear repeatedly in these pages. Yet there were valid reasons for excluding them from detailed consideration in this volume.

Catholic or Protestant in religion, clinging to their distinctive non-Indo-European language, self-consciously western in their traditional attitudes, passionately nationalist and convinced of the inferiority of other races, Hungarians usually angrily repudiated any suggestion that they were a Balkan people. Indeed, with the creation of the rump state of modern Hungary after the First World War at the Treaty of Trianon, and the loss of Croatia and Transylvania to Yugoslavia and Rumania, the centuries-old domination of the Magyars over regions specifically Balkan came to an end. As constituted after 1920, and with its economy becoming increasingly diversified, Hungary for most purposes was a central European state.

Although in some respects Greece was closely tied to its northern neighbors, our group of four states, it should properly be considered a Mediterranean rather than a Balkan country. Its long indented coastline, together with the relative poverty of its resources, led its people to seek their fortunes in shipping, and made them the leaders in the Mediterranean carrying trade. For this reason, among others, the Greeks became more cosmopolitan than any other people of southeast Europe, and the problems of Greece were intimately bound up with opinions formed and decisions taken, for example, among Greeks in Egypt or in the United States. Moreover, the differences between Greece and our four countries were accentuated in the last decade by the fact that first the British and then the Americans, by defeating and restraining the Greek Communists, succeeded in preserving Greece from absorption into the Soviet sphere. Greece was a western beachhead in eastern Europe. In this book our consideration of Greek matters will therefore be limited first to the question of the profound Greek influence in the Balkan area, and second to the relations between the various regimes of modern Greece and those of our four countries.

The centuries-long domination by the Turks left a permanent mark on the Balkan states. Moreover, the strategic issue of the Black Sea straits was closely related to the geographic position of the new Soviet satellites, Rumania and Bulgaria. Yet Turkey, properly considered, was not a Balkan country. After the last outer husks of the Ottoman Empire were stripped away from the Turkish kernel at the end of the First World War, the new Turkey abandoned all territorial ambition in Europe, where it held only the small region known as eastern Thrace and the great city of Istanbul. The exchange of population with Greece in the early 1920's reflected the nationalism of the new Turkish state, and was part of a drive toward Turkish homogeneity. While Istanbul itself still included its Greek, Bulgarian, Armenian, and Latin Christian minorities, the Turkish capital was moved to Ankara, high in the Anatolian plateau, and this in itself symbolized the fact that Turkey had become an Asian rather than a European nation. No doubt the dramatic and sweeping reforms of the externals of Turkish life made the country the most advanced of all the nations of the Middle East; but these reforms had perhaps not gone so deep as enthusiastic admirers of Kemal Pasha sometimes suggested. Strong vestiges of the old Ottoman ways remained. Unlike all the other countries so far mentioned, Turkey had no substantial indigenous Communist movement which could act as advance agent for the USSR. For this reason, doubtless, in addition to the aid given by the United States, Turkey, like Greece, and unlike the Balkan states, remained on the western side of the iron curtain.

Together, our four countries formed a significant unit. As peasant countries, they faced generally similar economic problems. Three — Yugoslavia,

Rumania, and Bulgaria—were Danubian states, and under normal circumstances were drawn together by the fact that the great trade artery of eastern Europe flowed through their territory and linked them to each other. Politically, all four were creations of the nineteenth and twentieth centuries; to a large extent they were products of the disintegration of the Ottoman Empire in Europe, and of the international diplomacy devised to deal with this development. Of the roughly 40,000,000 inhabitants, perhaps 27,000,000 were members of the Orthodox Church, which helped to lend a certain similarity to their patterns of culture, despite the presence of significant Roman Catholic, Uniate, Muslim, Jewish, and Protestant minorities. In all four, as a result of historical experience, violent nationalism had become a feature both of domestic cultural life and of international political behavior. All four had repeatedly found themselves involved in the rivalries of the European great powers, and had experienced varying forms and degrees of intervention in their domestic affairs. None had ever known a sufficiently long breathing-space to develop strong native traditions of democratic government.

Yet even within our four countries the diversities were impressive. Yugoslavia and Bulgaria were largely Slavic, and their people spoke a Slavic language, while Rumanian was essentially a Latin tongue, and the Rumanians an ethnic riddle. The Albanian language was Indo-European like the rest, but not closely related to any other tongue at present spoken; those who speak it were said to be descended from the ancient Illyrians. Two of the countries, Yugoslavia and Rumania, within their present boundaries were the much larger descendants of earlier states (Serbia, the Rumanian "Old Kingdom" or *Regat*) which had expanded from a nucleus at first only autonomous until they included in an independent nation all or most of the territory they once claimed. Bulgaria, on the other hand, was never able to achieve the frontiers planned for it on paper before it had come into existence, and this fact profoundly affected its foreign policies. And Albania achieved independence largely because the powers wished to keep its territory out of the hands of its neighbors. Albanian national consciousness developed very late, and in a form much weaker than that found elsewhere in the Balkans. But in the period immediately following World War II all four countries lay wholly within the new Soviet sphere in southeast Europe, while the defection of Yugoslavia in 1948 attracted the attention of the west to the lessons that might be learned in the Balkans. Albania, Bulgaria, Rumania, and Yugoslavia might, then, reasonably be considered together and alone.

Chapter 2

THE SCENE: A DESCRIPTION OF THE BALKAN COUNTRIES

1. Geography: the Land

THE WORD "BALKAN" MEANS MOUNTAIN IN TURKISH. The Balkan mountains proper, the range which gives the entire region its name, are geologically the eastward-running extension of the great curving mountain range which sweeps down through Rumania in a great reverse S, and is known there as the Carpathians or Transylvanian Alps.

East of the first member of this reverse S-curve lies the province called Moldavia; south of its second member lies the province called Wallachia.[1] Under the Turks these two were autonomous principalities each with its own capital, Moldavia at Iași, Wallachia at Bucharest. They united in 1862 to form Rumania — the Old Kingdom or Regat — with its capital at Bucharest. Corn and wheat are grown extensively in the Old Kingdom, usually under primitive conditions; the rich soil of the Danubian plain in Wallachia is among the best in the world. Also in Wallachia, north of Bucharest and south of the Carpathians, lie the Rumanian oil fields, centering around the refinery city of Ploești, several times bombed by the United States Army Air Forces during the last war.

On the other side of the Carpathians, lying within the curve made by the first two members of the reverse S, is the roughly triangular province of Transylvania, partly enclosed on its third side by the Ore mountains, running from north to south. Transylvania is a hilly region, with forested slopes, upland pastures, and occasional fertile valleys. Lumber and hides, cattle and mineral resources (lead and gold in small amounts) are its distinctive products. The name Transylvania is often loosely used to include adjacent Rumanian regions, in particular the land to the southwest called the Banat, one of the richest farm areas in Europe, closely linked economically with the neighboring Yugoslav Banat, and centering about the city of Timișoara (Temesvar).

Transylvania's chief claim to interest is the variety of its population, which for many centuries, in addition to the Rumanians, now a majority, has included large Magyar, German, and Jewish groups, as well as another people called Szeklers, related to the Magyars and found only in Transylvania. The religious diversity is even more striking than the ethnic: here there live Ortho-

[1] Because the name Wallach or Vlach as applied to Rumanians by foreigners has acquired insulting overtones, modern Rumanians did not like the traditional name Wallachia for their southern principality. They preferred to call its western portion Oltenia, after the river Olt, flowing south into the Danube; and its much larger eastern portion Muntenia (mountainland), after the foothills of the Carpathians which fringe its northwest border.

dox, Uniate, Roman Catholic, Lutheran, Calvinist, Unitarian, and Jewish groups. In the past autonomous or ruled by the Habsburgs from Vienna, Transylvania in more modern times has been a source of heated quarrels between Hungary and Rumania, and, as a result of the most recent peace treaties, is now once more entirely inside Rumania. Because of its mixed population and varied history, its cities usually have at least three names: Rumanian, Magyar, and German. Its capital is the substantially Magyar center of Cluj (Kolozsvar, Klausenburg).

At the westernmost point of the second curve of the reverse S, the Danube flows directly through the Transylvanian Alps at the bottom of a deep gorge. Here are the celebrated and picturesque Iron Gates, mighty cliffs on which there can still be deciphered inscriptions carved by the orders of the Roman Emperor Trajan, who first brought western civilization to Rumania. The line of the mountains divides the middle basin of the Danube, lying in Hungary and Yugoslavia, from the lower basin, the richly productive agricultural plain, through which the river now flows eastward, serving for more than two hundred miles as the frontier between the fertile cornfields of Wallachia in Rumania on the north and the only slightly less productive agricultural plain of northern Bulgaria on the south. The terrain of northern Bulgaria shelves upward, as one moves south from the river, into the Balkan range, the third member of the reverse S, running eastward parallel to the river almost to the Black Sea. High in the Balkans is Tirnovo, fortress capital of one of the medieval Bulgarian Empires, and site in 1879 of the first Bulgarian constituent assembly, which adopted the document known as the Tirnovo Constitution.

Less than a hundred miles from the Black Sea, the Danube takes almost a right-angled turn to the north, flows wholly inside Rumania for almost a hundred miles, and then, turning abruptly east once more, emerges in the Black Sea through a series of muddy channels and mouths not unlike the deltas of the Mississippi and the Nile. The delta and the whole lower course of the river are rich in fisheries; the caviar from delta sturgeon is excellent. Lying between the river and the sea is the roughly oblong territory called the Dobrudja, higher ground than the remainder of the plain, a region whose division between Rumania and Bulgaria has in the past been a source of disagreement. The Dobrudja has often been called an ethnographic museum, so diverse are the peoples who until very recent times have lived there: Rumanians, Bulgarians, Greeks, Jews, Germans, Turks both Muslim and Christian, Tartars, and a number of Russians mostly belonging to odd religious sects.

Along the course of the Danube from the Iron Gates to the Black Sea are a number of river ports, which have grown up around former Turkish fortified positions on both the Bulgarian and Rumanian shores. The Rumanian town of Giurgiu, for example, opposite the Bulgarian town of Ruse, has served as an oil port. On the northern course of the river lie the Rumanian ports of Braila and Galați, both of which can accommodate ocean-going as well as river-vessels. On the Black Sea coast of the Dobrudja lies Rumania's only seaport, Constanța, through which grain and petroleum, coming by pipe line from the oil-fields, are normally exported. It was at Constanța, then called Tomis, that the great Latin poet Ovid spent his unhappy last years in exile; with their enthusiasm for everything Latin, the Rumanians have commemorated his sojourn by a large statue in a Constanța public square named after him. Near Galați, where the Danube takes its last turn before entering the sea, it is only about forty miles from the curve of the Carpathians. Between Galați and Focșani in the foothills of the mountains there runs a line of fortifications, along which the Rumanian armies were expected to stand to resist the Soviet invasion in 1944.

The Pruth, flowing into the Danube from the north, marks the eastern boundary of Moldavia, and separates it from the neighboring province of Bessarabia (capital Kishinev; Rumanian, Chișinau). Often in the past in dispute between Russia and Rumania, and now a part of the USSR, its name derives from the old Rumanian family of Basarab. Bessarabia is bounded on the south by the course of the Danube in its last lap toward the sea, and on the east by the course of the Dniester. The USSR has also annexed the northernmost region of Moldavia, the northern part of the former Rumanian province called the Bukovina, or beech-forest, with its Ukrainian or Ruthenian minority.

Despite the long Black Sea and Adriatic coastlines, the emphasis in the Balkan region has never been on maritime pursuits. In the west the mountain formations, in the east the almost land-locked character of the Black Sea itself have helped to keep sea-faring and sea-borne commerce at a relatively low level. The natural outlet for the southern and central Balkan region is the Greek Aegean port of Saloniki. Here during the years between the wars the Yugoslavs had a privileged status which they regained after 1948. Greek possession of the entire Aegean coast has often aroused Bulgarian jealousy and animosity: the Bulgarians have maintained that they require an Aegean outlet, and seized Greek Aegean territory during the last war. It is the mountains, however, not the sea, that give the land and the people their character.

Indeed, there are mountains everywhere, except for three important areas of low-lying fertile ground. First, there is a portion of the rich middle Danube basin, lying partly north of the river in northeast Yugoslavia and southwest Rumania. In Yugoslavia this region is still known north of the Danube by its name of the Voyvodina, or Dukedom, given it in Habsburg times. The Voyvodina is subdivided into three districts called Baranya, Bachka, and Banat, the last meaning a Habsburg province governed by a Ban or governor. The frontier divides the Yugoslav Banat from the portion of the former Habsburg Banat now in Rumania. Before World War I, the entire Voyvodina, including both the present Yugoslav and Rumanian portions of the Banat, was part of Hungary. The Voyvodina is the most productive agricultural region of all southeast Europe, with crops of wheat, corn, and sugar beets; before World War II intensive agriculture was far advanced, agricultural industries were well developed, and the railroad system was adequate. The Yugoslav Banat is divided from the Bachka by the waters of the Tisza (Theiss) which flows south from Hungary into Yugoslavia to join the Danube not far below the important Danube provincial city of Novi Sad, and not far above the Yugoslav capital, Belgrade.

South of the Danube, the fertile plain, lying wholly in Yugoslavia, is watered by two parallel tributaries to the great river, the Drava and the Sava, both of which rise high in the mountains at the northwest corner of the country. The Drava flows into the Danube near the western border of the Voyvodina, the Sava farther to the south and east at Belgrade, capital first of Serbia, and after 1920 of Yugoslavia. Belgrade's strategic position at the confluence of the Sava and Danube has made it a key fort since ancient times; the Romans called it Singidunum; there are few positions in Europe which have been so often besieged.

The region lying between the Drava and the Sava is known as Slavonia, today administratively part of the Federal Republic of Croatia; while the adjacent region immediately to the east, lying between the Danube and the Sava, is called Srem (a Slavic adaptation of the ancient Roman name, Syrmium), and is administratively part of the Federal Republic of Serbia. Portions of these areas are hilly and forested; but there are no outcroppings of mountains; fruit is grown and stock is raised; and the valley of the Sava is particularly fertile. The low-lying region extends westward into Croatia proper, whose handsome capital city of Zagreb (in Habsburg times Agram) lies just north of the upper Sava, at the northern extremity of the last fertile pocket in the mountains. South of the Sava there rise the low hills of northern Bosnia, a corn- and pig-raising area. A little to the east lies the "forest" region of Serbia (the Shumadiya), a quadrilateral region bounded by rivers on all four sides. In the early nineteenth century the dense woods of the Shumadiya sheltered the Serb rebels against Turkish rule, and the area is regarded as the heart of the Serbian independence movement. The forests are mostly gone, and the region produces cereals and fruit, especially plums, in the rolling lowlands, while in the hills cattle and pigs are raised. Swine-raising is the traditional occupation of the Serbs, whose first liberator, Karageorge, was a rich pig farmer. In the early twentieth century Serbia fought and won the celebrated "pig war" with Austria, an economic struggle over foreign trade issues. Together all these contiguous areas of Yugoslavia form the largest continuous non-mountainous section of the Balkan peninsula. Geographically they are an extension of the great Hungarian plain to the north.

The second largest non-mountainous region of the peninsula lies in Bulgaria, south of the Balkan mountains and north of the Rhodope range, and forms a very roughly triangular funnel-shaped area, widening as it runs east to the low-lying seacoast of the Black Sea. This region is formed in part by the valley of the Maritsa River, rising in the lofty Rila mountains south of Sofia, the Bulgarian capital, and flowing east and south across the Turkish and

Greek frontiers, and into the Aegean Sea. In Bulgaria the Maritsa valley broadens out in the region around the important city of Plovdiv (Philippopolis), then contracts, and finally broadens again as it approaches the Turkish border. Closed on the north by the Balkan range, the valley is shut off on the south by the massive and rugged Rhodopes, which, like the Balkans, become lower as they move east, and cease altogether some distance from the Black Sea. The upper Maritsa valley is often barren and hilly; in the lower reaches rice and tobacco are grown, and there are extensive fruit orchards.

The remainder of the non-mountainous region of central and eastern Bulgaria is called by geographers the "sub-Balkan depression" or "inter-Balkan valley." This begins as the narrow valley of the Tundja River, which runs eastward from the southern foothills of the Balkan range, and lies between the Balkans proper (called "the old mountains"—*Stara Planina*—by the Bulgarians) and the lower range of the *Sredna Gora* to the south. This is the celebrated "valley of roses," where the flowers are cultivated and their petals distilled for the essence, which serves as the base for perfume. Rose oil is a very valuable commodity, a kilogram selling regularly for almost a thousand dollars. The Tundja turns south to meet the Maritsa at Adrianople on the Turkish side of the frontier. On the Bulgarian Black Sea coast lies the important port of Burgas, now the largest in the country, having displaced its rival, Varna, lately renamed Stalin.

The third non-mountainous area is the Albanian coastal plain, partly marshy, partly fertile, extending varying distances inland from the Adriatic Sea up to the forbidding mountains behind it, from the shores of Lake Scutari, lying athwart the Yugoslav-Albanian frontier to the north, in an irregular crescent all the way to the port of Valona in the south. The plain includes the entire low-lying coast line, with its ports of Durazzo (Durres) and Valona, and extends inland to the capital city of Tirana. South of Tirana lies the valley of the Shkumbi River, flowing west into the Adriatic; this is regarded as the boundary between northern and southern Albania, each portion having its distinctive dialect, cultural traditions, and characteristic economic patterns.

With these exceptions, the Balkan peninsula is almost entirely mountainous. Indeed it is often impossible to distinguish separate ranges and folds, so tortured does the surface of the earth appear to be. Yet it is useful to single out what are perhaps the most prominent features of the mountain formations. It is only in this way that we can understand the lines of communication across the peninsula, which have contributed so immeasurably to its history, political and military.

Beginning in the northwest corner of the peninsula, we find a range of mountains which runs southeast along the Adriatic coast through all of Yugoslavia, and continues south through Albania behind the coastal plain. This formation also continues on in Greece and even reappears on the Greek islands of the Mediterranean, on Crete, and on the mainland of Asia Minor.

It is called the Dinaric chain. At its northern extreme, it joins the Julian Alps, the easternmost extension of the Alps, which, together with the Karawanken range, enclose the northwest frontier of Yugoslavia, and are the dominant geographic feature of Yugoslavia's northwest province: Slovenia. Slovenia was long a part of the Habsburg Empire, and is still linked with neighboring Austria, where there is a Slovene minority. In the Slovene mountains the Sava takes its rise, and on it lies the Slovene capital Lyublyana (Laibach), which has a distinctly central European air. This is Alpine, not Balkan country; here in the mountains is the beautiful Lake Bled, where the Yugoslav royal family had its summer home, now inherited by Tito. The Slovene valleys have coal deposits; timber is taken from the forested slopes; and above the forests abundant pasturage feeds the dairy cattle.

Northwest of Lyublyana the Dinaric chain begins. It consists of two zones, one higher and inland, broad and spreading, geologically related to the Alps and consisting of various types of rock, the other somewhat lower, coastal, and formed almost entirely of limestone, or karst. The inner zone is well-watered, and has much good forest, with pasture above. The coastal karst is in the main bare and treeless and waterless. It extends along the Adriatic at varying distances from the sea; in the north the mountains seem to rise directly out of the water; this is the case along the Croatian coast and behind the port of Fiume (Riyeka), temporarily seized for Italy after the First World War by the chauvinist poet D'Annunzio. To the southeast, the mountains are farther inland, shutting off a narrow strip of coastal lowland from the interior of the country.

This coastal strip is the celebrated Dalmatia. So formidable is the mountain barrier to communications inland that Dalmatia's associations throughout much of its history have been with Italy across the Adriatic rather than with interior Slavic lands. The mainland and the islands lying off the Dalmatian coast provide some of the most magnificent scenery in the world, enhanced by a unique architecture which developed in Dalmatia under Venetian influence, but which shows a native genius of its own. Along this coast, among others, lie the Dalmatian cities of Zadar (Zara), Split (Spalato), and Dubrovnik (Ragusa). Zara, which formerly had over 10,000 Italian inhabitants, was awarded to Italy after the First World War, and to Yugoslavia after the Second. Split (Spalato) is a modern port, the most important on the eastern shore of the Adriatic, and is also celebrated as the site of the huge palace of the late-third-century Roman Emperor Diocletian, in and around the remains of which a substantial portion of the city's population live. Dubrovnik (Ragusa), a small stone city surrounded by massive walls, was for many centuries an independent republic. Beautifully preserved, despite a series of violent earthquakes in the seventeenth century, Dubrovnik is today a kind of living museum, one of Yugoslavia's great tourist attractions.

The Dalmatian coast is a great breeder of sailors, and Dalmatians have sailed in all the world's merchant navies. On the Pacific Coast of the United

States and in South America many of the most lucrative fishing fleets are owned and manned by seamen of Dalmatian origin. Ruled by the Habsburgs between the departure of Napoleon and World War I, the Dalmatians are mostly Croats, and Dalmatia is part of Tito's Federal Republic of Croatia. Producing little in the way of grain, Dalmatia, with its Mediterranean climate, grows some olives, grapes, and citrus fruits. It is a deficit food area; but it includes most of Yugoslavia's resources of bauxite, the valuable ore from which aluminum is extracted.

Down the coast from Dubrovnik lies the famous fiord of Kotor (Boka Kotorska, Bocche di Cattaro), a jagged inlet of the Adriatic, where the sea flows between lofty limestone peaks through a series of bays of varying widths which open into each other at different angles until it finally reaches the innermost harbor of Kotor, once an Austrian naval base. Despite its splendid anchorage, Kotor is of little use as a port, since the mountains rise steeply behind it and cut it off, except by a steep winding road, from the hinterland which it might otherwise serve.

The barren karst ridges are separated by basins in the limestone called *polye;* here settlements are possible because springs of water flow out of the limestone, and the basins catch and can hold some of the rain, which elsewhere in this area disappears into the ground, although it falls in torrents. In the karst region, almost all the rivers are invisible, since they flow under and through the limestone.

The inner zone of the Dinaric chain literally covers almost all of three of the traditional provinces of Yugoslavia: Bosnia, Hertsegovina, and Montenegro, which are increasingly mountainous and wild as one moves from northwest to southeast. The rugged country of Bosnia is good for grazing; tobacco and corn are grown in the lowlands, and oats, flax, and hemp at the higher levels. Salt deposits have led to the beginnings of a chemical industry; and iron and other minerals are also mined. Hertsegovina is more precipitous, much of it being formed of limestone, so that the mountains are starker and barer than those of Bosnia. It includes the picturesque valley and gorge of the Neretva, which has cut its way through the limestone as one of the few rivers above ground, and which flows south and slightly west into the Adriatic.

Bosnia and Hertsegovina are the centers of the Muslim population of Yugoslavia, except for Albania and Turkey the only considerable group of Muslims in Europe. The great majority is not Turkish by origin, but consists of Serbs or Croats who centuries ago adopted Islam as their religion. In Bosnia-Hertsegovina about 30 per cent of the population is Muslim. Mosques lend an eastern aspect to the towns and villages of the provinces.

The chief city of Bosnia is Sarayevo, where the Archduke was murdered in 1914, a town filled with reminiscences both of Turkish days and of Austrian rule. Typically Habsburg public buildings blend oddly with the domes of the mosques. The chief city of Hertsegovina is Mostar, celebrated for its ancient

Turkish bridge over the Neretva, and for the singular costume of its Muslim women, now forbidden. This was a curious all-enveloping oversize hooded woolen cloak, found nowhere else in Europe. Bosnia and Hertsegovina are usually thought of together; together they were occupied by the Austrians in 1878 and annexed in 1908; after a period in the nineteen-twenties and thirties in which they lost their identity, they are once more together as one of the Federal Republics in Tito's Yugoslavia.

Still more desolate is Montenegro (Tsrna Gora), the Black Mountain. From the air, Montenegro looks like the mountains of the moon: a tumbling wilderness of massive rock rising precipitous and forbidding, and extending in all directions. Forests grow on some of the slopes, and there is a small patch of lowland around Lake Scutari (Shkodra, Skadar) lying between Montenegro and Albania; here stands the town of Podgoritsa, lately renamed Titograd, and now the capital. Otherwise, the entire province is barren, with tiny hollows of green cultivation in bowls made by the rock. The old capital, Tsetinye, little more than a village, is reached by a famous motor road, which crawls in a series of breath-taking hairpin turns up over Mount Lovchen from the Adriatic coast at Kotor.

Into these fastnesses the Ottoman Turks were never able to penetrate for more than brief raids; and Montenegro remained a free and independent Serb state through all the centuries when the rest of the peninsula was subjected to Turkish rule. War against the Turks was the chief occupation of its men, and back-breaking labor the occupation of its women; and the price it has paid for its devotion to the spirit of liberty has been high. Despite its absorption after the First World War into the modern state of Yugoslavia, Montenegro has remained in a kind of Homeric age, primitive and backward in the modern world, with violence as its answer to all problems, simple or complex. Traditionally devoted to Russia, the rural Montenegrins have become the most Communist of all the peoples of Yugoslavia. Yet they are even more devoted to their leaders, and several of Tito's immediate aides and enthusiastic supporters in his policy of opposition to Moscow are Montenegrins.

Lying to the east of Montenegro proper is the small mountainous region known in the days before the First World War as the Sanjak of Novibazar. The Austrians made use of this area as a buffer between Montenegro and Serbia to prevent the two Serb states from uniting. The Sanjak has now been divided by Tito between the two Federal Republics of Montenegro and Serbia, each receiving the portions nearest its own frontiers.

From Montenegro the Dinaric chain continues from north to south the entire length of Albania, rising inland from the coastal plain. The mountains then cross the Greek frontier.

There remains the barren and mountainous area politically divided into the southern portions of Serbia, the so-called Kossovo-Metohiya region, the Yugoslav Federal Republic of Macedonia, and western Bulgaria. In this area the Dinaric chain meets both the lofty Rhodope system of southwest Bulgaria and the lower Carpathian-Balkan chain sweeping down from the north. Here lie buried the copper, lead, zinc, chrome, manganese, and other mineral resources of Yugoslavia. The chief geographical features of the region are the valleys of the rivers: the Morava, Vardar, Struma, and Nishava.

The Morava rises in the south Serbian mountains and flows north across Serbia until it enters the Danube east of Belgrade, passing through the town of Nish on its way. The Vardar, taking its rise in the Shar Planina south of the town of Prizren, not far from the sources of the Morava, flows south instead of north, so that the valleys of the two are almost continuous. Cutting across Macedonia, the Vardar flows past the Macedonian capital city of Skoplye, all the way across the Greek frontier and into the Aegean not far from the major port of Saloniki. The Nishava flows into the Morava from the east at Nish; its valley leads into the mountain passes which bring the traveler to Sofia, the capital of Bulgaria, beautifully situated in a pocket among the mountains. The Struma, rising south of Sofia, flows south through southwestern Bulgaria across the Greek frontier and eventually into the Aegean. South of Sofia and east of the Struma looms the highest portion of the Rhodopes, the Rila massif. Here there rises the famous monastery of St. John of Rila, now closed, once one of the great sights of the whole Balkan peninsula.

The entire region here described is linked by history and geography to the adjacent portions of Greece lying across the frontiers. Much of it is loosely known as Macedonia: its natural Aegean outlet is Saloniki, and its mixed population includes Vlachs, Armenians, Turks, and Greeks, as well as Albanians, Serbs, and Bulgarians. It is now generally agreed that the indigenous Slav population is neither Serbian nor Bulgarian but speaks a dialect somewhere between the two. Often in the past the source of grave international disagreement between Yugoslavia and Bulgaria, the Macedonian problem took on new bitterness after 1948. Parallel Greek-Bulgarian and Greek-Albanian disputes also continued unabated, with Greek extremists claiming most of Bulgaria and Albania, and Bulgarian extremists half of Greece. Even the Yugoslav-Albanian dispute revived over Kossovo, the region lying northeast of the Albanian frontier inside Yugoslavia. Partly in Yugoslav territory also at the extreme southwest corner of the country lie the lakes of Ohrid and Prespa. From Lake Ohrid, scene of the earliest Christian missionary efforts in the Balkans and once the site of the mediaeval Bulgarian Patriarchate, flows the Black Drin, the chief river of Albania.

2. The Impact of Geography on History

The far-flung mountain formations of the peninsula tended to divide the people of one valley from those of the next, and thus to foster local particularism and local hatreds. But the historic paradox of the Balkan region lay in the fact that the mountains served as a barrier chiefly to the settled inhabitants. For the traveler, for the army on the move, there were well-defined lines of passage, main avenues of communication leading into the heart of the peninsula and across the mountain barriers. Unlike the Iberian peninsula, cut off from continental Europe by the Pyrenees, unlike the Italian peninsula, cut off from continental Europe by the Alps, the Balkan peninsula lies open on the north, and the valleys of the Danube and of its tributaries have always provided an easy means of access from central Europe.

Across the mountain ranges proper the main avenues are two, one leading east and west, the other north and south. From Belgrade, the east-west route goes up the Morava to Nish, and then up the Nishava and over the Dragoman Pass to Sofia, down the Maritsa to Plovdiv (Philippopolis) and Edirne (Adrianople), and thence across eastern Thrace to Istanbul (Byzantium, Constantinople). The north-south route runs from Belgrade to Nish once more, and thence up the Morava and down the Vardar to Skoplye and Saloniki. In addition to these main avenues, the Romans built a great road beginning at Durazzo on the Adriatic coast of Albania and Macedonia to Saloniki, whence passage on to Istanbul is easy. During the middle ages the armies of Crusaders, crossing Europe on land to fight the infidel in Palestine, might get as far as Belgrade along any one of a number of routes. But from Belgrade on, they were forced into the only avenue of approach to the east: Nish, Plovdiv, Adrianople, Byzantium. A few centuries later, when the Turks began from Asia their conquest of the Balkan peninsula in the opposite direction, they were forced to move west and north along the two great avenues, to seize the strategic lines of approach as an essential first step to establishing secure control over the peninsula. All historical examples tend to show that, considered from the outside, the Balkan peninsula is a link, a physical bridge, rather than a barrier between east and west.

In modern times, the Nish-Plovdiv-Istanbul and Nish-Skoplye-Saloniki routes have remained, as they must always remain, the chief thoroughfares. It is through these valleys and over these passes that the roads and railroads run. In the First World War, the allied armies inflicted the first major defeat upon the Germans by marching north from Saloniki along the Vardar and Morava valleys to Nish and Belgrade. During the Second World War, guerrillas repeatedly cut the railroad running south through these valleys, which was carrying supplies south to Saloniki for transshipment across the Mediterranean to Marshal Rommel in North Africa. The Germans themselves attributed their loss of the North African campaign in no small measure to Partisan attacks on this vital Balkan rail line.

Because of these two factors taken together — inner fragmentation and outer accessibility — the Balkan countries were unusually subject to outside influences. On the one hand, the inhabitants were not able to unite to resist outside pressure; on the other, outsiders could easily enforce their will. So the peoples of our four countries, separated from each other and divided among themselves, were deeply affected by the radiations of military power and of political, economic, cultural, and religious influence which emanated from certain great centers of Europe, from which armies, diplomats, merchants, scholars, and priests always found it easy to penetrate into the heart of the peninsula.

The Byzantium of the Greeks, the Istanbul of the Turks — terminus of the great east-west route across the peninsula, but also guardian of the Straits and thus mistress both of the route to Asia and of the Black Sea — sent out a blaze of influence, along the valleys of the Maritsa, the Nishava, and the Morava, covering all of Bulgaria and Serbia, north along the Black Sea coast, and up the lower valley of the Danube to the Iron Gates, across the whole Wallachian plain, and over the wide expanse of Moldavia and Bessarabia. The same Greek and Turkish influences radiated north from Saloniki up the Vardar and Morava, saturating all of Macedonia.

From Vienna and Budapest the Habsburg imperial and Roman Catholic clerical and German cultural and Magyar chauvinist influences radiated down the middle valley of the Danube almost to Belgrade, over the whole Pannonian plain from Zagreb to Timișoara, and over Transylvania to the Carpathian wall. Venetian mercantile influences radiated down the east shores of the Adriatic, to be turned back behind the coastal strip only by the limestone karst, rising forbiddingly a short way inland; and more recently Mussolini's revived imperial legions were impelled across the Strait of Otranto to debouch upon the Albanian coastal plain and to meet their defeat at the hands of the Greeks in the rugged peaks of southern Albania. So the physical geography helped to shape history in the Balkans.

Byzantium, Vienna, Budapest, Venice, shone like great searchlights sending out level beams of light and heat, which penetrated up the valleys, through the passes, and across the plains. These beams were halted only as they advanced farther from their source and encountered effective mountain barriers or met the fierce glare of a beam sent out by a nearer rival beacon. Thus Montenegro was but faintly illuminated by the light sent out from Constantinople. In the Bosnian hills, the Turkish and the Habsburg beams petered out together. Belgrade, for all its vaunted modernity, remained in 1955 recognizably Byzantine and Turkish in atmosphere, while Zemun, just across the river, where the Belgrade airport now stands, remained Habsburg, and was still the Semlin of a century ago, the frontier station between the Austrian and Turkish Empires.

To the American of the 1950's, those extraordinary conglomerations, the Habsburg and Ottoman Empires, were no longer realities. They seemed as dead as ancient Egypt. We seldom stopped to consider that it was only three short decades since their disruption and disappearance. But old men in Dubrovnik or in Cernauți, having lived since 1920 under the Yugoslav or Rumanian monarchies, under Italian, German, or Russian occupation, and under native Communist regimes, would shake their heads and tell you that things had never been right since the "Austrians" left. The faces of old men in Valona or Skoplye would light up with pleasure at the sound of a word of

Turkish. It was mostly old men who were nostalgic in 1955 for the good old days, which seemed good only by contrast with the bitter present. For an American it was important to remember that it was only yesterday when the great beacons were dimmed and went out.

These nearby capitals were the main centers of radiation. Yet because the Balkan peninsula is a link rather than a barrier, open rather than shut, other forces emanating from remoter centers also played their vital part in the formation of our four countries, especially during the last century and a half.

The influence of France, for example, shone from far-off western Europe. Napoleon's brief occupation of the Dalmatian coast and the able government of his Marshal Marmont there, in the so-called "Illyrian Provinces," stimulated the Yugoslav movement for union and independence in Crotia and Slovenia. Even more impressive was the position France assumed in the minds of Balkan intellectuals as the source of liberal political ideas, as well as of national sentiment. This was perhaps particularly striking in Rumania, where, with the dawn of national consciousness in the late eighteenth century, the people realized that they were speaking a Latin language, and soon afterward came to regard France as the eldest and most glorious of the Latin countries. In the mid-nineteenth century, Rumanian revolutionary leaders, anxious to throw off the Turkish yoke, received asylum in France; Paris was their second home. In accordance with his ideas of national self-determination, Napoleon III sponsored Rumanian independence, and was partly responsible for its achievement. Upper-class Rumanians, the sole articulate and literate class, had French tutors for their children, and later sent their sons to Paris to the University. France became the spiritual home of Rumanians so trained; often they would deprecate and sneer at their own country.

Rivaling and surpassing French influence especially in the years after 1933 was that of Nazi Germany, now emerging as the dominant state on the continent. A highly industrialized country, Germany needed the food surplus and raw materials of the Balkan countries. By a clever program of purchasing, the Germans succeeded in becoming first the best, and later almost the only, customer for the produce of the Balkan states. When they had achieved this position, they began to force the Balkan countries to accept large quantities of little-needed goods (aspirin and harmonicas) in exchange. Despite the unpopularity of these methods, the Balkan countries were unable to resist them, since their economy had become too firmly linked to that of Germany. Moreover, long-range Nazi plans for acquiring "living-space" in eastern Europe demanded that the Balkan countries be absorbed into the "new order." The presence of large German minorities in Rumania and Yugoslavia assisted Hitler in his drive to the southeast. The existence of a large Jewish minority in Rumania, and the prevalence there of anti-Semitism, led to the rise of powerful political parties enthusiastically Nazi in complexion. Between the wars, the German universities shared with the French the task of educating young Balkan intellectuals. But nowhere in the Balkans were the Germans popular;

their defeat in the war put an end to their brief but dismal period of supremacy. Yet for economic reasons, Germany is likely in the future to play again a significant role in the southeast.

Britain also traditionally played a role in the Balkans. British interests in the Mediterranean communications-line to the Levant and India required that no great power potentially hostile to Britain should emerge onto the shores of that sea. So, throughout the nineteenth century, British influence was generally thrown into the scale on behalf of the decaying Ottoman Empire, in order to maintain the status quo: it was important to keep the weak Turkish power—friendly to Britain, highly conservative, and an excellent customer for British goods—in control of the Straits and of large parts of the Balkan peninsula. Liberal sentiment in Britain usually opposed this policy, which involved the continued subjection of the Balkan Christian peoples to Turkish rule. Occasionally, as during the Greek Revolution in the 1820's and the Turkish massacres of Bulgarians in the 1870's, the strength of this sentiment interfered with the continuity of British pro-Turkish policy. But as a result of the dominant policy, Britain, unlike France and Germany, had no following to speak of in our Balkan countries.[2] In 1955, the British were still definitely unpopular, for example, with Bulgarian nationalists, who blamed them for the refusal of the Congress of Berlin in 1878 to sanction the creation of the "greater Bulgaria" of which the nationalists continued to dream.

This British policy in the Balkans was, of course, largely designed to combat the advance of Russia: this was the underlying motive for British diplomacy on the "eastern question" before 1914, and was the chief cause of the Crimean War. But at moments when it appeared that Germany, rather than Russia, would emerge as the dominant continental power, British policy turned to collaboration with Russia against Germany, even at the cost of temporarily abandoning hostility to Russian Mediterranean aims. Thus, during World War I, when Germany, Austria-Hungary, and Turkey were allied, and it was these Central Powers which controlled the Straits and much of the Balkan peninsula, Britain not only engaged in both the ill-fated Gallipoli expedition and the successful drive north from Saloniki as a means of breaking the Central Powers' hold, but also agreed to allow Russia to occupy Istanbul and the Straits after the war. It was only the Russian defeat, followed by the Bolshevik revolution and withdrawal from the war, that rendered this promise a dead letter. And similarly, in World War II, Britain was allied with Russia in the struggle against German domination of the continent, including the Balkan peninsula and the Mediterranean; and Churchill, as we shall see, was inclined to make concessions to Soviet ambitions in the Balkans.

But after the war, of course, with the emergence of Soviet Russia as the dominant power in the Balkans, Britain renewed her opposition to Russian emergence in the Mediterranean, and clung desperately to the last footholds in Greece and at the Straits. This policy we in the United States inherited in

[2] As distinct from Greece, where pro-British sentiment is still widespread.

1947 directly from Britain. Our interests coincided with those of Britain in preserving the Mediterranean communications-line from domination by a potentially hostile continental great power. Viewed in this light, the Truman doctrine of aid to Greece and Turkey against the Communist and Soviet threat appeared as the historic successor to British Balkan diplomacy and military action during the nineteenth century.

In Russia, whether Tsarist or Bolshevik, the drive to expand toward the Mediterranean, though pursued with varying degrees of vigor at different times, was after the early eighteenth century a fundamental part of foreign policy. It was always accompanied by efforts to enlist the peoples of the Balkans in its service. To the Slavs Russia appealed as the great Slav power, to which they might look for affection and support. To the members of the Orthodox Church, whether Slav or not, Russia appealed as the heir to Byzantium and the last stronghold of an independent Orthodox hierarchy.

Pro-Russian sentiment in the Balkan countries usually varied directly with the distance of Russian representatives: the farther away the Russians were, the more sympathy they could command among the native peoples; the nearer they came, the more they were disliked. Thus the Greeks and the Montenegrins during much of the eighteenth and early nineteenth centuries were convinced that in Russia lay their salvation from the Turks. This delusion persisted in Montenegro, which the Russians never helped with troops; it was markedly weakened in Greece after a number of ineffective expeditions and betrayals. As for the people of the Danubian principalities (Rumania), who repeatedly had to experience Russian military occupation in the course of the numerous eighteenth- and nineteenth-century Russian wars against Turkey, pro-Russian sentiment there was always far weaker than anywhere else in the area. So too, the Bulgarians, liberated by the Russians in 1877–78, and for a time enthusiastically pro-Russian, grew quickly weary of the arrogance of the Tsar's emissaries in their country, were alienated by Russian misconduct, and withdrew from the Russian sphere. The Serbs also suffered many a disillusionment at the hands of Tsarist Russia, as Tito's propagandists were not slow to recall after the break with Stalin.

There was a brief hiatus during the early period of the Bolshevik regime, when the Soviet leaders confidently expected world revolution, and therefore abandoned the traditional effort to create spheres of Russian influence. They were also fighting a desperate internal struggle for survival. But soon the Russian drive for influence in the Balkan region manifested itself once more, with a recurrence of many of its characteristic and traditional features. Together with their new instrument of penetration, the Communist Parties, a vastly effective weapon in view of Balkan economic and political conditions, the Russian still made use of Pan-Slav Congresses to appeal to Slavs, and of the Orthodox Church to appeal to the Orthodox. And again their efforts met with some popular success, *until* their armies and agents put in an appearance. Experience of the Red Army, in 1944 and later, disillusioned many of the most enthusiastic Bulgarians and Yugoslavs, and confirmed the Rumanians in their already vigorous anti-Russian and anti-Communist attitude. By 1948 the efforts of the Russians to control and direct the policies of Yugoslavia had lost them Tito, their most powerful supporter in the whole Balkan region. Yet what the Tsars could never accomplish with the means at their disposal the USSR at least temporarily achieved in Bulgaria, Rumania, and Albania by the instrumentality of the Communist Parties.

These phenomena could not, of course, be explained on a geographic basis alone, but geographical understanding remained an indispensable prelude to any consideration of the subtler economic and political factors. Russia's expansion into the Balkans was in part at least a function of the Russian wish for security along the western Soviet frontiers, and of the concomitant wish to control the Straits, thus simultaneously obtaining warm water ports and challenging the British domination of the Mediterranean. Their success in dominating the Balkan region since World War II was in no small measure attributable to geography: the western allies hesitated to make massive wartime landings in the peninsula, especially on the Adriatic coast, because of the inaccessibility of the hinterland and the difficulties of supplying a campaign inland across the Dinaric chain. This time, they could not start, as they had during World War I, from Saloniki and march up the Vardar and down the Morava because the Germans were in full occupation of Greece, Saloniki included. Moreover the American planners of the strategy of war were convinced that the place for the western allies to strike their main blow at Hitler was in France.

The Russians, on the other hand, not excluded from the continent as were Britain and the United States, but fighting a land war from the east, invaded Moldavia, forced the Galați-Focșani line, produced a Rumanian surrender and change of sides, and with Rumanian assistance crossed the passes of the Carpathians into Transylvania, moving on westward into the Hungarian plain to defeat the Germans and Magyars at Budapest. A few days after the Rumanian surrender, the Russians crossed the Danube into Bulgaria, meeting no resistance and knocking that country out of the war in a few hours. With a "friendly" government in office in Sofia, they moved on with Bulgarian assistance over the passes and up the valleys to Nish and Belgrade and a junction with the Yugoslav Partisan resistance movement, dominated by Communists, which in turn was the complete master of the Albanian Partisans. From then until the Yugoslav defection in June 1948, the USSR controlled our four countries. After their loss of Yugoslavia, the Russians tightened their control over the other three. The geography of the peninsula had once more made its inevitable contribution to military, and subsequently to political, history.

Chapter 3

THE CHARACTERS, IN THE ORDER OF THEIR APPEARANCE: THE PEOPLES OF THE BALKANS

THE POSITION OF THE BALKAN PENINSULA and the structure of its land have always invited outside invasions. Waves of people coming by land from west, north, and east, coming by sea from west, south, and east have flooded it again and again since the beginning of recorded time. Some waves retreated, leaving little permanent effect; others temporarily left a deep impression which was effaced or modified by a succeeding wave; still others made a lasting mark. This succession of human waves produced a mixture of peoples of quite extraordinary complexity and interest. No group of the present inhabitants of our four countries could avoid receiving the impress of the peoples whom it found upon its arrival in the Balkan area. None could continue its residence there unaffected by further pressures applied by new arrivals. All of the peoples we shall encounter were in their time invaders. All were repeatedly invaded. In widely varying degrees each was molded by previous settlers and by later attackers. The present ethnic structure has been created by a long and complex process of stratification.

As with the rest of Europe, the Balkan peninsula first emerged from complete historic darkness into a misty period for which our surviving evidence is chiefly archaeological and anthropological. The peoples whom we discern at first, when the curtain begins to go up on history, at the end of the Bronze Age and the beginning of the Iron Age, perhaps about 1000 B.C., are two: the Illyrians living in the western half of the area, and the Thracians in the eastern.

1. Illyrians and Albanians

Archaeologists associate the Illyrians with what they call the Hallstatt culture, after a place in Austria where extensive remains were found. The Illyrians carried this culture southeast into what is now Yugoslavia, where they gave their name to the whole eastern Adriatic littoral as far south as Durazzo, and inland to the Morava. As early as the seventh century B.C. the Greeks had some commercial colonies along the Illyrian coast and among the islands. By the end of the third century B.C. the Illyrians were united into a state of their own with its center at Scutari (Shkodra, Skadar) on the lake, including parts of northern Albania and of Montenegro and Hertsegovina. Conquered by Rome after several wars, during which they were at one time led by a woman, Queen Teuta, the Illyrians saw their land become a Roman province in 168 B.C. But the Dalmatians, an Illyrian tribe, held out against Rome for a considerable time thereafter, and even after their surrender in 46 B.C. remained rebellious.

The Illyrians resisted both Greek penetration and Roman conquest. When finally absorbed into the Roman Empire, however, they proved, with the passage of centuries, extraordinarily valuable to the state. For many centuries the best troops of the Roman armies were supplied by Illyria. Diocletian (284–305) the great Roman Emperor who preserved the Roman Empire by transforming its institutions, was an Illyrian. So was Constantine (324–337), who completed Diocletian's work by transferring the capital from Rome to Byzantium and accepting Christianity. So, very likely, was Justinian (527–565), remembered for his sustained attempt to reconstitute the Empire on its old territorial basis, as well as for the codification of the Roman law and for the building of Santa Sophia, greatest of Byzantine churches.

Just as the Illyrians, who were unable to maintain a unified state of their own, served and ruled Rome and Byzantium, so the Albanians, their probable descendants, who have not as yet been able for long to maintain a unified state of their own, served and ruled the Ottoman Empire. For centuries they supplied the most reliable troops to the Turkish armies. The Köprülüs, an Albanian family, provided no fewer than four Grand Viziers to the Turkish Sultans at a period in the seventeenth century when the future of their state hung in the balance; and by their administrative skill assured its survival. Mehemet Ali, an Albanian tobacconist, rose through the ranks of the Turkish army in the early nineteenth century to become Ottoman governor and then independent ruler of Egypt, and the founder of the Egyptian ruling house which ended just the other day with Farouk. And when the Ottoman Empire crashed into ruins, at the end of World War I, it was Kemal Pasha, later called Atatürk, at least part Albanian, who led the forces resisting disintegration, and built a new Turkey from the debris of the old.

Except for the emergence of occasional distinguished individuals, however, the modern Albanians as a people had no recorded history over the long centuries of Roman, Byzantine, and Turkish domination, and emerged from relative obscurity only in the nineteenth century. Throughout the entire middle ages we scarcely hear of them, although documents survive telling us of the commercial or strategic interest in the Albanian coast displayed by Byzantines, Normans, Venetians, and others. For a while in the fourteenth century some Albanians lived under Serbian rule, and we have contemporary witness to the fact that they detested it. When the Turkish conquest began in the fifteenth century, it was fiercely resisted for a while by the hero who is perhaps the most celebrated of all Albanian history: Skanderbeg, or George Castriota, a dramatic figure who has won the interest and attention of Europeans ever since his own day. But even Skanderbeg's almost legendary exploits against the Turks did not avail.

In order to continue in possession of their landed property, in order to be allowed to acquire property, a large number of Albanians, particularly in the southern part of the country, was converted to Islam. The population today (perhaps a million and a quarter in number), has remained about 70 per cent Muslim. The orthodox Muslims among them were called, as everywhere else, Sunnis. Beginning at least as early as the eighteenth century, however, and almost certainly long before, there penetrated into Albania the teachings of a mystic sect of Islam, the Bektashi dervishes, probably founded in the late thirteenth century in Anatolia but apparently retaining some features of the pre-Islamic religion of the Turks in central Asia. By contrast with the rigid prescriptions of orthodox Islam, Bektashism was liberal in its attitude toward social questions. Women, for example, played their part in Bektashi ceremonies unveiled and on a basis of equality; and wine was used, contrary to the prescriptions of the Koran. Bektashism was humorously tolerant both of Muslim orthodoxy and of other faiths: it placed its emphasis upon the individual man. At the same time it was a secret cult, and many of its doctrines and practices were intended to be shrouded in mystery.

This extraordinary sect took deep roots both in Turkey and in Albania. With its abolition by the government in Turkey (1925), Albania became its main stronghold in the modern world. In our time, perhaps a third of the Muslims of Albania (more than 200,000) belonged to the sect; during the short period of modern Albanian history it was always recognized as one of the official religions of the country. Its leaders played an important role in the Albanian nationalist movement, and were in some measure responsible for the unusual degree of tolerance traditionally demonstrated by Albanians in the matter of religion. Lord Byron, who was one of the first westerners to visit Albania in the early nineteenth century, at a time when another of the remarkable Albanians of history, Ali Pasha, had made himself virtually independent ruler of Albania, together with the adjacent portion of northern Greece known as Epirus,[1] remarked on this tolerance of the Albanians. Elsewhere in the Turkish Empire, he says, a man would declare himself to be either Muslim or Christian, when asked what he was; the Albanian would reply only that he was an Albanian. Frequently, in the south at least, one branch of a family was Muslim, and another Christian. They would sometimes celebrate their religious holidays together.

The Christians of the country, roughly 30 per cent of the entire population, were about two-thirds Orthodox, living in the southern and central portion, and about one-third Roman Catholic, living altogether in the north. The Orthodox represented the descendants of those Albanians who refused to accept Islam at the time of the Turkish conquest, and continued in the faith of their ancestors. Often, but by no means always, they formed the agricultural laboring class in the south, working on the estates of the Muslim *beys*. The Catholics also were Christians before the Turks, but were converted by

[1] Byron and his companion, Hobhouse, set the fashion; and for a time almost no adventurous young Englishman performed the grand tour without paying his respects to Ali Pasha at Yannina.

Rome rather than Byzantium. That this population remained Catholic may be attributed to far more recent missionary activity, some of it under Austrian or Italian auspices, conducted by the Franciscan and Jesuit orders, chiefly the former.

North of the Shkumbi river, the population, Muslim and Roman Catholic alike, was known by the name of Gheg; south of the river, by the name of Tosk. Despite differences in dialect, Ghegs and Tosks were both Albanian-speaking; and both groups regarded themselves as Albanians, "sons of the eagle," which was the meaning of the Albanian name for the country, Shquiperia. The large minority of Albanians, perhaps amounting to 600,000 people, living across the northern and eastern border in Yugoslavia, was also Gheg, and almost entirely Muslim.

The great contrast, however, between Gheg and Tosk lay in their social systems. The Ghegs, living in the lofty mountains of the north, relatively inaccessible to outside influence, and never completely conquered or controlled by the Turks, preserved an extraordinarily primitive tribal society, not altogether unlike that of Scotland in the seventeenth century and earlier. They governed themselves by customs of immemorial antiquity: for example, the children of certain clans had to marry the children of certain others. Designed originally to prevent marital relations within the clan, which were regarded as incestuous, this system actually produced inbreeding within a few generations.

Anthropologists found the Ghegs of particular interest because of the light they shed upon the ethnic type called "Dinaric": "a tall convex-nosed, long-faced population inhabiting the mountain zone which stretches from Switzerland to Albania,"[2] with numerous regional sub-types. Many of the tribes preserved oral traditions with respect to their founding: usually a distant ancestor was said to have fled to the hills to escape the Turks. Among the Ghegs, until very recent years, it was the rule for the chief of the clan to exercise patriarchal powers over its members, arranging their marriages, judging their quarrels, and punishing them without question.

The most notorious practice of the Ghegs was that of the blood-feud, governed by a rigid code. A large variety of offenses toward women demanded blood: the marriage of one's betrothed to another,[3] the abduction of a wife, and adultery. Any blow called for blood, and so of course did the murder of a relative. The rules governing the feuds varied slightly from place to place; but in general men might not be shot when accompanied by a woman, or when encountered in company, or when an oath of peace (the *bessa*) had been exchanged and was in force. A man who failed to carry out the prescribed vengeance on his enemy or on his enemy's relatives was the object of such

[2] Carlton Coon, *The Races of Europe* (New York: Macmillan, 1939), p. 601.

[3] Women were betrothed in infancy; if, when grown, a girl did not wish to marry the man of her parents' choice, she had to swear perpetual virginity. A blood-feud started if she married another man.

scorn in the community that he could in effect not continue to live there; while a man who did carry out the vengeance was liable to be shot in turn by the relatives of the victim. This might continue indefinitely for years unless the matter were compounded by a tribal council. Moreover, if the blood-feud were within the tribe, as it frequently was, the tribe itself must punish one who killed his enemies by burning his house and destroying his property. If he became a fugitive he must be given hospitality wherever he applied for it.

The ancient law governing these feuds was generally attributed to the fifteenth-century Lek Dukagjin, and was called the Law of Lek. Allegiance to its provisions far outweighed the nominal loyalty to the church among Catholic tribesmen. In some parts of northern Albania perhaps 20 per cent of the annual male death rate in the 1920's was caused by the blood-feud. Sometimes young boys of seven or eight were shot. In this period strenuous efforts were made by King Zog to put down blood-feuds. But this almost surely did not have any permanent effect, since during the Second World War members of the tribes participated in one wing or another of the resistance movement, and must have got back into their old habits again. Western observers have not been able to visit northern Albania since the last war, but it is highly probable that the blood-feud still continues there, and that allegiance to the Law of Lek will not be abandoned until substantial social advance is registered in the country at large.

In northern Albania, the people tattooed themselves in the patterns which were found on ancient Illyrian artifacts. All men wore and cherished their moustaches. Both men and women had their heads shaved during childhood, and retained only a specially shaped patch or fringe of hair. The first shaving of the child's hair, which took place at about the age of two, was felt to be a more important ceremony than baptism; and the man who was invited to perform it was regarded as a kind of godfather. The families of those related by this shaving tie might not intermarry. Neither might those related by blood-brotherhood, which was cemented between friends by a ceremony involving blood-mingling and blood-drinking. Such blood-brotherhood might be sworn between Christian and Muslim as well as between members of the same faith. Despite the general religious tolerance, there was a widespread belief among Christians that Muslims had a special unpleasant smell; and there prevailed a general unwillingness, which could occasionally be surmounted by a sufficiently lucrative offer, to sell Christian girls into marriage with Muslims.[4] Belief in vampires, in various forms of spirits, in the evil eye, and in the existence everywhere of buried treasures was widespread. Infants were tightly swaddled, and cradled in a way that perhaps contributed to the characteristic flattening of their skulls; they were almost smothered beneath heavy felt blankets, and left unwashed. Infant mortality was high. Corpses were

[4] The Muslims of the far north are all Sunnis, the softening and liberalizing Bektashi influence not having penetrated north of Kruya.

buried with coins in their mouths. Throughout northern Albania sheep and goat-raising was the prevalent form of economic life, since not enough grain could be raised for subsistence. The people cut some timber, but took little care to prevent forest fires, which frequently raged unchecked.

Over the centuries there was always a regular flow of people moving in both directions between northern Albania and Montenegro, a Serbian land. Until recently, several of the north Albanian tribes spoke Serbian. Many of the customs and practices recorded of the Ghegs might in fact be of ancient Serbian origin, and could be found closely paralleled in Montenegro. The very large Albanian population of the Kossovo region, inside the political frontiers of Yugoslavia, was racially similar to the population of northern Albania proper; in Kossovo, however, there were no Catholics, and the Albanians were all Sunni Muslims, with the possible exception of some who had "Serbized," and adopted the Orthodox faith.

The low value set upon human life, and the humor with which killing was regarded, the miserable position of women, the neglect of children, all this was repugnant to men trained in more western, less primitive, patterns of thought. But these were only the less attractive aspects of people still living in their heroic age, and at the same time sunk in poverty and ridden by disease. So might life have seemed in the shabby halls of the poorer chiefs who accompanied the Achaeans to Troy, or in the remoter and less fertile sheep-raising regions of Iceland in the year 1000. There were of course more attractive aspects of such a society: an unquestioning open-handed generous hospitality and an eagerness to make every effort for the comfort of the guest.[5]

Anthropologically much less homogeneous than the Ghegs, the Tosks of Albania south of the Shkumbi were prevailingly of the "Alpine" rather than the "Dinaric" type: spherical head, high and bulbous forehead, round face, nose lacking the high bridge characteristic of the Dinaric. The Tosks more closely resembled their Greek neighbors and enemies across the border; indeed, a Greek minority lived among them, and in the past few centuries untold thousands of Tosks moved south to settle in Greece, where most of them were gradually assimilated. The male Tosks of Albania traditionally wore the short

[5] Recently, a sociologist of Croatian origin, now teaching in an American university, has christened this primitive group of behavior-patterns "Dinaric," and applied it in effect to all the Serbs of Yugoslavia in general. (Dinko Tomasic, *Personality and Culture in Eastern European Politics* [New York: George W. Stewart Inc., 1948]. Despite its grandiose title, the book deals almost exclusively with Yugoslavia.) This was incorrect and seriously misleading. Americans who encounter this book should remember that for years Croatian intellectuals bent every effort to prove that the Serb was somehow eastern and inferior; this most recent book was an attempt to continue this futile and tendentious line of argument. Actually the term "Dinaric" was properly applicable to nothing human except a certain shape of skull; and the practices which we have been considering were to be found only in northern Albania and in Montenegro. They could be related to past Serbian practices through popular poetry, through which we might learn that the Serbs too passed through a heroic age; but this did not make the behavior patterns "Dinaric" or permit the formulation of modern political generalizations, any more than the present-day remote descendants of the Homeric or Norse heroes can properly be labeled "Dinaric" in their folkways and political behavior.

pleated petticoat, the *fustanella,* which Americans usually associated with the Greek Evzone uniform, but which was originally an Albanian garment, and which the Albanians preferred to wear dirty, "clean-petticoat" being a term of reproach. The Tosks lived mostly in compact villages, in contrast to the scattered houses of North Albania. Unlike the Ghegs, they emigrated to other lands, chiefly the United States. In the early twentieth century they frequently left home in order to earn enough money to return and buy land. More recently, Albanians tended to remain in the United States, and to become citizens. Thus the Ghegs had never left their highland fastnesses; while the Tosks, although backward by western European standards, were much like other Balkan peoples, and included a considerable number of returned emigrants, who had brought back certain acquaintance with the industrial civilization of the west. A few sent their children to European intellectual centers for their education. The result was that when foreign ideas entered Albania at all, they usually penetrated via the south.

The economy of southern Albania was also different from that of the north. It was agricultural rather than pastoral; and until the advent of the present Communist regime, was characterized by large estates belonging to powerful Muslim landowners, and often worked by Christian labor, the whole system a direct outgrowth of Ottoman practice. Among the Tosks, the ancient tribal system had largely disappeared; with it went the blood-feud, only a pale reflection of the custom as it existed in the north.

2. *Thracians, Dacians, Romans, Rumanians, and Vlachs*

The second of our original peoples, the Thracians, appeared in Homer using the same sort of weapons as his Greek Achaeans, and Herodotus regarded them as the largest of all nations after the Indians. At the time when the Illyrians were moving into the Balkans, the Thracians already seem to have been living in the entire region north of the Aegean Sea (to the Danube and even beyond) and east of the Morava to the Black Sea coast, where the Greeks had important commercial settlements. Towards the northern part of Thrace lived a branch of the Thracians called Getae, and still farther north across the Danube in Transylvania and the eastern Carpathians were their close relatives, the Dacians. As early as 900 B.C. there was some sort of successful political organization in Thrace. In the fifth century B.C. there was a Thracian kingdom in the Maritsa valley; but disunion among the tribal chieftains made it possible in the fourth century for the Macedonians to assert their hegemony in Thrace.

During the third century B.C. the Macedonian rulers in Thrace were challenged by a wave of Celtic invaders, now spreading all over Europe from their original home in south Germany and Austria, and carrying with them the characteristic culture which succeeded the Hallstatt in about 500 B.C. and is called the La Tène, after a site in Switzerland. These Celts established a short-lived state in what is now central Bulgaria. After its fall a new independent Thracian kingdom was created, whose whole political outlook was altered when the Romans conquered Macedonia in 148 B.C. Thenceforward Rome asserted its authority over Thrace.

North of the Danube, the Dacian relatives of the Thracians were exposed to the inroads of the Scythians, a mysterious people, quite probably Iranians, who seem to have been largely absorbed in Transylvania by the Dacians. Then, after an initial defeat by Alexander the Great himself, the Dacians were repeatedly successful during the third century against Macedonian invaders from the south, only to be overrun by the Celtic invasion and the La Tène culture which it everywhere brought with it. In the first century A.D., the Dacians, under their leader Burebista, formed a substantial state in Transylvania, extending westward into what is now Czechoslovakia and southward into Thrace. Although Burebista's state collapsed after his death, the Romans had been badly scared; the whole Danube frontier of the Empire, as it took shape, seemed to be increasingly threatened by the possibility of a Dacian revival. The Romans felt obliged to undertake a whole series of punitive measures, including the use of further Iranian tribes, as a restraining force against the Dacians.

None the less, about 85 A.D., a new ruler, Decebalus, emerged as the leader of a revived and menacing Dacian state with its capital in the Haţeg valley of Transylvania at the town of Sarmizegetuza. The course of the wars between Decebalus and the Romans was indecisive until the great soldier-Emperor Trajan undertook two campaigns against the Dacians. The first, in 101, ended in a mild peace, but the second, in 106, ended in a fierce punitive slaughter of the Dacians[6] and in the suicide of Decebalus. These campaigns scotched the Dacian menace.

They are commemorated in the celebrated spiral sculptured frieze which winds its way around Trajan's column in Rome, almost our only source for the progress of the campaigns and for the costume and appearance of the Dacians. On the column we can see the Dacian nobles wearing brimless felt hats much like those of the Scythians, and the bare-headed Dacian peasantry. Now Dacia too became a Roman province, including Transylvania and Oltenia (western Wallachia); Wallachia east of the Olt and all of Moldavia remained outside the Roman Empire.

Thus by the beginning of the second century A.D. a future mélange of peoples in the Balkan peninsula was already predictable. If the Illyrian stock survived in the Albanians, if the Thracian stock, whether pure or Getic or Dacian, survived in the Rumanians and other modern inhabitants of the Balkans, it must necessarily have been heavily diluted, even before 200 A.D., by Scythian and other Iranian elements as well as by Celtic and Roman. It is of

[6] Hungarian scholars, for reasons which we shall shortly discuss, argue that this slaughter totally exterminated the Dacians, but this view appears too extreme, and cannot be substantiated.

course the Roman diluent of which we can be especially sure: Albanian was heavily influenced by Latin, while Rumanian is a Latin language.

In the third century A.D., suffering from a variety of internal disorders and menaced by a Gothic invasion, the Roman Empire was forced to retrench; and the earliest retrenchment naturally took place at just the point where the most advanced conquest had been scored: Dacia. In 271, the Emperor Aurelian withdrew the Roman legions from Dacia; and it seems fairly certain that at the same time he withdrew with them a substantial portion of the population, settling them in the province of Moesia (northern Bulgaria) south of the Danube. This act has aroused furious controversy in our own day.

Rumanian historians, regarding themselves as the descendants of the Daco-Roman population, and determined to make good their historic claim to Transylvania, the ancient Dacia, maintained that Trajan could not have massacred all the Dacians in 106, and that Aurelian could not have withdrawn the entire population of the province in 271. They argued that Aurelian left behind a mixed population of Romanized Dacians, or Daco-Romans, or Rumanians, speaking, after one hundred and sixty-five years of Roman occupation, a Latin tongue which had replaced the original Thracian. Hungarian historians, on the other hand, wishing to challenge the Rumanian claim to Transylvania, maintained, in the first place, that Trajan killed off all the Dacians, and, in the second, that Aurelian withdrew any that might have been left. They explained the presence of Rumanians, Latin-speaking people, in modern Transylvania, where they were a majority of the population, by a much later reverse migration, beginning in the thirteenth century, north again across the Danube into Wallachia and Moldavia, and thence across the Carpathians back into Transylvania once more. Thus the Hungarians argued that Rumanians were late-comers to Transylvania, and cleared the way for their own claims, since their ancestors, the Magyars, a people of Asiatic origin, had arrived in Europe at the very end of the ninth century, and soon afterwards took possession of the province.

Indeed, historical materials were so scanty that one might look in vain for documentary traces of the Latinized Dacians, or Rumanians, in Transylvania during the centuries between Aurelian's withdrawal of the legions in 271 and the late thirteenth century about one thousand years later. This put the burden of proof upon the Rumanians, who argued that, all this time, while one invader after another swept over the land, their ancestors, the descendants of the Romanized Dacians, had stayed in the high Carpathians and pastured their flocks, avoiding trouble, and simply surviving. They added that, instead of moving west and north into Transylvania from the other side of the Carpathians in the thirteenth century, the movement was the other way: many of the Rumanians left Transylvania and moved east and south across the mountains in order ultimately to found the Moldavian and Wallachian principalities.

Impossible as it was to prove beyond doubt, the likelihood was that the Rumanian version of these events was true in part, and that some at least of the mixed Daco-Roman population of Transylvania held out all through the centuries in their mountain fastnesses. This controversy might have only academic interest were it not that politicians in southeast Europe regularly used historical argument to support or to attack territorial claims; and were not these claims so powerful a cause of international strife. It thus became of importance to know what the rival twentieth-century parties to the dispute were saying about Aurelian and the long-dead Daco-Romans, who did or did not accompany the retreat of the legions into Moesia.

In 1955, it made no difference who had got to Transylvania first. The fact remained that the majority of the population there was now Rumanian, as was recognized in the Treaty of Trianon (1920), which awarded the entire province to Rumania, and again in the peace treaties after the Second World War.

While there might be valid arguments for minor adjustments of these frontiers in favor of Hungary, the retrocession to the Magyars of any substantial portion of the land would appear to be out of accord with the principle of self-determination. Nobody thought of asking the Magyars themselves to go back to Central Asia, or of ousting the Anglo-Saxon population from the British Isles and returning it to the coasts of Germany, merely because these peoples had not always lived where they lived now. Yet as recently as 1940, Hitler, doubtless for reasons of his own, allowed himself to be persuaded by the Magyar historical arguments, and ceded to Hungary the northern portion of Transylvania, which the allies then returned to Rumania in 1944. Dormant in 1955, since both Rumania and Hungary unwillingly found themselves within the Soviet zone, with Transylvania firmly in the possession of Rumania, the disagreement over this province could at any moment be revived by the USSR as a means of bringing pressure on Rumania. If Rumania and Hungary should be rescued from their Communist masters, the rival claims to Transylvania would at once be posed by both sides, and the western world would again hear much about Aurelian and Daco-Roman continuity.

In addition to the Latin-speaking Rumanians north of the Danube in Moldavia, Wallachia, and Transylvania, widely scattered groups of Latin-speaking people lived elsewhere in the peninsula. Their dialects varied, but all were close to modern Rumanian. These people were called Vlachs, a word much disliked by Rumanians, closely allied to our terms Welsh and Walloon, deriving from a Gothic root meaning foreigner. The Rumanians preferred to call these Balkan kinsmen of theirs Arumanians; they were also called Kutzovlachs, or lame Vlachs, and Tsintsars, the last being an apparent attempt to imitate the sound of their language, in which *ts* occurs frequently. In northern Greece and Macedonia these Vlachs pursued their traditional occupation of cattle-raising. They practiced transhumance, taking their flocks to the lofty mountain pastures in summer, and coming down into the valleys in winter. Other Vlach groups existed in the Balkan mountains in northern Bulgaria, in the Istrian peninsula, in Dalmatia, and in the corner of Yugoslavia across the border from Rumania at the Iron Gates of the Danube, where they were called Vlashi.

We need not worry much about the ethnic origin of the Balkan Vlachs: Rome, we know, conquered and governed the entire Balkan peninsula; it would be remarkable indeed if a Latin tongue, sign of Roman domination, had not survived widespread. Occasionally these nomad Vlachs, illiterate and without national consciousness as most of them were, unwittingly played an important part in modern international politics. In the early twentieth century, for example, at a time when Macedonia was still part of the Ottoman Empire, and all the adjacent independent states of the Balkans — Greece, Bulgaria, and Serbia — were competing fiercely by secular and clerical propaganda and by force for the loyalty of its mixed population, in the hope of annexing the territory eventually, the Rumanian government began to take an interest in the Macedonian Vlachs. No responsible Rumanian believed that Rumania would ever annex Macedonia, but Rumanian statesmen hoped that by the very act of renouncing, at some future date, all desire to do so, Rumania might gain international credit, and might then proceed to push some other territorial project of whose fulfillment there was a good chance. Thus the Rumanian government subsidized Vlach schools, and sent Rumanian clerics to preach to the Vlach nomads, as a kind of gamble.

Just as the modern Albanians appeared to be descendants of the Illyrians, so the Rumanians and the Balkan Vlachs appeared to be Romanized Dacians or Thracians. In all cases, of course, a large variety of subsequent influences had been brought to bear. Anthropologically, the Rumanians varied: on the plains, they were not as broad-headed as the full-fledged Dinaric or Alpine types. Both of these were, however, found in the Carpathians. In northernmost Moldavia (Bukovina) lived some mountaineers anthropologically almost indistinguishable from the Ghegs of northern Albania. The Balkan Vlachs, as might be expected, were not racially homogeneous, and tended to conform in each region where they lived to the normal ethnic types of the majorities settled there.

Just as the Albanians lived through long centuries without a history of their own, there were great gaps, shorter in time but more mysterious, in the history of the Rumanians. The Rumanians engaged in migrations, although we cannot tell precisely at what times, in what numbers, or in what directions. The Gothic invasions of the third and fourth centuries which left some striking traces in Dacia, were followed by a whole series of others, including both Slavs and Turks. These kept the region north of the Danube, on both sides of the Carpathians, in turmoil for a thousand years, and must still further have affected the stubborn Latin-speaking ancestors of the modern Rumanians.

Western students agreed that modern Rumanians were often shrewd and capable: the peasants demonstrated a considerable ability, developed over centuries and encountered in all Balkan peoples, to resist unwelcome pressures and to avoid unwelcome taxes. The urban intellectuals displayed great capacities in all fields of scholarly research. At the same time, Rumanians seemed lazier than the other Balkan peoples: most commerce and much industrial development in Rumania was in the past initiated and undertaken by Germans, Jews, Greeks, and Armenians, but particularly by Jews. Politically the most famous Rumanian characteristic was corruption, which always plagued the country. The Rumanian police once jailed a newly arrived foreign newspaper correspondent because he attempted to change his money legally at the bank instead of patronizing the black market. He must, they concluded, have discovered a new racket of some sort, and they wanted him in safe custody until they could figure out what it could be. Contracts for highways, bridges, railroads, and public buildings traditionally brought such large percentages of graft into the pockets of their lucky recipients and of the political friends who arranged the matter for them that frequently the public work in question never was built at all; the money simply vanished instead. Passports, licenses, documents of all sorts were regularly for sale openly and illegally in government offices; in fact with enough money and enough of an acquaintance there was nothing in the country which was not for sale.

With these qualities there went a gaiety and charm, a natural courtesy and hospitality which won the heart of many a visitor. Rumanians, it is agreed, were often frivolous: even the most serious matters were occasions for a joke. They were also less violent than the other Balkan peoples. When the members of the opposition during the last war contemplated assassinating the pro-Nazi dictator and his aides, they tried to find a Slav to do the job. Yet the outbreak of terrorism against the Jews during the heyday of the Iron Guard in 1940 and 1941 was as horrible as anything of its kind in recent history. In the years before the war Rumanians became accustomed to political assassination and murder as a political weapon, while in their invasion of Russia they committed ghastly atrocities.

Peştele de la cap s'impute, "the fish grows rotten from the head," there is always corruption at the top, was a Rumanian proverb which crisply stated the basic social problem of modern Rumania: alone among our four countries it had, until the Communists took over, a really privileged ruling group, small in numbers but entrenched in wealth and power, utterly corrupt and indifferent to the welfare of the mass of the population. The members of this class were sometimes brilliantly able, but often cynical and devoted chiefly to the pursuit of their own pleasures. This social system Rumania inherited from its Turkish past and its former Greek rulers: the national historical experience produced this small group at one end of the social scale and the millions of poverty-stricken peasants at the other with almost nothing Rumanian in between.

3. Asians and Slavs

About 800 B.C. Chinese sources tell us of a people in Mongolia whom they call the Hsung-Nu, who increased their power and prestige over about a thousand years until the Chinese defeated them so completely that they determined to migrate to the west. They last appear in Chinese sources about the year A.D. 170; a little more than two hundred years later, we find a people called Huns on the southern steppes of Russia. The interim is dark and much disputed: had the Hsung-Nu spent the intervening two centuries crossing the vast expanse of Asia, before emerging into the orbit of the Byzantine historians, who know them as the Huns? Or were the Huns a completely different people? Whatever the answer, the Huns were the first of the Asiatics who began now to enter Europe in waves, and who spoke non-Indo-European languages of the so-called Ural-Altaic group, akin to modern Turkish.

Repeatedly, in the thousand years which followed the Hunnic attack on Europe, a new Asiatic people would rise to prominence somewhere in central Asia, and, pushed by the wish for conquest or by economic and political conditions on the steppe, would burst into Europe, often producing a serious disruption of population there. The vast fourth- and fifth-century movements of the Germanic peoples into the Roman Empire, which we call the barbarian invasions, were in some measure touched off by the Huns. Our descriptions of the Huns, of the Avars in the sixth century, of the Bulgars in the seventh, of the Magyars in the ninth, of the Pechenegs, Uzes, and Cumans in the eleventh and twelfth, and of the Mongols in the thirteenth, show that all these peoples had certain striking similarities. They were typical Asiatic nomads, generally Mongoloid in appearance, living in felt tents, eating meat and cheese, drinking milk and fermented drinks made from milk, and raiding far and wide on horseback. When we note that all these Asiatic peoples without exception flooded into Moldavia and Wallachia, and that other non-Asiatics did the same, it becomes easier to understand the "disappearance" from our sources of the harassed ancestors of the Rumanians.

Sometimes these Asiatic peoples established headquarters somewhere in Europe and kept less warlike peoples in servitude for a period, eventually to have their "Empires" disintegrate and disappear into the steppes of southern Russia, or beyond, back into central Asia, whence they came. This was true of the Huns, who were established in Hungary, and raided in all directions until a defeat suffered in France in 451, followed by the death of their leader Attila, led to their withdrawal. It was also true of the Huns' kinsmen, the Avars, later arrivals on the scene, who vanished after a defeat inflicted on them by Charlemagne in the late eighth century. This defeat disrupted the loosely knit "Empire" they had created, which had temporarily held most of the peoples of eastern Europe in thrall. Among the people so enslaved by the Avars were the Slavs.

North of the Carpathians and east of the Vistula, stretching east to the Dnieper, lies the area where, scholars think, the Indo-European-speaking Slavs had their original home. The name itself is something of a mystery, perhaps derived from a root meaning *speech* or *word,* but more likely from the name of a place whose whereabouts we no longer know. From this original home, the Slavs began slowly to disperse west, east, and south during the first century A.D.; from the westward migration have come the Poles, the Czechs, and the islands of Slavic population in eastern Germany; from the eastward migration the Russians, Ukrainians, and White Russians, and from the southward migration, the Slavs of the Balkans. Apparently the Slavs had begun to reach the basins of the Danube and the Sava as early as the second century; but their migration was slow and not a mass movement; it was not until the sixth century that the Slavs fully occupied the middle and lower Danube basins on both sides of the Carpathians. The Danube was the frontier of the east Roman or Byzantine Empire, and the Slavs begin now to appear in Byzantine sources.

The Byzantine historian Procopius, for example, tells us that the Slavs could not agree to be ruled by one man: "They have lived from of old under a democracy," he writes, "and consequently everything which involves their welfare, whether for good or ill, is referred to the people."[7] Procopius also reports that the Slavs worshiped forest and river spirits and a god of lightning, that they lived generally in widely separated miserable hovels, but that they were constantly changing their place of abode. This description seems to show that the Slavs in the sixth century were in a stage intermediate between nomadism and settled agricultural life. The entire area north of the Danube, so far as Procopius knew, was in their hands. This is the period when Slavic influence must have been actively affecting the Romanized Dacians, a period from which their country got many of its place-names and their basically Latin language many of the Slavic words which still appear in modern Rumanian.

Slavic migration southward toward and across the Danube frontier of the Byzantine Empire was not a sudden invasion of the kind which could be repelled in battle, but a slow and inexorable infiltration, which could be retarded by a consistent policy of frontier defenses, but which apparently could not be arrested, any more than the movement of a glacier. The Slavs seem not to have been a nation, but a group of scattered related tribes, often at odds with each other. They seem not to have attempted full-scale military campaigns or formal siege operations; they advanced irregularly. During the sixth century they crossed the Danube. Against them the Byzantines adopted a variety of defense measures, but the Slavs just kept on coming.

Istria and Illyria, the entire Adriatic littoral, all of the interior of the peninsula, and Greece itself were occupied by the Slavs during the seventh century, when they penetrated as far as the southernmost regions of Greece,

[7] Procopius, *History of the Wars,* VII, xiv, 22; tr. H. B. Dewing, (London and New York: Loeb Classical Library), IV, 269.

and even crossed over to Crete on raids. Slavic place-names in Greece testify to their presence; indeed they controlled Greece proper until roughly 800. In Greece, however, as in modern Rumania, the Slavs were absorbed by the native population. The Greek language survived, far less affected by Slavic occupation than the Rumanian. The Slavs did become the dominant people in the entire area of the Balkans now known as Yugoslavia (land of the south Slavs) and Bulgaria. Although the language spoken today in this region from the Adriatic to the Black Sea seems to change rather gradually as the modern traveler crosses the territory from west to east, the written language can be divided into three main groups, Slovenian, Serbo-Croat, and Bulgarian.

The Slovenes, whose language is clearly distinct from the others, inhabit the northwest corner of the peninsula; they were independent for about a century after 650; but were conquered first by the Avars, then by the Bavarians, and finally by Charlemagne in 778; and from then until the end of the First World War they remained under Teutonic domination, Frankish and later Austrian. In due course, they were converted to Christianity from the west, and became Roman Catholics, which they remain. Those who know the Slovenes best regard them as the least turbulent and volatile of the south Slav peoples. They were deeply affected by the cosmopolitan culture of the Habsburg Empire, and were certainly the most literate and well-read of all the south Slavic peoples. Since the conclusion of the peace treaty with Italy after World War II there were perhaps 1,400,000 Slovenes in Yugoslavia, with perhaps 100,000 still in Italy and 80,000 in Austria.

Even earlier than the arrival of the Slovenes, the Croats and Serbs, who speak substantially the same language, with slight dialectical differences, had made their appearance along the Adriatic coast. The Croats were associated with the Dalmatian littoral and with the region immediately southeast of Slovenia; here they, like the Slovenes, came under Frankish influence. Despite a period of independence in the tenth and eleventh centuries, the Croats eventually found their kingdom absorbed in 1102 by the rising power of the Hungarians. Thenceforward Croatia was a Hungarian province, with its own local governor, or Ban, with a certain legal and constitutional claim to theoretical independence, and with a privileged nobility. Much of Dalmatia was in dispute during those centuries between Hungary and Venice, but, despite the exercise of overlordship by both powers, the cities, especially Ragusa (Dubrovnik), retained municipal liberty. When the Hungarians were defeated by the Turks in 1526, the crown of Croatia became attached to the Habsburg dynasty. The Croats were Roman Catholic, and used the Latin alphabet to write their language.

They were separated from the Serbs by no very clear geographical line; indeed in the regions of Bosnia and Hertsegovina, where the peoples were inextricably mixed, religion was the only test of the difference between them, since the Serbs became converted to Christianity in its Orthodox form, officially accepting it in the thirteenth century from the Byzantine Patriarch then in residence in Asia Minor. They used the Cyrillic alphabet to write their language. In general, they occupied the region to the east and south of the Croats. The direction of the mountain ranges and of the river valleys impelled them toward expansion southward. In addition to the inhabitants of Serbia proper, the Montenegrins and all Orthodox inhabitants of Bosnia, Hertsegovina, and Croatia were counted as Serbs. Whether the Muslims were Serbs or Croats was hotly disputed.

South of the Serbs and west of the Bulgarians lived the Macedonian Slavs, speaking a dialect somewhere between Serbo-Croat and Bulgarian. It was impossible to make any sort of accurate general judgment as to their racial affinities or their national emotions. Torn by past political quarrels between Serb and Bulgar states, they still lived divided. The majority in 1955 inhabited "Vardar" Macedonia, now Tito's Federal Republic of Macedonia within Yugoslavia. Across the Bulgarian border, in the Pirin district, thousands more Macedonian Slavs lived under Bulgarian rule.

The easternmost Slavic people of the peninsula were the Bulgarians. We do not know by what special name the Slavs of this area may have called themselves in the period of the migration. Soon after their arrival in the peninsula, another of the fierce Mongoloid invading peoples from Asia, the Bulgars, crossed the Danube and conquered the Slavic people they found in residence. The land is still called Bulgaria after these Hunnic Bulgars, although they were absorbed by the Slavic substratum within two centuries of their arrival.

Actual evidence of the absorption survived. The ancient Bulgar language which, written in Greek letters, had at first been used in all inscriptions, fell out of use. Contemporary historians began to refer to the *Slavic* companions of the Bulgarian ruler; and the names of magnates were clearly Slavic. The Bulgarian aristocracy seems to have resented the efforts of their ruler, the Khan, to establish himself as supreme lord over them, since as nomads they were traditionally used to weaker forms of control. But the Khans actually created a Slavic aristocracy to serve as counterweight to the Bulgarians, and in this way hastened the assimilative process. It is clear that in sheer numbers the Slavic population was vastly greater than the Bulgarian.

The modern Bulgarians were thus a Slavic people, with a strain of Asiatic which they had long since thoroughly assimilated. Occasionally a traveler to Bulgaria might encounter a single completely Mongoloid-appearing individual, who spoke Bulgarian and was not a member of the Tartar or any other Asiatic minority group. It was, however, entirely unsafe to assume that such a person was a "throwback" to the ancient Bulgarians, in view of the fact that repeatedly during the middle ages the country was overrun by other Turkic peoples; and that Pecheneg or Cuman ancestry would be at least as good a guess. The inhabitants of one group of villages near Sofia, the so-called *Shopi,* were popularly supposed to be descendants of the Pechenegs. The modern Bulgarians were Orthodox Christians. Their conversion came earlier than that of any other

Slavic people, and constituted a landmark in the history of relations between the churches of the east and west.

These then were the Slavic peoples of the Balkans, who displaced and absorbed the original Illyrians (except for the Albanians) and the original Thracians (except for the Rumanians and Vlachs). The Slovenes, advanced and cultivated, were sometimes called the Czechs of Yugoslavia because of their diligence and talents. The Croats traditionally regarded themselves as highly civilized westerners, and tended to think of the Serbs as highly uncivilized easterners. The Serbs, on the other hand, ignoring the fact that the Croats were often in bitter opposition to alien misgovernment, traditionally scorned the Croats for their long period of subjection to the Hungarians. They affected to despise the highly vaunted Croatian culture, and pointed instead to their own Serb struggle against the Turks. Mutual suspicion and dislike between the two peoples poisoned the whole period between the wars, the first twenty years of Yugoslavia's national existence, and was crystallized in specific political and economic issues.

Yet both peoples, perhaps particularly the Serbs, impressed the foreigner as volatile, excitable, vivacious, violent, and deeply suspicious of the intentions of others, but often with a magnificent air of dignity and nobility. The Bulgarians seemed much quieter. Hardy, thrifty, strenuous, silent people, often dour, they were persistent and steady. "The Bulgarian will hunt the hare in an ox-cart," ran a proverb, "and catch him," a saying quite vivid to anybody who had seen the typical Balkan ox-cart, a lumbering creaking rig, drawn by a docile hulking beast and moving at a snail's pace down the road. Though slow to anger, the Bulgarians when aroused were hard to calm; their political history was full of dogged ruthlessness. They were as deadly earnest as the Rumanians were frivolous, and often carried their intensity to excess, especially in matters of bloody political revenge.

4. Minorities: Magyars, Germans, Jews, Turks

We have now made the acquaintance of all the principal peoples of our four Balkan countries: Albanians, Rumanians, Serbs, Croats, Slovenes, and Bulgarians, and have discovered when and under what circumstances each settled in its present home. We have also encountered the close relatives of the Rumanians, the Balkan Vlachs, and the close relatives of Bulgarians and Serbs, the Macedonian Slavs. The political frontiers between countries were lines chosen for strategic and economic and psychological reasons. They usually had to be drawn without full consideration to the ethnic origins of the people affected. Thus there were still Albanian and Rumanian minorities in Yugoslavia, and Serb and Croat minorities in Rumania. But in addition to these minorities in one country consisting of ethnic groups primarily associated with another country, there were substantial minority groups of non-Balkan peoples.

Of these the Magyars were certainly among the most important, numerically and historically. A people related to the Finns, the Magyars, when they first appear in our sources, were a tribe called the Ugri, living between the Volga and the Ural mountains. Speaking a Finno-Ugric (Uralic) language, somewhat influenced by Turkish tribes (Altaic), the Magyars invaded Europe late in the ninth century, and made their headquarters in the Hungarian plain, where they have ever since resided. Here in Hungary Germans and Slavs mingled with the Magyars, as did other Asiatics, including remnants of Huns and Avars. Christianized from Rome about the year 1000, the Magyars became the dominant people, and their language the dominant language in the area. In this respect the developments in Hungary contrasted sharply with those in Bulgaria, where, as we have seen, the Ural-Altaic tongue of the conquerors was ousted by the Indo-European tongue of the conquered. Indeed, if we except the Finns as indigenous and the Turks as peripheral to Europe, the Magyars were the only Asiatics who managed to maintain their language, surrounded as they were by Indo-European tongues. To the casual observer there was nothing "Asiatic" about the appearance of the modern Hungarian; the judgment of anthropologists, however, was that "Hungary fits into the racial boundaries of the countries which surround her, without sharp transitions; at the same time she provides a refuge in Europe for a minor central Asiatic survival." [8]

Early in their occupation of the great plain, the Magyars conquered Transylvania. They sent out one of their princes as governor, and planted colonists to hold the eastern frontier against other Asiatic intruders. These were called Szeklers (Siculi, Szekely, Secui) or frontiersmen. After the Mongolian invasions of the mid-thirteenth century, the Szeklers came to occupy the deepest bend of the Carpathians, the outermost easternmost curve of Transylvania.[9] Their descendants, Magyar-speaking, and in all respects Magyar, but slightly differentiated for having been dwellers in a frontier outpost since the early twelfth century, were still there in 1955, though their lands now lay in the heart of Rumania.

During the middle ages, the Magyars regarded the Szeklers as a privileged people. Traditionally, they were all noble; no Szekler was a serf, which distinguished them from all of the other inhabitants of medieval Hungary. Technically all Szeklers were exempt from taxation, although on special occasions they might be asked for a gift. Traces of class distinction, however, mostly economic, might be seen in the different types of military service for which individuals among them were held responsible. They held much of their land in common. Although feudal practices spread among the Szeklers in later years, these never took such deep root as among the Magyars. Down

[8] Coon, *The Races of Europe*, p. 586.

[9] I cannot accept the statement of later mediaeval Hungarian sources, which would make of the Szeklers descendants of Attila's Huns, or the views of certain scholars who regard them as Bulgarians settled in Transylvania before the Magyar conquest.

into modern times the Szeklers preserved a strong feeling of individuality and independence. Coupled with this went a dislike for their kinsmen, the Magyars, as well as for the other peoples of the province, notably the Rumanians.

After Transylvania was awarded to Rumania in 1920, the Rumanian government sent out Rumanian officials from the Old Kingdom to man the Szekler post offices, tax-collecting agencies, and other organs of government—officials most of whom did not speak the language of the people among whom they were serving, and whose conduct was often arrogant. For these officers the Szeklers had a name, which roughly and politely translated would mean "a-stinker-from-Bucharest." In August 1940, after twenty years of Rumanian government, Hungary was given northern Transylvania by Hitler in the Vienna Award; and the new boundary was so drawn as to give to Hungary the three administrative districts inhabited primarily by Szeklers. Instantly the Magyars took over the government, and sent their own officials out from Hungary. After a brief experience of these, the Szeklers, whose Magyar language is agglutinative, and adds elements to old words to form new ones, were discovered to have modified in this way their old term for an official. Politely translated the new word would mean "a-stinker-from-Bucharest-from-Budapest."

A small group of Szeklers, numbering about 20,000, lived until 1940 in northern Bukovina, where their ancestors had fled after a massacre in Transylvania in the eighteenth century. In 1940, when the area was taken over by the USSR, they were transferred to Hungary by agreement between Hungary and Rumania before the cession took place. During the war, they and other Magyars were briefly settled in the Yugoslav Bachka.

In addition to the Szeklers, whom all censuses count as Magyars, and who total perhaps 550,000 to 700,000, there were, in 1930, 600,000 to 800,000 other Magyars in Transylvania (including the Banat). Between the Magyar conquest in the eleventh century and 1920, the Magyar nobility were the lords of the land. Except for privileges granted to the Szeklers and Germans, all political power, together with complete exemption from taxation, belonged to the Magyar nobles; all financial burdens rested on the shoulders of the peasantry, always Magyar in part, but, during the last two centuries at least, Rumanian in majority. Traces of the Rumanians, whom the Magyars called Vlachs, appear in the sources as early as the thirteenth century. During the nineteenth and twentieth centuries, the non-privileged Rumanian majority, mostly peasant, fought to remove the political, cultural, economic, and religious disabilities which the Magyars had for centuries placed on them. But their aim was not accomplished until the annexation of the entire province by Rumania in 1920. Thereafter the Rumanians in their turn began to mistreat the Magyars. When Transylvania was divided in 1940, 160,000 Magyars left the southern portion, still in Rumania, and moved to the north, now in Hungary. Most of these were probably re-absorbed into Rumania in 1945, when northern Transylvania was restored. Thus the Magyar minority in Rumania was a remnant of a former ruling race, although most of its members in Transylvania in 1955 were, as the majority always was, peasants. The present Communist-dominated regime in Rumania, as we shall see, did its best to conciliate the Magyar minority.

In Yugoslavia too, the Magyar minority was a remnant of the people who formerly ruled over the territories where they now resided. There were still more than half a million of them, mostly in the Voyvodina, where they formed perhaps a quarter of the population. A couple of districts in the northern Bachka had a Magyar majority; as a whole the Bachka was about 35 per cent Magyar, the other portions of the Voyvodina considerably less. The Magyars were mostly peasants, whose ancestors settled in these regions during the nineteenth century. In addition, there were Magyars in Croatia, perhaps 60,000 in all, and about 25,000 in an adjacent part of Slovenia.

At its creation after World War I, Yugoslavia was bound by treaty to observe minority rights, but its government failed to do so. In the Voyvodina particularly, the Magyar language was discriminated against, and so were separate Magyar schools. It should be said in extenuation that the Magyars themselves had in the period of their dominance used language and schools as a weapon against their Slavic and Rumanian minorities, and had persistently and often brutally tried to enforce the universal use of Magyar. Under the circumstances it would have been superhuman forbearance on the part of the Yugoslavs or Rumanians to refrain from using the same weapons when their turn came. Many small Magyar peasants were thrown completely out of work by the Yugoslav agrarian reform laws of 1920, which divided up among the Yugoslav peasantry the large estates formerly owned by Magyar nobles. The Magyar peasant now had to rent land from the new proprietors, or become a member of a landless proletariat. Political and cultural discrimination were regularly practiced, as we shall see.

The Hungarian state during these years appeared to be far more interested in the bad treatment Magyars were allegedly receiving from Rumanians and Czechs than in their fate at the hand of the Yugoslavs. But in 1941, as allies of Hitler, the Hungarians annexed Bachka and Baranya in the Voyvodina, and small areas in Slovenia and Croatia. They committed numerous atrocities against the Serbs, including a savage massacre in the Voyvodina. Moreover, they expelled many Serbs, and settled the Bukovina Szeklers and other Magyar peasants in their place, including some moved from Croatia. These were withdrawn by the Hungarian government as the Russian armies advanced in 1944. The Yugoslavs reoccupied the regions, and were charged in their turn with having committed atrocities against the Magyar inhabitants. In September 1946 an agreement was concluded between the then friendly Stalinist governments of Yugoslavia and Hungary whereby 40,000 Magyars in Yugoslavia were to be exchanged for an equal number of Yugoslavs in Hungary. But hundreds of thousands of Magyars still lived in Yugoslavia in 1955, and remained a potential source of friction between Hungary and Yugoslavia.

Until the recent war, the second most important minority group in the Balkans was the Germans. Many fewer in numbers today, they had in the past played an important role in Rumania and Yugoslavia. In Rumania, the largest German groups were two: the so-called "Saxons" of Transylvania proper, numbering about a quarter of a million, and the so-called "Swabians" in the Banat, only a few thousand less in number. The "Saxons" (who did not come from Saxony) followed the Szeklers into the country in the twelfth century, and were invited for the same purpose: to guard the frontiers.[10] They were granted self-government under a Count of their own choice, and exemption from all tolls and dues in exchange for the payment of a certain fixed sum, collected among themselves. In this way, in the early thirteenth century, the Saxons became the third privileged "nation" of Transylvania alongside the Magyars and the Szeklers. After the Mongol invasions and the Szekler move into the Carpathian bend, the surplus German population settled the land the Szeklers had abandoned.

From then on until 1945 they were virtually free to develop the traditions and attitudes of a self-contained enclave, almost a state within a state. A highly exclusive group, they looked with disdain upon the other nationalities among whom they lived, particularly the Rumanians, whom they regarded as a lower order of human being. Rarely intermarrying with other groups, they kept their inheritance intact in the countryside through voluntary limitation of the size of their families; and became the most prosperous of the peasants in all Rumania. In the cities they came to the fore first as merchants and traders, and then as manufacturers. In such important towns as Brașov (Kronstadt) and Sibiu (Herrmannstadt, Nagyszeben) they owned most of the shops, banks, and factories; and ran their own newspapers. Converted to the Lutheran faith during the sixteenth century, they had their own churches, choral societies, bookshops, and associations sponsoring research into their own history.

The Banat "Swabians" were descendants of settlers colonized in the region by the Habsburgs in the eighteenth century. Vis-à-vis the Rumanian population, their position was not quite so well established as that of the "Saxons," but generally they too had the best rural farms and the best urban businesses. The "Swabians" were Roman Catholics.

In addition to these two main groups of Germans, there were in prewar Rumania more than 150,000 others in Bessarabia, Bukovina, and the Dobrudja. Most of those in Bessarabia and northern Bukovina were returned to Germany in 1940 after the USSR had annexed these areas, by agreement between Hitler and Stalin, during their period of alliance. Those in southern Bukovina and in

[10] For a brief period (1211–1225) the Teutonic Knights, a German crusading order, were granted by charter the entire southeast border of the country: the so-called Burzenland or Țara Bârsei, in the neighborhood of the city of Brașov (Kronstadt, Brasso, now Stalin) south of the Szeklers. The arrogance of the Knights proved too much for the Hungarian state, and they were expelled, but other Germans continued to flock into Transylvania and to settle there.

the Dobrudja were returned to Germany by terms of an agreement between the German and Rumanian governments.

Groups so compact and culturally self-conscious and with so strong a sense of national superiority as the Transylvania "Saxons" and Banat "Swabians," however, fell easy prey to the ideas of Hitler. During the thirties they became almost unanimously Nazi. Under pressure from Berlin, the Rumanian government granted them more and more privileges until they were in the position of enjoying all the benefits of citizenship but sharing none of the responsibilities. When the German armies passed through Transylvania on their way east, the "Saxons" gave them a memorable welcome: 73,000 "Saxon" men joined the Nazi SS troops instead of the Rumanian armies; in Sibiu alone, it was reported in 1944, three hundred girls proudly had illegitimate children by German soldiers.

When the German armies retreated through Transylvania on their way west in 1944, perhaps 200,000 "Saxons" and "Swabians" left Rumania with them. As late as December 1944, however, after the Russian armies had overrun Transylvania and the first great fear of them had evaporated, many of the "Saxons" continued to live on in an unreal world, convinced that Hitler could not lose the war. At that date they could still be visited in Sibiu, for instance, in their large and handsome city-houses, some of the most luxurious built in the style of Hitler's own Berghof at Berchtesgaden, and richly furnished in the taste of the German bourgeoisie, looking out at the Carpathians through great panes of plate glass. Here, while their cities were actually under Soviet occupation, they dispensed coffee and cake to the first American officers to visit the area, and complained that some of their extra automobiles had been requisitioned by the authorities.

Only a few weeks later the Soviet military moved against these "Saxons"; together with the "Swabians" they were singled out for punishment. All males between the ages of seventeen and forty-five and females between eighteen and thirty who did not have children under one year of age were simply deported in trains to an unknown destination. The total number of those affected was estimated at 70,000. It is known that large numbers were sent to the Don Basin to work in the coal mines; a few, the ill or the pregnant, have returned, and have told what they dared about the hardships of the life. After the deportations came property confiscations. These gravely upset the economy of the entire region because the Germans had key positions and a degree of technical skill possessed by no other element in the population. Many of the farms, carefully tended for centuries by the frugal Germans, were turned over to Gypsies and other members of the landless proletariat who could not and would not farm them properly.

The Rumanian government of the time, not yet completely controlled by the Soviet Union, although only about a month of grace yet remained to it, protested against this act of the occupying power. The protest was not based on any wish to be soft with the Germans, for whose pro-Nazi behavior many Rumanians had only contempt; it was based on the illegality of the Russian act and the precedent set. If Soviet officers could deport any one group of Rumanian citizens there was nothing to stop them from deporting any other group. At the time, the Rumanians still cherished the hope that they would not be completely dominated by the USSR; the hope was doomed to early disappointment. The protest was rejected by the Russian authorities, as was the parallel action of the American and British members of the Allied Control Commission. The Russians pretended to think that all such protests reflected pro-German or pro-Nazi sentiments on the part of the Rumanians, Americans, or Britons who sponsored them. In May 1947 the Rumanian government, by now completely in the Russian orbit, began further expulsions of Germans to Austria and Germany. But there were still almost half a million in Rumania in 1955.

In Yugoslavia before the war there were about 570,000 Germans, of whom the largest group (300,000) lived in the Voyvodina across the line from the Swabians of the Rumanian Banat. Like the Swabians, they were descendants of the colonies planted by the Habsburgs during the eighteenth century. They lived mostly in their own villages and were, as everywhere, the most prosperous elements in the community. The fringes of this Voyvodina settlement overlapped into Croatia-Slavonia and Srem, where there were about 150,000 Germans. The other main groups were in Slovenia, where the city of Maribor was heavily German, as were certain other towns, and where the concentration was mostly urban, totaling about 30,000, and in Bosnia (15,000), where they were peasants.

Between the wars, the Germans, like the Magyars, at first experienced discrimination with regard to schools, and to the securing of adequate political representation. Pressure from Germany procured the German "Volksgruppe" numerous privileges especially in the Voyvodina; in Slovenia the Germans were severely restrained in the towns, their parent country, Austria, not protesting.

When Germany occupied Yugoslavia, the Germans annexed all of northern Slovenia and ruthlessly persecuted the Slovene population. Meanwhile, the Banat, in which most of the German minority was concentrated, was made a virtually autonomous administrative unit under German military control, in which the *Volksdeutsch* controlled the administration entirely. Inside the newly founded Axis puppet-state of Croatia the rest of the Germans (170,000) became a specially privileged group, except for about 20,000 who had been living in isolated communities in Bosnia, which was made part of the Croatian state. These Germans, who had been recent immigrants, were sent back to Germany by agreement.

After reoccupying all their prewar territory in 1944 and 1945, the Yugoslavs expelled those Germans who had not already fled. Perhaps 250,000 left with the German armies; about 100,000 more were sent to the USSR for forced labor; the remainder began to be ousted in 1947. The German minority in

Yugoslavia thus virtually disappeared. Into the German farms in the richly productive Voyvodina, thus made available for settlement, colonists were brought from the deficit areas of the country, with bad results for the economy, as we shall see.

The Jewish minority in the Balkans before World War II was numerous only in Rumania, where it numbered approximately 800,000 or well over 5 per cent of the population. Some families had lived in the country for centuries, but the majority were immigrants from Poland who came into Rumania during the nineteenth century, and in a new wave of immigration after the First World War. As in Poland and Russia, Jews could not become landowners in Rumania, and therefore tended to settle in the cities. By 1848 at least half the population of Iași, for example, was already Jewish. The Jews were often successful in commerce, and they cared deeply for education, sending their children, where at all possible, into the universities, and giving them professional training. As a result, they occupied posts in journalism, in finance, in law, and in medicine out of proportion to their numerical percentage of the population. In the countryside, especially in Moldavia, they often became proprietors of the village tavern, and sold liquor and loaned money to the peasants. The rates they charged were often usurious. They also gradually assumed the position of middlemen between the landlord and his peasants. As in other parts of Eastern Europe, their success in fields into which the native population lacked the energy, the training, or the imagination to enter created strong anti-Semitic prejudice against them both among Rumanian intellectuals and among the population at large.

The problem of Rumanian discrimination against the Jews was one which had attracted the attention of the powers ever since the Rumanians won first autonomy and then independence in the nineteenth century. The first Rumanian Constitution of 1866 made it illegal for foreign Jews to obtain Rumanian citizenship, a provision designed to prevent their becoming the majority in large areas of Moldavia. Western European Jews enlisted the authorities in France and England and Germany against this, and the Congress of Berlin in 1878 required that the Rumanians admit Jews to citizenship and its privileges as the price for independence. The Rumanians bitterly resented this measure, and managed to evade its full consequences. Hatred of the Jews was a strong part of Rumanian life at every level: for example, the major peasant uprising of 1907 began with anti-Semitic outrages. The acquisition of Transylvania brought in more tens of thousands of Jews, most of whom, moreover, were patriotic pro-Magyars. Organized political anti-Semitism emerged strongly in Rumania during the 1920's and especially after the depression, when it was further stimulated by Hitler's success, and during the Second World War it became national policy. Most of the 372,000 Rumanian Jews who survived deportation and massacre, therefore, had strong Zionist leanings.

The Communists, who very soon succeeded the pro-Nazis as rulers of Rumania, hated and fought Zionism for political reasons.

In Yugoslavia before the war there were about 80,000 Jews, settled chiefly in Belgrade, Sarayevo, and Zagreb. Most of them were of Spanish or Portuguese (Sephardic) origins, and their families had lived in these cities for centuries. Except for the doctrinaire Croatian extreme nationalists, there was little anti-Semitism in the country. But the war brought German occupation, and the supremacy of these Croatian anti-Semites. As a result, the Yugoslav Jews experienced the horrors of deportation and extermination. Only about 14,000 survived the war, and in 1948–49 more than half of these left to settle in Israel. By 1955 there were perhaps 6,000 Jews left in the country, living in their old centers, but hardly enough to continue the traditional community life. Yugoslav policy permitted emigration, and extended to any Jews who chose to remain religious toleration within the framework of the Tito regime's religious laws.

In Bulgaria, the Jewish minority before World War II numbered only 47,000. Anti-Semitism was never a public issue, and despite German pressure and the maintenance of the German alliance, the Bulgarian authorities never permitted Jewish deportations to the extermination camps. The Jews survived the war, but virtually all of them left for Israel in the years immediately afterwards. In Albania, there were only a few scattered Jews at any time.

The only other minority of any size in the Balkan countries was the Turkish, which was distinguished from the native Muslims. There were almost 600,000 in Bulgaria before 1940, when about 150,000 more were added by the acquisition of the southern Dobrudja from Rumania. The treatment of the Turks raised important political questions in the postwar period, and these will be considered in Chapter 13 below. In Yugoslavia, there were about 175,000 Turks living in Macedonia, chiefly east of the Vardar. They presented no particular social or political problem. In Rumania, the cession of the southern Dobrudja removed all but a few thousand Turks.[11]

In the Balkan world of 1955, the minority problems had lost some of their old importance as a result of the adoption of Soviet nationality policies toward those minorities who remained. But old antagonisms did not die down, and in the Communist persecution of Jews in Rumania and of Turks in Bulgaria one could see the old story repeating itself. Moreover, after Tito's expulsion

[11] For completeness, we should note the presence of smaller minorities in all the countries. These were Gypsies (perhaps 200,000 in Rumania, 140,000 in Bulgaria, and a few thousand in Yugoslavia), Czechs and Slovaks (more than 150,000 in Yugoslavia), Ukrainians (a few thousand remaining in Rumania since the cession of Bessarabia and northern Bukovina, 40,000 in Yugoslavia), Armenians (perhaps 30,000 each in Rumania and Bulgaria), and smaller numbers of Greeks and Tartars in Rumania and Bulgaria, and of Russians in all three countries. But the presence of the smaller minority groups should not lead the observer to conclude that the Balkans were a kind of ethnographic zoo. In the past, the Magyars, Germans, and Jews had provided the most important minority problems in three of our countries, in addition to those provided by the Albanians in Yugoslavia, and the Macedonian Slavs in Yugoslavia and Bulgaria.

from the Cominform, every one of his Stalinist neighbors—Albanians, Bulgarians, Rumanians, and Hungarians—used the minority question as a form of political warfare. Kossovo, Macedonia, the Banat, and the Bachka again became for a while almost as sensitive as they had been in the old days of rampant nationalism. One could not understand Balkan affairs past or present without a close acquaintance with the minorities and their traditions.

Chapter 4

THE LEGACY OF DEAD EMPIRES: FROM THE FOURTH CENTURY TO THE EIGHTEENTH

1. Byzantium

ON THE ELEVENTH OF MAY IN THE YEAR A.D. 330, the Roman Emperor Constantine dedicated the Greek city of Byzantium as the new capital of the Roman Empire. From then on, for eleven hundred years and more, the city was Constantine's city, Constantinople. His act was a dramatic abandonment, even a repudiation, of the old capital, pagan Rome. The new Christian city was to become the very symbol of the new faith. By the time the first of the Slavic invaders had begun to infiltrate the Balkan peninsula, Greek was displacing Latin as the official language of the eastern Roman Empire. But the Greeks of Byzantium never forgot that they were lords of the Roman inheritance. They called themselves Romans, and their empire the Roman Empire. Indeed their rulers, down to 1453, when the Turks finally put an end to Byzantium, were the direct successors of Augustus, and their capital was "new Rome." While the Germanic barbarians were deflected away from the new Rome on the Bosporus, they fell in all their force upon the lands of the old Rome in the west. The western Empire decayed and disintegrated; the Empire in the east stood fast.

From Rome, Byzantium inherited the prestige of empire, and the pretensions to world-power. Though its frontiers might fluctuate, and though provinces might be lost, the Byzantine Empire considered itself "ecumenical," the legitimate ruler over the whole inhabited world. From the ancient orient and the Hellenistic states the Roman Empire took many of the external trappings of absolutism, gilding the Emperor's hair, approaching him with extraordinary abasement and great ceremony, and elevating him to godhood. After Constantine had been converted to Christianity, the Emperor was no longer God, of course, but he was still the anointed of God on earth. Christianity added its own luster to his extraordinary powers and pretensions: the Emperor, crowned in Santa Sophia by the highest dignitary of the Orthodox Church, the Patriarch, made a solemn promise to defend the Christian faith.

His divinely awarded powers entailed immense earthly responsibilities. The only recourse against an unworthy emperor was rebellion and deposition. Though an individual emperor might be, and at Byzantium often was, overthrown by conspiracy, autocracy as an institution was not challenged.

Compassed round by a code of etiquette so rigid and complex that it governed every waking moment of the year, responsible for all law and justice, master of his subjects, who were all literally his "slaves," resident of a "sacred palace" which was the nerve-center of the state, the Emperor was also "equal to the apostles," pronouncing on matters of doctrine, giving the decisions of churchmen the force of law, and taking the initiative for the reform of the church. In old Rome, the absence of an emperor permitted the bishop of the town to assert temporal as well as spiritual power, and, in short, to become Pope. In new Rome, no Pope could arise to dispute the temporal sword, and even the spiritual sword was wielded by the Emperor and Patriarch together. When the Emperor went to battle, he went as the champion of the faith, protected by an icon of the Virgin.

This ideology and political behavior had a splendid house. Byzantium, washed by the Sea of Marmora and the Golden Horn, was defended on the land side by a massive series of walls and ditches, with great towers every few feet, constantly improved and kept in repair by the emperors. It became the symbol of impregnability, as wave after wave of invaders broke against its defenses. Not until 1204 were they breached, and by then the internal political and economic structure was far gone in decay. For almost nine hundred years the walls held fast. But the defender of Europe against the barbarian was also the great market for the world. Grain, salt, wine, furs, hides, and slaves from the countries around the shores of the Black Sea and from the Caucasus; spices, jewels, silk from the east; ivory and slaves from Africa poured into the city, and were sold there to merchants from the west. The emperors maintained a monopoly over the manufacture of silk and of purple dye and gold embroidery. Their gold coinage remained standard and stable for seven hundred years. Their revenues were enormous, their taxation system elaborate and efficient. Byzantium glowed with marbles and mosaics, cloth of gold and precious stones, its magnificent churches were redolent of incense. Its economic power matched its political claims, and its physical beauty and strength suited well with both.

BYZANTIUM AND THE BULGARIANS

The weight of the tradition of Rome and of the east, the power of army and navy, the skill of diplomacy, the great absorptive power of the Greek genius, and the glitter of external show made Byzantium "the city" to all barbarians who came within its orbit. In the Balkans, the most important of these were the Bulgarians, who had now conquered the Slavs north of the Balkans, and had founded a state of their own. In 811 the Bulgarian ruler, Khan Krum, defeated the Byzantine Emperor Nicephorus I, killed him in battle, took his skull, and had it hollowed out and lined with silver to use as a drinking cup. Nicephorus was the first Roman Emperor to die in battle since the year 378. Krum's people still lived in huts, sacrificed horses and dogs to the sun and moon, and led a thoroughly primitive life. But their leaders were clever men, who realized that they would have to become converted to Christianity if they wished to advance the cause of their state.

Though they were dazzled by Byzantium, they feared its power, and tried at first to negotiate with the distant Roman Catholic Germans and with the papacy. In the end, however, Byzantium won the competition to convert the Bulgarians. It was nearer than Rome and better able to exert military pressure. More important, the Bulgarians knew all about Byzantine magnificence and power, while Rome was distant and had less magic. Finally, the Byzantines did not insist on the use of Greek in the liturgy, while the Roman Church required Latin. Indeed, a pair of Byzantine missionaries had already invented a Slavic alphabet for use in translating the holy books into Slavic for the Moravians, ancestors of the Czechs of today. One of their pupils, St. Clement, brought the alphabet and Christian teaching in Slavic to Bulgaria, which in the 860's became converted to Orthodox Christianity from Byzantium.

The conversion of the Bulgarians to Orthodoxy did not mean that friendly relations were to obtain between Byzantium and Bulgaria. Indeed, the conversion whetted the appetites of the Bulgarian rulers for more power and prestige. What they sought was nothing less than the imperial title, and the national patriarchate which went with it, because "without a Patriarch a ruler is no Emperor." Under Tsar (Caesar) Simeon, himself the product of a Byzantine education, there began a bitter war, lasting about a century, down to 1018, during which the Bulgarians tried to establish themselves as emperors in Constantinople itself. At one moment during the conflict, the Byzantines gave one of the Bulgarian rulers a Byzantine princess in marriage, and granted him what he thought to be an imperial title, but with reservations, since in the official Byzantine view the Byzantine Emperor was the only true one.

Toward the end of the tenth century, the center of Bulgarian power shifted from the banks of the Danube far to the west, to Macedonia around Lakes Prespa and Ohrid. Ohrid was the site of the Bulgarian Patriarchate. From this region, the Bulgarian ruler Samuel sent out a great expedition against the Byzantines, whose Emperor Basil II, in 1014, captured about 15,000 Bulgarian prisoners, blinded ninety-nine of every hundred, and allowed the hundredth man to keep the sight of one eye, to lead the others back to Bulgaria. Samuel fell dead at the horrid sight of his blinded warriors. Basil II took the appropriate title of the "Bulgar-slayer," by which the Greeks still affectionately remember him. The great war was over soon afterwards. From 1018, Byzantium ruled Bulgaria as a conquered province for a period of almost two centuries. Despite an occasional revolt, the Bulgarians made no new successful effort to gain independence until 1186.

Then a "second" Bulgarian Empire grew up as the result of a determined attack on the Byzantines led by the Vlach element, which had long since been gaining in numbers in Bulgaria. Once again, there was a flirtation with Rome, which failed because of the papal demands on the Bulgarians; once again, the native rulers assumed an imperial title, and created their own patriarchate. But by now, the glories of Byzantium had shrunk. The throne of Constantinople had become a prize in a prolonged and bitter struggle between the landed aristocracy of Asia Minor and the imperial civil servants. The constant warfare had helped sap the military and economic strength of the state. And the conflict between Byzantium and the Roman Catholic west had become ever more acute.

BYZANTIUM AND THE ROMAN CATHOLIC WEST

As early as the eighth century, the Byzantine emperors and the popes had quarreled fiercely over the south Italian lands and the Balkan provinces. The popes had decided that the defense of Italy against Muslims and Lombards would be more effective if entrusted to the Christianized German Franks, on whose representative, Charlemagne, they conferred in 800 the title of Roman Emperor. Though the Roman Church and the Church of Constantinople differed on some points of doctrine and ritual, these differences might never have been noticed and would surely not have led to schism had it not been for the political questions at issue. During the dispute over who would convert the Bulgarians, the Pope excommunicated the Byzantine Patriarch for refusing to return the Balkan region to papal jurisdiction. When a series of weak popes allowed the prestige of the papacy to decline in the tenth century, the Byzantines became used to ignoring Rome. When a vigorous church reform movement restored papal strength in the eleventh century, the Byzantines did not properly estimate the transformation. The reformed papacy allied itself with the Norman invaders of southern Italy, who captured the region from the Byzantines, and restored papal authority there. This situation, coupled with the doctrinal disputes, led to a schism in 1054 between the Roman Catholic and Orthodox churches, a schism which, with only the briefest and most artificial interludes of reunion, has lasted into our own day.

Meanwhile, the westerners, or "Latins," had come to know and dislike the Byzantine Greeks, whom they regarded as effeminate and treacherous. The Greeks for their part regarded the Latins as savage, fickle, and violent. This mutual dislike swelled to a furious pitch during the eleventh and twelfth centuries, as the Italian city-states, especially Venice, took over more and more of the commerce of Byzantium in exchange for naval assistance to the emperors, beset by Normans and by Turks. The influence of the hated Latins penetrated deeply into the Byzantine Empire; local anarchy became the rule; and finally, in 1204, a crusading expedition in Venetian ships captured Constantinople, set up a Latin Empire there, and drove the Greeks into exile. The Latins fanned out, took most of Greece and the islands of the Aegean, and imported the western feudal way of life, which had already made considerable headway on Greek soil.

The ousted Greeks returned across the Straits from Asia Minor in 1261, only fifty-seven years later, and in turn drove the Latins from Constantinople, re-establishing there a Byzantine Empire which lasted down to 1453. The success of the Greeks was partly owing to papal loss of interest in the Latin Empire, which had proved able neither to heal the schism with the Orthodox church nor to serve as the base for a successful crusade against the Muslims. The Greeks also owed something to the assistance of the Genoese, deadly rivals of Venice. The restored Byzantine Empire, though the scene of a remarkable cultural and artistic flowering, was in its last two centuries only another small Balkan state. Civil wars raged between rival claimants to the Byzantine throne. The Latins clung to much of Greece. Bulgarians and Serbs maintained their own kingdoms in the Balkans. But despite their new weakness, the Byzantines maintained their pretensions to world-power. And such was the prestige which they had accumulated over the centuries that their Balkan neighbors largely accepted their own image of their empire.

BYZANTIUM AND THE SERBS

This was demonstrated by the Serbs, who now rose in their turn to create a powerful state of their own. In the early thirteenth century, the Serbs repeated the earlier performance of the Bulgarians: a preliminary flirtation with Rome, but subsequent acceptance of Orthodox Christianity from the Byzantines, who permitted the Slavic liturgy and authorized an autonomous Serbian Patriarchate. In the mid-fourteenth century, the greatest of the mediaeval Serbian rulers, Stephen Dushan, crowned himself Emperor of the Serbs *and the Romans,* and was quite possibly on the verge of capturing Constantinople, when he suddenly died in 1355. Though his Empire did not cohere after his death, his ancestors and he had expanded from Serbia and overrun much of Macedonia and western Bulgaria. Thus three times in the middle ages, the native Balkan peoples paid the Byzantine Empire the supreme compliment of imitation; *the* city and the things it stood for exercised just as compelling an attraction over the Serbs in the fourteenth century as they had over the Bulgarians in the ninth.

From Dushan's celebrated law-code and other sources, we know a good deal more about mediaeval Serbian society than about mediaeval Bulgarian society. Serbian agriculture flourished, and the Serbs exported their flour. Moreover, their mines, known since Roman times, were once again exploited, and some German colonists were imported to help produce the gold, silver, copper, and tin which made the country and its rulers rich. Their wealth enabled the Serbian rulers to hire mercenary soldiers to supplement their own military manpower. Great churches and monasteries arose on Serbian soil, adorned with magnificent frescoes, executed under Byzantine influence, but displaying extraordinary native talent and originality. But it was still a simple rural society, in which the king was little more than the superior tribal chieftain, and in which the powers of both the local chieftains and the king himself were limited by assemblies, in which the nobles, clergy, and delegates of the people met to consider pressing problems. On the land, the large patriarchal household, or *zadruga,* in which whole families of relatives shared a homestead and coöperated in the fields, was the rule. Its members accepted the authority of the eldest male, the "father" of them all, but voiced their own opinions freely.

The mediaeval Balkan empires left behind a legacy of fierce pride in the modern Bulgarians and Serbs. In the nineteenth century, when national sentiment awoke in the Balkan peoples after some centuries of subjugation to the Turks, the achievements of these remote ancestors aroused compelling interest. Unfortunately, Stephen Dushan had ruled for the Serbs in the fourteenth century much of the same land which Samuel had ruled for the Bulgarians in the eleventh. Thus the new nationalists, claiming the frontiers of their mediaeval predecessors, found themselves in hopeless conflict over Macedonia. Similarly, the Greeks could claim virtually all of the Balkan peninsula as a former part of Byzantine territory. The impelling drive of these sentiments must not be overemphasized; but it also should not be forgotten. To peoples starved of history, suddenly conscious of national identity, trying to acquire heroic traditions, the deeds of princes long since dead assumed enormous importance. Joan of Arc, Queen Elizabeth I, George Washington still aroused emotions in French, English, and American hearts. But they had never been forgotten, and their nations had enjoyed a continuous national history. It was the very fact that Samuel and Dushan had been forgotten, and then discovered anew by peoples whose national history had been interrupted, that helped lend such violence to Balkan national rivalries.

2. *The Ottoman Empire*

Byzantium exercised its powers of attraction not only on the Balkan peoples but also on the Turks of Asia Minor, across the Straits. There, the Seljuk Turkish state, established in the eleventh century, was disintegrating, and the luckiest and ablest of its heirs were the Osmanli or Ottoman Turks, called after their leader, Osman, who died in 1326. Moving westward in Asia Minor, the Ottoman Turks settled in the province of Bithynia, immediately across the Straits from Constantinople, which had served as the base for the Greek reconquest of 1261. Economic and political unrest, the result of Byzantine neglect, led the discontented Greek population of the region gradually to turn to the Turks, whose Muslim creed was at the time not fanatical. Popular Islam and popular Christianity had much in common. When a city was taken, the Christian population either paid a tax or was converted. By 1337, the cities of Bithynia were Ottoman; the population was becoming a Greek-Turkish amalgam; and the Turks were learning settled ways and Byzantine administrative practice from the Greeks. In the 1340's, one of the parties to the rivalry for the Byzantine throne invited the Turks into Europe as mercenaries. In the early 1350's, they obtained a European base, and not long afterwards their conquest of the Balkans began.

Leaving Byzantium with its walls behind their lines, they took Adrianople in 1361. They made this Thracian city their capital in 1365, transferring from Brusa in Asia Minor, and becoming primarily a European state. The Byzantine Emperor did homage to them, and they pushed on into Bulgaria, winning a decisive battle in 1371. They campaigned successfully in Macedonia in the 1370's, taking Sofia in 1385 and Tirnovo itself in 1393, and so put an end to Bulgarian independence until 1878, and to the Bulgarian patriarchate until 1953. Nish fell in 1386, and the Ottoman Turks now defeated the Serbs in the celebrated battle of Kossovo at the end of June 1389.

This proved to be the decisive battle of Serbian history. The Serb ruler, Prince Lazar, who had already done homage to the Turks, had decided to rebel against them, because the Turkish Sultan, Murad, had executed some Serbian soldiers whom Lazar had sent him. What actually happened on the battlefield is in some ways still obscure. We know that both Lazar and Sultan Murad were killed, but we cannot be certain precisely under what circumstances.[1] The Serbs have always celebrated the defeat as their national holiday, on June 28, St. Vitus' day, Vidovdan. Around the battle there grew up a large tradition of oral folk-poetry, dramatic and moving. The singer told how St. Elias, in the form of a falcon, offered Lazar his choice between an earthly and a heavenly kingdom. If he should choose the earthly kingdom, he would defeat the Turks. If he should choose the heavenly kingdom, he would be defeated, but should build a church as token of his future salvation. He chose a heavenly kingdom, and was killed. The singer thus consoled his listeners for the centuries of servitude under the Turks by reminding them that spiritual values were superior to material values. This transformed the disgrace into a triumph. The Kossovo-mystique was to become a fundamentally important part of Serbian national psychology.

THE FALL OF CONSTANTINOPLE; THE TURKISH ADVANCE IN EUROPE

After Kossovo came a halt in the Ottoman conquest of the Balkans, as operations in Asia claimed the attention of the new Sultan, and the Turks repelled a crusade from the west. In 1402, a Tartar conqueror, Timur or Tamerlane, inflicted a severe setback upon the Turks, and delayed their further

[1] The folklore which tells of treachery on the part of Lazar's son-in-law, Vuk Brankovich, cannot be substantiated. At the time, there was even some doubt who had won, because both commanders were dead, and the King of Bosnia, Tvrtko, an ally of the Serbs, claimed that the Turks had been defeated. His letters claiming a Christian victory started celebrations in Florence and Paris, where the Italians and French were watching Turkish progress westward with alarm. Actually, though the Turks did not impose immediate full-scale occupation upon the Serbs, the battle was a Turkish victory.

progress for a good many years. But the inability of eastern and western Christians to unite in the face of the Turkish onslaught made the eventual outcome certain. It was not military or economic incapacity alone that prevented such an alliance, but the legacy of hatred left from the Latin conquest of Constantinople that led many Byzantines to prefer the Turks to the hated westerner. In 1453, the Ottoman Turks under Mohammed II, the Conqueror (Mehmet Fatih), took Constantinople itself after a celebrated siege. The last Byzantine Emperor, Constantine XI, perished in the fight.

Mohammed II took up once again the conquest of the Balkans. He put an end to the autonomous status of Serbia in 1459, though the Hungarians were able to deny him the possession of Belgrade itself. The Orthodox population of the Serbian fortress-capital at Smederevo on the Danube opened the gates to the Turks rather than accept a Roman Catholic ruler. The old religious division among the Christians continued to contribute to Ottoman success.

There followed the turn of Bosnia. Here, in a land torn by civil war, the religious situation was unique. A substantial proportion of the population belonged to a heretical church, called Bogomil or Patarene. Bogomilism was the lineal descendant both of a heresy which had arisen in early Christianity, the Gnostic, and of the dualist religion of the Manichaeans, followers of Mani, who in the third and fourth centuries had competed with the Christians in the Mediterranean world. From Asia Minor, the doctrine passed to Thrace, Bulgaria, Bosnia, northern Italy, and southern France. Essentially an effort to explain the existence of evil in a world made by a good God, Bogomilism taught that the devil had created man's body. Its adherents preached asceticism, and repudiated the Christian sacraments. In Bosnia, battleground between Orthodox Serbs and Roman Catholic Hungarians, where each sect persecuted the other, many of the nobles adopted Bogomilism as a badge of patriotism.

In the 1440's, a Bogomil, King of Bosnia, elected by the magnates, turned Roman Catholic in order to get help from the papacy against the advancing Turks. The Bogomil population deeply resented his change of faith, and did not resist the Turks, who conquered the province in 1463, and twenty years later subdued Hertsegovina as well. Finding that the Turks regarded them as Christians like the Orthodox or Catholics, and that conversion to Islam was the only way to keep their estates, most of the Bogomil nobles seem to have become converts to the Muslim faith. Islam had some tenets which were not unlike those of Bogomilism; conversion brought great economic advantage; and Bogomilism had in any case been an expression of Bosnian nationalism. Now that the patriots no longer had a country of their own to defend, and could still keep on fighting the Roman Church, conversion to Islam was not difficult. Whatever the reason, the two provinces became largely Muslim, and the native Slavic nobles kept their lands.

Bosnia and Hertsegovina thus presented a picture strikingly different from that in the rest of the Balkan area so far conquered by the Turks, where the Christians kept their religion, and the conquerors displaced the native aristocracy and reduced all of the natives to the same level. Down until modern times, Bosnia and Hertsegovina had a native aristocracy, ethnically and linguistically little different from the Serbs or Croats across the border, but Muslim in religion, and holding on to their lands, worked for them largely by their fellow-Slavs who had remained Christian. The Serbs and Bulgarians remained Orthodox, and their aristocracy lost its lands and disappeared as a class. The Croats, whose territory the Turks never occupied, remained Catholic, but under Magyar domination, and had an aristocracy largely Magyar or Magyarized. But in Bosnia and Hertsegovina today there are about 900,000 Slavic Muslims, more than 40 per cent of the population of the area, the descendants of those who turned Muslim in the fifteenth century, in all probability mostly from Bogomilism.

After Bosnia, the Turks moved against Albania, where for some years they met with the determined resistance of George Castriota or Skanderbeg, the Albanian national hero. Educated at the Sultan's court, Skanderbeg turned against the Turks, created a league of Albanian chieftains against them, received subsidies from south Italian and Venetian governments, and won the epithet from the Pope of "athlete and battler for the Christian name." After his death in 1467, his league fell apart, and the Turkish conquest of Albania followed. Meanwhile, the Turks had also driven the last heirs of Byzantium and the last Latin rulers from the mainland of Greece, and from many of the islands. They had also begun the battle against the Christian princes of Wallachia and Moldavia, north of the Danube, two principalities which had come into existence in the fourteenth century, partly as a result of Rumanian migration from Transylvania under pressure from the Catholic Magyars. Here the national hero, who stood off the Turks for almost fifty years, was Stephen the Great of Moldavia (1457–1504). He raised a free peasant militia, and with it succeeded in holding the line of the Danube against the Turks. When Mohammed II died in 1481, all of our four Balkan countries except for Rumania, Montenegro, portions of northern Bosnia then under Hungary, the city of Belgrade, and the other Hungarian lands in Croatia and Dalmatia, had fallen to the Turks.

After Stephen died, his successors acknowledged Turkish overlordship, and the Danubian principalities, though never occupied in force by the Turks, none the less became part of their empire. But it was the great Sultan Suleiman the Magnificent (1520–1566) who, after an interval of expansion in Asia and the conquest of Egypt, pushed the European advance still farther, taking Belgrade in 1521, and crossing the Danube into Hungary. He defeated the Magyars at Mohacs in 1526, took Buda, and besieged but failed to take Vienna itself. He obtained recognition as ruler of most of Hungary, and this proved to mark the extreme outpost of Turkish advance.

OTTOMAN INSTITUTIONS

The institutions of the Ottoman Empire and the statecraft by which its fabric was held together were a complex amalgam, to which the theocratic traditions of Islam, the ancient central Asian tribal concepts of an elective kingship, and the Persian concept of a divine hereditary monarchy all made their contribution. Since the Persian tradition had also influenced Byzantium, it is hard to say, when confronted with similarities between Ottoman and Byzantine practices, whether the Turks were borrowing from the Byzantines or whether both had borrowed from the Persians. At any rate, the Turkish autocracy, with the autocrat immured in the sacred palace, living a life governed by rigorous protocol, surrounded by eunuchs, regarding all his subjects as his slaves, and decked out with all the splendid external trappings of God's agent on earth, the one true monarch in the world, resembled its Byzantine predecessor. In the Ottoman system of military land-holdings, scholars saw an outgrowth of a Byzantine prototype. The relationship between the Sultan and the Sheikh-ul-Islam, head of the Muslim men of the faith, was closely comparable to the relationship between the Byzantine Emperor and the Patriarch. The "capitulations" or trade treaties with the western European states of which the first was signed in 1536 with France, gave the westerners commercial privileges closely resembling those which the Byzantines had once extended to Venice and Genoa. Towards all foreigners, moreover, the Sultans preserved the attitude of complete superiority to barbarians which had characterized the Byzantines. They adopted the Byzantine ceremonies at the reception of ambassadors, which were designed to humiliate and impress the beholder. And when one of the best of all the grand viziers was told that his ally the King of France had defeated his enemy the King of Spain, he said only, "What matters it to me whether the Dog worries the Hog or the Hog the Dog?"

The most striking feature of Ottoman society was the advancement of slaves to the highest position within the state. Except for the Sultan himself, all Ottoman high officials, civil and military, were slaves. They were the children of Christian subjects of the Sultan, selected in their early youth for their promise, and specially educated for the Sultan's service. They owed to him all advancement, and he could instantly discharge or kill them any time he chose. Some of these slave-officials were selected from Christian prisoners of war, some were bought or received as presents. But at least a third were obtained through the notorious *devshirme,* or tribute of children, levied in the Balkan provinces of the Ottoman Empire. The practice, we now know, began as early as the 1390's, but was probably not regularized until the fifteenth century. Every four years, down to the seventeenth century, special officials, each with a quota of places to fill, visited the Balkan villages, and picked out the strongest and most intelligent youths between the ages of ten and twenty. The practice of course brought anguish to many families; but in many a poverty-stricken village some parents may have looked upon the unlimited opportunity for a career as a privilege for their sons.

All the youths then had to embrace Islam, as a kind of naturalization process to entitle them to government employment. No born Muslim could ever in theory be recruited into the system, because no born Muslim could ever be enslaved. Thus only born Christians could enter the system, and in theory no child of a member of it would be eligible. Most of the recruits apparently accepted the change of faith. They then received a careful education, during which the most promising were repeatedly weeded out and advanced until the cream of the crop became pages in the Sultan's own household, from which they advanced into military or administrative posts. Thus the Balkan Christians furnished many of the top officials of the Ottoman Empire. A typical success-story was that of Mehmet Sokolli, born Sokolovich in the south Slav lands, who graduated from the page corps as a gate-keeper, advanced to chief taster to the Sultan, moved on into the cavalry and became a general, commanded the picked corps of the janissaries, served as provincial governor in Europe and in Egypt, and passed through the three grades of vizier, finishing as grand vizier, or prime minister to the Sultan. At lower levels of ability, of course, men scored less spectacular success. The Sultan's harem was also made up of slaves, usually Christian-born, one of whom always bore the heir to the throne, so that each new sultan was always by birth half slave.

WEAKNESS AND DECLINE

There were many weaknesses inherent in the system. Its effectiveness depended upon the character of the individual sultan, who was all-powerful. But each sultan was brought up in the harem, which tended to produce weaklings, drunkards, debauchees, and men of little worldly wisdom. Moreover, the rigid exclusion of Muslims gave way early, and born Muslims, who could not be regarded as slaves, filtered into the system. Incompetent sultans and insubordinate soldiers sped the ruin of the state. The sale of offices and bribery bred corruption. The legal concepts of Islam were too inflexible to permit change and modernization. Christians outside the system often had no chance to serve the state, and remained *rayas* or human cattle, subject to the whim of their Muslim masters. The Empire became so large that it was unwieldy and difficult to manage. Trade routes shifted, and cut down on the value of Ottoman commerce. Before the sixteenth century was over, the Empire had entered upon the first of several long periods of gradual decline, which extended, with occasional temporary reversals or halts, down through the seventeenth and eighteenth centuries. In 1622, after a period of internal anarchy, the English ambassador wrote to his government:

> . . . the Turkish empire is become, like an old body, crazed through many vices . . . . all the territory of the Grand Signor is dispeopled for want of justice, or rather by violent oppressions, so much as in his best parts of Greece and Natolia a man may ride three, and four, and sometimes six daies, and not

find a village to feed him and his horse . . . . the revenew is so lessened that there sufficeth not to pay the souldiour and to maynteyne the court.[2]

The seventeenth century saw the Ottoman Empire engaged in a series of exhausting wars against the Habsburgs, during which even the most dramatic Turkish advances, such as that to Vienna in 1683, proved illusory because they contributed to the further weakening of the state. In a sustained counter-offensive, the Habsburgs drove the Turks behind the frontiers of Suleiman the Magnificent. Toward the end of the century Russia emerged as the great new threat to Turkish security, and there began the long series of Russo-Turkish wars which were to characterize the whole eighteenth and nineteenth centuries. Both the Habsburg advances and the Russian appearance on the scene profoundly affected the Christian subject peoples of the Balkans.

3. The Subject Peoples

THE GREEKS

At the time of the conquest of Constantinople, Mohammed II decided that the easiest way to administer the affairs of his Orthodox subjects would be to turn them over largely to the Byzantine Patriarch. Since many if not most Byzantines regarded the whole Turkish conquest as preferable to Roman Catholic domination, it was not difficult for the Sultan to reach an understanding with the Patriarch. The Greeks, like the other Christians, had to pay the head-tax and to contribute their children to the *devshirme.* They ran the same danger as the others when an occasional fanatic Sultan contemplated the extermination of all Christians. The conditions under which they lived varied greatly in different parts of the Empire. But in the capital, Constantinople itself, the Greeks came to enjoy a special status. The Patriarchate was located in a quarter of the city called the Phanar, after a lighthouse, and the Greeks who lived there were called Phanariots. The office of Patriarch gave them ecclesiastical jurisdiction over all the Christian peoples. The Patriarchate had its own system of civil courts to settle all cases arising between Christians. The office, like all Turkish posts, was for sale, and changed hands frequently. Corruption entered in early, as the patriarchs themselves sold bishoprics and lesser offices, and the bishops would use their courts as a source of revenue, often buying from the Muslim officials the right to judge certain kinds of cases.

In addition to their domination over the hierarchy in the Balkans, the Greeks, like the Jews and Armenians, only with even greater success, exercised their great commercial skills. As early as the sixteenth century, rich Greek merchant families began to appear, many of them taking the names of former Byzantine imperial or noble houses, to whom they claimed to be related. Colonies of Greek traders, subjects of the Sultan, sprang up in the

[2] *The Negotiations of Sir Thomas Roe, in His Embassy to the Ottoman Porte from the Years 1621 to 1628 Inclusive* (London, 1740), pp. 22, 67.

seaports and trading towns of Europe. In the 1560's, Suleiman and his successors employed one of these merchants to operate the fisheries and salt concessions of the Empire, as well as the customs houses, and he played a considerable role in Ottoman political intrigue. A century later, when the Ottoman Empire found itself deeply involved in diplomatic negotiations with the powers of Europe, a Greek appeared in the office of "grand dragoman of the Porte," chief interpreter. The post grew to be of critical importance, amounting almost to a ministry of foreign affairs. Greeks held it steadily from the 1660's to the 1820's. They also served regularly as grand dragomans of the fleet, a kind of executive deputyship to the Grand Admiral. The living descendants of the old Byzantines were becoming more and more powerful in the Ottoman successor-state.

PHANARIOT INFLUENCE

In addition, the Phanariot Greeks played an ever-increasing role in the principalities of Moldavia and Wallachia. Though the Turkish conquerors had promised not to build mosques on the soil of the principalities or to interfere with the princely elections or the exercise of the Christian religion, the Sultans exacted a heavy tribute from the native princes in exchange. The nobility came to exercise much of the power, and severely oppressed the Rumanian peasants, while a series of improbable and wicked rulers succeeded each other on the thrones of Bucharest and Iași. In the principalities, the great estates grew in size and their owners formed a class of hereditary magnates absent in the other Balkan countries which the Turks controlled directly, while the free peasantry decayed, and serfdom became the characteristic feature of society: a pattern much closer to that prevalent in Poland, Hungary, and Russia itself, but with special peculiarities. Chief among these was the Phanariot Greek performance of the role of middlemen between the various rival candidates for the two princely thrones and their master, the Sultan. Interested in the money to be made from the cheap and rich agricultural produce of the principalities, many Phanariots intermarried with the Rumanian aristocracy. Pious Orthodox Christians, the Rumanian nobility gave great gifts of land to monastic foundations, "dedicated" and thus subordinate to Greek monastic institutions on Ottoman soil.

Thus Greek influence usually controlled the choice of prince in Rumania, dominated commercial life, and permeated the church. The Greek language became fashionable, and began to displace Slavic in the liturgy. This was easier because Slavic itself was of course not the native tongue; yet, since few of the clergy knew Greek, the effort to impose it stimulated, in the long run, the development of a native Rumanian liturgy. Greek was the court language at Bucharest and Iași, but by the end of the seventeenth century Rumanian was coming into its own in the ordinary church services, and the first Rumanian books began to appear, printed in the Cyrillic alphabet but written in the native tongue. When the Habsburg counteroffensive began to drive the

Turks back in the years after 1683, Greek influence grew ever stronger in Rumania; and finally, after the native princes had tried to bring in the Russians to replace the Turks, the Sultan began in 1711 and 1714 to appoint Phanariots to the princely thrones, and continued the practice for well over a century.

During the "Phanariot period" in Moldavia and Wallachia, the Greek princes showed an extraordinary ability to milk their subjects. Twelve families supplied the thirty-three different individuals who ruled the principalities, with seventy-seven changes of regime. The native nobility was for the most part meekly subservient, while the peasants were sunk deep in miserable serfdom. Invested by the Sultan, each successive Greek prince was his absolute slave; but in Bucharest and Iași acted as absolute despots. Their luxurious courts aped the Ottoman court in ceremony, and the Ottoman court was itself in many ways a reflection of Byzantium. Arriving burdened with debt for the vast sum he had spent to buy the throne, each new prince hastened to squeeze his subjects as dry as possible as soon as possible, lest he fail to recoup his investment before he should be replaced. Cheating on all contracts, the princes would charge the state with expenses for nonexistent workmen and public works. They would forbid the legal importation of desirable commodities, and then arrange to smuggle them in and control their sales at high prices. They speculated in foreign currencies, sold offices, deposed churchmen, and pocketed the revenue of the vacant sees. At Constantinople they kept an agent, usually one of their relatives, to handle their relations with the Sultan. Every spring, the Greek merchants and their agents would drive off half a million Rumanian sheep to Constantinople, paying only nominal sums. If balked, they would denounce the prince to eager ears at the Turkish court, accusing him of intrigue with the Austrians or Russians.

Meanwhile, the peasants would burn down their houses to avoid the hearth or house-tax, or kill their cattle to avoid a cow-tax. Between the peasantry on the one hand and the Greek extortionists and the native nobility on the other, there was no middle class. The principalities had very few towns, no public education. The capitals themselves were a collection of hovels and palaces surrounded by a sea of mud. A few Armenians and Jews and Macedonian Slavs ate the crumbs which the Greeks let fall. In spite of the superb natural resources of the region, this atrocious system depressed Rumanian life to an extraordinarily low level, even for the Balkans. Though the Turkish loss of the Crimea to Russia in 1783 made the Rumanian lands more important than ever as a source of food for Constantinople, maladministration kept its people in miserable poverty and lessened its value to its masters. During the eighteenth century an occasional enlightened Phanariot ruler, and periodic Austrian and Russian occupations, provided some relief but did not alter the picture. The national experience under Ottoman and Phanariot domination could not help but determine the character of future Rumanian social, political, economic, and cultural development.

SERBIA AND MONTENEGRO

In Serbia, the Turks were the landlords, and the Christians the peasantry, which gave the population a far greater sense of national unity. Usually, the landlord was an absentee, a holder of a Serbian village who lived in a nearby town. If he proved unjust, his peasant tenants could in theory appeal to the Turkish government representative in Belgrade, the Pasha, for justice. Each village was still governed in most respects by the traditional head-man or *knez,* and groups of villages by an elected *obor-knez,* representing the Christians in their dealing with the Turkish authorities, and responsible to them. The preservation of this Serbian machinery of local government, after the central government had vanished, provided one nucleus around which eventual rebellion might coalesce. Another was provided by the outlaws, or *haiduks.* Serbia was always famous, like Greece, for its bands of brigands living in the mountains and preying on travelers.

Moreover, the Serbian church, with its Patriarchate at Pech, continued to serve as a reminder of the national identity. The Greek Patriarch at first had authority over it, but exercised it indirectly through the Archbishop of Ohrid, who, though Greek, could sometimes be prevailed upon not to disregard Serbian interests. Yet many Serbian manuscripts and other Slavic writings were destroyed by Greek fanaticism. In 1557, the Grand Vizier Sokolli, himself a Serb by birth, restored the autonomy of the Serbian Patriarchate, and made his own brother Patriarch: an example of a successful product of the slave-system remembering the people from whom he had sprung. In 1593, the Serbs staged a major revolt against the Turks, which continued to 1606, a sure sign that national feeling was still keenly alive.

Suffering under Turkish domination had from the beginning led large numbers of Serbs to migrate northward across the Danube into the Hungarian lands, in the hope of finding better treatment. During the Austrian offensive after 1683, many Serbs helped the invaders, and the Austrians issued proclamations urging revolution against the Turks. Although the Serbs soon found that they disliked the Roman Catholic Austrians as much as they had disliked all Roman Catholics since their own conversion to Orthodoxy, the Austrian Emperor promised them religious toleration if they migrated into his territory. When the Austrians had to retreat from Serbia in 1690, the Serbian Patriarch, Arseniye, feared Turkish vengeance, and himself led a mass colonization movement of Serbs into south Hungary, perhaps 100,000 strong. This migration gave its future Slavic majority to much of what was then southern Hungary, and is now part of Yugoslavia. A new Serbian Patriarchate now arose outside the Turkish dominions at Karlovtsi on the Danube. Though the Serbs always maintained that they had been promised self-government as well, it seems probable that the Austrians never intended more than to let them fight in the Habsburg armies under their own military commander or *voevod,* who would also serve as civil governor. Excellent soldiers, these

Serbs proved of great value to the Austrian armies. The region and much neighboring territory became known as the "military frontier," and served as the border defense zone of the Habsburg dominions against the Turks.

The Serbs who remained in Serbia to suffer the persecution of the angry Turks, as they returned to full occupation after 1690, always referred to their fellow-Serbs across the Danube as the *Prechani:* those on the other side of the river. Despite some Roman Catholic persecution, the Prechani Serbs lived a better life than those in Serbia. Their lands were very fertile. They engaged in commerce, and grew interested in education and learning. They remained devoted to their church. Their contacts with their less fortunate brothers across the Danube never ceased, and they were to influence them profoundly in times to come. Meanwhile, in Serbia proper, the Turks at first permitted the Patriarchate of Pech to exist, but after 1739 the Phanariots became more prominent in the Serbian church, trying to impose Greek as they had in Rumania; and in 1766 the Ottoman government abolished the Patriarchate, and put the Serbian church directly under the authority of the Greek Patriarch at Constantinople. He deposed all the Serbian bishops, and expelled many of the lower clergy from their parishes. At the same time, the justice which a Serb could hitherto occasionally obtain from the Ottoman authorities now vanished, as the whole Turkish system was breaking down, and the government sent thousands of unruly troops to Serbia just to get them out of the capital. These janissaries, now a hereditary corporation, oppressed Turks and Serbs alike, and would not obey the local Ottoman authorities. Their chiefs, or *Dahis,* as they were called, acted as robber barons, and extorted money and produce from the population at will, shooting whoever resisted. Between them, the *Dahi* and the Greek priest made life hideous in Serbia in the eighteenth century. All the more, the lot of the Prechani seemed enviable.

Montenegro alone continued free from Turkish domination, but only through constant warfare. Early in the sixteenth century, it acquired a unique form of government, a Prince-Bishopric. Each prince was also a bishop. The monks elected the *Vladika,* as he was called, and he served as the center for the fanatical national patriotism. Beginning in 1696, the throne passed from uncle to nephew in the Petrovich-Nyegush family. Montenegrin history is chiefly the savage story of the perpetual struggle with the Turks.

BULGARIA

The Bulgarians, as closest to Constantinople of all the Balkan peoples, and as the inhabitants of what might be called the primary security zone of the Ottoman Empire, probably fared better during the first centuries of Turkish domination than in the last of Byzantine. Except for some few thousand Bogomiles, who were converted to Islam, as they were in Bosnia, the people kept their Orthodox Christian faith. They paid only the head-tax and their contribution to the children-tribute. But in the seventeenth century, Greek influence began to grow, and the Turks authorized the Roman Catholic

Austrians to build churches on Turkish soil. For a brief period Catholicism became the center of an abortive nationalist effort to rouse the Bulgarians against their masters. By the eighteenth century, the attempt had failed, and full Phanariot cultural domination had set in, with the Slavonic liturgy forbidden, and all schools and monasteries centers for propagating the Greek language and Byzantine culture. Greek merchants had a substantial hold on the economic life of Bulgaria. Some Bulgarians "Grecized" in order to enjoy the privileges which the Greeks enjoyed. The Bulgarian language was regarded as barbaric, and when it was written it was often put into the Greek alphabet. Only the monastery of Rila inside Bulgaria and the monastery of Zographou on Mount Athos held out against the Greeks.

A few lines of connection to the west were maintained by travelers to the Habsburg lands or to Ragusa (Dubrovnik), whose independent and prosperous town-commonwealth maintained colonies of merchants scattered through Bulgaria. The Prechani Serbs, with their Patriarchate at Karlovtsi and their not dissimilar language and traditions, attracted some Bulgarian students to their schools. Thus in this period the ideas of the outside world filtered in to the Bulgarians largely through Serbian intermediaries, and Karlovtsi served as an inspiration to all south Slavs under the Turks. Yet the ordinary Bulgarian peasant was little if at all affected by such intellectual currents. He lived in ignorance, and in relative misery, persecuted by Greek and by Turk.

CONDITIONS IN THE BALKANS AND THEIR IMPACT ON THE PEOPLE

The corruption of the Turkish system was accompanied by unpredictable violence and misrule, which led to the depopulation of entire districts. An eighteenth-century Turkish writer of a book of counsel for public officials denounced bribery and oppression as causing the flight of the peasantry from their fields. The Christian travelers from western Europe also painted a discouraging picture:

> The insolence of the horse and foot is insupportable, for in their marches from one country to another, parties of twenty or thirty men . . . live upon free quarter and extort money and clothes from the poor vassals, taking their children to sell for slaves, especially the Bulgarians and the Serbians, and the people of Bosnia and Albania . . . so that, rather than be exposed to so much misery and license of the soldiery, the poor people choose to abandon their dwellings and wander into other cities or seek refuge in the mountains or woods of the country.[3]

The long centuries of domination by the Byzantine Empire and its Ottoman successor-state must be held responsible for many of the characteristic features of the Balkan countries. The destruction of the native aristocracy in Bulgaria and Serbia led to the development of strongly egalitarian peasant

[3] Paul Rycaut, *The Present State of the Ottoman Empire* (London, 1668), p. 170.

societies, with strong democratic tendencies, one of whose striking manifestations was the outspoken eloquence of the individual peasant. The native churches served as the preservers of the old traditions over the centuries of bondage. Though often passive, often dominated by the Greeks, the clergy, and the clergy alone, none the less had access to the books which preserved the memory of ancient national achievement.

Persecution bred the outlaw tradition, and made a natural hero out of the brigand; but successful careers in brigandage required pragmatic rather than moral decisions. So the outlaws were easily adaptable, collaborated when necessary with the authorities, playing the endless Balkan game of cops and robbers in the mountains, and freely committing what might elsewhere have been regarded as treachery in order to survive to fight another day. Without a clear understanding of this background, nobody could understand the story of Mihailovich in our own times. At the same time, the fantastic corruption of Ottoman and Phanariot administration produced the firm conviction that everything was for sale. It was no wonder that the *baksheesh* mentality persisted. There was no chance to breed a tradition of political responsibility. Moreover, social responsibility — *noblesse oblige* — did not blossom in the hearts of the native Rumanian nobles, or the converted native Bosnian aristocracy, or the Albanian *beys*. Toward their inferiors they were unrelenting oppressors, and a strong streak of violent cruelty ran through their behavior. Later, when a small upper class distinguished by wealth rather than by blood came into existence, it too would lack the sense of *richesse oblige*.

Among the peasantry, the experience bred a deep-seated distrust of government in general. Government meant tax-collectors, soldiers billeted in their houses and abusing them and their families, the loss of their crops to wicked agents, and possible starvation. They hid their crops and cursed their government, and developed, for mere self-preservation, a harsh suspicion of all men's motives: they had been fooled before. It was their land which gave them their livelihood, to which they clung. Those who dwelt in cities, especially those who came from the capital, they instinctively hated. Except for their land and their church they had nothing, and the Greeks from time to time seemed to be taking their church away. Out of this mentality there came of course the attitude of the Balkan peasant in our own day both toward many of those who wanted to teach him scientific agriculture, whom he instinctively suspected, and toward those who wanted to take his farm away and collectivize it, whom he utterly and passionately loathed.

4. The Habsburg Regions. Croatia and Ragusa

By the end of the eighteenth century, the historic experience of the Orthodox Balkan peoples had given their behavior a characteristic stamp. The Catholics in Slovenia, Croatia, and Dalmatia had a different fate. The Slovenes, absorbed by the advancing Germans as early as the time of Charlemagne, lived with apparent contentment under the Habsburgs. The Croatians, who had a kingdom of their own in the early middle ages, were conquered by the Magyars in 1102. Magyars and Venetians contended for the Dalmatian coast, where Venice established its trading stations in the towns, and ruled the land as a colonial power, setting its characteristic impress on the native architecture and painting. Even Ragusa, independent for most of its existence, spent the thirteenth and half of the fourteenth century under Venetian domination.

The exact constitutional relationship of Croatia to Hungary for many centuries provided the lawyers and politicians with a hot subject for dispute. Was Croatia a vassal-state, Hungarian by right of conquest? Or was it a partner of the Hungarians by its free election of the Hungarian King as its own? It seems improbable that any final answer can be given to these twin questions, and it is certain that, if the truth about the year 1102 could be discovered, it would have only limited relevance for the centuries to follow. The Magyars oppressed the Croats when they could; the Croat nobles maintained what autonomy they could, governing their own internal affairs and oppressing their own peasantry without much interference. But the Slavonia-Srem portion of Croatia, between the Sava and the Drava, most of the time belonged to Hungary outright, until the Turks flooded over much of it. When the Turks defeated the Magyars at Mohacs in 1526, and seized so much of the Hungarian lands, the Croat nobility put the province under the possession of the Habsburg Emperor, who was also King of what was left of Hungary.

As the outpost against the Turks, and the mother of good fighting men, Croatia was too important to Vienna to be permitted to go its own way. The Habsburgs restricted the rights of the ancient Croatian parliament or estates, and chopped off ever larger portions of the area over which the estates had jurisdiction, in order to form the "military frontiers," over which the Emperor himself exercised direct authority. As the Habsburg counteroffensive against the Turks pushed southeastward in the years after 1683, and Hungary and Slavonia-Srem were liberated, the border territories with their new Serb immigrants into Croatia and the Voyvodina were added to the "military frontiers." Germans too were settled here, in Croatia itself and in the Banat. The mixed population of northern Yugoslavia in modern times directly reflected the defense policies of the Habsburg Empire in the late seventeenth and early eighteenth centuries. To the orthodox immigrants, the tradition of a free or at least autonomous Croatia with its own parliament meant nothing. Their loyalty ran directly to the Emperor who had offered them hospitality, and for the Roman Catholic Croats and especially for the Magyars they had little use.

As for the Croat nobles themselves, many of them cherished the illusory hope that Vienna would help them against Budapest, and, in the eighteenth-century struggles between Austria and Hungary, they sided with Austria. Others, more Magyarized, especially members of the nobility, regarded Vienna and its centralizing ways with hatred, and hoped for complete union with Hungary. Still others hoped to play Austrians and Magyars off against each other, and to preserve and enhance Croat autonomy. The social pattern of Croatia was much like that in feudal Hungary; Latin was the language of administration, church, school, and polite letters. When the Magyars tried to enforce their own language in Croatia toward the end of the eighteenth century, the Croat nobles defended Latin, but began to realize the usefulness of their own tongue for the peasantry, as a defense against the Magyars. Though not the victims of the sort of oppression undergone by the other Balkan peoples, the Croat nobles experienced the frustrations and disappointments inseparable from their role as frontier provincials. It was no wonder that they developed feeling of great sensitivity about their own importance, and that, when their attention fell upon their Serbian brothers suffering under the Turks, they should readily adopt toward them the scornful attitude which their own Magyar masters felt toward all non-Magyar peoples.

Only at Ragusa (Dubrovnik) was there an active center of independent South Slav Catholics. With leases on some of the Serbian gold mines, and colonies of merchants scattered all across the Ottoman Empire, the Ragusans paid tribute to the Turks, but maintained their own commercial republic. Much like a pocket-Venice, the city was ruled by a tight patrician oligarchy, which carefully preserved rigorous class-distinctions, and limited its elected Duke to the briefest of terms in office. The Republic's ships (the word "argosy" is derived from the name of Ragusa) sailed all over the Mediterranean and on to India. In Ragusa, a splendid school of poets and dramatists arose during the sixteenth century, under the influence of the Italian Renaissance, but writing in the vernacular Slavic tongue. It was the great earthquake of 1667 which opened the period of its decline. Different as they were, Ragusa and Montenegro, by preserving a precarious independence, demonstrated throughout the centuries while the south Slavs were dominated by foreign empires that Catholic and Orthodox branches of the race alike possessed a strong native capacity both for warfare and for the arts of peace.

Chapter 5

NATIONAL AWAKENING AND THE ACHIEVEMENT OF INDEPENDENCE: FROM THE EIGHTEENTH CENTURY THROUGH WORLD WAR I

1. Austrians, Russians, and Subject Peoples, 1683–1791

ASIDE FROM THEIR EXPERIENCE OF GREEKS AND TURKS, the Balkan peoples as a whole during the early centuries of Ottoman domination had little contact with the outside world. It was not until the Habsburg counteroffensive after 1683 that they once more encountered their Austrian neighbors. Almost at once, the Orthodox found that they did not like the Roman Catholics any more than they had in the fifteenth century, when they had submitted to the Turks rather than accept Catholic domination. By the turn of the eighteenth century, less than twenty years after the counteroffensive began, the Orthodox peoples of the Balkans had begun to look to Russia, second home of orthodoxy after the fall of Byzantium, as a counterweight to the Catholics and the Turks: "We all pray with tears," says a Serb appeal to Moscow in 1698, "for the sovereign monarch to save us from the Papists and Jesuits who rage against the Orthodox more than they do against the Turks. The secular war may finish sometime, but the Jesuit war never."[1]

In 1711, Peter the Great, planning a new campaign against the Turks, used the ancient standard of Constantine the Great, with a cross and the inscription "under this sign thou shalt conquer." This vision Constantine had allegedly seen in 311; it had led him to adopt Christianity. Peter's Ragusan adviser drafted a manifesto to the Balkan Christians urging them to fight for faith and fatherland, and to drive the descendants of Mohammed out into the Arabian sands and deserts. The Russians were self-consciously lending their campaign all the trappings of a crusade for orthodoxy on the Byzantine pattern. The Montenegrins rose, as might have been expected, but Peter's campaign failed in the Danubian principalities. It marked the beginning, however, of a long period during which the subject Orthodox peoples would look toward Russia, and Russia would exploit their sentiments. In the early portion of the eighteenth century, Russia and Austria were allied and Russia was very far away; so that the Balkan Orthodox could not expect and did not receive genuine aid and comfort against either Turks or Catholics.

But Austro-Russian mutual jealousy grew into rivalry during the eighteenth century. In 1739, though allied with Russia against the Turks, the Austrians hastily concluded a peace because the Russians were scoring too many military successes. They thus freed a large Turkish army, and obliged the Russians also to end the war. When Catherine the Great fought the Turks again, her armies in 1768 and 1769 invaded and occupied Moldavia and Wallachia, bringing with them Russian manifestoes proclaiming that "the barbarous domination of the Turks seeks to fling into the abyss of impiety the souls of the Christians who live in Moldavia, Wallachia, Bulgaria, Bosnia, Hertsegovina, Macedonia, and the other provinces of the Ottoman Empire." From Constantinople the Sultan issued a decree that all Moldavians or Wallachians who submitted to the Russians were to be slaughtered and their wives and children sold into slavery. No doubt this drove many of them to take the oath of allegiance to the Russians, out of fear of what the Turks would do if they returned. Russian agents were also busy in Greece and Montenegro.

Indeed, the Empress sent a fleet from the Baltic around Europe and into the Mediterranean to make landings in Greece and join the Greeks in a great

[1] Cited by B. H. Sumner, *Peter the Great and the Ottoman Empire* (Oxford, 1949), p. 34.

uprising against the Turks. So badly planned was the effort, however, and so few were the Russian forces available, that they soon sailed away, leaving the Greeks who had helped them to the tender mercies of the Turks. In the treaty of Kuchuk Kainardji, which concluded this war in 1774, the Sultan was compelled to promise to protect the Christian religion and its churches. He would also permit the Russians to make representations on behalf of a new Orthodox church to be built in Constantinople, and to "remonstrate" in behalf of the principalities. So alarmed were the Austrians at this progress of the Russians that they planned to seize most of the Balkan region when the expected Ottoman collapse should take place. In 1775, they demanded and received the Bukovina from the Sultan, and this Rumanian province remained in Habsburg hands until the end of World War I.

During the 1780's, Catherine the Great hatched her celebrated "Greek project": to drive the Turks from Europe, and to restore the Byzantine Empire, with a Russian prince on the throne. One of Catherine's grandchildren was christened Constantine for the purpose. In preparation for his future post, the Russians hired Greek nurses to teach him the language. Recognizing that such an extension of Russian power would be impossible without Austrian agreement, the Russian Empress also proposed to set up an independent Kingdom of Dacia, including Moldavia, Wallachia, and Bessarabia, proposing for the throne her lover and general, Potemkin. The Austrians claimed as their share the entire western portion of the Balkans, including Belgrade, and the southern peninsula of Greece. In the war which followed, these grandiose plans were thwarted by Austrian military failure. Moreover, the western powers of Europe succeeded in bringing such pressure that the Russians called off the war, which ended in 1792 with the "Greek project" a failure.

By the end of the eighteenth century, then, the Russians had been actively and on the whole successfully campaigning against the Turks for well over a hundred years, and had agreed with the Austrians to divide the Balkan lands between them. The native peoples had for some time been exposed to their powerful eastern and western neighbors, and Habsburg and Russian influences had penetrated deeply into the peninsula. No longer isolated, the Balkan peoples began to be exposed as well to the contemporary European currents of thought. By the last half of the eighteenth century, national feeling was awakening everywhere in the peninsula except among the loyal Muslims in the Albanian and Bosnian fastnesses.

2. *National Consciousness*

In 1791, when it was clear that the Russians and Austrians would make peace without annexing the principalities, a group of native Wallachian nobles sent them an appeal. Fearful of being restored to Phanariot domination, they declared that there was such a thing as the Wallachian nation, and urged that they should be given the right to elect their native princes and maintain their native army, a kind of national militia, which would enable Wallachia to stay neutral in all future wars. This was an authentic nationalist plea, voiced by a nobility conscious once again of its Wallachian character.

But it was an isolated document, and the chief stimulus to the growth of Rumanian nationalism came from Transylvania. In this province, disputed between Habsburgs and Turks during the seventeenth century, there had been all during the middle ages three privileged nations: the Magyars, the Szeklers, and the "Saxons." Since the Protestant Reformation had won a large number of former Catholics to the various forms of Protestantism, there were also four "accepted" religions: the Roman Catholic, the Calvinist (Magyars), the Unitarian (Magyars), and the Lutheran ("Saxons"). The fourth nation, the Vlachs, or Rumanians, by now in all probability a majority of the population, had no privileges, and suffered persecution. Its religion, the Orthodox, was not "accepted." In the 1690's, the Roman Church gave the Rumanians a chance to win religious liberty by recognizing papal supremacy, and making a few changes in the creed, but allowing them to keep their Rumanian liturgy, and not enforcing celibacy upon their priests. They might elect their own bishop, and their clergy would be free of serfdom and feudal dues. In 1698, the Rumanian clergy in Transylvania accepted the Union, and their Metropolitan thus became a "Uniate"; there was now a sixth church in Transylvania. Those Rumanians who remained Orthodox had a difficult time indeed, and in 1759 were put under Serbian jurisdiction.

Oddly enough, it was the Transylvanian Uniate Church, an invention of foreigners designed to make the Rumanians quietly subordinate to the Habsburgs, which became the fountainhead of Rumanian national feeling. Its clergy proved to be fiery patriots, bombarding Vienna with memoranda on the suffering of their people from the manifest injustices of the Magyar system in Transylvania. As early as 1737, their Bishop spoke in the name of the Wallach *gens,* or nation, kept in "Egyptian bondage under the bloody lash." To this the Magyars replied that there was only a Wallach *plebs,* or rabble, whose function in society was that of moths in clothing. Uniate Rumanian nationalism received great stimulus from the journeying of their young theological students to Rome. There they saw the column of Trajan recording the Roman conquest of Dacia (Transylvania). And on the column they could discern the sculptured Dacians of nearly 2,000 years before, wearing the tall fur hats which the Rumanian peasants still wore in their own day and do in our own. In the seminaries of Rome, they studied, of course, in Latin, and at once realized that they had been speaking a Latin dialect all their lives.

The Rumanian Uniate seminarians awoke with a start to their national identity. They leaped to the conclusion that they were Daco-Romans, descendants of the ancient Dacians mixed with the Roman legions who had occupied the country. From being a persecuted and despised minority, they had suddenly acquired not only a sense of nationhood but also the most respectable possible historical ancestors. Their language suddenly became to them their "dearest treasure." In 1780, two of them produced the first Rumanian grammar, a book which the casual student might think harmless. With it, however, modern Rumanian nationalism received its first great stimulus. It led to the dropping of the Cyrillic alphabet and the adoption of Latin letters for their Latin tongue. It stimulated the Rumanians of Transylvania to put forth ever louder claims that they were the original inhabitants of the country, who had been neglected and persecuted for centuries, and who had a better right to rule it than anybody else. This provoked the most violent response from the Magyars in a quarrel which continued into our own day.

In Transylvania, in 1791, the Rumanian Uniate and Orthodox clergy united in presenting to the court of Vienna a memorandum called *Supplex Libellus Valachorum,* the beseeching pamphlet of the Vlachs. In it they put forward a full national program: emphasizing their antiquity, they demanded full equality for their clergy and laity; they wanted a proportional share in public office for Rumanians, and the use of Rumanian place-names in districts where the population was Rumanian. It took well over a century of further suffering before the demands were fulfilled. But the new national spirit, first aroused in Transylvania, crossed the Carpathians, and provided the miserable Rumanians of Ottoman and Phanariot-dominated Wallachia and Moldavia with their first modern consciousness of nationhood.

Among the Serbs too, the sense of national identity, kept alive by the church during the years of Ottoman domination, grew apace during the last quarter of the eighteenth century under the impulse provided by literary and linguistic scholars. The *Prechani* Serbs played the same role vis-à-vis the Serbs of Serbia proper as the Transylvanian Uniates vis-à-vis the Rumanians of the principalities. Yovan Rayich, born in 1726, educated abroad in Vienna, Russia, and the monasteries of Mount Athos, produced in 1796 a four-volume history of the Serbian people, which even illiterate Serbs prized as somehow a patriotic possession.

Dositej Obradovich, some fifteen years younger, who began his career as an Orthodox monk, escaped from the monastery, and sought his education not only on Athos, from the Greeks in Smyrna, in Vienna, Venice, and Constantinople, but also in Russia and Germany and France and England. He earned his living as a teacher of languages, obtained the patronage of Serbs living abroad, became a disciple of the eighteenth-century enlightenment and a great admirer of the Habsburg Emperor Joseph II, and determined to give the Serbian people books in their own language. He translated many works, and produced in 1783–1788 his autobiography, which some authorities still regard as the most important single work of Serbian prose literature. Over the barrier of religion and tradition, he clearly saw the intimate kinship between Croat and Serb; he had more than a glimmer of the "Yugoslav idea." Caring little for the traditions or folkways of the people, he wanted to westernize them. The Orthodox clergy thought of him as a dangerous atheist, but he ended his days as the first Minister of Education in the first autonomous Serbian state, and taught the son of its ruler, Karageorge.

The Bulgarians too produced their cleric who called them to an awareness of themselves. In the Serbian monastery on Mount Athos, Father Paissy, a deeply pious monk, not nearly so much affected by the outside eighteenth-century world which molded Obradovich, whom he had known in person, completed in 1762 his *Slavo-Bulgarian History of the Bulgarian Peoples, their Emperors and their Saints.* He summoned the Bulgarians to remember their medieval Empire, and to love their fatherland and especially their language. Those who despised Bulgarian and preferred Greek Paissy dismissed as a disgrace to the name Bulgarian. Paissy too had done research for his book in Karlovtsi, among the *Prechani* Serbs. His work was not printed until 1841, but it circulated in manuscript. Simple in style, it appealed to the few Bulgarians who read it, and deserves to be remembered as the first monument to awakening Bulgarian nationalism.

3. The South-Slav Movement toward Liberty, 1804–1875

The first Balkan revolution against the Ottoman Empire was that of the Serbs. Despite their growing sense of nationality, the uprising, which began in 1804, was not at first a national uprising at all. It began as a protest against the bad behavior of the *dahis* in the Ottoman *pashalik* of Belgrade. Since these dahis were themselves in revolt against the Sultan, having killed the Sultan's appointee as pasha in 1801, and having decided to execute all the leading Serbs, the movement against them was, paradoxically enough, in its inception a movement on behalf of the Sultan. Karageorge Petrovich, leader of the uprising, was a pig-farmer and head of a moderately prosperous family, who had served in the Austrian army, and whose energy and decision commanded the loyalty of the peasants. Having defeated the dahis, the Serbs asked the Sultan to allow them to choose a chief *knez* to serve as intermediary between the Turkish representative in Belgrade and the local knezes, and to permit them to obtain a guarantee of this status from a foreign power: they were in touch with both Russians and Austrians.

When the Turks failed to grant these requests, the movement turned into a genuine revolution. Though the Russians gave some help, they soon let the Serbs down. Karageorge himself leaned toward the Austrians, but a strong pro-Russian party grew up under the leadership of Milan Obrenovich. Obrenovich died, perhaps poisoned at Karageorge's order, in 1810. Thus Austro-Russian rivalry and Karageorge-Obrenovich rivalry, both of which were to characterize Serbian history well into the twentieth century, made their appearance before the new state had even achieved autonomy. Indeed, the Turks returned to control the country after Karageorge's emotional collapse and flight into Austria (1813). It took a second revolution, led by Milosh

Obrenovich, half-brother of Milan, who was chosen supreme knez in 1817, to attain liberation. But the path had now been blazed. The Greek revolution of the 1820's, the intervention of the powers of Europe, and the Russo-Turkish war of 1827–1828 benefited the Serbs, and in 1830 Milosh was recognized by the Sultan as prince of an autonomous principality. His state was still tributary to the Sultan, and a large Turkish garrison remained in Belgrade. It remained to transform autonomy into independence.

During the period of the first Serbian uprising, Napoleon, the general in command of the French revolutionary armies, had arrived in southeast Europe. Not only had the French precipitated the Russo-Turkish war of 1806–1812, and a new Russian occupation of the principalities, by persuading the Sultan to remove pro-Russian princes there, but they had put an end to the ancient Venetian republic and then "liberated" its colony, the Ionian islands. More important, Napoleon himself had campaigned in Dalmatia, terminating the Ragusan republic in 1806, and establishing the entire Dalmatian coast and Slovenia as the "Illyrian provinces." In "Illyria" Napoleon's officials tried to introduce administration, law, and education on the French pattern. The chief monuments to the occupation, however, were the excellent network of roads, and the legacy of the "Illyrian idea," which remained one of the main sources of modern Yugoslav nationalism.

Down to the late 1850's, Serbia was the only one of our Balkan provinces to have achieved autonomy. We need not follow in detail its turbulent political history and changes of dynasty between the two rival families of Karageorgevich and Obrenovich. Its political life was characterized by faction, maladministration, unsuccessful efforts at constitutionalism, and inefficiencies: all quite natural in a new state suffering from a lack of trained personnel, and from the intervention of foreign powers in its internal political affairs. Its population was only a little over a million. By the 1860's, Belgrade had well over 25,000 inhabitants; the other towns were simply overgrown villages. Pig-raising was the main occupation of the inhabitants, but cattle and sheep also thrived. Corn and plums, used to make the famous *slivovitsa*, were the staple agricultural products. Importing salt from Wallachia, coffee from Turkey, necessary manufactured goods from Austria, and religious articles from Russia, the country was prosperous in a simple rural fashion. The roads, built by forced labor under the oppressive regime of Milosh Obrenovich, were well-constructed but badly maintained. In the 1840's and 1850's the introduction of steamboats on the Danube brought Serbia into closer touch with the west. Lacking national minorities and an aristocracy, the Serbs formed a homogeneous patriarchal society, in which a few merchants were beginning to grow rich. Education was primitive to a degree, and most of the teachers were *Prechani,* trained in the Budapest classical tradition, and trying to interest their Serbian peasant pupils in Virgil and Horace. But students soon began to travel abroad, and in the 1850's most of the officials of the government had been educated in the west, chiefly Paris.

Second only to Obradovich in the influence he exerted on Serbian cultural life, Vuk Karadjich brought to Serbia the romantic nationalist passion for the native language and folkways which was a nineteenth-century commonplace elsewhere. Born in 1787, and educated in a monastery as a child, he fled to Austria after the collapse of Karageorge in 1813, and spent most of his life abroad. In Vienna, he met the great Slavonic scholar Kopitar. He taught Kopitar the Serbian peasant tongue, and Kopitar taught him philology and scholarly techniques. Karadjich collected and published Serbian folk-ballads, issued a Serbian grammar, a Serb-Latin-German dictionary, and collections of folk tales and proverbs. He tried with great success to purge the language of Church Slavonic or Russian influences, and to bring the written forms close to the spoken tongue of the people. But the collection of the extraordinary ballads and oral epics sung by the Serbian and other south-Slav singers, commemorating the heroic deeds of historical or legendary warriors, was his most lasting contribution. More passionate and far more political-minded than Obradovich, Karadjich, though very influential, had not succeeded by his death in 1864 in imposing his favorite west-Serbian dialect as the literary language, nor had he made official his phonetic spelling, because he included in his alphabet the Latin letter *j,* which to the suspicious Orthodox smacked of Roman Catholic influences.

In the 1830's, the Croatians too developed a movement toward linguistic self-consciousness, called at first "Illyrian" after Napoleon's name for his short-lived Balkan provinces. Its chief spokesman, Ljudevit Gaj, some two decades younger than Karadjich, advocated that the Croats adopt as their literary language the same dialect which Karadjich had been pressing on the Serbs. Gaj was successful where Karadjich had failed; so that the differences in dialect persisted, as the Serbs clung to a more eastern form of the language. Though separated by their alphabets and by the rather unimportant differences in dialect, the Serbs and Croats were brought closer by the "Illyrian" movement, which in its political aspects aimed at a union between the two and the Slovenes. It was natural that in the 1840's the leaders changed the name of their movement to "south Slav," or "Yugoslav."

From the 1840's on, this concept of a federal union, or Yugoslavia, found itself facing a rival concept, sponsored by the Serbian statesman Garashanin and others, which favored the re-creation of Stephen Dushan's fourteenth-century Serbian Empire, and stressed the sacred role of Serbia in the creation of a south-Slav union. Garashanin believed that promises of religious toleration would attract the Croats and Slovenes. Instead of "Yugoslavia," Garashanin envisaged a "greater Serbia." The conflict between these two conceptions of the manner in which south Slav unity was to be achieved forms one of the main themes of Balkan history down into our own times.

The Hungarian Revolution of 1848 profoundly affected the south Slavs and the Rumanians. Though liberal parliamentarians in politics, the leaders of the Magyar rebellion against the Habsburgs were intransigently nationalist, and planned to Magyarize their Rumanian and Slavic minorities. Unable to coöperate with the rebels, the Croats fought against them in the service of the Habsburg Empire, and so did the Prechani Serbs. Deeply sympathetic with their fellow-south-Slavs, the Serbs of Serbia proper wanted to go to war against the Hungarian revolution too. Had it not been for pressure from both Russians and Turks, they might have done so. As it was, the Serbian government stayed out of the war, but arms and volunteers flooded over the frontiers to help the anti-Magyar cause. Once the Hungarians had been defeated, the victorious Croats and Serbs of the Habsburg Empire received but shabby rewards for their services to Vienna. Their aspirations were not met, they were ruled harshly from Vienna; and, in 1867, when the Austrians were forced by circumstances to conclude their famous "Ausgleich" with the Hungarians creating the Dual Monarchy, they simply turned Croatia back to the Magyars.

Led by the celebrated and enlightened Roman Catholic Bishop Strossmayer, cultivated and strongly liberal in his views, the Croat nationalists were deeply disappointed. Strossmayer had hoped that Vienna would make Croatia and Dalmatia autonomous inside the Habsburg Empire, and that the new south Slav province would be so well administered and so free that in time it would attract all other south Slavs; thus Serbia and the Bulgarians would eventually join it, under the benevolent aegis of Vienna. This scheme, which was of course a modified Yugoslavia, would certainly have been difficult enough had Habsburg rule been enlightened and imaginative. As things were, it was impossible. The Croats instead obtained a compromise of their own with the Magyars in 1868, which gave Croat delegates certain representation in Budapest and Vienna, permitted them to use Croatian as an official language, and left them control of their church, courts, and police. Taxation, however, rested with Hungary. This was an extraordinarily liberal settlement. Croatian intellectual life flourished, as Strossmayer founded schools, a Catholic seminary, a learned academy, a university, and an art museum. Zagreb became one of the great centers of Slavic culture.

But most Croats felt great dissatisfaction with their political lot. The "Party of the Right," led by a politician named Starchevich, now emerged as the proponent of complete autonomy for Croatia. With none of Strossmayer's gentleness, the rightists were much more violent Croatian nationalists, scorning as inferior the Serbs and other non-Catholic south Slavs, whom Strossmayer had hoped to attract. Starchevich became the most successful native politician. But the franchise in Croatia permitted only about 2 per cent of the population to vote. As a result, the Starchevich party had only a few representatives in the parliament, or Sabor. The pro-Magyar nobles and their small unrepresentative "Unionist" party, together with the Magyar-appointed Ban or governor, dominated the situation.

In Serbia, the accession of Michael Obrenovich in 1860 brought to the throne the first truly competent ruler. He curbed the illegality and personal feuding that had characterized the country's politics. He converted what had been a virtual oligarchy managed by a seventeen-man Senate into a constitutional monarchy in which the popularly chosen *Skupshtina,* or assembly, had superior authority. He instituted a regular conscript army to replace the irregular *levée,* and collected an income tax to support it. By skillful diplomacy, he was able to secure the departure in 1867 of the Turkish garrisons from Belgrade and the other fortresses of Serbia, where their presence had been a constant danger and reminder of inferiority. Though the Turkish flag still flew next to the Serbian flag on the fortress at Belgrade, this was a comparatively harmless token of a submission growing ever more nominal.

Michael Obrenovich's ambitions were even more extensive than his achievements. Having watched the liberation of Italy under the leadership of the little state of Piedmont, he began to think of Serbia as the Piedmont of the Balkans. Foreseeing the need of a new war of liberation against the Turks, he negotiated with the Greeks, Rumanians, and Bulgarians, and planned to create a Balkan League, and eventually a confederation of the Balkans. In support of his plans, there was founded in 1867 a semi-secret nationalist Serbian society called *Omladina* (*Youth*). In part a literary and cultural group which managed its own publishing house, it also served in its more clandestine aspects as a sounding board for Michael's plans.

In the story of his negotiations with the neighboring peoples the student can discern the seeds of many future Balkan territorial rivalries. The Greeks and the Serbs could not agree on the future of Macedonia, while the Bulgarians claimed it as well. The Serbs and the Rumanians planned to divide the region which should have become an independent Bulgaria. The Greeks and the Bulgarians both claimed Thrace. The shrewd Russian Ambassador to Constantinople, Ignatyev, predicted at the time that, once the struggle with the Turks should be ended, the Christian peoples would fall to fighting among themselves. In any case, Michael was assassinated in 1868. After his death, Omladina virtually dissolved, its left wing emerging as an ancestor of the future Serbian Socialist Party, itself an ancestor of Tito's present Communists, and the right wing continuing to occupy itself with nationalist ambitions.

In Serbia as in Croatia, the years after 1868 saw the emergence of the first political parties. Far more numerous and powerful than the socialists were the Liberals and Radicals. The names had little to do with their programs, a phenomenon which would become standard in the Balkans. The Liberals were chiefly distinguished by their wish to centralize the power of the state, the Radicals by their advocacy of local authority and by their passionate nationalism. Their leaders kept alive, into a period during which the throne was increasingly unstable, the ideas of Michael Obrenovich.

Serbia now began to feel the impact of the modern west. Determined to introduce railroads and gas-lighting, aping Parisian or Viennese manners, the ruling group still used the old Turkish formulas for government. Members of the developing class of the rich merchants, called *charshiya,* from the

Turkish word for market-place, allied themselves with rival politicians. At one time in the 1870's one great Belgrade magnate had as his sons-in-law the Prince's military aide, the Minister of the Interior, the Serbian agent at the Porte, and a member of the Regency. His chief rival had as *his* sons-in-law the Ministers of War and Finance, and the President of the Skupshtina. Such alliances brought profit to all concerned.

4. The Freeing of Rumania

It took the Rumanians of the principalities twenty-six years longer than the Serbs before they attained the autonomous status which Milosh Obrenovich had won in 1830. There had been a Rumanian revolt in 1821, under Tudor Vladimirescu, former officer in the Russian army, who had come to know and admire Karageorge. Proclaiming his hostility to the Phanariots and the landlords, he had raised the countryside against the Greek forces of Alexander Ypsilanti, who had tried to begin the Greek Revolution in Rumania. Vladimirescu bitterly resented the Greeks, and was eventually captured and killed by Ypsilanti, whose own efforts soon afterwards failed. It was not a native uprising but outside intervention by the great powers which brought to the principalities improved administration and eventually autonomy.

The Treaty of Adrianople, which the Russians imposed on the Ottoman Empire in 1829, required that the princes be elected by the native nobility of Wallachia and Moldavia, for life terms. The princes obtained control over their own internal affairs, and might maintain their own militia. Though the Phanariot period was now over, the Rumanians had actually exchanged Turkish domination for Russian. In 1831 and 1832 the Russian commander there, Count Paul Kisselev, gave the Rumanians a kind of constitution called the *règlement organique*. The exactly similar regulations governing both principalities made their eventual union far easier than it would otherwise have been.

Each principality obtained its own assembly, made up of noble and merchant representatives. The nobles' proprietorship over the land received "constitutional" recognition, and their authority over their peasant serfs expanded, as the serfs' freedom of movement was restricted and their own holdings were cut in size. A single direct tax on every peasant replaced the irregular, outmoded, and unpredictable taxes which the nobles had been used to levy. This let the peasant know where he stood and regularized his obligations. With the end of the Turkish control over the principalities came a boom in the Black Sea grain trade, as western Europe showed a great eagerness for grain exports. Prices of land and wheat soared, and the nobles became ever more prosperous. Even after the Russians withdrew in 1834, their influence remained pervasive.

There now began efforts at modernization. The new prince of Moldavia, Michael Sturdza, wiped out brigandage, built roads and bridges, instituted the first postal system, and founded the first hospitals, high schools, and academy at Iași. French influence, which had already manifested itself under the Phanariots, now spread into both principalities, partly from Transylvania, where the Rumanian intellectuals admired Napoleon, and partly through the efforts of Rumanians educated in Paris. With the translation of the French romantics into Rumanian came aspirations for freedom and unity. Most of the handful of Francophile Rumanian intellectuals were idealistic, democratic, and nationalistic.

When the news of the Paris revolution of February 1848 reached Iași, a few of these young men tried to make a revolution in Moldavia, but they were quickly dispersed. In Wallachia, on the other hand, the city population was more deeply interested in following the lead of the intellectuals. In Transylvania, stirring assemblies of Rumanians were demanding freedom from Magyar rule, and this too stimulated the Wallachians. In the face of opposition, the rebels managed to set up a short-lived republic in Wallachia. Exposed to the threat of Russian attack and possible Turkish reprisal, the Wallachian republican regime failed to secure the support of the peasantry. Reluctant to abolish the feudal dues, but hoping that the landowners themselves would see the wisdom of such an act, they summoned a commission to discuss it, but failed to push it through. In the end, both Russians and Turks intervened to put down the republican regime. The princes were now to be restored, with seven-year terms of office.

In Transylvania, which the Hungarian rebels pronounced annexed to Hungary, large mass-meetings of Rumanians proclaimed their full national and personal rights. But Magyar intransigence drove the Rumanians the way of the Croats, and Avram Iancu, the chief Rumanian military leader in Transylvania, loyally supported the Habsburgs. Governed from Vienna after the revolution was over, the Rumanians gained none of the privileges which the Emperor had promised them. In 1867, the Dual Monarchy restored Transylvania to the Magyars, and the Rumanians there were subjected to renewed oppression.

One of the important causes of the Crimean war of 1854–1856 was a new Russian occupation of the principalities, undertaken to bring pressure on the Turks. After the British, French, Italians, and Turks had defeated the Russians, the Peace of Paris of 1856 restored the privileges which the Peace of Adrianople had granted to the principalities, and further stipulated that no one power (meaning Russia) should henceforth claim an exclusive protectorate over them. Still subject to the Turks, the Rumanian nationalists, who had been vigorous supporters of the French Revolution of 1848, now embraced Napoleon III, and by bombarding him with memoranda, won him to the Rumanian cause: part of his continent-wide effort to secure the self-determination of peoples. The Peace of Paris provided that a special commission of the powers would study the future status of the principalities.

After much pulling and hauling among the powers, long delays, charges of bad faith, and a major European crisis, the powers held elections in the principalities in 1857, which registered great majorities for union. In 1858, the powers agreed that the principalities were to be "united," but were to continue to have two princes and two assemblies, with a common central commission and court of appeal. Now both Moldavia and Wallachia proceeded to elect the same prince, Alexander Cuza, an honest but not especially prominent officer of thirty-nine. The Rumanians had outsmarted the powers, who had never foreseen such a performance, and had therefore not troubled to make it illegal. The principalities were finally autonomous and united under a single prince, and Cuza governed them from 1859 to 1866.

By able diplomacy he succeeded in obtaining permission to unify his two assemblies, and financial and judicial organs. The first Rumanian political parties emerged, the conservatives being the party of the great landowners, and the liberals favoring agrarian reform. This was the major issue in Rumania, and in 1864 Cuza simply rammed through a new constitution enfranchising the peasantry, and giving the prince the power to legislate. He followed this with an agrarian reform bill emancipating the peasantry from serfdom, and abolishing feudal dues, much in the manner of the Russian emancipation law of 1861. State bonds compensated the former proprietor of serfs, and the peasants had to make annual payments for fifteen years. As in Russia, a peasant's holding was usually too small to enable him to live decently, and the payments were more than he could afford. The nobles continued to possess much of the forest and pasture land.

Cuza also managed to obtain for the state the "dedicated" monastery lands which had belonged to monastic foundations outside Rumania, and which sent abroad enormous annual sums in revenue. He passed a sweeping law making education compulsory — so sweeping that all its provisions could not possibly be put into effect, but at least recognizing that education was the obligation of the state. But Cuza's regime was redolent of scandal; he lived an irregular personal life, and conservatives and liberals united in 1866 to obtain his abdication and replace him with a German prince, Charles of Hohenzollern-Sigmaringen. Charles was elected in a comic opera plebiscite by a vote of 685,969 to 224, and arrived in Rumania after a comic opera voyage, disguised as a salesman in blue goggles, traveling second class on a Danube River steamboat to elude the vigilance of the Austrian police. He obtained a new constitution, modeled on that of Belgium, with a bicameral legislature, a class system of voting, and a special Rumanian provision making it impossible for foreign Jews to be naturalized. The Sultan accepted the new prince, and the Rumanian dynasty was well-launched. By the 1870's Rumania, like Serbia, had become virtually free, but was still cursed by political and economic backwardness.

5. *The Freeing of Bulgaria*

Because the Bulgarians were so close to the Ottoman capital, and suffered the most consistent oppression from Turkish and Greek misrule, their liberation was delayed well beyond that of Serbia and Rumania. In the Russo-Turkish war of 1827–1829, which brought to the other two peoples a substantial improvement in their position, Bulgarian bands participated; but when the war was over, the Russians made no comparable effort on behalf of the Bulgarians. The Turks successfully put down three minor insurrections before 1851.

Bulgarian society in the nineteenth century was simple, the peasantry either contributing a certain amount of produce and labor annually to their village authorities for the benefit of the Turkish landlords, or serving the landlord directly as share-croppers, or as landless day-laborers on the landlord's land. A small class of gentry, the *chorbashi,* often peasants by origin, accumulated money as moneylenders, and served as intermediaries between the Turkish authorities and the population. Sometimes they collected the taxes. Though helpful to the authorities, many of the chorbashi also helped the educational movement in their country, and exhibited feelings of Bulgarian patriotism. In the small towns along the main trade routes, a commercial class grew up, engaged in the sale of native textiles, metal work, and preserved meat. A system of gilds, or privileged corporations of merchants and artisans, flourished in these towns. Under their own master and council, the gilds regulated the behavior of their members and supported schools and churches from their treasuries. They too provided a source of leadership in the struggle to take the national church out of Greek hands, and then to free the country from the Turks. Bulgarian colonies of merchants also settled abroad, in Braila, Bucharest, Odessa, and Smyrna, as well as Constantinople.

In the 1830's, with the foundation of the first school at Gabrovo, there began a lively intellectual movement. Within ten years the number of schools was fifty; they used books printed in Serbia. Western ideas penetrated the country along several clearly visible channels. American missionaries, arriving in the 1850's, founded schools and Congregational and Methodist churches, but put the chief emphasis of their work on education and social service, rather than on proselytizing. These kind and intelligent and selfless men and women proved an inspiration to many Bulgarians. Polish refugees from the Revolution of 1848 brought the popular ideas of nationalism and liberalism. The beginnings and development of the rose-oil industry led a few Bulgarians to Paris, and opened the way for direct French influence.

On the islands of the Aegean were Greek schools, which Bulgarian students attended, and where they also found themselves exposed to the new ideas. The Prechani Serbs, who had been so important in educating the Serbs of Serbia, also exerted direct and indirect influence on Bulgarians who went to Karlovtsi or Belgrade. Farther west, in Prague and Vienna, the Slavs of the Habsburg monarchy were studying Slavic origins. Even in Constantinople, some 30,000–40,000 Bulgarians plied the trades of tailor or gardener or shopkeeper, and many of them sent their sons to the French *lycée* opened by the Sultan himself in 1868, or to the American college, founded as early as 1840, which became Robert College in 1860. Perhaps the most important influence of all was Russian, exerted through the seminary at Odessa, which established scholarships for Bulgarian students beginning in 1840. Though most of the Russian sponsors of educating Bulgarians in the decades that followed hoped to train a generation of young south Slavs who would be loyal to Tsarist Russia, and would some day help the Tsar to overthrow the Turks, most of the Bulgarian students emerged as revolutionaries, deeply affected by the populist current then sweeping Russian student and intellectual circles.

Inside the Ottoman Empire itself, during the period from the 1820's to the 1870's, the spirit of reform was active, and the reformers were struggling against the entrenched system to improve the administration and westernize the state, while attempting to give members of the Christian minority equal rights and equal responsibilities. A major manifesto enunciating these principles was issued in 1856. In the propitious atmosphere which this generated, the Bulgarians strove to obtain a church free from Greek control. Interestingly enough, one of their methods was negotiation with Rome, just as it had been during the middle ages, and the papacy consecrated a Bishop of a Bulgarian Uniate Church. But, like the early Bulgarians, those in the nineteenth century really wanted their own Orthodox establishment. A Greek insurrection on the island of Crete in 1866 rendered the Turkish authorities thoroughly dissatisfied with the Greeks in general, and in 1870 the Turks consented to the creation of an autonomous Bulgarian church, under an "Exarch." Except for mentioning the name of the Greek Patriarch at Constantinople in his prayers, and certain other minor ecclesiastical matters, the Exarch was the subject of the Sultan, and not of the Patriarch.

Initially the Bulgarian Exarchate included only the Turkish province (Vilayet) of the Danube: that is to say, northern Bulgaria. But it was envisioned that other areas might join if two-thirds of the inhabitants voted to do so. In 1872 a plebiscite in Macedonia and Thrace resulted in an extension of the Exarchate to these territories, although it is doubtful whether two-thirds of the population really voted in that sense. Many Macedonian Slavs preferred the Greek church. The extension of the exarchate greatly alarmed the Greek and the Serbian churches and governments, and the appointment of the first Exarch was delayed some time. The Bulgarian church had now become a political question of the first importance, and the long years of conflict over Macedonia were foreshadowed.

In these years too, Bulgarian revolutionaries were debating the nature of their future state. In Bucharest a secret committee was formed in 1866; its first leader, Rakovsky, was rather a conservative, favoring a western constitutional monarchy. The second, Karavelov, succeeded him in 1867. Rejecting the idea of a dual monarchy between Bulgaria and Turkey on the Austro-Hungarian model, he favored a federation among the Balkan Christian peoples with a common parliament and separate administration. Only in such a union, he maintained, would the Balkan peoples become strong enough to resist Russian domination, which he greatly and rightly feared. Genuinely democratic, and a great admirer of the United States and of Switzerland, Karavelov is sometimes wrongly claimed by the leftists as an ancestor of their own. He retired in 1874, and died five years later. His successor, Hristo Botiev, was indeed a social revolutionary, with somewhat anarchist rather than Marxist leanings. He was to be killed in 1875, when the Bulgarian uprising began, and is now a hero of the present-day Communist rulers of Bulgaria. The Bulgarian revolutionaries, then, varied in their political views, and had no definitive plan for organizing the new country when it should come into existence.

It was the great Balkan crisis of 1875–1878, culminating in another Russo-Turkish War and in the decisions of the Congress of Berlin, that produced Bulgarian autonomy, and profoundly altered the balance of power in the region. The crisis began in Bosnia, where Ottoman tax-collectors continued to be as unpopular as ever, especially as Serbian propaganda for union flowed across the frontier. A visit paid by the Austrian Emperor in 1875 to his province of Dalmatia, during which he received delegations made up of Catholics from Bosnia-Hertsegovina, touched off the actual uprising. This soon spread to Bulgaria, and by the spring of 1876, the Turks, in putting down the Bulgarians, had committed the celebrated "Bulgarian atrocities," killing perhaps 10,000 men, women, and children in standard Ottoman punitive style.

Despite the efforts of the powers, Serbia and Montenegro entered the war against Turkey. This was the moment when the Russian Pan-Slav movement was at its height. The Serbian commander-in-chief himself was a Russian Pan-Slav, and Russian public opinion was warmly behind him and his forces. When the Turks proceeded to defeat the Serbs, Russian aid and volunteers poured into Serbia. England, traditionally pro-Turkish, out of a wish to protect imperial communications, could not this time help Turkey against the Russians as she had done in the Crimean War, because the Liberal Party under Gladstone made a political issue of the Bulgarian "atrocities," and tied the hands of Disraeli's Conservative government. So the Russians eventually entered the war, having first made sure of Austrian benevolent neutrality by promising Bosnia and Hertsegovina to Vienna as the price.

The Russian armies crossed Rumania, whose prince now proclaimed full independence, and joined the Russians as an ally. The Turks were defeated, and on March 3, 1878, the Russians required them to sign the Treaty of San Stefano, a strongly Pan-Slav document. The Turks agreed to recognize both Serbia and Rumania as independent. The Russians agreed to give Rumania the southern Dobrudja in exchange for the restoration of southern Bessarabia, which had been awarded to the Rumanians after the Russian defeat in the Crimean War. Most important, the San Stefano treaty provided for the creation of a large autonomous Bulgaria, including most of Macedonia. The new state would have an elected prince, tributary to the Sultan, and Russia would occupy it for two years. Moreover, it would be the biggest state in the Balkans. It would hopelessly shatter Turkish territory in Europe into unconnected fragments. It was not essentially unsound ethnically, since many of the inhabitants of Macedonia in 1878 certainly thought of themselves as Bulgarian. The treaty did, however, violate an agreement with Austria, by which the Russians had promised not to create a large Bulgaria.

The powers, especially England, were certain that the new state would be a mere Russian satellite. At the Congress of Berlin, the powers of Europe modified the Treaty of San Stefano beyond recognition. The big Bulgaria was not created. Instead, the Macedonian portion went back to the Turks. The rest was divided into two provinces. North of the Balkan mountains would be a politically autonomous principality of Bulgaria, with its capital at Sofia. For nine months, until an assembly should have prepared a constitution, a Russian commissioner would govern Bulgaria. South of the Balkans, the new province of Eastern Rumelia, including Plovdiv and Burgas, was put under the direct political and military authority of the Sultan. Eastern Rumelia was to be administered by a Christian prince, to be selected by the Sultan with the approval of the powers for a period of five years. Austria obtained the right to occupy Bosnia and Hertsegovina, over which the Sultan retained sovereignty.

6. *From the Congress of Berlin to the Formation of the Balkan League (1878–1912)*

The Berlin settlement left the Russians deeply disappointed at having fought a severe war for comparatively little gain. It also gave the Bulgarian nationalists a permanent wound. They were deprived of their large Bulgaria before it had even had the chance to come into existence. The frontiers of San Stefano became an ideal after which several generations of Bulgarian politicians deeply yearned. They chiefly blamed the English for their disappointment. Many of the policies adopted by the Bulgarian state down into our own day can be explained in terms of efforts to reach the frontier of which they felt deprived. The Serbs, although recompensed by independence and the obtaining of Nish and other territories, were bitterly opposed to the Habsburg occupation of Bosnia-Hertsegovina, while the Rumanians felt cheated at giving up southern Bessarabia. It was of course the Ottoman Empire which had suffered most by the new partition, but the Congress left a legacy of dissatisfaction throughout the Balkan region.

In the years following the Congress of Berlin, the leadership of the Rumanian Liberal Party, the Bratianu family, strongly supported the growth of an urban middle class, giving little attention to the methods by which its members made their money. Though representing the interests of the large landowners, the Conservatives, when in office, were hardly distinguishable from the Liberals. Certain efforts were made by both parties to enable the peasant to buy land from the state reserves, but the large landowners were the chief beneficiaries. In foreign policy, both the King and his ministers leaned toward Germany, as insurance against the Russian threat, and Rumania became secretly linked with the triple alliance of Germany–Austria-Hungary–Italy, despite the widespread pro-French feeling in the country. The alliance prevented Rumania from doing anything to play upon the rapidly rising discontent of the Rumanian minority in Transylvania, where Magyar persecution raged unchecked. But public sympathy with oppressed fellow-Rumanians grew steadily stronger and more articulate.

Prosperity ruled, as the petroleum resources began to be exploited. The railroad network grew; canals, bridges, and new harbors improved transport and commercial opportunity, major scandals accompanying each new advance. Yet the overwhelming majority of the citizenry, the peasants, lived in misery and ignorance. In 1907, influenced by the Russian revolution of 1905, the Rumanian peasantry in Moldavia rose in revolt, as the more far-sighted among Rumanians had long been predicting. Turning first against the Jewish middlemen, the peasants directed their hatred against the landlords also, by pillaging the large estates and beginning a march on the capital. It took full-scale military action by the regular army, and the slaughter of at least 10,000 peasants to restore order.[2] After the uprising only minor palliative measures were passed, and the landlords' essential powers remained intact. The Rumanian peasant did not share in the national prosperity, and his condition was pitiful when compared to that of the Serbian or Bulgarian peasant, who owned his own land, and helped to govern his native country.

After the Congress of Berlin, Prince Milan Obrenovich, disillusioned by the Russian abandonment of Bosnia-Hertsegovina to the Austrians, and the apparent partiality of the Russians for Bulgaria, signed a treaty with Austria, which virtually made Serbia an Austrian client state, since the Serbs could not conclude a political agreement with any other power without consulting Vienna first. While the Rumanian alliance with Germany and Austria did not impede national policy, Serbia, tied to Austria alone, did not for some years regain freedom of action.

In Bulgaria, the Russians assisted the Bulgarian notables in their debates on a constitution, modeled on the one Serbia had adopted in 1869. A "Grand National Assembly" (Sobranie) would vote on special problems like the election of a prince or constitutional change, while a "National Assembly" only half the size would deal with routine legislative business. The constitution, adopted at Tirnovo in 1879, was a thoroughly democratic document, so far as

[2] The present Communist regime has published the official documents: M. Roller, *Rascoala Ţaranilor din 1907*, 3 vols., Documente şi Marturi pentru Istoria României (Bucarest: Editura de Stat, 1948–49).

suffrage and civil liberties were concerned, but gave the prince a sort of veto-power over legislation. Moreover, it included no safeguard against its own suspension.

Alexander of Battenberg, a German prince related to the Tsar and the English ruling house, came to the throne as first Prince. He found himself in difficulty with the Russians, who had many civil officials in the country. All officers in the Bulgarian army above the rank of lieutenant were Russians. The native liberals supported the Prince in his effort to whittle down Russian influence. The Russians, for example, wanted the Bulgarian railroad lines linked to Russia and not to Vienna. For a brief period in the 1880's, St. Petersburg actually sent two Russian generals to Bulgaria, one of whom served as Prime Minister and the other as Minister of War. Needless to say, such open domination was unpopular in the country.

When the inhabitants of Eastern Rumelia staged a bloodless coup in 1885, and proclaimed their union with Bulgaria, Alexander of Battenberg was faced with the choice between offending the powers, including Russia, by accepting, and offending his nationalist subjects by refusing. He accepted; the Russians withdrew their army officers; the Bulgarian army, with its lieutenants now all promoted, defeated a Serbian attack, and it looked as if the Bulgarians would march to Belgrade. This crisis was averted and a settlement reached, but in 1886 the Russians succeeded in kidnaping Alexander, and eventually in forcing his resignation. His successor was Prince Ferdinand of Coburg, a cynical officer in the Austrian army. Ferdinand's election almost precipitated a Russian-Austrian war.

During the 1880's there began the active rivalry among Bulgarians, Serbs, and Greeks for the Turkish province of Macedonia. Determined to make good the losses of the Berlin Congress, the Bulgarian government spent vast sums on founding schools in the province, designed to teach the pupils that they were Bulgarian. The fact that most of the inhabitants had voted themselves ecclesiastical subjects of the exarchate assisted the Bulgarian effort. Deprived of Bosnia and Hertsegovina and defeated by Bulgaria in war, the Serbs too now founded patriotic societies to agitate in Macedonia, in order to convince the population that they were truly Serbian. Greeks and Rumanians also played the game, the Rumanians chiefly in the hope that they would obtain diplomatic bargaining power by calling the attention of the powers to the Vlachs in Macedonia.

Conditions in Macedonia deeply affected Bulgarian internal politics, as about 100,000 Macedonians immigrated into Bulgaria by the mid-1890's, including about half the population of Sofia itself. When the Turks temporarily suspended the Bulgarian schools in Macedonia in 1894, the ensuing agitation among the Macedonians led to the dismissal and assassination of the Prime Minister, Stambulov, a very talented politician. In 1895, the Macedonian exiles founded their own Supreme Committee, the so-called "external" organization, because its leadership lived in Bulgaria. In 1896, came the "internal" Macedonian Revolutionary Organization, known as IMRO, which proceeded in secret to organize Macedonia itself according to military districts, levied its own taxes on the population, drafted recruits, and administered its own extremely rough justice, all in a province which was still part of the Ottoman Empire. From a war of propaganda, the Macedonian rivalry became a war of rifles, kidnapings, bomb outrages, and terrorist raids on the peasant population. Open battles between the IMRO and the Serbs, Greeks, and Turkish regulars became the order of the day. Within the Macedonian terrorist organization, there were always two major parties. One party always intended that Bulgaria should annex Macedonia, and worked with the Bulgarian army and right-wing politicians. The other party hoped to create a sizable new autonomous Macedonian state including the Turkish vilayets of Kossovo, Monastir, and Saloniki. In later decades this party would come to believe that an autonomous Macedonia could survive only as a member of a Balkan Federation, which they would therefore strongly support. Some of them would become Communists.

In the great Ilinden (Elias' day) rebellion of August 2, 1903, IMRO demanded complete autonomy for Macedonia backed by a general guarantee from the powers. The powers, indeed, were increasingly concerned at the situation in Macedonia. War threatened, and both Russian and Austrian prestige and interests would be involved. At Mürzsteg, they agreed on a program of reforms, which they imposed on the Sultan. Russian and Austrian "assessors" would inspect the region with the Ottoman military commander. The *gendarmerie* would be reorganized by a staff of European officers representing all the powers. Russian, Austrian, French, Italian, and British zones were created, and a German took over the task of inspection of the schools. The largest remaining area of Ottoman domination in Europe had now become the scene not only of fierce rivalry between the recently liberated nationalities but also of great-power intervention to preserve the peace. In the fate of the Mürzsteg program and in Macedonian developments after 1903 lay the key to great changes in Turkey and in the Balkan world.

During these years in Serbia, Russian influence was hard at work to undermine the special position of Austria. By 1900, considerable success had crowned the Russian efforts, as the Tsar alone looked with favor on the marriage of Milan's son, King Alexander Obrenovich, to Draga Mashin, a Serbian lady with a somewhat dubious past. The marriage itself outraged many Serbs, especially as the King repeatedly showed a predilection for personal rule, and the Queen, who was incapable of bearing children, pretended to be pregnant, arousing the widespread fear that she would introduce into the palace a child which she would then pass off as her own. When her pregnancy proved false, the fear spread that her brother would be proclaimed the heir to the throne. Failure to pay the army promptly alienated the officer corps. The public found Alexander inept in foreign policy as well. Propaganda in favor of the representative of the rival dynasty, Peter Karageorgevich, began to circulate in

Serbia. Peter had fought bravely in the Bosnian uprising of 1875, and had since lived in Geneva.

Officers and civilians now hatched a conspiracy, whose leaders were in touch with Peter Karageorgevich. It culminated in June 1903 with the notorious invasion of the royal palace in Belgrade by a group of army officers, who murdered Alexander and Draga, and threw their mutilated bodies out of the window. Several prominent politicians also lost their lives. A new constitution was adopted. Peter Karageorgevich, a fundamentally decent and liberal man of sixty, who had translated John Stuart Mill's *On Liberty* into Serbian, was the beneficiary of these sensational and bloody events. Although he was prepared to abide by the constitution, and to maintain the policy of friendship with Russia and with the other Balkan countries, he found the powers of Europe at first reluctant to recognize him because of the atrocities which had led to his elevation. Russia was busy with a war against Japan in the far east.

Peter therefore turned to Bulgaria, and the two countries reached a cultural and economic accord, and planned a political alliance as well. When the Austrians learned that Serbs and Bulgarians were planning a tariff agreement, they demanded the right to pass on its contents. When the Serbs refused, the Austrians closed their frontiers to Serbian livestock. This touched off the celebrated "pig war" of the years 1906–07, an Austrian effort to bring Serbia back into line by severe economic pressure. The Serbs found other markets for their produce, and the effort hurt the Austrians more than the Serbs. But, even after the frontier was reopened, the Austrians continued to exert political pressure. They announced their intention of building a railroad through the Sanjak of Novipazar and south to Saloniki, which would have given them a line running between Serbia and Montenegro, effectively preventing the eventual union of the two Serbian states. Serbs and Russians countered this with a project for a railroad running from the Danube to the Adriatic. Though nothing came of either project, these developments of the years between 1904 and 1908 greatly increased Balkan tensions. Moreover, the Serbian-Bulgarian negotiations had been thwarted, and the Bulgarian Prime Minister who had been responsible for the treaties of 1904 was assassinated.

In the key year 1908, there took place the Young Turk Revolution, which began among the army officers stationed in Macedonia, and which led to the adoption of a constitution by the Ottoman Empire, and to a brief period of good feeling between the Turks and their Christian subjects. It was not long, however, before the Young Turks showed themselves to be more nationalist than liberal. The Austrian monarchy decided to take advantage of the crisis to annex the provinces of Bosnia and Hertsegovina, which they had now been occupying for thirty years. They arranged that at the same time Prince Ferdinand of Bulgaria would proclaim his full independence from Turkey, and would follow the Serbian and Rumanian rulers in taking the title of King (actually "Tsar of the Bulgarians," to remind his subjects of his mediaeval forerunners).

In order that two such drastic further assaults upon the Ottoman Empire should not create a major international crisis, it was of course necessary to have Russian consent. This the Austrians thought they had obtained by agreeing to open the Black Sea Straits to Russian warships. But Russian Pan-Slav officials did not support the Russian Foreign Minister in his willingness to see the Austrians take over Bosnia and Hertsegovina. They wanted instead to form a Balkan League under Turkish leadership as a block to further Austrian advances. Moreover, England was unwilling to deal the Young Turk government a further blow by supporting the Straits program of her new ally, Russia. Thus the Russians could not obtain what they wanted, and believed themselves betrayed by the Austrians. As a result, Europe was severely rocked by the "Bosnian" crisis. The Russians supported the Serbs, who vigorously protested against the annexation of Bosnia and Hertsegovina, and mobilized their army. Balkan tensions might well have precipitated a major war, had it not been that the Russians were not yet prepared to fight. They backed down, and the Serbs had to follow suit.

In addition to those Russians who wanted to obtain the opening of the Straits by securing the consent of the other powers, and those who wanted to create a Turkish-sponsored Balkan League against Austria, there were others who wanted to create a Balkan League without Turkey, and directed against both Turkey and Austria. It was this third policy which eventually triumphed. Under their aegis, and stimulated by the Italian attack on Turkey in Tripoli in 1911, a Balkan League of this sort gradually took shape.

The key problem was to bring Serbia and Bulgaria together over Macedonia. This was of course a difficult matter, in view of the powerful and uncompromising secret societies in both countries. Not only were the Macedonian organizations active in Bulgaria, but in Serbia the assassins of Alexander and Draga formed two successive organizations to obtain Serbian aims. The first, *Narodna Obrana* (National Defense), formed just before the Austrian annexation of Bosnia, to carry on Serb propaganda, put its emphasis on cultural activities. The second, *Uyedinyenye ili Smrt* (Union or Death), founded in 1911, was an overlapping organization, devoted to terrorism, and often called the Black Hand. Its leader, Dragutin Dimitriyevich, known as "Apis," was a Serbian army colonel, and its aims extended not only to Bosnia-Hertsegovina but also to Macedonia: it planned to unite all Serbs under Belgrade.

In the face of opposition from the secret societies, the Bulgarian and Serbian governments signed a treaty in 1912. In the event of their driving the Turks from Macedonia, they agreed to administer all conquered territory jointly for a period of three months. Thereafter, Serbia would obtain the Sanjak of Novipazar and the region north and west of the Shar mountains. Bulgaria would get the region east of the Rhodopes and the Struma. The large area in between would be autonomous if possible. If not, it would be further subdivided into three parts, with Bulgaria getting the largest easternmost share,

Serbia getting Monastir, and the Tsar of Russia determining the fate of the central section including Skoplye. The provisions showed how crucial the Macedonian problem was, and how difficult to settle in any way which would be satisfactory to the powers. This treaty was followed by Greek-Bulgarian, Bulgarian-Montenegrin, and Serbian-Montenegrin alliances. There was no Greek-Serbian alliance, and Bulgaria thus remained the pivot, linked to the other three.

7. *The Albanian National Awakening*

Before this Balkan League, so full of menace to the Ottoman Empire, had been completed, the Turks found themselves in deep trouble in Albania. Here, the national awakening had been delayed longer than anywhere else in the Balkans. It was not until the sessions of the Congress of Berlin in 1878 that the Albanians as such made themselves felt in Europe. The Berlin settlement awarded to Montenegro substantial areas whose population was in fact Albanian, while the Greeks were claiming the region of Korcha, which they regarded as "northern Epirus," the extension of their northwest province. Ironically enough, it was the Sultan himself, sure of his loyal Muslim Albanian subjects, who stimulated them now to protest against the territorial award to Montenegro. A League for the Defense of the Albanian Nation, usually called the "League of Prizren," after the town where it was founded, sent a memorandum to Disraeli, declaring that Albanians would fight to keep their territory in the Ottoman Empire. They asked that all Albanians be united in one province, to be governed from Monastir by a Turkish governor-general, who would be advised by an Albanian committee, to be elected by universal suffrage. Albanian would be the language of administration. To this and other demands the Congress of Berlin paid no attention, Bismarck simply stating flatly that there was no such thing as an Albanian nationality.

The Albanians, however, effectively prevented the Montenegrins from taking the lands which the Congress had assigned them. In the end, it took a naval demonstration by the six great powers of Europe to force the cession of the Adriatic port of Dulcigno (Ulcinj) to Montenegro. The League of Prizren, which the Turks had first encouraged, now alarmed them, and the Ottoman authorities arrested and exiled its leaders. By 1881 the League, though proscribed, had effectively called the attention of several distinguished European observers to the existence of the Albanian people. It had also shown its devotion to the national language, as all other Balkan national movements had done in their early days.

In Albania in the last quarter of the nineteenth century, the Muslim population, about 70 per cent of the whole, received what schooling was available only in the Turkish language. The Orthodox population, about 20 per cent of the whole, living largely in the south, had Greek schools. Only among the small Roman Catholic minority in the north, where both the Franciscans and the Jesuits had founded schools in Scutari, was there any opportunity to study in the native language. Indeed, Albanian was not yet in fact a written tongue, and there was considerable doubt whether Greek or Latin characters should be used in printing it. Some Bible translations of the early nineteenth century had appeared in the Greek alphabet. The British and Foreign Bible Society, on the other hand, which maintained offices in Monastir, printed a Latin-alphabet Bible and the first dictionary in the 1860's.

In 1879, the Albanians resident in Constantinople formed a Society for the Development of the Albanian Language, which used a mixed alphabet, largely Latin. It published its own periodical, and issued an inspirational pamphlet on the past, present, and future of Albania. Suppressed after the Turks had shut down the League of Prizren, the society transferred its headquarters to Bucharest in 1884. Like the Bulgarians twenty years earlier, the Albanians found refuge in Rumania, and continued their cultural nationalist activities there. The Greeks as well as the Turks participated in the persecution of Albanian culture. In 1886, the Patriarch of Constantinople threatened to excommunicate anybody found reading or writing Albanian. There were, however, two American-sponsored schools in Korcha, one for boys, and one for girls, where the native language was openly taught, and whose pupils clandestinely taught their families and friends to read and write it. The decade of the 1880's was the seed-time of nationalism for the least advanced of the Balkan peoples.

By the early years of the twentieth century, an anti-Turkish Albanian newspaper was appearing in Brussels, under the editorship of the distinguished Ismail Kemal Bey Vlora, and the League of Prizren carried on many secret activities inside Albania itself. The Young Turk revolution and the proclamation of the constitution and equality of all the subjects of the Ottoman Empire encouraged the Albanian nationalists to emerge from hiding. Ismail Kemal Bey Vlora returned to the country, and was elected to the Turkish Parliament, and an Albanian Congress at Monastir voted to use the Latin alphabet for the native language. But the Young Turks soon disillusioned the Albanians by their adoption of a policy of brutal Ottomanization and repression.[3]

By 1909, guerrilla operations against the Turks were in full swing, and in 1911 there was a large-scale rebellion. In these troubled waters, the eager Montenegrins gladly fished. The Serb Black Hand Society also stimulated the rebels. Thus Turkish folly alienated the Albanians, the only previously reliable European subjects of the Sultan, at the very moment when a Bulgarian-Serb-Greek-Montenegrin League stood ready for the attack.

8. The Balkan Wars and the Albanian Frontiers

In the summer of 1912 the first Balkan War began. Within a month, the Turks were pushed back to the defense of Constantinople. The Balkan armies

[3] They legalized the bastinado for certain offenses, legislated against carrying rifles, a practice dear to Albanian hearts, restricted the press, tried to impose the Arabic alphabet, tried to introduce conscription, and officially denied that there was any such thing as an Albanian nationality.

had overrun all Turkey in Europe except for Scutari, which the Montenegrins were besieging; Janina, which the Greeks were besieging; and Adrianople, which the Bulgarians were besieging. All three of these were eventually taken, but the powers did not let the Montenegrins keep Scutari. The Serbs took all northern Albania, and reached the Adriatic at Durazzo. It soon became clear that the Balkan states would not be allowed to dispose according to their own wishes of the territories they had conquered. Both Austria and Italy were irreconcilably opposed to a Serbian outlet on the Adriatic. Instead, they both favored the creation of an Albanian state. The Austrians feared that a Serbian Adriatic port would in fact be a Russian port. They foresaw that Slavic agitation would spread into their Dalmatian province and into the Magyars' Croatian satellite, thus posing a threat to the very existence of the Habsburg monarchy.

By the Treaty of London, which ended the first Balkan War on May 30, 1913, the Turks surrendered all their possessions in Europe west of a line drawn from Enos on the Aegean to Midia on the Black Sea. The process of fragmentation, which had begun with the Serbian revolt of 1804, had now reduced Turkish territory in Europe to a tiny fragment. The great powers undertook to draw the boundaries of a new Albanian state, to include Scutari on the north, but with no fixed borders either north or south. Moreover, the new country had no government. During the first Balkan War, Ismail Kemal Bey Vlora had proclaimed Albanian independence, and set up a mixed Christian-Muslim government with himself as president. But the powers had not given him recognition, and now decided that Albania should be an independent sovereign hereditary principality with a prince to be chosen within six months by the powers themselves. Meanwhile, an international commission administered the country.

The collapse of the Balkan League and the outbreak of the second Balkan War, however, jeopardized all plans for the area. Rumania and the Balkan allies were growing more and more hostile to Bulgaria. The Rumanian cause for grievance was that the Bulgarians had been willing to give them only the Danube town of Silistria, although Bulgarian territorial gain had been so material. Apparently the Rumanians did not stop to consider that the Bulgarians had won their gains by shedding their blood, and that their own demands virtually constituted blackmail. Even worse were Serbian-Bulgarian relations. When the Serbs learned that the powers were not going to permit them to keep their north Albanian gains, or to have their outlet on the Adriatic, they asked the Bulgarians to reconsider the territorial provisions of their pact, and to give them a larger share of Macedonia. This the Bulgarians refused to do. Moreover, there had never been any firm territorial agreement between Bulgaria and Greece. As a result both states were claiming Saloniki and other parts of Macedonia. Now the Serbs and Greeks, both angry at Bulgaria, reached an agreement of their own, dividing all Macedonia west of the Vardar between them, and deciding to fight the Bulgarians if they would not arbitrate.

The Montenegrins joined the new alliance, and it was clear that the Rumanians would also attack Bulgaria when the new war broke out.

This it did when the Bulgarian armies in Macedonia attacked both Serbs and Greeks. The Bulgarians put themselves in the wrong by this act of aggression, which was probably intended only as a demonstration, but which now, in June 1913, launched a second Balkan War. Not only the Rumanians but the Turks also joined the fighting against the Bulgarians. Within a month, the fighting was over. By the Treaty of Bucharest of July 30, 1913, Serbia obtained the Monastir region of Macedonia, while Greece got Saloniki and Kavalla. The Rumanians obtained the northern Dobrudja, and by a later settlement the Turks regained Adrianople and Thrace to the Maritsa. For a second time, the territories for which the Bulgarian nationalists longed had in large part been denied to them. Serbia and Montenegro divided the Sanjak of Novipazar, and obtained a common frontier.

Meanwhile, the powers were painfully trying to draw the frontiers of the new Albania, in the face of desperate Serb attempts to stay on the soil they had conquered. Finally, the Austrians, without notifying the other powers, sent the Serbs an ultimatum to get out of Albania within a week. The Serbs reluctantly withdrew, but bitterly resented the high-handed methods of the Austrians. Vienna, however, received firm support from the German Kaiser, who remarked at the time (October 26, 1913): "When His Majesty Emperor Franz Joseph demands something, the Serbian government must give way, and if it does not then Belgrade will be bombarded and occupied until the will of His Majesty is fulfilled. And of this you can be certain, that I stand behind you, and am ready to draw the saber whenever your action makes it necessary."[4] It was perhaps little wonder if this incendiary talk encouraged the Austrian Foreign Minister, Berchtold, to think highly of the policy of ultimatums to Serbia. The point is worth stressing, since the outbreak of World War I was then less than a year in the future.

In spite of all their efforts, the powers failed to draw frontiers for Albania. The winter weather of 1913–14 forced cessation of the work of the commission in the north; soon after it resumed in the spring of 1914, the war broke out. In the south, Greek troops occupied the country, and Greece strove to dominate the area. Here too, despite negotiations, and a protocol of December 1913, awarding "northern Epirus" to Albania in principle, the affair hung fire until after the outbreak of the war. Meanwhile, a German Prince, Wilhelm zu Wied, had been chosen as Prince of Albania. Inside the country, Essad Pasha had rebelled against Ismail Kemal Bey Vlora, and taken over most of the central portion of the country with a capital at Durazzo. Both of these governments finally gave up their powers to the allied control commission, and Wilhelm landed in Durazzo in March 1914. But while Austria wanted the

[4] Quoted in E. C. Helmreich, *The Diplomacy of the Balkan Wars, 1912–1913* (Cambridge, Massachusetts and London, 1938), p. 428.

new Albania to be strong and serve primarily as a block to Serbian advance, Italy wanted it weak to permit Italian domination of the Adriatic. Wilhelm never controlled much of his turbulent country, and after the outbreak of war, deserted by the powers who alone could have kept him in office, he left Albania, after about six months of miserable rule. The wildest anarchy followed.

Thus the Balkan Wars liberated all of southeast Europe except eastern Thrace from Ottoman domination, but produced their own crop of difficult Balkan problems. After all their victories, the Bulgarians were now restricted to a short stretch of the Aegean coast line, and smoldered with resentment against their former Balkan partners, who remained determined not to permit any territorial revisions in Bulgaria's favor. Cut off from the Adriatic, the Serbs were more bitter than ever against Austria, the power which had also annexed Bosnia-Hertsegovina, and were fully determined to fight a "second round" against the Habsburg Monarchy. Torn between the Serbs and the Greeks, preferring the Turks to either, given a prince who meant nothing to any of them, the Albanians suffered a collapse of all internal order.

9. Croatia and Bosnia to 1914

In these years during which the Ottoman Empire in the Balkans finally disintegrated, the south Slavs of the Habsburg lands also reached a feverish pitch of discontent. Chafing under Magyar domination, the Croats were furious at the Hungarian seizure of the thriving port of Fiume, which they regarded as lost Croatian territory. The Magyar governors tried their best to foster the antagonism between the Croats and the Serbian population of Croatia, putting Serbs into local offices. When Starchevich died, his son-in-law, Dr. Josip Frank, ironically enough a Jew by birth, took over the "Party of the Right," and called it now the "Party of the Pure Right," becoming more intransigently nationalist than ever. These leaders the Magyar government jailed, but Croat-Serb rioting recurred repeatedly. About 1900, Stepan Radich founded the Croatian Peasant Party, which favored not only liberation from Hungary, but also the social emancipation of the peasantry, and the end of Magyar landlordism.

By 1903, Serbs and Croats in Croatia were beginning to coöperate against the Magyars. Inspired by the teaching of Thomas G. Masaryk, the learned Czech statesman, under whom many south Slavs studied in Prague, both groups began to combine democratic views with their nationalism. The Serbs of Croatia supported the Croats in their demand for Dalmatia. When the Magyar Railway Servants Act of 1907 required all workers on the railroads to speak Magyar, the Croats began to boycott Hungarian goods. The Governor retaliated by arresting some fifty-odd Serbs and Croats, and trying them on charges of conspiring to unite Croatia and Bosnia with Serbia. The evidence was ridiculously inadequate; the defendants, though condemned, obtained a reversal of the verdict on appeal to a higher court. But these Zagreb trials of 1909 gave the Slavic press an opportunity to denounce the government. So did the case in the same year of the Austrian historian Friedjung, who charged in the Vienna press that the politicians in Croatia were conspiring to join Serbia. Friedjung was forced in court to admit that his documentary sources were forgeries. Thus the Habsburg monarchy, both Austrian and Hungarian portions, compiled a miserably bad record of dealing with its south Slav inhabitants. In 1912, a Bosnian student studying at Zagreb tried to assassinate the Hungarian Governor of Croatia. The student was a member of one of the Belgrade secret societies. He received praise in the Belgrade press. In 1913 and again in 1914, disgruntled Slavs, one of them a Bosnian, took pot-shots at the Governor's successor. These acts appeared in retrospect to be rehearsals for another assassination in which the bullet was to find its target.

In Bosnia and Hertsegovina, despite the efficient and enlightened rule of Baron Kallay between 1881 and 1903, the preservation of Habsburg rule depended entirely upon the local garrison. The Serbs were deeply affected by propaganda from Belgrade. The Croats wanted to join Croatia. The Muslims, though favored by the Austrians, who made no effort to change the system of land tenure, resented the departure of the Turks. The annexation of 1908, by apparently closing the doors to any of these solutions, added to the depth and sullenness of the resentment. The heir to the Habsburg throne, Archduke Franz Ferdinand, had a considerable appreciation of these facts. He favored the abolition of the dual monarchy, and its replacement by a triple monarchy in which the south Slavs would have the same status as the Austrians and Magyars. The Vienna and Budapest die-hards naturally opposed such a solution. So did the Serbian and Croatian patriots.

The rest of the story is all too familiar. Franz Ferdinand visited Sarayevo on June 28 (St. Vitus' Day, the anniversary of Kossovo) 1914. A young Bosnian student in Belgrade crossed the frontier and killed him with weapons from the Serbian state arsenal. The exact degree to which Apis was implicated is unclear, nor do we know whether the Serbian Cabinet was aware of the plan, although in a general way and on his own initiative the Serbian Minister in Vienna had warned that the appearance of Franz Ferdinand in Sarayevo might lead to trouble. The Austrian ultimatum which followed demanded that the Serbs permit Austrian officials to join the investigation of the crime and the suppression of the secret societies. It was so harsh that it was probably intended to be rejected. The Serbian reply went a long way toward compliance. Even the Germans thought that negotiation would clear up the remaining points at issue. But the Austrians declared war. In a short time, the Russians were mobilizing to back the Serbs; the Germans were mobilizing to back the Austrians, and the great powers were at war: Germany, Austria-Hungary, and Turkey against Russia, France, Great Britain, and eventually Italy and the United States.

10. The First World War and the Territorial Settlements

Here we can only review summarily the military and political developments in the Balkan countries during the war. The Serbs, with great losses, repelled two Austrian invasions, and by the end of 1914 had cleared their soil of the invader. Both allies and central powers bid for the support of the Bulgarians and Rumanians. To Bulgaria the allies eventually offered much of Macedonia, compensating the Serbs by a promise of Bosnia-Hertsegovina and Adriatic outlets. But the Bulgarians preferred the German side, since the Germans did not share the allied obligations to the Serbs. Entering the war in October 1915, the Bulgarians together with German and Austrian forces, drove the Serb armies westward in a retreat through the dead of winter across Albania and on to the Greek island of Corfu, where the survivors rested and regrouped. King Peter accompanied his troops. The allied forces which had been landed at Saloniki were unable to provide help to the Serbs. Their campaign northward did not begin until the end of 1916, and was not immediately effective. Austrians and Italians fought each other in the mountains of Albania.

It was the allies who won the auction for Rumania, promising Transylvania, the Banat, and Bukovina, a glittering offer which the central powers could not meet, since the territories were all parts of the dual monarchy. In August 1916, the Rumanians attacked, but the central powers beat them back, and occupied most of the country with all its rich resources. By early 1918, the Rumanians withdrew from the war, and made peace with the central powers, turning over all of the Dobrudja to Bulgaria, giving Austria-Hungary control of the strategic passes of the Carpathians, and Germany a ninety-year lease on the oil wells. In Bessarabia, however, the Rumanian population, taking advantage of the defeat of Russia, elected an assembly which proclaimed union with Rumania. Despite Russian protests, the central powers recognized this territorial gain.

In the fall of 1918, the reorganized armies of the allies, based on Saloniki, and including the re-formed Serbian forces, knocked the Bulgarians out of the war, and forced them to conclude an armistice which demobilized their army and left their territory free for allied operations. When the allied forces crossed the Danube into Rumania, the Rumanians came back into the war on the allied side. The Serbs cleared all of their country of the enemy, and advanced into the Banat, while the Italians took over Albania. As the Habsburg Empire disintegrated, politics, never abandoned even during the hottest military operations, took over the center of the stage.

During the war, the Serbs settled in bloody fashion a still mysterious high-level military and political quarrel of their own. Apis and two others were tried at Saloniki and shot in 1917, on charges of attempting to assassinate the heir to the throne, Prince Alexander, then acting as regent for his father. It is not clear whether the veteran Black Hand conspirators were destroyed by a rival army and political clique called the White Hand, and deeply involved in the murder of King Alexander Obrenovich in 1903, or whether it was felt advisable that men who knew too much about the Archduke's assassination should be removed.

Whatever the truth of this ugly business, in which Prince Alexander was heavily implicated, the most important wartime development was the growth of a program for unity among the southern Slavs. Alexander proclaimed the Yugoslav ideal in 1916, and a Yugoslav Committee operating in London commanded the support of many Croats and Slovenes as well as Serbs. In July 1917 on Corfu, the Serbian Premier Pashich and the Croatian President of the Yugoslav Committee, Dr. Ante Trumbich, signed an agreement providing that all south Slavs should join in a new kingdom under Alexander Karageorgevich. Serbs, Croats, Slovenes, and Montenegrins would have a degree of autonomy to be determined by the new constitution. Radich, leader of the Croatian Peasant Party, supported the decision, with some reservations. He would have liked to see the Bulgarians in the new state, and he would have preferred the republican form of government. The Italians, to whom the secret Treaty of London (1915) had promised much of Dalmatia, as a price for entry into the war on the allied side, found themselves faced with determined south Slav opposition. At a Congress of Oppressed Nationalities at Rome, including Czech, Polish, Rumanian, and Yugoslav delegates, the Italians in the spring of 1918 informally agreed to recognize Yugoslav self-determination. Still the Yugoslavs felt hurried into proclaiming their new state in order to forestall Italian territorial claims. After Croatian and Montenegrin bodies had acted, King Alexander became King of the new state of Serbs, Croats, and Slovenes on December 4, 1918.

The Yugoslavs had been correct in their haste and their apprehension of danger from Italy. The Italians wanted not only all that the London Treaty had promised them but Fiume as well, which the flamboyant adventurer, D'Annunzio, was to occupy briefly in 1919 with a private proto-fascist army. It was President Wilson, at the Peace Conference, who refused to accept the London Treaty; and the Conference ended, after many stormy moments spent discussing the Italo-Yugoslav frontier, without a settlement of the subject. Not until October 1920 did the Treaty of Rapallo between Italy and Yugoslavia draw the frontier. Italy obtained most of Istria, four of the Dalmatian islands, and the city of Zara (Zadar). Fiume became a free city, which Mussolini's fascists were to seize in March 1921. Only in March 1924 did Yugoslavia concede Fiume, obtaining the neighboring Porto Barros. Frightened of a united south Slav state across the Adriatic, the Italians alienated the Yugoslavs. The whole quarrel left a legacy of bitterness which would last through and after the Second World War, when the question would focus on Trieste, not on Fiume.

A less critical but sensitive problem was provided by the new frontier with Austria. The Yugoslav claims to the region of Klagenfurt were rejected by a plebiscite held in October 1920, in which a Slovene majority voted for union with Austria. With Hungary, the Treaty of Trianon of June 1920 gave Yugoslavia the Voyvodina, except part of the Banat, with a large Magyar and German minority. The remainder of the Banat went to Rumania. The frontier drawn then is the one which has been restored today. With Bulgaria, the new frontier was planned to give the Yugoslavs certain strategic salients for defense, but Macedonia remained divided.

The new state was more territorially than the most patriotic Serb could have imagined. Great areas of Macedonia, all Bosnia and Hertsegovina, all the Habsburg south Slav lands except for what had fallen to Italy now came under the jurisdiction of Belgrade. The new Yugoslavia should have been a satisfied state. But the preparation for such growth was inadequate. To the Serbs it appeared that all they now had to do was govern the rest of their compatriots. To the others, it seemed that they had exchanged one form of bondage for another. The future of the new state was to be stormy indeed.

Rumania too acquired virtually all the territories to which Rumanian nationalists had any claim. As Austria-Hungary disintegrated in 1918, the Transylvanian Rumanians, rejecting a last-minute offer of full equality from the desperate Magyars, overwhelmingly supported a resolution adopted at Alba Iulia on December 1, 1918, calling for union of all Rumanians in one state. Modeled on the mass-meetings of 1848, the new assembly also declared that in the new Rumania all nationalities should have the right to use their languages freely, all institutions should be entirely democratic, basic civil liberties should be guaranteed, and radical agrarian reform should put an end to the outmoded system of land tenure and peasant society. Iuliu Maniu, a Uniate lawyer, who had served since the early years of the century as deputy in the Hungarian Parliament at Budapest, and had distinguished himself as an opponent of all the Magyar measures oppressing his fellow-Rumanians of Transylvania, emerged as elected chief of the Transylvanians. Rumanian armies entered Transylvania, and invaded Hungary itself during the Bela Kun Bolshevik regime. In the summer of 1919, Rumanian troops entered Budapest, where they indulged in all the sweet pleasures of revenge on their ancient enemies. They did not leave, despite the protests of their own allies, until early 1920, when they took with them great quantities of Hungarian goods.

The Peace Treaties, as ultimately signed, awarded to Rumania not only Transylvania proper with its half-million Szeklers in a compact mass in the bend of the Carpathians, but Maramureș, Crișana, and the eastern Banat. The westernmost strip of this region had a large Magyar population, and was assigned to Rumania for strategic reasons; but the extreme Rumanian claim for a western boundary on the Theiss was rejected. Bukovina too returned to Rumania after almost a century and a half under Habsburg rule. As for Bessarabia, its acquisition by Rumania continued for a considerable time to be *de facto* only. The Soviet government never recognized the loss of the province, and the other powers agreed to recognize Rumanian possession in 1920, but delayed ratification until 1924, in the case of England and France, and 1927 in the case of Italy. The division of the Banat with the Serbs was negotiated directly.

As in the case of the new Yugoslavia, territorial satiation brought the new "greater" Rumania its own serious problems. The Ottoman and Phanariot tradition of the Old Kingdom (Regat) was now combined in one state with the Habsburg and Magyar tradition of Transylvania, much as in the case of Serbia and Croatia. In addition, there was Bukovina, which had always been well-run from Vienna, and Bessarabia, which had been both neglected and oppressed under Tsarist rule. The grave social and economic problem presented by the large estates and the oppressed conditions of the peasantry urgently demanded an immediate answer, if the Rumanians were not again to experience, as they had in 1907, their own imitation of a Russian revolution.

Bulgaria, the loser at the Congress of Berlin and in the second Balkan War, lost for the third time as the result of the World War. Not only were the frontiers with Yugoslavia somewhat revised in favor of the Yugoslavs, but the Greeks now received the entire Aegean coast line, and Bulgaria had only its Black Sea outlets. Refugees from the areas awarded to Greece and Yugoslavia made the atmosphere of Bulgarian politics even tenser with irredentist longing than ever. Relations with the Balkan neighbors remained hostile. The foreign tensions were at least matched by those in domestic political and economic life.

Albania suffered political partition during the war. The Treaty of London of 1915 envisaged Italian possession of Valona and a portion of the nearby coastal area. Serbia and Montenegro would obtain much of the northern portion, and Greece much of the south. The tiny central Albanian area remaining would be an autonomous state, but Italy would "represent" it in its relations with other powers. This dark future for Albanian nationalists was modified during the war by declarations that Albania should be unified and independent but under Italian protection. When the war actually ended, however, the Italians were in occupation of most of the country, with the French at Korcha and Scutari. An Albanian provisional government eventually was formed, despite Italian opposition. At the Peace Conference, Serbs, Greeks, and Italians all put in their territorial claims. Especially after it became clear to the Italians that they were not going to get all of Dalmatia, they felt it necessary to assert ever more loudly their claims to Albania.

Essentially, it was Wilson's insistence on the principle of self-determination that led to eventual Italian capitulation on the subject, but first an Albanian National Congress had met at Lushnja in January 1920, and decided to hold general elections for a national parliament, which should nominate a Cabinet. By March 1920, the first regular Albanian parliament had been elected, and a government under Suleiman Bey Delvine had been formed. The Minister of the Interior was a young Muslim chieftain of the Mati tribe, who had distinguished himself during the war. His name was Ahmed Bey Zogu. Since

Wilhelm zu Wied had never formally abdicated, Albania was still nominally a monarchy. A council of regency was therefore appointed with four members: a Bektashi, a Sunni, a Roman Catholic, and an Orthodox. In the south, native Albanians were appointed to be prefects and sub-prefects in the administrative districts laid out by the French and Italian occupiers.

The formation of a government in Albania and the disinclination of the Italians to go on fighting led to the withdrawal of troops. By August 1920, Italy recognized the Albanian government at Tirana, and signed a treaty by which Italians retained only the island of Saseno off Valona. In December 1920, Albania was admitted to the League of Nations. Though the country was both sovereign and independent, and so recognized, it still had no exact boundary lines, and these had to wait until 1926 and 1927. Moreover, the problem of establishing a stable state in the face of Italian and Yugoslav intrigues would prove extraordinarily difficult.

Chapter 6

FROM THE FIRST WORLD WAR TO THE SECOND

VIEWED IN RETROSPECT, the period between the wars was too short a time for the Balkan countries to work out their destinies satisfactorily. Imported constitutions, liberal though they might be, did not reflect the true levels of political maturity which the area had achieved. Cynical politicians flouted them with impunity, and substituted manipulation and rigging for genuine consultation of public opinion. Everywhere, experiments in free government failed. But this was the period when western liberal institutions were being repudiated in more advanced states as well. Scarcely was war damage mended when depression struck. In depression's train came irresistible internal and external pressures. As a whole, the Balkan peoples were insufficiently educated; they lacked the will to defend institutions which were not indigenous, and were all too often a sham. Even more than most other Europeans, they were trapped in a dreadful century whose motive power they did not understand.

1. Social Structure and Political Expression

THE RULING GROUPS AND THEIR POLITICAL PARTIES

The war and the immediate postwar years brought substantial social change to those Balkan landowning aristocracies which had survived: the Rumanian, the Bosnian, and the Croatian. In 1917, ten years after the slaughter of the peasants in the revolt of 1907, the Rumanian government found itself defeated in war, its country occupied by the Germans, and its peasant soldiers exposed to the news of a successful revolution in Russia, across the frontier. The King in person promised them land and a larger role in politics. In 1918, the promise was fulfilled. We shall examine later the provisions of the land reform and its economic implications. Here we must note that the large landowners became reduced to the level of a small gentry. This gentry, together with the small urban business and professional and urban class, formed the dominant class in Rumanian political and social life. The day of the great "boyar" was over. The same development took place in the Habsburg lands of Yugoslavia. Only in southern Albania did the old system prevail. Here the powerful beys kept both their lands and their influence. But the postwar land reform gave Rumania and all Yugoslavia a social pattern far more like that of Serbia and Bulgaria than it had previously been.

Numerically, of course, the new amalgam which formed the ruling group was very small compared to the peasantry. It was largely recruited from among the sons of peasants who had obtained higher education, and stayed in the cities to enter the civil service, the professions, or business, rather than return to the farm. Politics was closely linked with law and university teaching. The professions were overcrowded, especially the law, and Balkan capitals were often full of unemployed intellectuals or would-be intellectuals, spoiled for the farm by their education and their pride, and living their lives on the edge of bitter penury. This tended to make them extremists, seeking to alter by one violent means or another a society which had been so unjust to them. In the Balkans, political parties were more often a matter of personal following than of program and organizational or educational endeavor. Personal magnetism and demagogic skill brought more than one such unemployed intellectual forward as the leader of a successful right-wing or left-wing political group. These were the men on the fringe of the ruling class.

In the center of the picture were the successful commercial and professional people. Though often only one generation from the peasant village, this ruling group of the Balkan middle classes had little interest in the welfare of the peasantry as such. Having arranged for land reform, the politicians of this class felt they had done their duty. Education for the peasant, even agronomical education, could wait; roads and transportation to the market could wait; even farm implements and credits could wait. The politicians proceeded to put their energies and their resources into industrialization. And their tax policies hit the peasant every time. Import duties on agricultural machinery and implements went up so far as to put these necessities beyond the reach of the peasantry. Yet the prices paid for the peasant's own produce remained low. He paid for the industrialization, which, as we shall see, did not advance far enough to benefit him, and his standard of living was wretched. The Liberal Party of the Bratianus in Rumania, the (Serbian) Radical Party of the wartime Serb Premier Pashich in the new Yugoslavia were outstanding examples of parties which represented the new ruling group. They became the more important because the parties which had represented the point of view of the great landlord in Rumania and Croatia naturally disappeared with the disappearance of the landlord class.

Passionately nationalist, adept in rigging elections and all the shadier tricks of Balkan politics, making the state responsible for economic progress and therefore identifying national interest with the new industrial interest, these parties were in many ways responsible for the continued corruption which all observers noted in the Balkan countries. The American reader should not make the mistake of confusing the developments here described with our own concepts of "free private enterprise." We consider that competition is the essence of industrial development. The Rumanian Liberals, the Serbian Radicals, and their counterparts operated by state subsidy to favored industries and favored individuals, who expressed their gratitude by political contributions. The bureaucracy swelled enormously, and its members were as dependent upon business as business was upon the politicians.

THE PEASANTS AND THE "PEASANT" PARTIES

The reader will ask at once whether the downtrodden peasantry in countries where universal suffrage was the rule could not make its displeasure felt through the use of the ballot, no matter how the party in power might choose to stuff the ballot boxes and announce rigged results. The answer is a complicated one. In the first place, the Balkan peasant was not prepared by his historic experiences to understand the complicated problems of twentieth-century society. His political outlook was focused on his own interests: the wish for land, the need for credit to work it successfully, and the hope for reduced taxes.

One could explain to him that industrialization would eventually help his country to improve his lot, but to grasp this required a great effort, and in the interval he saw the city-dwellers enriching themselves (and often ostentatiously displaying their wealth) while he remained poor. The technical problems as to where the capital was to come from could not concern him at all. It was little wonder that he regarded his new government as simply the latest installment in a long history of hoax and persecution. Usually docile and suspicious by nature, the Balkan peasant now allowed his docility to become political apathy, his suspicion to become increased resentment of the town-dweller, the official, and the politician.

Yet there were political parties in the Balkan countries which claimed to represent the peasant point of view. In the Old Kingdom of Rumania, a radical agrarian movement led by Ion Mihalache, himself a peasant by birth but a schoolteacher by profession, had culminated just after the war in the formation of a Peasant Party; the party ideology harked back in some degree to the populist views expressed in the first decade of the twentieth century by Constantin Stere, a Bessarabian nobleman who had been associated with the populist revolutionaries in his native province while it was part of Russia. The Russian populists (*narodniks*) had been anti-Marxist socialists, cherishing a deep, often mystical, belief in the peasantry as the class whose communal institutions provided the means for Russia to avoid capitalist development as it had taken place in the west. Some believed in industrialization, others did not; but all glorified the peasant. Many populists were intellectuals, who had a sense of ancestral guilt at the thought of the way in which their country and the privileges of the leisure class had been built up on the labor of the peasant, and they conceived themselves as owing the peasantry a great debt which they must pay.

Stere's views reflected these attitudes of the Russian populist. Unlike the Russian Social Revolutionary Party, however, which also grew from a populist origin, Stere argued that Rumania could now never industrialize, since the more advanced countries had already captured all the markets. What he wanted was a rural democracy based on peasant villages, strengthened by coöperation, and industrialized only to the extent to which idle peasant labor might be used during the winter months in household industry. He also envisaged crafts and small industry, and favored the nationalization of existing large industry, such as petroleum. Against the Marxists, who contended that the good Rumanian society must wait upon successful revolution in the west, he argued that the peasantry itself could furnish leaders and transform Rumania into a kind of Balkan Denmark. In his nationalism and his anti-capitalism, he sometimes let a note of anti-Semitism appear.

Much less visionary than Stere, Mihalache put his own emphasis on the complete destruction of large estates, and the establishment of coöperation. A practical politician rather than a theorist, he did not rule out industry for Rumania as an eventual source of wealth for all classes, but concentrated upon the immediate practical issues. The chief economic theoretician of the party, Madgearu, no longer fought against the concept of industrialization, but pointed to the peasant's preponderant numerical position, and his important role both as producer and as consumer. As citizen, the peasant could, if he were articulate politically, prevent the financial oligarchy from dominating the country, whether through democratic forms or through dictatorship when the left seemed to threaten. Mihalache's and Madgearu's radical peasant democracy reached its expression in the twenties, just at the time when extremist movements were pushing such concepts to the wall everywhere in Europe.

In 1926, the Peasant Party of the Old Kingdom fused with the National Party of Transylvania, led by the distinguished Iuliu Maniu, whom we have already encountered as a deputy at Budapest standing up for the rights of the Rumanians in Transylvania against their Magyar oppressors. Because most of the Transylvanian Rumanians were peasants, and had Hungarian landlords, Maniu's party favored land reform as part of its defense of Rumanians. But the national rather than the peasant program was always more important to these Transylvanian politicians, none of whom was himself a peasant. Indeed, before its merger with the Peasant Party, the Transylvanian National Party had already absorbed one wing of the Old Conservative Party, which had represented the landlords. Some of the Peasants were disturbed at the conservative viewpoint of the Transylvanians. The merger was one factor diluting the peasant ideology of men like Mihalache, which had in any case, however, grown more temperate with time. The whole party lost its fire. It also lost what peasant character it had had. Though Mihalache wore peasant costume on all occasions, appearing at Bucharest cocktail parties in his long white woolen drawers, most of his colleagues in the party were city men and professionals. When they came to power, they paid little attention to agriculture; and the main feature of their policies was actually the friendly welcome they extended to foreign capital in Rumanian industry, in contrast to the Liberal policy of favoring a native industry entirely dependent on native investment. As political representative of the peasantry, the Rumanian National Peasant Party was inadequate.

In Yugoslavia, both Serbs and Croats had peasant parties also. The Serbian Democratic Party, in origin an offshoot of the Radicals, preserved a good deal more of the Radicals' original concern with peasant problems than the parent organization, but essentially its emphasis was the same. The Agrarian Party, on the other hand, pitched its appeal to the peasants. Its leadership, however, remained in the hands of city people: business and professional men. Though it had considerable support among the radical peasantry of Bosnia and Hertsegovina, its success with the voters never reached the level of the Radicals or the Democrats, which itself is the best evidence that the peasants failed to identify the interests of their class with the Agrarian program or the Agrarian leadership. In the last years before the war, the left-wing Agrarians, under Dragolyub Yovanovich, revived radical populist programs. But it was Stepan Radich's Croatian Peasant Party which alone in Yugoslavia deserved to be compared to the Rumanian National Peasants, as a party at least in its inception truly devoted to peasant interests. Indeed, it preserved its character somewhat more successfully than its Rumanian opposite number.

Radich was himself a peasant, an extraordinary orator, and a believer in a peasant state. It was his brother Ante who was the more consistent theorist, the brains of the peasant movement, but Ante died before the creation of Yugoslavia. Stepan was a strong Croat partisan, and properly suspected the expansionist tendencies of the Serbian dynasty, bureaucracy, and nationalist politicians. Combined with this mystical passion for the Croat peasantry went an astonishing capacity for changing his mind, an inability to formulate clear demands or to stick to them, and a willingness to obstruct rather than to bargain. By visiting Moscow in 1924, Radich produced the false impression that he was perhaps some sort of agrarian Bolshevik. Like Maniu in Rumania, his strength lay in opposition, and he rarely seems to have asked himself whether this was the way to gain his ends. Some of the ablest and most intellectual Serbs in Croatia, under the leadership of Svetozar Pribichevich, formed in

1927 the Independent Democratic Party, which was restricted to Serbs living in Croatia, and which was one of the most liberal and democratic of all Yugoslav political formations. The Independent Democrats collaborated with Radich, in opposition to the Serb-centered tendencies of Belgrade.

Even before Radich was assassinated on the floor of the Parliament (Skupshtina) in 1928, the Croat Peasant Party had begun to lose its purely agrarian character. The widespread support it enjoyed among the peasantry tempted professional men and city politicians to capitalize on the failure of genuine peasant leadership to materialize. Most peasants were too busy and insufficiently educated to go in successfully for actual political leadership. Moreover, the old middle-class parties of prewar Croatia with its restricted franchise were now simply swamped in the high tide of universal suffrage. Unable to conquer the Peasant Party, they joined it, and made it something quite comparable to the Rumanian National Peasant Party and quite distant from the peasants themselves. It became chiefly a mouthpiece of Croat national discontent with Serbian maladministration. Radich's successor, Vlatko Machek, himself a lawyer, cared deeply for the fate of the peasant, but was unable to weld together in an effective political instrument the left wing of his party, true to its radical peasant principles, and its right wing of city people. The right wing paid lip-service only, and sometimes not even that, to the old program of the Radich brothers, and cared more for sabotaging the "Yugoslav idea" than for the interests of the peasant. Many of the far right members now looked back with nostalgia to the good old Habsburg days, and lamented the loss of Croatian ties with Catholic Central Europe. In their views they came close to the Starchevich-Frank line of Croatian political thinking, and were far removed from the Strossmayer-Radich-Machek line.

In Bulgaria, unlike Rumania and Croatia, the large estate had not existed. Here, Alexander Stamboliisky, a peasant and a passionate peasant ideologist, had founded a Peasant Party before the war. He had also opposed the participation of Bulgaria in the war on the German (i.e., anti-Russian) side. Postwar disillusionment with wartime defeat brought him into power. Alone among the peasant leaders, the Bulgarians got a chance, though a brief one, to put their ideas to the immediate test. Further land-reform made the country more egalitarian than ever. Compulsory education began to deal with the problem of illiteracy. A progressive income tax produced a budget surplus. A compulsory labor law drafted all young Bulgarians for one year of useful work for the state.

But Stamboliisky was personally authoritarian; his enthusiastic love for his fellow-peasants was matched by his enthusiastic hatred for the city, and the people who lived and worked there. Then too, his fellow-Agrarians were not up to his own high standards of efficiency and moral behavior. It was no wonder, of course, that untrained peasants should have abused high office and engaged in corrupt practices, or that politicians were suddenly dazed by their first experience of power. This was an example of what the Communists call a "lack of cadres." Combined with the ruthlessness of the Prime Minister and the scandalous behavior of many of his henchmen went a high-minded but unpopular foreign policy. Stamboliisky was an apostle of close relations between Bulgaria and Yugoslavia, as an initial step toward Balkan Federation and a union of all South Slavs. He was responsible for the Nish Convention of 1923, which provided for joint Bulgarian-Yugoslav measures to prevent disorder on their common frontier. But his theories extended to all of peasant Europe.

With the support of Czech Agrarian leaders, Stamboliisky sponsored an International Bureau of Agriculture, called the Green International, signifying its opposition to the Red or Communist International. With offices at Prague, the Green International strove during the twenties to initiate widespread coöperation among the peasant parties of Europe, western as well as eastern. The Rumanian National Peasant Party initially viewed it with some suspicion as a Slavic organization, and felt that progress must begin within each individual country. They eventually joined it, however, as did the Croatian Peasant Party, and other European peasant parties. Though the agrarian leaders thus established contact with each other, and exchanged information and ideas, the forces of industrialism and communism against which they were fighting were too strong to be effectively combated. The governments of the eastern European peasant states also tried to coördinate their economic policies in the face of the industrial states, and to get a better deal in international trade. But this movement, with which the Green International had little to do, collapsed as a result of the depression.

Probably few Bulgarians knew or cared deeply about the Green International. But all knew about Stamboliisky's wooing of the Yugoslavs. Recently defeated by Serbia, and still smarting under the loss of Macedonian territory, most Bulgarians, especially the highly organized Macedonian terrorist organizations, violently opposed such policies, while the short-sightedness of the Yugoslav government prevented their reaching any fulfillment. The city-dwellers, the Macedonians and pro-Macedonians, the army, the King of Bulgaria, Boris, who succeeded his father Ferdinand at the end of the war, all opposed Stamboliisky. A *coup d'état* in 1923 ended in his murder and the destruction of much of his work by his right-wing successor, Alexander Tsankov. The Communists, who might have helped Stamboliisky and his party, refrained until it was too late. Thereafter, Bulgarian Agrarians of the Stamboliisky stamp mostly went into exile or into hiding. A more conservative wing of the party continued to operate openly, and to engage in party politics. When allowed to return in 1933, the radicals succeeded in founding a newspaper, *Pladne* (Noon), which publicized their doctrines. But it was not until the Second World War that the Agrarians again played a critical role in Bulgarian public life. Then, for the second time, the result was tragedy.

Whereas in Rumania and Croatia the Peasant Parties became urbanized and almost unrecognizable, in Bulgaria many of their members remained peasant revolutionaries.

THE WORKERS AND THE MARXIST PARTIES

The growth of industry, though not far advanced in any of the Balkan countries, had produced by the end of World War I a distinct urban working class in Yugoslavia, Rumania, and Bulgaria. Very few in numbers everywhere, Balkan factory workers were of course recruited from the peasantry. Since, as we shall see, rural overpopulation was a ubiquitous problem, the labor supply remained large, and wages low. In undeveloped industry, seasonal work was also a characteristic feature, the peasant leaving home for the winter months, and earning in town the cash needed to supplement his income from the farm. Except for the petroleum industry in Rumania, and for the railroad workers and printers in all the countries, there was very little "class-consciousness" among the Balkan workers. If the history of Communist movements teaches us anything, it is that countries with undeveloped industry and a large measure of agrarian discontent often produce a few skillful politicians and conspirators who can create mass support for Communist parties without much help from the small "proletariat" or the trades unions. In Yugoslavia and Bulgaria, the prevalence of peasant discontent, together with the widespread popularity of Russia, helped to account for the growth of substantial Communist movements in the absence of any substantial industrial working class. A Communist vote was a protest vote. In Rumania, where the peasants were more apathetic and the feeling for Russia was hatred and fear, the Communist movement remained very small indeed; instead, demagogues of the right were able to win the protest votes.

The ancestors of the Yugoslav Communist Party were the Croatian, Slovenian, and Serbian Social Democratic Parties. The first, developing in the Habsburg monarchy, was under the influence of Central European Marxists and Anarchists, and as a party, dates from 1894. It had a considerable following among the peasants, as well as among the printers and other workers. It met with short shrift at the hands of the Magyar governor, not emerging from a period underground until 1906. Its program was generally "reformist": the improvement of working conditions and the increase of political freedom, and it did not hesitate to coöperate with the "bourgeois" parties. The Slovene Social Democrats too were under the influence of their elder brothers in Vienna, but had their own organization after 1896, and their own newspapers.

In Serbia, the socialist movement did not take on a Marxist character until the 1890's. During the first decade of the twentieth century, internal quarrels raged over the questions whether to coöperate with the "bourgeois" parties, whether to try to dominate the labor unions, and whether to accept peasants as members. The faction which opposed coöperation with the bourgeois parties, but favored an effort to dominate the trade movements and the admission of peasants as members won the fight. Tito has praised the winning faction as the most truly Marxist, and pointed to the fact that the Serbian Social Democrats were among the few Marxist Parties in the national parliaments of Europe who refused to vote for credits for the pursuit of the First World War. In Bosnia and Hertsegovina also, a Social Democratic Party developed under Austrian occupation, especially in the first decade of the twentieth century, when it led strikes among tobacco-workers and others for shorter hours and higher wages.

Inspired by the October Revolution in the USSR, the Serbian Social Democratic Party took the lead in bringing about a fusion of the other social democratic movements in 1919 and 1920. Repudiating the "social chauvinists" who had supported the war and the Second International, the new Socialist Workers Party of Yugoslavia (Communist) joined the Comintern. At the Second Congress at Vukovar in 1920, the party expelled right-wing and center elements, and adopted a program calling for a Yugoslav Soviet Republic, with its own people's army, the expropriation and socialization of industry and commerce, protection of the workers' jobs, socialization of public health facilities, compulsory education, separation of church and state, and the cancellation of workers' taxes.

Looking back in 1948, Tito strongly criticized the Vukovar program on three grounds. The Communists had not grasped the importance of the "national" question: the efforts of the Serbs to transform Yugoslavia into the greater Serbia they had always dreamed of, and the resistance of the other nationalities, especially the Croats. Failing to exploit this grievance by taking a firm position on national autonomies, the Communists in 1920, by their endorsement of "national unity," actually seemed to support the great Serbs themselves. Moreover, the Vukovar program erred with regard to the question of land reform, not specifically enunciating a program of land-distribution among the poorer peasants. Third, the cancellation of workers' taxes, and program for support of the state by taxes from the wealthy ran counter to a proper plan for the elimination of capitalism. Of these criticisms no doubt all were justified from the point of view of a doctrinaire Communist speaking in 1948; the most cogent, however, from the point of view of practical politics, was surely the first, since the national question dominated all Yugoslav politics between the wars, and the Communist Party failed to capitalize on it.

From the first, the government of the Kingdom of the Serbs, Croats and Slovenes strove to repress the Communist Party. Its chief enemy was the Minister of the Interior, Milorad Drashkovich, whose ministry controlled the police. None the less, the party won a series of municipal elections in important towns, including both Belgrade and Zagreb, and in the nation-wide elections to the Skupshtina of November 1920, polled some 200,000 votes, and won 58 of the 419 seats in that body. At the time, the party membership was less than one-third the number of votes which it polled—a clear demonstration that many Yugoslavs were voting the Communist ticket simply as a protest against the regime. Moreover, the strength of the party was smallest in the more industrialized province of Slovenia, and largest in rural Macedonia and Montenegro. The party also fomented strikes and took a leading role in widespread public demonstrations against foreign intervention in Soviet Russia and Bela Kun's Hungary. The government denied the Communist deputies their seats in the Skupshtina, closed the Communist press, and took other repressive measures. These culminated in 1921, after a Bosnian Communist had assassinated Drashkovich, with the outlawing of the party. The same law for the security of the state forbade Communist or anarchist propaganda, strikes by public employees (which included railroad workers), and Communist political activity by trades unions. This effectively muzzled the Communists, who went underground, and remained there until World War II. Their effort to create a legal "front" party, called the "Independent Workers of Yugoslavia," proved a failure in 1923, when it polled fewer than 10 per cent as many votes as the Communists in 1920. A small group of former right-wing and center members, who had been purged by the Communists themselves, continued to operate as a legal Socialist Party, but never commanded any significant public support.

Underground, and no longer able to serve as the channel for non-party voters' discontent, the Communist Party of Yugoslavia lost its popular following, and much of its early membership. It now experienced years of factional strife. This reflected the conflicts raging in the USSR at the same period; indeed, the CPY had become a faithful tool of Moscow. It was, however, not sufficiently faithful to imitate the early Soviet policy of secession and autonomy for the minorities, and thus it lost what political opportunity it might otherwise have seized, since this was the issue which in these years chiefly interested Yugoslavs. On the other hand, it is difficult to accept in full the justice of Tito's criticism of Sima Markovich, the Yugoslav party boss in these years, since we cannot tell how seriously it would have hurt the Party in Serbia if it had supported Croat separatism. At the time, Stalin and the Russians kept urging the CPY leaders to seize this issue, and thus explode the Kingdom of Serbs, Croats, and Slovenes from within. But it seems likely that many of the Yugoslav Communists were Yugoslavs first, and hesitated before embarking on a path that would lead to the shattering of a state of which they had dreamed. By 1926, Markovich's reluctance had been temporarily overcome, and the party endorsed secession.

But now the reflection of the Stalin purge of Trotskyites and Bukharinites, his enemies of the left and of the right, appeared in Yugoslavia. Tito, then a young party leader in Zagreb, begged for guidance from the Comintern, going over the heads of his superiors. In 1928, Moscow asserted its authority, purged Markovich, installed a new leadership including Tito, and forced an endorsement of secession, not only for the Croats, Slovenes, Macedonians, and Montenegrins, but even for the Hungarian and Albanian minorities. With many of the leaders, including Tito, in jail, the party fell on evil days. Its sponsorship of a hopeless revolt against King Alexander in the early thirties cost it many activists. In 1932, Milan Gorkich, whose real name was Chizhinsky, and who was probably a Czech, took over as leader. With the Moscow adoption (1935) of the popular front line against the rise of fascism, the CPY, acting on orders, scrapped secessionism as a policy. Its leadership, having got the word from Stalin, declared that the rise of Hitler made secessionism impossible, and that Yugoslavia must continue unified, while the state was "reorganized" peacefully. In other words, Moscow estimated that the breakup of Yugoslavia, which would have benefited the USSR in the 1920's, would benefit Hitler in the 1930's.

In 1937, Gorkich was purged as a Trotskyite, and Tito became Secretary-General. He was regarded as a loyal Stalinist. A Zagreb metal-worker named Josip Broz, whose Party name was "Walter," he had been taken prisoner by the Russian armies in the First World War, and had played a part in the Bolshevik Revolution. He now began the job of building the CPY underground. It was small, but it could count on the anti-Mussolini and anti-Hitler sympathies of many Yugoslavs. Intellectuals of all ages, and especially university students flocked to join or at least to sympathize. The Spanish Civil War brought military experience to many young activists. The whole atmosphere of the Popular Front period all over the world was favorable to the growth of pro-Communist sympathies among those who disliked fascism. So skillful was Tito's clandestine operation that the Fifth Party Conference could be held in Zagreb in 1940, with 105 delegates participating and no arrests made by the ubiquitous and efficient police. Tito spent to some purpose the four years between his election as Secretary-General and the engulfment of Yugoslavia in war. His whole organization was entirely loyal to Moscow, and Moscow doubtless regarded him as one of its most capable disciples.

In Bulgaria too, communism dated back to the last decades of the nineteenth century. Founded in 1891, the Social Democratic Party soon found itself split between two factions, the "narrows" (*tesni*) and the "broads" (*shiroki*). The tesni, whose leader was the venerated Dimiter Blagoev, were stanch "anti-reformist" Marxists, and opposed all coöperation with non-working-class parties, while the shiroki took the opposite position. To the tesni today's Bulgarian Communists give the credit for insistence on class warfare, leading a large miners' strike in 1906, and pushing the movement for an eight-hour working day and social legislation. These improved working conditions and other reforms are not of course Bolshevik goals, and the Bulgarian Communist historians make it clear that the tesni were not true Leninist Bolsheviks, though their opposition to Menshevism and their strong party discipline entitled them to respect. They did not, for instance, realize that capitalism had reached its final "imperialist" phase. They therefore could not become the "vanguard of the working class," and lead a revolution. Nor did they understand Lenin's thesis about the revolutionary usefulness of the peasantry as an ally of the proletariat, and so they mistakenly kept on regarding the peasantry as hopelessly conservative. In 1903, the tesni split away from the shiroki; both continued to be members of the Second International, though the tesni opposed the Balkan Wars, which the shiroki supported. In 1912, the tesni received 10,000 votes in a general election (at a time when they had some 3,000 members), but they had no representatives in the Sobranie.

The widespread national discontent following Bulgaria's loss of the second Balkan War led to many more votes for tesni candidates. By the outbreak of World War I, they had eleven deputies in the Sobranie. They protested against the Second International's support for the war, and voted against credits for the Bulgarian government at the end of 1915, when Bulgaria came into the war. They favored a federation of Balkan republics. Their leaders, including a printer and trades-union leader named Georgi Dimitrov, then in his late twenties, went to jail. The new defeat gave the tesni increased opportunity, since they had predicted it. They were of course affected by the successful Bolshevik Revolution in Russia. In 1919, they broke with the Second International, joined the Third (Comintern), set up in Moscow, and took the name of Bulgarian Communist Party.

In 1948 Georgi Dimitrov said that, if the tesni had taken proper advantage of conditions in Bulgaria, they might have made a successful revolution in 1919 by forging an alliance of discontented troops and discontented peasantry. As it was, they elected 44 deputies out of a total of 236. They fomented strikes, which Stamboliisky suppressed, and captured a large number of municipal city councils in elections. Indeed, they became very strong among civil servants, trades unions, and in some coöperatives. When the anti-Stamboliisky forces staged their coup in June 1923, the Communists stood idly by. They explained their action on the grounds of Stamboliisky's earlier anti-Communist activities, including the suppression of strikes. But later they declared that their failure to join the peasants, led by Stamboliisky's Agrarians, against the forces of the right, had constituted a signal historic error. They had "underestimated their own strength among the masses, and the masses' hatred for fascism and for the crown." Moreover, they had failed to follow Lenin's policy of a "united front," preached in 1921.

Rebuked by the Comintern, they tried to lock the barn door after the horse had been stolen. Failing to obtain substantial help from non-Communists, the Bolshevik wing of the Bulgarian leadership, under Dimitrov and Vasil Kolarov, staged a revolt anyhow. Without the help of the Agrarians, whom Tsankov had already smashed, the effort failed in September 1923, and Tsankov, in true Bulgarian style, now put on a genuine "white terror," slaughtering many thousand Communists, and driving the leaders from Bulgaria. In 1924, he banned the party, which thus lost its Sobranie delegates. Dimitrov and Kolarov both fled to Russia, where they took high office in the Comintern. Others set up headquarters in Vienna, and began to publish a newspaper favoring Balkan Federation, to begin with a sovietized Bulgaria, and urging worker-peasant coöperation. In the effort to secure help from the Agrarians, Dimitrov in 1924 approached one of the leading "Pladne" group, Kosta Todorov, who later reported in his autobiography how he had refused an offer to join in a common Agrarian-Communist revolution in Bulgaria, because he suspected that the Communists had no intention of sharing power.

But plotting continued, and the militants among the Communists now took to acts of individual terrorism, which in theory do not form part of Communist practice. These reached their height with the spectacular bomb explosion in Sofia Cathedral in April 1925, which killed 125 persons attending funeral services for a leading Bulgarian general assassinated by the Communists the day before. For more than two decades thereafter, the Communists repeatedly denied all responsibility for the outrage. But in his speech to the party on December 19, 1948, Dimitrov himself acknowledged that the Communists had perpetrated it, as everybody in Bulgaria had thought from the beginning. He considered it an "error" by the "ultra-left" members of the party, equal to that of those who had stood by while the Agrarian regime of Stamboliisky had been liquidated. In any case, the explosion touched off a wave of anti-Communist activities by the government, and it is clear that the party was seriously crippled.

A "front" party called the Worker's Party became legally active in 1927, secretly manipulated by the Communists. During these years, Dimitrov opposed both those whom he called Trotskyite left-wingers, who kept talking and planning in terms of immediate revolution, and the Social Democrats, whom he called Mensheviks and reformers. The depression and widespread unemployment strengthened the hands of the Communists in the early thirties, despite steady pursuit by the police. In 1932, Communists won control of the Sofia city council, but were not allowed to take their seats. Favorable publicity came to the Communists during the celebrated Reichstag Fire Trial in Germany in 1933, when Dimitrov himself became a kind of hero of the anti-Nazi world by his defiance of Goering in the courtroom. The various Bulgarian governments continued their anti-Communist activities; but the Popular Front anti-fascist policy of 1935 and the succeeding years proved a success in Bulgaria. The Bulgarian Communists, for the moment making noises like good liberals, were demanding that King Boris restore the abrogated Tirnovo Constitution with its guarantees of civil liberties, and urging a variety of other democratic measures.

After an initial coolness, the Agrarians and Social Democrats joined the Popular Front, and allowed their youth organizations to be merged with that of the Communists. By the time of the 1938 elections, the Front won 63 seats in the Sobranie out of 160; and only the markedly unfair electoral law prevented their having many more. However, since the Communists themselves had no direct candidates for office, one may ask whether the Bulgarian "Popular Front" was not, politically speaking, a surrender to the Agrarians and Social Democrats, to whom the Communists turned over their voter-support. The "Constitutional Bloc," which was the name chosen by the Bulgarian Popular Front, did not represent a Communist political triumph. In the trades unions also, the government's own union organizations competed, on the whole successfully, with the Communists.

Thus, by the time of the Soviet-German Pact of 1939, which abruptly terminated the Popular Front period everywhere, communism in Bulgaria was stronger than anywhere else in the Balkans, but the Communist Party as such represented no particular threat to the state. Part of the strength lay in the extraordinary national affection for the USSR. In the period of German-Soviet friendship, King Boris himself reached trade and other agreements with the USSR. Whenever the Communists tried to organize pro-Russian demonstrations, they found their work done for them by the population, which would scream itself hoarse with delight at the arrival of a Soviet soccer team, whether the Communists urged them to or not. The Communists were able to profit by this entirely nondoctrinal popular sentiment. Moreover, the Bulgarians, Dimitrov, Kolarov, and several others, played a role in international communism quite out of proportion to Bulgaria's size or importance, or, it may be said, to their own capacities. This loaned the Bulgarian Party a quite fortuitous prestige. Its history up to the German attack on the USSR was one of missed opportunities and blunders, quite apart from its oversupply of the usual Communist cynicism and violence.

In Rumania, the first Marxist ideas came from across the Russian frontier. Russian revolutionaries used Iași as a refuge in the 1870's, until the Russian government brought pressure on the Rumanian government to stop their activities. Beginning with 1875, Constantine Dobrogeanu-Gherea, who was a Russian Jew by birth, produced a flood of articles and books popularizing Marxism. After the usual preliminary discussion groups and clubs, the Social Democratic Party was founded in 1893, a reformist and antirevolutionary organization consisting mostly of intellectuals, although striving to work among both trade unionists and peasants. The effort petered out in controversy by the end of the century. Ion Nadejde, editor of the party newspaper, and several others joined the Liberals. The party revived after the Russian Revolution of 1905, but stoutly opposed the peasant uprising of 1907. The active leader of the movement was now Christian Rakovsky, a Bulgarian by birth.

A distinguished contribution to Marxist literature was made by Dobrogeanu-Gherea in 1910, with the publication of his book *Neoiobagia* (Neo-Serfdom). By this term, the author described society in Rumania, which he regarded as a curious mixture of western political liberalism and the old Ottoman-Phanariot manorial economy. On an inadequate plot of land, the peasant was still subject to the proprietor, despite the façade of free institutions provided by the constitution. As a true Marxist, Dobrogeanu-Gherea preached industrialization and the development of capitalism, as the necessary first step away from feudalism and toward socialism. He did not believe that the Social Democrats should agitate among the peasants. The very moderation of his views made it certain that few strong revolutionaries would be attracted by them, while there was always a Liberal Party for the true bourgeois. In 1952, the Rumanian Communist Premier, Gheorghe Gheorghiu-Dej, denounced Dobrogeanu-Gherea as a Menshevik and opportunist who had failed to realize the revolutionary potentialities in the small Rumanian proletariat and in the peasantry, a pupil of the western European Social Democrats, and not at all a Leninist. The "debilitating influences" of Dobrogeanu-Gherea's views were not fully exorcised, according to Gheorghiu-Dej, until 1932.

The Rumanian Social Democrats opposed participation in the Balkan Wars and World War I, deploring the inaction of the Second International, and succeeding in producing an antiwar demonstration by the workers at Galaţi. The government cracked down on them. In 1917, Rakovsky and much of the Rumanian movement became deeply involved in the Bolshevik Revolution. Rakovsky went from one important post to another in the service of the USSR. Inside Rumania, when the fighting stopped, the government continued to control the Marxists, and in 1920 easily suppressed a general strike attempted by the Social Democrats and the unions, in protest against the martial law under which the country still was governed. Thereafter, in 1921, the party split, the moderates continuing as the Social Democratic Party, while the Bolsheviks formed their own Communist Party, adhering to the Third International. Those who voted for affiliation were promptly arrested. In 1952, Gheorghiu-Dej attributed the failure of the strike to the "treachery" of the moderates, who assisted the "capitalist hangman (Prime Minister General Averescu)." To him, of course, the Social Democrats were thereafter mere "agents of the bourgeoisie."

In Rumania between the wars, the tiny Communist Party led a precarious and inglorious life. It was outlawed in 1924. Comintern directives forced it to favor the detachment of all the provinces newly won, a policy most unpopular in a country of rampant nationalism, and one which obtained for the Rumanian Communists the correct reputation of being mere agents of the Soviet Union. The Comintern criticized its deviations, and required it to oppose the National Peasant Party, while at the same time forcing it to denounce all other political groups in the country. Only after the 1935 shift to the Popular Front did the Communists try to coöperate with other parties. Meanwhile, such affairs as the Griviţa railway-workers' strike in 1933, which the government put down by force, had removed all chance for even limited toleration of the Communists. No popular front was possible, and the country moved down the path toward a dictatorship of the extreme right.

The Rumanian Social Democrats were all the time a legal party with its roots in the still weak trades unions. They conceived their role in terms of Dobrogeanu-Gherea's ideas: speeding the advent of capitalism, and meanwhile furthering the education of the masses. They remained a small and ineffective party, and many of their leaders collaborated with the agencies which were transforming Rumania into an out-and-out fascist state. Such a man as Lotar Radaceanu, distinguished by his lack of principle, was useful to the Rumanian fascists, and after World War II he was to prove of value to the Communists as well. As a whole, the party never could make up its mind between the orthodox Marxist position that the peasantry was too hopelessly conservative by nature to constitute a possible ally for Social Democrats, and the obviously expedient Leninist tactic of seeking support among the discontented in the countryside.

POLITICAL FORMATIONS OF THE RIGHT

The interwar period of Balkan independence produced, in addition to the "bourgeois," peasant, and socialist parties, political groupings of the extreme right. In Rumania, there emerged a true "fascist" party, the Iron Guard, which commanded considerable popular support. In Croatia, the Ustasha movement, though illegal, and largely devoted to terrorism, shared many of the features of a "fascist" party. In Bulgaria, the IMRO, entirely terrorist, and not a political party at all properly speaking, none the less deserves consideration here, since its activities dominated all Bulgarian political life for many years. In addition, as the efforts at constitutionalism collapsed under the impact of the depression, the examples set by Italy and Germany, and the fear of the left, royal dictatorships emerged in Yugoslavia, Bulgaria, and Rumania. Each of these countries produced its crop of opportunist politicians who were ready to support a system of government in which the dominating elements were the King, the police, and the army. Such "big business" as existed usually lent its assistance. Many of these politicians had links with right-wing political groupings, or even launched "fascist" parties of their own, but none of these had deep roots in the country.

In Rumania, the indecision, incompetence, and corruption of the political parties early produced a sense of frustration with the constitutional system. Fear of Russia, as the powerful neighbor which had so often occupied Rumanian territory in the past, and which had never abandoned its claim to Bessarabia, combined with fear of communism, now the official religion of the USSR. A tradition of passionate nationalism, dating back to the days when Rumania was yearning to unite all Rumanians into one great state, survived the achievement in 1920 of all except the most extreme of Rumanian territorial aims, and became even more intense as the public discovered that the mere acquisition of the "lost provinces" did not lead to any particular changes in the national life. A fierce anti-Semitism, arising from social and economic causes which we have already explored, was endemic in the country, and led, as early as the late nineteenth century, to Professor Alexander Cuza's writing of numerous articles against the Jews. Indeed, there was a current in populism itself, which led the believers in a peasant state and the haters of industrialism to associate the advent of all these new-fangled evils with the Jews and the Marxists, and to lump Jews and Marxists together as enemies. Rumanians of all social classes and of any or no degree of education, of all Christian sects and all professions, hated Jews, and were prone to blame them for the troubles of the country. In the Hitler period, when anti-Semitism became fashionable in Europe, the Rumanians often claimed to have invented it.

Under all the circumstances, it would have been extraordinary if politicians had not arisen, ready to trick out Rumanian nationalism with a few radical phrases to win mass support, and to drape it in mystical garments. It would be a mistake to attribute the success of Rumanian "fascism" to the Italian or German examples, or to the money which first Mussolini's and later Hitler's diplomatic representatives readily advanced to help Rumanian "fascists" meet their financial needs. It is true that the Iron Guard borrowed the external trappings of fascism and Nazism: colored shirts, a private army, special war-cries and ceremonies, and efforts at mass hypnosis. Even then, the peculiar Orthodox religious overtones of the leaders' pronouncements and public performances were purely Rumanian. And the Iron Guardists did not need to borrow from anybody the hatred of democracy, liberalism, parliamentary institutions, or the Jews. The depression brought peasant misery to help the Guardist movement.

Early in the 1920's, Cuza's ideas gained headway among university students. His "League of Christian Defense," founded in 1923, was the first political party with anti-Semitism as its chief plank. One of his most ardent and active organizers was Corneliu Zelea Codreanu, then in his early twenties, born in Iași of a German mother and (in all probability) of a Polish or Ukrainian father, and thus, like Hitler or Stalin, an outsider in the country whose passionate champion he claimed to be. His "Legion of the Archangel Michael" was originally the youth organization of Cuza's party. In 1924, Codreanu murdered the police chief of Iași for attempting to curb his movement, and was acquitted in a widely publicized trial. Soon afterward, he took his legion out of Cuza's party, which was insufficiently revolutionary for him. The military branch of his movement, founded in 1930, he called the Iron Guard, the name which was thereafter often applied to the movement as a whole.

Both Peasant Party and Liberal Party premiers tried to dissolve the Guard, and in 1933 the Guardist gangsters assassinated Premier Duca. Codreanu was once more acquitted, and gave his party in 1934 a new name: "'All for the Fatherland (Totul pentru Țara)." With green shirts and little bags of Rumanian soil around their necks, his followers strode through the streets booted and in uniform. To the peasants they denounced the imitative shoddy pseudo-western "civilization" of Bucharest, and called for a return to true Rumanian peasant simplicity, in an unspoiled land, where everybody wore gaily embroidered peasant costume, cultivated his garden plot, sang the national songs, and had swept out the debris of the alien world outside, beginning with the Jew, the symbol of all that was foreign, all that was connected with money, all that was on the one hand plutocratic and on the other communistic. Glorying in its murders, the Guards held macabre burial and memorial services for its own martyrs, digging up their corpses and announcing the ascension of their souls to heaven, exhibiting a frenzied cult of necrophilia. Despite its fascist slogans and trappings, the Guard repudiated Mussolini's corporatism. Its leaders were not economists or indeed thinkers on any subject. They were visceral and not intellectual. They attracted some members of the old nobility, "superfluous" university graduates, misfits, and thugs.

By 1937, the Guard polled about one-sixth of the votes cast in a national election. Codreanu proclaimed his sympathy with Hitler and Mussolini, and his intention to repudiate the Rumanian alliances with the west when he should come to power. It may have been for this reason that King Carol determined to come to grips with the Guard by stealing its thunder. In any case, the king had long since, as we shall see, embarked on a program of building a royal dictatorship. After the elections of 1937, he put in as premier Octavian Goga, a Transylvanian poet, and head of the "National Christian Party," another anti-Semitic group including the remnants of Cuza's party, less popular and less revolutionary than the Iron Guard, and therefore less dangerous. The short-lived Goga government soon led to outright royal authoritarian rule. King Carol outlawed the Guard, arrested Codreanu, and jailed him, and in November 1938 had him and thirteen other Guardist leaders shot "while attempting to escape." The Guard retaliated in the usual way, by murdering the Prime Minister, Armand Calinescu, in September 1939. Carol then took severe reprisals against the Guard. By the time of the outbreak of the Second World War, there could be no doubt that the movement, now led by Codreanu's lieutenant, Horia Sima, had been brought to heel. But there could also be no doubt that it reflected the political wishes of many Rumanians, and had achieved a genuine and not a spurious following.

The Iron Guard was far and away the biggest and most successful Balkan fascist party. The Croatian Ustasha movement differed from it in many respects, but shared its intransigence and its generally "fascist" coloring. An outgrowth of the Starchevich-Frank parties of extreme Croatian nationalists, the Ustasha (rebels) had strong Roman Catholic clerical leanings. Their movement grew in strength as a result of the general sense among Croats that the Serbs were dominating the new Kingdom of the Serbs, Croats, and Slovenes, and that Croatian aspirations were receiving no hearing. Illegal, the Ustasha operated underground in the country. Their leader, Ante Pavelich, lived abroad, mostly in Italy, where Mussolini subsidized him as part of a general project for bringing about the disintegration of Yugoslavia from within. The Hungarians too, who were in close touch with the Italians, and who hoped to get back territories lost to the Yugoslavs, gave shelter to Pavelich's men, who trained picked groups of terrorist assassins in special camps on both Italian and Hungarian soil. Since any enemy of Serbia was a friend of Pavelich, he also cultivated close relations with the Macedonian terrorists (IMRO) in Bulgaria. Pavelich published abroad Croatian newspapers denouncing Alexander, calling for an independent Croatia, and instigating terrorism. The chief fruit of all this was the assassination of King Alexander of Yugoslavia in Marseilles in 1934. The murderer was actually an IMRO man, but he had close links with the Ustasha and with the Italian and Hungarian subsidizers of subversion in Yugoslavia.

IMRO itself could not be called a fascist party. Indeed, fascism as such hardly manifested itself in Bulgaria. From the early 1920's on, IMRO bands raiding into Yugoslavia poisoned the relations between Sofia and Belgrade. We have already noticed IMRO's part in the murder of Stamboliisky, and its close connection with army and government circles. When its leader, Todor Alexandrov, in 1924 endorsed the project of a Balkan Federation, then favored both by Radich and by Moscow, he was murdered, presumably by fellow-IMRO men in the pay of the government, who inclined to the Bulgarian view that Macedonia must become part of Bulgaria, rather than an autonomous unit in a Balkan federation. Alexandrov's successor, Ivan ("Vancho") Mihailov, took the official Bulgarian view, and the Bulgarian government winked at those of his activities which they did not sponsor and subsidize. Among these the shooting down of members of the rival "federation" wing of IMRO, led by General Protogerov, loomed large. Protogerov himself was murdered in 1928, and Sofia streets were rendered hideous and dangerous by the constant exchange of bullets between the two wings of IMRO. Mussolini supported the Bulgarian government, and in all probability supplied the funds with which the Macedonians terrorized the Yugoslavs and each other. It was not until 1934 that a military dictatorship took the matter of IMRO in hand, and used the army against their strongholds in the southeast portion of the country. During the years between 1934 and the outbreak of war, IMRO's role was greatly reduced.

Finally, in reviewing right-wing Balkan movements, we must say a word about the Slovene Clerical Party, which was neither fascist, like the Iron Guard, nor terrorist like the Ustasha and IMRO. Very strong in the countryside, where the priests had taken the lead in helping to form peasant coöperatives, the Slovene Clericals were really a Central European clerical party which by fortune found itself in the Balkans. Its attitudes had been formed, like those of the Austrian Christian Socialists, in Habsburg times. In Slovenia, the standard of living and of literacy were far higher than elsewhere in Yugoslavia. The Clericals wanted to cement the closest possible relations with the

Vatican. They favored autonomy for Slovenia within Yugoslavia, and therefore on the whole supported their Croatian fellow-citizens in their program for Croatian autonomy. They feared and hated the left, and were violently anti-Bolshevik. Their leaders, including Msgr. Koroshets, were to play a role in Yugoslavia out of proportion to their number: a tribute to their education, their ability, and their articulateness. Except for the Clericals, the Slovene political spectrum presented a familiar picture: Liberals (conservative anti-clerical city-dwellers), Social Democrats (workers in the towns), and a few Communists (mostly young intellectuals), all were active.

2. *Internal Politics*

It is against this background that we may consider the internal political developments in Yugoslavia, Rumania, and Bulgaria during the interwar years. Though the national experiences of the three Balkan states were in general discouragingly similar, the story varied greatly in detail from one to another. Everywhere, the national past loomed large as the conditioning factor in the present. Everywhere, the sense of frustration grew, as it became clearer and clearer that the independence for which the Balkan countries had hoped so long was actually a fiction, and that their ultimate fates depended upon events they could not control in a world far removed from southeast Europe. Just as the Byzantine, Ottoman, Habsburg, or Venetian powers had governed the destinies of the peninsula in the past, and the diplomatic and territorial rivalries among the powers of the modern world had determined the moment at which the native peoples won their freedom and the form it took, so, in this new chapter of their history, it was a depression beginning in the United States, the rise of fascism in Germany and Italy, and the consolidation of communism in Russia which fixed the pattern of their tragedy.

YUGOSLAVIA

In Yugoslavia, the years between 1918 and 1929 saw the failure of democratic constitutional government. The continued crisis in relations with Italy over the Istrian frontier postponed the first elections until November 1920. In the interim, the old Serbian Skupshtina, elected in 1911, was the only parliament in the country. Croatian, Slovenian, and Bosnian provincial governments continued to function. From the first, there was a head-on clash between the Serbian Radicals, under Pashich, who was determined to make the new state a highly centralized "greater Serbia," and the Croat Peasants, under Radich, who was equally determined to make it a federalized state, and, if possible, a republic. The Constituent Assembly, elected in November 1920 to make a constitution for the new state, considered a variety of plans. The Croatian scheme would have given to six provincial governments all powers except the minimum (foreign affairs, military affairs, posts, money, and the like) essential for the central government. The Serbian Democrats would have had nine provinces, each with a governor-general representing the central government, to which they would have given more extensive powers than the Croat Peasants envisaged.

In this situation, Radich's decision that his followers should abstain from voting enabled Pashich to put through a highly centralized constitution. He won a majority for it only by making a deal with the Muslim landlords of Bosnia-Hertsegovina, to whom he promised compensation for their land. Prince-Regent Alexander took the oath of allegiance to the new constitution on June 28, 1921, St. Vitus' Day (Vidovdan): the anniversary of the Battle of Kossovo. The constitution is always called the Vidovdan Constitution. It was in some ways an extension to the whole Kingdom of the Serbs, Croats, and Slovenes of the Serbian Constitution of 1903. Of course, the Roman Catholic and Muslim and Jewish faiths were granted recognition and toleration, as well as the Orthodox. Moreover, the constitution established free manhood suffrage, eliminating financial requirements for the vote, gave labor the right to organize, and supported social legislation. But the rights of the government to control press, speech, and assembly were far more extensive in the new constitution than in the Serbian document: "notwithstanding the customary phrases of western liberalism incorporated in the supreme law, the police power of the government is without practical limits."[1]

The Serb Democrats, as well as the Croat Peasants, opposed the constitution, but Radich would not coöperate with the Serbian opposition. His efforts to create a Croatian Republic could lead nowhere, and the murder of Stamboliisky in Bulgaria in June 1923 put an end to the hopes for a Green International. For a time, Radich was actually in prison. In 1924, he performed the most peculiar gyrations of his peculiar career. First, he seemed to accept the wishes of the moderates among his followers, changed the name of his party to "Croat Peasant Club," and allowed it to participate in the Skupshtina, which meant the acceptance of the constitution. It looked as if the Croat Peasants would now join the Serbian Democrats and Agrarians and the Slovenes and Muslims in opposition. But the wily Pashich made his own deal direct with Radich, whom he released from prison, and who now joined his former chief enemies, Pashich and the Serbian Radicals. Pashich died in 1926, and thereafter the crown permitted no comparable political figure to make an appearance. Radich now moved back into opposition, allying himself with Svetozar Pribichevich and the Independent Serb Democrats (Serbs from Croatia, the old Prechani). To the accompaniment of this seemingly meaningless political minuet, the politicians cynically enriched themselves, and principles apparently disappeared in a kaleidoscope of political "combinations" and a welter of corruption.

The period ended in gunfire. On the floor of the Skupshtina (June 20, 1928), a fanatical Montenegrin shot down Radich and his nephew, as well as a third Croat Peasant Party deputy. The infuriated Croats quit the Skupshtina, and for a brief period Alexander had a Slovene Premier, Msgr.

[1] C. A. Beard and G. Radin, *The Balkan Pivot: Yugoslavia* (New York, 1929), p. 55.

Koroshets, leader of the Clericals. Radich's successor, Machek, demanded as the price of Croatian return to political life a federal state so loose that each of the provinces would have controlled its own army and the postal and telegraphic services on its own territory. Anarchy would surely have been the result. So Alexander now determined to take affairs into his own hands. In January 1929, he suddenly abolished the Vidovdan Constitution and proclaimed a royal dictatorship. The King now had supreme power, subject to no constitutional restraints. He made the laws, commanded the army, nominated all officials, declared war, and made peace. He was irremovable. Simultaneously, he decreed the end of freedom of person, of press, of speech, of assembly. A death sentence was prescribed for any attempt to overthrow the government, for spreading propaganda aimed at the existing social order, and for relations with any revolutionary organizations abroad. The new Premier was General Petar Zhivkovich, who as a lieutenant in 1903 had opened the palace gates to the conspiratorial assassins of King Alexander Obrenovich and Queen Draga, and who, as the chief of the mysterious "White Hand," had helped Alexander liquidate the Black Hand at Saloniki in 1917.

Educated in prewar St. Petersburg, where he had been a member of the imperial pages' corps, Alexander doubtless had authoritarian leanings, and not much political flexibility. On the other hand, one cannot doubt his patriotism for his whole people, and not just for the Serbs. He now strove by all means in his power to wipe out the old national loyalties which had made so precarious and so hideous the political life of the Kingdom of the Serbs, Croats, and Slovenes. First, he forbade the existence of any political parties which were "tribal" or religious. This automatically outlawed any group calling itself "Serbian," "Croatian," "Slovene," or "Muslim." Then he officially changed the name of the state to "Yugoslavia" (October 1929), even going to the length of re-dedicating Serb battle flags as Yugoslav. Erasing from the map the lines of the historic provinces, he divided Yugoslavia into nine "governments" (banovinas) mostly named after the rivers.[2] This did deliberate violence to all provincial tradition. Alexander set the seal on his own actions by promulgating a new constitution in 1931, legalizing his own position, and creating a legislature which could not help but be his puppet, since he appointed half the upper house, which shared power with the elected Skupshtina. Any party winning a plurality in an election automatically received two-thirds of the seats in the Skupshtina. The new constitution reached into the judicial sphere, abolishing the irremovability of judges, one of the precious gains of past Serbian constitutional struggles, and undermining the

[2] The *Drava* Banovina roughly coincided with Slovenia, the *Sava* with Croatia-Slavonia, the *Danube* with the Voyvodina, Srem, and north central Serbia including Belgrade; the *Primorje* (littoral) with Dalmatia and much of Hertsegovina, the *Vrbas* with northwest Bosnia, the *Drina* with the rest of Bosnia and western Serbia, the *Zeta* with the rest of Hertsegovina, Dubrovnik, Kotor, Montenegro, the Sanjak, and part of Kossovo-Metohiya; the *Morava* with eastern and southern Serbia, and the *Vardar* with Macedonia and the rest of Kossovo-Metohiya.

independence of the courts. Alexander's police state had now sanctioned itself.

From then until his assassination in October 1934, the King ruled through subservient politicians. His failure to do anything to appease the Croats played into the hands of the extremists, and the Ustasha movement gained rapidly. Machek went to jail; Slovene and Muslim leaders were interned. Police brutality and the arrest of political opponents were standard features of the royal dictatorship. Dozens of examples could be found of well-known Croats or Macedonians arrested, tortured, or killed.[3] Each atrocity bred a counter-atrocity. Not only Croats but "communists" suffered at the hands of the regime. The term was loosely applied to any critic of the regime, and the very looseness of its application helped the Communists, since the regime became widely unpopular, and many who opposed it accepted the label communist without any devotion to or even any knowledge of Communist principles. The University of Belgrade became a hotbed of "communism," that is to say, opposition to King Alexander, although there were many true Communists as well among the students. The Serbs suffered greatly under the dictatorship, but to the Croats it seemed a Serbian regime, since Serbian police operated in Croatian cities, and Serbian politicians held high office. It was the IMRO-Ustasha assassin, Georgiev, Vancho Mihailov's chauffeur, who, with Hungarian and Italian backing, murdered Alexander on a visit to Marseilles, which he had undertaken in order to strengthen Yugoslav ties with France and the Little Entente. It is said that, at the time of his death, Alexander had decided that the dictatorship was a failure, and had resolved to restore representative government.

The murder was greeted with dismay all over Yugoslavia, even by those who loathed the regime, and who had fought it. Only the Croat extremists took any satisfaction in the act. Alexander's son, Peter, was then aged eleven; the King's will appointed a three-man regency: King Alexander's cousin, Prince Paul Karageorgevich, and two distinguished citizens, a Serbian physician, and a Croatian government official. Prince Paul failed to take advantage of the national mood of conciliation, and continued in Alexander's dictatorial path, though he did let Machek out of jail. Some hope was aroused by the elections of 1935, which returned a huge opposition vote, despite corruption. Then too, Paul was willing to negotiate with Machek, who was now prepared to accept a far more limited autonomy for Croatia than he had demanded in 1928. The public, oddly enough, also hailed the appointment of Milan Stoyadinovich as Premier in June 1935. Stoyadinovich, a businessman with experience as former Finance Minister, was considered a moderate, who would pursue negotiations with the Croats. Slovenes and Muslims joined his

[3] A police agent tried to kill Svetozar Pribichevich in 1929; others did kill a pro-Hungarian scholar of Albanian history, Professor Milan Šufflay, in 1931; others beat up the Croatian novelist, Budak.

Cabinet. Indeed, he united his own wing of the Radicals with the Slovene Clericals and the Muslims in a new party called the Yugoslav Radical Union.

The expected domestic restoration of liberties did not take place, however. Instead, Stoyadinovich, under direction from Prince Paul, carried on a flirtation with the Hitler regime in Germany. Prince Paul himself was hardly a Serb at all, except through the blood of his father. His mother had been a Russian noblewoman, and he inherited from her a hatred of communism quite equal to Alexander's own. Educated in England, a connoisseur of painting, married to a Greek princess who was half-Russian, Paul found Yugoslav domestic politics stormy and boring, and thought of himself as a gifted negotiator in foreign policy. This led him to conclude pacts with Bulgaria and Italy in 1936 and 1937, without consulting Yugoslavia's Czech and Rumanian allies of the Little Entente. Hitler, Goering, von Neurath, and other leading functionaries of the Nazi regime wooed Yugoslavia with flattering pronouncements, to which Prince Paul listened complacently. Responsible Serbs, devoted to the pro-French and pro-Entente policies of King Alexander, worried lest they find their country cut adrift from its traditional friends and linked in a dangerous alliance with its traditional enemies. Their fears had the justification that both Prince Paul and Msgr. Koroshets, the Slovene Clerical leader, deeply distrusted the "popular front" movement, so powerful in France, and looked with great suspicion on the French and Czech treaties with the USSR.

It was amidst this alarm that Stoyadinovich in 1937 presented to the Skupshtina a draft Concordat between Yugoslavia and the Vatican, which, in fact, had been approved by Alexander before his death. The announcement of the planned agreement produced an outburst of Serbian public demonstration, led by Orthodox clergymen, some of whom were roughly handled by the police. In the midst of the excitement, the Orthodox Patriarch died, and rumors spread that he had been poisoned by the Catholics. The government had to withdraw the Concordat in deference to outraged public opinion, which quite wrongly suspected the whole arrangement as a step toward an alliance with Italy.

Soon afterwards, Machek and his Independent Serbian Democratic allies reached an understanding with the Serbian opposition, which by now included the Agrarians, the Democrats, and the anti-Stoyadinovich Radicals. All of them agreed on the need for a new constitution which should supersede Alexander's authoritarian document of 1931. This coalition represented a substantial majority of all Yugoslavs. When Prince Paul rejected its program — on the excuse that nothing could be done until the King should come of age, which would not be until 1941 — the fear spread that Paul had an ambition to seize the crown for himself. Actually, he probably only wanted to enjoy his virtually unlimited power a while longer. This he managed to do. But public opinion clearly supported the opposition. Never had Serb-Croat friendship on the popular level been so close. Machek was hailed by a crowd of 50,000 Serbs when he visited Belgrade in August 1938. The throng of ordinary Serbian peasants cheered him to the echo when he denounced the police terror. The government, however, hesitated to reach an agreement with the Croats.

In 1937 and 1938, despite reassuring visits to Paris and London, Stoyadinovich also paid quite unreassuring visits to Rome and Berlin. The pro-German attitude of Paul and Stoyadinovich gained in strength with the Nazi occupation of Austria in the spring of 1938, and the Munich crisis leading to the dismemberment of Czechoslovakia in the fall of that year. Paul attributed the fall of the Czechs to their alliance with Russia, and the inaction of the French to their victimization by Communists. In the Axis he saw the bulwark against the USSR. In the elections held in December 1938, the government managed, through the usual fraudulent techniques, to defeat the opposition, although by a narrow margin. As a result, Stoyadinovich and Paul automatically obtained an enormous majority in the Skupshtina. There was by now a truly fascist Serbian political party, led by Dimitriye Lyotich, but it won not a single seat in the elections, although Stoyadinovich interested himself in its welfare. Early in 1939, Paul decided to dump Stoyadinovich. Some had thought of Stoyadinovich as a candidate for dictator of Yugoslavia, partly because he stationed, among crowds listening to his speeches, agents who hailed him vociferously as "leader." Now everybody realized that he had all along been merely the tool of Prince Paul.

His successor, Dragisha Tsvetkovich, was commanded to reach terms with Machek. Prague fell to the Germans in March 1939, and even Prince Paul realized that in the intensifying crisis it would be well for the Yugoslavs to settle the Serb-Croat problem that had racked the Kingdom since its foundations, and not to permit Pavelich's Ustasha to capitalize further on Croat discontent. The negotiations dragged on for months. The final agreement (*Sporazum*) was reached on August 26, 1939, the day before the signature of the Hitler-Stalin pact which let loose World War II. Prince Paul succeeded in separating the whole question of Croat claims from the question of liberalizing the constitution. He made his concessions to Machek and not to Machek's allies of the united opposition; the Serbian Democrats, Agrarians, and anti-Paul Radicals were furious. Machek concluded the agreement, which did not meet the wishes of any group except the Croat Peasant Party, largely because he realized that war would soon break out, and that it was urgent to counter Pavelich's appeal in Croatia.

By the terms of the "Sporazum," the Sava and Primorje Banovinas, and parts of Bosnia, were united in a new Croatian Banovina. The territory involved included about 4,500,000 people, of whom more than 850,000 were Orthodox Serbs, and more than 150,000 Muslims. Croatia won substantial autonomy within Yugoslavia. It would have its own diet, the traditional Croatian Sabor, to deal with all problems other than foreign and military affairs, commerce, and transportation. The Regent was to appoint a Ban, or governor, who would have considerable powers. Paul appointed Machek's choice, Dr. Ivan Shubashich, a Zagreb lawyer, who was to play an important part in Yugoslav politics during and immediately after the war. Machek himself entered the Tsvetkovich Cabinet as Vice-Premier, with three other Croatian Peasant Party representatives, and two Independent Serb Democrats. But the rest of the Serbian opposition (all from Serbia proper) remained outside the coalition.

Superficially, the Sporazum had healed an old and dreadful wound. Actually, however, it probably caused as much discontent as pleasure. The Croats wanted still more territory. The Serbs, who thought of themselves as those who had sacrificed most to create Yugoslavia, now saw the Croats obtain autonomy and rights which were denied to them. There was much demand for a "Serbian Banovina," since historic Serbia was still split up among the artificial administrative units created by Alexander. The Serbian opposition, in its frustration, began to denounce the Croats, and to appeal to the national hatred which had died down while the two peoples had suffered equally under the regime's oppression. Terrorists in Croatia began to murder Serbs. The new autonomy had brought with it no social reform; so the peasants were still governed by the townsfolk, and the party of Radich was dominated by the bourgeoisie. In order to woo the Pavelich extremists, Machek's own followers made violent anti-Serb speeches, which the Serbs could then quote, and point to as a clear sign of Croat ingratitude.

Yugoslavia thus reached the moment when a new World War was about to break out, with its two most important nationalities substantially unreconciled, and civil liberties denied to all its population, as they had been for a decade. Its government did not command the loyalty of a substantial portion of the public, which looked with undisguised dismay upon the efforts at rapprochement with Germany and Italy. Underground, the Ustashe were waiting their chance. So were the Communists, their ranks swollen by many who cared nothing for Marxism and knew less about it, but hated oppression and wanted liberty. Their leadership was in the hands of a clever skillful group of doctrinaire Marxist-Leninist-Stalinists, who had studied war and revolution with Comrade Walter, soon to emerge in his incarnation as Tito.

RUMANIA

Rumania, as the other territorially satisfied Balkan state to emerge from World War I with greatly expanded frontiers, also quickly learned that satisfaction of traditional territorial demands did not in itself bring contentment or prosperity. Bessarabia and Transylvania suffered economically not only from the cutting of the historic ties with Russia and Hungary but also from the centralized financial and banking system by which the politicians of the Regat — especially the Liberals — unified the provinces and exploited them. In 1920, the King ousted the Transylvanian Peasant Premier Vaida-Voevod, elected after the war, and installed the war hero, General Averescu, whose double mission was to help the landowners avoid a truly radical agrarian reform, and to suppress what appeared to be danger from the socialists on the left. His premiership saw the adoption of land-reform laws, which we shall analyze below. His lack of party support led to his fall with his mission accomplished. Early in 1922, the Liberal Party came to power, where it remained for most of the next six years.

Though corrupt and unpopular, the Liberals met with no united opposition, and were able to rig elections to their own advantage. Their new constitution, adopted in 1923, made Rumania a strongly centralized state. Although the question of provincial autonomy never reached the pitch of the Croatian question in Yugoslavia, the Transylvanians in particular resented the degree to which they were governed from Bucharest. The measures guaranteeing civil liberties were so worded that in practice it was easy to limit their exercise. The two-chamber legislature included a lower house elected by universal male suffrage, and an upper house, some of whose members were elected by citizens over forty and by corporate groups like city-councils, universities, and the like, and some of whom held their posts by virtue of former political service or position in the church, the courts, the army, or the royal family. The national assembly could appoint members of district and local governing bodies. The crown had a good deal of power, and the constitution provided for the establishment of martial law in an emergency.

Occasional leftist and other disorders punctuated the period of Liberal rule, strengthening their hands rather than otherwise. Communist propaganda found some willing listeners in Bessarabia, partly as a result of incompetent Rumanian administration. When Prince Carol, the heir to the throne, left the country with his mistress, the celebrated Madame Lupescu, his father, King Ferdinand, demanded that Carol come back alone. Carol refused, and in late 1925 abdicated in favor of his son Michael, still an infant. The Transylvanian Nationalists and the Peasants protested that they had not been consulted about the regency which would govern for Michael after Ferdinand should have died. As their position grew more shaky, the Liberals bolstered it with an electoral law even worse than Alexander's later effort in Yugoslavia. It provided that a party winning a plurality of 40 per cent or more became automatically a majority party. It would receive 50 per cent of the seats in the assembly, plus a percentage of extra seats equal to its percentage of the vote. If a party obtained a plurality by polling 40 per cent of the votes, it would capture 50 per cent of the seats, plus 20 per cent more, or 40 per cent of the other 50 per cent, and would thus have a total of 70 per cent of the seats.

The years 1926 and 1927 provided an interlude in Liberal rule, during which General Averescu, and a non-party ministry under Prince Știrbey (allegedly the father of all Queen Marie's children except Carol), successively held office. The period was notable for an excessively corrupt election and for the Liberals' success in driving from office the Știrbey Cabinet, which had some dissident Peasant Party members. The way in which the election law worked is vividly indicated by the figures for the elections of 1926 and 1927. In the first, managed by Averescu, Averescu won 52 per cent of the vote; in the second, managed by the Liberals, Averescu won not even the necessary 2 per cent to seat representatives in the chamber. Even in volatile Rumania, the loss of 50 per cent of the electorate during a single year reflected not popular sentiment but skillful manipulation at the polls. The death of King Ferdinand permitted the National Peasants to make an issue of the regency, on which they had not been consulted. They also were strong enough to harass and effectually prevent the Liberals from obtaining a necessary foreign loan. At the end of 1928, the Liberals fell from power, and Maniu, leader of the National Peasants, became Premier. For some months past, he had been denouncing the government, and had summoned and harangued a huge mass meeting of peasants to demonstrate his political strength.

Liberal economic policies had included deflation, in an unsuccessful effort to stabilize the currency, the imposition of high tariffs to protect industry, the exaction of high export duties to provide ready cash, and encouragement of industry. In all of this, the Liberals regarded the foreigner with some suspicion, unwilling for a long time to use a foreign loan to help the currency, and guarding by statute against foreign capital investments of more than 40 per cent in Rumanian industry. Agriculture they neglected, making no provision for credits, and pressing the peasants to pay up for the land they had received, but using the payments for ready cash and not to amortize the bonds held by the expropriated landowners. Both the tariffs and the export duties also hurt the peasants. The Liberals did pass measures making it more difficult for peasants to sell their holdings, and thus tried to prevent the drift of land away from the small proprietor. They also set up Chambers of Agriculture, parallel to Chambers of Commerce, which were to assist the peasants, but which did not represent the poorer peasantry (the majority). These Chambers never had enough money to carry out a genuine program, and were involved at once in politics, since they had the right, as corporate bodies, to elect Senators. A leading western authority says that the Liberals' economic policies were

> based upon a strong nationalism and upon a greatly simplified view of the nature of economic progress. . . . They were unwilling . . . to accept the consequences of a free economy; they feared it would keep Rumania a weak agrarian state at the mercy of foreign capital and unable to provide the needs for its own defense. But they were not fully aware of the far-reaching consequences of a policy of forced industrialization. . . .

which "would have involved a long-range program of organized forced savings quite beyond their powers. . . . Under the best of circumstances, it would be difficult to persuade a peasant electorate that agriculture should pay for the advancement of industry. In Rumania, with a very primitive peasantry on the one hand and a not very public-minded group of industrialists on the other, it was impossible, especially when there was a large and articulate Peasant party vociferously criticizing 'artificial industries.'"[4]

[4] Henry L. Roberts, *Rumania* (New Haven, 1951), pp. 128–129.

Maniu's National Peasants stayed in office for two disappointing but crucial years. The elections, which were fair, gave them an 80 per cent vote, and a resulting overwhelming majority in the chamber. Though they had denounced the election law, they did not repeal it, now that it was benefiting them. Constitutionalism, foreign capital, and assistance to agriculture were the main features of the Peasant program. The effort to create stronger local government caused the withdrawal of the opposition from the assembly. Communist infiltration harassed the government from the left. The regime put down a coal-mining strike by using troops, and inflicting casualties on the striking miners, but later blamed both management and labor, and dismissed those responsible for violence. Police brutality persisted, and scandal continued. Though the foreign capital was forthcoming, bad harvests, the beginning of the depression, and the fall of grain prices kept the economy in crisis. The Peasant Party insisted on appointing a new Regent to replace one who had died, in precisely the same fashion as that for which they had previously bitterly reproached the Liberals. In by-elections, the Peasants began to show signs of weakness, and extreme right or left candidates polled large votes.

The crisis was precipitated by the sudden return of Carol in June 1930. Maniu, who favored the action, to ensure dynastic continuity, resigned, but quickly came back as Premier. It was probable that public opinion welcomed the return of the prince, who soon became king legally. Maniu made his own approval conditional upon Carol's achieving a reconciliation with his wife, and abandoning Madame Lupescu. It is not clear whether Carol had promised to do this or not. At any rate, Madame Lupescu soon returned to Rumania, and resumed her position as Carol's mistress. Maniu thereupon resigned, and refused to participate in his own party's government, which lasted only until the end of 1930. Quite probably Carol had broken his promise to Maniu. But the puritanism which had made Maniu exact it, and which now led him to withdraw from active direction of affairs, was quite un-Rumanian and unrealistic. Accustomed to playing the role of opposition deputy in the Budapest Parliament, Maniu probably felt more comfortable when protesting against something than when striving to put through a positive program. He abandoned his own party, which had had a mandate from a large majority of the people, and the King quickly obtained its resignation.

It is doubtful whether the National Peasants could have stayed in office very long even without Carol's return, since the depression was already producing misery among their constituents. Moreover, their economic policies in office emphasized industrial, commercial, and financial programs rather than agricultural ones. No more land was distributed. No effort was made to consolidate peasant holdings into compact farms instead of scattered strips of land. The National Peasants did make easier the sale of landed property, with the expectation that the more energetic and able peasant would build up prosperous farms, but without much regard to the feebler and less efficient, who would go to the wall when he sold his farm. From the Communist point of view, of course, this process was the creation of "kulaks." The government did try also to further the coöperative movement by legislation, and to improve agricultural credit. But none of their actions helped the really poor peasant. In lowering the tariffs, on the other hand, they improved the lot of the peasantry, and in welcoming foreign capital without restriction they strove to loosen up the tight industrial situation of the Liberals' period of office. But their entire program and performance vividly illustrated their transformation from a peasant party into a middle-class party with vestiges of concern for the peasants.

From his return in late 1930 to the outbreak of the Second World War, King Carol himself was the most important Rumanian politician. Clever but superficial and unscrupulous, he moved by degrees into a position where he could imitate Alexander of Yugoslavia and Boris of Bulgaria in trying the increasingly fashionable Balkan expedient of a royal dictatorship. The King's old tutor, the extraordinarily prolific historian and writer on political affairs, Nicolae Iorga, became Premier, and in 1931 engineered an election, in which the National Peasants, recipients of 80 per cent of the ballots in 1927, now got only 15 per cent. By mid-1932 the government was out under a barrage of attacks from all political parties, and the National Peasants came back. Vaida-Voevod and Maniu alternated as premiers, Vaida resigning out of disapproval over the government's effort to negotiate with the USSR, Maniu out of inability to get along with Carol, and Vaida returning in January 1933. Violent labor unrest punctuated this period, the government using violence to quell the Communist-inspired strikes. Vaida, indeed, was moving far to the right, wooing the Iron Guard, and focusing his attention on the need of fighting the Communists rather than on a constructive program. He failed to put through his only positive policy: to exclude the Magyars of his native Transylvania from government posts. At the end of 1933 the Liberals came back. The Iron Guard promptly shot Premier Duca, who was succeeded by Gheorghe Tatarescu.

During the next few years, Carol, operating through Tatarescu, managed affairs to an increasing degree. The regime strove to capture for itself some of the enthusiasm which was now contributing to the growing strength of the Iron Guard. For the time being, the Guard itself, in its new guise as the *Totul pentru Țara* party, was allowed to operate, but Carol founded his own youth movement as a challenge to its appeal. The rise of Hitler and the obvious hesitation of the western powers in the face of it led to a sense of uneasiness about Rumanian commitments to France and the Little Entente, and to a sharpening sense of Russia as the enemy. The skillful Foreign Minister, Nicolae Titulescu, who had for years directed Rumanian foreign policy on the basis of intimacy with the west and an eventual reconciliation with the USSR, fell from office in 1936. Increasingly, the pro-German views of the Rumanian extreme right wing, together with their domestic fascism and anti-Semitism were receiving a respectful ear at court.

At the end of 1937, Tatarescu's term came to an end, and in the elections of November of that year, Maniu made an electoral pact with the Iron Guard. Communist propaganda on this subject always maintains that this demonstrated Maniu's lack of democratic principles. The pact, however, was a limited and technical one. It did not involve the merging of the two parties or the use of joint lists of candidates. It was designed to combine the technical forces of the two parties to combat Tatarescu's expected effort to rig the election and falsify the returns. But it did depress the idealists among the supporters of Maniu, who had always thought of him as so pure that he would rather be defeated than treat with the devil. At any rate, the result of the pact was that the Maniu-Guardist combination did prevent Tatarescu from winning the election. With no party having the 40 per cent of the votes necessary to get the bonus in the assembly, Carol turned for his new Premier to Octavian Goga, leader of the violently anti-Semitic National Christian Patry, which had polled some 9 per cent of the vote. The King explained that the Liberals had not won enough votes (36 per cent), and that he did not want to summon the Iron Guard to power (16 per cent). He might have added that Maniu's personal hostility to him prevented his giving the nod to the National Peasants (20 per cent).

He also might have pointed out that he hoped a few weeks of the Goga regime would produce a public revulsion, and enable him to seize power himself. In any case, the anti-Semitic policies of the Goga regime, in which General Ion Antonescu, later dictator of the country, appeared for the first time, made it the object of wide protests from abroad, and the ensuing economic dislocation was all that Carol could have hoped. Having neutralized the Peasants through his long feud with Maniu, and split the Liberals by using the tractable Tatarescu, Carol was now in position to take over. He established early in 1938, a "government of National Union," with the Patriarch of the Orthodox Church, Miron Cristea, as Premier. As an ideological model, if one may dignify Carol's views with such a term, the King had Germany, and especially Mussolini's corporate Italy before him.

Rumanian economic policies had long supported corporatism in practice. The failure of the Viennese Kredit-Anstalt in 1931 had proved a landmark in all European financial history. No more capital flowed to Rumania. As credit stopped, the state financial position, hit also by the continued fall in grain prices, which had begun in 1929, became extremely insecure. The peasants could no longer meet the payments on the land distributed in the 1920's. Nor could the larger proprietors pay their obligations. A moratorium had to be voted for agricultural debts, and various measures were undertaken to reduce their amounts. The government tried to support grain prices, and sought in vain to get better markets. As recovery began about 1934, the government focused on industrialization. It was the National Bank and the state which provided the finance for the new heavy industries, a natural response to the depression in agriculture. Moreover, the international situation called for armaments in quantity, and Rumania began to manufacture her own. King Carol invested his own personal fortune very heavily in the operations undertaken now by heavy industry, especially by the celebrated Tweedledum and Tweedledee of Rumanian business: Nicolae Malaxa, a Greek, and Max Aușnit, a Jew. High tariffs protected the new enterprises. These ate up available capital. Agriculture and the individual peasant both suffered, although the government continued to protect farm prices, and began to support, with help from Germany, a policy of diversifying agriculture by planting cash crops. Dictatorship and forced-draft industrialization had come to Rumania together.

Carol produced a new constitution early in 1938, which abolished the political parties, and increased his own powers greatly. Instead of universal suffrage, the law sanctioned voting only by occupations, thus imitating the Italian corporative forms. It forbade a citizen to advocate any change in the form of government. The King alone could amend the constitution, and choose and dismiss ministers. He now launched his attack on the Iron Guard, whose course we have briefly indicated above. At the end of 1938, he created a single party, the National Renaissance Front, equipped with all the usual paraphernalia of fascist parties. The whole performance could be interpreted as an effort both to appease the rising fascist forces in the country, and to stay in command of them.

Specifically, the Iron Guard threatened the King, not only because it was independent and perhaps uncontrollable, but also because its leaders were so uncompromisingly pro-German. Carol hoped to avoid total commitment to the German cause, at least until it was clear that the Germans would certainly win. German influence was growing in the economic field. Soon after Munich Carol visited England and Germany both. In March 1939, the Rumanian government concluded an economic agreement with the Germans, possibly in part to soothe Hitler, who was angry at Carol's rough treatment of the Iron Guard. Germany promised to help diversify Rumanian agriculture, and to assist in the setting up of joint companies for petroleum and other minerals, to help finance the expansion, and to supply arms. The agreement offered Rumania considerable economic benefits, but it was of course designed by the Germans as part of their scheme to guarantee their new armies food and fuel from southeast Europe. Before long, the benefits which German help might have brought Rumania were swallowed up in war. It was of course the Hitler-Stalin pact which knocked the props out from under Carol's policy. Rumania was now again caught between the European giants.

BULGARIA

We have already seen how Bulgaria emerged from the First World War defeated. The insurgent Agrarians were beaten in their attempt to march on Sofia in 1919 only with the help of German troops. But popular sentiment was too strong for King Ferdinand, who abdicated in October, and was succeeded by his son Boris, called Boris III. Stamboliisky had already received the benefit of an amnesty, and became Prime Minister. His achievements, deficiencies, and downfall have already been chronicled. The degree to which Boris may have sponsored or approved the army and IMRO in their liquidation of the Agrarian regime is still unknown; but there was much hostility between the King and the redoubtable peasant Prime Minister, and it is at least sure that Boris did not mourn Stamboliisky.

The Tsankov regime, with its strenuous police efforts against the rambunctious Communists, and with IMRO running wild both in the Yugoslav frontier region and in the streets of Sofia, formed a period of disorder. Tsankov's successor as Premier in 1925, Liapchev, made no important changes. Italy was subsidizing not only IMRO but also King Boris himself, who married an Italian princess in 1930. A shift of regimes in 1931 and a period of rule by Democrats and right-wing Agrarians did not alter the nature of the problem. The uncontrollable activities of IMRO dominated political life, while the depression led to a revival of Communist strength.

The *coup d'état* which altered the situation finally took place in May 1934. It was master-minded by a small group of army officers, active in a so-called "military league," not unlike the associations which the Serbian military had formed before World War I, but smaller and more exclusive. The leader was Colonel Damian Velchev, born in 1881, a graduate of the St. Petersburg Military Academy, and pro-ally in the First World War. He had helped materially to organize the Tsankov coup against Stamboliisky in 1923, but cannot be held responsible for the terror which followed it. Abstaining from political office himself, he had put one of his chief supporters, Kimon Georgiev, into the Cabinet. He contented himself with the post of Commandant at the Sofia Military Academy, where he exerted a powerful influence over the younger generation of army officers. Though he had been hostile to Stamboliisky, Velchev shared the view that Bulgarian-Yugoslav relations must be close and friendly, and deeply disapproved of the constant crisis which IMRO's activities were provoking. Very close ties existed between Velchev and the intellectuals and politicians who produced a periodical called *Zveno* (The Link). This group, not a political party in the ordinary sense, is often called the "Zveno" group. During 1933, Velchev had prevailed on King Boris to undertake measures against IMRO. Sofia became quieter, but the IMRO stronghold in the Petrich district on the Yugoslav frontier continued undisturbed. Together with the squabbling between Mushanov's Democrats and Gichev's right-wing Agrarians this convinced Velchev that the time for forceful political action had arrived.

On May 19, 1934, Velchev's "military league" and Zveno, with their overlapping memberships, seized power in a quiet well-managed coup. Mushanov suddenly found he was no longer Premier. Once again, Velchev himself took no office, but allowed Georgiev to serve as Premier. Enemies of Zveno have called it fascist, but the term is inaccurate. There was about the *Zvenari* none of the mysticism or fanaticism of the Iron Guard or Ustasha. They were essentially military-minded military men, with a passion for neatness and an inability to tolerate messes. There could be no doubt that Bulgarian political life was a mess. Moreover, the Zveno people did not represent a social class: they were not for or against the bourgeoisie, the peasants, or the workers; great landowners and industrial barons they could not represent, because there were none in Bulgaria. As army officers, they leaned to authoritarian behavior. They were militant patriots, but believed in friendly relations with Yugoslavia, and with the USSR. While they shared with all European fascists their disillusionment with parliamentary institutions and party politics, they were not fascists but a group of political technicians without any social basis in the Bulgarian population.

The Zveno dictatorship lasted less than a year. It abolished political parties and labor unions, in which the Communists and Social Democrats had enjoyed considerable influence, and replaced them by "corporative" unions without political leanings. It tried to adjust the balance as between the country and the town, by assisting professional men, especially physicians, to leave the cities and work in the country districts, where they were badly needed. It tried to enlarge the credit facilities available to the population by founding a new credit bank. It planned an educational reform, with emphasis on technology. Most important, the Zvenari cleaned up the IMRO, using the army against it without hesitation, capturing many of its leaders, and compelling Vancho Mihailov himself to flee to Turkey. As an immediate corollary to this decisive action against the Macedonian terrorists came improved relations with Yugoslavia. By now, ten years after Stamboliisky's murder, Bulgarian public opinion had swung around to his way of thinking. Experience of IMRO atrocities had convinced many Bulgarians that IMRO must be wrong, and that good relations with the ancient "Serb" enemy would be best for Bulgaria. A month before the IMRO-Ustasha-Italian-Hungarian plotters killed King Alexander of Yugoslavia in October 1934, he visited Sofia, and was warmly received.

But King Boris was the ultimate gainer by the Zveno coup. He took advantage of a disagreement between Velchev and the Cabinet to oust Georgiev. In mid-1935, Velchev fled to Yugoslavia; he returned illegally in the fall, and was tried on a charge of conspiring to overthrow the monarchy and to replace it with a republic. Sentenced to death, Velchev found his sentence commuted to life imprisonment. King Boris now took over. From early 1935 until his mysterious death in 1943, during the Second World War, Boris governed Bulgaria as dictator. He kept the Zveno ban on political parties, governing through subservient politicians and making full use of the police. The army he purged of Velchevites, and made loyal to himself. Though King Boris would not allow IMRO to resume its terrorist activities, he relaxed the rigorous proscription under which the Zveno regime had placed the IMRO leadership, and would consult with individual Macedonians.

Despite the efforts of Bulgarian official propaganda to create at home and abroad a picture of Boris as simple, unassuming, sparing in his personal expenses, and preferring above all to spend his time driving a locomotive, he seems rather to have been a true son of his father, Ferdinand of Coburg. Shrewd, cynical, quiet, and ruthless, he apparently never felt very deeply about matters of principle, and decided that after all it would be easiest to govern the country with an iron hand. He did, however, make certain concessions to public opinion. In January 1937, for example, he concluded a pact of "eternal" friendship with Yugoslavia, which, as one of Prince Paul's and Stoyadinovich's advances toward the enemies of the Entente, alarmed Yugoslavia's allies, Rumania and Czechoslovakia. Thus, while Boris' pact looked like a continuation of the pro-Yugoslav policies of Stamboliisky and Velchev, it should be thought of rather as a Yugoslav rapprochement with the Axis than a Bulgarian rapprochement with the Entente. A pact which the French would have welcomed if Velchev had negotiated it was now hailed with pleasure in Berlin. Hitler's Foreign Office hoped to use Bulgaria as a magnet to pull Yugoslavia the rest of the way out of her old associations and into the Axis camp.

Domestically, the years of Boris' ascendancy brought few notable events. We need notice here only the national elections of early 1938, the first in seven years. The way was paved by the holding of municipal and communal elections in 1937, in which for the first time some women had the vote. Though the central government continued to appoint the mayors and prefects, the population elected the city and county councils. Boris did not restore civil liberties for either these or the national elections, which were held for a Sobranie reduced in number to 160 members after a redistricting of the country. Married, widowed, and divorced women obtained the vote. Though the political parties were not allowed to resume activities as such, their leaders could run for office, and electioneer. The semi-managed election gave Boris a little less than two-thirds of the seats, which gave the opposition a substantial voice. The government soon expelled the Communists and "Pladne" Agrarians.

Thus Bulgaria reached the period of the Second World War under a tight police dictatorship imposed after a period of unequaled turbulence. The absence of great social and economic cleavages in the country had not protected it from violence which outdid anything Rumania or even Yugoslavia could show. Here, where there were almost no "class distinctions," and no minority problem comparable to those in Rumania or Yugoslavia, there were hatreds on every hand. One generation removed from the village, the army, the civil servants, the businessmen, and the intellectuals knew perfectly well that there were already too many of them, and strove to keep the peasantry out in the country. The peasants never forgave the townsmen for destroying Stamboliisky. The workers and many intellectuals dreamed of a Communist revolution and eventually of union with the USSR. Both wings of IMRO contained some idealists, but far more brigands, who terrorized the peasants on the Bulgarian side of the frontier as much as those on the Yugoslav side. Long lines of concrete blockhouses and barbed-wire entanglements grew up along this boundary line passing through the desolate goat-pasture that the nationalists of both countries so desperately wanted. An "eternal" friendship pact between the two governments reflected the interests of both peoples, but the cynicism with which it was concluded made it possible to predict the resumption of hostility at the first suitable moment. In foreign relations as in domestic affairs, the Bulgarian record between the wars was as disappointing as that of the other Balkan states.

ALBANIA

Caught between Yugoslavia and Italy, unable to sustain itself economically without a foreign patron, several stages behind the other Balkan countries in educational evolution and political experience, Albania started its nineteen-year-long period of independence with severe, perhaps insurmountable, handicaps. Only six months after the League of Nations had recognized Albanian autonomy, one of the leading Gheg chieftains, the Roman Catholic Gjon Markagjoni, led his Mirdita tribesmen in a revolt against the authority of the four-man inter-denominational Regency and the Albanian Parliament. The Parliament was a bicameral assembly, with a Senate appointed from among its own members by the Congress of Lushnija, and an elected Chamber of Deputies with one deputy for each 12,000 inhabitants and an additional member representing the Albanian emigrants in the United States. The Yugoslavs gave military support to Markagjoni's "Republic of Mirdita," whose center was on Yugoslav territory in Prizren, and only the threatened intervention of the League of Nations led to a Yugoslav withdrawal. The Markagjoni republic disappeared by the end of 1921.

Meanwhile there were emerging the earliest political parties in Albanian history: the delay itself reflects the country's lag behind its neighbors. As usual, the names of the two parties had little if anything to do with their programs. In Albania, more even than elsewhere, the parties were loose groupings of prominent personalities, temporarily allied for their own purposes. Thus, the Popular Party included the Orthodox Bishop of Durazzo, Fan S. Noli, a Harvard graduate, who had returned to Albania much impressed with western ideas. A learned and talented man, Noli was to become the translator of much of Shakespeare into Albanian, and the author of numerous books. Also a member of this party was Ahmet Bey Zogu, whom we have encountered as the brave and vigorous young Muslim leader of the Mati tribe during the war. The rival party, though called "Progressive," was essentially the party of the landholding Muslim Beys of the south, whose main platform was firm opposition to any possible plan for taking away their lands and giving them to the peasantry. The leader of the Progressives was a rich and powerful landowner named Shefqet Bey Verlaci. To find even a partial parallel elsewhere to the Albanian Progressives one would have had to turn to the Bosnian landlords or perhaps to the old Rumanian Conservatives of pre-World War days. Yet the Progressives too had the loyalty of certain far more enlightened men than

Shefqet Verlaci, including Mehdi Bey Frasheri, a distinguished and well-educated man who thoroughly understood Albanian problems.

In this unstable situation, with the Ghegs as such standing aloof from both political parties, and giving support to a group which wanted to unite all Albanian factions in a "Sacred Union," Albanian governments changed frequently. There were five between July and December 1921. The fifth was that of the Popular Party leader, Xhafer Ypi, with Zogu as Minister of the Interior, and Bishop Noli as Foreign Minister. Early in 1922, the enemies of the Ypi government openly attacked Tirana, and the entire government fled, except for Zogu, who stayed behind, and defeated the attacking armies, thus saving the day for the government. Noli had earlier resigned, out of disapproval of Zogu's authoritarian methods in attempting to disarm the Albanians of the lowlands. The impermanence and unreliability of Albanian political alignments was now vividly demonstrated, as Zogu announced his engagement to be married to the daughter of Shefqet Verlaci, the moving spirit of the "Progressive" Beys' party. Since power determined position, Zogu now moved into the Premiership, as of December 1922. It was taken for granted that the Beys had bought him.

A realignment of political forces therefore took place, with Noli and the other westernizers forming an Opposition Party of Democrats, including all Zogu's enemies, while Zogu's followers now formed a Government Party. Zogu's enemies of course included not only those who hated him on ideological grounds, but also those whom he had not found it possible to reward. Their political views ranged from Noli's program to modernize the country overnight to extreme Ottoman-type conservatism. They could unite only on opposing Zogu, and on this could summon considerable support from the population. The Orthodox peasants of the south were eager for agrarian reform and freedom from domination by the Beys. All Zogu did was abolish the title of Bey, and make it illegal for a landlord to evict a tenant who had fulfilled his obligations. The inhabitants of Scutari were disappointed that their city had not become the capital of the country. Many nationalists were displeased with the government for not continuing to dispute with Yugoslavia the Kossovo region, where so many tens of thousands of Albanians lived under Yugoslav domination, and the Kossovo Committee, formed to fight for the area, was quite active in opposition to Zogu. Indeed, both Yugoslavs and Greeks oppressed their Albanian subjects.

But a flood of foreign advisers now helped the new state get under way. A Dutchman in the treasury, an English officer in the Ministry of the Interior, a German engineer in the Ministry of Public Works, an Italian agricultural expert as director of the agricultural school at Lushnja, an Austrian general as reorganizer of the army, all worked at their tasks. The Sunnis, in solemn Congress, cut their last ties with Istanbul, by declaring formally that there had been no Caliph since Mohammed himself. They also forbade polygamy, and made the wearing of the veil by women a voluntary matter. Early in 1924, there took place elections for a constituent assembly, which had been planned since 1920. The body chosen was also to serve as parliament until a constitution should have been adopted. There were ninety-five members, with Zogu controlling forty, Noli thirty-five, and the Popular Party the remaining twenty. Although Zogu had brought some public order, his policies were neither sufficiently aggressive in foreign affairs nor sufficiently liberal in domestic affairs to win him support. Moreover, finances were in a bad state, and the Dutch financial adviser now urged higher income taxes, more days of labor given free to the state, a heavy cut in the bureaucracy, and the abolition of the army, which was too small to be useful, but big enough to eat up funds. Zogu had to resign in February 1924, but his prospective father-in-law, Verlaci, succeeded him. Before resigning, Zogu was wounded in three places by the bullets of a would-be assassin.

The assassin was a member of the most radical wing of the opposition, the "Union of Young Albanians." The leader of this Union, Avni Rustemi, was murdered in the street outside the parliament building in May 1924. Noli and his followers attributed the assassination to Zogu's Mati tribesmen, who believed in the vendetta. The Opposition now withdrew from Parliament on the not altogether unreasonable pretext that Tirana was too close to Mati for safety. From north and south the discontented now advanced on Tirana. By July, the insurgents had won; Zogu had fled to Yugoslavia; and Noli was Premier. His program called for order, the end of feudalism, reform, pruning of the bureaucracy, strengthening of local government, balancing the budget, help for the peasants, a welcome for foreign capital, and improvements in the judiciary, transportation, public health, and education. He realized how ambitious this was, and how difficult it would be to put it through. He was never to have the opportunity, partly through his own fault.

Noli's regime set up a special tribunal, which passed death sentences in absentia on Zogu, Verlaci, and others, and confiscated their property. Moreover, many of those who had followed Noli when it was a question of ousting Zogu and Verlaci were by no means agreed on the sweeping program of reform. Then too, Noli did not get the outside assistance which alone could keep Albania afloat. At the League of Nations, he showed himself bitterly critical of parliaments, as institutions devoted to the overproduction of hot air. With a good deal of justice, Noli severely criticized the League of Nations for failing to secure a final settlement of Albanian frontiers. Disorder still raged on both the Yugoslav and Greek borders. A republican, Noli found himself opposed by many monarchists. A proponent of land reform, he aroused the opposition of the beys; and—so he himself later declared—when he failed to carry out the reforms, he lost the support of the peasantry. His scrupulously honest handling of finances, however, resulted in a balanced budget.

In Yugoslavia meanwhile, Zogu received some Yugoslav and some White Russian refugee troops as support for a counterstroke. The Yugoslav government was hoping for a pretext to intervene and restore Zogu, in order to secure for itself the disputed points along the frontiers. When Noli's regime recognized the USSR, and Moscow sent a representative, the Yugoslavs charged that the Albanians were moving toward Bolshevism. In December, the Yugoslav-backed forces crossed the frontier, and by the twenty-fourth Zogu was back in Tirana, Noli and his Cabinet having left for Italy. Italian support was not forthcoming for the enemies of Zogu, despite the obvious role which Yugoslavia had played in ousting them. Probably the Italians already had wind of Zogu's view that Italy was preferable to Yugoslavia as a protector.

Early in 1925, Zogu formed a new government; what was left of the Assembly proclaimed a republic. On January 31, Zogu was elected President for a seven-year term, and soon afterwards Albania adopted a new constitution. The new Senate was to have eighteen members, twelve elected and six appointed by the President. The Chamber would have fifty-seven elected members. The President had unconditional veto powers, and the sole right to call for elections or to initiate constitutional change. He had already removed all former members of the Opposition from responsible posts in the army and civil service, and replaced them by men loyal to him. Noli, who had indeed usurped power illegally, was charged with misappropriating public funds. Zogu exiled and imprisoned some of his enemies. One of Noli's right-hand men was murdered in Italy by an Albanian who may well have been an agent of Zogu. In any case, the new President now had the good will both of Yugoslavia and of Italy.

That of Yugoslavia he soon lost. What he had promised the Yugoslavs with regard to the disputed frontier points is not known, but they certainly seem to have expected that they could now take over unimpeded. But once in power, Zogu continued to press Albanian claims. The whole matter hung fire for some time, but Albania eventually ceded the points in question, in exchange for some minor frontier rectifications in her favor. The final settlement was signed on July 30, 1926. It was, however, Italy which Zogu had chosen as his protector. In May 1925, there began a process of Italian penetration with Albanian consent which would culminate fourteen years later in occupation and annexation. The first agreement permitted the Italians to carry out prospecting and to exploit Albanian mineral resources. Soon afterward, the Albanian parliament agreed that the Italians should found the Albanian National Bank, acting as the Albanian Treasury, but with a main office in Rome and effectively controlled by Italian banks. Italian shipping companies obtained a monopoly on freight and passenger transport to and from Albania. The SVEA (Society for the Economic Development of Albania) began in late 1925 to advance loans to the Albanian government at high rates of interest, the money to be spent on transportation, public works, and agriculture.

Political demands did not lag far behind the Italian economic advance. In mid-1926, the Italians asked, among other things, that their special interests in Albania receive formal recognition, and that Italian instructors be accepted for the army and police. Zogu tried to evade acceptance, and secured at least temporary British backing and postponement of the demands. But in November an uprising broke out among the tribesmen of the north. It was suppressed, but not before Zogu had concluded the Treaty of Tirana with Italy. It is not clear, and not very important, whether the Italians had stirred up the revolt to achieve their purposes, or whether the Yugoslavs were behind it. In any case, the new treaty with Italy provided only that the maintenance of the Albanian *status quo* (political, juridical, and territorial) was to the interests of both powers. Neither state would conclude with any other state an agreement prejudicial to this mutual interest. In a supplementary statement, the Italians agreed not to intervene in Albanian internal affairs without a specific Albanian invitation. The signing of the treaty precipitated a storm of protest in Yugoslavia, but the Albanians, with Mussolini's backing, blandly offered to conclude a precisely similar pact with Belgrade. The Yugoslavs did not respond to this overture, and relations continued to be strained. The arrest by the Albanian government in early 1927 of an Albanian citizen allegedly engaged in espionage for Yugoslavia led to recriminations, a crisis, and a break in diplomatic relations between Belgrade and Tirana, but by July the intervention of the powers had restored calm.

In November 1927, Albanian-Italian relations were further cemented by a defensive alliance, an answer to the Franco-Yugoslav pact of a few days earlier. This brought General Pariani and forty-odd Italian officers into Albania to train the army. The government bought from Italy large quantities of arms. The Albanians also allowed Italian experts to train young men in para-military youth groups modeled on Mussolini's *ballila* system. It is true that the Albanian gendarmerie was under the direction of British officers, but these were retired from the British services, and hired and paid by the Albanian government, while the Italians were on active duty. A new penal code was modeled on that of Italy, while the new civil code was modeled on that of France. Both replaced outmoded Ottoman systems. The concept of civil marriage and the possibility of divorce aroused opposition from the Roman Catholics, but both codes were adopted.

With order largely restored, and enforced by Zogu's decrees forbidding the vendetta and the promiscuous carrying of weapons, the President moved to make himself King. He managed this in constitutional fashion, securing the assembly's consent to its own dissolution and the election of a new constituent body, which dutifully amended the Constitution and created Zogu King Zog I (September 1, 1928). A few Albanians remained loyal to Prince William of Wied, who was still alive. There was also a good deal of criticism because Zog called himself "King of the Albanians," implying authority over Albanians outside the borders of the country. But recognition from the states of the world was soon forthcoming. The new monarchical constitution left Zog's powers much what they had been, but abolished the senate, and created a one-chamber parliament of fifty-six members, one for every 15,000 inhabitants.

The new king ended his engagement to Shefqet Verlaci's daughter. He could not now afford to alienate the population by alliance with the Beys, or to alienate the other Beys by honoring one of their number. Offended, Verlaci stopped supporting Zog, and began to plot against him. Eventually he was exiled. In a land of blood feuds, Zog had of course a great number of personal enemies, whom Albanian mores required to try to kill him. He was surrounded by guards, and made few public appearances. On a visit to Vienna in 1931 Zog and his attendants fought a gun duel with assassins on the steps of the opera house.

Though Zog ordered the tribesmen disarmed, and the government collected 180,000 rifles during his reign, he let his own tribe, the Mati, and their allies, the Dibra, keep their weapons. He kept the British officers in charge of the gendarmerie in the face of all possible Italian pressure to remove them. The army, though always under 10,000 in size, was a serious drain on the exchequer, and the exclusive Italian domination over its training rapidly alienated many of the public. Public opinion indeed, became steadily more anti-Italian.

When the Tirana Treaty of 1926 expired in 1931, Zog refused to renew it. In 1932 and 1933, Albania could not pay the interest on the SVEA loan, and the Italians put on the screws. They now demanded that Zog put Italians in as directors of the gendarmerie, join a customs union with Italy, give Italy control of the sugar and telegraph and electricity monopolies, teach Italian in all Albanian schools, and admit Italian colonists. Though in debt and faced with the loss of further financial assistance, Zog refused (early 1933). He ordered the most rigid economy, cutting the budget by almost 30 per cent, and abandoning his own personal income for a year. He dismissed a good many Italian advisers, and nationalized the Catholic schools in the north, previously largely run by Italians. He opened negotiations for an economic agreement with Yugoslavia. By June 1934, Albanians and Yugoslavs had signed a trade treaty; Mussolini had suspended all promised payments; and Zog had substituted French for Italian as the language to be taught at the best school in the country, the high school or lycée at Korcha. The Italians now sent a squadron of warships to demonstrate off the Albanian coast, and the Albanian authorities allowed the forces to land unarmed. The whole attempt to intimidate the Albanians failed completely.

Mussolini, about to become involved in his Ethiopian adventure, now returned to conciliatory methods, and determined to buy Zog back. In early 1935, he advanced 3,000,000 gold francs to the Albanian government as a gift. Zog's success in putting down two local revolts completed the conviction of Mussolini that he must reach a new agreement. Late in 1935, Zogu installed a wholly new regime, consisting mostly of young men, but with Mehdi Frasheri, the enlightened Bektashi Bey, as Premier. The new government obtained from Italy a commitment to meet the financial obligations Mussolini had assumed toward Albania, and to grant new loans, for the improvement of the harbor at Durazzo and for other purposes. The Italians returned as "friends" but in smaller numbers than before.

Zog's regime was a curious mixture of Ottoman corruption with strivings toward westernization and improvement. That harbor at Durazzo, of course, had already been improved at such cost that one would have expected it to have had installations as impressive as those along the Hudson or the Thames. That it continued to need improvement was suggestive of the way in which funds vanished in the Balkans. In the sense that all of Zog's ministers were completely subservient to him, came and went at his bidding, and cultivated apparent views of their own only to be useful to him (there was a "pro-Italian" team used for negotiating with Mussolini, for example), they were reminiscent of the royal servants of Alexander of Yugoslavia, Boris of Bulgaria, and Carol of Rumania. But the illiteracy of the population and the economic and social backwardness of the country distinguished Albania in the interwar period from the other Balkan states. It was still rather like a poor and remote Ottoman province.

Except for Mehdi Frasheri, the government which Zog put into power in 1935 was made up of men who had received their education since liberation from Turkey. And Mehdi Frasheri himself was the most distinguished sort of Turkish public servant, with a long record of honest and selfless service both to the Ottoman Empire and to Albania. But the repeated local uprisings and the persistence of assassination as a political instrument made the way hard for the few enlightened Albanians. Zog himself kept at his side an Ottoman type of favorite in the person of Abdur-Rahman Krosi, an inveterate briber and corrupter and plotter. The Frasheri regime fell in 1936, before it had succeeded in its favorite project of improving agricultural education and establishing an agricultural bank. Zog removed it because he wanted his "pro-Italian" team in office. He also had been embarrassed by the publication in the local press of one of the lists of candidates for the new elections whose election he was secretly supporting.

Once the Ethiopian war was over, the Italians became involved in Spain. But by the spring of 1939 that adventure too had been successfully completed. German aggression in central Europe, recently climaxed by the occupation of Prague in violation of the Munich agreement, had outshone Italian achievements. Mussolini determined to put an end to Zog's kingdom. When Zog refused once more to accept large sums of money in exchange for full Italian penetration and colonization of Albania, Mussolini invaded the country on April 7, 1939. It made no difference that Mussolini's son-in-law Count Ciano, had, only a little over a year before, acted as best man on the occasion of Zog's wedding to Geraldine Apponyi, half Magyar noblewoman, half American, or that Queen Geraldine had just produced an infant son and heir, named, of course, Skander. Though the Italians met with vigorous resistance, especially at Durazzo, the Albanians had to submit. Queen Geraldine and her baby and later Zog fled to Greece, and eventually made their way to London. Shefqet Verlaci returned to the country to serve as collaborationist premier in a fascist government. King Victor Emmanuel took the title of King of Albania. The country was turned into a province of Italy, and was intended to serve as a base for further Italian expansion toward Greece.

The brief experiment in independence had ended in tragedy. It need not perhaps have been so, had there been more time for the Albanians to adjust themselves to the twentieth century. But the entire society of Albania was probably unable to produce a government much more effective than Zog's had been. He had to get economic help somewhere. Italy offered it. The arrangement might have proved continuously profitable for both sides had it not been for Mussolini's dreams of conquest. Given these, not even Plato's Republic could have survived Italian all-out attack. Zog, far from a philosopher-King, had negotiated with the Italians over some fifteen years in the only way he knew: he had yielded when he had to, resisted when he could, made a good thing out of both. When time ran out, he was caught, as many a better man was, by fascist aggression. The qualities of courage and hospitality which distinguish the Albanians proved that there was a magnificent foundation for a healthy country in a world that was not predatory. This world had never come into existence, and the Albanians had never had their chance.

3. Balkan Territorial Issues

During the interwar years, despite the efforts of the peacemakers, territorial issues remained to trouble the relations of the Balkan countries, with each other and with their neighbors. These questions could not be solved in a way satisfactory to both sides. Nor was it easy to say in any case where justice lay. The nations deprived of territory by the peace treaties (Bulgaria, Hungary) looked with longing across their new frontiers toward lands which had once been theirs. We have already had occasion to observe the way in which the Macedonian problem dominated Bulgarian political life, both internal and external. Hungary too breathed irredentism. All tourists in Budapest saw the enormous statue of Hungary mourning the lost provinces, north, east, south, and west, and the great map, laid out in flower-beds in the public park, showing in different-colored blossoms the territories relinquished to Austria, Czechoslovakia, Yugoslavia, and Rumania. Between the wars the national motto became the celebrated *Nem, nem, soha* (No, no, never). Revisionist propaganda flowed from the presses in all the languages of western Europe, often convincing the unwary foreigner, who had little knowledge of Hungary's black record with her minorities, that the Magyars had experienced grave injustice.

Transylvania separated Hungary and Rumania; Bessarabia separated Rumania and the USSR; Macedonia separated not only Bulgaria and Yugoslavia but Bulgaria and Greece; Kossovo separated Albania and Yugoslavia; "southern Albania" or "northern Epirus" separated Albania and Greece; Istria separated Yugoslavia and Italy; Carinthia separated Yugoslavia and Austria; the Voyvodina separated Yugoslavia and Hungary. Less important but still genuine issues over the Dobrudja and the Banat separated Rumania from Bulgaria and Yugoslavia respectively. World War II was to bring all these territorial questions up for new settlement.

TRANSYLVANIA

In Transylvania, the large Magyar minority, well over a quarter of the total population, had lorded it over the Rumanians for at least seven hundred years, and still had the feeling of belonging to a master race. In the interwar years, the Rumanians did not deprive the Magyars of their schools or newspapers and periodicals in their own languages. The importation of Hungarian literary materials from Hungary was permitted. The Bucharest regimes did, however, require all civil servants to pass a Rumanian language examination, and often used this to discriminate unfairly against Magyar applicants. The Rumanians tended to make Transylvania pay more than its share of taxes, and to ignore the province when it came to road-building. The Magyar peasantry suffered from Rumanian bad government, but then so did all Rumanians. But it was Magyar irredentism that kept the question alive, an irredentism growing ever stronger with the growing triumphs of Hitler and Mussolini. As Hungary fell more and more into the orbit of the Axis, the Hungarian regimes brought more and more pressure on the Germans and Italians for a readjustment of the Rumanian frontier. Nothing could be done until the outbreak of the Second World War had upset the peace settlements of the first, but it was only a short time thereafter before the Hungarians had succeeded in obtaining a new settlement in their favor.

BESSARABIA

Bessarabia had changed hands repeatedly during the nineteenth century. The Russians took it from the Turks in 1812; Moldavia obtained the southern portion in 1856; this reverted to Russia in 1878; and the Rumanians acquired the whole province in 1917–18. All during the period before the First World War, this was one of the most backward of Russian provinces. The native Bessarabian nobility had an extraordinarily conservative point of view, and the peasantry continued in ignorance and apathy. When the Tsarist government was overthrown in February 1917, a revolutionary peasant movement existed, but it was the more conservative nationalist Moldavians who summoned the council which declared for union with Rumania in the fall of 1917. This council opposed Russia and the Bolshevik regime, which took power in October, and Rumanian troops backed it up by ousting the local soviets, which the reds had established. The peasants had seized a good deal of land before the province was joined with Rumania, and thus agrarian reform took a different course in this province from that followed elsewhere in Rumania.

The population of roughly 3,000,000, of whom a little over half was Rumanian, and about a quarter Ukrainian or Russian, gave the Russians no basis for demanding the return of the province. But they never recognized Rumanian possession. Soviet desire for the return of Bessarabia was doubtless based only in part on questions of prestige. It must have rested largely on the important strategic position of the province, controlling the mouths of the Danube, and serving as a buffer against attack from the west, as well as providing a suitable base for further advance toward the Straits and the Balkans. In the interwar years, there were no diplomatic or commercial relations between Rumania and the USSR until 1934 and 1935, when ambassadors were exchanged. A commercial agreement was concluded in 1936, but the volume of trade remained very small, and public opinion in Rumania extremely cool. More revealing was the steady Soviet effort to infiltrate Bessarabia: smuggling of agents, arms, and propaganda across the Dniester, which culminated in the "revolution" at Tatar Bunar in September 1924. This was put down by the Rumanian government. Even after relations had been renewed they were soured by the defection early in 1938 of a Soviet diplomat in Bucharest. The question of Bessarabia never arose officially, but the Rumanians were keenly aware of the Soviet attitude on the subject. None the less, the province was perhaps the worst-governed of all Rumanian provinces in the interwar years, which is to say that it was very badly governed indeed.

MACEDONIA

As to Macedonia, the Yugoslav government, which controlled most of it, called its portion first "south Serbia," and then the Vardar Banovina. Both names symbolized the "Serbizing" policy of Belgrade. New Serbian colonists were sent in to dilute the Macedonian language and sentiments of the area. Otherwise, it was largely neglected, despite its backwardness and the obvious need for transportation, public works, educational institutions, agricultural improvements, and exploration for new natural resources. The government position was that there was no such thing as a Macedonian; there were only Serbs. It often arrested local Macedonians whom it accused of sympathy with the perpetual IMRO raids. It created more such sympathy than it crushed. After the long years of terror and strained relations, the Zveno suppression of IMRO led to so great an improvement in Bulgarian-Yugoslav relations that it survived even King Alexander's assassination by a Macedonian. As the German-Italian alliance fused into the Axis in the late thirties, the Macedonian question became temporarily less critical. It was the Axis hope to win both Yugoslavs and Bulgarians to their camp. Only the ultimate refusal of Yugoslavia to be won, led, as we shall see, to the reopening of the issue by the Germans in favor of the Bulgarians.

Bulgarian occupation forces in Greek Macedonia during the First World War had compiled a record of brutality extraordinary even for this area, deporting some 42,000 Greeks to Bulgaria. After the war, Greeks and Bulgarians concluded an agreement by which Greeks in Bulgaria and Bulgarians in Greece might go to the other country if they chose, and take their movable property with them. A League of Nations Commission was to sell their real estate and liquidate their claims. IMRO, however, was dismayed at the thought of the Slav minority, on which it based its claims to Greek territory, moving into Bulgaria. Other factors delayed the migrations, but by the early 1930's about 52,000 Slavs had left Greece for Bulgaria, and about 25,000 Greeks had left Bulgaria for Greece. There were almost no Slavs left in Greek eastern Macedonia. West of the Vardar, however, near the Yugoslav frontier, a Slavic-speaking population continued to live in Greece. These the Greeks agreed in 1924 to treat as a Bulgarian minority; but the Yugoslavs immediately objected to the term Bulgarian, because it implied to them that their own Macedonians might be so called or so regarded. So the agreement was dropped, and the Greek government treated its roughly 100,000 Slavic-speaking Macedonian subjects not as a minority but as Greeks, and without discrimination. At the same time, the influx of Greeks from Turkey and the departure of Turks turned the area into a more solidly Greek region than it had ever previously been.

This movement of populations lessened the tension between Greece and Bulgaria, since not even IMRO could justify raids into eastern Macedonian territory where there were no Slavs. This helped keep IMRO's attacks concentrated against Yugoslavia, which was so much more vulnerable to them than Greece. There were, however, Greek-Bulgarian frontier incidents, of varying degrees of seriousness. A further question was provided by the question of Yugoslav and Bulgarian use of the great Aegean port of Saloniki, the natural outlet for all of Macedonia, and claimed for a Macedonian state by its proponents. A Greek-Serbian agreement of 1914 had provided for a Serbian free zone in the port, and negotiations in the early twenties led in 1925 to a Greek lease to the Yugoslavs of such a zone for a period of fifty years. Though an integral part of Greece, it was to be subject to Yugoslav customs officials, and would be managed by the Yugoslavs. But the Yugoslavs pushed for outright cession of the Zone, and for its enlargement. There were also disputes over freight rates. Several times on the point of settlement, the problem actually hung fire until early 1929, when the Zone was enlarged, and freight rates adjusted, but Greek sovereignty retained. The Yugoslavs were not satisfied, however, and used the Zone very little. The Bulgarians for their part in 1923 and 1926 flatly refused a Greek offer of a zone on similar terms. It was clear that the Bulgarian regime did not want to accept anything from Greece, however advantageous to themselves, which would seem to imply any surrender of their claim on an Aegean outlet of their own in western Thrace. Despite their best efforts, the Greeks could rest easy with respect to neither Yugoslav nor Bulgarian ambitions to possess Saloniki.

Obviously a region with future revolutionary possibilities, Macedonia in the interwar period deeply interested the Communists. The USSR on the whole favored the claim of Bulgaria to the province. There was at first no effort to organize a Macedonian Communist Party as distinct from the Yugoslav, Bulgarian, and Greek parties. The Comintern regarded Bulgaria as the one Balkan country which in the early twenties might be ready for its revolution, and it worked to create Macedonian support for the revolution when it should come, negotiating with a good many IMRO leaders, and flattering IMRO with public approval of its policies and support for a Macedonian Republic inside a Balkan Federation. IMRO responded warmly to the wooing in 1924, and a kind of common front of IMRO and Communists seemed on the point of emerging. The Comintern blasted the errors of their own Greek and Yugoslav parties for not supporting an independent Macedonia. But the IMRO leaders who had flirted with the Communists soon either repudiated their signatures on a common manifesto or were murdered, or both. The Communist effort to capture IMRO had been thwarted. Subsequent Comintern experiments with a "United IMRO" to carry on the old line proved a failure. In 1929, Moscow was still calling for Communist coöperation with the national movements, and now urged partisan warfare as a means of touching off revolutions.

The Greek Communist Party in these years actually split on the question of autonomous Macedonia. But the Yugoslav Party found itself given a loophole by Stalin himself. In an address in March 1925, Stalin declared that, while the Macedonian minority would have a right to secede from a future Soviet Yugoslavia, it *would not be obliged to secede,* if it preferred to stay. This was to provide the Yugoslav Communists with valuable ammunition for use against their Bulgarian opposite numbers in the years of the Second World War and later. As with all problems, the Comintern line was determined by the Soviet interpretation of the USSR's own interests. When it became clear by 1934 that Hitler had assumed for his own purposes the leadership of those who wanted to revise the peace treaties, the USSR abandoned its own revisionism. With it went the essentially revisionist Macedonian policy, whose chief purpose was to explode the Balkan countries from within. This enabled the Bulgarian, Yugoslav, and Greek Communist Parties to go their own ways, the Bulgarians still secretly eager to acquire Macedonia, the Yugoslavs and Greeks each eager to keep their own share.

KOSSOVO

The term Kossovo is loosely applied to the whole area of Yugoslavia across the frontiers from Albania, in which Albanians lived.[5] The present Tito regime calls this Kossovo-Metohiya.[6] There could be no doubt that the overwhelming majority of the approximately 600,000 inhabitants was Albanian and Muslim. Relatively fertile, the area served as an important source of grain supply for Albania proper, and as a market for the Albanian villagers across the frontier. The Albanian population was, however, of comparatively recent

[5] The term sometimes refers to the whole *polye* or plain where the Serbs met their historic defeat in 1389, sometimes to the old Turkish *vilayet* or province, which extended quite far to the east, sometimes to one of the Albanian prefectures.

[6] For our purposes, it includes a strip along the northwestern frontier of Albania with Montenegro, with the Adriatic port of Ulcinj (Dulcigno), the Gusinye-Plav district, the Metohiya plain, the southern part of the Kossovo plain, the Shar Planina, the upper Vardar valley, headwaters of the Black Drina, and the neighborhood of Lakes Ohrid and Prespa.

date for the Balkans, going back only to the sixteenth and seventeenth centuries, when the Serbs had migrated north out of the Ottoman Empire and into Habsburg territory. For the Serbs, the region included the site not only of their Patriarchate at Pech but also of the battle of 1389, towards which they felt somewhat the same way as Americans might feel about Valley Forge.

We have noted the long debates and delays over the Albanian northern frontiers. Although the Conference of Ambassadors in 1913 had agreed that the area in question would belong to Serbia, the World War and disputes over points of detail prevented the conclusion of an Albanian-Yugoslav frontier agreement until 1926. Meanwhile, Yugoslav behavior in the Kossovo area had not been such as to discourage Albanian irredentist claims. The Belgrade government made a concerted effort to settle the land with Serbian colonists, after dividing the estates of the Albanian landowners. But agricultural and health conditions in the area were wretched, and many of the colonists eventually departed. The policy had, moreover, involved much injustice to the Albanian inhabitants, who saw their religious property confiscated, and whom the Serbian police frequently mistreated. Often the Yugoslav officials would confiscate the central portion of a farm, leaving the owner with a divided property which was hard to cultivate. The Albanians were often unable to meet the strict Yugoslav requirements for written title-deeds to their land, as this was a region where tradition and not documents proved possession. The Yugoslavs closed the Albanian schools, despite protests made at the League of Nations by Albanian priests. With a Turkish repatriation agreement as pretext, Yugoslav authorities simply deported many Albanians to Turkey, although they did not wish to leave. When they arrived in Turkey, they either had to accept Turkish citizenship or undergo a new deportation.

The Albanian regime, though naturally sympathetic to the plight of fellow-Albanians in Yugoslavia, had not the strength to make an issue of the problem. Efforts to repatriate some of the wretched Kossovars were not a success. As Zog became more and more dependent on Italy, Yugoslavia acted more and more severely in Kossovo. In the area itself, the "Kossovo Committee" acted as a clandestine focus for discontent, favoring annexation to Albania. The committee, financed by some of the richer Beys, issued propaganda for a "greater Albania," tried to keep Albanians from registering or reporting for military service in the Yugoslav army, and, when war came, preached desertion. The issue, like the others here passed in review, thus smoldered right inside the lid of Pandora's Box. When Mussolini and Hitler opened the box, it was one of the first to emerge.

"NORTHERN EPIRUS"

At the other end of Albania, the two Albanian prefectures of Korcha and Gjinokaster (Koritza and Argyrokastron), with a population of some quarter million, provided a major source of friction with Greece. Greek nationalists called the area "northern Epirus," and claimed it as their own. To Albanians, it was simply southern Albania. As early as 1913, the Greeks pointed to Turkish census statistics of earlier years, which classified most of the inhabitants of northern Epirus as *Rumi,* and declared that this proved them Greek. The Albanians answered, quite correctly, that it only proved them Orthodox Christians, since the Turks used the term for all Orthodox without distinction as to language or nationality. To the Greek assertion that the churches and schools in the area used the Greek language, the Albanians answered, again rightly, that this was only because the Ottoman regulations forbade the use of the Albanian vernacular. The Conferences of Ambassadors required the Greek troops to withdraw from the area; but the Greeks apparently sponsored an insurrection and the establishment of an "autonomous" government before they departed. Of course, the war prevented a settlement of the question, and Greek claims were pressed again in 1919, but were eventually set aside.

Greece delayed recognition of Albanian independence until 1922, and then made reservations regarding the frontiers. In a variety of ways, the Greeks kept the tension alive. Albanians from the disputed prefectures traveling in Greece found themselves deprived of their Albanian passports and forced to accept Greek ones. Greek forces occupied part of the area, cutting off Korcha from its hinterland. Impartial observers do report, however, that there was some pro-Greek feeling among Orthodox Albanian inhabitants of the area in 1922 and 1923. In the first place, they were concerned at the emergence of Zogu as the most powerful man in the state, and feared, as it turned out without foundation, that Muslim domination might bring discrimination against Christians. In the second place, they longed for the agrarian reforms which would liberate them from the Beys, and feared they might not obtain them from Zogu; and in this fear they were entirely justified. Moreover, they felt that much of their tax-money was being spent in poorer parts of the country. But apparently in most cases these various sources of discontent did not make the southern Albanian Orthodox Christians eager for union with Greece. The Albanian regime treated the Greek minority of the region (perhaps about 30,000) with consideration, subsidizing for them their own schools, while the Greeks severely discriminated against their own Albanian minority (the "Chams") in southern Epirus (or Chamuria).

In August 1923, the Italian General Tellini, who was the chairman of the international commission engaged in drawing the southern frontier of Albania, was murdered with three other Italians, just after the commission had decided that all the villages near Korcha which the Greeks still occupied were to be awarded to Albania. The crime was brought home to the Greeks; Mussolini, compounding evil, bombarded and seized Corfu in revenge. Finally, the Conference required Greece to apologize and perform various humiliating acts of compensation. But the explosive northern Epirus question had virtually touched off a war. Despite the alarming friction generated by the episode, the Greeks did not withdraw from the villages in question until October 1924, and then only after all sorts of pressure had been brought to bear. Greek-

Albanian tension continued high, especially as the Greeks tended to regard their own Muslim Albanian minority as Turks, and to deport them to Turkey in accordance with the Greek-Turkish agreement for an exchange of populations. In 1925, the Albanians were threatening to expel their Greek minority in reprisal.

The year 1926, however, cleared the air. The Greek Premier, remarking that "super-patriotism is as dangerous as patriotism is beneficial," dissolved the Greek societies agitating for the annexation of northern Epirus. In October 1926, Greeks and Albanians signed a series of agreements. From then on, the "north Epirus" issue slumbered for a time, although Greek treatment of the Chams did not improve. The Italian occupation of Albania in 1939, however, and the launching of the invasion of Greece from Albanian bases in 1940, together with the heroic defense of the Greeks, provided, as we shall see, the Greek "super-patriots" with a pretext for renewing their demands. The resistance of the Albanian Communists to any cession of southern Albanian territory probably helped them recruit support for their Partisan movement during the Second World War. Though often in abeyance, the problem, like the others, arose after the war in the Greek claims at the Peace Conference of 1946, reappeared during the Greek Communist rebellion of 1946–1949, and is still with us, affecting the relationships of the nations in the new Balkan Pact.

ISTRIA

Though important and complicated and much discussed, virtually all Balkan territorial issues appeared simple by comparison with the Istrian problem. The region in question marks the southernmost part of the frontier zone between Slavs and non-Slavs which runs across all Europe irregularly from north to south. It includes the Istrian peninsula and the regions to the immediate north of it both in Italy and in Yugoslavia. One of the most authoritative students of the problems of the area[7] prefers to call the whole area the Julian region, since both Italians and Yugoslavs use the term. Disputed since Roman times as a frontier land, it became more important in the middle ages with the development of Venetian commerce, and was the focus of Venetian, Habsburg, and occasional Turkish pressures. Later, as we saw, the Napoleonic occupation provided a stimulus for Slovene nationalism. Though there was a fringe of Italian population in Trieste and along the western and southwestern shores of the Istrian peninsula, the inhabitants of the hinterland were Slovene or Croat. This was the result of a phenomenon, familiar all over eastern Europe, whereby the native people of an area are the rural population, while foreigners come in and build the cities. Just as the Transylvanian towns and the Baltic towns were German, in a countryside of Rumanians and Magyars or of Latvians and Esthonians, so the Istrian towns were Italian in a countryside of Slavs. And, when Slavs came to town they often learned Italian and became assimilated in order to carry on their business.

[7] A. E. Moodie, *The Italo-Yugoslav Boundary* (London, 1945).

With the ruin of Napoleon, the Habsburgs took over his Kingdom of Illyria, and made frequent changes in the administrative structure, in an effort to produce stability. But a Slovenian literary and national awakening was now well under way. The peasantry, emancipated from serfdom in 1849, slowly acquired their own credit organizations, bought their lands, and freed themselves from debt, through hard work and intelligent organization. With the attainment of Italian independence and unification, Italian nationalists were eager to liberate from the Habsburgs the many Italians living under their domination in addition to those of Istria; but from the first Istria too became part of their irredenta, and part of their own conception of their proper natural boundaries.

It was during the nineteenth century that Trieste and Fiume, both ancient cities but of limited importance, began to grow into great ports. Baron Bruck, the Austrian Minister of Commerce in the mid-nineteenth century, undertook the development of Trieste as the major outlet for Austrian trade, building docks and railroads to the town to make it a great commercial center. Fiume served in a similar capacity for Hungary. Both were deliberate creations rather than natural growths, and were assisted by the opening of the Suez Canal in 1869, and the ensuing boom of Mediterranean trade. Neither developed local industries. By 1913 the annual volume of shipping for Trieste was almost five and a half million tons. It served Austria, southern Germany, the Czech lands, and Slovenia. The Hungarians, despite the vehement protests of Croatian nationalists, used Fiume in the same way, building railroads to it in the 1870's; its tonnage reached more than six million in 1912. It served Hungary and Croatia.

The two ports were to a certain extent rivals, but Trieste suffered more than Fiume from the competition of the north German ports as an outlet for central Europe. Even at the height of Trieste's usefulness to Austria, it handled only a little more than one-fifth of Austrian overseas imports. Neither port served Italy to any notable extent, nor did either have the appropriate Italian rail connections. It was Austrian and Hungarian money that created the shipping and insurance companies which grew up in the ports. Though the population of both ports spoke Italian, this was the maritime language of the Habsburg Empire, and, despite the substantial number of Italian immigrants, many Italian-speakers were Italians neither by sentiment nor by birth, but Austrians. Because the Austrian census listed people according to the language they ordinarily spoke, many Slovenes or Germans were listed as Italian. The agitation for Trieste in Italy was therefore somewhat artificial, as was also shown by the maintenance of an Italian alliance with the Habsburg Empire down to and after the outbreak of the war.

As we know, the conflict between the terms of the Treaty of London of 1915 and the Wilsonian principle of self-determination almost disrupted the Peace Conference. In the end, the negotiations over the boundary between Italy and Yugoslavia had to be carried on not by the great powers in concert but between the Italians and Yugoslavs. Final settlement was not achieved until 1924. Though the Italians did not get Dalmatia, they obtained even more territory in the Julian region than the Treaty of London had assigned to them. Italian arguments were based on strategic considerations: the wish to obtain a good defensive line in the northeast; and economic considerations: the wish to control the Central European trade outlets of Trieste and Fiume. Yugoslav arguments were based on demographic considerations: the wish to absorb into the new state almost 500,000 Slovenes and Croats, as well as on their need for a northern Adriatic port. The line as drawn cut the Julian region in two, and gave the Italians the half-million Slavs the Yugoslavs wanted, though the Yugoslavs received port facilities at Fiume.

In the interwar years, the Italians sought vainly to maintain the commerce of Trieste and Fiume. Even in 1924, the best year of the period, total traffic through Trieste failed to reach the 1913 level, while in the depression years volume shrank to about one-sixth of 1913. The case of Fiume was even worse: even the best year (1929) was less than half 1913. By the mid-thirties, the town was a ghost port. The competition of the German North Sea ports was in part responsible, but Italian tariffs also played a considerable role. Moreover, the Yugoslavs developed Split, Dubrovnik, and Shibenik as their own Adriatic ports, and did not use the old outlets. Their hostility to Italy helped render the Italian territorial gains unprofitable.

The Italian Fascist regime in Istria persecuted the Yugoslav minority. It gradually excluded them from the Italian Parliament, by rigged election laws and terrorism.[8] Similarly, the provincial and communal administrations excluded Slavs. The Italians closed all private Slovene and Croatian schools, and almost half of the public schools. In those that remained they first prescribed compulsory Italian, and then began a gradual process of introducing Italian as the exclusive language of education, completed by 1930. Similar regulations applied to religious instruction. The teachers were discharged and replaced by Italians. Special Italian kindergartens sought to convert the younger Slovene and Croat children into little Italians. Though the Italians claimed officially that instruction in Slovene and Croatian continued as school subjects, the object seems to have been not to permit the Slavs to learn their own language but to educate a few Italian officials in Slavic sufficiently to enable them to govern the Julian region. Slovene and Croatian were banned in the law courts and in the public services; they were forbidden even as the language of public conversation in certain cases. Signs in foreign languages were ruinously taxed. Public monuments and tombstones with Slavic inscriptions were desecrated. Slavic children were compelled to belong to Fascist youth organizations.

The regime purged Slavic officials and civil servants; it abolished Slavic labor unions, and forced their members into the Fascist Syndicates; it made

[8] There were five deputies in the 1921 Parliament, only two in the second one, of 1924, and none in the third, of 1929.

possible the removal of Slavic lawyers and doctors from their professions for acting in any manner contrary to the national interest, a clause which might be applied for almost any action, such as wishing to baptize a child with a Slavic Christian name. It persecuted and then abolished Slavic cultural societies. When the Slovene Club in Trieste was burned down in 1920 with the loss of many lives, the local Fascist paper boasted of the deed, and declared that Trieste was "purified at last." The Italian government suppressed the Slavic press in 1930, after years of increasingly rigorous regulations aimed at it. It censored Slavic books, and sought to collect and destroy Slavic primers for children. It changed Slavic place-names to Italian ones, it forced parents to confer Italian baptismal names upon their children, and Italianized Slavic surnames. Though the Slavs were overwhelmingly Roman Catholic, they had

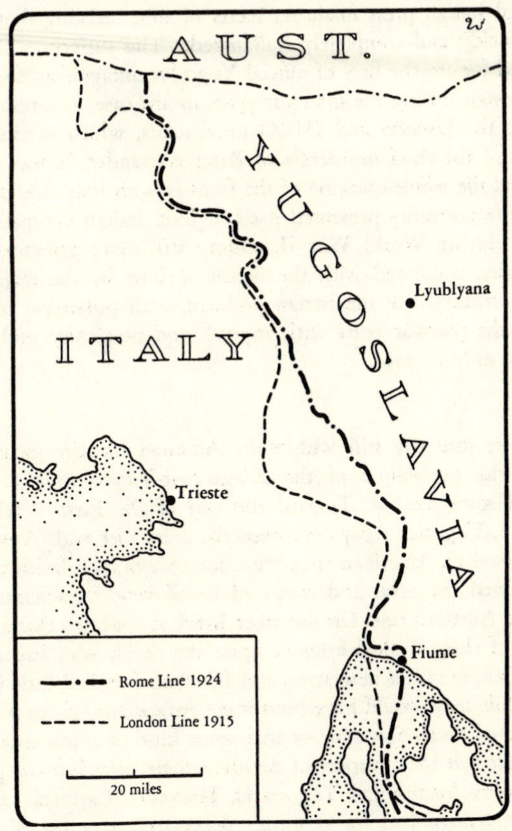

The Italo-Yugoslav Boundary Before 1939

for centuries been accustomed to the liturgy in the Church Slavonic or Croatian versions. Italians mistreated and deported Slavic priests, ruthlessly persecuting their fellow-Catholics.

On the economic side, the Slavs suffered from the loss of their former markets for farm produce, from the heavy taxes, which were farmed out to private individuals to collect, from the dissolution of their agricultural coöperatives, and from deliberate Italian attempts to colonize the region with Italians. About 100,000 Croats and Slovenes migrated during the 1920's and 1930's: 70,000 to Yugoslavia, and the rest to South America, France, and Belgium. Though much of the terror which the Slavs of the Julian March experienced in these years of Italian Fascist rule extended also to all anti-Fascist Italians, Mussolini's regime was impelled, in the case of the Slavs, by a fixed intention to denationalize them.

The official Italian press made no secret of this, insisting that the region should be "quickly and completely Italianized." The sufferings of the Slavic minority added fuel to the fires of official Yugoslav antagonism for Italy. This was strong enough during the interwar years in any case, as a result of Italian sponsorship of the Ustasha and IMRO movements, which in the end made Mussolini one of the chief murderers of King Alexander. It was of course to be expected that the whole question of the frontier with Italy would arise again as soon as the opportunity presented itself. It took Italian occupation of parts of Yugoslavia during World War II, adding still more grievances, and the Partisan victories, combined with the defeat of Italy by the major allies, to create the opportunity. But the Istrian problem, with possession of Trieste as its core, filled the postwar years with anguish and perplexity, and achieved a new settlement only in 1954.

CARINTHIA

The Slovene minority still within the Austrian frontier formed perhaps two-thirds of the population of the Klagenfurt-Villach area of Carinthia, and numbered some 120,000. Toward the end of the First World War, in November 1918, Yugoslav troops occupied the area, met with Austrian resistance, and accepted an American suggestion for temporary administration. The Yugoslavs claimed the area, and many of its Slovene inhabitants had been unhappy under Austrian rule. On the other hand, it appeared that a substantial number, even of these, looked askance upon the Serbs, who had emerged as the dominant people in the new state, and felt that they had little in common with them. While they would have been more enthusiastic about a union with a Croat-dominated south Slav state or with some kind of autonomous Slovenia, they also hesitated at the prospect of dividing their own beloved province of Carinthia between Austria and Yugoslavia. Moreover, Carinthia was an area in which the Germans had for centuries dominated over the Slovenes both economically and culturally, sometimes descending to open persecution, at other times simply discriminating against the Slovene language and denying the Slovenes the right to use it in their own schools. Slovenes were timid about expressing their views, and were in many cases cowed by the Germans.

Under Yugoslav pressure, the French and British at the Peace Conference favored dividing the Klagenfurt basin, giving the most Slovene portions to Yugoslavia; the Americans favored leaving the whole area in Austria. It was decided that there should be a plebiscite in the entire basin to decide its fate. The Yugoslavs were furious, and advanced their troops. Eventually, over Yugoslav protests, the Allies decided to divide the area into two Zones. If the first, which was the most thoroughly Slovene, voted to stay Austrian, there would be no plebiscite in the other, less Slovene, region. If the first voted for union with Yugoslavia, there would be a plebiscite also in the second. Meanwhile Yugoslavia administered the first Zone, favoring the Slovenes, and cutting off communications with the second Zone, and the Austrians founded propaganda organizations to urge the rejection of any proposal to divide Carinthia. The actual plebiscite, on October 10, 1920, however, was held under satisfactory conditions. More than 95 per cent of those entitled to vote in Zone I did so.

The Austrians won 59 per cent of the total vote. This made a plebiscite unnecessary in Zone II. Ten thousand Slovenes had voted not to join Yugoslavia. The Yugoslavs had had a substantial advantage in administering the zone, and still the population had voted them down. Actually, the division of the province apparently gave the voters a foretaste of the economic difficulty they might expect if an international frontier were to be drawn running through it. A leading Yugoslav authority on the subject attributed the success of the Austrian cause to the votes of Slovenes who favored the Germans, partly out of their traditional fear and awe of them, partly because, though they spoke Slovene, they felt as Carinthians. Yugoslavia had adopted compulsory military service; the new Austria had abandoned it; so it had proved effective propaganda to tell the Slovenes that if they opted for union with Yugoslavia they would soon find their menfolk on army duty in darkest Macedonia.

In the years which followed, the Yugoslavs accused the Austrians of continuing and intensifying their persecution of Slovenes, and of totally failing to live up to their promises of nondiscrimination. Only the actively pro-German Slovenes enjoyed equal economic and political opportunity. Known Slovene nationalists were dismissed without pensions; their cultural societies were closed; there were arrests, attacks on priests, and numerous instances of violence. All Austrian parties opposed a cultural autonomy bill in 1927, which the Yugoslavs hoped to get through the Austrian parliament. The leading German organization, the Heimatbund, had members of all political views, united on anti-Slovene principles, but growing more and more Nazi during the early 1930's. The use of the Slovene language in the schools was gradually diminished. The Yugoslav government tried on occasion to use the German minority in Yugoslavia as hostages for the good treatment of Slovenes in Carinthia.

After Hitler took over Austria in the spring of 1938, persecution sharpened rapidly. Small Slovene children were drafted into German-language kindergartens, and all the instruments of the Nazi police state were deployed against the Slovenes. When the Second World War came, the pro-Yugoslav Slovenes formed a resistance-movement, and soon were linked with Tito's Partisans. It was clear that the Yugoslavs would reassert their claim to the Slovenian part of Carinthia even though, when last consulted, the population had decisively preferred not to join Yugoslavia.

VOYVODINA

In the ethnically thoroughly mixed area of the Voyvodina, with its large Magyar and German minorities, and its smaller Rumanian minority, the interwar years bred future trouble. Owing its name to the brief period of twelve years between 1848 and 1860 when the Habsburgs had granted the Serbs their wish for an autonomous Dukedom, or Voyvodina, the area had been under Magyar rule since 1867. The Serbs of the province prospered, and maintained their own schools and their celebrated cultural society in Novi Sad, the Serbian Queen Bee (Srpska Matitsa). Those who felt inclined could migrate to Serbia, where they were always welcome, and where Prechani cultural influence, as we saw, was always high. Serb military occupation at the end of the war was followed by annexation, and adjustment of the frontier with Rumania to give Bucharest Timișoara.

Yugoslav administration of the former Hungarian territories was about as bad as Italian administration of the Julian region, and much resembled it. No local elections were held before 1927, and King Alexander's dictatorship of 1929 ended all local government. Until 1929 an extra tax, levied on the region because it had not been ravaged during the war, added to the burdens of the whole population. The Serbs of the area became almost separatist in their opposition to Belgrade, and often voted for Machek's Croatian Peasant Party in protest, as did the Independent Serbs of Croatia. The Magyars, however, suffered far worse. They only once obtained seats in the Skupshtina, and then (1927) only three. They had to put up with Serbian as the language of administration. Magyar civil servants, on the railroads and elsewhere, were discharged in favor of Serbian substitutes. All street signs, business stationery, and shopkeepers' books had to be in Serbian; conversations in public had to be conducted in Serbian. Clubs and societies were closed. The Serbs took over all the Magyar institutes of higher education, and permitted the Magyars too few kindergartens and elementary schools for their numbers. Croatian priests were substituted for Magyar in the Roman Catholic churches. The minority, including the Magyar-speaking Jews, simmered in discontent, and remained loyal to Hungary. Here too was a situation ready to become explosive with the first defeat of the Yugoslavs and the first opportunity for Budapest.

4. *The Little Entente and the Balkan Entente*

The rehearsal of this long list of territorial grievances should not create the impression that all Balkan foreign relations during the interwar period were chaotically hostile. Though the reopening of these old sores was always a danger, much progress was actually scored in the direction of a Balkan understanding. An eventual confederation was in the minds of all the diplomats, and received warm support from the allied powers, including the United States. The League of Nations recognized the validity and usefulness of regional understandings. The gravest problem was of course presented by the fact that Bulgaria and Hungary were determinedly revisionist, and the other countries equally opposed to all revision. The common interest which the southeastern European nations had in mutual understanding at times seemed reduced to their common wish to hold Bulgaria and Hungary down. Yet this negative aspect of the foreign relations of the interwar years should not obscure the positive work accomplished by Balkan diplomats.

By mid-1921, Rumania and Yugoslavia were linked to each other and both to Czechoslovakia by treaty. This was the Little Entente, which played an important role in keeping southeast Europe relatively stable. In 1924, the French signed an alliance with the Czechs, and followed this in 1926 and 1927 by similar pacts with Rumania and Yugoslavia. These more or less balanced Mussolini's friendships with Hungary and Bulgaria, his sponsorship of the IMRO and of the Ustashe, and his steadily increasing domination over Albania. The depression, the Japanese disregard for the League, and the rise of Hitler posed a clear threat to collective security as well as to the individual members of the Entente.

Their spokesman was the Czech, Beneš, who pressed in vain for League measures against Japan in 1931. Within two weeks after Hitler became Chancellor, the Little Entente adopted a new constitution, which set up a permanent council of the Foreign Ministers of the three countries, to meet three times a year. All three powers would have to approve any change in the political or economic relations of any of the members with any outside state. Efforts were made in the economic sphere as well, and the Entente established a permanent secretariat. The Entente resisted Mussolini's proposal of a Four Power Pact, which would have made the four great western European powers arbiters of the continent; and the French declined to sell their partners out.

Meanwhile, in the Balkans proper, beginning in 1930, Yugoslavia and Rumania had been participating in a series of conferences with Greece, Turkey, and Bulgaria. They established a Balkan Chamber of Commerce and Industry at Istanbul in 1931, a Balkan Medical Union, and an Agricultural Chamber in 1933. The conferences drafted a political pact, a pact creating a Balkan Customs Union, and a program of social and cultural coöperation.

These remained ideals, however, as the hostility, especially between Bulgaria and Yugoslavia, could not be quickly overcome. In 1933, Alexander of Yugoslavia took the initiative in easing relations with Bulgaria, inviting King Boris to Belgrade, and making subsequent visits to Rumania, Bulgaria, Turkey, and Greece. This led on February 9, 1934 to the signing of a Balkan Pact, including Rumania, Yugoslavia, Greece, and Turkey, but not Bulgaria or Albania. Since it provided for the mutual defense by all four countries of the frontiers of any one of the four, a Bulgarian signature would have meant renunciation of all hope of territorial gain. Though the members were at pains to declare that the pact was not directed at any nation, and aimed only to protect Balkan frontiers against Balkan aggression, the only Balkan states omitted were Bulgaria and Albania.

This showed that Bulgaria could never expect any of its neighbors to listen sympathetically to any of its territorial pleas, and that Greece had by no means abandoned its hope of acquiring Albanian territory. Despite these grave weaknesses, the Balkan Pact did serve notice that the four signers hoped to resist aggression collectively. They followed the Pact by a Balkan Entente, with its own Permanent Council and Economic Advisory Council, and began to put into effect some of the recommendations which the earlier conferences had made. The murder of King Alexander might well have opened southeast Europe to Mussolini, as he surely hoped it would, had not Yugoslavia been firmly linked to both Little Entente and Balkan Entente, and receiving full support from its allies.

Beginning in 1936, the Entente set up a Marine Commission, signed an aviation agreement, and took steps toward a central European union of postal, telegraphic, and telephonic systems. All sorts of commercial and financial understandings were reached. But the Ethiopian affair of 1935 and the League's decision to apply sanctions to Italy, after the Hoare-Laval effort at appeasement had been repudiated, not only revealed the weakness of France as a force against aggression but also affected the Ententes directly. The sanctions policy cost the Balkan countries heavily in foreign trade with Italy, and the Germans now began their great campaign to capture the foreign trade of the southeast. In this they were helped, as we saw, by the dangerously wavering policies of Prince Paul and Stoyadinovich, the growth of the Iron Guard and the incapacity of Carol, and Boris' ouster of Zveno and assumption of personal rule. Each German and Italian success — in the Rhineland, in Spain, in the formation of the Axis — weakened the Little Entente and the Balkan Entente, if only indirectly.

The Yugoslav-Bulgarian Pact of January 1937 might superficially appear to have been a step in the right direction: toward breaking the isolation of Bulgaria among her neighbors. But the trouble was that Paul and Stoyadinovich had made the pact without informing any of their fellow-Entente powers. Not only did this violate the constitution of the Little Entente, but it rendered the Balkan Pact questionable: "eternal friendship" with Bulgaria was all very well, but how did it square with Yugoslavia's obligations to help any other Balkan state which might become the victim of Bulgarian aggression? Stoyadinovich also recognized the Italian conquests in Ethiopia without consultation. Though both Ententes continued to meet, their fabric had been strained. It was too late to link them with Bulgaria and Hungary in the proper way to prevent further aggression. The Austrian crisis aroused further fears, and the Czech crisis of 1938 exploded the Little Entente by removing one of the members. Though the Little Entente tried at the last minute to obtain Hungarian support for Czechoslovakia, the Hungarians preferred to deal with Hitler. The Rumanians and Yugoslavs, however, would have stood by their obligations if the French had stood by theirs. It was the defection of France, the policy of Munich, and the sell-out of Czechoslovakia which led both Yugoslavia and Rumania to try to appease the Axis on their own. As for the Balkan Entente, its members did reach agreement in July 1938 with Bulgaria, agreeing that Boris might rearm, in exchange for a pledge of his peaceful intentions. Yet, though the Entente went on meeting, until war had come and after, the weakness of England and France and the strength of Germany and Italy dominated its existence during the last year of hideous suspense before war actually came.

When Hitler occupied Prague in March 1939, completing the disruption of Czechoslovakia, and cynically violating the Munich agreement, the French and English governments recognized the futility of their policy of trying to negotiate with the Nazis, and to appease an unappeasable man. In an effort to shore up the eastern European countries which seemed most immediately threatened, they now guaranteed the independence and integrity of Poland, Greece, and Rumania. To this the Germans and Russians replied with the Hitler-Stalin pact of August, followed almost immediately by the German invasion of Poland and the launching of the Second World War. A secret annex to the pact included virtual German consent to Soviet annexation of Bessarabia. Though the outbreak of war did not immediately touch the Balkan region, it was not long before Stalin's efforts to implement this clause set in motion the train of events which once more brought fighting and agony to southeast Europe.

Chapter 7

THE BALKAN ECONOMY

ABOUT 80 PER CENT of the sixteen million Rumanians and seven million Bulgarians, 75 per cent of the sixteen million Yugoslavs, and perhaps 90 per cent of the million-plus Albanians were in 1939 engaged in agriculture or stockraising. Yet only 54 per cent of the Bulgarian national income, 49 per cent of the Rumanian, and 48 per cent of the Yugoslav before the war was derived from agricultural pursuits. These colorless statistical sentences described the way of life of perhaps 35,000,000 people, the daily toil, the hopes, the fears, the ever-present problems. They explained popular attitudes, superstitions, and native institutions. Concealed in these sentences lay the challenge still facing the Russians and native Communists in their efforts to dominate southeast Europe.

With some exceptions, notably the inhabitants of the rich region of the Rumanian Banat and of the adjacent Yugoslav Voyvodina, the overwhelming majority of the Balkan peasants in recent times lived in poverty: poverty which varied in degree, but poverty nevertheless, not only by comparison with the standards of the United States or of western Europe but by comparison with authoritative estimates of the minimum needed to support life. Western visitors to the Balkan countries frequently saw very little of this, since they often stayed in the capital cities in comfort, conversing with those who could speak a western language. The visitor in prewar and wartime Bucharest, for example, was dazzled by the luxurious houses, the glittering cars, the superb restaurants with the endless supplies of caviar and whipped cream, the ostentatious display of jewels and Paris dresses at parties. Yet only an infinitesimally small proportion of the Rumanian people ever enjoyed this way of life. Their wealth was sometimes inherited from generations of landowners, sometimes made in business in more recent times, sometimes abstracted from the public funds. It was often invested abroad in dollars or in Swiss francs. In prewar Belgrade a smaller and less fashionable but similar group existed, here almost all newly rich from the sale of concessions to foreign investors and from various forms of commercial and political activity. Sofia was far less showy, but here there lived a solid comfortable bourgeoisie in clean, well-built apartment houses amid green parks, with a fine university and handsome public buildings and well-swept boulevards paved with yellow brick. In Tirana, not even the strenuous building activities of the Italian conquerors who poured money into public structures after 1939 could conceal Albania's wretchedness and primitiveness.

It was almost easier to understand the Balkan countries by *not* visiting the capital cities. The Balkan countries were poor. The peasant was burdened and bent and often broken by the weight of poverty. The dust and dung of a Moldavian or Bosnian village were worlds away from the plate-glass store windows of Bucharest or Belgrade, but far more typical and far more meaningful.

Balkan peasant poverty was a complex phenomenon; it had a number of closely related aspects; it could be explained by a number of interdependent factors. When a student tried to consider solutions or palliatives he found that these too were closely related. Each proposed solution raised new problems of its own, and apparently only a combination of them all might in theory be expected to provide any considerable improvement. Indeed, a study of the

Balkan economies involved one in a morass of inadequate information and unreliable statistics.

Balkan peasant poverty arose in part from all the following factors: poor soil, the prevalence of dwarf and divided landholdings, poor equipment and techniques, poor communications, insufficient capital, and the concentration upon cereal crops to the neglect of cash and fodder crops. These conditions produced a low level of purchasing power and a low standard of living. This in turn had a bad effect on public health. All of these phenomena were in some ways symptoms of one great central problem: there were too many people living on the land in relation to what the land produced. This was the evil of overpopulation. Its twin was underemployment: there was often not enough for the peasant population to do. Even when they all worked hard their labor was insufficiently productive.

Some of the remedies and palliatives often suggested were the regrouping of landholdings, irrigation and drainage projects, the introduction of fodder crops for livestock and the substitution for cereals of crops with higher yields, improvement of the communication network, technical education, the extension and improvement of coöperative movements, and, by Communists, the collectivization of agriculture. To deal with overpopulation most authorities recommended both emigration and industrialization. The Communists put particular emphasis on the latter, no doubt in part at least for their own political purposes. Since the industrial proletariat which, according to their theories, ought to have been essential to their rise to power, actually scarcely existed in the Balkan countries, they felt they must create it. By 1939, when World War II broke out, many of these remedies had already been tried, to some extent at least, but the poverty and misery remained, and it was apparent that a suitable overall formula had never been found and might not exist.

1. Small Holdings and "Land Reform"

Large areas of our four countries consisted of poor soil, divided into parcels too small to enable the peasant to wring subsistence from them. Virtually all Yugoslavia south of the Sava fell into this category. Here the population in 1939 had an average of less than one-half hectare of arable land per head, considerably less than half the minimum estimated as adequate for subsistence.[1] Poorest of all was the Bosnian forest region, where the Muslim peasantry lived under the most primitive conditions imaginable. In all this portion of Yugoslavia the only relatively prosperous areas were some of the valleys of Serbia proper, tucked away amid the poorer mountain regions. Transylvania too had bad soil; only a quarter of the land was arable; again, the holdings were very small; there were frequent crop failures, and in bad years starvation lurked nearby.

In the mountains of the Balkans — that is to say almost everywhere — fer-

[1] One hectare is about two and a half acres.

tile valley land was at such a premium that every villager needed a small share. High in the hills and perhaps far away from his arable valley strip he might have another lot, this time perhaps vineyard or only pasture. Elsewhere he might have still other holdings. When he died, his land was divided equally among his sons; each must of course receive some arable in the valley and some of the poorer land in the hills. In one generation, a man's property, often too small to begin with, might become a collection of tiny strips, separated by long distances, and totally uneconomical to work. Sometimes a peasant held forty, fifty, or even more tiny plots, several miles apart, all adding up to one inadequate holding. The dwarf and divided holding had by 1939 become characteristic of the Balkan countries.

Regroupment of these holdings into larger and more economic units was very difficult, since somebody was sure to be left with all the less good land, while somebody else got the more productive fragments. In parts of Bulgaria, where the problem was perhaps a bit easier than in Yugoslavia south of the Sava or in Transylvania, regroupment had been voted before the war, and put into effect. In other parts of Bulgaria the issue was as serious as it was elsewhere.

The dwarf holding did not produce enough to feed the family of the proprietor. Besides, he had to sell some of his crop to enable him to buy minimal necessities: kerosene, matches, and salt, as well as to raise the cash to pay his taxes. In recent decades peasants tended to buy more and more of their clothes as well, especially shoes. In order to earn enough to buy the remainder of the food necessary for the family, some member or members of it had to work off the holding, either on a larger plot belonging to somebody else or as seasonal laborers in industry, if such employment offered itself. Occasionally but rarely, this turned out to be lucrative; and before the Communists took over, in Transylvania particularly, one could find villages where the small holding had proved a blessing in disguise, since outside work had brought more prosperity and higher standards to the village than agriculture alone would have done. But these were only the exceptions that proved the rule: that grinding bitter poverty accompanied the dwarf holding.

Before World War I, the small individual peasant holding prevailed only in Serbia, Bulgaria, and northern Albania. Elsewhere, in the Yugoslav lands under the Habsburgs, in southern Albania, in Transylvania, and throughout Rumania, much of the land belonged before 1918 to large proprietors, on whose estates the peasants, often landless themselves, labored. In Rumania, for example, nearly 40 per cent of the land consisted of estates over 500 hectares in size, and nearly 50 per cent of estates over 100. Thus, fewer than 1 per cent of the landowners of the country owned nearly half the land. In both Rumania and the Habsburg parts of Yugoslavia, these big estates were divided by agrarian reform laws put into effect after the war. In Albania, reform was projected but not put into effect. It was only after such reforms that the small holding became universal. Such division of large holdings was often considered an end in itself, especially by those who prided themselves on liberal political ideas. Yet it raised as many problems as it settled.

It was the outbreak, late in 1917, of the Bolshevik Revolution in Russia, characterized by peasant seizure of large estates, which precipitated the passage of the agrarian reform law in Rumania. Aware that the economic structure of their country was much like that of Tsarist Russia, and conscious that peasant discontent might well take the same course in Rumania, the Rumanian King and politicians attempted to avert revolution by promising reform. The urban middle-class political opponents of the conservative landlords were eager to destroy their economic power, and this provided an additional stimulus. Passed for political reasons while the country was still at war, the new law gave preferential treatment to war-veterans, war-wounded, war-widows, and war-orphans. It was thus markedly political in substance.

Yet the government did expropriate a great deal of land: 6,000,000 hectares, of which almost 4,000,000 was actually distributed to 1,393,000 peasant families, almost 70 per cent of those having a claim to land (i.e., peasants with lots of five to seven hectares or smaller). The revolutionary danger was averted. But the process was extremely slow. In 1940, there remained some estates which had not yet been reduced in size, and almost a million hectares of land expropriated but not yet distributed. By 1930, only 7.4 per cent of the arable land was in holdings over 500 hectares; 85 per cent was in holdings under 100 hectares, 60 per cent under 10 hectares, and 35.8 per cent under five hectares, a dwarf holding. This 35.8 per cent of the cultivated land represented 75 per cent of the holdings.

The big estates were thus dealt a severe blow. A considerable social transformation had been accomplished by the transfer of almost half of the land in the country. Some former landless sharecroppers became independent landholders. But the result was to multiply the number of uneconomic small holdings. A shortage of agricultural implements was one of the immediate outgrowths of the reform. Whereas a big estate could be worked with relatively few implements, the very same property, when divided up among individual proprietors, required many more; those peasants who possessed them were jealous of their use, and sometimes the former owner of the estate removed the equipment which had previously been used to work the land. This was notably the case in Transylvania, where the government often colonized the newly confiscated land with peasants who had come from other parts of Rumania, and who therefore did not know how many ploughs and other implements they might expect to receive. Newly settled peasants would often go into debt in their effort to buy or hire necessary equipment, and would sometimes be forced to mortgage or sell their land. In this or other ways a number of large estates came into being once more, sometimes in the possession of the former proprietor himself. There were also many new medium-sized estates. Moreover, in accordance with traditional Rumanian practice, the land reform law was quite often corruptly administered: certain proprietors were allowed to keep their estates, or a larger percentage of their land than that to which they were legally entitled, or at least to engage in protracted lawsuits. The distribution of the land, begun in 1918, was by no means complete when World War II began in 1939. In view of this, we can understand why, by the end of World War II, a certain demand had arisen in Rumania for a new "land reform." Although further distribution of small plots could only make economic conditions worse, the formula of "land for the peasants" retained its magic, misleading strength.

In Yugoslavia, the agrarian reform after the First World War took place in the Voyvodina and in parts of Croatia and Bosnia-Hertsegovina, where the land had previously belonged to great proprietors, almost all non-Slavs or Muslims. During the war, peasants in many of these areas simply seized the land; so that the law passed by the new Yugoslav state in 1919 often merely regularized a process which had already taken place. By this law all estates of more than 300 hectares of cultivated land, or more than 500 hectares in all, were divided up among the peasants, either by allotment to families already settled on the estate or by the colonization of new groups of small-holders. Estates not yet seized by the peasants were gradually distributed. In this way the Slovene and Croatian lands newly taken over from the Habsburg Empire were given a pattern of land-tenure much like that prevalent in Serbia. The dwarf holding of less than five hectares became characteristic. By 1931, the estate of more than one hundred hectares had almost disappeared, and about 70 per cent of the holdings were smaller than five hectares. Temporary economic dislocation and a fall in crop yields, sometimes very serious, was caused by the breakup of the large farms, which had formerly been well-managed. Draft animals and equipment became scarce, and processing industries declined. Even despite the subsequent addition to the total cultivated area of a further half million hectares in Macedonia, previously not farmed, the small holding became the characteristic feature of all Yugoslavia, as it had already been in Serbia and Bulgaria, and as it was becoming in Rumania.

In Albania, unlike the other countries, only a small portion (11 per cent) of the total area was cultivated in 1938; and of this a little less than half was devoted to vineyards, olive trees, and fruit orchards, the rest being tilled. One-third of the total area of the country was pasture, and more than a third forest. Five per cent was water surface and marsh, and 6 per cent classed as altogether uncultivable. This left another 11 per cent, an area equal to that under cultivation, which might have been tilled, and was potentially productive. Most of Albanian farming was always extremely primitive. It was subsistence-farming, and the individual peasant family tended to be virtually self-sufficient. Livestock was more important than agriculture: grain had to be imported in amounts depending on the harvest, while hides, cheeses, eggs, and live animals were the chief exports.

While it would be impossible to defend the social injustice characteristic of the system of large estates, it would be equally impossible to pretend that the mere division of the land and the establishment of the peasant as an independent proprietor had come close to solving the agrarian question, or that "land reform" did not aggravate other perennial difficulties. There was simply not enough arable land to give every individual peasant household a holding sufficiently large and fertile to support its members. Or, put another way, there were too many peasant households for the extent and fertility of the soil. In the 1930's, 62 per cent of Bulgarian farms, 68 per cent of Yugoslav farms, and 80 per cent of Rumanian farms were under five hectares in size. This amounted to about 30 per cent of the arable in Bulgaria and Yugoslavia, and almost 44 per cent in Rumania. The density of farm population per square kilometer of arable was 67 in Albania, 82 in Bulgaria, 75 in Rumania, and 104 in Yugoslavia. Agricultural experts felt that the optimum would be no more than 50.

2. *Diversification, Communications, Irrigation, Education*

Even in those parts of the Balkan area where the soil was rich, the methods of production were backward. This was vividly illustrated, for example, in the Danube plain of Wallachia, where the peasant had the famous black earth to work with. Characteristically, he stuck exclusively to wheat and corn production, alternating these two cereal crops, without even a fallow period for the fields. Despite its fertility, the region was very dry. Therefore, in order to avoid loss of his crop, the peasant had to plant early, and get the harvest in before the summer drought. This he often failed to do, with disastrous results. He wasted manure instead of using it for fertilizer; he had almost no agricultural machinery, and ploughed, harvested, and threshed by antiquated methods. His livestock, miserably fed on cornstalks, consisted almost exclusively of work animals. There was little stock breeding for meat consumption or for the market. Indeed, during the years between the World Wars, livestock production fell off, as cereal cultivation was extended. The peasant of Wallachia lived almost entirely on corn meal, a diet which left him prey to a variety of deficiency diseases, widespread among the population. In the even more densely populated and less fertile region in the Carpathian foothills above the plain, and in Moldavia, the situation was still worse. If the peasant had a dwarf holding, the chances were but one in ten that he had a plough of his own. If he did not own one, he had to hire one from a richer neighbor, and this he could not afford either to do or not to do.

The practical difference between an educated western European farm population, working with advanced methods under the stimulus of nearby urban markets, and the backward farm population of the Balkans was clearly indicated, for example, by the statistics on wheat crop yields per hectare during the thirties in Denmark (29.2 quintals per hectare) as compared with Bulgaria (11.9 quintals), Rumania (9.1 quintals), and Yugoslavia (11 quintals).

In some contrast to the Rumanian portion of the Danube plain was the Bulgarian portion north of the Balkan mountains. Though the soil was somewhat less good, the peasants were more enterprising. By 1939, they had introduced some green crops, and had undertaken the breeding of livestock. Elsewhere in Bulgaria, efforts had been made to get away from the extensive agriculture characteristic of the other Balkan countries, and to introduce cash crops, which would pay more per unit than cereals. This shift to intensive cultivation had taken place between the Balkan range and the Rhodope, where tobacco and roses, grapes and vegetables, sugar beets, soya beans, and oil-seed plants like sunflowers were produced. In southeast Bulgaria, grapes were grown.

Although this prewar Bulgarian attempt to diversify agriculture was the most significant in the Balkan region, both Rumania and Yugoslavia also experimented with raising such crops. Over 80 per cent of Rumanian arable land was used for grain, 5 per cent for fodder, and 8 per cent for all other crops. The most important of these others were sugar beets, sunflowers, and soya beans; both oil-seed crops were begun in the thirties by German corporations, and both were grown chiefly in Bessarabia, now part of the USSR. Thus postwar Rumania lost most of what little intensive agriculture prewar Rumania had. In Yugoslavia, despite government encouragement, the cultivation of such crops was retarded by overpopulation, which, as we have seen, makes for the almost exclusive sowing of grains. In the thirties, the Germans joined the Yugoslav government in sponsoring oil-seed crops, which took a sharp turn upward. In the Voyvodina, sugar beet was also grown to an extent sufficient to meet local sugar requirements. Fruit, chiefly plums and prunes, was produced in quantities sufficient for substantial export; a little wine and olive oil were exported from Dalmatia, and some tobacco from Macedonia. Diversification and intensification, however, had not proceeded nearly as far as was desirable; nor, in view of the population picture, could they have been expected to proceed much farther.

While intensification overcame some of the problems of prewar Balkan agriculture, it too raised new problems. For one thing, intensive farming created a demand for seasonal labor. Seasonal employees, taken on mostly at harvest-time, were badly paid, in view of the large labor supply, and had little employment at other times of the year. They became a landless proletariat, barely able to keep alive. While the acuteness of the overpopulation problem was somewhat softened by intensification practices (since these men might not have been employed at all had it not been for the new crops), the problem was only transformed, not solved. In addition, steady profitable export of the specialty crops depended upon the tariff policies adopted by other countries. There was always the danger that the profits from a flourishing crop might be wiped out by an unforeseen tariff imposed by a customer nation. This risk discouraged the investment of capital in the new crops and in their processing, and tended to drive the peasants back to cereal production for consumption. It was no accident that the growing of specialty crops in the Balkans made its greatest advance under the influence of German orders and German investments, in the period of the 1930's, when the Nazis were trying to turn the Balkan countries into their own agricultural back yard.

The absence of good communications too played an important part in keeping Balkan agriculture backward. This cut the peasant off from his natural market in the villages, in the larger towns, and in the deficit agricultural regions. Wherever better communications were introduced, the pattern of peasant life was improved; the peasant was brought close enough to his market to tempt him to diversify his crop, and to introduce the more profitable intensive cultivation. But it was difficult and expensive to move the surplus produce of the Yugoslav Voyvodina, for example, into the deficit area of Dalmatia.

Rumania inherited, with her new provinces acquired after the war, communication lines which proved to be nothing more than the end-portions of lines whose main length lay still within Hungary, Russia, and Bulgaria. It became imperative to link these new lines with existing Rumanian communications, and to gear the road and rail systems in with the vitally important Danube river water-route, and with the seaport of Constanța. Equipment damaged during the war had to be repaired or replaced. Most of the Rumanian railroads remained single-track; and communications between the peasant producer and the town consumer remained difficult. Moreover, badly planned freight-rate schedules charged the peasant too heavily for transporting his agricultural surplus. The peasant, who should have been the best client of the railroad system, and should have supplied it with the funds to improve itself, was therefore inhibited from using it. This was somewhat but not much alleviated by the introduction of better highways and bus-lines. In addition, the land routes were allowed to compete with the cheaper water-route, instead of supplementing it. Few departments of the national life gave more opportunity for the indulgence of the national vice of corrupt management than the roads and railroads.

In Bulgaria the mountainous structure of the country dictated that the chief rail and road connections run east and west rather than north and south, although there were a few lines which crossed the Balkan range. The most important function of the railroads was to connect the centers of the interior (Sofia, Plovdiv, and others) with the Black Sea ports of Varna and Burgas. The absence of railroad communications between Bulgaria and Rumania was a source of difficulty and delay. There were no bridges over the Danube, and it was therefore necessary to transship goods to a ferry on one side of the river and back again to rail on the other side. Most of the Bulgarian lines were single-track, but on the whole the communications systems of Rumania and Bulgaria were better than that of Yugoslavia.

Albanian communications were among the least developed in Europe: as a result, even fertile areas produced only for consumption, since there was no efficient and economical way of moving surplus into a deficit area. There were no railroads, properly speaking; but a number of short narrow-gauge lines were in use in connection with the mining industry. Roads were few and badly surfaced; the large number of streams made many bridges necessary. There were about 1,000 motor vehicles in 1939, including bus-lines running between the more important towns. Port facilities at Durazzo and Valona remained inadequate.

The difficulties of the fertile Wallachian plain could probably have been alleviated, and the crop-yields increased by an estimated 50 per cent — a level which would perhaps have eliminated overpopulation — had irrigation been introduced to remove the hazards of drought, and had fodder crops been cultivated for the feeding of livestock. Irrigation, however, required the investment of large sums of money, which no private or public agency was ever able or willing to advance, since the return would necessarily be slow and small, from the point of view of an investor. Irrigation would have provided only one of the manifold advantages that would have resulted if the "TVA on the Danube," occasionally referred to in the United States as if it were a joke, could ever have been established. The great amount of electric power which could have been made available by the harnessing of Balkan rivers would have enabled industrialization to proceed rapidly and efficiently, and might well have made up for the shortage of coal which was one factor that delayed such industrial development.

Although it would not have met the problem of overpopulation, as it might in Wallachia, irrigation would also have proved beneficial in Dalmatia and Montenegro; while in the Danube delta region and in the Albanian coastal plain large-scale drainage operations were called for. For many years, for example, the drainage of Lake Scutari, lying partly in Yugoslavia and partly in Albania, was discussed, as a desirable step which would make available for agriculture about 18,000 hectares of very fertile soil.

To succeed, any such undertakings as these in the realm of public works would have needed to be accompanied by widespread efforts at education of the peasants in new methods. This meant more than merely ending illiteracy; it meant devising a system of education which would keep the able farmers interested and happy on the farm. It meant attracting the intellectual to the countryside. This problem was on the whole neglected by Balkan governments in the years between the wars until the deepening international crisis had made it too late to hope for major accomplishments. The Rumanian government sponsored university-level agricultural education in the major urban centers, and an Institute of Agronomic Research, which studied the soil and its needs and the improvement of plant varieties. Wheat and corn conferences were held, and propaganda efforts made among the peasants. Private initiative, though active, could not hope to complete the task by itself. The most interesting and thoroughgoing efforts were those made, beginning in the twenties, by Dumitrie Gusti, a leading Rumanian sociologist. Gusti sent to the villages teams of investigators to do field research into the conditions of the peasantry. These men, trained in the different disciplines of the social sciences, and working closely together, hoped not only to study the peasants, but to stimulate them to improve their own position, and to take a wider interest not only in advanced agricultural techniques, but also in the wider fields of general culture.

Gusti's people founded "cultural centers" in 2,600 villages, where the local teachers, priests, and agents of the government worked with the peasants on all sorts of tasks, ranging from the building of clinics and libraries to the promotion of better farm practices and better public health. Leaders of the centers were trained from among the peasantry itself. Beginning in 1934, smaller teams, including advanced scholars and students in agronomy, medicine, and veterinary medicine, went to the villages to study local needs and to try to fulfill them, to work patiently with the peasant through the cultural centers, and to demonstrate the superiority of modern techniques.

In various ways, the Rumanian government assisted the work, and in 1938 passed a law of Social Service, which made it compulsory for all intellectuals (of whom only one year's military service was required rather than the usual two) to spend an additional three months on such social service work among the peasants. Every effort was made to acquaint the urban intellectuals with the nature of Gusti's enterprise, and to arouse in them the appropriate enthusiasm for its continuance and furtherance, by no means an easy task in view of the traditional lack of interest in the peasant. Gusti's remarkable effort was interrupted by the war before it could achieve its ends, and it is difficult to measure the advances for which it was responsible.

It pointed the way toward alleviation of the peasant's lot in a country where the introduction of advanced methods would really have served to raise the standards, in view of the excellence of the soil. Moreover, it was unique in our countries, where in most cases the educated peasant, by the very process of becoming educated, left the farm behind him to run as it had always run, and entered one of the overcrowded professions in the cities. Gusti's program was certainly a healthy instance of the Balkan intellectual's realizing his social responsibility. Whatever one may think of a law compelling "social service" (and certainly the Rumania of King Carol in 1938 was on its way to becoming a thoroughly authoritarian state), the fact remains that the original conception of voluntary assistance to be rendered the peasant by the scholar and the student was both noble and practical. Finally, the approach of Professor Gusti was particularly fruitful, in that it took into account the fundamental importance of peasant psychology. The Balkan peasant looked with suspicion upon those who wanted to "civilize" him from above and bring improvements to him from the outside. Centuries of experience with the tax-collector and the usurer had taught the peasant to expect no good of emissaries from the capital. Gusti's whole effort was designed to counteract and dilute this suspicion. He worked to give the peasant confidence in himself, and help him help himself.

But even these measures — of diversification and intensification, of improved communications, of irrigation or drainage, and of education — which alone would have made the richer areas productive enough to support their inhabitants, would have been of little avail in the poorer areas, especially in Yugoslavia south of the Sava or in Transylvania. Indeed, in Transylvania, farming methods were already far in advance of those in the Wallachian plain; Transylvanian livestock, for example, included the water-buffalo, which needed but little feed, and whose cows gave milk, with which the peasant might vary the dangerous monotony of a cereal diet. Here some pigs were raised and pork occasionally eaten; here crops were rotated, with oats following the corn or potatoes, which followed wheat; and here fertilizers were widely used. Despite relatively advanced techniques, however, Transylvania simply could not produce adequate yields.

In these areas, and to a considerable extent in Moldavia and Bulgaria as well, the output of the soil would have been adequate for subsistence only if many fewer people had lived on it, and if the individual holdings had been correspondingly larger, irrespective of the methods of cultivation used. In Wallachia, adequate output for the agricultural population could be assured only by a drastic change in methods. So the student found himself back facing the problem of rural overpopulation, a condition aggravated by the high birth-rate during the twenties and thirties.

3. Coöperation

One of the most obvious devices for overcoming problems too great to handle alone was coöperation with others in the same situation. In the American tradition, neighbors helped each other build new houses or barns, helped each other make furniture or quilts, husk each other's corn, and the like. In the primitive days of Turkish domination, Bulgarian peasants would assist each other in dragging or guiding the plough, an instrument too heavy to be handled alone. Indeed, the south Slav historic tradition was distinguished for a form of social organism in which coöperation was the very keynote of existence: the *zadruga,* or communal multiple family, an institution much studied by scholars, who have engaged in controversy about its origins and its meaning.

The zadruga was defined by the chief authority on the subject as "a household composed of two or more biological or small families, closely related by blood or adoption, owning its means of production communally, producing and consuming its means of livelihood jointly, and regulating the control of its property, labor, and livelihood communally."[2] It was, of course, a feature of the old rural society; and with the gradual growth of cities, the adoption of written national codes of law, and the development of an exchange economy, the zadrugas began to disappear, especially the larger ones, which had formerly consisted of as many as sixty members. The smaller units of four to twenty-five members continued to exist in many places in Yugoslavia and Bulgaria, and were visited and studied even as late as the years immediately before the Second World War.

Many claims, some of which seem extravagant, have been made for the zadruga by its devotees, according to their own political and social predilections: a recent French scholar, for example, argued that the superior cohesion shown by the Yugoslav Partisans as guerrillas against the Germans during World War II might be attributed to the fact that the Partisans were recruited in family groups, and that they had carried over from the zadruga a strong sense of collective responsibility. He saw in certain laws of the new Communist Yugoslav state, those on marriage, which provided for the absolute equality of both partners, and those on inheritance (which were not even drafted when he wrote!) direct outgrowths of the zadruga experience, and argued that they were based on the customary law which regulated the zadruga.[3] Another sociologist regarded the zadruga as the symbol of gentleness and indifference to political power, and identified its members closely with the Croatian peasantry; he sharply distinguished it from what he called the Dinaric society, characterized by violence and military and political ambition, whose members he identified with the Serbs and with the aggressive Partisans, neither of whom he happened to like.[4] These two writers on the zadruga were able to find in it either the essence or the antithesis of the present Yugoslav system, according to their prejudices. Both positions were extreme.

It does seem reasonable, however, to point out that in the zadruga coöperation was the mutual order of the day: work both in the fields and in the house, both male and female, was assigned by agreement; no individual member owned any of the land, or indeed any property except his personal effects; none of the land could be disposed of except by joint decision; communal meals, a communal dwelling house, communal arrangements for the care of the children; communal decisions on matters of importance, election by the community of a chief who could be dismissed by the community—these were some of the fundamental features of the zadruga. It seems to have provided a natural base for coöperation as a movement among the peasantry, since it overrode the jealous feelings of possessiveness often inherent in individual ownership. This is not to imply that the coöperative movement in the

[2] Philip E. Mosely, "The Peasant Family: the Zadruga, or Communal Joint-Family in the Balkans," *The Cultural Approach to History,* ed. Caroline F. Ware (New York, 1940), p. 95.

[3] Émile Sicard, *Problèmes familiaux chez les Slaves du Sud* (Paris, 1947).

[4] Dinko Tomasic, *Personality and Culture in Eastern European Politics* (New York: George W. Stewart, Inc., 1948).

south Slav countries grew out of the zadruga, or took the zadruga's place as it began to disappear; it is merely suggested that the widespread previous existence of so coöperative an institution may have created a predisposition among the peasants to welcome and understand and participate in other coöperative forms.

The modern coöperative was an association formed on a voluntary basis by a group of individuals who wished to assist each other to perform together some economic function which they were unable to perform singly. They shared the risks and the profits in proportion to the investment of money or effort. In theory, the employees and managers of the coöperative were salaried, and received no part of the profits. Coöperatives in the Balkan countries before the war varied widely in type. A small proportion were associations of producers. Only about a third of these were actually engaged in coöperative production; the other two-thirds were engaged in the sale of produce. These coöperatives were to be found dealing chiefly with specialty crops, rather than with cereal production, and could not assist in solving the central questions of the economy. Others were purchase and sale coöperatives, which marketed produce and bought necessary implements and seeds for the peasants. Some ran factories connected with food-processing industries; some developed resources of water-power and electricity. There were also varying combinations of these functions. But by far the most common form of coöperative society was the credit coöperative, designed to furnish credit facilities to the peasant. Before the Second World War 46 per cent of the Yugoslav coöperatives, 58 per cent of the Bulgarian coöperatives, and 73 per cent of the Rumanian coöperatives were of this type.

Probably the oldest and certainly the most widely developed coöperative movement in the Balkan area was that of Bulgaria. It is usually said to have started in the 1860's, before liberation from the Turks, when an enlightened Turkish governor founded what were called General Utility Bureaus, designed to provide credit for the peasants, and thus to protect them from usurious moneylenders. At first, certain lands in each district were cultivated coöperatively, and the produce sold; the proceeds were then used to buy the necessary goods. This method of fund-raising, however, was early abandoned in favor of a levy in kind imposed upon every member. Beginning in 1894, the government intervened to exert centralized control over these credit societies. Eventually the governing body became the Agricultural Bank, whose directors were named by the government, and which became the chief source of credit. Local coöperatives continued to multiply, and formed in 1907 the first Union of Agricultural Societies, which continued, with splits and other vicissitudes, down to the Second World War.

The political parties took advantage of the obvious need for spreading the coöperative movement, after the Balkan Wars and the First World War. During the period 1918–1939, the Bulgarian Social Democrats, for example, founded the large coöperative organization called *Napred* (Forward), which had a textile factory, a flour mill, and other valuable installations. Another large organization supplied electricity to certain villages and towns. Critical observers during the interwar period believed that the credit coöperatives were too much engaged in speculative activities, and diverted available funds from productive to consumptive purposes. Moreover, although it originated as a rural movement, the Bulgarian coöperative movement became centered in the cities; its concentration upon the extension of credit prevented it from being sufficiently active in the critical fields of production and marketing. It did not undertake the pooling of the small holdings for purposes of cultivation; it neglected many of the opportunities for developing commercial farming and for educating the peasants in new techniques. The accompanying table showed the type, number, and membership of Bulgarian coöperatives in 1939.[5]

TABLE 1

Type	Number	Membership
Production	735	200,223
Commercial	278	114,713
Credit	2,386	472,983
Insurance	9	151,747
Public works, health, and art	30	16,949
Unions and Centrals	64	9,534
Total	3,502	966,149

Before the formation of Yugoslavia, coöperative movements grew up separately in the former Habsburg lands (Slovenia and Croatia), and in Serbia proper. In general, it may be said that the Habsburg regions devoted more attention to the movement. Here the Catholic priests took an interest in promoting the welfare of the peasants, while the Orthodox clergy of Serbia were far less active. In Slovenia, for example, the coöperative movement dates back to the 1890's. Here the two most important coöperatives were associated with the two chief political parties, Clericals and Liberals. These were credit societies, each with its central bank, and each maintaining a wholesale trading organization for the purchase of farm implements and feed. They also marketed the produce of the affiliated local societies. In this advanced portion of the future Yugoslavia, the only region in which dairy farming developed as a leading agricultural pursuit, the coöperatives built cheese factories, and installed pasteurizing equipment.

Before the creation of Yugoslavia, the same pattern held true for Croatia. In the Voyvodina also, there was a Central Agricultural Bank, which furnished credit, and to which the local German coöperatives in particular were affiliated.

[5] *Statisticheski Godishnik na Tsarstvo Bŭlgariya,* XXXII (Sofia, 1940), p. 608.

In this period, before 1920, it has been estimated that the coöperatives handled 74 per cent of the credit operations in Slovenia, 40 per cent in Croatia, and only 24 per cent in Serbia.

After the formation of Yugoslavia, there were thirty-seven different federations of coöperative societies, including three Serb, three Slovene, and six Croat federations, and a German and Czech federation, as well as others divided by religion or political party. The new Serb-dominated state attempted to coördinate the activities of the coöperatives in all parts of the country, an effort which met with resistance on the part of the Slovene and Croat societies, who rightly suspected that this was part of a general Serbian drive to control all coöperative agencies in the nation. Despite the failure of the state to substitute a central Agrarian Bank, granting its own credits directly and by-passing the federations of coöperatives, state support was essential for the movement. The state, for example, exempted the coöperative federations from taxes, granted them credits, and guaranteed them a share in agricultural exports. In exchange for this necessary economic aid, the state required political subservience.

In the twenties, Serbia made its chief contribution to the coöperative movement: the health coöperatives. These supplied the villages, where public health was often at a low ebb, with resident doctors, with dispensaries, and occasionally with midwives. By means of voluntary labor, they sometimes built "health houses" as headquarters for these efforts. In the thirties, more than a quarter of a million persons belonged to the 114 member societies of the Union of Health Coöperatives.

In 1935, the Croat Peasant Party created an economic branch in the form of a coöperative. By the outbreak of the war it had almost a quarter of a million members in over five thousand village branches. Similar movements on a smaller scale followed in Slovenia in 1937, and in Serbia in 1939. These societies strove to keep farm prices up, organized fairs, made wholesale purchases of necessities, arranged for mass vaccination of cattle (reducing veterinary costs seven-eighths), collectively sprayed fruit trees and otherwise removed pests, bargained collectively on behalf of the village with owners of machinery and proprietors of mills, with electrification enterprises, and with large landowners, and supplied food collectively to regions experiencing shortages.

In 1940, just before the war came to the Balkans, the Yugoslav government initiated a system of tractor stations to supply tractors to the peasants at low rates. It is not possible to estimate the degree to which this improved agricultural conditions.

In Rumania the coöperative movement had no particular roots in ancient forms of social organization as it had in the Slav countries. It took its start, however, in the 1890's, arising, as in Bulgaria and Yugoslavia, from the need for credit in the villages. Credit societies were always the most numerous, although soon there were other kinds as well. Early in the twentieth century, the government reached out and took control; and by a series of laws in 1903, 1905, and 1908, established overall requirements for the organization and functioning of credit and other coöperatives. The state could dismiss officials of the coöperatives of whose acts it disapproved, and could dissolve individual societies if it saw fit. A central Bank coördinated activities.

When greater Rumania was formed after the First World War, the regulations governing coöperatives in the Old Kingdom were extended to those which had grown up in the new provinces under their former regimes. A general law governing all coöperatives was passed in 1929, and modified in 1935 and 1938, nullifying efforts to increase "autonomy" by those dissatisfied with the large role of the state. The law required all new coöperatives to be licensed in advance by the state. Acting through the National Institute of Coöperation, a part of the Ministry of National Economy, the state would declare their purpose, and would regulate the recruitment of their members, the allotment of shares, the degree of responsibility of the members, and the distribution of profits. Coöperatives were tax-exempt during their first three years of existence and had preferential treatment thereafter. Minority groups were allowed to maintain their own coöperatives. The accompanying table gave figures for the number and membership of the various types of Rumanian coöperatives as of the end of 1936.[6]

TABLE 2

Type	Number	Members
I. Rumanian Organizations		
Credit	4,633	963,637
Production	192	23,336
Supply	355	42,793
Consumers	824	89,500
Purchase	179	18,435
Affermage (Arendare)	52	6,194
Forest	206	24,221
Total	6,441	1,168,206
II. Minority Organizations	1,171	233,010
Total	7,612	1,401,126

Even from this summary description of Balkan coöperatives as they existed prior to the war, it is clear that the state made a habit of intervening for its own political purposes in the affairs of these societies. Frequently a government would grant funds to a coöperative in exchange for the promise of a bloc of votes at the next election. Sometimes tax-exemption or financial aid would be extended on condition that the coöperative help certain classes of peasants rather than others: usually those who needed it least, but whose

[6] G. Mladenatz, "La Coopération," *La vie rurale en Romanie* (Bucharest, 1940), p. 97; XIVe Congrès Internationale de Sociologie.

political support was particularly desired. Coöperatives under the sponsorship of political parties, it is clear, could also be misdirected if their management placed political purposes ahead of economic ones. Moreover, individual entrepreneurs could set up what purported to be a peasant coöperative, and extract profit from it for their own benefit. In practice then, the Balkan coöperative often fell far short of the ideal of assisting the peasant to solve his problems.

The prevalence of mismanagement and of interference from outside sources quite often disillusioned the peasant with the coöperative venture. When the state began to dominate an undertaking, the individual peasant might well grow suspicious, unless the enterprise were still obviously conducted primarily in his interests. To the peasant it became just another example of people outside trying to get money from him for their own purposes; the coöperative was no longer his movement; it was something dreamed up by the tax-collectors and usurers who had always tried to fleece him. In its intervention, the Rumanian state actually made the local branches of coöperative organizations act as tax-gatherers; nothing could more quickly have convinced the peasant that the whole idea of coöperation was a fraud. On the other hand, it is very difficult to imagine a group of economically weak peasants — those who need coöperative effort most — achieving their purposes without aid from the state, or refusing the offer of state funds and privileges. The theoretical problem was to ensure honest management and a well-planned distribution of effort, with a minimum of exploitation and a maximum of assistance.

It would have helped the peasant more had the state improved transport and storage facilities as an aid to marketing, and undertaken public works in the realm of irrigation, drainage, public loans of necessary machinery, and electrification. If such efforts had been accompanied by education and by the encouragement of all the natural trends toward coöperation as preserved possibly in the memory of the zadruga, and certainly in the traditional communal ownership of pasture and forest-land, the coöperative venture might well have proved a more effective instrument for improving agricultural conditions. Ideally, all sectional and even national interests ought to have been subordinated to the interests of the entire Balkan region. Yet even under ideal circumstances a coöperative movement could only assist the development of peasant agriculture; it could not cure the problem of overpopulation.

4. Collectivization

One cold, dark night in late December 1944, I was standing with several other Americans outside the palace of the Orthodox Archbishop of Cluj, capital of Transylvania. He had sent a priest to the restaurant where we had been having dinner to invite us urgently to come to see him and hear his account of the Russian occupation of the city. Cluj was under a temporary administration installed by the Red Army, whose main body in that part of Europe was then across the border, several hundred kilometers to the west, besieging Budapest. There was a complete blackout because of the danger of German air raids, and the streets were patrolled by civilian guards, mostly Magyars, armed with rifles which they gleefully fired off in the general direction of any light they saw or any noise they heard. There was a rigid six P.M. curfew, after which anybody on the street might be shot with impunity. It was nearly seven.

Under the circumstances it will surprise nobody that we knocked vigorously at the Archbishop's gate and pulled violently at the Archbishop's bell-pull. After much knocking and ringing we heard through the gate the slow shuffle of a pair of felt slippers coming down the stairs inside the palace. As the steps came nearer we could hear the muttered grumbling of an aged Rumanian servant, complaining to himself as he came to let us in: "All right, all right, I'm coming," he was saying, "Where do they think they are, ringing like that? In a *Kolkhoz?*"

To this old man, as to millions of peasants all through the Balkan region, the word *kolkhoz,* the Russian term for a collective farm, had come to mean a place where people bossed you ruthlessly, and hurried and chivied you into doing things you did not want to do faster than you would ever be willing to do them. This attitude toward the collective was certainly in part a result of the propaganda against the Soviet system to which the Balkan peasant had for many years been subjected both by his own governments and by the Germans. But the propaganda fell on receptive ears: the Balkan peasant knew that in Russia the government had taken the peasant's land away from him, and he knew that many peasants had suffered and died in the process. This was enough for him. Collectivization meant tyranny, and he would resist it to the utmost, as indeed he had heard the Russian peasants themselves had resisted it.

In the Soviet Union, between 1929 and 1934, 18,000,000 individual peasant holdings were combined into 250,000 large units. This transformation, accomplished only by the application of the severest pressure, involved savage cruelty to the individual human being, the mass slaughter by the peasant of valuable and irreplaceable livestock, the burning of crops, a disastrous drop in yields, and millions of deaths by famine. Much of this tragedy, however, may not have been an inevitable corollary of the process of collectivization itself, but may have resulted rather from the doctrinaire methods by which the process was carried through. Had the peasants been permitted to keep their livestock, for example, when entering a collective, the slaughter would certainly have been avoided; indeed, the Soviet government itself tacitly admitted this mistake too late by changing its policy and permitting, as it still does, individual ownership of animals inside the collectives.

For an American it is hard to dissociate the theoretical economic objectives of agricultural collectivization from the mass frightfulness of the Soviet performance. The very word *collectivization* necessarily carries with it for us some of the connotations which *kolkhoz* had for the Archbishop's gatekeeper. Yet it may be helpful to examine the process separate from the ruthlessness with which the Russians put it into practice. What is collectivization supposed to do? Has it accomplished its purpose (at whatever cost) in the USSR? To what extent, if at all, could it rationally be instituted in the Balkan countries? Would it help the rural problems we have been considering?

In the USSR, collectivization was designed in the long run to mechanize the agriculture of the peasant village, and therefore to increase the output of food, in order to ensure a supply for the industrial population of the cities. It was also a device for the speedy colonization of previously uncultivated areas, as a relief for rural overpopulation. Before the Second World War, yields in the USSR had gone up only a little; livestock production had not been restored; and the increase in output which had taken place was due rather to the colonization of the new areas than to the collectivization of the old. Along with this resettlement, it was industrialization, the other essential feature of Soviet economic planning, which had been mainly responsible for the exodus from farm to city by 1941, and for the relief of rural overpopulation.

During a period of rapid forced industrialization, the Soviet state secured control of agricultural production at a time when there was nothing much to give the peasant in exchange for his crops. In theory, as industrialization advanced, consumers' goods were to become available, and the purchasing power of the peasant would be higher. For many reasons this did not happen in the USSR. Peasant purchasing power in the USSR remained low. Soviet peasant standards of living were by and large no higher than those of the Balkan peasant in 1939. If a period should ever come when Russian industry can increase its production of consumers' goods — that is to say a period of peace and low expenditure on armament — the peasant's standard of living will rise. In the long run (and entirely apart from the brutal methods by which it was introduced) Soviet agricultural policy might well turn out to have been appropriate for the USSR, although resettlement and industrialization, rather than the collectivization of the older villages, proved to be its most rewarding features.

But the Balkan countries had very little uncultivated land. Colonization and resettlement were impossible on any scale. Moreover, an observer in 1939 would have discounted the possibility in the Balkans of that rapid forced industrialization which had accompanied collectivization in Russia. The Balkan countries lacked, he would have said, the necessary industrial resources, the capital, and the skills; so the situation was not parallel to that in Russia, and whatever collectivization might have accomplished for the USSR it seemed unable to do in the Balkans. Yet the land was not appropriately utilized under individual ownership. A theoretician might suggest, therefore, that a policy retaining some features of a modified collectivization could conceivably have been applied profitably in southeast Europe. Certainly planned investment by the state in a large-scale public works program, accompanied by industrialization to the extent possible, and by mechanization of agriculture where appropriate, could have resulted in an improvement in the condition of the people.

5. *Emigration, Industrialization*

As economists and demographers have long pointed out, there are two sure ways of relieving rural overpopulation: large-scale emigration, removing the people from the region altogether, or large-scale industrialization, offering many new jobs away from the land. In the USSR, a land of vast undeveloped industrial resources, it was possible by ruthless methods to industrialize, keep manpower at home, and absorb the rural excess population. In the Balkans, where the resources were scantier and far less developed, it was emigration which traditionally presented itself as the solution.

Before World War I, many hundreds of thousands of emigrants left the Balkan countries for the United States in particular. The stream dried to a mere trickle in the twenties. By 1929, the American outlet had been virtually lost. After the depression of 1929, and during the period of crisis which followed, up to the outbreak of World War II, the number of emigrants overseas from the Balkan countries was just about balanced by the number of those returning. While France in the thirties took some tens of thousands (1931 was the peak year, with 31,433 Yugoslavs, 14,704 Rumanians, 4,919 Bulgarians), this was by no means enough. A flow of approximately 400,000 a year would have been necessary to deal with the overpopulation.

The possibilities for industrialization depended upon a variety of factors: the wealth of industrial resources of the region, the extent to which they were exploited, the availability of capital, resources in skilled manpower, and the pattern of foreign trade. These we must now survey, beginning with Yugoslavia, the best-endowed of the Balkan countries.

Even in Roman times, gold, silver, copper, and iron were mined in what is now Yugoslavia. Mineral resources provided much of the wealth of the mediaeval rulers of Serbia. Under the Turks, operations virtually ceased for five hundred years. In the nineteenth and twentieth centuries, the range of valuable minerals was widened by the beginnings of exploitation of coal, manganese, antimony, chromium, and bauxite (aluminum oxide). It was not, however, until the years between the wars that effective exploitation began. The output of coal tripled from 2,200,000 tons in 1919, to over 6,000,000 tons in 1939. Output of metallic ores, only 70,000 tons in 1919, rose by forty-five times in the next twenty years to a figure of 3,200,000 tons in 1939. It was clear that this was only a beginning.

It was foreign capital which made this upturn possible. And it was insufficient foreign capital which limited the output to the figures achieved. Yugoslavia was poor in domestic investment capital, especially private capital, and the Yugoslav state was the most important investor. About 60 per cent of the capital invested in industry was foreign; the French, the British, the Czechs, and the Swiss together accounted for 50 per cent. The Yugoslav state owned the two chief iron mines (90 per cent of production), about 40 per cent of the forest areas, the mines producing 25 per cent of the coal output. It also maintained a monopoly on tobacco, salt, silk; controlled iron and steel production and the manufacture of armaments; and invested heavily in the lumber, cellulose, sugar, and agricultural products industries.

Yet the lack of more capital prevented adequate development of the resources. In the first place, the skilled labor force could not be expanded to appropriate size: mining experts had to be imported to train domestic specialists, which was a slow process; and peasants tended to regard work in the mines as a seasonal occupation only. Lack of capital also hampered the development of adequate transportation facilities. In Serbia and Bosnia only occasional narrow-gauge spur railroad lines connected the mines with the main lines; many valuable deposits therefore went unworked.

As a result, despite the relatively fortunate position of Yugoslavia with respect to mineral resources, only 2 per cent of the national income in 1939 derived from this source. By 1939, the exploitation of industrial raw materials had barely begun; it was still necessary to export much of the metal in the form of ore, and to import finished metal. In mining, more than 75 per cent of investment was foreign, with the British owning about 41 per cent and the French about 28 per cent of the investments, and only about 23 per cent being native Yugoslav by 1937. The depression year of 1929 closed down some of the mines, and operations began again on a full scale only in 1935. Between 1935 and 1940 came the most productive five years of Yugoslav mining history. It was no accident that this period coincided with the aggressive Nazi economic policy in southeast Europe. Between 1937 and 1940, the German investment in Yugoslav mining rose from 1 per cent of all foreign capital to 20 per cent.

Three-quarters of the 160 mines operating in these years were engaged in mining coal. Of Yugoslav coal, about 95 per cent was lignite or brown coal, and the remaining small amount black bituminous coal. Wherever possible, domestic industries had to use the inferior lignite or brown coal. Almost all provinces of the country had some coal resources, but those in Bosnia-Hertsegovina (mostly state-owned even before the war), were believed to be the richest: deposits were estimated at 4,800 million tons, and only eighteen of the eighty deposits were worked. As in all other respects, it was Slovenia which was the most advanced in coal-mining and in transportation facilities, and which therefore had the largest output. The Slovene Trbovlye mine, the largest in the country, had at least fifty kilometers of underground workings and prewar outputs ranging up to 800,000 tons. With the exception of one mine in Bosnia and one in Slovenia, all the black coal deposits were in Serbia; and the Serbian output was on the increase. The black coal was used in large part for briquettes for heating homes. Railroads and industries were the largest consumers of coal; only a little over 1 per cent of the output was exported in 1939; in that year all of the 80,000 tons, not an important amount, went to Italy. The Yugoslavs, of course, had to import bituminous coal, of which they did not produce enough for their own needs; and anthracite and coke, of which they produced none. About 400,000 tons were imported in 1939, of which 232,000 were coke; these imports came from Germany (40 per cent), Czechoslovakia (30 per cent), Poland (15 per cent), and the remainder from Hungary, Britain, and Bulgaria.

In 1939, Yugoslavia produced 667,000 tons of iron ore. The chief iron deposits were in Bosnia (estimated total more than 250,000,000 tons). Eight iron mines were active in the late thirties, of which the two leading producers were Lyublya and Vares, the former state-owned and never worked to full capacity because operations depended wholly on demands for export, and the latter far smaller in output. Total exports of iron ore reached 385,000 tons in 1939; Hungary, Rumania, Germany, and Czechoslovakia in that order were the chief purchasers. There were four blast furnaces in Yugoslavia in 1939, and others were added in 1940, including a large one at Yesenitsa. Yet pig-iron output reached only 84,000 tons in 1939. Yugoslavia imported pig iron, as well as raw steel and other iron and steel products. The most important Yugoslav steel plant, Zenitsa (Bosnia), was enlarged in 1937; a new rolling mill was built and a Krupp electrical smelting furnace was installed to obviate the necessity of importing coke. Zenitsa's capacity was 220,000 tons annually of iron and steel products. The other chief steel plants were in Slovenia, to which the pig iron had to be brought from Austria. Other installations were built in Serbia. The total steel output of the country in 1939 was 235,000 tons.

The chief prewar mineral resources of Yugoslavia, however, were the nonferrous metals, of which copper was the most important, though being challenged by others. The mines at Maidanpek and at Bor in Serbia were the only ones worked; Bor was French-owned. With the copper, some gold and silver were also found. In 1939, almost a million tons of copper ore were mined at Bor, producing 43,000 tons of raw copper. Before 1936, Yugoslavia actually had to import some 3–4,000 tons of refined copper yearly; in that year the French company agreed, in exchange for an extension of its concession, to build a refinery for electrolytic copper with a capacity of 12,000 tons annually, enough for the needs of Czechoslovakia and Rumania as well as Yugoslavia. Copper concentrate also began to be produced after the refinery had been built in 1938. Together with the entire mine, it was placed under government supervision in 1940; output, export schedules, and investment in plant were to be determined by the Ministry of War. In the late thirties almost the entire output of raw copper was exported, the United States, Germany, and Belgium each taking about one-third; copper concentrate (about 500 tons in 1939) went to the United States alone. By 1939, Yugoslav imports of finished copper had decreased to 2,800 tons, and were largely in refined and sheet metal.

Yugoslavia also had highly valuable deposits of lead and zinc ore, the most important of which were the Trepcha mines in south Serbia, owned by the British until the war. Total deposits were estimated at 3,900,000 tons of ore, with an average zinc content of 6.4 per cent and lead content of 9.4 per cent. Less well-known and less exploited deposits existed in Slovenia and Bosnia. Trepcha had its own valuable equipment: the loading of the ore-cars was performed by machine, and the cars hauled by Diesel locomotives. Seven hundred thousand tons were mined in 1939 in Trepcha alone, about 775,000 in the country as a whole, but the figure was 100,000 tons below that of 1938. There were six smelters in the country, of varying capacities: 33,000 tons of lead and 6,300 tons of zinc metal were produced in 1940, a tripling of the lead output over 1939; and 87,000 tons of lead concentrate, as well as 56,000 tons of zinc concentrate (production of the latter had been as high as 95,000 tons in 1935). Until the mid-thirties most of these metals were exported as ores; after the erection of new smelters, the largest being that at Zvechan, on the main railroad line between Belgrade and Skoplye, they could be exported as metal. Belgium and Tunisia were the best customers for ore and concentrates, Hungary, Austria, and Rumania for the metals.

None of the metals so far considered formed any very appreciable percentage of world output in 1939, although Yugoslavia was first in Europe in lead and second in copper. The Yugoslav production of bauxite, however, had reached the rather impressive figure of 10 per cent of the world output in 1939; and vast resources still remained unexploited. The chief deposits of bauxite were located along the coast of the Adriatic in Dalmatia, in Hertsegovina, and in Montenegro. The Hertsegovinian deposits were richer in their content of aluminum oxide than the Dalmatian ones, but they were of course far less accessible to transport. Until 1937, when the first aluminum plant was built at Lozovats, near Shibenik on the Adriatic coast, none of the bauxite could be worked in Yugoslavia. Peak bauxite production before the war came in 1938, when 404,000 tons were mined; peak aluminum metal production came in 1940, when the Lozovats works turned out 2,800 tons. Another plant, scheduled for construction at Mostar in Hertsegovina, was never built. Almost all the bauxite produced was exported, a maximum of 388,000 tons in 1937, Germany taking almost the entire output, and the United States just beginning to buy in 1936. Sixteen hundred tons of aluminum metal were exported in 1939, mostly to Japan; but Yugoslavia still had to import some hundreds of tons for domestic consumption.

In addition to these nonferrous metals resources, Yugoslavia also had chrome, almost all in southern Serbia, the Orasye mines having belonged until the war to the British-owned Allatini company, with an output of 20,000 tons a year, about a third of total production for 1939. Toward the end of the thirties the chrome began to be used for domestic steel production, and exports fell off to some extent. The United States, as well as Sweden and Germany, bought chrome from Yugoslavia, the second largest chrome-producer on the continent. Pyrites for sulphur were also mined in Serbia, with a peak output of 150,000 tons in 1938, of which 132,000 tons were exported, chiefly to Germany, Czechoslovakia, and Hungary. Manganese mines existed in almost all the provinces, with those in Bosnia the most important before the war, and peak output reaching 10,600 tons in 1940. This was insufficient for Yugoslav domestic consumption, and the country imported 14,000 tons in 1939, mostly from South Africa, but also from Morocco and the USSR. Many unexploited deposits of this strategic mineral were known to exist.

Yugoslavia ranked first in Europe in the production of antimony. The smelters were small and antiquated. In 1940, 24,000 tons were mined and 1,700 tons of metal produced. Exports were small. The remainder was used for hardening in the manufacture of copper and lead alloys. Gold and silver were also produced, the Bor mine being responsible for some 80 per cent of the gold output, and Bor and Trepcha both producing silver. The amount of gold produced in 1940, 2,325 kg., was the fifth largest output in Europe. The output of silver (71,383 kg. in 1939) was the third largest. Magnesium was mined in Bosnia and Serbia: up to 40,000 tons were produced, the third largest output in Europe.

In 1939, the total installed capacity of electric power in Yugoslavia was 600,000 kilowatts, of which about one-third was hydroelectric. The output of electricity was more than a billion kilowatt hours. Nearly 90 per cent of the output was used in industry. In the whole country, there were only thirteen power stations with more than a 5,000 kilowatt capacity. The largest was the Kralyevats station in Dalmatia, with a capacity of 70,000 kilowatts. Potential water-power resources, however, were very great. One estimate maintained that capacity could be multiplied tenfold or more at maximum flow, reaching perhaps 7,000,000 kilowatts.

The lag in industrialization and electrification meant that light industry played a large role in the country's economy. Textile production employed more than any other single industrial branch (83,998 in 1936), while the forests (with 62,479) and the food industry (with 48,125) both had more workers than mining and metallurgy (47,259). The output of the food industry was worth more than that of any other (4,451 million dinars, as against 3,060 million for mining and metallurgy). But the very fact that the underdeveloped mineral resources were already second-ranking in value indicated how great the possibilities might be, given capital, trained technicians, and years of peace for rational development.

Elsewhere in the Balkans, Rumanian industry enjoyed the fullest development. In its petroleum resources Rumania possessed the most valuable single industrial asset of the whole region. Here too foreign capital had been largely responsible for development: both the prospecting for new wells and the building of refineries. Together, the English, French, and Belgians owned about two-thirds of the production, while the Standard Oil Company of New Jersey operated the Romano-Americana firm, which was alone responsible for 14 per cent. Peak production (8,700,000 tons) was reached in 1936. The country had more than enough refining capacity to handle the entire output. Rumanian services — railroads, industries, power-stations — depended upon petroleum to a greater extent than those of any other European country. Moreover, the volume exported in 1938 represented more than 43 per cent of the value of Rumanian exports. Both the internal economy and foreign trade thus leaned heavily on oil. Many western authorities believe that the high quality oil reserves in the fields were nearing exhaustion as early as the mid-1930's. Closely connected was the natural gas industry, producing 2,130 million cubic meters in 1938, and supplying 17 per cent of the country's fuel.

Rumanian coal, by contrast, was in short supply. A total of 2,396,000 tons was mined in 1938, but of this more than 2,000,000 tons was lignite or brown coal, of inferior quality, unsuitable for coking. This rendered the native iron and steel industry to a considerable degree dependent on imports of coke and coking coal. Production figures for 1938 included 139,000 tons of iron ore, 133,000 tons of pig iron, and 277,000 tons of steel. The biggest center for ferrous metallurgy was Reshița, with modern open-hearth plants. Rumania also produced small amounts of other metals: 60,200 tons of manganese in 1938, and small amounts of chrome, copper, molybdenum, zinc, lead, gold, and silver. Despite the resources in oil and water power, electrification was insufficiently advanced. Of almost 6,000,000 kilowatts estimated water-power resources, only 50,000 were exploited, supplying a mere 2 per cent of the country's electricity.

As in Yugoslavia, industry in Rumania employed only a small fraction of the population (a total of 289,117 in 1938). The oil industry, for all its importance, had fewer than 25,000 workers, while the forests employed 43,326, mining and metallurgy 51,321, and textiles 74,077. There were 250,000 cotton spindles and 153,000 wool spindles active in textile production in 1938. A student of the region would have put Rumania second to Yugoslavia in the Balkans, with regard to industrial potential.

Bulgarian industrial resources were meager by comparison with those of Yugoslavia. Fewer than 100,000 people were employed in industry in Bulgaria prior to the war. The main mineral resources were lignite and other coals (792,000 tons in 1938), which were sufficient for home consumption. In Bulgaria, handicrafts — tailoring, shoemaking, carpentering and the like — produced a greater revenue than industry, and employed 135,000 people, one-third again as many as industry. The chief industrial establishments produced consumers' goods: processed foods, tobacco, cotton and woolen cloth, shoes and overshoes, cigarettes, beer, and soap. Sunflower-seed oil was refined by Bulgarian refineries. There were about 1,200 plants of various sorts in the country in 1939, mostly small. Bulgaria produced very small amounts of iron (11,000 metric tons in 1938), lead, manganese, and chrome. It had no oil, made no steel, and was very incompletely electrified (430 million kilowatt hours in 1939).

Industry as the term is understood in the west was practically nonexistent in Albania. The chief mineral resource was oil, mostly located in Kucovo, and developed by the Italians, who took over in 1939 all the concessions of other foreign companies. A pipeline was constructed between Kucovo and the port of Valona, and oil taken to Italy for refining. Top production of 125,000 metric tons was reached in 1939; Albanian oil had a large sulphur and asphalt content but could be made to yield up to 80 per cent in gasoline. In addition to oil, Albania had bitumen (top production 10,110 metric tons in 1939), some lignite (top production 7,000 metric tons), and iron, chrome (production 14,300 metric tons), copper, bauxite, manganese, and gold in quantities unknown and little exploited. There was a cement factory in Scutari (Shkodra) and a brewery in Korcha (Koritza), as well as cigarette factories using local tobacco in Durres (Durazzo), Scutari, and other places. Water-power potential was very little developed, although resources were great.

Of the four Balkan countries, therefore, Yugoslavia led in industrialization, owing to the investment of foreign capital, and Rumania was not far behind, for the same reason. This development was far slower in Albania, where, by 1939, Italian exploitation of Albanian resources was just beginning as the country entered on virtually colonial status. Least of all had foreign investment come to Bulgaria, largely because domestic resources did not attract it. The foreign investors usually took too high a profit for the good of the country in question, and often exploited the native resources without much regard to the native economy as a whole. Many native citizens were galled at seeing their forests and mines pouring dividends into the pockets of foreigners, while their countrymen had to buy back at high prices the finished products of their own raw materials. None the less, it was foreign capital that made possible the substantial development which took place, created the jobs which to some extent relieved the pressure of agricultural overpopulation, and helped raise the level of the entire Balkan region. It is hard to imagine what the fate of the countries would have been without the foreign capital in question.

The value of Yugoslav foreign trade equaled one-quarter of Yugoslavia's national income, a clear indication of the important role which exports and imports played in the national economy. Agricultural and forest products accounted for about 70 per cent of the exports; the remainder was metals. Imports were chiefly finished goods. All through the 1930's, the country maintained a favorable trade balance, even in the depression. The government regulated foreign-trade policies, imposing substantial protective tariffs on imports, in order to protect Yugoslav industry. So high were the tariffs that the consumer often had to buy inferior native products, rather than pay the exorbitant prices for which foreign products had to be sold after the tariff had been imposed. We have already seen how Germany moved in on Balkan foreign trade in the thirties, helped considerably by the League policy of sanctions on Italy after the invasion of Ethiopia, and speeded still further during 1938 by Hitler's absorption of Austria and destruction of Czechoslovakia, the two most active trade partners after Germany. Even without Austria and the annexed portions of Czechoslovakia, Germany had more than one-third of Yugoslav foreign trade; no other country had even 10 per cent. When Germany took over control of Czechoslovakia, it obtained the chief sources of Yugoslav military equipment, and of textile yarns and coke, as well as control over the substantial Czech investments in the Yugoslav economy. Nazi power and influence was by no means wholly political, ideological, and emotional: by 1939, the fact was that the Germans were supplying about half of Yugoslavia's imports, and taking more than half of the country's exports. They had deeply penetrated the whole Yugoslav economy, and made the country in many ways dependent upon them. The outbreak of war only increased the dependency. It was little wonder that the Germans regarded Yugoslavia as virtually in their pockets.

The picture of Rumanian foreign trade was not dissimilar, except for the great asset of oil. Grain, timber, livestock, seeds, eggs, meat, fruit, and vegetables were the chief exports; iron and steel, textiles, machinery and metals, chemicals, motor vehicles, rubber, citrus fruits, coffee, and tea were the chief imports. The balance of trade was generally favorable, falling off to unfavorable only in 1929. The chief partners were the countries of Europe, outside the USSR, with Germany playing an ever more important role. By paying prices above those current in the world market for agricultural goods, Germany became, as with Yugoslavia, the customer for about half of Rumania's exports, and the supplier of about half its imports. In 1939, the two countries, whose developing political relationships we have already examined, were planning to put into effect a ten-year German-sponsored scheme for Rumanian economic development. Rumania had been even more deeply penetrated than Yugoslavia, and the destruction of the alliance system on which the two states had built their policies left them both prey to the Germans. It was only differences in the national character of the two peoples, and the profound differences in attitude toward the Soviet Union which could explain the contrast between the Rumanian and Yugoslav roles in the Second World War.

The case of Bulgaria was even more dramatic. In the interwar years, Bulgarian exports were overwhelmingly agricultural and specialty items. Tobacco, sugar, vegetables and fruits, animal products, and grains among them accounted for more than 90 per cent of exports. Machinery, metal goods, textiles, railroad cars and motor vehicles, resins and chemical products accounted for more than 80 per cent of imports. The balance of trade fluctuated markedly in the 1920's, but was favorable all through the 1930's, except for 1932. By 1939, Germany (including Austria and the Czech lands) was the partner in almost 75 per cent of Bulgarian foreign trade; Italy handled 6 per cent; and no other country had more than 3 per cent. If Yugoslavia and Rumania had been deeply penetrated, Bulgaria had become a virtual economic dependency of the Axis.

As for Albania, it was not only a dependency but a liability. The exports were petroleum, skins, cheese, livestock, and eggs. The imports were grain and other foodstuffs, as well as metal products and machinery. The balance of trade was never favorable; in 1939, the exports were worth only about one quarter as much as the imports. Italy took about 70 per cent of Albanian exports, and provided almost 40 per cent of her imports, as well as footing the annual bill for the remainder. These came from Yugoslavia (grain), Britain, the United States, and other countries.

6. Conclusion

The data which the economist had procured for us often vividly revealed the nature of life in the Balkan countries. In the 1930's, the annual dollar cash income per person was probably about sixty dollars. Real income per person, in terms of purchasing power, was perhaps a fifth of that in the British Isles. People did not get enough to eat: pellagra, rickets, scurvy, anemia, and tuberculosis were common; and infant mortality ranged up to almost 1,800 per 10,000 live births. Proteins, calcium, vitamins: things which Americans took for granted, were deficient in the Balkan diet, where milk, eggs, meat, and fats were lacking. One could translate such cold details of the "standard of living" into human behavior. In the Balkan countryside, people had learned to submit to fate, not to mourn too greatly at the death of a child or an old person, to meet the events of most days with resignation. Beneath the surface smoldered the sense of injury, for which the government and city-dwellers in general were held responsible.

Yet peasant life had its own quiet rewards. Men everywhere sang songs and told stories of the heroic deeds of ancestors or the wickedness of spirits. The dances too, men and women in a circle, were everywhere much the same, and often continued for hours on end. There was always alcoholic consolation for the men, to be bought of the village tavern-keeper, to whom the villagers were so often in debt. Carding and spinning bees provided social life for the women, and in some places served to bring young men and girls together in an easier and more natural social life than was available on other occasions. Peasant craftsmen made strikingly handsome objects in carved wood and pottery. Long after the drab "storeclothes" of the west had become conventional, the women produced for festive wear brilliantly embroidered garments which were traditional. The men exercised the authority in the family, and, in Montenegro, northern Albania, and parts of Bosnia-Hertsegovina, allowed the women to do much of the heavy work in the fields. But close students of Balkan family-relationships maintained that the subordinate role of the wife was more apparent than real, and that husbands consulted their wives on all important family and farm decisions. Fathers and mothers gave their children love and security.

But the strong and simple family ties, and the occasional flash of embroidery or note of song could not mitigate or conceal the harshness of the everyday life in 80 per cent or more of Balkan households. Many of the city-dwellers were concerned to perpetuate the myth of the happy carefree peasant dancing in his picturesque clothes, lifting his hat when his betters went by, content to be untroubled by the complicated problems of the world, and relying with touching devotion upon the wisdom of his benevolent government. Once a Rumanian businessman told me that the peasants were the strong backbone of the country, and that he would always be proud of their strength and their joyous rural life. A few sentences later, he was calling them "animals who can talk," and showing the utmost contempt for them, and even for Rumania itself. Government propaganda almost always echoed his first statement, and backed it up with photographs for tourist agencies. But the propaganda was often written by men who would fully have endorsed his second.

The Balkan countries had grievous problems. No known panacea or combination of panaceas would have turned them into prosperous Denmarks or Switzerlands. In a world in which the great powers had built effective machinery to keep the peace, there would have been time for Yugoslavs, Rumanians, Bulgarians, and Albanians to forget their own rivalries, to adjust to the impact of western industrialized society, to borrow from the richer countries the means to raise their own standards of living, while not losing the values of their own precious cultures. This was not the world of the twentieth century. But strong character and a deep sense of human values survived an almost intolerable fate. It was these and these alone that the people of the Balkans took with them into the catastrophe of the Second World War.

PART II

Since 1939

Chapter 8

THE WAR YEARS

1. From the Outbreak of War to the German Attack on the USSR. September 1939–June 1941

THE FRAGMENTATION OF RUMANIA AND ITS CONSEQUENCES

DURING THE FIRST TEN MONTHS of the Second World War, an unnatural calm prevailed in southeastern Europe. In the fall of 1939, Stalin and Hitler divided and crushed Poland, and the following spring the Germans occupied Denmark and Norway, overran Holland and Belgium, and conquered France. The remnants of the British armies were retreating toward Dunquerque. Stalin had miscalculated the strength of his dangerous ally, and may well have feared that the British would now make terms, and that the Germans would turn east against Russia. In any case, he felt it was high time to collect the territories which the secret annexes to the Soviet-German pact had promised to the USSR, among them Bessarabia. The secret annexes had "called attention" to the Soviet interest in the province, and the Germans had specifically stated that they had no political interest in it. As early as March 1940, Soviet Foreign Minister Molotov made a speech in which he referred openly to the Soviet wish to get Bessarabia back.

Now, on June 23, 1940, Molotov told the German Ambassador that the USSR was about to demand Bessarabia. But he also declared that the USSR intended to seize Bukovina, the "beech-forest," the northernmost region of Moldavia, which had been a Habsburg possession between 1775 and 1918 (before 1775 it had been Turkish). Here too there was a Ukrainian minority. But Bukovina had never been in Russian possession; the USSR had no prior claim to it, and the German-Soviet treaty had never mentioned it.

In the discussions with the Germans which followed immediately upon this unexpected announcement, the Russians reduced their claim to the northern portion of Bukovina, including the capital, the strategic city of Cernauți, with important rail and road communications to the territories which the USSR had recently taken from Poland. The Russians agreed to transfer the German minorities, and on June 26, 1940 they presented a twenty-four-hour ultimatum to Rumania demanding both Bessarabia and Northern Bukovina.

Now that France had collapsed before Hitler, and Hitler was allied with Stalin, Rumania was left helpless before the Russian demands. The German Minister advised King Carol to yield to the Soviet ultimatum. The Rumanian Foreign Minister, Gafencu, has given an account of the way in which Molotov, using a thick pencil, scrawled the new frontier on a map: the line he drew slopped over at the edges so that the Russians acquired several villages in Moldavia proper in addition to Northern Bukovina, as well as a substantial portion of the Danube delta outside the province of Bessarabia. The Russians flatly refused to accept anything less than this Molotov line.

The territorial losses to the USSR naturally strengthened still further Rumanian anti-Soviet sentiment, already strong. King Carol renounced the guarantees given Rumania in 1939 by France and England, declaring that he was bound by eternal friendship to Germany and Italy. Horia Sima and the other Iron Guard leaders got an unconditional amnesty, and the King promised that all those who had killed members of the Iron Guard would now be punished. He tried to tighten up still further his "National Renaissance Front," by abolishing all political parties other than the government party, now called the Party of the Nation, which all Rumanians except Jews and Communists were required to join within two weeks. Rumania was now no longer "corporate"; it was "totalitarian." Strongly pro-German Rumanians were appointed to the chief Cabinet posts: Ion Gigurtu, director of a Transylvanian gold-mining syndicate, became Prime Minister, and Mihai Manoilescu Foreign Minister. British and French subjects were maltreated and their properties seized.

By all these acts of subservience to the Nazis, King Carol tried to ingratiate himself and save his throne. But his country had other territorial bills to pay. First, Bulgaria demanded the return of the Southern Dobrudja, which Rumania had acquired in 1913 as the result of the second Balkan War. The province had never had a Rumanian majority despite considerable efforts at colonizing it with Rumanians, and it was a region about which few Rumanians had ever cared very deeply. Some rich people had beautiful villas at Balčik, on the seacoast, and Queen Marie's heart had been buried there at her request, but there seems to have been little sense of public outrage at the Treaty of Craiova (August 23, 1940) by which the southern Dobrudja was ceded to Bulgaria. Queen Marie's heart was transferred to Bran, in Transylvania.

Quite different, of course, was the public attitude toward Transylvania itself, which every Rumanian felt to be an integral part of his country. All during the winter of 1939–40, while the contractors cheated and got rid of their faulty materials, Rumanian conscript laborers had been dying by the hundred in a frantic effort to build a line of fortifications against Hungary, the "Imaginescu" line, as the Bucharest wits called it. The Hungarians now demanded large parts of Transylvania, and negotiations began in July under Axis auspices. Carol was willing to cede to Hungary a strip of land along the frontier, but the Hungarians wanted much more.

When discussions broke down, the Rumanian Foreign Minister, Manoilescu, was summoned to Vienna, where the Germans and Italians "arbitrated" the dispute, and drew a new frontier between Hungary and Rumania. Northern Transylvania, including the capital city of Cluj (Kolozsvar), was given to

Hungary, which obtained also the three Szekler districts, and thus had a long salient thrusting deep into the heart of Rumania. The new border could not be defended. Hungary had acquired more than a million Rumanians, but none the less remained dissatisfied.

Rumanian resistance in the ordinary sense was not possible; but King Carol could, in theory at least, have threatened to destroy the oil refineries, and thus render unavailable to the Germans the supplies on which they were counting from the Rumanian wells. This desperate gamble might conceivably have forced the Germans to reconsider, since the Hungarians could make no equally effective threat. But Carol did not take it, despite the overwhelming weight of public opinion, which favored resistance. The decisive factor was the threat made by the Soviet ambassador, who now spoke menacingly of a frontier incident which might require further intervention. It is probable that the Russians were trying in this indirect way to serve notice on their allies, the Germans, that they were still interested in the country which the Axis powers were now so busy carving up without consulting Moscow. But the immediate effect was to terrify the Rumanians into doing just what Hitler wanted them to do. They signed the Vienna Award, and Hungary took over Northern Transylvania.

The award provided that all public property and all officials would remain undisturbed pending a final peaceable settlement, but the Rumanian government immediately ordered all movable goods to be taken out of the northern part of the province before the Hungarians could arrive. Eyewitnesses report long lines of trucks and long freight trains rushing across the new frontier into southern Transylvania carrying furniture, school and hospital equipment, and the like. At the same time, the Rumanians expelled from southern Transylvania all government officials of Magyar origin, forcing them on forty-eight hours' notice to cross the frontier into the northern part of the province, and leave their property behind them except for what they could carry. Other Magyars in the Rumanian part of the dismembered province began to suffer severe persecution. On the other hand, the Hungarian authorities expelled many Rumanians from northern Transylvania under conditions equally barbarous, and persecuted those who remained. The natural hostility between Rumania and Hungary was thus highly exacerbated, and the Germans and Italians found themselves with a pair of allies who hated each other at least as much as they hated the Russians. Through the years of war on the eastern front which were to follow, nobody in Rumania, even the Communists, gave up the hope of regaining the lost northern portion of Transylvania. Nor did the Hungarians renounce their claims to the southern portion.

By the cumulative cessions to the USSR, to Bulgaria, and to Hungary, Rumania had in two months lost more than a third of its territory and about a third of its population. No shots had been fired, but war had none the less reached the Balkans. The crisis which ensued forced the abdication of King Carol on September 6, 1940. The armored railway car bearing him and Madame Lupescu into luxurious exile pulled out of the Bucharest terminal in a hail of Iron Guard bullets. Young King Michael succeeded his father for the second and last time. General Ion Antonescu, a competent officer with strong Iron Guard connections, who had been called to the Premiership in the last days of Carol's regime, continued in office, with the leader of the Guard, Horia Sima, as his deputy. Maniu and Bratianu, leaders of the National Peasant and National Liberal Parties, at first supported Antonescu, on condition that he abolish the dictatorship which the King had established. Instead, he tightened it.

The partial dismemberment of Rumania was of momentous importance not only for the Rumanians themselves, but also because it led directly to the first major disagreements between the Germans and the Russians. Immediately after the Vienna Award, pushed through without any consultation of Moscow, the Axis powers guaranteed the frontiers of Rumania. To the Russians this could mean only that Germany was now prepared to defend Rumania against further Soviet encroachment. They interpreted the guarantee as a warning to them, and an unfriendly act. Molotov indeed protested vigorously. Further disagreement manifested itself when the powers convened in Bucharest in October to discuss a new system of regulations for the Danube, of which the USSR had become a riparian state by the annexation of Bessarabia. The Russians insisted that the strategic delta be administered by a commission on which they and the Rumanians alone would be represented: in the circumstances, this would have turned the mouths of the Danube into Soviet territory. Germany, Italy, and Rumania demanded that the delta, like the remainder of the river's course, be under the authority of all the powers acting in consultation. After almost two months, the conference adjourned without reaching an agreement on this fundamental question.

Indeed, during October, German troops appeared in Rumania, on a mission to train the Rumanian army. Their arrival was followed within a few days by a treaty giving the German minority in Rumania a special "legal personality," whose "will" was expressed by the Nazi party, and which had allegiance to Germany. The "Volksdeutsch" had all the benefits of Rumanian citizenship but virtually none of its obligations. As the number of German troops increased over the months that followed, the Rumanian government offered the pretext that they were needed to protect the oil fields against British efforts at sabotage, an excuse hardly likely to reassure the Russians. These were the clouds which forecast the stormy end of the Russo-German alliance a few months later.

The months between Antonescu's accession in September 1940 and the coming of full-scale war to the Balkans in March 1941 were marked by two Iron Guard outbreaks. Though they were strongly represented in the government, and though Antonescu himself was wearing his green shirt and calling himself *Conducator* (Duce or Fuehrer), the radical elements in the Guard were discontented. They believed in the revolutionary slogans of their party, itched to see the Jews eliminated from Rumanian life, and yearned for vengeance on those who had opposed them and killed their founder and his entourage. What was the good of cabinet posts, if the old system continued unchanged and the old enemies walked the streets unmolested or were merely thrown into jail? The first disorders came in November 1940, when the Guard broke into the Jilava prison and massacred a group of more than sixty political prisoners who had been the chief instruments in carrying out the repression of their movement. The Guard now kidnaped and brutally mutilated and murdered the former Premier, Professor Nicolae Iorga, a one-man intellectual tradition in himself, who, though passionately chauvinist, had opposed the excesses of the Guard. Virgil Madgearu, a distinguished National Peasant Party economist, met the same fate. The Guard perpetrated numerous outrages against Jews.

What Hitler chiefly needed in Rumania was public order. His interests demanded that the economy should function smoothly, and that the greatest possible amounts of oil and agricultural produce be made available to the German armies. The Guard had served its purpose in the thirties as a pro-German subversive force in Carol's kingdom. The Germans could always count on its squads of toughs when they needed them. But now the revolutionary ideas of the radical guardists presented a danger, and the Germans fully supported Antonescu as he moved to disarm them. Feeling that their days were numbered, as the strength of the army regular units grew, the Guards broke loose in January 1941 in a violent uprising, accompanied by mass atrocities on the helpless Jews of the capital, some of whom were slaughtered, dissected, and hung on meat-hooks in the municipal slaughterhouse with insulting placards tied to their severed limbs. There were three days of violent fighting in Bucharest before the army and the Germans succeeded in crushing the Guard. Now the Antonescu dictatorship and the Germans held Rumania firmly in their grip. The regime made no change in the social or economic system of the country. It took measures against the Jews, but they suffered little physical violence, and their position was for the moment far better than in Germany or German-dominated Poland and Czechoslovakia.

MUSSOLINI'S FAILURE IN GREECE AND ITS CONSEQUENCES

While Germany had been winning dramatic victories, Italy's part in the war had so far been confined to the "stab in the back" delivered to the prostrate French after the Germans had defeated the French armies. Eager for military glory, but fearful that Hitler would restrain him, Mussolini launched an attack on Greece at the end of October 1940 without telling Hitler of his intentions until after the Italian troops had marched. Attacking from their Albanian base, the Italians scored some initial successes, but soon met with fierce resistance. Mussolini had hoped for a quick victory, which would have helped to raise Italian prestige to a level worthy of a junior Axis partner, but he underestimated the Greeks, who not only routed the Italians on Greek soil, but proceeded to advance northward into Albania, driving Mussolini's armies before them. The Greeks took the main cities of the Tosk region — Korcha and Gjinokaster; it seemed doubtful whether the Italians could hold the port of Valona. Indeed it looked as if the Italians might be driven out of Albania altogether, and as if Mussolini would suffer a complete disaster.

Naturally, the Albanians were delighted, and many Albanian units which had been mobilized into the Italian armies went over to the Greeks. King Zog, in exile in London, saluted the victories of the King of Greece, and offered to join his forces. British intelligence agents in Belgrade had for some months been hard at work among influential Albanian exiles and refugees in Yugoslavia, building a movement which at the proper moment should begin a revolution inside Albania and oust the Italians. The leaders of the British-sponsored organization were the Kryeziu brothers, Gani and Said, who commanded much support from Albanian tribesmen on both sides of the Yugoslav border. Gani was a professional soldier, who had served in the Yugoslav army; Said an intellectual, educated in Paris and a strong social-democrat in politics. Both were enemies of Zog.

To get the support of Zogists as well, the British brought from Turkey Abas Kupi, a Bektashi from Skanderbeg's own fortress of Kruya, north of Tirana, an experienced guerrilla, who had once fought Zog but had made his peace with him. As commander of the port of Durazzo (Durres) Abas Kupi had put up a brave resistance to the Italians in 1939; he commanded the confidence of thousands of tribesmen in his own part of Albania. Finally, the United Front of anti-Italian Albanian exiles formed by the British included an Albanian Communist, Mustafa Gjinishi. All sorts of contacts were established inside Albania, the Kossovo province forming an easy and natural base of operations for work among Albanians on the other side of the border. With the Greek victories, this United Front was ready to launch its revolution if the British delivered a supply of rifles. It seemed possible that the Italians would now be crushed between the Greeks advancing from the south and an Albanian uprising coming from the north.

But the Greek general staff did not approve the plan. Not only did they want the rifles for themselves, but many Greeks also still hoped to annex southern Albania. To accept the assistance of a native Albanian revolt would certainly make it more difficult in the future to annex Albanian territory. The plan for a revolt had to be abandoned. Moreover, the original Albanian enthusiasm for the advancing Greeks was greatly dampened by the chauvinism the Greeks displayed in the portions of Albania which they were occupying. One cannot say definitely that an Albanian revolt in the winter of 1940–41 would have completed the Italian rout, but it might well have made it more difficult for Mussolini to stabilize a front in central Albania, which he succeeded in doing. The stalled Italian armies were a constant source of humiliation to the Axis, and it became clear to Hitler that he would have to rescue Mussolini before he could feel secure that the British would not reappear on the continent in force in Greece.

To get at the Greeks, Hitler had to extend his sphere of influence in southeast Europe: Rumania was no longer enough: now it was a question of putting pressure on Bulgaria and Yugoslavia to permit the passage of German troops, a move which was sure to arouse the grave alarm if not the active hostility of the USSR. Indeed, when Molotov visited Berlin in November 1940, and Hitler offered the dazzling prospect of Soviet control over the Straits and an enormous sphere of influence to include the Persian gulf and the shores of the Indian Ocean (after Britain should have been defeated), Molotov listened politely but brought the conversation back to the Balkans. He demanded that Germany and Italy recognize that Bulgaria lay within the security zone of the Russian Black Sea boundaries, and that they accept the necessity of a mutual security pact between the USSR and Bulgaria, which, he declared, would in no way affect the internal regime of Bulgaria, her sovereignty or her independence.

To this Hitler answered evasively that he would have to consult the Italians and Bulgarians before assenting. He did not accept the Soviet demand for a pact with Bulgaria, but decided that his differences with Stalin were irreconcilable. On December 18, a little over a month after Molotov's visit, Hitler signed the instructions ordering his army high command to prepare operational plans for a campaign against Russia. German-Soviet relations, which had begun to deteriorate over the German guarantee to Rumania, now were dangerously strained because of the Russian effort to counter German influence in Rumania by the establishment of their own domination in Bulgaria.

So when the Germans began soon thereafter to press Bulgaria to adhere to the Axis, they were posing a direct threat to the Russian "security zone." The British representatives in Sofia tried hard to restrain King Boris from joining the Axis. President Roosevelt sent Colonel (later Major-General) William J. Donovan to Bulgaria to try to stiffen the will of the King against Germany. Mushanov and the Bulgarian Democrats also tried to influence King Boris against it. The Russians published an official statement opposing the entrance into Bulgaria of any foreign troops, and in their diplomatic correspondence with Germany warned that German occupation of Bulgaria might lead to Turkish entry into the war, and thus open the Straits to the British. But all these efforts failed. They are interesting as the first episode in which the Soviet Union and the western powers were arguing the same side of the question.

King Boris seems to have felt that southeast Europe would in future be dominated either by Germany or by Russia. He was of German origin, and deeply feared communism. He knew that Hitler intended to attack Greece, and that Bulgaria would get back the outlet to the Aegean which she had lost to Greece after the First World War, and other territories in Macedonia lost since the second Balkan War. So on March 1, 1941, he went to Vienna, signed the Axis pact, and committed Bulgaria to the German alliance. German troops poured into the country across the Danube. A couple of days in advance, the Germans told the Russians what was about to happen, adding that their troops were entering Bulgaria to keep the British out of Greece, and that Hitler had no intention of attacking Turkey. Molotov reiterated the Soviet view that Bulgaria lay in the Russian "security zone," and the Russians made their disapproval public in an official Tass communiqué.

Meanwhile, Yugoslavia was in torment. The establishment of the Croatian Banovina just one day before the conclusion of the Russo-German pact had lessened internal tension only slightly. Immediately upon the outbreak of the war, the Yugoslav regime declared its neutrality, but the German successes created a great sense of uneasiness. The Balkan Entente, meeting in Belgrade in February 1940, issued a windy communiqué, ill-concealing the fear of its members at the disappearance of Poland and Czechoslovakia and the end of the Little Entente.

In the spring of 1940, relations between Yugoslavia and the USSR were renewed after twenty years, and a trade delegation, a military delegation, and an ambassador followed each other to Moscow. Relations with Bulgaria too were growing closer. Stoyadinovich and his chief policeman were interned. Prince Paul was doing what he could to make his neutrality genuine. But the fall of France, the battle of Britain, the entry of the German troops into Rumania, and the Italian attack on Greece led to great public alarm and depression.

After Italian planes had bombed the Yugoslav Macedonian city of Bitolj, the Yugoslav regime considered helping the Greeks. The Germans, however, urged the Yugoslav government to seize Saloniki while the Greeks were busy in Albania; but this was an obvious trap to commit the Yugoslavs on the Axis side, and was declined. Moreover Paul refused a secret Turkish offer of an alliance, which if accepted might well have given pause to King Boris and delayed or prevented his yielding to Hitler. Had the Yugoslav government boldly joined hands with Greece and Turkey at this moment in the war, it is possible that both Bulgarians and Germans would have hesitated. But Paul kept the Turkish offer a dead secret, and the opportunity, if any, was lost. The only offer to which Paul did respond came from Budapest. The pact of "eternal friendship" reached with Hungary in December 1940 was Axis-inspired, and aroused little enthusiasm among Yugoslavs, whose wisdom was soon to be demonstrated.

In mid-February 1941 came the first summons to Berchtesgaden. Premier Tsvetkovich and Foreign Minister Tsintsar-Markovich offered to guarantee that Yugoslavia would not become an instrument of British policy against Germany, and Hitler asked that Yugoslavia adhere to the Axis pact. Prince Paul and the Cabinet clung to the hope that, if Yugoslavia adhered to the pact, the

Axis would not ask for Yugoslav troops, would not demand passage through Yugoslavia, and would guarantee Yugoslav territorial integrity. Though Paul refused to receive British Foreign Minister Anthony Eden in Belgrade, he did reach an agreement with the British and the Greeks to remove Stoyadinovich from his internment in Yugoslavia, and send him on first to Athens, and then to the British island of Mauritius, far off in the Indian Ocean and out of reach of the Germans, who thus lost a potential collaborator.

Personally unpopular with many leading politicians (four Serbs chose this moment to resign from the Cabinet because they foresaw the adherence of Yugoslavia to the Axis Pact), Prince Paul was deeply aware of Yugoslavia's military unpreparedness, which was in considerable part his own fault. He knew that neither the frontiers nor the capital could be defended in case of attack. With his own White Russian background, he may well have been lured by the prospect of a German attack on the USSR. It is sometimes said that Hitler dangled before Prince Paul the prospect of the Yugoslav or even the Russian throne. It is sure that Paul enjoyed his own dictatorial position, and knew that to yield to the pressure of anti-Axis public opinion would mean the dropping of the subservient Tsvetkovich and the establishment of a far more democratic regime. So he knuckled under to the Germans in the end, and on March 25, 1941, in Vienna, Tsvetkovich and Tsintsar-Markovich signed the Axis pact on behalf of Yugoslavia. Prince Paul had not even dared inform the Skupshtina, packed as it was in his favor, much less the general public, which heard the news only on the return of the ministers on March 26.

What happened next astonished the world and delighted the enemies of Hitler. A group of Serbian officers, mostly in the air force, of whom General Boris Mirkovich was the chief, led a *coup d'état* against Prince Paul. Tsvetkovich, Tsintsar-Markovich, and others were arrested. Young King Peter, still six months short of the legal age of eighteen, was proclaimed King, and Prince Paul was intercepted on his way to his country place, and soon after sent into exile in Kenya. Air-force Colonel Dushan Simovich became prime minister.

The new Cabinet included leading members of the Serb Radical, Democratic, and Agrarian parties, Dr. Machek, the leader of the Croatian Peasant Party, and three other leading Croats, two Slovene Clericals, a Bosnian Muslim, two Independent Serb Democrats (i.e., Serbs from Croatia), and two former premiers of Alexander's dictatorship, Bogolyub Yeftich and Petar Zhivkovich, leader of the White Hand. It was a representative group of elder statesmen. Government was now back in the hands of the Yugoslav political parties, and indeed this had been a major object of the coup.

Although the conspiracy was carried through by a small number of officers in the best tradition of Serbian plotting, there can be no doubt whatever that it expressed the popular will. The Belgrade streets were full of wildly enthusiastic mobs of Serbs chanting a doggerel verse: "better war than the pact, better death than slavery," and attacking German shops. It is difficult for those who did not live through the dark days of 1940 and 1941 to sense what a ray of light the news of the Serb coup let into the gloomy thoughts of all those in despair at the succession of easy Axis triumphs. As Prime Minister Churchill said at the time, Yugoslavia had found her soul. Under-Secretary of State Sumner Welles also praised the action. Though *Pravda* denied that the Russians had been in any way responsible for the coup, it congratulated the Yugoslavs. The contribution to the allied cause was by no means the last or the greatest which Yugoslavia was to render, but it stands as a splendid episode of human courage, and the Serbs alone deserve the credit.

Hitler was as furious as his enemies were pleased. The coup happened to coincide with the state visit of the Japanese Foreign Minister to Berlin, and his Nazi hosts could hardly have been more embarrassed. The German press instantly discovered a lot of imaginary atrocities, and railed against the Yugoslavs. The new Yugoslav government had no clearly defined policy. Churchill of course hoped it would invade Albania from the north and take the faltering Italians in the rear. But the government instead assured the Germans that it accepted the Vienna agreement, and would respect all existing treaties. It assured the British that Yugoslavia wished to make it clear that Germany bore the full responsibility for war if it should come. The Germans demanded compensation for damage done to the German shops during the riots in Belgrade, which was granted. They demanded that the Axis pact be ratified at once, which the Yugoslav government was prepared to do. They demanded immediate demobilization of the Yugoslav army, which could hardly be accepted.

While a plane stood ready to take Foreign Minister Ninchich to Berlin to discuss the questions at issue, and Prime Minister Simovich proclaimed Belgrade, Zagreb, and Ljubljana open cities, the Germans struck, on April 6, 1941. Without a declaration of war, and to the accompaniment of a statement blaming the whole affair on the British and on the "same people who drove the world into war by the Sarayevo murders," Hitler's air force began the bombing of Belgrade. A pact of friendship between Yugoslavia and the USSR, signed two hours before the German attack began, committed neither party to act in the event of aggression by a third party, and was therefore of no practical value, except to underline for Hitler Stalin's displeasure with the Germans. But the pact did include a guarantee of Yugoslav territorial integrity by the Soviet Union, which thus served notice that no future partition of the country would be acceptable.

The repeated savage bombardments of Belgrade, an open city, were soon followed by all-out invasion. Most of the German striking force came across the Bulgarian frontier. Other troops came from Hungary and Rumania. Italian and Hungarian troops participated, the latter in spite of the fact that the treaty of "eternal" friendship with the Yugoslavs was less than four months old. The Hungarian Prime Minister, Count Teleki, committed suicide in despair at what he rightly regarded as the loss of Hungarian honor. Within twelve days the whole Yugoslav army had been rolled up, owing to faulty troop dispositions, sabotage, bad equipment, and inferior communications. Serbian charges that Croat treachery played a part in the defeat certainly contained a germ of truth, although considerably exaggerated. The settlement with the Croats was far too recent to have eliminated anti-Serb sentiment and created a real loyalty to Yugoslavia. King Peter and the government fled, first to Greece, then to Palestine, and finally to London, where they arrived in June. Meanwhile, the British plan to sponsor a revolt in Albania, which the Simovich government had sponsored, had become a casualty of the German victory over Yugoslavia, and the leaders of the movement, who had crossed the Albanian frontier, separated, and went into hiding in various parts of the country.

Linking up with the Italians in Albania, the German armies now drove on into Greece, defeating the Greeks and the British expeditionary force, and completing the conquest of the Balkans in May by the spectacular attack on Crete, largely carried on with troops landed from gliders. The entire peninsula was now dominated by the Axis. But the campaign had cost Hitler heavily, especially in time: his attack on Russia had been delayed six to eight weeks. This turned out to be crucially important, since his armies were halted on the way to Moscow by winter, for which the Germans had made inadequate preparations.

During the weeks between the conquest of Crete and the invasion of the Soviet Union on June 22, 1941, the Russians strove mightily to avert Hitler's attack by a series of acts of appeasement, of which we need notice only one: in a frantic effort to please Hitler, Stalin expelled from Moscow the Yugoslav embassy, representing a country with which a few weeks before he had signed a treaty of nonaggression and friendship. But this craven act was without avail.

2. *Occupation and Resistance (1): Yugoslavia and Albania, Spring 1941 — Winter 1943*

THE DISMEMBERMENT OF YUGOSLAVIA

Now the Axis powers, before the end of 1941, proceeded to dismember Yugoslavia. Germany directly annexed two-thirds of Slovenia, with a population of over 900,000 people, extending the administration of the Austrian districts of Styria and Carinthia to include the newly conquered territory. Italy annexed most of the rest of Slovenia, centering on the capital, which became the "Provincia di Lubiana," with about 300,000 people. To Italy went also most of the Adriatic coast and islands, including Split and Kotor but not Dubrovnik, with a population of well over half a million, and all of Montenegro, with a population of more than 300,000. Initially the Italians called Montenegro an independent state. Setting up a native "Consulta Tecnica," they planned to put on the throne the grandson of the last King of independent Montenegro, Prince Mirko, nephew of the Queen of Italy. But Mirko refused, and though independence was proclaimed and King Victor Emmanuel III visited Tsetinye, he never named a regent, and the region was governed by Italy through an Italian military governor.

Hungary annexed small districts in Slovenia and Croatia, and the Bachka and Baranya regions of the Voyvodina, adding more than 900,000 people. To Italian-occupied Albania was awarded the Kossovo region and parts of Montenegro and Macedonia, with a population of more than 700,000. Bulgaria occupied the rest of Macedonia and portions of southern and eastern Serbia with a population of a million and a quarter. Though the Bulgarians treated Yugoslav Macedonia as annexed territory, the Germans did not permit formal annexation.

What was left of Yugoslavia was erected into two puppet states, Croatia and Serbia, but with quite different status in the Axis world. In Croatia the Germans would have liked to use Dr. Machek, leader of the overwhelmingly

Yugoslavia During World War II

popular Peasant Party, as ruler. But Machek refused to collaborate with them, and went into retirement. So the role of chief native subordinate to the Germans and Italians was given to the Ustasha leader, Ante Pavelich, who now became Poglavnik (Fuehrer). On a visit to Rome in May 1941, Pavelich was solemnly met at the station by Mussolini and Ciano. He also was received by Pope Pius XII, an incident for which the Vatican was severely criticized, but one which was allegedly not intended to imply official recognition.

Pavelich now offered the Crown of Croatia to the House of Savoy. King Victor Emmanuel of Italy nominated his second cousin, Aimone, Duke of Spoleto, younger brother of the Italian commander-in-chief in East Africa, the Duke of Aosta, to whose title Aimone succeeded in 1942. The Duke was to assume the "Crown of Zvonimir," and took the name of Tomislav II, both Tomislav and Zvonimir having ruled the mediaeval independent state of Croatia before the Magyars had taken it over. In fact, however, the Italian "King" never visited his kingdom (his wife was a sister of the King of Greece and strongly anti-German).

Thus, in practice, under the eye of Kasche, the German Minister, Pavelich ruled Croatia,[1] which had a storm-troop organization in the Ustasha (the regular army was called the *Domobranstvo* or Home Guard), an endlessly repeated slogan (*Za dom spreman,* For the fatherland—ready), membership in the three-power pact, and recognition from all the other Axis powers. In due course it declared war on the western allies and the USSR. Croatia thus became a typical Axis puppet, like independent Slovakia. Both were portions chopped out of Versailles-created successor states and now given a regime of native extremists. The cession of large Croatian areas to Italy was in some measure compensated by Hitler's award to Pavelich of all of Bosnia and Hertsegovina, with their large Serbian population and most of the Jews in Yugoslavia. Part of the Adriatic hinterland was under Italian military and, for a time, civil administration. The total population of "Croatia" was perhaps 7,000,000.

After several months of purely German military administration in Belgrade, in which some of the members of the Serbian Fascist Party (Zbor) assisted, the Germans announced in August 1941 the formation of a government for Serbia under General Milan Nedich. Nedich, who had served as Minister of War in 1938–40, appointed a cabinet to have competence only in those matters which were "the concern of the Serbs themselves." Unlike Croatia, therefore, puppet Serbia had no foreign ministry or regular army of

[1] Associated with him in the new regime initially were Slavko Kvaternik, a former officer of the Austrian army, whose father had been executed for treason to the Habsburgs, who now became field marshal and commander-in-chief of the army; and his son Eugene, immediate boss of the assassination of King Alexander in 1934, who took over the police, receiving instructions from Himmler in person. Others were the new Minister of Education, Mile Budak, a novelist, who had been beaten up on the streets of Zagreb in the early thirties by agents of the Belgrade regime, and who had in consequence developed an immoderate hatred for the Serbs; and Dr. Andriya Artukovich, a fanatical lawyer, who took over the Ministry of the Interior.

its own, and it was clear that the Germans regarded the Serbs as defeated enemies, the Croats as rewarded allies.

One of the chief tasks assigned to Nedich was the maintenance of order, which, as we shall see, meant participating in the fight against the resistance. For this purpose he had at his disposal a Serbian State Guard, a small force of local "volunteers" (*Dobrovoltsi*), and the followers of Kosta Pechanats, the commander of a traditional Serb irregular force known as Chetniks (from Cheta, a guerrilla band), who was loyal to Nedich and the Germans, and whose men must be distinguished from the anti-Axis Chetniks, whom we shall encounter shortly. Nedich called his regime the "Government of National Salvation," and no doubt thought of himself as loyal to King Peter, and as keeping alive some sort of Serbia to which the King would some day return. Later, as the German position deteriorated, Nedich secretly wrote, begging the King not to class him with Pavelich. Defenders of Nedich always insist that he be regarded not as a Quisling but as the Serb Pétain.

The real rulers of Serbia were the German military authorities, who retained final veto in all political, administrative, and economic matters, applied German and martial law, divided the country into fourteen districts, and installed a regular central and local military government, as well as bringing in the Gestapo. In some parts of eastern Serbia, they used Bulgarian troops for garrison duty. The Germans used Nedich to deflect some of the criticism of conditions, which would otherwise have fallen exclusively on themselves. Further, they governed dismembered Yugoslavia in some part by cleverly manipulating Croat-Serb antagonism, and for this purpose they needed a Serbian authority. The territory of the puppet Serb state was about the same as that of the old Kingdom of Serbia before the first Balkan War, with a population of something over 4,000,000.

Finally, the Banat, the only portion of the Voyvodina not annexed by Hungary, was in practice detached by the Germans from Serbia, although remaining nominally subject to Nedich for civil administration, and given into the hands of the local German minority, who ran it almost as a German republic. They formed about a quarter of its population of some 650,000, and supplied the manpower for a special SS Division.

In this elaborate way Yugoslavia was carved into separate fragments, each exploited for the conqueror. Tyranny raged everywhere. In the German-annexed portions of Slovenia the Germans made a systematic attempt to Germanize the population. They sent a great number of Slovene men to concentration camps, and packed their wives and children to the number of some 60,000 into freight cars and dumped them into Serbia, handing over their houses and farms to German colonists imported from the Reich. Slovene books in the libraries were publicly burned, and inscriptions in Slovene erased from all monuments, even the tombstones in the churchyards. Among the Slovenes left behind, the Germans, through the medium of the so-called Carinthian National Association, spread a systematic propaganda to the effect that they were in fact of German origin, and urged them to abandon their native language and national way of life and become Germans.

Even more savage were the ghastly Ustasha massacres of Jews and Serbs in "Croatia." The Jews of Zagreb and Sarayevo were killed or sent to concentration camps or deported to Poland for extermination. Ustasha gangs also slaughtered tens of thousands of Serbs. To some they offered the choice between conversion from Orthodoxy to Catholicism or instant death. Others were permitted to join a new and totally artificial "Croat Orthodox Church" with a Hitlerite White Russian at its head. In the mixed Serb-Croat villages, incredible scenes of violence took place, whole populations often being herded into Orthodox churches and burned alive. In this bloody work the Ustasha had the assistance of many of the Muslim population, who were from the first treated with special favor by the Pavelich authorities (a mosque was even opened in Zagreb), and who were eventually recruited into a special SS division of their own, which later in the war was reviewed and inspected by the Grand Mufti of Jerusalem.

It must also be recorded as a historic fact that certain members of the Croat Catholic hierarchy, notably Archbishop Sharich of Sarayevo, endorsed this butchery, and some members of the Franciscan order took an active part in the forced conversion of the Serbs and also in the massacres. As for the Archbishop of Zagreb, Stepinats, whose trial and sentence after the war have been a *cause célèbre,* he attended Ustasha ceremonies, belonged to the commission for the conversion of the Orthodox, and often appeared in public on ceremonial occasions with members of the regime, to which the newspaper of his archdiocese gave its support. It is known, however, that he deplored the excesses of Pavelich and his henchmen.

Sickening though these were, their victims were not as numerous as the Serbs in exile claimed them to be. The Yugoslav idea itself was put into jeopardy, as indeed the Axis and the Ustasha intended that it should be. Some patriotic Serbs abroad, maddened by the horrifying news from Croatia, and putting the blame on the whole Croat people instead of on the fanatical minority who followed Pavelich, now maintained either that Yugoslavia could never be reconstituted, or that any effort to do so must begin with a systematic massacre of at least a million Croats. Thousands of Serbs, fleeing Ustasha persecution, streamed over the border into German-occupied Serbia, where they added to the hatred already felt by their fellow-nationals for the Croats, fanning the flames of the old conflict, and perfectly suiting the German game. The massacres also had a profound effect upon the Yugoslav government in exile.

Elsewhere the dreary story varied only in degree. The Hungarians massacred at least 10,000 Serbs in Novi Sad and at other points in the Bachka in January 1942. Though the Italians in the Provincia di Lubiana were initially far milder than the Germans or Ustasha or Hungarians, the murder of their first collaborator, Natlachen, who had been a Yugoslav government official, and his replacement by General Leo Rupnik, who had served in both the Austrian and Yugoslav armies, led to a tightening tyranny, which increased with the growth of resistance. Here the Catholic hierarchy, under Bishop Rozman, was almost solidly collaborationist. In the regions annexed by the Albanians, their so-called Skanderbeg division, made up of members of the Albanian minority in Yugoslavia, massacred Serbs with impunity. Branches of the Albanian Fascist Party, itself under Italian direction, were set up. The Bulgarians behaved better than any other occupying force, but instead of giving autonomy to Vardar Macedonia (which the Macedonians had expected so fondly that many of them had actively welcomed the Bulgarians), they kept the region firmly under control from Sofia. They set up their own schools, founded a university in Skoplye, and a Bulgarian library, theater, and museum. This Bulgarian rather than Macedonian cultural nationalization soon disillusioned the population.

Though Germany and Italy were allies, their policies in Yugoslavia were somewhat divergent. Italy had for years supported Pavelich, and thus fed Croat nationalism, but Mussolini's annexation of Dalmatia and military occupation of large areas of Hertsegovina had humiliated and thwarted the Ustasha. The Italians now faced the prospect that the Croat leaders would in future make against Italy the claims which Italy had once encouraged them to make against the Yugoslav state. So the Italians gradually moved into a pro-Serb position to give them a weapon against the Croats. The Germans, on the other hand, who had for years hoped so much from Stoyadinovich and other Serb politicians, now felt that they had been betrayed by the Serb coup of Simovich, and had become anti-Serb, and pro-Croat. Thus friction often arose in the occupation. It became more marked as resistance grew.

RESISTANCE IN YUGOSLAVIA: MIHAILOVICH AND TITO

Resistance in Yugoslavia began even before defeat. The very rapidity of the German advance made it possible for many Yugoslav units to escape destruction or capture. Some of the soldiers went home, taking their arms with them, or hiding them in secret dumps. Others melted into the woods. Still others belonged to units which had not been fully mobilized before the capitulation to the Germans. They too kept or hid their weapons. As an act of favor toward Pavelich, the Germans set free thousands of Croat prisoners, and while he mobilized many of them into his own forces, he could not always count on their loyalty. Some, finding that the Germans and the Croat authorities were sending large drafts of forced laborers abroad, disappeared with their rifles. When the Ustasha massacres began, many Serbs fought back, or left their villages for the Bosnian mountains. Acts of sabotage became numerous; an ammunition train was blown up, a great munitions dump exploded, German officers were killed. In accordance with their usual practice, the German armies avenged each such incident by executing hundreds of hostages.

Drazha Mihailovich, Colonel on the General Staff of the Yugoslav army, was the highest-ranking of these irregular warriors. In the honored guerrilla tradition of Serbia, his men called themselves Chetniks. Mihailovich was a patriot, but a Serb rather than a Yugoslav patriot. He was deeply concerned that his people, the Serbs, should not be decimated by German or Croat reprisals, and that they should retain their numerical preponderance in Yugoslavia, which might be jeopardized by the bloody consequences of large-scale guerrilla warfare. Though he loathed the invaders, and especially in the earliest days after the defeat, ordered military and sabotage operations against them, his dominant idea soon became caution. He proposed to wait until British and American rescue forces should land in Yugoslavia, and then take command of a great *ustanak,* or uprising, which would drive the Germans and Italians out. Meanwhile, he organized sub-commands in widely scattered portions of the country, entrusting them to officers with whom, as it turned out, he was often to have little contact, and over whom he sometimes maintained only the slenderest control. His followers grew long beards, and wore the traditional Chetnik insignia of a skull and crossbones. Had an allied invasion come in 1941 or even in 1942, he would surely have welcomed it and given it every possible military assistance. But prolonged inaction, though perhaps prudent and politic, was not the meat for which most of the men in the woods were hungering.

Early in 1942, the government-in-exile in London made Mihailovich its official Commander-in-Chief of the Royal Armies in Yugoslavia, and appointed him Minister of War. This loaned him some additional authority, but only with those Yugoslavs who remained loyal to the government-in-exile. In fact, many were disgusted and angry with the politicians who had fled, and who were now issuing instructions from London to a people suffering the grim horrors of German and Italian occupation. Mihailovich's exploits were magnified beyond recognition by the publicity which the exiled Serb politicians spread in England and the United States, and this was all the easier because the memory of the heroic Serb coup of March 1941 was still fresh, and still provided the public in the west with almost its only instance of brave resistance to the enemy.

A second Yugoslav resistance movement, however, soon sprang up and early threatened the supremacy of Mihailovich. The Yugoslav Communist Party, illegal for years under the royal government, took the lead, and the Party's Secretary-General, Josip Broz, nicknamed Tito, commanded its activities. He called his forces Partisans, after the irregular units which had fought against Napoleon in Spain in 1808 and in Russia in 1812. The official Yugoslav Communist version of events insists that Tito ordered resistance even before the German attack on the Soviet Union. Whether or not the Partisans perpetrated acts of opposition to the occupiers before June 21, 1941, it seems highly probable that they were at least preparing to resist before that date. In any case, after June 21 the Communist leaders, dedicated to the Soviet cause, threw themselves into the struggle against the Germans and

Italians, feeling that every act of theirs which hurt the Axis helped the USSR. Many Yugoslav Communists, moreover, were Yugoslavs first and Communists second, and eagerly sought every opportunity to kill and harass the enemy. The activism of the Partisans struck a far more responsive chord in a great number of Yugoslavs than the passivity of Mihailovich. The peasants in the villages suffered grievously under the reprisals to which they were now exposed, as Mihailovich had feared. None the less, from the first, a thin trickle of Chetniks, who wanted to shoot at the Italians and Germans, flowed into the Partisan ranks, and the trickle constantly swelled during the years of occupation.

The Partisans welcomed such Chetnik recruits, and indeed recruits from all quarters, even Ustashe. In this way they put Mihailovich at a further disadvantage; the narrow nationalist ideology of the Pan-Serb attracted many fewer fighters than the carefully preserved fiction of the popular front against the enemy put forth by the Partisans. The Communists formed only a small fraction of Tito's forces, but they retained an iron grip on the commanding posts. Though their men wore the red star of communism on their hats, superposed it on the national flag, and saluted each other with the Communist clenched fist salute, the leaders carefully refrained for the moment from forcing Communist dogma down the throats of the ordinary Yugoslavs who made up their rank and file. They temporarily subordinated Marxism-Leninism-Stalinism to the "popular democracy" of a common struggle. Their slogan "Death to fascism, liberty to the people" evoked a genuine response. Women and youths served in their units side by side with men, and observers all reported the stern moralistic puritanism which usually held sway in the ranks. Clergy of all faiths were to be found among their numbers, one of their earliest and most proudly exhibited leaders being a Serb Orthodox priest, Father Vlada Zechevich, who had left Mihailovich in order to fight. In at least one instance, a Franciscan friar served as local commander of a Partisan detachment.

At the time of the Yugoslav defeat, Tito had been living under a false name in Zagreb. With forged papers he made his way to Belgrade, and organized the movement there: the local authorities of the royal government were to be destroyed wherever they still existed, and arms taken from the police. Provincial commanders were appointed: Edvard Kardelj, a Slovene schoolteacher and leading Marxist theoretician, for Slovenia; Milovan Djilas, a Montenegrin, for Montenegro; Svetozar Vukmanovich-Tempo for Bosnia-Hertsegovina. Serbia Tito reserved for himself. Thus, contrary to much Serb propaganda that the Partisan movement was Croat in origin, it actually got under way in the other provinces first. Though Tito was himself a Croat, he fully appreciated the importance of Serbia, and made it his first concern. Within a few weeks the Partisans had "liberated" a substantial amount of territory in Serbia, and Tito himself left Belgrade in September 1941 for this liberated area, not to return until 1944.

A few days later he had an interview with Mihailovich, the first of two, in addition to several conferences by telephone. Mihailovich expounded his theory of delay, and refused to agree to joint operations with the Partisans. Having forced the Germans to evacuate western Serbia, Tito set up headquarters at Uzhitse, its chief town, where he had the use of a rifle factory, which turned out several hundred weapons a day. The Partisans set up their own local institutions: so-called "people's councils" (*odbors*) modeled on the soviets in revolutionary Russia. From the village and the region, these councils reported to the newly formed National Committee of Liberation for Serbia. The Partisans opened schools, published a Communist newspaper, put on plays, and enthusiastically got up football (soccer) matches. More important, they extended their territorial holdings into Bosnia and Montenegro, so that couriers and troops could move from the Adriatic all the way to Belgrade by avoiding the Axis-controlled main towns. Indeed, the Partisans were able to provide an escort across Yugoslavia for the first British mission sent to assist Mihailovich.

As the Germans prepared to attack his Uzhitse "red republic," Tito sought out Mihailovich for the second time. He now proposed an agreement for joint operations, a joint command, a joint system of supply, joint division of booty, a joint commission for settling differences, voluntary mobilization, and even "the creation of provisional authorities . . . to consist of representatives of all political groups which were willing to fight the invaders."[2] In retrospect it is clear that Mihailovich would have done well to accept this offer. But he boggled at joint operations, voluntary mobilization, and the proposal to create provisional local authorities. None the less, Tito is said to have turned over to him, in exchange for a pledge to fight the Germans, 500 rifles from the Uzhitse factory. No agreement was reached, although the meeting was apparently friendly enough.

It is clear that Mihailovich was deeply suspicious of Tito. He loathed communism, and is said to have concluded from Tito's accent that his guest was a native Russian. Moreover, the frightful German massacre of some seven thousand Serbs at Kraguyevats on October 20, 1941 confirmed Mihailovich's view that German reprisals for guerrilla warfare would be so terrible as to threaten the Serb people with extermination. So he began to feel that it was the Communists, with their insistence on provoking reprisals, who were the greatest danger. He ordered them attacked at Uzhitse on November 2. The official Communist account maintains that the Chetniks were firing the very rifles which Tito had given them to use against the Germans. Though the Partisans surrounded the Chetniks, Tito allegedly ordered them not to press their victory because of a broadcast from Moscow, overheard by chance, which referred to Mihailovich as the leader of Yugoslav resistance.[3]

[2] Vladimir Dedijer, *Tito* (New York: Simon and Schuster, 1953), p. 165.

[3] Chetnik-Partisan relations were also embittered by a quarrel over the town of Pozhega, where the Chetniks had taken a Partisan commander off a train and shot him.

Civil war had begun, thus infinitely complicating the problems of Yugoslavia, already complex almost beyond human understanding. Here were two resistance movements, both extremely promising from the point of view of potential usefulness against the Germans, now irreconcilably at odds, one of them led by an officer soon to be War Minister of the government recognized by all the major allies, and the other by a fanatical Communist. In this tragic situation lay the origins of much bloodshed in Yugoslavia, much bewilderment and embarrassment in Washington, London, and Moscow, and much rejoicing among the Germans and Italians.

Indeed, a true picture of the Yugoslav situation was long denied to the west. It was rumored that Tito was not a man but a syndicate, that the initials T.I.T.O. stood for "Secret (Taina) International Terrorist Organization," and even that Tito was a woman. Commenting on these absurdities, a British paper sardonically suggested that the real answer to the riddle was that the Partisan movement strongly favored prohibition, and that the initials really stood for "Thrice-Intransigent Tee-totallers Onward." But in these early days the Partisans lacked publicity channels abroad. Churchill himself, no doubt influenced by the Serb propaganda emanating from the Yugoslav government-in-exile, clung until 1943 to the idea that the Partisans were Croatians operating in Croatia.

PARTISAN OPERATIONS AND ALLIED POLICY; AVNOJ

Actually their long war with the Germans and Italians, in which they distinguish seven major enemy "offensives," began in the fall and winter of 1941. The Germans drove the Partisans out of Uzhitse, in what in known as their first offensive. The Partisans retreated first to the Sanjak of Novibazar, from which they were driven by the second offensive (January 1942), and then to the east-Bosnian town of Focha. In the third offensive, they broke through an encirclement and moved supreme headquarters to western Bosnia (spring 1942). By fall, they were located in the town of Bihach. But this repeated movement of headquarters did not mean that the movement was on the wane. From 80,000 men at the end of 1941, it swelled to 150,000 in the fall of 1942. Its leadership wisely avoided pitched battles with superior German forces. Instead the Partisans eluded the enemy in the rough terrain, hit him and harassed him, and withdrew again.

And in the midst of military operations, Tito never forgot politics. At Bihach in the fall of 1942, he convened a congress of delegates, including representatives from several non-Communist political parties such as the Croatian Peasant Party and several Serbian parties, but with a Communist majority, which proceeded to elect an Anti-Fascist Council of the National Liberation of Yugoslavia (AVNOJ). He had wanted to elect a provisional government for the entire country, but Moscow restrained him. AVNOJ's program included the guarantee of equal rights to all the nationalities of Yugoslavia, respect for private property, and the postponement of any social change until national elections after the war had made known the popular will. It did provide, however, that in liberated territory "reactionary" authorities would be replaced by "popularly elected representatives." In this seemingly unexceptionable provision lay the seeds of future Communist domination of the local scene through "people's councils" (*odbors*).

In early 1943 the "fourth" Axis offensive, in which Chetnik troops participated, drove the Partisans southeast into Hertsegovina and Montenegro, where headquarters were located on rugged Mount Durmitor. In the midst of a fierce battle, at the height of the "fifth" offensive, the first British mission to Tito arrived, headed by Captain William Deakin, a history don at Oxford who had assisted Prime Minister Churchill in his historical writing. Deakin was wounded, and the Partisans again broke through, escaping to the north. The summer of 1943 also brought two events which were to prove decisive for the Partisan cause: the arrival by parachute of Fitzroy MacLean, a brilliant young alumnus of the Foreign Office with long experience in the USSR, and a good knowledge of Serbo-Croatian, as chief of the Allied Military Mission to Tito (he had one American with him); and the surrender of Italy to the western allies in September. Although Tito was at first extremely angry because he had not been informed in advance that the Italians were likely to surrender, the Partisans obtained great quantities of arms, and were able to use a certain number of Italian prisoners in various capacities. Even more important was MacLean's initial decision to recommend that the western allies send Tito arms and supplies. Supreme headquarters were now at Yaitse, in Bosnia.

This dry summary of Partisan operations in the first two years of the resistance conveys only faintly the drama of the action, which was punctuated by hairbreadth escapes in which Tito himself was often near capture or death. It fails completely to give a sense of the agony of the struggle: the armies were short of food and clothing, virtually without medicines, often very low on ammunition. Cold and hungry, they lived a hunted life. Every time they were attacked they had to retreat, taking their wounded with them, for it was the Axis practice to shoot all Partisan prisoners. Sometimes the starving forces staggering through the snow were subject to mass hallucinations. The record of the heroic performance of the Partisans has been described in detail by MacLean and by one of his officers, Stephen Clissold.

In Yaitse, political questions once more came to the fore. Tito wired Moscow on the eve of the Conference there of the Foreign Ministers of the big three, putting them on notice that the Partisans would not permit the King and the government-in-exile to return after the war because of their support for Mihailovich, whom he accused of collaborating with the Germans. He added that the National Liberation Committees headed by the anti-Fascist Councils were the only legal government of Yugoslavia. He also summoned the second session of AVNOJ, which set up the National Liberation Committee as a temporary cabinet or provisional government with Tito as Premier.

AVNOJ made Tito Marshal of Yugoslavia, and passed a resolution forbidding the King to return to the country, and postponing the whole question of the monarchy to a postwar election. Meanwhile, at Teheran, Roosevelt and Churchill, largely as a result of intelligence reports from inside Yugoslavia, had agreed to give large-scale military aid to the Partisans.

Though observers at the time did not doubt that Tito's bold political actions had the approval of Moscow, he had in fact acted without informing Stalin, and Stalin was very angry indeed. At the time, so Tito's official biographer declares, the Yugoslavs were puzzled by Stalin's anger: "not to create the National Committee, not to give the people in Yugoslavia a clear indication that they were fighting for a new Yugoslavia different in every way from the old Yugoslavia under the Karageorgevich dynasty, would have meant to renounce everything that had been achieved in two and a half years. It would have meant the end of the Yugoslav revolution."[4] Stalin probably feared that the United States and Britain would blame him for Tito's denunciation of the King, and might reconsider the decisions made at Teheran. No doubt, the willingness of Tito to act without Moscow approval augured that the Yugoslav revolution might later prove difficult for Moscow to manage.

Ironically enough, the western allies, convinced that Tito had Stalin's backing, and aware from their intelligence officers of the scope of the Partisan military effort, showed no alarm at the Yaitse political pronouncements, and the Soviet authorities, finding that their allies were more radical than they, officially announced that "events in Yugoslavia" were "positive facts that will contribute to the further successful struggle of the peoples of Yugoslavia against Hitlerite Germany," and bore witness "to the remarkable success of the new leaders of Yugoslavia in the cause of uniting all the people's forces of Yugoslavia." After these events at the end of 1943, it was clear that Tito had won his gamble. His movement was strong and growing. The western allies were about to make it stronger by stepping up their shipments of arms. Nobody had imposed any political conditions, or challenged the AVNOJ decisions. The contradictions between the AVNOJ decisions and the obligations of Britain and the United States to the Royal Yugoslav government were something for Churchill and Roosevelt, especially Churchill, to worry about. They need not concern Tito particularly. All that was asked of him was to go on doing what he fully intended to do in any case: kill Germans.

Now when we ask ourselves why so canny a politician and so convinced an enemy of communism as Churchill should have reached the decision to strengthen the hand of a dedicated Communist, we must seek the answer not only in the successes of Tito but in the failures of Mihailovich. The Chetnik forces had been strengthened by his appointment as Minister of War and by the BBC broadcasts in Serbo-Croatian, a chief source of news inside Yugoslavia, which had glorified his exploits. Guerrilla formations in other provinces, especially within the borders of Pavelich Croatia and Montenegro, now put

[4] Dedijer, *Tito*, pp. 209–210.

themselves under his command. But in these regions the Italians had made arrangements with many of these Serb bands to coöperate with them against the Partisans. Thus Mihailovich acquired subordinates who were already collaborating with the enemy. His belief that the Communists posed a greater threat than the Axis led him to turn a blind eye to this. Indeed, almost from the first, he had contacts with the Nedich puppet regime.

Mihailovich took active command of 15,000 Chetniks allied with the Italians in the Neretva valley in what the Partisans call the "fourth" offensive. He himself recommended to the government-in-exile that they award the Karageorge Star to Djevdjevich, a Hertsegovinian Chetnik officer deep in collaboration with the Italian General Roatta. Hitler personally wired Mussolini his objections to the Italian use of the Chetniks in the summer of 1943. As time wore on, Mihailovich found himself negotiating hopefully with nationalists in Hungary, Rumania, Bulgaria, Albania, and Greece, and before the end he was pushed into the position, ludicrous and horrible for a Serb nationalist, of negotiation with the Croat Ustasha. With the surrender of the Italians, the Chetniks soon found themselves allied with the Germans, as the Italians frantically sought protection from the Partisans against the efforts of the Germans to destroy them. More and more deeply Mihailovich was involved in the toils of collaboration. One of his closest personal friends and collaborators, Djurishich, simultaneously held a command for Nedich, and in 1943 tried to exterminate the Muslims, Croats, and pro-Partisans of the Sanjak. The massacres he perpetrated in this fantastic effort challenge comparison with the Ustasha-Muslim massacre of Serbs in Pavelich territory in 1941. The allied government could not remain in the dark forever: Mihailovich and his subordinate commanders were either inactive or fighting the Partisan forces who were fighting the Germans. As these facts became clearer, there was no choice for the allies: they had to support Tito; they had to abandon Mihailovich. So much was clear by the end of 1943, which finished with the "sixth" enemy offensive, driving Tito from Yaitse to Drvar, about 125 miles west, still in Bosnia.

Thus far we have concentrated our attention chiefly on Tito himself and the movements of his supreme headquarters. But the Partisan movement was active elsewhere as well.

SLOVENIA, MONTENEGRO, MACEDONIA

In Slovenia, the Partisans under Kardelj focused their efforts in the Italian-occupied Provincia di Lubiana, in view of the fierce German grip on the rest of the province. In Ljubljana itself the Slovene Communist secret police assassinated Clericals and collaborators. The Partisans preserved the core of the movement through a major Italian offensive, commanded by Rupnik and the Italian General Robotti, and launched by Mussolini himself in the spring of 1942. Weakened, Kardelj boldly moved headquarters nearer to the capital, in order to restore the prestige of the guerrillas. The courageous but somewhat simple-minded British liaison officer with the Slovene Partisan movement became a complete devotee. Mihailovich's agent in Slovenia, Major Novak, was at first deeply involved with the Clericals, and their so-called "White Guards," an anti-Partisan organization, and then formed his own "Blue Guard," which helped the Italians and the Whites in the offensive. In return he received an area of his own from the Italians. When Italy surrendered, the Whites and Blues were desperate, and were soon defeated by the Partisans, who executed all the prisoners they took. Immediately thereafter (October 1943), the local Communist-dominated committees of the "people's front" were summoned to send delegates to a Slovene assembly in Kochevye. Typical of similar Partisan-staged affairs, it included representatives of the Italian minorities in Slovenia, and the usual priest, to disarm the Clerical critic. Though the Germans were closing in once more, the Partisans had by the end of 1943 asserted themselves as the dominant resistance force in Slovenia.

In Montenegro, the Italians had initially leaned upon the support of the so-called "greens" (zelenashi), who had never accepted the original union of Montenegro with the other south-Slavs after the First World War. Strong only in the barren southern part of Montenegro, the "greens" were far less numerous and powerful than the "whites" (belashi), who had favored the union. On July 13, 1941, both Communists and Chetnik or nationalist forces arose and defeated the Italians, liberating the entire province except for the three chief garrison towns. Then Communists and nationalists fell out. The former, led by Djilas and Mosha Piyade (a Jewish intellectual, who had translated Marx into Serbian and learned Chinese while in the prisons of the royal regime), ruthlessly purged their own ranks, and by planting misleading evidence brought the reprisals of the Italians on the clans who would not join the Partisan movement. Nowhere were Communist excesses so ruthless as in Montenegro, where the leadership in these early phases completely ignored the popular front line so skillfully exploited elsewhere by Tito.

The disastrous results soon showed themselves when the Chetniks and Italians joined forces, and the Partisans were largely driven from the province, only to infiltrate back once more early in 1942, when, incorrigible, they even proclaimed Montenegro a part of the USSR. Here in the land where pro-Russian sentiment had since the seventeenth century been stronger than anywhere else in Europe, the twentieth-century Communists maintained the old tradition. But by June 1942 the Italians and Chetniks had triumphed a second time. Now the "greens" won the south, and the Chetniks the two other regions into which the province was divided. Tito, who as yet had no British mission, wrongly suspected that the British, as well as the excesses of zeal demonstrated by his own followers, were to blame for the Partisan defeat and for the transformation of Montenegro into a Chetnik stronghold, to which Mihailovich himself now made his way. Tito absorbed the remnants of the defeated Montenegrin partisans into his own forces, and withdrew from the province. It was not until after the Italian surrender that the Partisans were able to reassert themselves there; but then they captured and executed the leading Chetniks, and began again to do battle, this time with the Germans.

In Macedonia, that eternal Balkan sore spot of rival nationalisms, Bulgarian Communists and Yugoslav Communists proved as deeply chauvinist as if they had been old-fashioned bourgeois parties. Despite the Bulgarian occupation, from the first Tito hoped to assert the claim of his own Yugoslav Communist Party to operate in the province, and even to push across the old Bulgarian frontier into "Pirin" or Bulgarian Macedonia. He had long justly suspected the leader of the Yugoslav Communist Party in Macedonia, "Sharlo" (Metody Shatarov), of pro-Bulgarian sympathies. In April 1941 Sharlo dissolved the Yugoslav party and went off to Sofia, refusing to heed a summons to come to Belgrade. The Bulgarian party declared its sole right to operate in the province.

When Sharlo returned to Macedonia, he refused to circulate the Yugoslav Communist directive to conceal all arms from the occupying authorities, and Tito sent Lazar Kolishevsky, a Macedonian Communist, to Skoplye to combat Sharlo, and to push the Tito line of preparation for a general resistance. As soon as Russia was invaded, Tito formally expelled Sharlo, who issued his own call to the Macedonians, not for an armed uprising on the Yugoslav pattern, but only for boycott of the war against the USSR, in which Bulgaria, as a German satellite, might become involved. Making no reference to Yugoslavia, he referred only to "free Soviet Macedonia." The Bulgarian party supported Sharlo.

The Comintern now ruled that the Tito line of an armed struggle against the occupier was correct, and that the Bulgarian party must help the Yugoslavs, but added that the two parties must teach a common line on Macedonian self-determination. Though the Bulgarians accepted the ruling in principle, they kept Sharlo in Macedonia, and he and other Bulgarian Communist leaders continued their rivalry with Kolishevsky. The first Partisan units in Macedonia, formed by Kolishevsky, were liquidated late in 1942 by Bulgarian regulars. The authorities interned Kolishevsky, and Yugoslav Communist influence was greatly reduced. The Bulgarian Communists failed to raise new units, urging instead that local Communists enter the regular Bulgarian army when drafted, and thus presumably bore from within. This was the line of the Bulgarian, not of the Yugoslav, party.

Early in 1943, Tito sent to Macedonia Svetozar Vukmanovich (Tempo), a Montenegrin who had worked in Skoplye before. He sought Macedonian support for Tito by assuring the Macedonians that the Yugoslav party would look with pleasure on the eventual union of all Macedonia (Yugoslav, Bulgarian, and Greek) within the framework of a federal Yugoslavia. Meanwhile the Macedonians would have autonomy, and could use their own language freely. Since the Macedonian nationalists were by now thoroughly disillusioned with the Bulgarizing occupation forces, this approach won much support. Tempo was a skillful operator with long experience as a specialist in running illegal printing presses. He now harnessed the passionate Macedonian nationalism to the Yugoslav Communist movement.

Tempo decided to transfer the preparation of Partisan units from the tightly held Bulgarian portion of Macedonia to the western, Albanian-Italian, region, where the authorities were less efficient, and the peasantry was suffering from Albanian excesses. This activist policy paid dividends. Sharlo and the other Bulgarian Communists were withdrawn, and by August 1943, the former Regional Committee for Macedonia of the Yugoslav Communist Party had become the Central Committee of the Macedonian Communist Party. In conformity with the practice elsewhere, it busied itself with the creation of a "National Liberation Front" and decided to call an "Anti-Fascist Assembly." A Macedonian General Staff was founded, which issued manifestoes to the Macedonian people to win their freedom within the framework of Tito's Yugoslavia, and, be it noted, to achieve their unity (meaning acquisition of Bulgarian and Greek territory). The Yugoslavs had won, and the Bulgarians were in retreat.

In the Yaitse declaration of November 1943, no more was said about the achievement of Macedonian unity. This document, issued without the consent or foreknowledge of Moscow, was radical enough already without seeming to claim Greek and Bulgarian territory. It might be safe to make such claims in propaganda designed for Macedonian consumption, but it was more prudent to omit them from a document intended for the three major allies. So the Yaitse declaration confined itself to mentioning Macedonia as one of the future Yugoslav federal republics. That Moscow approved at least this much was made strikingly clear by the appearance on the Titoite Macedonian Anti-Fascist Council of Dimiter Vlahov, in his youth an IMRO man and Bulgarian official, but later for years Macedonian delegate to the Comintern, and proponent of a Balkan Soviet federation of which Macedonia should be one member. Vlahov was now a convert to the Tito solution. Despite the fact that Moscow publicly endorsed the Yaitse declaration, the Bulgarian party continued for some time to call for the old federation solution and to repudiate the Yugoslav line. No doubt it is true that the Bulgarian party was in part forced to take this position in order to maintain in existence its "Fatherland Front" coalition of bourgeois parties, which we shall shortly examine, but in part the nationalist instincts of the Bulgarian Communists themselves must also have been asserting themselves.

ALBANIA

In Albania, as we have seen, there were under King Zog's rule no political parties. As a doctrine, however, communism had won a few adherents especially in the towns of the south.[5] But it could hardly thrive amid a population largely Muslim, illiterate, agrarian, and governed by the rigorous security measures of King Zog. It exercised more influence, however, among some of the Albanians whom the regime had sent abroad to be educated and prepared for the civil service, and among the handful of other Albanians who could properly be called "intellectuals" in the continental sense. Dr. Sejfulla Malleshova, for example, who had once been secretary to Bishop Fan Noli, had been a party member even in the 1920's, had won the sobriquet of "Lame Kodra," the red poet, and had distinguished himself as a propagandist and conspirator. Mustafa Gjinishi, younger than Malleshova, had also been exiled in the twenties, and had lived in Paris.

Paris indeed had been a center for Albanian Communists. Here too had labored Lazar Fundo, originally a Vlach from Korcha, who worked both in Europe and in Asia for the Comintern during the twenties and thirties.[6] Apparently denounced by Malleshova during the purges as a right-wing deviationist, Fundo was cleared in Moscow, on the intervention of Georgi Dimitrov, and was sent back to Paris. But his visit to the USSR had convinced him that Stalin was murdering good Communists solely to enhance his own power, and Fundo now actually did become a deviationist. By 1939 he had become the arch-heretic of the Albanian movement, alleged leader of a Trotskyite faction, but apparently in truth a believer in social democracy. Arrested and interned by the Italians in the summer of 1939, he was in a concentration camp until 1943. Many of the Paris Albanian Communists had been shipped back to Albania by the Germans after the fall of France in 1940, and were left at large by the Italians during the period of the Soviet-German pact, since they were helping the Axis by denouncing the "imperialist" war.

It was the Yugoslavs who rescued the Albanian Communists from faction and impotence, established the first Albanian Communist Party, and gave its leaders the guidance for their resistance to the Italians. The story of this relationship from the Yugoslav point of view was published in Serbo-Croatian in 1949,[7] but so far as I know has never been made available in any summary in a western language. Yet the full implications are of major importance for recent Balkan history.

As early as 1939, the account runs, realizing that the Albanian Communist movement was ineffectual, Tito sent to Albania Miladin Popovich (party-name: Ali), Secretary of the district (oblast) committee of the Yugoslav

[5] Ali Kelmendi, for example, strove during the thirties to create class-consciousness among the working population of Korcha, and to lay the foundations for a future Communist Party. Imprisoned for a while, he lived in exile in Turkey and in France, and edited Albanian-language Communist papers. He died of tuberculosis before the outbreak of the Second World War.

[6] According to his own story as told to Julian Amery, he had once briefed Tito, who, he said, had been regarded in Moscow as distinguished for loyalty and courage rather than for brains.

[7] Vladimir Dedijer, *Jugoslovensko-Albanski Odnoši* (*1939–1948*) (Belgrade, 1949).

Communist Party for Kossovo-Metohiya (its headquarters were near Pech, Ipek). Popovich's mission was to explain the equivocal role of Fundo and to assist the Albanian comrades to build a party. When war came, Popovich was captured and interned near Elbasan. The Yugoslavs then sent Dushan Mugosha (party name: Sali or Duch), who made several trips to Albania in 1941, and who arranged for the Albanians to liberate Popovich from jail. Together, Popovich and Mugosha held meetings and conferences in Tirana with members of the Albanian Communist "groups."

Of these there were eight, two of which were "Trotskyite." The three most important were the "Korcha" group, the "Shkodra" group, and the "youth" group. The "Korcha" group, the oldest, included Kocho Tashko, a former diplomat who had served in Moscow, but was now in private employment; Koci Xoxe (Dzodze), tinsmith; Mihalj Lako, a worker; and Enver Hoxha (Hoja). Hoxha had studied in France and Belgium, had served as secretary of the Albanian Royal Legation in Brussels, and had taught in the French *lycée* in Korcha, but had now been expelled from state service, and was selling tobacco in Tirana. Others were Nako Spiro, son of the owner of a tobacco factory, and Djevdet Dodu, a teacher in Tirana. It was of this Korcha group, whose leaders now lived in Tirana, that Fundo had once been a member. Though ridden by "opportunism" and "social democratic" errors, this group appealed to the Yugoslav Communist envoys, because its membership had a better balance between intellectuals and workers than the others. It had also started organizations similar to trade unions, in which discussions were held, and the Yugoslavs thus concluded that it had more "contact with the masses" than the others. It had not yet, however, reached the "correct" conclusions with regard to fighting the Italians.

The "Shkodra" group was the one with which the Kos-Met committee had first come into contact, since its headquarters were immediately across the frontier from Yugoslavia, and it had repeatedly asked for assistance. Founded in 1938, it had included as one of its early members Zef Malje, who wrote a book on the economic development of Albania, in which he blamed "imperialist" intervention for delaying the growth of capitalism and the development of a proletariat, and maintained that revolution would be impossible so long as Albania remained at its then economic level. Others were Vasili Shanto, a bakery-worker, Fadil Hoxha, Emin Duraku, and, especially prominent, the carpenter Tuk Jakova, and the woman intellectual Liri Gega. The Yugoslav observers found the chief merit of this group in its contact with young people in the schools, and its issuance of an occasional manifesto.

"Youth" was more dubious; apparently its members impressed the Yugoslavs as little more than a gang of thieves with strong Trotskyite leanings, though undoubtedly brave, resolute, and eager for self-sacrifice. They seem to have engaged in robbery, bringing the proceeds in to the leadership. Membership included Hysni Kapo, an intellectual from Valona, Bedri Spahiu, an officer from Gjinokaster, Ramadan Citaku, privately employed, and Sadik

Staveleci, a student in a technical school. Alone among the groups, "youth" had some cells: three-man units or "troikas." Because recruitment into all three groups was by personal contact, there had never been any general Communist congresses. The "Fire" group in Tirana was of less interest.

The two Yugoslavs summoned a meeting in Tirana on November 8, 1941, attended by some twenty leaders of the three groups they considered most promising, and the Albanian Communist Party was now actually founded. A central committee of eleven was chosen, with Enver Hoxha as provisional secretary, at least two other members of the Korcha group, four from the Shkodra group, and two from "youth."[8] Immediately afterwards, a Communist youth organization was set up, with two members of the Central Committee in key places. The country was divided into regions and subregions for party organization, and demonstrations and rioting began at once, together with acts of sabotage, the assassination of Italian soldiers and police agents, and the formation of the first Partisan detachments. Inexperience greatly hampered these early endeavors. The official "History of the Communist Party of the Soviet Union (Bolshevik)" and "Foundations of Leninism," for instance, were unavailable, and had to be hastily translated into Albanian by comrades who knew English, Italian, and Serbian. The Albanians took over the Yugoslav slogan — "Death to fascism, liberty to the people," and wore the red star.

In May 1942, Dushan Mugosha came out to western Bosnia to report to Tito, and in September returned to Albania bearing a letter from Tito, in which he gave his Albanian comrades the line: build a common front of Communists and all Albanian nationalists and patriots willing to fight the enemy; work in the villages to recruit Partisan detachments; establish a clear line of authority between the appropriate party unit and each military unit.

In September 1942, at a conference at Peza, the Communist leadership met with leaders of "patriotic" elements who were strongly anti-Communist, representing the Ghegs of the north, among whom, save in Shkodra itself, communism had never commanded any support. These included Abas Kupi, whom the British had sponsored as a leader of the United Front in Belgrade before the invasion of Yugoslavia; Myslim Peza, an old enemy of Zog, who had been engaged in guerrilla activities for years in the north; Haxhi Lleshi of Dibra; two stalwart abbots of Bektashi monasteries or tekkés, Baba Faya Martaneshi and Baba Feza of Malakastre; Muharrem Bajraktar, a northern

[8] The first Central Committee and previous "group" affiliation was as follows: Enver Hoxha (Korcha), Ymer Dishnitsa (previous "group" unknown, but a doctor of medicine, young, who had studied in France and Belgium), Xhemal Shtafa (Shkodra), Ramadan Citaku ("youth"), Koci Xoxe (Korcha), Nako Spiro (Korcha), Kristo Temeljko (Shkodra), Tuk Jakova (Shkodra), Liri Gega (Shkodra), Bedri Spahiu ("youth"), Kadri Hoxha (previous "group" unknown). When Julian Amery wrote his most interesting book, *Sons of the Eagle* (London, 1948), dealing with his experiences among the Albanian nationalist resistance, he had no access to the materials summarized above. He wrote (p. 54): "Mystery still surrounds the beginnings of the Albanian Partisan movement," and was unable to give a coherent or accurate account.

tribal leader and former Zogist officer, and others. Together with the Communists they formed a National Liberation Movement (Levizje National Clirimtare), regularly abbreviated as LNC. A central council of ten members included both Communists and nationalists. But, as Amery explains, the tribal nature of the Gheg nationalist leaders' influence over their supporters rendered it necessary for them to spend most of their time with their constituents, preventing blood feuds among them and keeping their forces in being, while the Communists in practice determined the policies of the LNC. Moreover, the Communists were able to penetrate the forces of Baba Faya and of Myslim Peza, while Abas Kupi alone of the Gheg leaders kept Communist political commissars out of his forces.

The LNC union of Communists and nationalists in Albania did not, however, prevent the emergence of a purely nationalist resistance group, comparable to that of Mihailovich in Yugoslavia. Appearing also toward the end of 1942, this was called the Balli Kombetar (National Union), regularly abbreviated as BK. Most of its leaders were southerners, many of them landowners, usually opponents of Zog, and republicans. Some were liberal and democratic by western standards, such as Midhat Frasheri, a distinguished intellectual, with past experience in the Ottoman administration, but an enemy of Zog, who for some years had been running a bookshop in Tirana, and occasionally writing pamphlets. Though naturally anti-Soviet and pro-English and American, the Balli Kombetar none the less feared that an allied victory would mean the restoration of Kossovo to Yugoslavia; as nationalists, the leaders opposed and dreaded this. Moreover, as large owners of property, their enthusiasm for the rough and tumble of guerrilla warfare and its consequent destruction was somewhat limited. British liaison officers joined the Albanian resistance movements in early 1943, and reported on the high military morale of the Communist-led units, whose leaders were none the less deeply suspicious of the British, and clearly as much interested in the elimination of possible future political rivals in Albania as in killing Italians.

At every stage the Albanian Partisans had Yugoslav advice and help. On his trip to Macedonia in 1943, Tempo also came to Albania, and participated in military action as well as urging active opposition to the Balli Kombetar. As in Yugoslavia, village and town councils were set up in "liberated" territory; political commissars served in each unit. Dushan Mugosha and Miladin Popovich presided over the main decisions.

The allied victories of 1943 in Sicily and Italy led the Albanians to anticipate the Italian defeat, and to plan for their own political future. The Communists now began to direct most of their efforts to attacking the Balli Kombetar. With British encouragement, Abas Kupi tried to make peace between the two groups, which disagreed on the Kossovo question. The Communists, Yugoslav-dominated, could not approve of the nationalist program of annexing it. At Mukaj in July 1943, the LNC and BK representatives reached agreement, stimulated by the news of Mussolini's fall. Wild enthusiasm brought thousands of new recruits to the guerrilla forces, which had hitherto numbered perhaps eight or ten thousand in all. The five and a half Italian divisions soon disintegrated before the Partisan attacks; they were disarmed but not mistreated; the Communists occupied most of the main southern cities, except for Valona, which was a BK stronghold. The nationalist leaders of the LNC scored successes in the north.

But before the guerrillas could capture Tirana, and take complete control over the entire country, the Germans intervened. A parachute division landed and saved the capital. Moving both north and south against LNC nationalists and Communists as well as against BK, the Germans soon recaptured the main centers, and drove the guerrillas into the hills. With limited numbers of troops to use in policing Albania, the Germans now embarked on a "soft" policy for the country. The Italians had used a native quisling regime since their occupation in 1939. Now the Germans announced that after the war Albania would be independent. They set free many patriots imprisoned by the Italians, and, following the constitutional forms established after the departure of Prince Wilhelm zu Wied in 1914, established a four-man regency to act for a future king. They never specifically made any statement to the effect that Zog himself would be objectionable to them, and thus seemed to be leaving open the way to his restoration. In this way they made an effective bid for the support of Zogists. Then too, the Germans had no commitment with regard to the returning of Kossovo to Yugoslavia; so that all nationalists interested in keeping it — and they were legion — were also attracted to the German cause. In Kossovo itself, the Germans sponsored the so-called "Second League of Prizren," an organization devoted to Albania's retention of the territory.

The members of the regency were thoroughly honorable, and each represented one of the four religious groups in the country. Mehdi Frasheri, cousin of Midhat, the BK leader, enlightened and pro-western, was the Bektashi member; Fuad Dibra, the Sunni; Lef Nosi, the Orthodox Christian; and Rev. Anton Harapi, a Franciscan, the Roman Catholic. A new government was formed under the regency, also made up of moderate and respectable Albanians. Albanians in general had nothing against Germans, who had never oppressed them or acted "incorrectly." As a piece of political warfare, the German policy was a great success, since it strongly tempted all except the Communists to collaborate with them. German troops protected the coastal plain against a possible allied landing, held the principal towns and roads, and left the rest of the country pretty much alone. The forces of the government were mostly Kossovars under the direct control of the Minister of the Interior, Xhafer Deva, himself a strong Albanian nationalist from Kossovo, and the head of the "Second League of Prizren."

Faced with this new situation, Enver Hoxha and the Communists let the Mukaj agreement go by the board, and launched a series of attacks on the BK, forcing them back into the fringes of German-held territory, and consolidating their own administration of the areas which they occupied. The

BK leaders made contact with their like-minded friends in the Tirana government, hoping that a counterforce to the Communists could still be mobilized. And the Germans quickly seized the opportunity to rearm the BK forces and to use them against their Communist enemies. Now Hoxha was able to claim — and technically he was correct — that his nationalist enemies were collaborating with the Germans. BK was thus discredited in the eyes of the allies.

Hoxha and the Communists, by violating the Mukaj agreement, now drove Abas Kupi from the LNC. He had been perfectly willing to coöperate with the Communists so long as they truly formed a national front of all anti-Italian elements, and confined their efforts to liberation. But as a stanch Zogist, he now could do nothing except consolidate his support in the areas where he had a strong following — Kruya, his own home base, the Mati region, Zog's native area, and the neighborhood of Tirana itself. He now in December 1943 announced the formation of the so-called "Legality" (Legalitet) movement of Zogists. Though offered the opportunity, Hoxha flatly refused to collaborate with him, and Kupi thus became the leader of the only resistance movement which was both anti-German and anti-Communist.

CONCLUSION

By the end of 1943, then, Tito had transformed his Partisan movement into a massive army. With Bosnia as its center, it was holding down and harassing the Germans, whose attempts to extirpate it Tito had repeatedly foiled. In every province of the country, he had scored signal successes, not only over the Germans and the defeated Italians, but over the bewildering collection of native forces arrayed against him: Slovene blues, whites, and "Rupniks," Croatian Ustashe and Domobrantsi, Montenegrin greens, pro-Bulgarian Communists in Macedonia, and above all Mihailovich's Chetniks, scattered through Bosnia, Hertsegovina, Dalmatia, and Montenegro. Serbia, where the Partisan movement had begun, remained to be conquered, but even the combination of Nedich and Mihailovich could not prevent this crowning achievement.

And while still hard beset at home, Tito had seized the opportunity to reorganize the Albanian Communists, direct the formation of the first Albanian Communist Party, and teach its backward but willing leadership the lessons of the resistance. In Albania, Hoxha's armies had succeeded in forcing the BK into collaboration with the Germans, and Abas Kupi was the only native leader who stood between the Communists and complete victory. It is sometimes said that the USSR had taken a direct hand in organizing the movement in Albania, but this is apparently untrue. As late as 1946, Stalin allegedly professed himself to be almost totally uninformed about the personalities of the Albanian leaders, asked Tito for information about their internal disagreements, and agreed that Tito should continue to take care of difficulties within the Albanian party.

Everywhere, political activity had kept pace with military operations. From local people's councils and liberation committees, Tito had proceeded to form AVNOJ and a rudimentary future government. At Yaitse he had with some insolence warned the allies against commitments to the royal government. And he had got away with it.

The crowning irony was that the British and, in their wake, the Americans, had supported him more effectively and enthusiastically than had the USSR, whose only assistance had been the broadcasts from the so-called Free Yugoslavia Radio, located in Soviet Georgia. Stalin had repeatedly refused to send even token amounts of military supplies, each time alleging that the Soviet Union could spare nothing from its own struggle, and counseling patience and continued suffering. There were no Russian representatives in Yugoslavia. But Britain and the United States had sent first observers and then supplies, not of course in anything like the amounts which Tito would have liked, but still in useful quantities. More important, a trans-Adriatic supply-line was now being built up, and a regular flow could shortly be expected. Still more important, the western allies had convinced themselves that Mihailovich was collaborating with the enemy, and decided that they could no longer help him. The situation had changed completely since 1941, when the BBC had attributed Partisan successes to Mihailovich. Indeed, in 1943, on at least one important occasion, it attributed to the Partisans the demolition of an important bridge which the Chetniks had actually blown up under the prodding of allied representatives.

In retrospect, the historian can see that, though much remained to accomplish, Tito had won his struggle in Yugoslavia itself by the end of 1943. He now moved into the area of high allied diplomacy to assure himself that he could hold and extend his gains.

3. Occupation and Resistance (2): *Yugoslavia and Albania from the End of 1943 to the Liberation of Southeast Europe in the Fall of 1944*

TITO AND STALIN

According to the official biography of Tito, it was Radio Moscow's startling publicity in late 1941 for Mihailovich as leader of the Yugoslav resistance that led Tito, in the midst of a successful operation against the Chetniks, to issue to his subordinates, despite his disappointment, the following order: "We must not destroy Drazha Mihailovich although we have surrounded him. We must be careful not to cause difficulties in the foreign relations of the Soviet Union."[9] The anecdote illustrates Moscow's extreme caution in acknowledging Tito as its agent, a caution which did not disappear even with his successes. Not only did the Russians turn down the repeated requests for supplies, but they kept urging Tito to conceal even more thor-

[9] Dedijer, *Tito,* p. 168.

oughly the Communist character of his movement. In 1942 they complained that the British and the Royal Yugoslav government would suspect the Partisan movement "of acquiring a Communist character and aiming at the Sovietization of Yugoslavia." "Why," asked Moscow, "did you need to form a special Proletarian Brigade? . . . Are there really no other Yugoslav patriots, apart from the Communists and the Communist sympathizers, with whom you could join in a common struggle against the invaders?"[10]

At the same time, the Russians expressed doubts of Tito's charges that the government-in-exile was siding with the invaders. Moscow continued to refer to Mihailovich as a brave warrior against the Germans. Late in 1942, the Russians proposed to send a military mission and supplies to the Chetniks, but the royal government refused unless the Partisans were ordered not to attack the Chetniks, unless the Partisans were put under Mihailovich's command, and unless the radio and press campaign against Mihailovich should cease. On this, the Royal Yugoslav ambassador in the USSR commented: "Here in Russia, impossible to read or hear anything against Mihailovich. If there is a campaign in the foreign press, it is not reported here."[11] Tito's feelings must have been badly bruised when he was told that he was not making enough of an effort to hide his politics, but it is hard to visualize his state of mind when he discovered after the war that at a time when the existence of his whole movement was in jeopardy for lack of supplies, and the Russians were refusing his requests, they were actually offering supplies to Mihailovich. We have already seen how angry Stalin was at the news that Tito's Yaitse decision at the end of 1943 barred the King from returning.

Looking back at these wartime developments after their expulsion from the Cominform in 1948, the Yugoslav Communists interpreted Stalin's extremely cautious attitude toward the Partisan movement to mean that, while he was interested in the fight against the Germans, he was also determined to prevent the growth of any Communist movement which would have its own institutions and would not be entirely dependent on the USSR. They could explain in no other way the fact that Stalin played down the Partisans in all his propaganda, despite his receipt of full information daily from a secret transmitter located in Zagreb. Though this Yugoslav Communist interpretation may well have some validity, it is also entirely probable that Stalin, hard-pressed by the Germans, in desperate need of assistance from allies whom he did not know very well and whom he did not trust, felt it tremendously important in 1941, 1942, and 1943 to lull their suspicions. Imputing to Great Britain and to the United States an attitude as suspicious as his own, he seems to have feared that, if his allies should become convinced that he or his agents intended to communize Yugoslavia after the war, he might be subjected to unpleasant pressures. Perhaps he even feared that the western allies would cease to help him or make a deal with Hitler and change sides.

[10] *Tito,* p. 180.
[11] *Tito,* p. 182.

But by the end of 1943 he had seen the west adopt Tito. And in early 1944, assured by now that the alliance with the west would bring eventual victory over the Germans and thus save the USSR and his own regime, Stalin unbent toward Tito. For the first time he sent him a personal answer to a telegram. More important, he sent a Soviet military mission, headed by a general, whose members, symbolically enough, refused to parachute and could not land in Yugoslavia by plane because of heavy snow, so that they were brought in by British glider from Italy. Though their arrival was the occasion for great celebrations at Partisan headquarters, there was nothing much for them to do. Soon afterward (spring, 1944), Tito sent a military mission to Moscow, headed by Djilas. Though Stalin now arranged for some Russian planes to drop supplies to the Partisans, he was noncommittal about recognizing the Tito government as the legal government of the country. And he allegedly said to Djilas: "What do you need the red stars for? You are frightening the British. The form isn't important."[12] He was still maintaining his connections with the royal government, and even suggested that a Yugoslav brigade being formed in the USSR of refugees, Croat war-prisoners and deserters, and others should use the royal emblem, agreeing only under pressure to change it to the red star.

THE YUGOSLAV GOVERNMENT-IN-EXILE, THE ALLIES, AND THE RESISTANCE

Meanwhile, the British, having determined to give all-out military support to Tito, were trying somehow to reconcile the Yugoslav government-in-exile to their policies, and to bring King Peter and Tito into some sort of relationship. The government-in-exile, even when driven from Yugoslavia in 1941 under the hero of the Serb coup, General Dushan Simovich, had been made up largely of elderly politicians preoccupied with the traditional Serb-Croat rivalry. Few of the Serbs really accepted the *Sporazum* between Prince Paul and the Croats, and most of them looked on the war as a chance to aggrandize Serbia. They refused to commit themselves to recognize the Croatian Banovina, and blamed the Croats for the German victory. The Croats, on the other hand, would not help do the government's business in the absence of such a guarantee. The Ustasha massacres only inflamed opinion still more. The Serbian politicians spread anti-Croat propaganda everywhere, and became less "Yugoslav" and more "great Serb" in their outlook with each passing day. The politicians were backed up, or even outdone, by the diplomats, men who had been sent out under King Alexander or Prince Paul, and by the Serbian army officers gathered in the middle east. The Yugoslav Ambassador to the United States, for example, Constantin Fotich, who was a relative both of General Nedich and of Lyotich, leader of the Serbian Fascists, showed himself bitterly anti-Croat, and quite naturally acted as the spokesman for Serb nationalism.

General Simovich gave way as Premier first to Professor Slobodan Yovanovich (January 1942), who was succeeded by Milosh Trifunovich (June 1943),

[12] Dedijer, *Tito*, p. 215.

and soon after by Bozhidar Purich. Purich had been Minister to Paris, and his government was designed to eliminate political squabbling and install responsible technicians, but he was the son-in-law of Nikola Pashich himself, and hardly conciliatory to the Croats. All of the premiers and their governments were Serb chauvinists, clung doggedly to Mihailovich, and refused to make any effort to come to terms with the Partisans. Politicians voted themselves large salaries, King Peter's own being enormously larger than that of the President of the United States, while cash reserves melted away. American aid to the government-in-exile was limited chiefly to the gift of four Liberator bombers (October 1943), to be flown by Yugoslav aviators trained in the United States. The bomber-crews fought bravely, and three of the planes were shot down.

In 1942, the Yovanovich government had refused a Soviet offer of a treaty of mutual assistance, on the ground that small powers should not make such treaties with the major allies until after the war. At the end of 1943, however, Purich asked the Russians to conclude such a treaty, on the model of one already concluded with the Czechs. The Russians politely asked the government-in-exile to settle its factional differences first, a suggestion which was at first interpreted as meaning that Purich should make some sort of approach to Tito. But early in February 1944, Tass remarked that the Yugoslav government's offer of an alliance had caused amazement in the USSR, because of the "pro-fascist" role of General Mihailovich. Aware that the western allies were finished with Mihailovich, the Russians now hardened their own attitude toward his government. The Moscow press now launched a series of unbridled attacks on Mihailovich, coupled with fulsome praise of Tito. The ambassador of the royal government to the USSR resigned; Tito congratulated him, and appointed him to be his own representative in Moscow, the Soviet government giving him full diplomatic privileges, but simultaneously assuring the British that they would not sever connections with the royal government without giving suitable advance notice.

Meanwhile, Churchill, in personal correspondence with Tito for the first time, wrote reassuringly: the British would help Tito alone, but could not break relations with King Peter. In a general way, he urged that political enmities be forgotten. To this Tito replied that he fully understood the British relationship with the King, and added that he would try to avoid embarrassing the British by frequent propaganda attacks on Peter. Churchill now wrote that he had hesitated to ask King Peter to dismiss General Mihailovich as Minister of War only because this might seem tantamount to requiring the King to jettison his only loyal supporter; would the dismissal of Mihailovich, he asked, provide a better basis for relations between Peter and Tito? Though the question of the return of the dynasty must await liberation, Churchill agreed that an agreement between the King and Tito would bring the Partisans a good deal of support in Serbia, where they were weakest. But the British themselves had already weakened their bargaining power with Tito by assuring him that he alone would receive military support from them. They had thus deprived him of his chief incentive to work for an understanding with King Peter.

Soon thereafter (late February 1944), the British decided to withdraw their missions to Mihailovich, and cut off all supplies to him. The United States decided to maintain its own contacts with Mihailovich, partly for intelligence purposes, partly because the American air forces based in Italy were undertaking raids over central and southeast Europe, and it was necessary to encourage him to assist us in case planes were shot down and their crews landed in Yugoslavia. As things turned out, Mihailovich was extremely helpful in rescuing American aviators, and a fresh American mission was sent to him as late as the fall of 1944.

Meanwhile, in the spring, in a belated gesture designed to regain some allied support and to set up a rival to Tito's "government," Mihailovich held a large meeting in Gorni Milanovats, Serbia, attended by a variety of delegates from prewar Serbian parties, and formed a "Yugoslav Democratic Popular Union," which denounced Tito, declared that freedom must be won for the Serbian people, and elected Dr. Zhivko Topalovich as president. Topalovich had been the leader of the prewar Yugoslav Socialist Party, a small Serbian group, which the regime of King Alexander had used largely to counter the weight of Croat trade unionists, and to demonstrate that the "working class" of Serbia was allowed its own political life. Most of the other leading figures were great Serbs, and at least two had had intimate connections with the authoritarian Stoyadinovich. The whole effort was a rather pathetic effort at political warfare, which could not inspire renewed British confidence in Mihailovich. During these months, too, pro-Partisan sentiment became more and more manifest among the Yugoslav military and naval forces of the government-in-exile in Egypt and Libya, while General Dushan Simovich himself, leader of the coup of March 1941, but ousted as premier by rival great-Serb intriguers early in 1942, publicly announced his support for Tito, thus putting himself forward as possible head of a new government designed to bring about a working arrangement with the Partisans.

Early in March 1944, the King returned from Cairo to England, where he married Princess Alexandra of Greece, a step which he had long wished to take, and which had been approved by Mr. Churchill himself in one of his most pungent and entertaining "minutes,"[13] but which had been opposed by the politicians as "un-Serbian." The Communists took the opportunity to argue that Peter had put his personal happiness ahead of the national interest, and to launch in Serbia a song with the refrain "Tito fought while the King took a wife." For some weeks, politicking among the Yugoslavs not in office continued, as the British advised Peter to oust Purich, and to replace him with a moderate. Toward the end of April, Peter sent to the United States for Ivan Shubashich, Ban (governor) of the Croatian Banovina created by the Spora-

[13] Winston S. Churchill, *The Second World War*, V, *Closing the Ring* (Boston: Houghton Mifflin Company, 1951), 651–652.

zum, a Croat and follower of Machek. A moderate but not a strong man, Shubashich was finally appointed Premier on June 1, the first Croat ever to hold the office.

Expressing his admiration for "those fighting men and women, who, refusing to compromise with the enemy or his agents or to acquiesce in the enslavement of our beloved country, have banded themselves together to resist and fight the German invader," the King pleaded for unity and for the postponement of "all internal political issues until after the liberation of the country." The Shubashich government, Peter declared, could fulfill its task only "in collaboration with and support of all resistance elements in Yugoslavia. I have consequently directed the Ban of Croatia to establish relations with those elements before deciding upon the final composition of the government."[14] Thus the Purich regime, Mihailovich, and the great Serbs were dismissed together, and the King entrusted to Shubashich the negotiations with Tito, which, it was felt, must precede the formation of a government. Public opinion had been prepared for the dropping of Mihailovich by a speech in the House of Commons, in which Prime Minister Churchill declared: "He has not been fighting the enemy, and, moreover, some of his subordinates have been making accommodations with the enemy."[15]

THE ATTACK ON DRVAR, THE TITO-SHUBASHICH NEGOTIATIONS, THE PROBLEM OF SERBIA

During the last phases of these political maneuverings, the Germans launched a full-scale parachute attack on Tito's headquarters at Drvar. Tito himself barely escaped by climbing up the cliff in which his cave had been located. A British and an American newspaperman were captured, and the Germans claimed more than 6,000 prisoners. They massacred the civilian population of the district, which had been loyal to the Partisans. They captured Tito's brand-new uniform as Marshal of Yugoslavia with its Russian-made gold braid, and exhibited it in Vienna. These operations constituted the seventh and last "offensive." Tito himself was flown across the Adriatic to Bari, and then back to the Dalmatian island of Vis, which the British had decided to use as a main operational base for supplies to the Partisans. Vis now became the supreme headquarters of the Partisans. To Vis, after a session in Italy during which he interviewed Mihailovich's representative, Topalovich, Shubashich now came.[16]

On June 16, 1944, Tito and Shubashich reached a preliminary agreement: the new government which Shubashich was about to form should consist of

[14] *New York Times,* June 2, 1944.

[15] Fitzroy MacLean, *Eastern Approaches* (London, 1949), p. 438.

[16] Tito's followers have since reported that their chief held Shubashich responsible for the deaths of certain Croatian Communist leaders, who had been found in jail in 1941 by Pavelich and executed. Tito believed that Shubashich ought to have liberated the Communists and let them go into hiding before he himself fled the country. In any case, this grudge does not appear to have manifested itself at once.

"progressive democratic elements who were not compromised in the struggle against the National Liberation Movement," and its main task should be to organize aid to the National Liberation Army, to feed the population of Yugoslavia, and to coördinate the work of the missions abroad with the work inside the country. This clearly indicated that diplomats of great Serb leanings should be dropped. The two parties agreed jointly to appoint the organs for the continuation of the struggle, and "thereby facilitate the creation of a united representation as soon as possible." [17] They further agreed that the question of the monarchy would be settled after liberation, and Shubashich promised to issue a declaration recognizing the achievements of AVNOJ and its executive organ, the National Committee of Liberation, recognizing the Partisan army, and calling upon all Yugoslavs to join it. The agreement was to be made public as soon as Shubashich had formed a government. Though vague, this document was a step toward collaboration. Tito had made few concessions, and these grudgingly, but the stake of allied political recognition was a high one.

The great problem for the British and Shubashich now was to gain some Serb support for this agreement. It was suggested that Serbs enlisting in the liberation army might be allowed to wear the royal emblem, and Tito did not object. Shubashich's new government, announced early in July, included two Serbs, two Croats, and two Slovenes. Tito appointed two of its members himself, in accordance with the agreement, a Serb and a Slovene with no Communist associations and blameless records.[18] The other Serb, Sava Kosanovich, was also a member of the Independent Democratic Party. Both Serbs were from outside Serbia, and neither was regarded by the great Serb group as in any way representative of true Serbdom. Ambassador Fotich in Washington publicly refused to recognize the new regime, and declared his allegiance to the Mihailovich National Committee. The problem of winning Serb support continued to be as serious after the formation of the new government as before, and the King at one moment entertained the idea that he might appoint another Serb officer to Mihailovich's command, withdraw Mihailovich, and order his successor to coöperate with the Partisans. Mihailovich's National Committee reaffirmed its loyalty to the King, but announced a "negative attitude" toward the Shubashich government, and reserved "full liberty of action toward" it.

TITO AND CHURCHILL

The British now invited Tito to conferences at Allied Forces Headquarters at Caserta to discuss various military and operational problems with the theater commander, General Wilson, with Shubashich, and, they hoped, with King

[17] J. B. Tito, *Political Report of the Central Committee of the Communist Party of Yugoslavia* (Belgrade, 1948), pp. 113–114.

[18] Tito's appointees were Sreten Vukosavlyevich, an Independent Democrat (Serbs from outside Serbia proper) who was a native of the Sanjak, had been Professor at the University of Belgrade, and had accepted various positions in Partisan organizations, and Drago Marushich, a Slovene Agrarian, who had once been governor of Slovenia.

Peter as well. But at the last moment Tito refused to go to Italy, apparently under pressure from his fellow-Communists, who were deeply suspicious of any act which might lead to an agreement with the King, and did not relish their chief's leaving his headquarters on a summons from the British. Indeed, military and diplomatic success had by now given Tito something of a swelled head. He began to intimate that the two members of the new Cabinet whom he had selected were not truly "representative" of the Partisan movement (as indeed they were not, being non-Communists) but were only "respected" by the movement. Much was said about the need for AVNOJ confirmation of the arrangements just entered upon. But early in August, his initial hesitation actually overcome, Tito did consent to cross the Adriatic, and not only conferred at Caserta with Shubashich and General Wilson but also at Naples with Prime Minister Churchill himself, whose own account of the interview is now available.

Comfortable in white duck, Churchill affirmed his interest in the unity and independence of Yugoslavia. Sweltering but magnificent in his marshal's uniform, Tito repeated earlier statements that he had no intention of communizing the country, but declined to make an immediate public pronouncement to this effect for fear that it might seem to have been extracted from him, although he agreed to do so later. To suggestions that he meet with King Peter he replied that he had no objection in principle, but that the time had not yet come. He objected to Churchill's suggestion that the Partisans had not sufficiently recognized the "power and the rights" of the Serbian people, or that a "reconciliation" between the Serbs and the Partisans was essential. The two leaders also discussed the Istrian question, but reached no agreement. Tito and Shubashich agreed on a common use of the Yugoslav naval forces, and then returned to Vis to continue their discussions.

The picturesque details of the sessions are recorded by MacLean, in whose account we listen to Churchill himself warning Tito against collectivizing agriculture after the war:

> "My friend Marshal Stalin," he began [and I could see Tito sit up a little straighter at the mere mention of the name], "my friend Marshal Stalin told me the other day that his battle with the peasants had been a more perilous and formidable undertaking than the battle for Stalingrad. I hope that you, Marshal," [he added], "will think twice before you join such a battle with your sturdy Serbian peasantry." [19]

It is rewarding too to read the account written from the Yugoslav point of view by Dedijer, who gives a different impression of his chief's assurances on future communization:

"Churchill suddenly asked in the course of the conversation whether it was our intention to establish socialism in Yugoslavia on the Soviet model.

[19] MacLean, *Eastern Approaches,* pp. 465–466.

Tito's reply was that Soviet experience would be useful, but that we should take our own conditions into consideration."[20]

THE LAST PHASE OF THE FIGHTING

The Tito-Shubashich discussions on Vis looked toward a merger of their two governments into a single provisional Royal Yugoslav government, to remain in power until liberation and elections. But operations on the various fronts now changed the diplomatic picture. The Partisan campaign in Serbia had been going well. General Kocha Popovich, himself a Serb and the son of a Belgrade millionaire, but a Communist, was in command. Working northward from headquarters in the southern part of Serbia, Popovich made progress between April and August 1944 in overcoming the hostility of the Serbian peasants, still relatively prosperous in this area, and disinclined to take the risk of joining or aiding the guerrillas. In Serbia the terrain was far less favorable for Partisan operations than in Bosnia. But the cessation of allied supplies for Mihailovich and their steady flow to the Partisans impressed the population, who now saw where power would probably lie. Successful operations against the Germans brought captured weapons, and more recruits flocked in to take advantage of the amnesty offered by the Partisans to Chetniks and Nedich followers who would join them. And, as the end of occupation began to seem a real possibility and not a mirage, the Serbian mood, MacLean reports, swung strongly in favor of Tito and resistance to the enemy, especially as the Partisans played down the Communist character of their leadership, and publicized King Peter's summons to the Serbs to support Tito.

German opposition was beginning to crumble everywhere in the country. Pavelich Croatia was in a state of concentrated panic bordering on collapse. Bulgarian troops were beginning to surrender. Under MacLean's direction, the Partisans, supported by allied air-forces, everywhere coöperated in carrying out a campaign of blowing up key communications lines to prevent easy German withdrawal. Of course this military situation in Yugoslavia was the direct result of the allied advances in France and Italy, and the Russian advance into Poland and southeast Europe, where, on August 23, 1944, the Rumanians surrendered, and a little over two weeks later the Bulgarians too were out of the war.

On September 21, during the Soviet advances, Tito disappeared ("levanted," Churchill called it) from Vis without a word to the British. Leaving a guard on his cave to deceive the observers into thinking he was still there, he flew off in a Russian plane to Moscow. Annoyed and offended, the British at first concluded that Tito had gone to Serbia to take command of the campaign there; early in October, Stalin himself told Churchill in Moscow that Tito had been there. The Russians blamed the secrecy of the whole affair

[20] Dedijer, *Tito*, p. 228.

entirely on Tito: "The Russians attribute this graceless behavior to Tito's suspicious peasant upbringing, and say that they did not tell us out of respect for his wish for secrecy."[21] When MacLean told Tito of Churchill's displeasure, Tito remarked that Churchill had recently held a meeting with President Roosevelt, but had not previously informed Tito of his intentions.

In Moscow, according to Dedijer, Stalin and Tito agreed to coördinate Red army and Partisan operations for the liberation of Belgrade, after which Soviet forces could withdraw and proceed to their attack on Hungary. Otherwise, the conversation, as Tito reports it, was not particularly cordial. Stalin showed his resentment of Tito's telegrams during the war, and Tito dared to disagree with Stalin about the strength of the Serbian bourgeoisie, flatly opposing Stalin's suggestion that King Peter be restored, even when the boss assured him: "'You need not restore him forever. Take him back temporarily, and then you can slip a knife into his back at a suitable moment.'"[22] The liberation of Belgrade proceeded according to plan, and in the third week of October 1944 Tito returned as conqueror to the capital he had left as a conspirator a little more than three crowded years earlier. What remained was the mopping up of the remaining German forces, and the political maneuvering that would assure him of undisputed supremacy in the country.

ALBANIA

During 1944 the Albanian situation developed along parallel lines. In January the Germans defeated the LNC so decisively that only supplies of British arms permitted the regroupment of its detachments in the south. At the end of May 1944, Hoxha formed a provisional "government." Proceeding according to the model furnished by Tito, he summoned a congress at Permet attended by 250 delegates, who set up a cabinet with himself as prime minister. Communists held all but two of the eleven posts.[23] King Zog's return, like King Peter's in Yugoslavia, was declared a matter for after the war, but the Communists denounced him in unbridled terms. The new government, again imitating the Yugoslav example, then proceeded to reorganize its military forces, formally making Hoxha a Colonel-General and "Commander in Chief of the National Army of Liberation." The first division, on the model of the "Yugoslav proletarian brigade," was placed under the command of Colonel Mehmet Shehu, an active Communist, like many of the Yugoslav leaders a veteran of the Spanish civil war, and a man with an outstanding reputation for ferocious cruelty even among Albanians. Ahead of him lay a glittering future in the grim jungle of Communist politics.

[21] Churchill, *The Second World War,* VI, *Triumph and Tragedy* (Boston: Houghton Mifflin Company, 1953), 230.

[22] Dedijer, *Tito*, p. 233.

[23] Several of the ministers were members of the Central Committee of the Party; the government also included Sejfullah Maleshova, the "red poet," who seems somehow to have returned from France to Albania during 1943.

With its grip on the south hardly challenged, the LNC infiltrated the north. Meanwhile, Abas Kupi's Zogist forces in the central part of the country were quiescent. The British now determined to make every effort to arouse the Ghegs, especially Kupi, and to bring him and Hoxha together once more in an effective alliance against the Germans and their Albanian collaborators. The account of this effort, from April to November 1944, is splendidly told in Julian Amery's *Sons of the Eagle.*

Kupi and the other Zogist leaders were deeply anxious because the allies had not recognized Zog or admitted Albania to the United Nations; they deplored the British assistance to the Communist-led LNC; they were worried that Kossovo would be returned to Yugoslavia, and that southern Albania might be ceded to Greece; and before they would fight they wanted assurances on these subjects and the promise of arms. Kupi himself had contact with the German-sponsored Tirana government and with the BK, who were eager to collaborate with the allies. From the first, he doubted if Hoxha would hear of a reconciliation. He and the other royalists whom the British mission visited on long reconnaissance trips suspected that Albania had already been assigned by England to a future Soviet sphere of influence.[24]

Kupi's political demands could not be fulfilled, especially the granting of recognition to Zog and the guarantee on Kossovo. The Communists, who were fighting the Germans, were wholly opposed to Zog. Yugoslavia was an ally, and no commitment could be made with regard to Kossovo, a portion of its prewar territory. Albania could not be admitted to the UN, because there was no recognized Albanian government-in-exile, and could not be. The only promises which the British mission could make to Kupi were independence for Albania, and the delivery of arms as soon as the Zogists showed unmistakable intention of fighting the Germans. The chieftains in the north, however, wanted supplies of arms first, before they would rise in revolt. The one sure way to activate the Zogists seemed to be to obtain a direct telegraphic or radio command from Zog ordering his loyal supporters into the field. This the British mission tried in vain to procure. The LNC, moreover, was gradually moving north, and when they reached the Shkumbi, would attack the Zogists unless an agreement should previously have been reached. And the Germans, in Tirana, were organizing an anti-Communist front of Albanians, which the British mission was not strong enough to stop.

Though Abas Kupi was willing to go to Bari to discuss a truce with the Partisans, Hoxha flatly refused. By mid-July 1944, civil war was raging, and Kupi had been obliged to join forces with many northern Albanian tribesmen who had previously been "collaborationist." The British continued to supply

[24] Typical of the complex Albanian situation was the divided allegiance of the Elezi clan of Dibra, whose head, having fought both Italians and Germans in the past, was now a colonel in the Tirana government, while other relatives were in command of LNC detachments, and still others were dealing with Kupi and the British. Insurance for the clan against any eventuality was the key to their typically Balkan policy.

arms to the Partisans while they were attacking the Zogists, despite the urging of the mission with Kupi. As the summer wore on, no appropriate instructions came to the British mission from London or Italy. The Germans, preparing to withdraw from the country, began a campaign of executing all Albanians suspected of collaborating with the British or of holding British sympathies.

In the circumstances, the mission made an attempt to bring the Tirana forces together under Kupi for an all-out attack on the Germans. The German-sponsored government, for several months in the process of disintegration, now resigned. Its members, as well as the BK leaders, dispersed to rally what support they could. Tirana was left to the Germans with only a few Albanian politicians still collaborating. Far to the north, in July and August, Gani Bey Kryeziu, supported by British arms, attacked the Germans steadily.

The possibility was strong that the nationalist forces of the north would now rise in that revolt for which the British had been working. Facing this situation, which threatened to provide him with rivals for the eventual control of the country, Enver Hoxha now (late August) demanded that the British mission to Kupi be withdrawn, as assisting collaborationists, and even threatened to court-martial them if they fell into his hands. Though the British authorities at Bari forced Hoxha to retract this threat, they soon decided not to help Kupi, in order to avert trouble with Hoxha. The mission's effort to rally the nationalists thus failed, just at the moment when the BK leaders and powerful tribesmen who had helped the Germans were prepared to switch sides if encouraged. The Communists had won the political battle in Albania as they had in Yugoslavia.

And, as in Yugoslavia, the last days of the successful military and political struggle were signalized by the arrival of the first Russian officers at LNC headquarters. A full-fledged new Yugoslav military mission also appeared early in September. The anguish of the British mission with Kupi, whose hands had throughout remained clean of collaboration, and who had been loyal at all times, is recorded in dignified and moving fashion by Amery. As if symbolizing their triumph, an LNC unit in the north disarmed and mistreated a British officer, and captured and brutally murdered Lazar Fundo, the ex-Communist who had been acting as adviser to Gani Bey Kryeziu's brave guerrillas. It was only after an appeal to London that high British political and military authority approved Abas Kupi's own evacuation to Italy. By October 1944, the Communists ruled supreme in "liberated" Belgrade and Tirana.

4. The Axis Balkan Satellites in the War, June 1941–September 1944

RUMANIA

Rumania declared war on the USSR simultaneously with Germany, and Rumanian troops crossed the Soviet frontier on June 22, 1941, with the Germans. The war commanded, it is agreed, general public approval: the Soviet seizure of Bessarabia and northern Bukovina was less than a year old, and Rumanian opinion was bitterly anti-Russian. But when the lost territories had been reconquered within a few weeks, and the Rumanian armies crossed the Dniester onto Russian soil proper, doubts grew among moderate Rumanians. Maniu went on record by writing Antonescu that he opposed further advances of Rumanian troops as aggressive warfare, but the German hold on the country was too strong to permit Antonescu to halt his armies even had he wished to do so.

Moreover, he and many other Rumanian nationalists believed that Rumania and Hungary were now in a kind of competition for Hitler's favor, and that if the Rumanians performed better than the Hungarians on the eastern front, the Germans would reverse the Vienna award, and would return northern Transylvania. Though public opinion would doubtless have supported even more enthusiastically a war against Hungary for the reconquest of this lost territory, for the moment both countries were unable to avoid participation in the war on Russia, and it seems doubtful whether any large number of Rumanians strongly opposed it even after the armies had reached the Dniester.

After some thirty Rumanian divisions had conquered the area between the Dniester and the Bug including the major Soviet port of Odessa, the Germans (hoping that this might help to soothe the painful loss of Northern Transylvania) permitted Rumania first to occupy and then to annex the whole region, which was now named "Transnistria." Here Antonescu established a special military regime, under a governor directly responsible to him. Moreover, he did not restore the recovered territories to the regular organs of local government under the Ministry of the Interior, but appointed his own governors for Bessarabia and all of Bukovina, south as well as north.

In these two provinces there now took place severe oppression of Jews and other minority groups, who were accused of having favored the Soviet occupiers. Rumanian soldiers committed large-scale pogroms, expelling at least 200,000 Jews from their homes and dumping them across the Dniester into "Transnistria," where concentration camps awaited them. This province had always been one of the portions of Russia where the Jewish population was most numerous; so the "Transnistrian" Jews, especially those of Odessa, also suffered horribly under Rumanian occupation. Some of the most grisly aspects of life in this little-studied area and period can be found impressionistically and vividly described in Curzio Malaparte's gruesome work, *Kaput.* The Rumanians systematically plundered Transnistria; in the fall of 1944, I myself saw some of the Odessa trolleys running on the streets of Timisoara in the Banat, with their Russian markings still not painted out.

The Jews in the recovered and conquered regions suffered more than those in Rumania proper, where the government distinguished three categories of Jews: those who had been in Rumania since the end of 1918, or had been wounded or decorated in the First World War and their descendants, who escaped some of the discriminatory measures; and all others, who were now oppressed in a variety of ways. Decrees forbade Jews to own land, and required them to sell their shares in oil companies and other industries of national importance. They might not sell alcoholic drinks, a blow at the Jewish tavern-keeper, who was a familiar feature of the Moldavian village. The office of "Rumanization" expropriated much of their property. Jewish businessmen had to train Rumanian apprentices to take over their businesses as soon as practicable. Jews might not enter the professions, such as chemistry, journalism, and the stage; and only veterans of the First World War might practice law. Jewish doctors might attend Jewish patients only. Jews could not own radios, go to the movies, or own automobiles. They might not employ "Aryan" servants. They were issued special ration cards which were not honored until after all other customers had been served, and which entitled them to less food. The state schools and universities were closed to them. Even in their own schools, children might not receive training beyond the level of that usually given to a thirteen-year-old child. The severity of these decrees, obviously copied after the Nuremberg laws in Germany, was somewhat mitigated by the fact that Rumanian officials could often be bribed not to enforce them. But on the other hand, the Jews were forced to perform labor services, and the Rumanian press raged and ranted against them as viciously as the German. Moreover, when air-raids on Bucharest began in the spring of 1944, the police required "Aryan" credentials from those seeking shelter.

In 1941–42, Rumanian forces played a major part in the German Crimean campaign, and in the march on Stalingrad and the great siege there, but casualties mounted, reaching perhaps half a million in all. There is no question but that the Rumanian armies fought extremely well, and far exceeded Hitler's expectations. It was only after the disaster at Stalingrad that the Germans undertook to arm the Rumanian units in Russia with equipment comparable to their own, and to equip in Rumania itself tank divisions and a modern air force. Antonescu himself had the courage to stand up to Hitler on a good many specific questions; he refused to increase the number of Rumanian troops or to permit the use of Rumanians for garrison duty except for Transnistria and the Crimea. He never ceased to press Rumanian claims to all of Transylvania, and was extremely irritated when Goering on one occasion told him that most of the inhabitants were Saxons.

In addition to manpower, Rumania of course provided oil and grain, and all Rumanian industry worked for the war-effort. The Germans seized French and Belgian properties for themselves, and in Transylvania, members of the *Volksdeutsch* minority took over at low prices expropriated Jewish enterprises, which thus became virtually German holdings. But economic collaboration did not always run smoothly. The Germans pressed for greater quantities of goods and larger advance commitments, insisting that the Rumanian economy be geared to the total Axis war effort. But they could not pay for Rumanian deliveries either in goods or in gold. They argued that they needed their gold for the purchase of raw materials in neutral countries, and maintained that it would do no good in the vaults of the Rumanian National Bank, while the raw materials it bought abroad would speed the common victory. As inflation grew worse and worse in Rumania (by early 1944, prices had risen to more than seventeen times the 1939 level), the Rumanians felt increasingly that the Germans were exploiting them. It was with ill-grace that they consented to the German suggestion that Rumania's credit in Germany should be met in part with war materials and materials for railroad building, and in part should stay on the books until after the war.

Friction between Germany and Rumania was increased by the presence in Germany of Horia Sima and many other Iron Guardists, refugees from Antonescu but old friends of the German Gestapo. The Rumanian government feared that the Germans were secretly supporting Iron Guard political activity, and in January 1943, when Horia Sima escaped from German internment, and went to Italy, Antonescu was sure that Himmler had connived at the escape, if indeed he had not arranged it. Then too, there was the problem of the *Volksdeutsch* minority in Rumania. Until Stalingrad, the Germans had agreed that the *Volksdeutsch* should serve in the Rumanian army, although they did smuggle a few of them into Germany for war service or labor in war industry. But after Stalingrad, the German authorities demanded and got the right to call for "volunteers" among *Volksdeutsch* males under forty-five. In theory no compulsion was to be employed, but in practice the local *Volksdeutsch* organizations brought virtually irresistible pressure to bear, and some 80,000 "volunteers" went off to serve in the SS and in German war-plants.

Within the Rumanian regime itself, the Vice-Premier and Foreign Minister, Mihai Antonescu, no relative of the Marshal, proved himself a confirmed and somewhat frivolous intriguer. He liked the Germans less than the Italians, and, as the war dragged on, he sought through Bova Scoppa, the Italian Minister, to convince Mussolini that salvation would lie in a movement to withdraw Italy and the other allies of Germany from the war and to make a separate peace with the west. At one time in 1943, Mihai Antonescu so irritated the Rumanian Ambassador in Berlin, Bossy, that Bossy resigned. Mihai Antonescu, however, refused to accept the resignation, and for six months as Foreign Minister continued to address Bossy as ambassador, while Bossy steadfastly declined to act as such. This comedy of errors naturally made for increased difficulty between Bucharest and Berlin. The Germans of course soon found out about Mihai Antonescu's clumsy attempts at betrayal, and brought them to the attention of the Marshal, who is said to have berated his subordinate fiercely, and threatened to get rid of him. But apparently Mihai Antonescu begged so convincingly, and the ladies' camarilla, of which the Marshal's wife was a member, interceded so effectively that, after a diplomatic illness of one month, the Vice-Premier was restored to duty.

The Rumanian government in general believed that, after peace with the USSR should have been obtained, the Transylvanian question would probably precipitate a new war with Hungary, and both Antonescus therefore sought close diplomatic ties with the other anti-Magyar satellite states, Slovakia and Croatia, as insurance against such an eventuality. The Rumanians flooded the German foreign office with complaints about the behavior of the Hungarians in northern Transylvania, but these seem to have received as scant attention as the flood of Hungarian complaints about the behavior of the Rumanians in southern Transylvania. At one time, a mixed German-Italian commission visited both parts of the divided province, and reported that the complaints of both sides seemed fully justified; but here the matter rested.

The Rumanians, indeed, feared a Hungarian attack even while the fighting in Russia was at its height in 1942, and asked German permission to retain inside Rumania some of the war matériel which the Germans were supplying for the front. To this the Germans replied that matériel would henceforth be sent direct neither to Hungary nor to Rumania, but only to the staging areas for the Russian front, where it would be turned over directly to the troops of both powers. Transylvania, indeed, was an obsession with the Rumanians: according to Ion Gheorghe, Rumanian military attaché and later ambassador in Berlin, the Germans were astonished beyond words to discover that Rumanian troops fighting deep in the Caucasus, when asked what they were fighting for, replied "Transylvania." It was not until March 1944, however, when Hitler was furious at the Hungarian regime for attempting to negotiate with the allies, that he offered to return the lost part of Transylvania to Antonescu after the war. And although it was perfectly clear that Hitler had lost, and though Antonescu himself seems to have known it, the Rumanian Marshal was as delighted as a child with this absurd promise.[25]

All during the war, there continued to exist inside Rumania the "tolerated opposition" of Maniu and Bratianu, leaders of the National Peasant and National Liberal parties, forbidden to engage actively in politics, but in no way disturbed, and allowed to write occasional memoranda to the Premier, making known their views of the situation, which were often in strenuous opposition to his own. To these Antonescu would often reply, but this peculiar correspondence seems to have been written largely for the record rather than for any immediate political effect. According to Gheorghe, the Germans in the spring of 1943 captured documents which had passed between Maniu and the British, and demanded that Maniu be punished. But the Marshal replied that he had himself received from Maniu's intermediary a copy of the communication, and that Maniu was a "negative" politician who did not represent Rumanian opinion. No action was taken against Maniu.

Indeed, the universal Rumanian view was that war between Rumania and the western powers was a regrettable accident, and that it would be more gentlemanly if the western allies recognized this, and left Rumania alone. As the situation grew more threatening, with the repeated Axis defeats in the

[25] Ion Gheorghe, *Rumăniens Weg Zum Satellitenstaat* (Wels, 1952), *passim*. This work, by a man of strong Iron Guard sympathies, is to be read with all due skepticism.

USSR, Rumanians began to explore ways of making peace with the west, and enlisting the western powers to protect them against the Russians, always expressing incredulity that they should be regarded as full-fledged enemies. By mid-1943, peace-feelers from Rumanians were being put forth to the western allies in ever-increasing number in the chief neutral capitals: Lisbon, Stockholm, Berne, Ankara, Madrid. The effort was always the same: to persuade Britain and the United States to make a separate peace, and then to land forces in Rumania to keep the Russians out and to keep Bessarabia and northern Bukovina out of their hands. The entire Rumanian war effort was explained as an action undertaken to regain purely Rumanian territory which had been taken by the USSR. The first great American raid on the refinery-center of Ploești in August 1943 did not markedly affect the Rumanian attitude. When Cordell Hull, as Secretary of State, issued a stern warning to the German satellites, the Bucharest daily *Universul* wrote, on December 17, 1943, that the "great republic" which had set up the largest statue to liberty in the world should understand and sympathize with the Rumanian fight for the maintenance of territorial integrity.

It would serve no purpose to review here all the approaches to the western allies. The most important came early in March 1944, when former Premier Prince Barbu Știrbei went to Cairo via Istanbul with the consent of the government and of the tolerated opposition of Maniu and Bratianu. Though his mission was supposedly secret, it was immediately publicized in the press. Știrbei was received in Cairo by British and American representatives. They reported all discussions to the Soviet representative, who also saw Știrbei, and made it clear to him that the USSR would insist on retaining Bessarabia and northern Bukovina. The allies also demanded that the Rumanians collaborate in the war on Germany, free their allied prisoners and internees, agree to pay reparations, and assist all allied troop movements through Rumania. Northern Transylvania was to be returned to Rumania.

On April 3, 1944, Molotov issued a public statement, making clear Russian territorial demands, but otherwise guaranteeing Rumanian territorial integrity, the implication being that Rumania would recover northern Transylvania. Molotov further undertook not to change in any way "the existing social structure" of the country, although he declared that the Russian armies intended to pursue their enemies across Rumania. The Rumanian surrender was to be followed by an immediate declaration of war on Germany. A series of Anglo-American air-raids on Ploești and on Bucharest itself lent point to the urgency of the situation, and demonstrated the unity of the three major allies. These raids Antonescu denounced as an unprovoked attack on civilization by people whom Rumania had never harmed. He did not reply to the notice of the surrender terms transmitted from Cairo. Since the war, Soviet authorities have alleged that the western allies tried to negotiate secretly for a Rumanian surrender, and did not keep faith with Moscow. Nothing could be more untrue, although nothing would have pleased the Rumanians more. It was precisely the American and British insistence that Russia participate in all negotiations which so long delayed the Rumanian surrender.

Unwilling to believe that the western allies would permit the Soviet Union to occupy the country, and hoping for the landing of British and American troops in the Balkans, the regime and Maniu virtually suspended negotiations during May and June. Early in July, however, Maniu sent out Constantin Vișoianu, a professional diplomat associated in the past with Nicolae Titulescu, the most skillful Rumanian diplomat of the interwar period, who had been responsible for the resumption of relations with the USSR in 1934. Though Maniu was now allegedly planning a "revolt" against the regime, the Vișoianu mission did not advance discussions materially; indeed, the allied landings in France served to keep alive the mistaken belief that Rumania would obtain protection from the west against a Soviet occupation. In the light of hindsight, one may actively doubt whether earlier acceptance of the Russian terms would have helped Rumania in the long run. It was manifestly impossible for the United States or Britain to intervene with the USSR on behalf of an Axis satellite whose armies had invaded, devastated, and annexed Russian territory. It was clear that Soviet occupation was inevitable. Russian troops were by the third week in August deep in Moldavia.

Throughout the war, the Rumanian left, never strong either in numbers or in following, and outlawed by the government, had engaged in some clandestine political activity, although later Communist claims that they had conducted any sort of genuine resistance were absurdly exaggerated. The Communists had for some time in 1943 tried to persuade Maniu to include them in a united anti-German front. But, as faithful disciples of Stalin, the Communists could not join any effort to get back Bessarabia and northern Bukovina from the USSR, which Maniu at that time still insisted upon as necessary. The Communists and a few fellow-travelers, having failed with the truly representative Rumanian opposition leaders, then formed their own "Union of Patriots," which published a clandestine newspaper, *Romania Libera.* The government several times arrested groups accused of Communist activities, and there seems little doubt that the left had a number of clandestine radio-transmitters.

The most important Communist in Rumania was probably Lucretiu Patrașcanu, an intellectual and a lawyer, educated in the west, who had often acted as defense attorney for accused Communists on trial for subversive activities, and who had himself spent much time in jail.[26] Of the fellow-travelers, the most notable was Petru Groza, a wealthy Transylvanian businessman and politician, who had served in minor Cabinet posts in the late twenties and early thirties, and who had founded the so-called "Ploughmen's Front," a left-wing organization of peasants in Transylvania. Groza too had served a

[26] Patraşcanu's book, *Sous trois dictatures* (Paris, 1946), is an interesting analysis of Rumanian history in the late 1930's and early 1940's.

term in jail, but it had lasted only a month, and by his own account he had enjoyed many special privileges while there. But this did not prevent him from writing a lachrymose narrative of his fearful sufferings in confinement, which, he maintained, had taught him to abhor cruelty, and to favor the commonwealth of mankind, and especially good relations between Rumania and Hungary.[27] Educated in Budapest, Groza spoke fluent Magyar, and had many Hungarian friends. A poseur and publicity-seeker, a buffoon and a boor, Groza never earned the well-known Balkan epithet of a "serious" man. Yet some of his Transylvanian followers were truly idealistic, and he himself opportunistically preached a vague doctrine of worker-peasant coöperation which sounded a note welcome to Russian ears. Under the circumstances, his future was assured, at least for the short run. To the activity of the left Moscow had paid no overt attention until mid-March 1944, when the Soviet press praised the Union of Patriots and gave publicity to its program; this had no social content, and called only for the expulsion of the Germans, the overthrow of Antonescu, the formation of a "national" government, and the restoration of civil liberties.

As the situation grew more desperate in the spring and summer of 1944, the Union of Patriots renewed its contacts with Maniu and Bratianu. The small Social-Democratic Party, headed by C. Titel Petrescu, became the fourth member of a loose opposition coalition, all of whose members knew that Antonescu must be overthrown. But their discussions dragged on interminably, and in the end it was not they but young King Michael himself who acted. Never on really good terms with Antonescu, he had come, under his mother's guidance, to believe that the situation was desperate, and that his premier would have to go. Baron Stârcea-Mocsonyi, Marshal of the Court, a courageous and brilliant young man, educated in England, and Grigore Niculescu-Buzești, a foreign-office official who had run a kind of pro-allied and pro-Maniu information center under the nose of Mihai Antonescu all during the war, also were instrumental in precipitating action. Summoning the Marshal to the palace on August 23, the King informed him that he was dismissed, ordered him disarmed, and had him temporarily locked in the safe built to house the splendid royal stamp-collection, with which King Carol had fled the country.

Michael then issued a proclamation announcing that Rumania had accepted the allied surrender-terms, and that the war against the allies had come to an end, and ordering a cease-fire on the Russian front. He told his people that Rumanian integrity had been guaranteed, and that northern Transylvania would be restored. He also announced a new government of "national union." Headed by General Constantin Sanatescu, it included a large number of army officers in the important ministries, but the leaders of the opposition, Maniu, Bratianu, and Titel Petrescu, all became ministers without portfolio, and the

[27] *L'école du pouvoir* (Paris, 1947).

Communist Patrașcanu obtained the Ministry of Justice. Nicolescu-Buzești became Foreign Minister. Concentration camps were declared abolished, and all interned persons were to be released at once.

Within a couple of days the Russians were publicly promising collaboration, provided that the Rumanian armies would now declare war on Germany and attack the Hungarian troops in northern Transylvania. If they were to do so, the Russians would not disarm Rumanian units, but would keep them intact and join them in their operations. To this the King's new government responded by making the desired declaration of war. The Germans launched air-raids against Bucharest, and set up a Rumanian "government" under the refugee Iron Guard leader, Horia Sima, whom they had long been keeping in reserve for just such an emergency. The British and American air forces attacked the Germans in accordance with information furnished them by the Rumanians.

In this way, though much had been said in the weeks before the surrender about the massive fortifications of the Galați-Focșani line, the Rumanians in the end chose not to defend it. Their surrender immensely helped the advance of the Soviet armies, and their own troops now turned against the Hungarians and Germans. Soviet troops rolled unopposed into Bucharest and beyond.

What remained was the signing of the armistice. Știrbei and Vișoianu flew to Moscow from Cairo; a delegation of five others including Patrașcanu flew from Bucharest. Americans and British participated in the discussions, which were delayed until September 12, while Soviet troops made good their complete occupation of Rumania, to the consternation of the Rumanians, who declared that at Cairo they had been promised that the Russians would not enter certain zones. The Russians also took the Antonescus into their own custody. Before the armistice was even signed, clear evidences of Rumanian-Russian friction had thus manifested themselves.

The terms themselves provided for the boundaries foreseen in the preliminary discussions, leaving a loophole for possible minor adjustments of the pre-Vienna Award boundary with Hungary. Reparations were fixed at $300,000,000, payable in six equal annual installments, and Rumania was compelled to pay the bill for the Soviet operations on her territory. Rumania would repeal anti-Semitic legislation, release all pro-allied prisoners, ban fascist groups, and assist the Russians to arrest and try war-criminals. The Soviet High Command and the Rumanian authorities were to negotiate an agreement on control of the press and radio. All three allies would have representatives on an Allied Control Commission to be set up in Bucharest, but the constant references throughout the armistice to this body as operating under the "Allied (Soviet) Command" showed clearly where the preponderance of authority was to lie.

BULGARIA

The position of Bulgaria in 1941 was quite different from that of Rumania. No Bulgarian regime could have declared war on the USSR and survived, because of the traditional and almost universal pro-Russian sentiment in the country, a sentiment which often had nothing to do with communism. The Bulgarian government had joined the Axis under pressure from Hitler, but under equal pressure from the sentiment of Bulgarian nationalists, who felt that this was the time to fulfill their old territorial ambitions. As we have seen, the German Balkan campaigns of spring 1941 virtually fulfilled all of the Bulgarian irredentist demands at the expense of Yugoslavia and Greece, although final annexation, it was understood, must await the postwar settlement. Having sent their troops into these disputed territories, the Bulgarians were satisfied. In no need of Bulgarian manpower for the initial campaigns in Russia, and aware of the state of Bulgarian opinion, Hitler did not even ask that King Boris join him, and though there were many German units in the country, Hitler did not occupy Bulgaria.

Thus Bulgaria was neutral, but her regime under Prime Minister Bogdan Filov, a distinguished professor and scholar of the history of art, was certainly "neutral for Germany." The Bulgarian press and radio aped the Germans in denunciations of communism. The government gave the Germans full use of port facilities in Varna and Burgas, and closed the Soviet consulate at Varna so that the Russians could not spy on the Germans. The Bulgarians coöperated fully with the Germans, especially in secret police operations. Though the Germans could not pay for them, Bulgaria continued to make deliveries of foodstuffs and other goods to Germany.

There was even a small group of Bulgarians who wanted to go to war with Russia, including General Lukov, who was assassinated in February 1942, in the first of several murders of pro-German personages. These terrorist acts were attributed to the Communists, who were now rounded up by the police of the Minister of the Interior, Peter Gabrovsky, the most pro-Hitler man in the Cabinet, and one of the most feared and hated police chiefs even in Hitler's Europe until he left office in August 1943. Among the Communists arrested was Traicho Kostov, who for some reason was not executed. Not only Communists but other pro-Russian Bulgarians suffered from the vigilance of the police.

The Bulgarian government also showed its pro-German orientation by introducing a Commissariat for Jewish affairs, forbidding Jews to live in Sofia, and requiring the wearing of the yellow star of David. These measures, it should be noted, met with little response among the Bulgarian people. On the other hand, the Jews in Bulgaria, though many fewer in number than in Rumania, suffered as individuals almost as much. A certain amount of support for anti-Semitism came from the various extreme nationalist organizations, some of them para-military, and all of them blessed by the government: the legionnaires, Brannik, Ratnik, Otets Paissy, all of which united at the end of 1943.

At the end of August 1943 King Boris, who had just been on a visit to Hitler, died suddenly and mysteriously. Since the new King Simeon was only six years old, a three-man regency was set up, including Prince Cyril, Boris' brother and Simeon's uncle, Premier Filov, and the Minister of War, General Mihov. This procedure was unconstitutional: a special Grand National Sobranie, twice the size of the ordinary body, should have been elected but was not. Dobri Bozhilov succeeded Filov as Prime Minister.

Since the war the Bulgarian Communists have loudly boasted of the resistance to the Germans, even comparing the Bulgarian underground to the Yugoslav Partisan movement. These boasts were greatly exaggerated, though possibly not as much so as the claims made by the Communists in Rumania, where no resistance worthy of the name existed in fact. The Bulgarian Communists claim that the party's politburo organized a special military commission to direct sabotage immediately after the German attack on the USSR, and boast that they succeeded in disrupting communications, killing a good many individual Germans and pro-Hitler Bulgarians, and cutting production in the factories by 40 to 50 per cent. They assert that they infiltrated the ranks of the army, and popularized the slogan "not a single Bulgarian soldier on the eastern front," and that they ordered the party members among the occupation troops in Yugoslavia to desert to the Yugoslav Partisan movement. Very few, however, did so, which is something the Bulgarian Communists do not mention.

The Bulgarian Communists did form Partisan bands in the mountains, but these groups did not fight against Germans, since there were no Germans to fight, but against Bulgarian police and military units sent out to oppose them. The Communist claim that their Partisans tied down an "army" of 20,000 in the Sredna Gora in 1942–43 and a 100,000 man "army" in 1943–44 is highly inflated. Indeed the Communist claims contradict each other: they allege that most of the Bulgarian army was engaged in fighting the Communist Partisans, and at the same time that most of the Bulgarian army was deeply infiltrated by Communists. Those Bulgarian guerrilla units which were the most important were near the Yugoslav frontier, and received direction and assistance from the Yugoslav Partisans. Some of them received supplies from the British, and two British liaison officers were killed helping the Bulgarian Partisans. There were Communist political commissars with each Partisan unit.

In accordance with the Communist line everywhere, the leadership in Bulgaria sought to rally all those opposed to the Germans into a popular-front organization. In Bulgaria this was called the Fatherland Front (Otechestven Front), abbreviated as OF, and was formed in mid-1942. In addition to the Communists, the OF included the "Pladne" Agrarians, the Social Democrats, and Zveno, all of them legal parties, and thus at a certain disadvantage, since their leaders could not combine underground activity with ordinary politics. From the first, the Communists took the lead in the OF, but the other parties thoroughly approved of their resistance activities. These were also encouraged by a Soviet-controlled clandestine broadcasting station called Hristo Botiev after the nineteenth-century Bulgarian revolutionary. In addition to those groups actively engaged in the OF, the old Democratic Party was strongly anti-German, and its leader, Mushanov, led the "tolerated opposition" in the Sobranie. Thus Bulgaria continued to have the semblance of constitutional government, in contrast to Rumania, where parliamentary life had ended, and the opposition leaders had to act quite unofficially.

Though Bulgaria was neutral against the USSR, she was at war with Britain and the United States. Air-raids on Sofia began in November 1943, and were repeated in December and in the first months of 1944. These helped precipitate a political crisis, and stimulated the growth of pro-Russian sentiment, always strong, and now nurtured by a steady barrage of radio propaganda from Moscow. Public opinion surely favored abandonment of the Germans and the making of peace, but the government could not bring itself to face the possibility of full-scale German occupation, or run the risk of losing the Yugoslav and Greek territories so recently acquired. The Russian Ambassador to Bulgaria, Lavrishchev, applied diplomatic pressure on both the government and leaders of the tolerated opposition to try to push Bulgaria nearer to a change of sides. "Bulgarians," said Moscow Radio in May, "your time has come. You must make your choice and make it immediately." To every such threat and to every air-raid by the Americans and British the Germans replied with threats of their own, insisting, for example, on Bulgarian general mobilization, which had never yet taken place. The Russians demanded that the Bulgarians reopen the Soviet consulate at Varna and permit new ones at Burgas and Ruse, so that they could see for themselves what the Germans were doing in those ports. The Germans demanded that Bulgaria break diplomatic relations with the USSR.

The Bozhilov government finally succumbed on May 21, 1944, and was succeeded on June 1 by a new regime under Ivan Bagrianov, a former army officer and member of King Boris' personal staff, who had retired from the army and gone into agriculture and business. A member of the Agrarian Party, and an Agrarian deputy in the Sobranie, he had served as Minister of Agriculture between 1938 and 1941, but owed his political advancement rather to Boris' patronage than to any following of his own. His cabinet, like that of Bozhilov, was composed mostly of "technicians," but included a pro-German Macedonian surgeon, Stanishev, as Minister of the Interior. Stanishev belonged to the annexationist wing of IMRO. The new government, neither pro-German enough to suit Hitler nor anti-German enough to suit Stalin, faced the same pressures as the old. The balancing act between Germany and Russia continued. But it was clear that the Bagrianov government hoped to break with Germany at a moment when the Germans could no longer inflict punishment on Bulgaria.

As German forces withdrew, the Premier made a number of reassuring gestures toward the Jews, removed pro-Germans from the police forces, and granted amnesty to more than 15,000 political prisoners and relatives of members of the underground. He labored mightily to convince the Turks that his government was friendly toward Turkey and would under no circumstances attack her. As the Russian advance rolled on into Moldavia, Bagrianov on August 17 made a speech strongly hinting at an abandonment of the German alliance and affirming his government's love of peace. A few days later his Foreign Minister, Purvan Draganov, a former army officer, friend and illegitimate half-brother of King Boris, and wartime Minister to Spain, made another pacific statement to the effect that Bulgaria would withdraw from occupied Serbian and Greek territory, but that Thrace and Macedonia were Bulgarian. The statement showed clearly that the Bagrianov government was still seeking reassurances that Bulgaria might keep conquered territory, and was offering to evacuate only those areas which it had not intended to annex.

Soon afterwards, the Bulgarian government sent envoys to negotiate with the allies, choosing Stoicho Mushanov, nephew of the aging Democratic leader, and a member of the same party, who had been President of the Sobranie, and in that capacity had visited England officially in 1939; and Colonel Zhelezkov, military attaché in Ankara. They reached Cairo on August 30, 1944, a week after the Rumanian surrender. Here they negotiated with the British and American representatives, but not of course with the representative of the USSR, because Bulgaria had never been at war with Russia. The Russians, however, were kept fully informed of the discussions, and at the time thanked the western allies for their reports. All later statements by Soviet or other Communist sources to the effect that the western allies negotiated with the Bulgarians without informing Russia are untrue. While thanking Britain and the United States, however, the Russians strongly hinted to the Bulgarians that they should avail themselves of Russian "good offices" to get better terms, to which Bagrianov replied that Bulgaria was not at war with the USSR. The western allies demanded that Bulgaria break relations with Germany, intern all German nationals and disarm all German troops, evacuate all occupied Greek and Yugoslav territory, free allied prisoners, end discriminatory legislation, help arrest and try war criminals, return all allied (i.e., Greek and Yugoslav) property, assume the responsibility for payment of reparations, and fulfill whatever demands for demobilization, disarmament, and contribution to relief and rehabilitation might be required. The way was thus left open for Bulgarian cobelligerency against Germany.

While these terms were under discussion, the Regency on September 2 replaced the Bagrianov government. Moving definitely in the direction of the western allies, they now installed a Cabinet headed by Kosta Muraviev, a nephew of Alexander Stamboliisky and a member of his uncle's government in 1923, who had been exiled by Tsankov, returned in 1926 after the amnesty, and served in Mushanov's Cabinet in the early thirties. His political position seems to have been somewhere in the center of the Agrarian Party. Mushanov himself became Minister without Portfolio, and the remainder of the government consisted chiefly of Democrats and "right-wing" Agrarians. The new regime thus represented the "tolerated" opposition, and contained no elements of the OF resistance or left-wingers of any complexion. It was this which apparently doomed it. The Soviet Union was manifestly unwilling to allow moderates to run Bulgaria or the western allies to dictate the peace alone.

On September 4, the USSR suddenly declared war on Bulgaria, and *Pravda* demanded that the Bulgarian people "rid itself of the ruling clique." Muraviev at once asked for armistice terms, and within three days freed all political prisoners, and all allied prisoners, dissolved the political police, and declared war on Germany. But Russian troops marched into the country on September 8. The next day, the OF staged a coup, ousted the Muraviev government, and installed a new Cabinet, which in turn installed a new Regency. All ministers who had served since 1941 were arrested.

The new Cabinet was headed by Colonel Kimon Georgiev, one of the founders of Zveno, and Premier after the 1934 coup which his political club had led. Zveno also had two other posts, the Ministry of War, held by its leading figure, Colonel Damian Velchev, who had originally brought Zveno and the "military league of captains" together, and the Ministry of Propaganda, held by Dimo Kazasov, a journalist with a varied political career including membership in the Social-Democratic Party, service under Tsankov, and long membership in Zveno. There were several left-wing (Pladne) Agrarians including their leader, Nikola Petkov, who became Minister without Portfolio, three Social Democrats, and four Communists, including Anton Yugov, Minister of the Interior, and Mincho Neichev, Minister of Justice, both key ministries. Aside from the OF members, there were two representatives of the Democratic Party. The new Regency included a Communist, an Agrarian, and a political independent. Thus the Russians and their Bulgarian allies in the OF forced the issue, turned Bulgaria into a cobelligerent, made the negotiations in Cairo superfluous, and removed a Bulgarian government oriented primarily towards the United States and Britain. The Germans meanwhile sponsored a "Nationalist" government-in-exile under Tsankov, parallel to their Rumanian government under Horia Sima, and just as ineffective.

The OF regime and Tito now hailed each other as allies, and Bulgarian troops began to fight against the Germans in Yugoslavia, together with the Yugoslav Partisans and Russian forces. They played a considerable part in the last stages of liberating Yugoslavia from German occupation. Premier Georgiev promised to restore the Tirnovo constitution, and meanwhile promulgated a series of reforms establishing equal rights for women and separating church and state. The Communists issued reassuring statements, declaring that they had no intention of communizing the country. The Minister of War forbade the use of the Communist clenched fist salute in the army, or the display of the red flag unless Russian troops were being welcomed: the Russians and their domestic allies viewed the zeal of many Bulgarian Communists as premature.

During the remainder of September and most of October 1944, Bulgarian signing of an armistice was delayed, apparently in large part because of difficulty over arranging the evacuation of Bulgarian troops and civilians from Greek and especially from Yugoslav territory. The situation was complicated by the fact that the Bulgarian armies were actually fighting in Yugoslavia, and so could not in fact be withdrawn, and by the fact that Tito's men moved at once to incorporate Pirin (Bulgarian) Macedonia into their own federal republic of Macedonia formed in August. The OF government and the Bulgarian Communists could not permit this; they announced that Macedonians had the right to self-determination, but did not mention the Yugoslav Macedonian Republic. Secret negotiations between Tito and the Bulgarian Communist Vice-Premier, Dobri Terpeshev, and between Tempo, Kolishevski, and the Bulgarian Communists followed, in which the Bulgarians promised to give Pirin both cultural and administrative autonomy, and the Yugoslavs apparently agreed not to occupy the area at once. It was clearly a temporary compromise, and not helped by the fact that Tito bitterly distrusted Velchev, who had been in touch with Mihailovich. On October 9, the Yugoslav Radio announced the conclusion of a pact with Bulgaria providing for military collaboration and the peaceful settlement of outstanding questions.

The Bulgarians also showed great reluctance to leave Greek soil, and seem to have hoped that somehow Moscow might procure them those "easier" terms which the Russians had told Bagrianov could be obtained through them. In the end, however, the allies all insisted that the Bulgarians accede to the original requirement and evacuate Greek and Yugoslav territory, except for those troops actively fighting the Germans in Yugoslavia. On this basis the Bulgarian armistice was finally signed, in Moscow, like the Rumanian, on October 28, 1944. Except for the matter of cobelligerency, already determined by events, it embodied the Anglo-American demands presented in Cairo. As in the case of Rumania, it provided for an "Allied Control Commission" to function under the "general direction of the Allied (Soviet) High Command."

5. *The Great Powers and Southeast Europe*

So far in this account of the war years we have been considering the Balkan countries themselves and the relations of the major powers to one or another of them. By the fall of 1944 we have seen the Communists emerging everywhere in positions of strength. In Yugoslavia and Albania they had directed successful guerrilla movements which had already begun the process of transforming themselves into governments. In Rumania and Bulgaria they had joined political coalitions which had come to office with the German defeat in Russia and with the defection of the two countries from the Axis alliance. In Bulgaria where, in contrast to Rumania, they had dominated a resistance movement, they already held the key interior and justice ministries, which controlled the police and the courts. Although their future was by no means secure, it looked bright. Now we must abandon for a time this complex narrative, and seek the explanation for the course of events in the Balkans where so often in history the explanation has lain: in the decisions of the great powers among themselves and in their relationships to each other. It was Stalin, Churchill, and Roosevelt who in the end, by acts committed and omitted, determined the future of southeast Europe.

THE MILITARY DECISIONS

One of the chief reasons for the Communist successes was obviously military: it was the Soviet Union whose armies defeated and invaded Rumania and Bulgaria, and completed the expulsion of the Germans from Yugoslavia. There were no British or American troops in southeast Europe. This was the direct result of Anglo-American strategic planning of the war against Germany, in which the North African, Sicilian, and Italian campaigns were to be followed by the main cross-channel operation against the Germans in France, supported by a blow against southern France from the Mediterranean. It is often said that Prime Minister Churchill longed to invade the Balkans and that he struggled bitterly against the conception of the cross-channel blow as likely to lead to a repetition of the enormous casualties of the western front in the First World War. This Churchill in his own magnificent history of World War II steadily denies, and denounces as a legend.

A careful reading of Churchill's text, buttressed as it is at every point with the original documents, clearly demonstrates that he did not indeed favor any sort of major Balkan campaign for American and British troops. But it also shows quite clearly how the legend came to arise. Churchill did fear the casualties to be expected in northern France, but always accepted the cross-channel operation as an eventual necessity. But after a while he strongly opposed the ancillary invasion in southern France as unnecessary and wasteful of manpower and shipping strength. Even when he had to accept it, he persisted in trying to cut down the allotment of forces scheduled to undertake it. He had set his heart on two operations: the capture of the Dodecanese Islands, which he felt sure would make it possible to bring the Turks into the war, thus opening the Straits and the Black Sea to allied shipping, and enabling Britain and the United States to give the Russians "our right hand along the Danube";[28] and an invasion of central Europe from the head of the Adriatic through the Lyublyana gap, which would bring the forces of the western allies to Vienna ahead of the Russians, and which, though he does not say so, might well have brought them even farther to the east than Vienna. This operation was to be accompanied by strong material assistance to the Partisans across the Adriatic, which would have helped them clear Dalmatia of the enemy. He also expected that when the Germans withdrew from Greece it would be the forces of Great Britain and the United States that would help in the liberation. None of these three undertakings singly would have involved the forces of the western allies in a "Balkan" campaign, nor

[28] Churchill, *The Second World War,* V, *Closing the Ring* (Boston: Houghton Mifflin Company, 1951), 286.

indeed would all three of them together have done so. But many American authorities loosely spoke of his powerful pressure to obtain shipping and manpower for these operations as efforts to launch a campaign "in the Balkans."

In the event, the Aegean island campaign undertaken by the British in 1943 failed because insufficient supplies were allotted to it, and the Germans retook the islands of Cos, Leros, and Samos, which the British had initially seized. Turkey stayed out of the war until just before the very end, although at Teheran Stalin agreed to fight Bulgaria if the Turks came in and Bulgaria attacked Turkey. The Lyublyana gap operation depended entirely on an allied break-through into the Po valley and the seizure of the head of the Adriatic, from which any such venture would have had to be mounted. The German resistance in Italy, however, was so strong, and the Italian front was deprived of so many troops who were withdrawn for the operations in France, that Rome was not taken until June 1944. Even then, much heavy fighting lay ahead in Italy for the allies, who did not reach the take-off point for any hypothetical operation against Vienna until long after the Russians had forced the Rumanian surrender and begun to sweep into central Europe. Churchill's wishes were thus frustrated by the pursuit of what were essentially American military plans.

But it should be noted that Roosevelt himself, at Teheran in December 1943, raised the question of a trans-Adriatic drive, perhaps on his own initiative, perhaps under the influence of correspondence and discussion with Churchill. The Sherwood-Hopkins version of this episode is as follows:

> Roosevelt surprised and disturbed Hopkins by mentioning the possibility of an operation across the Adriatic for a drive, aided by Tito's Partisans, northeastward into Rumania to effect a junction with the Red Army advancing southward from the region of Odessa. Hopkins thereupon scribbled a note to Admiral King: "Who's promoting that Adriatic business that the President continually returns to?" To which King replied, "As far as I know, it's his own idea." Certainly nothing could be farther from the plans of the US Chiefs of Staff. Churchill was quick to associate himself with Roosevelt's suggestion. . . . Stalin then expressed the opinion that it would be unwise to scatter forces in various operations throughout the eastern Mediterranean . . . he favored simultaneous operations in Northern and Southern France. . . .[29]

The Churchill version of what Roosevelt said differs only in that it makes no specific mention of Rumania, and speaks instead of "moving from the head of the Adriatic towards the Danube."[30] This indicates that the President at least wanted to test Stalin's reaction to what he must have known was one of Churchill's favorite ideas. Whether he had any intention of pushing it we cannot know. In the event, however, the plan, great though its strategic and political merit may well have been, was not tried. Of Churchill's plans for southeast Europe only the British liberation of Greece actually took place.

[29] Robert E. Sherwood, *Roosevelt and Hopkins* (New York, 1948), pp. 780–781.

[30] Churchill, *The Second World War*, V, *Closing the Ring*, 349 ff.

Elsewhere in the Balkans, it was the Russians and their native Communist friends who had the arms and the armed men in the fall of 1944.

THE POLITICAL DECISIONS

But the grand strategy of the allied campaign against Germany, critical though it was in determining where actual power was to lie, was not alone responsible for the ease with which the Communists were able to take over. The major allies made political as well as military decisions. As early as December 1941, when Foreign Minister Eden visited Moscow, Stalin raised the question of future territorial arrangements:

> He suggested that Yugoslavia should be restored and even receive additional territory from Italy; that Albania should be reconstituted as an independent state. . . . Turkey might . . . receive certain districts in Bulgaria. . . . Stalin desired the restoration of the position in 1941, prior to the German attack, in respect of . . . Bessarabia. . . . Rumania should give special facilities for bases, etc., to the Soviet Union, receiving compensation from territory now occupied by Hungary.

Prime Minister Churchill reminded Eden that "We are bound to the United States not to enter into secret and special pacts. To approach President Roosevelt with these proposals would be to court a blank refusal and might cause lasting trouble on both sides."[31]

This mention of the United States, however, seems in part at least to have been intended to supply Mr. Eden with a graceful way of evading the whole territorial issue: Stalin was also asking that Britain recognize the Curzon line in Poland, the annexation of Finnish territory taken in 1941, and the annexation of the Baltic states, and this last demand Churchill himself strongly opposed. The British communicated the Russian demands to Washington, where the reaction was precisely what Churchill had predicted: "The Department of State," says Secretary Hull, ". . . took the position that the test of our good faith with regard to the Soviet Union should not be our willingness to agree to the recognition of extended Soviet frontiers at this time, but rather the degree of determination which we show loyally to carry out our promises to aid the Soviet Union with equipment and supplies." And behind this specific attitude lay an important fixed general principle:

"Our attitude had been predicated on our general policy not to recognize any territorial changes that had been made in European frontiers since the outbreak of the war, and not to enter into any territorial commitments that might hamper the proceedings of the post-war peace conference."[32]

By March 1942, Mr. Churchill was prepared to grant the Soviet demands. On March 7, 1942, he wired Roosevelt that "The increasing gravity of the

[31] Churchill, *The Second World War,* III, *The Grand Alliance* (Boston: Houghton Mifflin Company, 1950), 628.

[32] *The Memoirs of Cordell Hull* (New York, 1948), II, 1168.

war has led me to feel that the principles of the Atlantic Charter ought not to be construed so as to deny Russia the frontiers she occupied when Germany attacked her. . . . I hope . . . that you will be able to give us a free hand to sign the treaty which Stalin desires as soon as possible." [33] In the end, however, the State Department view prevailed, not only in Washington but also in London. On Molotov's visit to England in May 1942, after much discussion the Russians agreed to an Anglo-Soviet treaty in which no territorial provisions were included. Both Mr. Churchill and Mr. Hull report their deep feeling of relief, and it is perfectly clear from their accounts that it was the American insistence on the major principle which had won the day.

The only specifically Balkan territories which would have been involved in the proposed Anglo-Russian treaty, however, would have been Bessarabia and northern Bukovina, since there was in the end no Russian proposal to include any cessions of Bulgarian territory to Turkey, of Italian territory to Yugoslavia, or of Hungarian territory to Rumania. At one point, when it seemed that the British would not guarantee the June 1941 frontiers of the USSR, Molotov suggested that Russia's "special interests" in Rumania be recognized. This too was in the end omitted.

At various times in the months which followed, the British and Americans discussed the postwar settlement. Churchill favored a Danubian federation, "based on Vienna and doing something to fill the gap caused by the disappearance of the Austro-Hungarian Empire," and a Balkan federation, but his account contains no details of these plans, if indeed any were ever formulated.[34] It was not until the spring of 1944 that the major allies again discussed in detail their own future roles in the Balkans. By then, the Mediterranean had become a British theater, with the appointment of Eisenhower to command the scheduled assault on France. Churchill was alarmed at the Russian "Communist intrigues in Italy, Yugoslavia, and Greece," and wanted a showdown.

Mr. Eden made to the Russians a "general suggestion . . . that the USSR should temporarily regard Rumanian affairs as mainly their concern under war conditions while leaving Greece to us," and this the Russians on May 18, 1944 were prepared to accept if the United States approved. Churchill telegraphed Roosevelt as follows:

> There have recently been disquieting signs of a possible divergence of policy between ourselves and the Russians in regard to the Balkan countries, and in particular towards Greece. We therefore suggested to the Soviet Ambassador here that we should agree between ourselves as a practical matter that the Soviet Government would take the lead in Rumanian affairs, while we would take the lead in Greek affairs, each government giving the other

[33] Churchill, *The Second World War,* IV, *The Hinge of Fate* (Boston: Houghton Mifflin Company, 1950), 321.

[34] Churchill, *The Second World War,* IV, *The Hinge of Fate,* 803.

help in the respective countries. Such an arrangement would be a natural development of the existing military situation, since Rumania falls within the sphere of the Soviet armies and Greece within the Allied command under General (Sir Henry Maitland) Wilson in the Mediterranean. . . .

I hope you may feel able to give this proposal your blessing. We do not of course wish to carve up the Balkans into spheres of influence, and in agreeing to the arrangement we should make it clear that it applied only to war conditions and did not affect the rights and responsibilities which each of the Great Powers will have to exercise at the peace settlements and afterwards in regard to the whole of Europe. The arrangement would of course involve no change in the present collaboration between you and us in the formulation and execution of Allied policy towards these countries.[35]

It is clear that Churchill was deeply and justifiably concerned over the growing strength of communism in Greece, and Soviet intentions there. This is not the place to rehearse in detail the history of Greece under German occupation, which has been skillfully done by C. M. Woodhouse and W. H. McNeill.[36] It may be said, however, that the situation inside Greece had developed along lines not dissimilar to those we have already reviewed in Yugoslavia and Albania. A powerful Communist-dominated resistance army, the ELAS, under the political direction of a Communist-led "popular front" group of political leaders, the EAM, had outdistanced its various nationalist rivals, of which General Zervas' EDES was the most important but far inferior in number. There had been much fighting between the resistance groups, and British efforts to reconcile them met with only temporary success. The Greek government-in-exile, like the Yugoslav, was strongly anti-Communist, while the Greek Communists, like the Yugoslav, were determined to prevent the return of the King, and to rule the country themselves after liberation. Churchill cared deeply for the traditional Anglo-Greek alliance; he had a personal regard for the King; Britain had lost 40,000 men in 1941 defending Greece against the Germans; and above all Churchill was determined not to let Greece, with its key strategic position, fall to the Communists.

But the State Department saw in the proposal precisely what lay implicit in it, though Churchill had skillfully tried to counter the response before it should be forthcoming. Despite the vague language—"Take the lead in Rumanian affairs . . . take the lead in Greek affairs . . . each government giving the other help"—and despite the disarming references to a purely military agreement, and the specific denial of any intention to create spheres of influence, the proposal clearly held within it the germs of a division of the Balkans into British and Russian spheres. Secretary Hull was vigorously opposed to setting a precedent so contrary to the principles on which Amer-

[35] Churchill, *The Second World War*, VI, *Triumph and Tragedy*, 73–74.

[36] C. M. Woodhouse, *Apple of Discord* (London, n.d. but 1948); W. H. McNeill, *The Greek Dilemma* (Philadelphia and New York, 1947).

ican policy had been based, and so likely to "sow the seeds of future conflict."[37]

Churchill cabled the British Ambassador in Washington, Lord Halifax, on June 8:

> There is no question of spheres of influence. We all have to act together, but someone must be playing the hand. It seems reasonable that the Russians should deal with the Rumanians and Bulgarians, upon whom their armies are impinging, and that we should deal with the Greeks, who are in our assigned theatre, who are our old allies, and for whom we sacrificed 40,000 men in 1941. I have reason to believe the President is in entire agreement with the line I am taking about Greece. The same is true of Yugoslavia. I keep him constantly informed, but on the whole we, His Majesty's Government, are playing the hand, and have to be very careful to play it agreeably with the Russians.

He also referred to the difficulty of reaching decisions by "triangular or quadrangular telegraphing," and remarked that "we follow the lead of the United States in South America. . . ."[38]

This cable is of interest for several reasons. It reveals that Churchill was prepared to allow the Russians to "deal with" Bulgaria as well as Rumania, something which he had not yet communicated to the United States, or apparently even to the Russians. It shows that, despite his assurances to the President, he felt the whole question to be one in which the British were primarily concerned, and that he was growing impatient with having to get American approval for decisions in this theater. The South American parallel was certainly not apt: there was no war on the South American continent, and no question of putting any South American country into the sphere of any great power. The mention of Yugoslavia clearly referred to the efforts at reconciling Tito and King Peter, which were quite different from allowing any great power to "play the hand" there.

Moreover, in fact, Churchill's attitude toward the future of Yugoslavia differed markedly from his attitude toward the future of Greece. In Cairo, at the end of 1943, Fitzroy MacLean reports the following conversation:

> I now emphasized to Mr. Churchill the other points I had made in my report, namely, that in my view the Partisans, whether we helped them or not, would be the decisive political factor in Jugoslavia after the war and, secondly, that Tito and the other leaders of the Movement were openly and avowedly Communist and that the system which they would establish would inevitably be on Soviet lines and, in all probability, strongly oriented towards the Soviet Union. The Prime Minister's reply resolved my doubts.
>
> "Do you intend," he asked, "to make Jugoslavia your home after the war?"
>
> "No, Sir," I replied.

[37] Hull, *Memoirs*, II, 1452.

[38] Churchill, *The Second World War*, VI, *Triumph and Tragedy*, 74–75.

"Neither do I," he said. "And, that being so, the less you and I worry about the form of government they set up, the better. That is for them to decide." [39]

Now, it may well be unfair to put too much emphasis on one perhaps partly frivolous remark of the Prime Minister. But he never could have made, even in jest, such a remark about Greece. So it seems to be true that, for whatever reason, he regarded the eventual triumph of communism in Yugoslavia — though he strove mightily to avert it or dilute it — as posing a less serious threat to Britain than the triumph of communism in Greece, which he was determined to prevent at all costs. And he was not really much interested in the future of Bulgaria — "caitiff Bulgaria" as he once called it in a speech — or of Rumania: "I had never felt that our relations with Rumania and Bulgaria in the past called for any special sacrifices from us." [40] Churchill, it will be noted, tended to ascribe personal qualities to whole countries. In any case, he was first and foremost a political and military realist, and it was perfectly true in June 1944 that, as the military plans had developed, it would be the Soviet armies which would move into Rumania and Bulgaria.

President Roosevelt replied to him on June 11, 1944:

> we acknowledge that the military responsible Government in any given territory will inevitably make decisions required by military developments, but are convinced that the natural tendency for such decisions to extend to other than military fields would be strengthened by an agreement of the type suggested. In our opinion, this would certainly result in the persistence of differences between you and the Soviets and in the division of the Balkan region into spheres of influence. . . . We believe efforts should preferably be made to establish consultative machinery to dispel misunderstandings and restrain the tendency toward the development of exclusive spheres.[41]

To this Churchill replied in a long cable of protest, pointing out that any consultative committee would always be overruled by one of the heads of government, and that "Somebody must have the power to plan and to act." He set forth the realistic basis for his proposal:

> The Russians are ready to let us take the lead in Greece, which means that EAM and all its malice can be controlled by the national forces of Greece. Otherwise civil war and ruin to the land you care about so much . . . . considering that the Russians are about to invade Rumania in great force and are going to help Rumania recapture part of Transylvania . . . it would be a good thing to follow the Soviet leadership, considering that neither you nor we have any troops there at all, and that they probably will do what they like anyhow.

[39] MacLean, *Eastern Approaches*, pp. 402–403.

[40] Churchill, *The Second World War*, II, *Their Finest Hour* (Boston: Houghton Mifflin Company, 1949), 208.

[41] Churchill, *The Second World War*, VI, *Triumph and Tragedy*, 75.

He proposed that the arrangements suggested be given a three-month trial, after which they were to be subject to review by the three great powers. On June 13, President Roosevelt agreed to the three-month trial, adding that "We must be careful to make it clear that we are not establishing any post-war sphere of influence."[42]

Secretary Hull's *Memoirs* reveal that President Roosevelt agreed to this three-month trial arrangement contrary to the advice of the State Department. The Department had been shown Mr. Churchill's cable to Lord Halifax, and so knew that the Prime Minister was thinking of Bulgaria as well as Rumania, and Yugoslavia as well as Greece. Mr. Hull seems to have thought that Churchill was claiming the right for Britain to "play the hand" in Yugoslavia too, but this is belied by the text of the Churchill cable. In any case, the mention of two more countries confirmed Hull in his conviction that spheres of influence were being established. The President not only failed to consult the State Department about consenting to Churchill's proposal for a trial period of three months, but did not inform the Department that he had done so. Indeed, the Department, still going on the assumption that the United States objected to the whole arrangement, now gave the British Embassy a memorandum outlining the arguments against it and proposed instead the establishment of "adequate machinery for frank consultation regarding the Balkan region." Mr. Hull also called the President's attention to the fact that Bulgaria and Yugoslavia were involved in Mr. Churchill's planning, as well as Rumania and Greece.

It was not until June 26, when the American Ambassador to Greece, Lincoln MacVeagh, then in Cairo, cabled that his British opposite number had informed him that the United States had agreed to the proposal, that Mr. Hull was aware that the President must have acted on the matter privately. On Mr. Hull's inquiry, the President showed him a copy of his message to Churchill sent two weeks earlier. After giving his consent to the three-month trial, he had also forwarded to London the State Department's memorandum of objection. With it he had said that both he and the Department were worried about the Balkan region, and that he was disturbed because the British had taken up the entire matter with the Russians first, and had mentioned it to the Americans only after the Russians had asked whether the proposal had American approval.[43] To this Mr. Churchill replied that he could not admit he had done anything wrong in acting on his own to try to persuade the Russians "to quit boosting EAM and ramming it forward with all their force." He termed the whole proposal as "a temporary working arrangement for the better conduct of the war," and referred to an instance in which Roosevelt had communicated with the Russians without telling Churchill about it in

[42] Churchill, *The Second World War,* VI, *Triumph and Tragedy,* 75–77.
[43] Hull, *Memoirs,* II, 1455 ff.

advance. The interchange between President and Prime Minister on this subject now ended with an agreement to consult in future.[44]

About this entire episode of June 1944 one may comment that the President's failure to consult or inform the State Department was certainly a piece of bad administration, and resulted in embarrassment. More substantially, however, there arises the question as to the merit of the State Department position. "Spheres of influence" were considered to be anathema, and no arrangement creating such spheres was to receive American approval. This seems on the whole a rather abstract, not to say immature, view of international affairs: it is of course perfectly possible that spheres of influence, delineated by common agreement, and maintained by common consent, may contribute to keeping the peace instead of to destroying it. To condemn such arrangements in the abstract reflects the American mythology which distrusts secret diplomacy of all sorts.

If one is to sustain effectively the pious moral view that spheres of influence are *ipso facto* a "bad thing," then one must put forward some practical suggestion for a substitute. The State Department never got beyond the suggestion for establishing a committee through which the major powers might consult each other on the Balkans. And this suggestion, which might have worked in leisurely times of peace, had little merit in the hurried and troubled times of war, in which, as Churchill said, "events will always outstrip the changing situation."[45] Nor could any mere committee have dealt with so momentous a matter, for example, as a Russian decision to back the Communists in Greece, which was what really concerned Churchill. Only direct arrangements made by the heads of state could prove effective. In view of the military operations actually going on, such arrangements in fact necessarily constituted the establishment of spheres of influence, and nothing the State Department might say could affect the matter. The question was: were the spheres of influence to be established with or without prior agreement, in such a way as to maximize or to minimize the risks of great-power friction?

The Russians now consulted the State Department direct, and on July 15, 1944 Mr. Hull informed them that the United States approved the arrangement for a period of three months,

> our assent having been given in consideration of the present war strategy. Except for this overriding consideration, we pointed out, this Government would wish to make known its apprehension lest the proposed agreement might, by the natural tendency of such arrangements, lead to the division in fact of the Balkan region into spheres of influence.

This, the Secretary of State went on to say,

> could not but militate against the establishment and effective functioning of a

[44] Churchill, *The Second World War,* VI, *Triumph and Tragedy,* 77–78.
[45] Churchill, *The Second World War,* VI, *Triumph and Tragedy,* 75.

> broader system of general security in which all countries would have their part . . . . we supposed that the three months' trial period would enable the British and Soviet Governments to determine whether such an arrangement was practicable and efficacious as applying to war conditions only, without in any way affecting the rights and responsibilities which each of the three principal Allied nations would have to exercise during the period of the reëstablishment of peace, and afterwards, in regard to the whole of Europe. Finally, we assumed that the arrangement would have neither direct nor indirect validity as affecting the interests of this Government, or of other Governments associated with the three principal allies.

Mr. Hull concludes his account of the interchanges of May, June, and July 1944 by saying: "Events fully justified the apprehensions we entertained over this Anglo-Russian agreement, which duly entered into effect following the President's acquiescence."[46] Those who have written on the subject since Mr. Hull's *Memoirs* appeared have all assumed that this was right. Cordell Hull's successor as Secretary of State, Edward R. Stettinius, for example, writing as late as 1949, says that he believed the agreement to have been a serious mistake.[47]

In fact, however, the June agreement did *not* enter into effect. As Churchill makes clear, he wired Stalin on July 11 asking for the three months' trial period, now approved by the President. Stalin wired back on July 15 that he would take it up again when he had the American reply. This he seems not to have done. Churchill says:

> We were thus unable to reach any final agreement about dividing responsibilities in the Balkan peninsula. Early in August the Russians dispatched from Italy by a subterfuge a mission to ELAS in northern Greece. In the light of American official reluctance and of this instance of Russian bad faith, we abandoned our efforts to reach a major understanding until I met Stalin in Moscow three months later. By then much had happened on the Eastern Front.[48]

In the absence of memoir-literature from the Russian side, we can only speculate about the reasons for Stalin's behavior. But it presents few riddles. Why should he conclude an agreement, which the British were requesting, and which gave him the lead in Rumania? This, as Churchill remarked, he had anyhow. Why should he consent to deprive himself of his opportunity to play some sort of a hand in Greece, where the Communists were strong and the stake high? Perhaps the only reason for doing so would have been strong Anglo-American pressure. If he had seen that the two western allies were united, it is conceivable at least that he might have consented, no doubt with all the usual mental reservations, to exclude himself from Greece. But inquiry had shown the two allies divided. The United States, it is true, had con-

[46] Hull, II, 1457–1458.

[47] E. R. Stettinius, *Roosevelt and the Russians* (New York, 1949), p. 12.

[48] Churchill, *The Second World War*, VI, *Triumph and Tragedy*, 81.

sented, but only for three months, and then with a wealth of high-sounding reservations. So there was no need whatever to abandon the Greek Communists — a very strong card in the future game he would have to play with Churchill — in exchange for a free military hand for the next three months in Rumania, where he would in any case have literally millions of troops, and where England and the United States would in any case have none. Off "by subterfuge" went the Soviet mission to the EAM, and the future of the Balkans was not decided in the spring and early summer of 1944. It seems quite clear that by sticking to a principle, and an invalid one at that, the United States during these months helped prevent the conclusion of an agreement which might have saved Greece a good deal of agony later.

CHURCHILL IN MOSCOW, OCTOBER 1944: THE "PERCENTAGES" AGREEMENT

The next step was taken on Churchill's next visit to Moscow, on October 9, 1944, when he and Stalin, Eden, and Molotov conferred alone with their interpreters. Before the meeting, Roosevelt, at Hopkins' urging, wired Stalin reaffirming the interest of the United States in all questions which might arise, and declaring that in his view the Churchill-Stalin talks were merely preliminary to a three-power conference.[49] As to what then happened in Moscow, it seems best to quote Mr. Churchill's account direct:

> The moment was apt for business, so I said, "Let us settle about our affairs in the Balkans. Your armies are in Rumania and Bulgaria. We have interests, missions, and agents there. Don't let us get at cross-purposes in small ways. So far as Britain and Russia are concerned, how would it do for you to have ninety per cent predominance in Rumania, for us to have ninety per cent predominance in Greece, and go fifty-fifty about Yugoslavia?" While this was being translated I wrote out on a half-sheet of paper:
>
> Rumania
>
> | | |
> |---|---|
> | Russia | 90% |
> | The others | 10% |
>
> Greece
>
> | | |
> |---|---|
> | Great Britain (in accord with USA) | 90% |
> | Russia | 10% |
>
> | | |
> |---|---|
> | Yugoslavia | 50–50% |
> | Hungary | 50–50% |
>
> Bulgaria
>
> | | |
> |---|---|
> | Russia | 75% |
> | The others | 25% |
>
> I pushed this across to Stalin, who had by then heard the translation. There was a slight pause. Then he took his blue pencil and made a large tick upon

[49] Sherwood, *Roosevelt and Hopkins*, pp. 933–934.

> it, and passed it back to us. It was all settled in no more time than it takes to set down.
>
> Of course we had long and anxiously considered our point, and were only dealing with immediate war-time arrangements. All larger questions were reserved on both sides for what we then hoped would be a peace table when the war was won. After this there was a long silence. The pencilled paper lay in the centre of the table. At length I said, "Might it not be thought rather cynical if it seemed we had disposed of these issues, so fateful to millions of people, in such an offhand manner? Let us burn the paper." "No, you keep it," said Stalin.[50]

It is difficult to comment on this extraordinary episode. What, in fact, does such a term as "ninety per cent of the preponderance," mean? It cannot refer to numbers of troops, since the western allies were to have none in Rumania and Bulgaria. It cannot refer to numbers of diplomats or military representatives or intelligence agents or economic representatives. It cannot refer to political influence, since such questions are not accurately described in precise arithmetical terminology, and besides, Churchill assures us that "only immediate wartime arrangements" were under discussion. Perhaps the most we can make of the fateful sheet of paper is to conjecture that the numbers were intended only to dramatize the roles of the great powers: in Rumania, Britain would not interfere with Soviet activities, but by the 10 per cent figure simply kept a foot in the door to protect its own interests: the security of its agents, its citizens' investments in the oil fields, and the like. It is harder to see what the Russians' 10 per cent in Greece entitled them to do, since Soviet citizens had no investments there, and the smallness of the percentage could hardly have been interpreted as authorizing any support of the Communists. Why did Churchill ask for more of a say in Bulgaria than in Rumania? And how does a 25 per cent say really compare with a 10 per cent say? These questions must remain unanswered.

What did the agreement mean to Stalin? Did he ask himself how to apply concrete percentage figures to matters not susceptible of such treatment? Did he say to himself that the percentages were meaningless? Did he feel that the 10 per cent of the say which he retained in Greece gave him scope enough to back the Greek Communists and at least cause the British trouble, while the 10 per cent they retained in Rumania would enable them to do nothing? Did he accept a fifty-fifty division in Yugoslavia light-heartedly, believing that the predominant position already won by Tito would mean that Russia would in fact have preponderant influence there too? Did he accept the seventy-five, twenty-five arrangement in Bulgaria because he really felt that Britain had a right to two and a half times as much say in Bulgaria as in Rumania, or because the percentage divisions seemed so meaningless to him that it did not really make any difference whether one said "10 per cent" or "25 per cent" so long as the USSR had the larger fraction?

[50] Churchill, *The Second World War*, VI, *Triumph and Tragedy*, 227–228.

Churchill's own account has a curious inner inconsistency, which must have struck the reader. If the agreement dealt only with "immediate war-time arrangements," and if "all larger questions" were in fact "reserved on both sides for what we hoped would be a peace table when the war was won," why should anybody have criticized the undertaking as cynical? Why should Churchill refer to the "immediate war-time arrangements" as disposing of "those issues so fateful to millions of people" if indeed he expected that all really long-range problems would receive a fresh hearing later? I think we must conclude, however reluctantly, that the Prime Minister knew in his heart that it would be extremely difficult to lessen Russian influence anywhere, once it had established itself, and that his wish to burn the paper arose from apprehension that it might leak out, and that its true momentous impact upon the lives of the peoples of the Balkans might be realized. For, despite the number of questions which we have had to ask and leave unanswered, the one posed by Churchill answers itself: "Might not it be thought," he asked, "rather cynical?" The answer to that question is yes.

On the subject of this Balkan arrangement with the Russians, *the first which actually became operative,* Churchill wired Roosevelt from Moscow that he was having a full meeting of minds with Stalin, "so that we may prevent civil war breaking out in several countries, when probably you and I would be in sympathy with one side and U.J. [Uncle Joe] with the other," and that he would report all agreements.[51] But, though the piece of paper with the percentage figures had already been accepted, Churchill did not report its content. This he hinted at, but again without percentage figures, in a cable to Harry Hopkins.

Indeed, from the very first, the percentage figures, or possibly Stalin's instant acceptance of them, troubled Churchill. He drafted a letter to Stalin, *which he did not send,* but in which he wrote:

> These percentages which I have put down are no more than a method by which in our thoughts we can see how near we are together, and then decide upon the steps necessary to bring us into full agreement. As I said, they would be considered crude, and even callous, if they were exposed to the scrutiny of the Foreign Offices and diplomats all over the world. Therefore they could not be the basis of any public document, certainly not at the present time. They might however be a good guide for the conduct of our affairs. If we manage these affairs well, we shall perhaps prevent several civil wars and much bloodshed and strife in the small countries concerned.

He went on to say that Britain, despite its close relationship with the Kings of Greece and Yugoslavia, had no intention of imposing monarchical institutions on those countries. He was glad that Stalin had declared that he would not "change by force or by Communist propaganda the established

[51] Churchill, *The Second World War,* VI, *Triumph and Tragedy,* 229.

systems in the Balkan states." While both great powers of course opposed Fascism or Nazism in these countries,

> In principle I feel that Great Britain and Russia should feel easy about the internal government of these countries, and not worry about them or interfere with them once conditions of tranquility have been restored. . . . It is from this point of view that I have sought to adumbrate the degrees of interest which each of us takes in these countries with the full assent of the other and subject to the approval of the United States.

Finally, Churchill sought to warn Stalin against trying to impose communism in southeast Europe:

> No country wishes to go through the bloody revolution which will certainly be necessary in nearly every case before so drastic a change could be made in the life, habits, and outlook of their society. We feel we were right in interpreting your dissolution of the Comintern as a decision by the Soviet government not to interfere in the internal political affairs of other countries.[52]

This memorandum, never sent to Stalin, clearly reflects Churchill's malaise both at the percentage figures themselves and at the rapid Russian acceptance of them.

Indeed, the percentage figures needed explanation even to the British Cabinet, to which Churchill on October 12 cabled that:

> The system of percentages is not intended to prescribe the numbers sitting on commissions for the different Balkan countries, but rather to express the interest and sentiment with which the British and Soviet governments approach the problems of these countries, and so that they might reveal their minds to each other in some way that could be comprehended. It is not intended to be more than a guide, and of course in no way commits the United States, nor does it attempt to set up a rigid system of spheres of interest. It may, however, help the United States to see how their two principal Allies feel about these regions when the picture is presented as a whole.
>
> Thus it is seen that quite naturally Soviet Russia has vital interests in the countries bordering on the Black Sea, by one of whom, Rumania, she has been wantonly attacked with twenty-six divisions, and with the other of whom, Bulgaria, she has ancient ties. Great Britain feels it right to show particular respect to Russian views about these two countries and to the Soviet desire to take the lead in a practical way in guiding them in the name of the common cause.

There followed a summary of British interests in Greece, ending:

> Here it is understood that Great Britain will take the lead in a military sense and try to help the existing Royal Greek Government to establish itself in Athens upon as broad and united a basis as possible. Soviet Russia would be ready to concede this position and function to Great Britain in the same sort of way as Britain would recognize the intimate relationship between Russia

[52] Churchill, *The Second World War*, VI, *Triumph and Tragedy*, 231–232.

> and Rumania. This would prevent in Greece the growth of hostile factions waging civil war upon each other and involving the British and Russian governments in vexatious arguments and conflict of policy.

About Yugoslavia, Churchill cabled:

> Coming to the case of Yugoslavia, the numerical symbol 50–50 is intended to be the foundation of joint action and an agreed policy between the two powers now closely involved, so as to favor the creation of a united Yugoslavia after all elements there have been joined together to the utmost in driving out the Nazi invaders. It is intended to prevent, for instance, armed strife between Croats and Slovenes on the one side and powerful and numerous elements in Serbia on the other, and also to produce a joint and friendly policy towards Marshal Tito, while ensuring that weapons furnished to him are used against the common Nazi foe rather than for internal purposes. . . . It must be emphasized [Churchill concluded], that this broad disclosure of Soviet and British feelings in the countries mentioned above is only an interim guide for the immediate war-time future, and will be surveyed by the Great Powers when they meet at the armistice or peace table to make a general settlement of Europe.[53]

This masterly interpretation of the "cynical" and "crude" percentage figures goes a long way toward answering many of the objections which might legitimately be raised toward so cavalier a treatment of the Balkan countries. But we must emphasize here the fact that it was addressed only to the British Cabinet, where it doubtless allayed any doubts about the wisdom of the proposals. It was *not* addressed to Stalin, to whom Churchill's other explanatory memorandum was *not* sent, nor, so far as the record shows, did Stalin ever see or hear anything more than was contained on the original single sheet of paper with the percentages on it. This left Stalin free to interpret the figures as he chose. We cannot be sure how that was, but we can be sure that the figures did not mean to him what they meant to Churchill. It seems clear that Churchill sensed this, worried about it, and did nothing about it. Perhaps no agreement at all would have been better than this. Left without interpretation, the percentage figures virtually authorized the Russians to behave in ruthless fashion in Rumania and Bulgaria, while leaving intact their influence over Yugoslavia. Moreover, the negotiation entirely failed to prevent a dreadful civil war in Greece.

As to the United States, Mr. Hull tells us that cables from the Moscow and Ankara embassies reported the percentage figures, but he gives them incorrectly:

"Russia would have a 75/25 or 80/20 predominance in Bulgaria, Hungary, and Rumania, while Britain and Russia would share influence in Yugoslavia 50/50."[54] The failure to mention Greece and the very incorrectness in the embassy reports, printed in Hull's *Memoirs* as late as 1948, is testimony to

[53] Churchill, *The Second World War*, VI, *Triumph and Tragedy*, 233 ff.

[54] Hull, *Memoirs*, II, 1458.

the secrecy with which the original sheet of paper was preserved, and the inaccuracy of the accounts made available to the United States. Indeed, Stettinius in 1949 was still quoting these inaccurate figures.[55]

Hull goes on to comment: "Had we made such a determined fight against the Anglo-Russian agreement as we had made successfully against the proposed territorial clauses of the Anglo-Russian alliance in May 1942, it is possible that some of our later difficulties in the Balkans might not have arisen." [56] No such fight was apparently made. Despite the fact that President Roosevelt had specifically warned that the United States would have to reserve until a big three conference its approval for specific decisions reached between Stalin and Churchill, and despite Churchill's correct recognition that the percentages agreement did not bind the United States, no further discussion of the problem was held until the Yalta conference of February 1945. The United States at no time made concrete proposals for a substitute arrangement of any sort. The opportunity to do so went by default. This was because, by the time of Yalta, the British had already acted on the agreement in Greece, and the time to effect a change had passed.

THE GREEK CIVIL WAR AND THE YALTA MEETING

The British moved into Greece in October 1944, as German troops withdrew. London had previously sponsored the reorganization of the Greek government in exile, in which the EAM now had representatives, while ELAS remained overwhelmingly the strongest armed force in the devastated country. Its leaders did not observe the agreements which the EAM leaders had entered into. Yet they did not seize power at once, apparently because they thought they could get it later. As early as November 7, we find Churchill heading a minute to Eden as follows: "In my opinion, having paid the price we have to Russia for freedom of action in Greece, we should not hesitate to use British troops to support the Royal Hellenic Government. . . . I fully expect a clash with EAM, and we should not shrink from it, provided the ground is well chosen." [57]

It is impossible here to enter into the controversy over the immediate origins of the EAM uprisings, which began on December 3.[58] Suffice it to say that the clash Churchill expected took place, and proved indeed to require a full-fledged British military operation against the Greek Communist-led guerrilla forces, involving the transfer of more than two divisions of British troops from Italy, and serious disturbance of public opinion in the United States and

[55] Stettinius, *Roosevelt and the Russians,* pp. 12–13.

[56] Hull, II, 1458–1459.

[57] Churchill, *The Second World War,* VI, *Triumph and Tragedy,* 286–287.

[58] In addition to Mr. Churchill's sixth volume, and to the works of McNeill and Woodhouse previously cited, readers may wish to consult W. H. McNeill, "The Outbreak of Fighting in Athens, December 1944," and L. S. Stavrianos, "The Immediate Origin of the Battle of Athens," both in the *American Slavic and East European Review,* VIII (December 1949), as well as L. S. Stavrianos, *Greece* (Chicago, 1952). Stavrianos gives the EAM point of view.

in Britain itself. After severe fighting, the British defeated ELAS. A military agreement was reached on January 15, 1945, and a political agreement between the two sides at Varkiza on February 12, 1945. By that date the Yalta Conference had just concluded its sittings. Its communiqué was dated February 11.

We do not know whether the ELAS had the backing of Moscow for its attempt to take over Greece. Stalin may have said in effect to the Greek Communists: "Go ahead and try to take power if you think you can get away with it, but do not expect any overt support from us." In any event, as we shall see, Churchill himself believed that Stalin had lived up to the "percentages" agreement, and had abstained from any intervention in Greece. The British had had to use force against Greeks, in a tragic battle which saddened all who knew about it. But they had prevented the Communists from taking over. And, in so doing, Churchill was fully conscious that he had "paid the price to Russia for a free hand."

Now at Yalta, President Roosevelt produced a Declaration on Liberated Europe, drafted by the State Department, which had also proposed that a European High Commission be created to handle questions arising in these countries. Roosevelt rejected the idea of a High Commission, feeling, according to Stettinius, that the foreign ministers of the three big powers could handle such matters more satisfactorily in their periodic conferences. But he now presented the draft of the "Declaration." The body of the text included the following key passages:

> The establishment of order in Europe and the rebuilding of national economic life must be achieved by processes which will enable the liberated peoples to destroy the last vestiges of Nazism and Fascism and to create democratic institutions of their own choice. This is a Principle of the Atlantic Charter — the right of all people to choose the form of government under which they will live — the restoration of sovereign rights and self-government to those peoples who have been forcibly deprived of them by the aggressor nations.
>
> . . . . .
>
> To foster the conditions in which the liberated peoples may exercise such rights, the three governments will jointly assist the people in any European liberated state or former Axis satellite state in Europe where in their judgment conditions require, (a) to establish conditions of internal peace; (b) to carry out emergency measures for the relief of distressed peoples; (c) to form interim governmental authorities broadly representative of all democratic elements in the population and pledged to the earliest possible establishment through free elections of government responsive to the will of the people; and (d) to facilitate where necessary the holding of such elections.[59]

Stalin suggested that one sentence be added: "In this connection, support will be given to the political leaders of those countries who have taken an

[59] Stettinius, pp. 243 f.

active part in the struggle against the German invaders." He then "mischievously observed" that Churchill need have no anxiety that this amendment applied to Greece, to which Churchill replied that he had no anxiety about Greece, where he would welcome a Soviet observer. "The Marshal then remarked that he thought it would have been exceedingly dangerous had the Prime Minister allowed any but British forces to go to Greece," — surely a comment implying that Russian troops would have fought on the side of the ELAS — but added that he had complete confidence in British policy in Greece. Thus, by Stettinius' account, Stalin greeted the first appearance of the United States-sponsored Declaration on Liberated Europe with a reference to Greece and a scarcely veiled reminder to Churchill of the percentages bargain. In future discussions, the United States refused to accept Stalin's suggested addition, itself a clear bid for recognition of the Communist role in liberation movements not only in eastern but in western Europe. In the end, the Russians accepted the American draft, and the Declaration formed part of the Yalta communiqué on February 11, 1945.

The Declaration clearly had different meanings for the major powers. To the United States, it meant what it said, and implied that no major power would establish or attempt to establish a "sphere of influence" in Europe. To the Russians, so far as the Balkan countries were concerned, it was largely window-dressing; they clung to the percentages agreement. Having refrained from intervention while the British put down a Communist-led uprising in Greece, they had no intention now of forfeiting their own right to a "ninety per cent say" in Rumania and a "seventy-five per cent say" in Bulgaria. To the British the "Declaration" represented a better bargain in southeast Europe than the percentages agreements, since, if it were to be literally interpreted, it would restore them to a position in Rumania and Bulgaria which they had already abandoned. Yet the "Declaration," as we shall see, was also an embarrassment to the British: if taken seriously, as the United States took it, it required Churchill to insist on breaking the percentages bargain, by which he had already profited, and which he was prepared to keep; if disregarded in the Balkans, as the Russians planned to disregard it, it meant that the British had put their name to a document even more cynical than the percentages agreement, since this one was intended from the beginning to be ignored and violated. The test was to arise within three weeks after the "Declaration" had been published.

One further point perhaps needs to be made about the "Declaration on Liberated Europe." It contained terminology — "all democratic elements in the population," "free elections," "governments responsive to the will of the people" — which meant or could be made to mean different things to the three major allies. Both Americans and Englishmen understood and interpreted such language in terms of their own political traditions of civil liberties and the secret ballot. The Russians, although the western allies did not yet fully understand this, meant by "democratic" simply "pro-Russian," and differed widely from the west in their interpretation of "free" elections. To them no election which would have returned to power an anti-Communist government could be a free election. Yet a western-style free election held in early 1945 in any of the east-European countries except possibly Bulgaria would have returned an anti-Communist government.

So it was that the seeds of bitter misunderstanding were sown. As a result of military decisions, power in eastern Europe lay in the hands of the Russian army. In the Balkans, the percentages agreement had recognized the fact. The Yalta "Declaration," as things turned out, only clouded the issue.

Chapter 9

THE COMMUNISTS TAKE OVER: BALKAN POLITICS FROM THE FALL OF 1944 TO JUNE 1948

1. Politics at Home

YUGOSLAVIA

A FEW DAYS AFTER THE LIBERATION OF BELGRADE, Tito and Shubashich concluded a second agreement (November 1, 1944). It provided for a regency to act for the King until the long-envisioned plebiscite on the form of the future government should have been held. AVNOJ was to be enlarged by the addition of such members of the last Yugoslav Parliament of prewar days as had not been in any way compromised by collaboration with the enemy. This new legislative assembly would have all its acts ratified by a future constituent assembly. King Peter was profoundly disturbed by the agreement to create a regency, since the Yugoslav constitution did not provide for any such action at a time when the King was of age and in good health. The King requested Shubashich's resignation, but British pressure was too much for him. Despite a deadlock of several weeks on the identity of the new Regents, the King had to reappoint Shubashich as Premier. All hope that the royal view might receive support vanished when the big three, meeting at Yalta, issued as part of their final communiqué of February 11, 1945 an official recommendation to Tito and to Shubashich to put their agreement of November 1 into immediate effect.

On March 5, 1945 the three Regents, a Serb, a Croat, and a Slovene (all of them Tito's candidates but none of them a Communist), took their oaths in Belgrade. Shubashich and his Cabinet then handed in their resignations to the Regents, and Tito and his government handed in theirs to AVNOJ. On March 7, the new amalgamated government took office, Tito as Prime Minister and Minister of War, and Shubashich as Foreign Minister. Of the twenty-eight cabinet posts, only five were held by non-Tito representatives. These included Shubashich himself and Milan Grol, leader of the Serbian Democratic Party, who now became Deputy Prime Minister. Loyal Partisans held all key posts, and it was perfectly clear that Tito's acceptance of the so-called royal representatives was purely perfunctory. Tito announced that the new government would remain in office until a constituent assembly should have been chosen by universal suffrage and secret ballot.

But the locus of power was never in doubt. Even before the new government had been established, AVNOJ had set up an Economic Council, coordinating all economic activities of the state, and including all economic ministries and the defense ministry. It had also instituted a Supreme Court and a Public Prosecutor, both modeled on Soviet prototypes. And, soon after the new government took office, a decree created a Legislative Council, to consist of the Minister for the Constituent Assembly (Kardelj), the Minister of Justice, and the Ministers of the six federal units into which AVNOJ had divided Yugoslavia even during the war (Serbia, Croatia, Slovenia, Bosnia-Hertsegovina, Montenegro, Macedonia).

The requirement of the Tito-Shubashich agreement that AVNOJ be expanded by addition of members from the prewar Parliament was also specifically endorsed by the Yalta declaration. But the Parliament in question had been elected in 1938 under Stoyadinovich, according to the electoral laws of King Alexander's dictatorship, and had been dissolved in August 1939, at Machek's request, as unrepresentative. It had had no successor before the German invasion put an end to free Yugoslav political life. It was therefore extraordinarily easy for the Tito regime to maintain that virtually nobody in this body was entitled to join the new parliament. Nothing was done until after the end of the war. In August 1945 AVNOJ met, and after much negotiation finally added thirty-nine members of the old parliament, sixty-nine members of six non-Communist political parties, and thirteen men distinguished by their public careers. The 121 new members now joined AVNOJ, which became the National Provisional Parliament on August 10, 1945. In this way the Tito-Shubashich agreement of November 1, 1944 and the Yalta declaration on Yugoslavia received formal fulfillment.

The new parliament then passed three laws which regulated the elections for the long-planned Constituent Assembly. Women for the first time received the vote, as did all citizens over eighteen, and anybody, no matter what his age, who had fought in the Partisan armies. Those who had helped the enemy were disfranchised to the number of about a quarter of a million, or about 3 per cent of the electorate. The law set up electoral districts and local commissions on every administrative level. It permitted any group of one hundred citizens to submit a list of candidates. Voting was to be by secret ballot, in the form of rubber balls, which were to be placed in the box representing the list which the voter wished to support. He could put his hand into any number of boxes he chose, but would of course drop the ball only into the one he selected. This method was traditional in the Balkan countries, since it enabled illiterates to vote if election officials told them which box was which.

The government now launched its electoral campaign, complete with threats against the opposition, made up of the prewar parties and their leaders. One important factor preventing a free election was the activity of the secret police, founded during the war and patterned after that in the USSR. Its leader, Alexander Rankovich, a Montenegrin Communist, was one of Tito's closest collaborators. It was called first O.Z.Na (Section for the Defense of the People) and then U.D.Ba. (Administration for State Security), but whatever its initials, it behaved like its GPU, NKVD, MVD prototype. Though busy purging alleged collaborationists, it had plenty of time for the political opposition. Grol resigned from the government in August 1945, and Shubashich himself and his fellow-member of the local Peasant Party did so in September. Both objected to the provision of the electoral law which disfranchised "collaborators," since the government could now decide to disfranchise anybody it chose.

Grol and the former Serbian Radical leader Milosh Trifunovich, who came back to Yugoslavia from exile, planned to run a joint opposition slate of candidates. Typical of the government's violence was the slogan "Ballots for Tito, Bullets for Grol." At first, Grol was allowed to print and distribute a newspaper, *Demokratiya,* but gangs of Communist thugs attacked its vendors and burned the papers in the streets of Belgrade. A Croatian Peasant Party paper, begun in Zagreb by the widow of Radich, appeared only twice before the Communists suppressed it. Shubashich himself, who was ill, was kept under house-arrest, and even British official visitors were excluded. Grol and Trifunovich eventually decided to boycott the election, and when *Demokratiya* appealed to the electorate to do the same, it was suppressed, just before the elections, after about five weeks of publication. Thus the Serb Radicals, Agrarians, and Democrats, and the Croat Peasant Party all abstained and officially boycotted the election. In the light of hindsight, one may criticize the opposition for not uniting on an electoral list, and at least giving the population a chance to express its sentiments.

As it turned out, only the Popular Front (government) lists were available, although the regime provided special ballot boxes for those simply wishing to express their disapproval of these lists. Thus the Communists were able to disarm criticism that the election was unfair, since any opponent of the regime had only to vote against its lists of candidates, although he was not voting *for* anything or anybody. On November 11, 1945, the elections were held. Every effort was made to turn out the vote; invalids were transported to the polls, and Muslim women appeared in their veils. Western observers reported no disorder and no intimidation at the polls, but this was not necessary in view of the previous terrorism. Though the voting itself took place amid an atmosphere of celebration, one of the prevailing emotions was certainly fear. The regime reported that more than 88 per cent of the eligible electorate had voted, and that it had received more than 90 per cent of the ballots cast.

At its first meeting on November 29, 1945, the second anniversary of the Yaitse session of AVNOJ, the Constituent Assembly proceeded to declare Yugoslavia a republic, and to condemn King Peter as having supported collaborationists. With this act, of course, the regency simply disappeared as an institution, and the long constitutional process begun two years earlier was completed by the foundation of the Federal People's Republic of Yugoslavia. Tito's provisional government now received a vote of confidence, and the assembly proceeded to discuss the draft constitution which had been prepared by the government amid nation-wide publicity. Final adoption came on January 30, 1946. Thereupon the Constituent Assembly voted that it was itself the People's Assembly of the Federal People's Republic of Yugoslavia (hereafter FPRY). Tito proposed a new government, in which eleven of the twenty-one ministers were Communists and the other ten, though nominally members of other parties, safe fellow-travelers. The constitution put much emphasis on the sovereignty of the "people," but what had really happened was that the Communist-dominated coalition which had exercised power in practice since the triumph of Tito during the war had now legalized its authority and transformed itself into a constitutional regime.

The People's Assembly consisted of two houses, a Federal Chamber and a Chamber of Nationalities. The Federal Chamber was to have one representative for every 50,000 inhabitants, or 348 members. The Chamber of Nationalities, modeled on that in the Soviet Union, was to have thirty representatives from each of the six federal republics, plus twenty from the "autonomous region" of the Voyvodina and fifteen from the "autonomous province" of Kossovo-Metohiya, which were both portions of the Serbian federal republic, but received special status because of their respective Magyar and Albanian minorities. The total membership was thus 215. Elected for a four-year term, the two houses sat separately, and had equal powers. Ordinarily they were to meet only twice a year, on April 15 and October 15. Their sessions were devoted to rubber-stamping the work of other institutions.

The Presidium of the People's Assembly actually exercised far more influence on legislation than the assembly itself. Elected by a joint session of the two chambers, it included a President, six Vice-Presidents, one from each republic, and not more than thirty members. It was this inner body which, as in the USSR, acted for the Federal Assembly at any time when the Federal Assembly was not in session. The first President of the Presidium was Dr. Ivan Ribar, an elderly non-Communist but pro-Partisan Croatian intellectual, whose son, Lola, killed during the war, had been one of the heroes of the resistance, a Communist, and a close associate of Tito. As President of the Presidium, Dr. Ribar was in effect President of Yugoslavia, but the office had little real power. The Presidium itself, however, appointed and relieved

Cabinet ministers, acted as a final court of constitutional review (a Supreme Court existed to review decisions to determine whether they conformed to federal law, but could not declare such federal law unconstitutional), reviewed the constitutions of the six federal republics, and issued virtually all legislation. But it was of course not the only law-making body, since the Cabinet, which it appointed, and which was responsible to it when the Federal Assembly was not in session, could also pass laws in theory requiring the approval of the Assembly.

The Cabinet included two classes of ministries, federal and federal-republican. The federal ministries dealt with matters affecting the entire nation: foreign affairs, defense, foreign trade, transportation, the post office, and the like. The federal-republican ministries dealt with the corresponding ministries of the six republics to coördinate their effects in such matters as the interior, justice, finance, industry, mines, agriculture, forestry, and the like. In addition to the ministries, the Cabinet controlled all other phases of life through commissions and committees: the Federal Planning Commission, the Federal Control Commission, the committees on education, on "science, art and culture," on religion, education, and social welfare, and the Office of the Public Prosecutor.

As in the Soviet Union, the determining factor was the Communist Party, which completely controlled all the constitutional organs. Though the "People's Front" consisted in theory of the Socialist, Democratic, Republican, and Agrarian parties of Serbia, the Croat Peasant Party, and the Independent Serb Democrats, as well as the Communists, none except the Communist Party had any political organization of its own; all consisted of former members who collaborated with the Communists. In Rumania and Bulgaria, as we shall see, it was necessary for the Communists after the war to split the other political parties, and then to accept a pro-Communist splinter as the "true" party. In Yugoslavia, because the Communists had dominated the resistance and its political organs, they had an easier time manufacturing their "Front," and controlling it completely from the first. As a careful observer remarked as early as 1947:

> Josip Broz-Tito is not only premier of Yugoslavia but minister of national defense, commander-in-chief of the Yugoslav Army, Marshal of Yugoslavia, representative to the People's Assembly, member of the Presidium, as well as head of the Popular Front of Yugoslavia and chief of the Communist party. His Communist comrades are similarly distributed in proportionally subordinate positions in all of these and similar organizations. Thus, in a country so completely dominated by a single party, a Communist-controlled cabinet can hardly expect, or does it receive, any opposition from a Communist-dominated Presidium elected by a Communist-dominated People's Assembly consisting of representatives of a Communist-dominated People's Front.[1]

[1] M. B. Petrovich, "The Central Government of Yugoslavia," *Political Science Quarterly,* LXII (1947), 527.

Students of the Soviet system will have observed the administrative similarity, approaching identity, between it and the Yugoslav system we have been sketching. The Yugoslav Constitution reflected the Stalin Constitution of 1936; the People's Assembly was parallel to the Supreme Soviet with its two chambers; the Presidium with its ornamental president, the federal and federal-republican ministries, and the interlocking role of party and government all corresponded to their Russian prototypes. The Popular Front alone survived the war as a native Yugoslav device to enlist the support of non-Communists, but this was presumably intended to be temporary. The pyramid of people's councils elected at each administrative level closely reflected the soviets of the USSR, and indeed were established in the countryside during World War II in conscious imitation of what had happened in Russia in 1917. Originally they had commanded a good deal of popular enthusiasm, but after the war the central government reached out to dominate them, and to bring them into complete harmony with Belgrade's policies, for which they now became mere sounding boards. The councils at every level, from the lowest to the People's Assembly itself, elected judges. And assisting the Party at every level were the Communist youth organizations, organizations of "anti-fascist" women, the trade unions, and the management boards of factories and coöperatives.

The constitution of Yugoslavia guaranteed the right of private property. This provision was clearly intended to be temporary, and to allay suspicion until economic planning had reached the point where nationalization and collectivization were thought desirable. The constitution also guaranteed freedom of speech, association, assembly, and religion, and the inviolability of the home, the right to work, and the right to leisure. But these provisions were window-dressing only, since the constitution specifically declared it illegal to use these civil liberties for the purpose "of changing or infringing the constitutional order with an anti-democratic purpose." The government and its police and judicial organs were of course the sole judge as to what constituted such "anti-democratic purpose." So police invaded the home with impunity, and dragged away for secret trial and sentence many a citizen accused of nothing but opposition, or the exercise of those very liberties which the constitution guaranteed.

In addition to the thousands of trials and punishments of which the public never heard, one of the features of life in Yugoslavia was a series of widely publicized major trials. The first, and in some ways the most dramatic, was that of General Mihailovich, who was captured in Bosnia with the handful of his remaining followers in March 1946. The trial, which began on June 10, was reminiscent of those conducted in the USSR: the State Prosecutor played the role of Vyshinsky in hectoring the accused; the defendant had insufficient time to study an enormously long and detailed indictment. Though weary and exhausted, Mihailovich did not "confess" to all the charges brought against him. Unless one is willing to stipulate that all the documentary evidence was manufactured by the Communists, one must concede that the evidence of collaboration with the enemy was convincing. Often the collaboration was carried on without Mihailovich's direct knowledge, and it is clear that he had very little control over many of his subordinate commanders. The motivation of his behavior was complicated indeed, and the Communists neither understood nor sympathized with the tragic confusion of a man who

> found myself in a whirl of events and intrigues. I found myself in a whirl of events and strivings. I was confronted with the aims and tendencies of my own government. I was surrounded with all possible intelligence services, the British Intelligence Service, the Gestapo, and all the intelligence services of the world. Destiny was merciless towards me when it threw me into the most difficult whirlwinds. I wanted much, I began much, but the whirlwind, the world whirlwind, carried me and my work away.[2]

On July 17, Mihailovich was shot.

In the same month, Dr. Dragolyub Yovanovich, a member of the People's Assembly on the Popular Front list, made a speech strongly criticizing the government. Yovanovich, who had been educated in France, had served in the prewar period as professor of agricultural economics at the University of Belgrade. He had been a member of the left wing of the Serbian Agrarian Party, had been imprisoned under the dictatorship in 1932 for anti-state activities, and in 1939 had founded his own Popular Peasant Party, which had some following among the Serbian peasantry especially in his native district of Pirot, but had not had time to become widely known or strongly entrenched before the war. Like Radich or Stamboliisky, Yovanovich was a left-wing agrarian who favored peasant coöperatives, a Balkan federation, and close relations with Russia, but opposed communism as such. Though sympathetic to the Partisans during the war, he was at one time said to have led his own resistance group in Pirot. He now declared that the peasants were not getting enough representation, that the public prosecutor had too much power, and that it was unwise to depend exclusively upon the USSR in foreign affairs. He was given a grim lesson in democracy by the regime, which ousted him from the Serbian Assembly, and from his university post, forced his by now docile People's Peasant Party to expel him, deprived him of his seat in the People's Assembly, and eventually in September 1947 brought him to trial. He was charged with collaborating with British agents in the organization of a peasant opposition to the regime, and was sentenced to nine years' imprisonment. This trial represented one of the high points of Yugoslav Communist injustice and undemocratic behavior.[3]

[2] *The Trial of Dragoljub-Draža Mihailović* (Belgrade, 1946), p. 499.

[3] In 1947 and 1948 there were other similar trials of political opponents, including Milosh Trifunovich, the Serb Radical leader; Boris Furlan, a Slovene Progressive; Franyo Gazhi, a left-wing member of the Croatian Peasant Party; and Tomo Yanchikovich, a Croat Peasant. Moreover, the regime arrested and brought to trial groups of guerrillas operating against the state, some of them allegedly infiltrated by Pavelich supporters from Italy and, according to the Yugoslav government charges, equipped with radio receivers by the American intelligence services.

In the spring of 1948 came the first evidence of difficulties within the Yugoslav Communist Party itself. It had all along been the policy of the party to keep its own organization a secret. Even the names of its Politburo were not published, and the public was left to conjecture as to the exact positions of its real bosses, although everybody knew that Tito, Kardelj, Vukmanovich-Tempo, Piyade, Rankovich, Djilas, and others were among them. In March 1948 two of the Ministers known to be Communists, Sreten Zhuyovich-Tsrni (the black or swarthy one), Minister of Finance, and Andriya Hebrang, Minister of Light Industry, failed to appear at the sessions of the People's Assembly which met to discuss the budget. Without naming them, Kardelj in a speech referred to certain members of the Financial Planning Commission who had manifested an "incorrect attitude." Soon after came the announcement that Zhuyovich and Hebrang had been expelled from the party, and sent to prison.

But the real meaning of the internal dissension was hidden until June. The Yugoslav government had been judged so loyal a satellite of the USSR that the new Communist Information Bureau or Cominform, set up in September 1947, had established its offices and was publishing its newspaper in Belgrade. Now the world learned with amazement that Tito and his colleagues had in fact been engaged in a great quarrel with the Russians, and were now solemnly excommunicated. This momentous news marked the opening of an entirely new phase both in the history of southeast Europe and in that of world communism.

ALBANIA

Meanwhile, in Albania, Tito's pupils were imitating their master as faithfully as conditions permitted. The LNC changed its name to the Democratic Front, and tried and executed all the BK and Zogist leaders it could catch. Bedri Spahiu, one of the earliest Communist leaders, acted as prosecutor, and the trials were designed to cast the gravest possible aspersions on the western allies, especially the British. Unlike Yugoslavia, where the Tito-Shubashich agreements had made possible a legal continuity of regime, Albania still had no government which the allies had recognized. A British military mission under Brigadier Hodgson arrived in Tirana in March 1945, and in the same month Mr. Stettinius as Secretary of State declared that the United States planned to send diplomatic observers into the country. But, though Hoxha professed great anxiety for recognition, he treated allied personnel with suspicion and calculated rudeness, and delayed for some time the signing of the proposed agreement for UNRRA assistance.

In a country where there were only a couple of thousand real Communists, Hoxha tried to maintain control by introducing into all government agencies the equivalent of political commissars (*pergjegjes*). The front conducted an election on the Yugoslav model (December 2, 1945): 92 per cent of the electorate voted, and 93 per cent of their votes were cast for the Front's list.

There was no other, but, as in Yugoslavia, facilities were provided for the expression of disapproval. The resulting constituent assembly met in January 1946, declared Albania a republic, and produced a constitution modeled on those of the USSR and Yugoslavia, except that in Albania there was no need for a chamber of nationalities, so that the assembly was unicameral.

Unlike the Yugoslav party, however, the Albanian Communists were ridden by faction. At a meeting of the plenum at Berat in November 1944, Hoxha was criticized for favoring the "intellectuals," and showing an intolerant attitude toward the "proletarian" members of the party. Koci Xoxe emerged on this occasion as Hoxha's opponent. His particular target was Liri Gega, the leading Albanian woman Communist, a North Albanian, member of the first committee of national liberation and of the party Central Committee, and leader of the "anti-fascist women's front," Minister of the Interior, and Colonel on the General Staff. She was now expelled from the Central Committee. One of the Yugoslav emissaries strongly and successfully opposed Nako Spiro, also a friend of Hoxha and an "intellectual," in his bid for office as member of the Central Committee. Dishnitsa and Malleshova were also named as belonging to this "clique" of intellectuals.

The Yugoslavs sided with Xoxe and the "proletarians" against Hoxha and the "intellectuals." As Secretary of the Central Committee and head of the secret police, Xoxe, with Yugoslav backing, continued this feud in the interval before the Cominform break, picking off the "intellectuals" and apparently making an attempt to isolate Hoxha himself. Though Spiro was supposedly a friend of Hoxha, he was the author of a highly critical biographical sketch of him, which the Yugoslavs have reprinted with some satisfaction. One of the "signs of error" for which the Yugoslavs were looking among the Albanian comrades was of course any support for "ethnic Albania," the nationalist desire for the Kossovo region, a human longing which some Albanian Communists could not repress.

The French-educated "intellectuals" were too western-oriented. Hoxha himself let fall some ill-considered works of praise for de Gaulle and for France as the "cradle of liberty." The vigilant Yugoslavs and Xoxe were on the watch for any such failure to appreciate that only the Soviet Union and Yugoslavia were the possessors of the truth. Worse yet, the government resumed relations with Italy, repatriated by agreement Italians still in Albania, and allowed Albanians to study in Italy. Some of the "intellectuals" even referred to "brotherhood" between Italy and Albania, which clearly proved them "fascists." Moreover, there even seemed to be among some of them a leaning toward the United States.

At the fifth plenum on February 21, 1946, the "proletarians," led by Xoxe, expelled Malleshova from the Politburo and the Central Committee, as guilty of advocating a "liberal completely opportunist policy with regard to the relations which our country should have with the Anglo-American imperialist countries." In the spring of 1947, Malleshova was expelled from the party.

Dishnitsa, one of whose great sins was the conclusion of the (violated) Mukaj agreement of 1943 to join forces with the Zogists, had been ousted from the party Central Committee in 1944 for that wicked act at the urgent pressure of the Yugoslav, Dushan Mugosha, but Hoxha had none the less made him Minister of Health. Xoxe drove him from the party at the same time as Malleshova in 1947.

Nako Spiro, head of the Communist youth organization during the war, a member of the Politburo and Minister of National Economy, was not an "open" pro-westerner like Malleshova but a "secret" one. His sins were truly unforgivable: hostility to Yugoslavia, opposition to the various economic agreements between the two countries, "sabotage" of the Durazzo-Peqin railroad, which was in course of construction with Yugoslav materials and technical aid, agitation against Yugoslavia in the Albanian youth brigade building the railroad, opposition to the Five-Year Plan, and favoring Albanian self-sufficiency and economic development without Yugoslavia. Under the circumstances it was surely no wonder that Spiro should have been found dead, killed "while cleaning his revolver" before the meeting of the eighth plenum of the party, or that the plenum should have denounced him, or that a later announcement should have declared him a suicide, who was "conscious of his treason."

Of all the East European Communist Parties, the Albanian was the only one not invited to participate in the formation of the Cominform in 1947. One may conjecture that the immaturity of the party and the relative unimportance of Albania itself may have been the reason for this. On the other hand, it seems at least equally plausible that Stalin and Zhdanov from the first intended the Cominform in part as an instrument to coerce the unruly Yugoslavs, and that the Albanian party was too much under Yugoslav influence to serve as an effective member of the new organization. If Dedijer's official biography may be believed, Stalin asked Tito in 1946 about the Albanian party and its internal problems, reporting that Hoxha was very anxious to come to Moscow, "but they do not want to let Enver come alone; they want to send Kochi Dzodze (Xoxe) with him, as a sort of control." Tito replied that he had never seen Hoxha, that the leaders of the Albanian party were young, and that he was not aware of deep disagreements among them.

The conversation allegedly continued as follows:

> STALIN: "We are constantly putting off their coming. What do you think; should we receive them here in Moscow? It seems to me there is no need to do so. It would now be unpleasant for them to come, both for themselves and for us. Better if we helped them through you. But, nevertheless, things aren't in order in the Albanian Politburo."
>
> RANKOVICH: "There are no matters of import, except that the comrades in the Albanian Politburo do not consider Enver Hoxha a sufficiently firm Party man and always endeavor to have Kochi Dzodze going about with him as the eldest member of the Party in the Politburo. During the April plenum (1946) they discussed the Party line, especially in relation to Yugoslavia and the

Soviet Union, and exposed some errors, and, holding Seyfoul Maleshov (Sejfulla Malleshova) responsible, evicted him from the Politburo. The leadership has been more compact since."

TITO: "We can settle those questions with them."

STALIN: "Good." [4]

Always supposing this dialogue to be truly accurate, we can conclude that the Yugoslavs were highly secretive with Stalin in answer to his questions: they said nothing about the division between the "intellectuals" and the "proletarians," and nothing about the "pro-western" orientation of the former, even though we know from their own publications that they were aware of the feud, and participating actively in it. They apparently were determined to hold on to the Albanian party as their own satellite, and it is at least plausible that Stalin's questions were not so naïve as they seem, and that he was trying to test precisely this point. In 1947, again according to Dedijer, Stalin asked Kardelj still more about the Albanians; in fact, Dedijer says, he was always asking about them.

This time the conversation allegedly went as follows:

Stalin suddenly asked: "How are things with the Albanians? Enver Hoxha has complained about your political advisers in their army, he says they are weakening discipline or something of the sort."

KARDELJ: "That is news to us. They said nothing to us about it."

STALIN: "What is the origin of the Albanians?"

KARDELJ: "They are descendants of the Illyrians."

STALIN: "I remember Tito told me they are related to the Basques."

KARDELJ: "Yes, that's right."

STALIN: "They seem to be rather backward and primitive people."

AMBASSADOR VLADIMIR POPOVIC: "But they are very brave and faithful."

STALIN: "Yes, they can be as faithful as a dog; that is one of the traits of the primitive. Our Chuvashi were the same. The Russian tsars always took them for their bodyguard." . . . "Do you know Enver well? What is your opinion of him? Is he a consistent man? Will he remain with us to the end?"

KARDELJ: "Our opinion is that he is good and honest on the whole, although he has certain characteristics of a petty bourgeois intellectual. He has a good war record and the people love him. But he lacks Marxist-Leninist training. Still, we think that he will hold on. But we consider that the best and most consistent man there is Kochi Dzodze, a worker, although he also lacks training."

STALIN: "They had some disagreement?"

KARDELJ: "That's all settled now."

STALIN to MOLOTOV: "What do you think?"

MOLOTOV: "I think that the opinion of the Yugoslavs is right. I saw Hoxha in Paris. He is very handsome and leaves a good impression. He is quite cultured, but you feel Western influence in his upbringing."

[4] Dedijer, *Tito,* p. 273.

Dedijer goes on to say that all this time agents of the Soviet Union were "provoking a conflict between Enver Hoxha and Kochi Dzodze, and constantly intriguing against Yugoslavia."[5]

This may well be true; if so, while the Yugoslavs were backing Xoxe, the USSR and its agents were clearly backing Hoxha. Surely Stalin's innocence was a pretense, and he was putting the Yugoslavs to the test. Neither here nor in other fields did they pass it.

RUMANIA

In Rumania and Bulgaria, the Communists were in a different position. In one sense they were at a disadvantage: they had to deal with the other political parties of the country in a true coalition, and had not established during the war local and central government institutions of their own. In another sense they had an advantage: Soviet troops were in occupation of their countries, and could give them full backing.

Indeed, there now returned to Rumania from the USSR several prominent Rumanian Communists, who had been in exile in Moscow for varying periods. One of these was the notorious Ana Pauker, daughter of a Moldavian Rabbi, who had allegedly turned in her own husband as a Trotskyite. She had played an important part in clandestine Rumanian Communist activities in the twenties and thirties, and had been arrested in 1932 and sentenced in 1934 to ten years in jail. In 1940, the Rumanian government "exchanged" her and others for Rumanians captured by the Russians in their occupation of Bessarabia. The war years she spent in the Soviet Union, where she broadcast in Rumanian over the Moscow radio. She was active in organizing and indoctrinating a special division of Rumanian troops, formed from prisoners of war captured by the Russians, and christened the Tudor Vladimirescu division, after the peasant leader of the Rumanian uprising of the early 1820's. It marched into Rumania with the Russian armies, and fought against the Hungarians and Germans.[6]

Another "Moscow" Communist who now returned was Vasile Luca, a Szekler from Transylvania, whose name was often given its Magyar form Laszlo Lukas. A Communist leader in the Rumanian trade unions, he had been "liberated" when the Russians occupied northern Bukovina, and under their first occupation in 1940–41 was made deputy mayor of Cernauți, where he was allegedly in charge of deporting Rumanians from the province. He then became a major in the Soviet army. On his return, he began to edit the party newspaper *Scânteia* (*The Spark*, cf. *Iskra*). A third returner was Emil Bodnaraş, a half-Ukrainian Rumanian citizen from the Bukovina, whose real name may have been Bodnarenko or Bodnariuk, and who is also said to have

[5] Dedijer, *Tito*, p. 303.

[6] A second Soviet-indoctrinated Rumanian division was formed somewhat later and named "Horia, Cloşca, and Crişan" after three Transylvanian peasant rebels of the 1780's. It did not participate in the war.

used the name Spataru. Graduate of a Rumanian military academy, and a regular army officer, he had allegedly deserted to Russia, and served the Communist cause as spy and organizer of party cells in Rumania. Though he had been arrested in Rumania, he had escaped to the USSR. His role was that of party strong-man and organizer of armed squads of toughs.

These three all suffered from the same liability: none of them was a real ethnic Rumanian. In a party with fewer than 2,000 members, the chief Rumanian leader, except for the intellectual Patrașcanu, was Gheorghe Gheorghiu-Dej, a Rumanian railway worker, who had served as Secretary-General of the Communist-dominated railway-workers union in the late twenties and early thirties. It was Gheorghiu-Dej who had led the famous Grivița strike of the railway workshops in Bucharest in February 1933. He too had spent much time in jail, adding to his own surname of Gheorghiu the name of the Transylvanian town of Dej, where he had been imprisoned. It is said that, while in prison in the thirties, Gheorghiu-Dej led an intrigue against the Secretary-General of the Communist Party known as Foris, whom he accused of being a fascist spy. Ana Pauker, Vasile Luca, and other leading Communists are supposed to have joined Gheorghiu-Dej in this maneuver; Gheorghiu-Dej was in prison at the time of the Soviet "liberation"; he is said to have brought about the execution of Foris in jail, and to have emerged to join his fellow-Communist activists entering the country with the conquering Soviet armies.

With the Soviet armies on the soil of Rumania, and Moscow enjoying 90 per cent of the "say" by the Churchill-Stalin agreement, it was unlikely, to say the least, that these activists would content themselves with Patrașcanu's Ministry of Justice, which was the only political post they held in the first Sanatescu government, and was actually far more than they deserved either from the point of view of the political support they commanded or of their achievements during the war. They now embarked on a campaign of harassment and political pressure which was to culminate in early March 1945 with overt Russian interference and the establishment of a purely pro-Soviet regime.

To rally some support from non-Communist Rumanians, they used four chief "front" organizations. The Union of Patriots (Uniunea Patrioților) was designed for professional men, chiefly liberals and opportunists, who none the less hesitated to take the plunge and join the party itself. Groza's Ploughmen's Front (Frontul Plugarilor) had initially been founded for peasants in Transylvania, where it was now revived, but also operated in the Regat. Though it recruited some real support, most of its officers were Communists, and many of its rank and file Iron Guardists. The Patriotic Defense (Apararea Patriotica), ostensibly a social-welfare organization, raised funds for wounded soldiers, victims of famine, and the like. It also commanded a militia of its own, consisting of armed workers. Its agents virtually extorted large contributions from all who could pay, and the resources were certainly used for party purposes. The ARLUS, or society for friendship with the Soviet Union, the first of what would be a whole series of such organizations in eastern and southeastern Europe, ostensibly acted as sponsor of cultural exhibitions and banquets celebrating the new comradeship with the USSR, but was largely also a fund-raising outfit, membership in which gave businessmen the opportunity to stay in the good graces of the regime.

The Communists had the further advantage that the Rumanian conservative parties were whole-heartedly anti-Russian, and a good many of their members continued to assume that the western allies would somehow intervene in Rumania and protect the country from Soviet pressure. Failing to appraise the situation realistically, they did not push for purges of pro-Germans and war-criminals, and some in high positions did what they could to evade the Russian demands for material assistance in the war against Germany. With this unmistakable trend as an excuse, the Communists were able to engineer a split in the loose four-party opposition bloc. They and the Social Democrats, together with the Union of Patriots, the Ploughmen's Front, and the reactivated trade-unions, in which Gheorghiu-Dej and his fellow-Communist Gheorghe Apostol were very active, split away in October 1944 from the National Peasants and National Liberals, and formed a so-called National Democratic Front (FND).

Early in November 1944, the first Sanatescu government gave way to a second, which included far more politicians and fewer generals. Constantin Vișoianu, who had been Maniu's emissary to Cairo, and had signed the armistice in Moscow, became Foreign Minister, and a number of Liberals and Peasants also took office. But the left also greatly increased its representation, Gheorghiu-Dej taking the portfolio of communications, Groza of the Ploughmen's Front becoming Vice Premier, and a number of left-wing Social Democrats also obtaining ministries. Neither Maniu nor Bratianu, who had been ministers without portfolio, held office in the new Cabinet. Nicolae Penescu, a National Peasant, was Minister of the Interior.

It was on this key ministry, which controlled the police, the rural gendarmerie, and the appointments of local prefects and mayors, that the Communists now concentrated their fire. "Spontaneous" demonstrations of workmen taken out of factories and of unemployed who were paid a tiny sum a day for their "services" were now organized to parade the streets of Bucharest carrying banners and shouting "Down with Penescu." The Moscow Radio accused both Maniu and Bratianu of obstructing the fulfillment of the armistice terms. In one of the demonstrations a couple of workers were allegedly killed by the police, and Ana Pauker took the opportunity to blame Penescu. Early in December Sanatescu resigned. His successor as Prime Minister, General Nicolae Radescu, was another nonpolitical general. During the war, he had courageously written an angry letter to the German Ambassador, Von Killinger, protesting against the German domination over the country, and the Germans had punished him by internment. Radescu himself took over the Ministry of the Interior, which meant that the left had succeeded in ousting Penescu. More important, a Communist under-secretary, Teohari Georgescu, was now appointed to that ministry, which represented a further gain for the left. The other ministers were about the same as their predecessors. The new government came to office apparently strengthened by a promise of a political truce.

During December 1944 the Radescu government managed to get a certain amount of business done. It repealed anti-Jewish legislation dating back to 1938, and passed a decree calling for the arrest of war criminals. One of the major difficulties facing the regime was that its authority scarcely extended beyond Wallachia and southern Transylvania. In Moldavia the Antonescu-appointed authorities had fled from the Russian advance, and the Russians had replaced them with officials of their own choosing, mostly Communists, including many Jews. In northern Transylvania, liberated from the Hungarians in October and November, the Russians declared that the Rumanian authorities initially sent out from Bucharest had engaged largely in arming the Rumanian peasants and inciting them to persecute the Magyars. It is true that armed Rumanians, called by the Hungarians and Russians "Maniu guards" (although they often had only the most tenuous connection if any with the National Peasant Party), did go about shooting and terrorizing Hungarians. It is also understandable that after four years of Hungarian domination, most Rumanians in northern Transylvania were itching for revenge, and that the politicians of the National Peasant Party and others had no interest in curbing excesses.

At any rate, the Russians, declaring that public order was necessary to the conduct of the war, expelled the first Bucharest appointees from the area early in November. This gave rise to a great crop of rumors in the capital that the Russians intended not to return northern Transylvania to Rumania but to create a Soviet republic there. Under the sponsorship of the Russians, but chiefly under the immediate influence of local left-wing Rumanians and Hungarians, most localities proceeded to choose their authorities by "acclamation," a procedure which usually resulted in the installation of men satisfactory to the left. Thus conditions in Moldavia and northern Transylvania were such that the Radescu government was virtually powerless there, and depended entirely upon Russian good will if it were ever to reassert Rumanian authority.

In January 1945, Ana Pauker and Gheorghiu-Dej went on a trip to Moscow. Here they apparently got orders or permission to push the FND bloc's program. Once again crisis raged. On January 27, the left leadership called for a new government, declaring Radescu a reactionary, and announcing that only the FND could command the confidence of the Soviet Union, and, it hinted, obtain the return of northern Transylvania by applying a "democratic" policy toward the Magyar minority. The left also demanded immediate agrarian reform: the confiscation of all properties larger than fifty hectares, and the distribution of all lands belonging to "war-criminals." No mention was made of an earlier demand: that large industries and major banks be nationalized; apparently the Russians felt that the time was not yet ripe for anything so radical and so likely to alarm the moderates and, possibly, the British and American members of the Allied Control Commission in Bucharest. The left now began to use a new and most effective instrument: through its control of the printers' union, it prevented the publication of National Peasant and National Liberal newspapers.

Radescu himself bravely fought against the intimidation from the left. When his statements were not printed by the Communist-dominated printers' union, he determined to make a speech in a Bucharest theater. When the Communists packed the theater, he moved the speech to another one, and broadcast an address in which he appealed for order, and came out against an immediate agrarian reform. In the Premier's own ministry of the interior, the Communist under-secretary, Teohari Georgescu, countered by demanding that the officials of the ministry pay no attention to Radescu, and urging the peasants simply to seize the land. There can be no doubt that Radescu was a strong patriot, who justly feared what was about to happen to his country. He might have served it better, however, and even managed to cling to office, had he remembered that he was a "nonpolitical" appointee, who technically ought not to have taken a stand on the program of the left, although he was free to take steps for the preservation of order. His emergence in a "political" role as leader of the opposition to the left — which had helped appoint him — actually weakened rather than strengthened his moral position. But the decision had in any case apparently been made elsewhere.

There was a final crisis on February 24, when several people were killed after a National Democratic Front demonstration in Bucharest. The Communists maintained that the troops under Radescu's orders had fired on the demonstrators when they moved toward the Ministry of the Interior. Radescu flatly denied the truth of this: the troops, he declared, were under orders not to fire, and the bullets had come from a truckful of Communist toughs. When the bullets were extracted from the unfortunate victims they proved to be of a caliber not in use in the Rumanian army. That night Radescu delivered a broadcast in which he referred to Pauker and Luca as "horrible hyenas" and "foreigners without God or country," a clear reference to the Jewish origins of one and the Hungarian origins of the other. The left press in return indulged in comparable vituperation, calling Radescu a murderer.

A couple of days later, on February 27, Soviet Deputy Commissar Vyshinsky arrived in Bucharest, and put on a performance which has since become notorious. Telling the King that Radescu was unable to maintain order, Vyshinsky demanded that the King dismiss him. The following day, when the King told Vyshinsky that he was consulting with his ministers on the question of a successor, Vyshinsky gave him two hours and five minutes to announce the name. He pounded the table and slammed the door so hard on leaving the room that the plaster of the wall cracked. He refused to accept the King's suggestion of Prince Ştirbey as premier, and declared that Groza was the only choice who would be acceptable to the USSR. Moreover, when Groza gave the King his purely FND slate of ministers and the King declined to accept it, Vyshinsky told him that such refusal was an act unfriendly to the USSR, and that unless the King swallowed the entire Groza cabinet by noon the next day, Rumania might cease to exist as a sovereign state.

Under this pressure the King yielded, and by March 6, 1945, the country knew the worst. The Groza Cabinet included not one single member of the National Peasant or National Liberal Parties. Instead, in addition to the Communists and their fellow-travelers of the front groups, Groza and his left-wing advisers had chosen as Vice Premier and Foreign Minister Gheorghiu Tatarescu, a "dissident" member of the Liberal Party, twice premier under King Carol, a discredited and dishonest politician of the most opportunist sort, deeply tinged with anti-Semitism, and responsible among other notorious acts for the massacre of peasants by the police at Tatar Bunar in Bessarabia in the mid-thirties. Pro-German and utterly unscrupulous, Tatarescu might well have been hanged as a war criminal instead of receiving a post in the cabinet; but this was precisely why the Russians chose him. Nobody could possibly call him a Communist, and yet the Russians had as complete control over him as if he were, because they could at any moment "remember" his record, and drag him off to jail.

There were three or four other such "dissident" Liberals, and three "dissident" Peasants representing nobody but themselves, but enabling the Russians to claim that the Cabinet was representative. Here we encounter an early instance of a technique with which the world was to become all too familiar in the satellite countries: the isolation from a recognized political party of a few opportunists who would collaborate with the Communists. These would then be hailed as constituting the party in question, and its genuine members could be disregarded and eventually persecuted. Such were the "Liberals," "Peasants," and "Socialists," in the Groza Cabinet. The Minister of Cults, Father Burducea, was a priest who had formerly been a vigorous Iron Guardist. The Groza government also included Teohari Georgescu as Minister of the Interior. The Communist Party had now obtained the ministry it had sought for months. Groza declared that the Russians had told him they would restore northern Transylvania, and within three days they did so. The writ of Bucharest ran again in this province, but it was now a safely left-wing writ. Groza further announced that he would push agrarian reform and the punishment of war criminals.

Indeed, now that the USSR had a Rumanian government made to its order, it turned over to the Groza authorities the four chief Rumanian "war-criminals," Marshal Antonescu, Mihai Antonescu, and two Generals. They were tried in May, and executed in June 1945. After testifying at their trial,

Maniu, in leaving the courtroom, shook the hands of both Antonescus, a gesture which he later explained as a necessary Christian farewell to two human beings in deep trouble. Maniu's act enabled the Communists to identify him with the Antonescus, whereas he had actually opposed their regime.

The unilateral intervention of the Russians in Rumanian internal affairs in February-March 1945 seemed to the United States a clear violation of the Yalta declaration on liberated Europe. Churchill of course thought so too; but was hesitant to protest because of the percentages agreement.

> We were hampered in our protests because Eden and I during our October visit to Moscow had recognized that Russia should have a largely predominant voice in Rumania and Bulgaria while we took the lead in Greece. Stalin had kept very strictly to this understanding during the six weeks fighting against the Communists and E.L.A.S. in Athens, in spite of the fact that all this was most disagreeable to him and to those around him. . . . He had subscribed to the principles of Yalta, and they were now being trampled down in Rumania. But if I pressed him too much he might say, "I did not interfere with your action in Greece; why do you not give me the same latitude in Rumania?" [7]

Churchill was also concerned for fear that a protest on the Rumanian development might jeopardize a settlement on Poland, which was then in the course of discussion among the big three. Roosevelt himself also felt that Rumania was a poor test case. As the later Secretary of State, James F. Byrnes, reports:

> Great Britain and the United States had no armed forces in Rumania. It was under the exclusive control of the Red Army. The President knew that the Soviets had to maintain a line of communication from the homeland through Rumania to their armies in Germany. We knew the Soviets would claim the action taken was necessary to protect their armies. . . .[8]

But, despite the British embarrassment and the American reluctance, it is clear that Rumania had provided the first source of major disagreement between the Russians and the western allies, just as it had provided the first test of the earlier alliance between the Russians and Hitler. Soon there were other causes for Soviet-western friction; but Vyshinsky's activities in Rumania only three weeks after Yalta were the beginning. It was now clear that the Russians would pay no heed to the "Declaration on Liberated Europe," and that they harked back to the percentages agreement as their real guide for action.

For some time the course of Rumanian internal politics continued to be largely determined by the relationship among the three major powers. The first conference after President Roosevelt's death and the end of the war in Europe was held at Potsdam (July 17–August 2, 1945). When Churchill and Stalin dined together on the night of July 18, Stalin revealed how dismayed he had been to find that the percentages agreement had not been binding on the United States:

[7] Churchill, *The Second World War*, VI, *Triumph and Tragedy*, 420.
[8] J. F. Byrnes, *Speaking Frankly* (New York, 1947), p. 53.

"Stalin also said that he had been hurt by the American demand for a change of Government in Rumania and Bulgaria. He was not meddling in Greek affairs, and it was unjust of them. I said I had not yet seen the American proposals."[9]

Soon afterwards, the United States delegation presented a paper maintaining that the Yalta declaration had not been properly carried out in Rumania or Bulgaria. Stalin instantly produced a memorandum attacking British behavior in Greece. The Russians wanted the western powers to join them in diplomatic recognition of the Groza government. To all the western protests about the difficulties put in the way of the western representatives in Rumania, the Russians countered with complaints about the ill-treatment allegedly accorded to their own representatives in Italy. Though refusing to allow the western allies to assist in the supervision of Rumanian elections, the Russians were willing to ease up on the restrictions of the movements of allied representatives and on the censorship of newspaper correspondence. The first Potsdam declaration on southeast Europe proclaimed that the Council of Foreign Ministers would prepare peace treaties for Rumania and Bulgaria, and that these would be concluded with "recognized democratic governments." Moreover, the three governments agreed to "examine . . . the establishment of diplomatic relations . . . to the extent possible prior to the conclusion of peace treaties. . . ." Two days after the close of the Potsdam conference, the Russians accorded the Groza government diplomatic recognition.

It was clear that nothing had been settled. The new British Foreign Minister, Ernest Bevin (the Labor Party had won the elections held during the Potsdam Conference), declared in the House of Commons on August 20, however, that the Rumanian, Bulgarian, and Hungarian governments were not "sufficiently representative to meet the requirements of diplomatic relations." King Michael now declared that the wording of the Potsdam declaration made it obligatory for the Groza government to resign, since it was not a "recognized democratic government." He asked for American, British, and Russian assistance in forming a new cabinet which should be acceptable to the west, as Groza's clearly was not. Both the Rumanian left and the Russians instantly assumed that the King was receiving American and British support for his action, although in fact this was not the case. Groza refused to resign, visited Moscow, received full Russian backing, and returned to Bucharest. King Michael retired to the royal summer palace at Sinaia, and refused to sign any decrees. Groza tried to pretend that no serious rift had taken place. *Izvestia* denounced the United States and Britain for plotting with the King.

The impasse continued through the conference of foreign ministers which met in London from September 11 through October 3, 1945. Here Molotov told the press that the Rumanian government was democratic (if democratic meant "pro-Russian," this was true) and that it enjoyed the support of the majority of the people (which was manifestly false). While the western allies

[9] Churchill, *The Second World War*, VI, *Triumph and Tragedy*, 636.

could not accept this view, both had long agreed that the Russians were reasonable in demanding "friendly" governments in the states along their frontiers. Byrnes reiterated this view in a broadcast made not long after the London conference had ended in disagreement, and added that the United States would never intrigue against the USSR by supporting groups hostile to Moscow. Yet the harsh fact of the matter was that any election in Rumania conducted in a way such as to seem "free" to the west would surely have returned an overwhelmingly anti-Soviet regime to power. Rumanian opinion was purely and simply anti-Russian, and if consulted, as the Yalta "Declaration" required it be consulted, this would have been clearly manifest. The Russians, who had never taken the Yalta declaration seriously, and who had instead counted on the percentages agreement, would presumably never have subscribed to the Yalta declaration had they realized that the Americans and British intended to hold them to it. But their own "correct" abstention from interference in Greece had encouraged them to believe that there would be no objection to their adoption of their own methods of insuring a "friendly" government in Rumania.

When instead they found that the United States, which had never been bound by the percentages agreement, chose to regard the Yalta declaration as the true policy instead, and when they found that the British, though somewhat embarrassed, joined the United States in forgetting the "percentages" agreement and insisting on the fulfillment of the Yalta declaration, they were apparently both surprised and chagrined. On the level of efficient conduct of government operations, one may criticize all three great powers: Britain for proposing the original percentages agreement and then for not making it abundantly clear at Yalta that it had been superseded; the United States for not vigorously opposing the percentages agreement and for pretending at Yalta that it did not exist; and the Russians for not inquiring whether their allies were really as cynical as they, and truly intended the percentages agreement to operate after the Yalta declaration had been issued. But even if all three governments had conducted their business efficiently, the nature of Rumanian public opinion could not have been altered: a freely elected Rumanian government would have been an anti-Soviet government.

In Rumania early in November 1945 there were demonstrations of strong loyalty to the King on his birthday. The crowds apparently were peaceful until fired upon by Communist workers brought up in trucks and by the Tudor Vladimirescu division. The violence led to the arrest and interrogation of a number of leaders of the Peasant and Liberal parties. Though these men were innocent of organizing a specific demonstration against the government, the very assembly of the crowd was an act of protest against the unrepresentative and Soviet-dominated regime and of support for its opponents.

After the failure of the London conference, Secretary Byrnes appointed Mark Ethridge, editor of the Louisville *Courier-Journal,* to visit Rumania and Bulgaria, and report on conditions. The appointment was made partly to answer Molotov's repeated assertions that the American government was ill-informed on the Balkan countries, and partly to obtain a reliable report from an experienced journalist to supplement the dispatches of the professional diplomats. The Ethridge report on Rumania, submitted in early December, strongly supported the other information at the disposal of our government.

Finally, in December 1945 at their conference in Moscow, the three foreign ministers reached an apparent compromise. The Russians agreed to join the other two powers in advising the King that one National Peasant Party member and one National Liberal Party member should be added to the existing cabinet. These two new members of the government were to be "truly representative" members of the parties, a clear indication that the western powers would not accept members of the dissident splinter groups which the Communists had been sponsoring. When the government had been recognized by the addition of these two representatives, it was to announce the holding of free and unfettered elections as soon as possible, and was to guarantee the preservation of civil liberties. The fulfillment of this new arrangement was entrusted to a three-man team of Vyshinsky and the American and British ambassadors to the USSR, W. Averell Harriman and Sir Archibald Clark-Kerr. As soon as the commission notified the three powers that the Groza government had fulfilled the requirements, the United States and Britain would grant it diplomatic recognition.

The compromise was obviously from the first a Russian victory. The two new representatives were not necessarily to hold portfolios, and would easily be neutralized in a cabinet of twenty-odd ministers of the FND. Recognition was to precede the holding of elections; so the United States and Britain gave up in advance any leverage which they might otherwise have exercised to enforce the provision that the elections were to be free and unfettered. The very certainty that free elections would have returned an anti-Russian government to power made it certain that no such elections would be held. The two representatives of the "historical" parties were chosen: Emil Hațieganu for the National Peasants, and Mihai Romniceanu for the National Liberals. They held no portfolios, and their FND colleagues simply ignored them. Groza gave oral assurances that concentration camps had been closed and that there were fewer than ten political prisoners in the entire country. The United States and Britain recognized the Groza government early in February 1946.

Now the western allies were entitled to expect that preparations for the "free" elections would go forward with all speed, and that the elections themselves might be held sometime in the spring of 1946. But the Communists had apparently no intention of living up to the Moscow agreement. Although the Peasant and Liberal parties were allowed to print their newspapers, there was much interference with the distribution, and it was often impossible to buy them outside the capital. Thugs invaded opposition political meetings and beat up those who attended; arrests multiplied. Protests from the United

States and Britain were simply ignored. The government could not hold even a rigged election until it had intimidated and disrupted the opposition as much as possible.[10]

The electoral law gave every advantage to the Communists. Polls were set up in factories and barracks, where FND agents could bring direct pressure on workers and soldiers. Electoral lists were hastily compiled so that no real check could be made on inaccuracies. Women were enfranchised for the first time, and fascists, Iron Guardists, and those who had of their own free will fought against the "allies" were disfranchised. The new assembly was to be a single chamber with 414 members, and would have a four-year term of office.

Meanwhile all conceivable pressure was brought to bear on the Socialist party of Titel Petrescu to run a common list of candidates with the Communists. This party, claiming some 600,000 members after the war, commanded a good deal of support among the workers. Ever since the formation of the FND bloc, to which the Socialists had adhered, the Communists had been working to subvert Petrescu's party by infiltrating its own agents. Their work was made easier by the presence on the party's central committee of a good many politicians who had collaborated with Antonescu and the Germans, written articles against the USSR, and the like, who were therefore compromised, vulnerable, and fit tools for the Communists. On March 10, 1946 a party conference met to consider the Communist demands.[11] The tactics successfully split the Socialists, the pro-Communist wing agreeing to common lists, and Petrescu endeavoring without much success to organize his own party, which should be independent. Tatarescu's dissident "Liberals" also naturally agreed to run on common lists with the Communists.

On the eve of the elections, the western allies protested once more against these practices, but the Groza government rejected the protests, since the USSR had not joined in them, adding that the United States and Britain were guilty of unwarranted interference in Rumanian internal affairs. On November 19, 1946, the Rumanian people went to the polls in an election in which every fraudulent, violent, and unscrupulous device ever used in the Balkans was brought into full play. The government announced that 89 per cent of the electorate (almost 7,000,000 voters) had given it a great majority. It reported 880,000 votes for the National Peasant Party and 289,000 for the Liberals. In the new assembly the Peasants got thirty-two seats, the Liberals three. The rest of

[10] In August, Nicolae Penescu, the former National Peasant Minister of the Interior and a special Communist target, now secretary general of his party, was wounded and his private secretary killed. One of Maniu's relatives was also injured. The two Cabinet Ministers, Romniceanu and Haţieganu, were also harassed. A detailed account of the atrocious behavior of the left during the months before the elections is available in *Rumania under the Soviet Yoke* (Boston: Meador, 1949) a book by Reuben H. Markham, an American journalist who was eye-witness to what he reports.

[11] A member of the party, D. G. R. Serbanescu, has fully described the techniques used by the Communists to pack the meeting and even to silence Petrescu himself. See *Ciel Rouge sur la Roumanie* (Paris: Sipuco, 1952).

the 414 members were leftists.[12] Romniceanu and Hațieganu resigned from the government, which thus reverted to a pure FND body, and though the United States and Britain both declared that the elections had not fulfilled the assurances which the allies had required of and obtained from the Rumanian government, the new assembly convened on December 1, 1946.

The western allies had lost the struggle for Rumania. In retrospect it is clear that only a threat of force could have won it. In 1946, with the war against the Axis so fresh in their experience, and hope for world peace in coöperation with the USSR still strong in their minds, neither the American nor the British public would have supported any measures stronger than the ineffectual ones which were actually taken. Yet this was never fully clear to the Rumanian public, and the friends of the west and enemies of the USSR in Rumania had been cruelly exposed to vengeance by the series of protests from the west which kept alive their hopes that they could avoid what proved to be an inevitable fate. The Peace Treaty with Rumania, signed in February 1947, only gave legal sanction to the existing state of affairs. It is true that Article 3 required the Rumanian government to guarantee for all its subjects "the enjoyment of human rights and of the fundamental freedoms, including freedom of expression, of press, of publication, of religious worship, of political opinion, and of public meeting." In practice, however, Article 3 remained a dead letter, and every one of its provisions has been systematically violated ever since.

During the year following the elections, the Groza government, with Soviet backing, proceeded methodically to smash the political opposition. In June 1947 began the attack on the National Peasant Party. After the arrests of smaller fry, Ion Mihalache, long one of Maniu's chief lieutenants, was arrested in July, just as he was about to flee the country by air with Penescu and others. Maniu himself and most of the party leadership were also taken into custody. The party was outlawed. Deprived of parliamentary immunity, Maniu and the others were tried in November, before a court over which there presided, ominously enough, Colonel Petrescu, who had been in charge of all prisons and concentration camps under Antonescu.

Maniu, Mihalache, and seventeen others were accused of conspiring with two American intelligence officers named Hall and Hamilton to organize clandestine activity against the government and to set up American air bases in Rumania. The whole trial was designed to cast the United States, as well as the Rumanian opposition, into disrepute. The National Peasant leaders certainly opposed the Groza government, and looked to the United States for sympathy. There were quite possibly contacts between the intelligence officers

[12] Communists 73, Socialists 75, Ploughmen's Front 70, and scattering votes to the smaller dissident groups, including 29 seats for the so-called Hungarian Popular Party (Madosz) of Transylvania, which was also completely Communist-dominated, and 26 seats for the so-called National Popular Party, a new group formed from the old Union of Patriots by the Communists.

and members of the party. Maniu himself declared that he considered the Groza government illegal, and admitted that he had hoped to send some of his followers abroad to organize opposition there. He maintained that he was acting in accordance with the article of the Peace Treaty which guaranteed freedom of political action. One of Maniu's aids, Serdici, testified against him, swearing that Maniu had ordered him to inquire of the American Legation if the time had yet arrived for underground opposition to the Groza regime, to which, he said, the answer had been no. The outcome was a foregone conclusion: Maniu and Mihalache were sentenced to hard labor for life, which was commuted to solitary confinement in consideration of their age. The others received lesser sentences. The United States government publicly declared that the charges against its officials were false insinuations.

Meanwhile, Tatarescu as foreign minister courted attack from the government. The diplomatic service was still full of anti-Groza elements. Moreover, Tatarescu had actually written a memorandum attacking the government's economic policies and its extreme repression, as well as prison conditions. He urged that foreign capital be better treated. In the summer of 1947, this was tantamount to a veiled plea for the Marshall plan, or at any rate could be so interpreted. Under the circumstances, one can hardly avoid paying tribute to the courage of Tatarescu. First the Communists forced out the old-line foreign-office employees, and in November dismissed Tatarescu himself, and with him the other "dissident" Liberals. They had served their purpose. It was now that the three "Moscow" Communists assumed office for the first time. Ana Pauker succeeded Tatarescu in the Foreign Ministry, Vasile Luca became Minister of Finance, and shortly afterwards Bodnaraș became Minister of War.

During these same months, the Communists proceeded to do away with the Socialist Party by fusing it with their own. Though Titel Petrescu and his followers in the Independent Socialist Party, which they had formed at the time of the elections, resisted for some months, their efforts were of course futile. The United Workers Party, as the new fusion was called, declared itself to be the "vanguard of the working class," emphasized its Marxist-Leninist ideology, and proclaimed its close ties with the USSR and the "new democracies" in its neighboring countries, and its "brotherly solidarity" with the "victims of imperialist policy" in Greece and elsewhere. Titel Petrescu's own party was dissolved, and he himself was arrested in May 1948 on charges that his party had illegally distributed leaflets. He has never been tried. In the consolidation process, the Ploughmen's Front also absorbed a substantial portion of the "dissident" National Peasants. The new "Popular Democratic Front" as reorganized in the spring of 1948 thus included the new United Workers Party (Communists plus "dissident" socialists), the Ploughmen's Front, the National Popular Party (formerly the Union of Patriots), and the Hungarian People's Union (Madosz).

Before the process of reorganization was complete, however, the Communists needed to remove one great anachronism: the King. Immensely popular especially since the coup of August 1944, he had even been awarded the highly expensive ruby-studded Soviet Order of Victory in July 1945, as a tribute to his personal bravery in taking his country out of the war against the allies. But only a few weeks later he was defying Groza, refusing to sign decrees, and earning still more popularity, as shown by the demonstration on his birthday November 8, 1945. Even had he proved content to serve as a figurehead, he could hardly have hoped to keep his throne in a Communist country. In November 1947, he visited England for the wedding of Princess Elizabeth and the Duke of Edinburgh. He met and became engaged to Princess Anne of Bourbon-Parma. When he returned to Bucharest, he found that Ana Pauker and the other members of the government opposed the marriage, allegedly on the ground of expense, but quite probably because it would have offered opportunities for a show of popular enthusiasm. They now required Michael to abdicate. His proclamation of December 30, 1947 declared that a monarchy represented a serious impediment to Rumania's development, and left it to the "Rumanian people" to choose the new form of government. Some months later in exile, he declared the abdication invalid, as having been signed under duress.

The "people" moved rapidly to transform Rumania into a republic. Dissolving the assembly, the government called for elections for a new body to approve a new constitution. This time (March 1948) the government obtained 405 of the 414 seats, only tiny groups of "dissident" peasants and liberals filling the other nine. The assembly then (April 13, 1948) unanimously approved the new constitution, creating the Rumanian People's Republic (RPR). Modeled of course upon the Stalin constitution of 1936, the new Rumanian document presented little worthy of extended comment. It recognized the right of private property and flatly declared that "the land belongs to those who till it. The state protects the peasant holding. It encourages and maintains rural coöperation. With a view to stimulating agriculture the State can create agricultural enterprises which are the property of the state." It decreed minority and nationality rights, and guaranteed freedom of religion, press, opinion, assembly, processions, and demonstrations. But "citizens enjoy the right of association and organization if the aim is not directed against the democratic order established by the Constitution. Any Fascist or anti-democratic [i.e., anti-Communist] association is forbidden and punished by the law." The government reorganized itself: it instituted three vice-premiers, each with coördinating functions over lesser economic or social ministries. The personnel, however, remained unchanged.

There had, however, been one major political development even before the constitution was approved and the republic proclaimed. This was the disgrace of the Communist Minister of Justice, Patrașcanu. Doubtless suspect to the "Muscovites" as western-educated, Patrașcanu had apparently manifested nationalist leanings on the question of the Magyar minority. Despite all the illegal actions of which he had been guilty as Minister of Justice, he was regarded, even by westerners, as a "moderate" Communist, and it seems probable that he regretted the complete subservience of Rumania to the USSR. At any rate, he was removed from office, and jailed in February 1948. Teohari Georgescu, who had reputedly been his closest friend, denounced him as a Menshevik who had befriended war criminals and capitalists. Gheorghiu-Dej said that Patraşcanu had become a "victim of bourgeois ideology" and had "detached himself from the masses." He was replaced by Avram Bunaciu, known as a fanatical Communist. Thus in the period between the surrender of August 23, 1944 and the spring of 1948, the tiny Rumanian Communist Party, working with the assistance of Russian advisers and supported by the presence of Russian troops, had ousted, destroyed, and replaced the political opposition, transformed the monarchy into a republic, and made itself the ruler of Rumania. It had even conducted, in the Patraşcanu case, its own modest purge. It was hardly any wonder that, when Tito was expelled from the Cominform in June 1948, the Russians moved its headquarters from Belgrade to Bucharest.

BULGARIA

In Bulgaria the Communists had advantages which they did not enjoy in Rumania. They were substantially stronger in number, and commanded a good deal more respect as the leaders of the genuine though overestimated OF resistance movement during the war. Moreover, the generally pro-Russian sentiments of the Bulgarian public contrasted sharply with the strongly anti-Russian views of the Rumanians. In Bulgaria, the Communists started out after the OF coup of September 9, 1944 with both the Ministries of Justice and Interior, while in Rumania their opponents succeeded in keeping the interior portfolio until March 6, 1945, even though the Communists had installed their man Teohari Georgescu as Under-Secretary.

On the major postwar question of punishing "war-criminals," for instance, the left in Rumania was dilatory and ineffectual, partly because it did not control both police and courts; partly because many Rumanians had really been guilty of "war crimes," and the whole public *felt* guilty and lived in apprehension of what might befall them; partly because the Communists were busy recruiting former Iron Guardists and other extreme pro-German elements to strengthen their own feeble rank and file; partly perhaps just because they were Rumanians. In Bulgaria, on the other hand, where real pro-German sentiment had been far less vigorous, and genuine "war-crimes" by western standards almost nonexistent, the regime moved rapidly and with grim efficiency about the work of "epuration."

Setting up special "People's Courts," the OF government began in December 1944 the trial of the three ex-Regents, former Premier Filov, Prince Cyril, and General Mihov, thirty-eight cabinet ministers who had held office in the wartime governments, and 130 deputies from the wartime Sobranies. The

Regents and cabinet ministers were accused of supporting the ambitions of King Boris and the Coburg dynasty and making Bulgaria a slave to Germany, supporting Hitler's ambitions, crimes against the Bulgarian state and people, including the dispatch of Bulgarian workers to Germany, support of the anti-Semitic laws, and inhuman reprisals against the resistance. The deputies faced charges of approving the wartime policies of the regime, including the declaration of war against the United States and Britain, the occupation of Greek and Yugoslav territory, and the German use of Bulgaria as a base against Britain.

The courts sentenced to death and executed the regents and former premiers Bozhilov and Bagrianov, even though it had been Bagrianov who first sought to free the country from its ties to Germany. The former Minister of the Interior, Gabrovsky, twenty-five other cabinet ministers, and sixty-eight of the deputies suffered the same fate. The regime imposed many lesser sentences. Even the members of the anti-German Muraviev government suffered, Muraviev receiving a life-sentence, apparently for preferring the United States and Britain to the USSR. Nikola Mushanov, aged leader of the Democrats and of the "tolerated opposition," and Atanas Burov and Dimiter Gichev, equally innocent, received jail sentences. All this seemed to indicate that the Communist-dominated courts were more interested in discrediting their pro-western political opponents than in justice.

But the headline trials were by no means the only ones. All over the country, the regime set up its people's courts with their powers of execution without appeal. In a country still at war, no moderating influences manifested themselves to restrain the Communists at their bloody work. They now settled a lot of old political scores under the convenient cover of eagerness to punish war-criminals. The official summary of the victims as of March 1945 already ran to 2,138 executed, and 1,940 sentenced to twenty-year terms out of a total of 10,897 tried. Even if one accepts these official figures (and they are probably far too small), this was the severest purge in all of occupied Europe, and took place in the country where there were fewer "war-criminals" than any other. By March 1945, when the Bulgarian Communists were already proudly announcing their grim totals in the thousands, the Rumanians had not yet been permitted to try even the Antonescus themselves.

The Bulgarian Communists also got off to a head-start in the political "task" of attacking, splitting, and neutralizing the other political parties. The chief rivals were the Agrarians, corresponding to the Rumanian National Peasants, and the Socialists, since the former Democrats, corresponding to the Rumanian National Liberals, were not members of the OF or allowed political activity. Zveno, though it now transformed itself into a political party — the "Peoples Union Zveno" — remained more of a high-level political pressure group among the military, whose members collaborated with the Communists, than a genuine party with a popular following. The Agrarians, commanding as they did a very widespread loyalty among the peasants in a peasant country, presented the Communists with their chief target; the Socialists, strong among the urban workers, especially those organized in trade unions, were less of a problem, both numerically and ideologically.

Soon after the OF coup of September 9, 1944, Dr. Georgi M. Dimitrov, member of the "Pladne" wing of the Agrarian Party, returned to Bulgaria. Because his full name is exactly the same as that of the chief Bulgarian Communist, then still in Moscow, I shall hereafter refer to him by his nickname, "Gemeto," by which he was known both to his supporters and to his enemies. "Gemeto" had spent the war years in Cairo and Istanbul, where he had been in British service. This gave the Communists and his other political opponents the opportunity, which they were not slow to seize, to accuse him of being a British agent, and to try to discredit him as a representative of foreign interests. "Gemeto" became Secretary of the Agrarian Union (as the party was known) but did not take a cabinet post.

He found himself dissatisfied with the close collaboration between his fellow-Agrarians and the Communists, with the number of cabinet posts held by his party, which he felt to be disproportionately small, and especially with the Communist efforts in many villages to make political inroads on the strength of the Agrarians. As Secretary of the party, "Gemeto" had the duty of organizing its units on the local level, and it was here that he often found himself blocked by the local Communist-dominated OF "committees." Though he backed the OF, he took the position that Bulgaria must maintain close ties with the west as well as with the USSR. In December, when the British put down the ELAS uprising in Greece, the Bulgarian Communists used this as part of their effort to dispose of "Gemeto." On January 21, 1945, "Gemeto" resigned as secretary of the party, and was succeeded by Nikola Petkov.

Petkov's father, Dimiter, had been educated in Russia, wounded at Shipka in 1877, active as a Liberal reformer, and assassinated as Prime Minister in 1906. His elder brother, Petko, had been anti-German in the First World War, had worked closely with the Agrarian leader Stamboliisky, whom he succeeded as head of the Agrarians, and had been assassinated in June 1924 by Macedonian terrorists who disapproved of the Stamboliisky policy of friendship with Yugoslavia. Nikola Petkov lived in exile in Paris until 1931, but thereafter became an energetic leader of the Pladne agrarians. Anti-German, he had spent some time in internment before and during the war. After 1941 he emerged as leader of the Agrarian wing of the OF resistance, and member of the OF Executive Committee. He had become Vice-Premier and Minister without Portfolio in the OF Cabinet on its foundation, and was the editor of the Agrarian newspaper *Zemedelsko Zname* (*The Agrarian Banner*). He strongly favored collaboration with the Communists as the one way to cure the rural-urban hostility which cursed Bulgaria. In fact, the Agrarian supreme council, after the resignation of "Gemeto" and Petkov's appointment, called for "strengthening the fighting alliance between workers and peasants," and for tying Bulgarian foreign policy unbreakably to that of the USSR.

But the Communists could not be satisfied with collaboration, so long as the Agrarian Party kept any claim to its own identity and program. The Bulgarian "Muscovites," of whom Georgi Dimitrov and Vasil Kolarov were the most prominent, had not returned from the USSR, as had the Rumanians. For the moment it seemed that there were enough native Bulgarian Communists on the ground to manage the affairs of the party. But in March 1945 the OF held a congress in Sofia, and elected Dimitrov and Kolarov to its national committee. The Communists had already named Dimitrov president of their own Central Committee, and had sponsored a good deal of clamor for his return. But as yet he remained in Moscow, the sage of the party, with a world-wide reputation, consulted on Bulgarian developments and sending authoritative telegrams on every conceivable occasion. A Pan-Slav Congress in Sofia and a visit by delegates of Russian Orthodox clerics served to keep pro-Russian manifestations virtually constant.

The question of Bulgarian elections, as required in the Yalta declaration of February 1945, now preoccupied the Communists, and they stepped up their efforts to establish their own political dominance. They demanded a common OF list of candidates for the future assembly, with a prearranged ratio of seats to be allotted to the various parties making up the coalition. Needless to say, the Communists were planning to make sure that they themselves would obtain at least half the seats in the new assembly. The Agrarians and Zveno both wanted to have their own separate lists. Though ready to collaborate with the Communists, Petkov was not willing to submerge the identity of his party. The Communists, moreover, were working steadily to dominate the trades unions and displace their Social Democratic rivals. They also demanded a single "anti-fascist" youth organization, while the Agrarians fought for the maintenance of separate party youth organizations. All through the spring, this issue remained acute, while the Communists continued to blast "Gemeto," and Petkov showed himself unwilling to yield to their pressure. In May, "Gemeto," in fear for his life, took refuge in the home of the American political representative, Maynard Barnes, who granted him asylum. Four months later, as a result of strenuous American diplomatic representations, the Bulgarian government permitted him to go into exile.

In May also, the Communists produced their own Agrarian collaborator, ready to head the splinter group, which they would then recognize. He was Alexander Obbov, opportunist former right-wing member of the party. By packing the congress of the Agrarian Union with Obbovites and their own supporters, the Communists succeeded in ousting Petkov from control of the party and in taking over *Zemedelsko Zname*. Petkov lost the party secretaryship, but remained in the government and the OF. In June the Communists arrested Petkov's private secretary. He instantly demanded her release. The Communist Minister of the Interior, Yugov, told him that the militia would soon let her go, but three days later he announced that she had committed suicide, just as she was about to confess that the Agrarians had been plotting against the OF regime. This atrocity was only the harbinger of worse to come. As arrests continued, Petkov and the Agrarians loyal to him resigned from the government and the OF in August. Obbovite Agrarians replaced them in the Cabinet, which thus ostensibly continued to have Agrarian representation. But the overwhelming majority of the Agrarian Party supported Petkov. The Obbovites, like the "dissident" Liberals and Peasants in Rumania, represented nobody but themselves and their Communist masters.

The Communists also split the Social Democrats. One wing under Krustu Pastuhov had always refused to enter the OF. Among those who had, Obbov's role was played by Dimiter Neikov, who led a wing prepared to collaborate with the Communists. Grigor Cheshmedjiev, leader of those who had up to now taken part in the OF and in the government, was forced out. Neikov's followers took over the party newspaper, *Narod,* in May and the party organization in July. Cheshmedjiev resigned, and soon afterwards died, his place as leader being taken by Kosta Lulchev. The Communist election campaign continued amid mounting terror. The departure from the OF of the real Agrarians and Socialists meant that their spurious substitutes would take their places on the OF joint lists for the elections, scheduled for August. Though the OF had certainly been largely representative of Bulgarian political opinion in September 1944, Communist ruthlessness had rendered it virtually a Communist mouthpiece by August 1945. Only Zveno remained little disturbed, doubtless owing to the relatively small popular support commanded by its leaders. Its day of reckoning lay ahead.

Under the circumstances, the western allies concluded that the Yalta free election provision would hardly be properly observed if the Bulgarians held their elections as scheduled on August 26. Petkov had officially protested to the American and British representatives in Sofia. The United States and Britain in turn protested not only to the OF government but to Moscow, after the close of the Potsdam Conference in early August. Mr. Byrnes's otherwise illuminating book makes no mention of the matter, but in fact the Russians agreed to tell the Bulgarian government through their member on the Allied Control Commission that they did not object to the postponement of the elections. On election day itself, August 26, 1945, the OF announced that the elections were off until November 18. The Communists had suffered a temporary setback.

During the interval, in October, the Ethridge mission visited Sofia on its fact-finding errand. Its members found that the OF had taken certain steps to improve political conditions, recognizing the political existence of the opposition parties—Petkov's Agrarians, Lulchev's Socialists, and even Mushanov's Democrats—and permitting them to print and distribute their newspapers. But the OF still kept the opposition off the air, and refused to give up its monopoly of radio time. This manifestly unfair tactic alone would probably not have deterred Petkov and the other opposition leaders from participating in the elections. But the threat of police terror still hung over them, and the

Communists were openly prophesying doom for all who voted against the OF list. Having no faith in the intentions of the government after the elections, Petkov and his fellow-opposition leaders now declined to put forward their tickets. Moreover, like the Rumanian opposition at a slightly later date, they probably overestimated the support they could hope to receive from the western allies. In the midst of the campaign, Georgi Dimitrov arrived from Moscow (November 7). He indicated to the members of the Ethridge mission that he had come to lend further strength to the regime, and made it quite clear to them that the Communist concessions were only a temporary tactic until the Bulgarian Peace Treaty should have been concluded. In the hope of discovering the real intentions of the Russians, the Ethridge mission proceeded from Sofia to Moscow a week before the scheduled date of the new elections.

As Mr. Ethridge and Professor C. E. Black of Princeton University indicate in their account of the episode, they hoped that the Russians might be convinced that the United States would not recognize a Bulgarian government elected under the existing conditions, and might therefore agree to postpone the elections long enough to enable all four OF parties to run separate lists. Meanwhile the Americans hoped to broaden the government by the inclusion of genuine Agrarian and Socialist ministers, and to restrain the instruments of terror. To the firm report of the Ethridge mission that they had found the Bulgarian Communists violating the terms of the Yalta declaration, that the OF had ceased to be representative as a result of Communist tactics, and that the Russians seemed to be reaching out for exclusive power in Bulgaria, Mr. Vyshinsky replied that his information was different:

> Excesses had doubtless been committed by both sides, but fundamentally conditions in Bulgaria were no different from those in any democratic country. Vyshinsky saw no relevance in the fact that the Bulgarian Chief of Staff had served for twenty years as an officer in the Red Army. If Dimitrov had sent telegrams from Moscow giving advice to the Fatherland Front, he had only been expressing his views as a private citizen as was his right. If the Fatherland Front was dominated by the Communists, so was the British Government dominated by the Labor Party.[13]

Vyshinsky was clearly not interested in postponing the elections for a second time, though he did not positively rule out a postponement if the Bulgarian government should again ask the USSR for its opinion on the question. Though the Sofia regime would certainly not ask the question without advance Russian approval, it seemed to the Americans worth while to make the effort. So the State Department informed the Bulgarian government of the unfavorable findings of the Ethridge mission, and made it clear that the United States did not believe that the elections would be free or would produce a representative government, which would deserve American recognition.

[13] Raymond Dennett and Joseph E. Johnson, editors, *Negotiating with the Russians* (World Peace Foundation, 1951), p. 193.

The Sofia government did not ask for the Soviet opinion; the elections were held, with the opposition abstaining. They produced an 86 per cent majority for the government. The second-ranking Bulgarian Communist, Vasil Kolarov, who had spent years in Moscow, became President of the Sobranie.

At the Moscow Conference in December 1945, Mr. Byrnes raised with Molotov and Stalin the problem of Bulgaria, proposing that the Bulgarian and Rumanian governments be reorganized "to include all leading democratic elements."[14] Molotov declared that the USSR considered that free elections had taken place in Bulgaria, and that therefore no interference should take place. Byrnes had not ordered the Ethridge report published. It surely would have given the American public a great deal of information not yet available to them on the Soviet methods of taking over ostensibly sovereign states. So, in conversing with Stalin, Byrnes said that if Stalin refused to do anything about the Balkan countries, he would be compelled to publish the Ethridge report. To this Stalin answered that if the Ethridge report were published he would ask Ilya Ehrenburg, one of the chief Soviet journalistic hatchet-men, "who was also an impartial man and had visited those countries, to publish his views."

But Stalin eventually consented to advise the Bulgarian government to add to its cabinet "two truly representative members of two important political parties not then represented," who should be "really suitable, and will work loyally with the Government." The decision was parallel to the one taken as regarded Rumania, but whereas the Rumanian decision was to be implemented by the Vyshinsky-Harriman-Clark-Kerr trio, Stalin made different arrangements for Bulgaria, because the election had already been held there. He declared that no pressure could be brought, and insisted that the Soviet Union should handle the problem alone. The final communiqué (December 27, 1945) made it clear that the United States and Britain would not recognize the Bulgarian government until they were "convinced that this friendly advice has been accepted by the Bulgarian Government and the said additional representatives have been included in its body. . . ."

In January 1946, therefore, began a period of negotiations between government and opposition. The OF at this time would have been willing to admit Petkov and Lulchev themselves into the cabinet, which might well have made more of a difference in the course of events in Bulgaria than the admission of the far less influential Hațieganu and Romniceanu had done in Rumania. But just because they were powerful, Petkov and Lulchev were determined either to deal the Communist domination a real blow or else to abstain from participating in the government. They wanted to annul the elections of November, and even to recapture the Ministries of Justice and the Interior. They relied heavily on the influence of the western allies. Vyshinsky himself visited Sofia in January in an effort to persuade Petkov and Lulchev to join the government without conditions. He told them that the enforcement of the

[14] Byrnes, *Speaking Frankly*, p. 116.

Moscow conference decision was in Russian hands, and that this decision had not envisaged the making of any conditions by the opposition. In effect, he told them to take it or leave it: enter the government or stay out, but stop bargaining.

This the opposition leaders refused to do. Indeed, by March 1946, they had prevailed upon the OF government to agree to give the Ministry of Justice to a member of the opposition, and to put a Petkov Agrarian and a Lulchev Socialist into the Ministry of the Interior as under-secretaries to the Communist Minister, Yugov. One of these under-secretaries was to have charge of the militia, and the other of local government. Moreover, the government agreed to hold new free elections with each of the parties having its own lists. These were real concessions; it seems that the OF so badly wanted recognition by the western allies that it was prepared to accept what would surely have proved to be two serious political defeats. But apparently the concessions were too great. At the last moment, the Russians vetoed the agreement. It never went into effect, and the deadlock continued. Instead of giving the Bulgarian government the "friendly" advice to add two opposition members, as Stalin was bound by the Moscow conference decision to do, the Russians prevented it from making the necessary concessions, which it would otherwise have been willing to do. In retrospect, the first three months of 1946 thus emerge as a decisive period in postwar Bulgarian political development.

The summer of 1946 saw the postponed but inevitable Communist attack on Zveno. Though General Damian Velchev, its founder, whose remarkable political career we have already examined, had ostensibly resigned from the party when he became Minister of War in the OF government, the Communists were correct in judging him to be the moving spirit of Zveno and in singling him out as their most important target. Their press began to denounce him as responsible for the suppression of Stamboliisky's government in 1923 (although their own role on that occasion had been far from glorious), and to cite against him his known correspondence with Mihailovich. They cut down on his powers as Minister of War by making the Cabinet collectively responsible for the army. They arrested his aide, who, like Petkov's secretary, "died" while in custody, presumably from torture inflicted on him in an effort to get him to denounce Velchev. Finally they accepted his resignation on the grounds of health, and appointed him Minister to Switzerland, where he had the good judgment to remain until his death in 1954. After the removal of Velchev, the drive went out of Zveno, although Kimon Georgiev remained in office as Prime Minister for a while longer.

The Communists now moved against the monarchy, which was far less popular in Bulgaria than in Rumania. Young King Simeon was only a child, and his father and grandfather had not endeared themselves to the people by taking Bulgaria into two wars on the side opposite to the Russians and losing both. Unlike Michael, who had himself ordered the arrest of Antonescu and had stood out against the left, Simeon had had no opportunity to ingratiate himself with the Bulgarians. The propaganda campaign which the Communists now launched against the monarchy was hardly necessary. A plebiscite (September 8, 1946) produced the predictable huge majority for a republic, and King Simeon and his mother, Princess Ioanna, went into exile. They received some $20,000,000 for the royal properties in the country, which were now confiscated.

In October, after the usual campaign of propaganda and terror, there followed elections for a new assembly, this time a "Grand" National Sobranie, twice the usual size, designed to give the country a new constitution. Fighting bravely against the Communists, the opposition put up candidates, but a large number of the leading Petkov Agrarians and Lulchev Socialists were arrested and jailed before the election, while the collaborating Obbov Agrarians and Neikov Socialists of course ran on the OF ticket. The OF obtained 78 per cent of the vote and the opposition 22 per cent.[15] Neither the opposition nor the western allies believed that the elections had been freely conducted, and recognition was still withheld. Georgi Dimitrov himself now moved into the Premiership, and the Communists held more posts than ever before. They were preparing themselves to give even their allies in the OF only token representation in the Cabinet.

In the Grand National Sobranie, Petkov took the leadership of the opposition deputies, and proceeded now, on the floor of Parliament, to defy the Communists with almost reckless bravery. Dimitrov himself had "reminded" the opposition of the fate of Mihailovich, and it was perfectly clear what lay ahead. But Petkov, though foreseeing his fate, boldly denounced his former Communist allies:

> They threaten, they intimidate, they arrest, they beat people up, they send our supporters to concentration camps, they kill our members, and then say they are willing to coöperate with us. The Prime Minister has said that the Opposition are under instruction from international reaction — Britain and America. . . . The Opposition is waiting for the Prime Minister to prove these allegations. . . . Tell us the truth, Mr. Dimitrov. Back your charges with facts. Our parliamentary immunity, our liberty, our fate, and our very heads are at your disposal and anyhow within your power.[16]

In response to the threats of the Communists against his life, made on the floor of the Sobranie, Petkov virtually challenged them to shoot him. In January 1947, he taunted Dimitrov as follows:

"Let me remind you that I have never been a citizen of a foreign country, nor have I been in foreign service," to which Dimitrov replied: "I was a citizen

[15] In the new Grand National Sobranie the Communists had 277 seats, the Obbov Agrarians 69, the Neikov Socialists 9, Zveno 8, and the opposition 101, a total of 364 for the OF, made up of 92 Petkov Agrarians and 9 Lulchev Socialists.

[16] December 4, 1946: Michael Padev, *Dimitrov Wastes No Bullets* (London, 1948), pp. 46–47.

of the great Soviet Union . . . an honor and a privilege," and the exchange continued:

> PETKOV: "You became a Bulgarian subject two days before the elections. This was officially announced from Moscow."
> DIMITROV: "I'll teach you a lesson soon."
> PETKOV: "For more than twenty years you were officially a foreign subject and in the service of a foreign state."[17]

Petkov did not limit himself to attacks on Communist methods and personalities. He objected, for example, in April 1947 that the budget for the police had soared above the level it had reached at the very height of the pro-German regime during the war.

For six months Petkov conducted this desperate, and, as he well knew, hopeless, fight for political decency. His newspaper continually published ringing defenses of freedom and attacks on those who were destroying it. Some of these are memorable documents from a literary point of view; all are dignified and moving. One excerpt here will have to suffice:

> If men in power destroy the liberty of speech and Press, any excess soon becomes permissible. Such men proclaim themselves infallible, and decide the fate of peoples arbitrarily, without any control on their actions. The citizens of such a state cease to be a society of thinking men and become a flock of sheep, with no opinions or ideas of their own. Once freedom is destroyed, all other foundations of human society crumble into ruins. A flock of two-legged sheep, even if they look like people, and are well-fed and well-shod, is not a society of human beings.[18]

By the end of April 1947, the Communists were furious with the continued proclamations of the truth. They did not want to suppress Petkov's paper because the Peace Treaty with Bulgaria, adopted by the three great powers in February 1947, had still to be ratified, and they could not yet afford to violate its requirement of a free press. So they got the printers' union to refuse to print it, and the *Strela* organization, which had the state monopoly on distributing newspapers, to refuse to circulate it. Petkov instantly wrote to Dimitrov, who had started his own career in a print-shop, declaring that this form of censorship was purely unconstitutional, and demanding that, if his paper was actually "harmful to Bulgarian interests," it should be officially banned. Of course there was no answer, and the paper never again appeared. All this time, the Communists were preparing to incriminate him in "conspiracies." They had arrested in 1946 some members of alleged military conspiratorial groups. They tortured their victims into implicating Petkov. On June 6, 1947, the Communist militia arrested Petkov himself on the floor of the Sobranie, amid the screams of his enemies and his friends.

The Communists tried Petkov in August 1947 before a "People's Court"

[17] Padev, p. 49.
[18] Padev, p. 55.

consisting of three Communist judges. They accused him of preparing a *coup d'état,* and of having urged certain army officers to conspire against the state. They refused to allow defense witnesses to testify, excluding their testimony as "not of essential importance." They organized demonstrations all over Bulgaria, demanding a death-sentence. They produced various "intimidated witnesses to testify against Petkov. They reported conversations with people who had been dead at the time. Careful analysis of the testimony at the trial reveals dozens of discrepancies and absurdities. There was no proof whatever that Petkov was conspiring to overthrow the government by force. His sin lay in his parliamentary opposition to it. Petkov did not confess. He declared that he was on trial for his political views. His judges sentenced him to death. His appeal to the Supreme Court of Cassation, consisting of four Communist judges, was rejected.

The British and American governments protested against the sentence of death passed against Petkov. They asked that the Bulgarian government suspend the sentence and permit the Allied Control Commission to review the case. The Bulgarian Government refused the plea. On September 23, 1947, Petkov was hanged, to the accompaniment of that abominable chorus of howls with which the Communist press greets the destruction of an enemy: the Executive Committee of the Bulgarian Trade Unions passed a resolution commenting "To a dog, a dog's death," and Sofia Radio gave this wide publicity. The United States protested; the British government in an official note to Bulgaria called the execution "judicial murder." Later, in January 1948, Georgi Dimitrov, who himself had been saved from the Nazis by the intervention of world opinion in the Reichstag Fire Trial of 1933, made in the Sobranie the following statement to the Social Democrats:

> As you remember from this rostrum I many times warned your political allies from Nikola Petkov's group. They did not listen to me. They took no notice of all my warnings. They broke their heads, and their leader is now under the ground. You should now think it over, lest you share their fate. . . . When the trial against Nikola Petkov began you said "The court will not dare to sentence him to death. It would be too horrible. Both Washington and London will rise against it in order to stop it." I said then: "Nobody can stop it. Those who may try to intervene from abroad will only worsen the position of the accused and his friends." What happened? What I said would happen. The court fulfilled its role, fulfilled the will of the people and sentenced the traitor to death.
>
> Then you said: "If they execute the death sentence, the glass of patience will overflow. The whole world will rise against it, and all its wrath will fall on the back of the Bulgarian people."
>
> Of course, if there had been no interference from abroad, if they had not tried to dictate to the sovereign court, the head of Petkov could have been saved. Yes, it could have been saved. His death sentence could have been commuted to another sentence. But when they tried to blackmail the Bulgarian

people and question the authority of a sovereign court, it became necessary for the death sentence to be executed. And it was executed.

What happened then? Who rose against it in the country? Where were the demonstrations, the mutinies with which we were threatened? Nothing like that happened.

And what happened abroad? Not even decent diplomatic notes were delivered, which could have been expected. No one raised a hand in defense of Petkov. Some people in the West shouted for a while, but soon quietened (*sic*) down. . . . The whole incident was soon forgotten.[19]

This blustering menacing speech reveals how bitterly the Communists resented western intervention, and how determined they were to free themselves from it and to discredit the United States and Britain. The United States had recognized the Bulgarian government a week after Petkov was hanged; Dimitrov's estimate of the power of the west to influence events in Bulgaria seems not inaccurate.

Some three weeks after Petkov was hanged, Dimitrov, visiting in the USSR, produced a "confession" in which Petkov admitted that all his political activity had been an error, undertaken with the support of the "imperialist states," and "exploited" by "international imperialistic reaction." He implicated Lulchev, Mushanov, and other pro-western politicians. But the fact that the Communists could publish the "confession" only posthumously, and its free use of all the Communist jargon would be enough to stamp it as a forgery. Still later, the Communists produced a "second page" of the "confession," when they wanted to smear another prominent Bulgarian.[20]

In accordance with the threat posed in Dimitrov's speech in the Sobranie quoted above, the Communists now turned on the Lulchev Socialists. Even after the hanging of Petkov, the Socialists opposed the OF government, voting against the new constitution put through in December 1947 and against the budget for 1948. In July 1948, Lulchev and six of his nine fellow Socialist deputies were arrested, and Lulchev sentenced to fifteen years' imprisonment. As he was already an old man, this was equivalent to a death-sentence. Crippled by the arrest of their brave and independent leaders,[21] the opposition Socialists no longer presented a threat, and the collaborating Neikov-ites joined forces with the Communists at the end of 1948, disappearing as an independent political party. There remained only a fraction of the Zveno,

[19] Padev, p. 153.

[20] Professor Venelin Ganev, notable constitutional lawyer, former regent of the OF's own appointing, who had hoped to testify for Petkov but whom they had prevented from doing so. Conveniently they "found" the "second page," and sent Ganev off to internment in a distant village, after depriving him of his university post and his pension. He too opposed the Communists. General Stanchev, hero of the resistance, and long-time foe of the monarchy, received a life-sentence for opposing Communist arrests of army officers.

[21] Krustu Pastuhov, head of the faction which had never collaborated with the Communists, had already been put in jail for "spreading rumors calculated to weaken military discipline."

and the Obbov collaborationist agrarians. Both were completely under Communist control. Outside the OF no political voice could be raised.

The constitution of December 1947 was modeled on that of the Soviet Union. The Communists and their allies greatly modified a first draft which would have created a republic with a President elected every four years, who should have the role and powers of a head of state, and which included the very broad and liberal bill of rights that had distinguished the Tirnovo Constitution of 1879. The Communist draft, which was of course the one adopted, eliminated the President as head of state. It gave his role to the Presidium of the National Assembly (a President, two Vice-Presidents, a Secretary and fifteen members), just like the Yugoslav Constitution which we have already examined. Where the earlier draft had required a national referendum before changes could be made in the constitution, the draft actually adopted placed this power in the hands of a two-thirds majority of the assembly: that is to say, in the hands of the Communists.

As in Yugoslavia, the constitution created not only seventeen ministries but a State Planning Commission, a State Control Commission, and a committee for science, art, and culture. It put local power into the hands of city and county people's councils, to be elected every three years. The National Assembly was to elect the Supreme Court and the Attorney General of the People's Republic (People's Prosecutor), and he in turn was to have the right to appoint and discharge all other prosecutors. As in all the People's Republics, civil liberties were guaranteed by the constitution. As in all of them, the constitution took away with one article what it granted in the next:

> The law forbids and punishes the formation of and participation in organizations the aim of which is to deprive the Bulgarian people of the rights and liberties gained by the national uprising of 9th September 1944 and guaranteed by the present Constitution, or to encroach on those rights and liberties, or to imperil the national independence and State sovereignty of the country; or organizations which openly or secretly propagate fascist and anti-democratic ideology or facilitate imperialist aggression.[22]

By the spring of 1948, the Bulgarian Communists had gone a long way toward making their country over in the image of their big brother.

2. *Politics Abroad: Yugoslav Ambitions*

The revolutionary drive which had swept Tito into power as the chief of a successful guerrilla movement did not stop at the borders of prewar Yugoslavia. Yugoslav ambitions extended beyond those borders, to the Italian province of Venezia Giulia on the northwest, with its mixed Slavic and Italian population and its great port of Trieste. They extended also to Pirin Mace-

[22] Conveniently translated in full in A. Gyorgy, *Governments of Danubian Europe* (New York, 1949), p. 337.

donia on the southeast, with Bulgaria beyond, to Greek Macedonia on the south, with Greece beyond, and to Albania on the southwest. Aside from the relations of the great powers to Rumania and Bulgaria, the chief developments in Balkan foreign relations during the period between the end of the war and June 1948 were determined by the Yugoslav push for power. In the west, the United States and Great Britain managed to blunt the Yugoslav ambitions short of their ultimate goals. Elsewhere, Tito's ambitions and his independence in pursuing them aroused the suspicions of his teacher and master in Moscow. What Churchill, Attlee and Bevin, Truman and Byrnes did to Tito against Russian opposition in the west and in Greece, Stalin and Molotov did to him elsewhere.

ISTRIA AND CARINTHIA

At the Yaitse session of AVNOJ in November 1943, the Yugoslav Partisans had announced that the Italian province of Venezia Giulia, with the city of Trieste, was annexed to Yugoslavia. The allies, of course, did not accept this action. When Tito had visited Italy in August 1944, Churchill had shown him a memorandum on allied military intentions with regard to Istria. This document made it clear that the western allies intended to set up allied military government in the area, and that they would need to be supplied through the port of Trieste. Churchill declared that the Yugoslavs might present their claims to Istria at the peace conference or at a meeting of the powers. In fact, Churchill was determined that the British should safely hold the head of the Adriatic, including Trieste, and that they should push on to Vienna as fast as possible. During the early months of 1945, as the Germans withdrew, the Partisans established themselves in Istria, and threatened to take Trieste.

On April 27, 1945, Churchill cabled Mr. Truman, who had been President only a couple of weeks:

> The late President always attached great importance to Trieste, which he thought should be an international port forming an outlet into the Adriatic from all the regions of the Danube basin. There are many points to consider about this, but that there should be an outlet to the south seems of interest to the trade of many states involved. The great thing is to be there before Tito's guerrillas are in occupation. Therefore it does not seem to me that there is a minute to wait. The actual status of Trieste can be determined at leisure.[23]

Field Marshal Alexander, who had discussed the matter with Tito in Belgrade, now found the Yugoslavs in a much stronger military position than he had then expected them to occupy. Partisan forces had taken most of Istria, and by May 1, 1945 were fighting inside Trieste itself. A head-on clash between the Yugoslavs and the allied forces seemed a strong possibility. Alexander

[23] Churchill, *The Second World War*, VI, *Triumph and Tragedy*, 552.

reminded Churchill that the Yugoslavs would doubtless enjoy Russian backing, and that the British armed forces had a high admiration for the Partisans, and would hardly welcome combat against them.

On May 2, New Zealand troops under General Freyberg occupied the dock area of the town. Local tension ran very high. Alexander made it clear that Tito wanted a promise that he would be allowed to incorporate Trieste in Yugoslavia at a later date, which Churchill of course refused. On May 12, after the surrender of the Germans in western Europe, President Truman cabled Churchill entirely supporting the policy of firmness toward the Yugoslavs in Trieste, but a few days later he seemed more worried about the possibility of war with the Yugoslavs, and indicated that he felt it right to use allied troops against them only if they actually attacked. He agreed, however, to a show of military and aerial strength in the area, as a deterrent to any rash act by the Yugoslavs, whose behavior had been such as thoroughly to antagonize the allied troops.

On June 9, 1945, the Yugoslavs, yielding reluctantly to a virtual ultimatum, accepted a line of demarcation running roughly north and south and then westward to the sea south of Trieste. It was called the "Morgan line," after the British General who was chief of the Allied General Staff in the Mediterranean. The Yugoslavs withdrew behind this line, leaving the city of Trieste to the allies. Relations between the Yugoslavs on the east side of the Morgan line and the allied forces on the west side continued to be hostile. In one of his exchanges with the Yugoslavs the irritated Field Marshal Alexander compared Tito's conduct to that of Hitler or Mussolini. One can certainly sympathize with Alexander's irritation, but the comparison infuriated the Yugoslavs, who had just spent four years of great hardship fighting the Germans and Italians.

Stalin cabled Churchill on June 21, giving the Yugoslavs the first overt support they had yet received from him, and complaining of Alexander's language. On June 23, Churchill replied in a scorching message:

> Our joint idea at the Kremlin in October was that the Yugoslav business should work out around 50–50 Russian and British influence. In fact it is at present more like 90–10, and even in that poor 10 we have been subjected to violent pressure by Marshal Tito. So violent was this pressure that the United States and His Majesty's Government had to put in motion many hundreds of thousands of troops in order to prevent themselves from being attacked by Marshal Tito. . . .
>
> I do not consider that it can be said that Marshal Tito has conquered all this territory. It has been conquered by the movements of far greater forces both in the west and in the east which compelled the strategic retreat of the Germans from the Balkans. . . .
>
> We think that any permanent territorial changes should be settled at the peace table. . . .
>
> The actual wording of Field Marshal Alexander's telegram has been largely taken from the President's draft. We do not see why we should be

pushed around everywhere, especially by people we have helped, and helped before you were able to make any contact with them. . . .

It seems to me that a Russianized frontier running from Lübeck through Eisenach to Trieste and down to Albania is a matter which requires a very great deal of argument conducted between good friends. . . .[24]

Churchill's words show that he still considered the percentages agreement to be in force, that he did not hesitate to remind Stalin of British responsibility for Tito's wartime successes, and that he opposed a Russian-dominated base at the head of the Adriatic. At Potsdam, on July 18, Churchill and Stalin dined together, and the "argument among friends" continued:

I then spoke of the difficulties in Yugoslavia, where we had no material ambitions, but there had been the fifty-fifty arrangement. It was now ninety-nine to one against Britain. Stalin protested that the proportions were 90 per cent British, 10 per cent Yugoslav, and 0 per cent Russian interests. The Soviet Government often did not know what Tito was about to do. . . .

I then said how anxious people were about Russia's intentions. I drew a line from the North Cape to Albania, and named the capitals east of that line which were in Russian hands. It looked as if Russia were rolling on westward. Stalin said he had no such intention.[25]

The conversation is more interesting as revealing Stalin's early distrust of Tito than as marking any change in the positions of the powers on the issues involved, including Trieste.

These positions remained the same, and the "argument" continued at the London Conference in September 1945, when the Foreign Ministers met to consider the peace treaty with Italy. As signers of the armistice with Italy, the French participated in these debates together with the Russians, British, and Americans. Both Yugoslav and Italian representatives presented their cases. Molotov supported and the other Ministers opposed the Yugoslav claims to all of Istria including Trieste. The conferees were able to agree only that Trieste should be a free port and that the Italo-Yugoslav frontier should be "in the main the ethnic line, leaving a minimum under alien rule."

Further, Mr. Byrnes suggested and the others agreed that a commission of experts from the four powers should visit the area and that each recommend the line which seemed to him best to conform to this description in view of local geographic and economic factors. In January 1946, the Deputies of the Ministers, meeting in London, appointed the commission of experts. Even on this, there was disagreement. The Russians wanted to direct the experts not to visit most of Istria because it was already earmarked for award to Yugoslavia, but yielded to the majority point of view.

From early March to early April 1946, the four experts (the American was Professor Philip E. Mosely of Columbia University) traveled throughout

[24] Churchill, *The Second World War,* VI, *Triumph and Tragedy,* 560–561.
[25] Churchill, *The Second World War,* VI, *Triumph and Tragedy,* 636.

Istria, interviewing people on the spot. They checked statistics as far as this was possible, and east of the Morgan line witnessed the "spontaneous" Yugoslav demonstrations demanding that the area be awarded to them. When they got back to London, the four experts presented a joint report as to conditions, but made four separate recommendations for the new frontier.

The Russian line ran far to the west of the others, giving Yugoslavia not

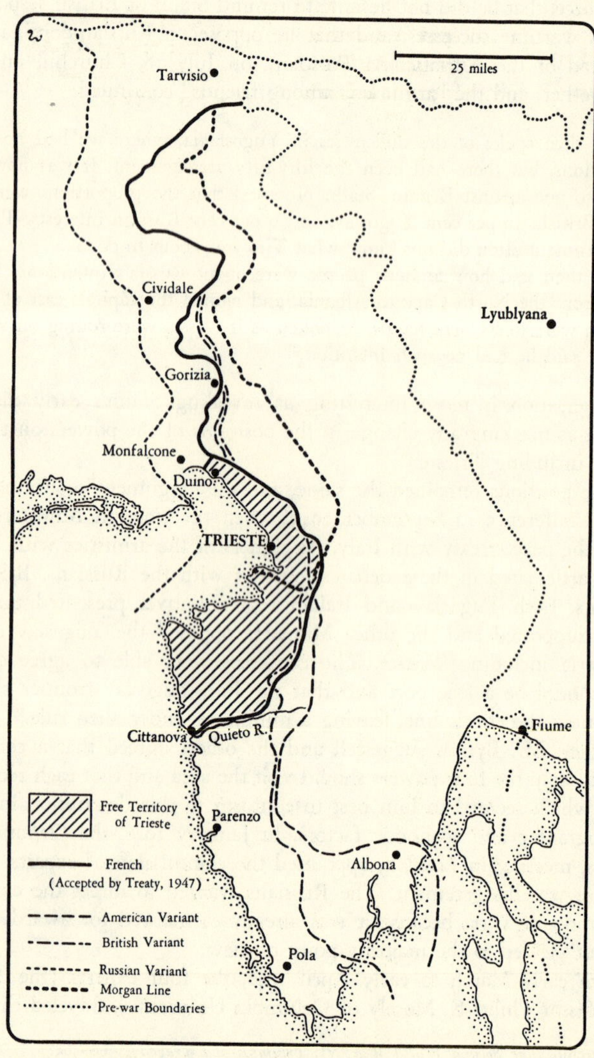

Proposals for Istrian Boundary, 1947

only all of Venezia Giulia including Trieste and Gorizia, but also Tarvisio, Cividale, Monfalcone, and Cittanova. The American, British, and French lines coincided roughly in the north, where they followed the old pre-World War I boundary between Italy and the Habsburg dominions. All three left to Italy not only the four cities which the Russians would have awarded to Yugoslavia, but also Gorizia and Trieste. To the south the lines diverged. Both the British and Americans would have given Italy the southwestern corner of Istria, including Pola and Parenzo, and the American line would have given Italy the southeastern corner of the peninsula as well, including Albona, and the Arsa coal mines. The French line, diverging from the others, followed the Quieto River to the sea, and thus awarded both southwest and southeast Istria to the Yugoslavs, who would obtain Parenzo and Pola and Albona.

From the ethnic point of view, the Russian recommendation would have given Yugoslavia almost half a million Italians, and Italy no Yugoslavs. The American recommendation would have given Yugoslavia about 50,000 Italians, and Italy more than 150,000 Yugoslavs; and the British recommendation would have given Yugoslavia a few more Italians, and Italy a few less Yugoslavs. Ethnically, the French recommendation was the most nearly evenly balanced: Yugoslavia would obtain 130,000 Italians, Italy 115,000 Yugoslavs. All these population figures in this area can be only rough approximations.

The Foreign Ministers now met in Paris, and early in May 1946 heard once more the claims of Vice-Premier Kardelj of Yugoslavia and Premier de Gasperi of Italy. Molotov again fully supported the Yugoslav claims, arguing that Trieste in Italian hands would serve as a base for Italian aggression against the Yugoslavs. To deprive Yugoslavia of Trieste would be unjust punishment. Pointing out that it was hardly punishment to give the Yugoslavs an area which they had never before possessed, with a population of more than 300,000 people, Mr. Byrnes offered to compromise by accepting the French line, which gave Yugoslavia still more territory and people, and recommended that a plebiscite be held in the disputed area. Molotov refused to accept these suggestions, and tried to use them as the basis for further bargaining. But the Americans and the other western allies had now reached the limit of their concessions. Georges Bidault, the French Foreign Minister, now proposed a temporary international regime for Trieste. The Russians continued to demand the city for Yugoslavia.

Flatly refusing to accept Yugoslav sovereignty over Trieste, Mr. Byrnes also rejected on June 22, 1946 a Russian proposal that the powers declare Trieste and the surrounding countryside an autonomous state under Yugoslav sovereignty, to be governed by a statute which the four great powers would draft.

> With Yugoslav sovereignty and a Yugoslav governor [said Mr. Byrnes], there would be little for the representatives of the four powers to do and there would be no connection whatever with the United Nations. The United States cannot accept Yugoslav sovereignty over the Trieste area. I recognize

> that the Soviet Union cannot accept Italian sovereignty. We are willing, therefore, to consider any proposal that offers a way out—either United Nations administration as proposed by Mr. Bidault or leaving the issue to the peace conference for decision. I prefer the latter, for then the responsibility will rest upon the twenty-one nations.[26]

Molotov now seems to have accepted the principle of an autonomous territory of Trieste. Negotiations then continued, with Molotov first proposing a scheme, which, Mr. Byrnes reports, "cut the port off from its shipyards, . . . severed the city from its water supply, and placed its power transformers in Yugoslavia. He wanted four-power rather than United Nations supervision. We refused to budge from our position that responsibility should lie with the Security Council. . . ."

Early in July 1946, the Russians accepted a new French compromise suggestion. This made the French line the frontier of Yugoslavia, and created to the west of it the "free territory of Trieste," including, beside Trieste itself, the towns of Duino to the north and Cittanova on the south, a roughly crescent-shaped area, across which ran the Morgan line. The portion to the south and east of the Morgan line, including Cittanova, was in Yugoslav hands. This would soon become "Zone B." The region north and west of the Morgan line, including Duino and Trieste itself, was in allied hands. This would soon become "Zone A." The Foreign Ministers did not at this meeting spell out the form of international government which they intended to install in the "free territory." The settlement deeply hurt both Italians and Yugoslavs, and did not please any of the great powers. It was defended, however, as the only compromise on which the big four could agree, and as a necessary preliminary to a peace conference and the signing of the treaties.

The Yugoslavs indeed felt angry not only at the decision, but at the Russians for not supporting their claims to the bitter end, and especially for not telling them in advance about the compromise on Trieste before agreeing to it. The night before Molotov accepted the French proposals, he spent the evening with Kardelj, but did not hint in any way what he had in mind. The next day, when Molotov told him that he had accepted the French compromise, Kardelj felt betrayed. According to the Yugoslav diplomat, Alesh Bebler, a western diplomat later said to him: "If Molotov had stuck to it for only another week, you would have got at least Gorizia," a suggestion which seems highly improbable from Byrnes's account. Later, Bebler himself complained to Molotov that the treaty left Slovenia cut off from the sea. According to Bebler, Molotov replied, "Is it your idea that every township should have its own seacoast?" a remark which Bebler bitterly resented,[27] but which, on the whole seems quite reasonable, in view of the long stretch of Istrian seacoast which the French line gave to Yugoslavia.

[26] Byrnes, *Speaking Frankly*, p. 133.

[27] A. Bebler, "Trois rencontres avec Molotov," *Questions Actuelles du Socialisme*, 16 (January-February, 1953), pp. 50–52.

At the Paris Peace Conference which followed, opening late in July, the other countries accepted the boundaries proposed by the big four. But the four presented separate recommendations for the statute to govern the free territory. The USSR wanted as far as possible to cripple the future governor by rigorously circumscribing his authority. The Russians also recommended a customs union between Yugoslavia and the free territory, partial Yugoslav administration of the railroads, and free settlement and employment of the citizens of both on the territory of either. This would have virtually given the city to the Yugoslavs after all.

The western allies, on the other hand, proposed to give the new governor very considerable powers to control the police, to maintain order, to declare a state of siege, and to protect human rights. They feared to create a new situation like that in the 1930's which had rendered the High Commissioner of the Free City of Danzig, appointed by the League of Nations, powerless to resist the Nazis. The Conference wrangled over the two opposing concepts, and finally adopted a French compromise close to the American and British view. When the Yugoslavs threatened not to sign any Italian treaty embodying this compromise, the Conference pressed an American-sponsored article excluding any state which refused to ratify the treaty from sharing in the benefits or rights which it conferred. While the Peace Conference was in session, a serious incident imposed severe additional strain upon the relations between the United States and Yugoslavia.

American military transport planes at this period flying between Rome and Vienna followed a route over the Italian city of Udine and the Austrian city of Klagenfurt. A straight line between these two points passes through the northwest corner of Yugoslavia, and official American orders to the pilots required them to avoid Yugoslav territory. But the region is mountainous. In bad weather it was easy for the pilots to stray over Yugoslav territory, and in any case the pilots were naturally tempted to cut across the corner of Yugoslavia and avoid certain dangerous mountain passes. Ordinarily a friendly state would have raised no objections, but the Yugoslavs were highly suspicious, belligerent, and distressed at theii impending loss of Trieste, which they attributed largely to American influence. They complained of 176 American "violations" of their frontiers. On August 9, 1946, Yugoslav fighter planes forced down an American transport plane, and wounded a Turkish passenger. The Yugoslavs interned the eight other men aboard in Belgrade, and prevented them from communicating with American officials. Ten days later, on August 19, they shot down a second plane, this time killing the five Americans aboard. To a State Department request for information, Tito replied by a bristling speech in which he accused the United States of sending "squadrons" of military planes over Yugoslavia.

Mr. Byrnes, in Paris, told Kardelj that the United States, if the situation had been reversed, would have taken all pains to look after the crew of a lost

Yugoslav plane, and would never have been guilty of firing upon it. When the Yugoslav replies were unsatisfactory, the State Department notified the Tito regime that, unless they released the eight men interned and saw them safely out of Yugoslavia within forty-eight hours, the United States would refer the case for action to the Security Council of the United Nations. A member of the American delegation shortly afterwards observed Molotov apparently urging Kardelj to see that his government acted properly. In any case, the Yugoslavs complied, and later agreed to pay indemnities to the families of the five Americans killed in the other plane. The American display of firmness had brought the incident to a close, and the form of its ultimatum had shown that Washington respected the newly established organs of international security, and did not rely on unilateral punitive measures. But the outrageous slaughter of unarmed Americans in an unarmed plane by a supposedly friendly power had deeply stirred American public opinion, already anti-Yugoslav because of the warlike behavior of Tito's people over Trieste, and thoroughly suspicious also that the trial of Mihailovich that same summer had been a piece of Communist brutality.

The Conference closed on October 15, 1946, with the Yugoslavs absent and still threatening not to sign an Italian treaty embodying the Trieste recommendations. At New York, in November, they were still arguing their case in the same way, but Mr. Byrnes flatly refused to negotiate further. In December, Molotov accepted the French-sponsored compromise on the government of the free territory. In January 1947, the United Nations Security Council agreed to accept responsibility for governing Trieste, and on February 10, 1947 the Italian treaty embodying the Trieste settlement was signed in Paris, together with the treaties with Rumania, Bulgaria, Hungary, and Finland. Yugoslavia signed the Italian treaty, despite the long months of protest.

For more than a year following the signature of the Italian treaty, the great powers discussed in the Security Council the appointment of a governor for the free territory. The Russians vetoed all candidates put forward by the United States, Great Britain, or France. The western allies vetoed all candidates put forward by the USSR. Paralyzed, the Security Council never could appoint a governor, and the newborn free territory proved to have been stillborn. Meanwhile, the Yugoslavs continued to occupy Zone B, while across the Morgan line to the north and west British and American forces occupied and administered Zone A, including the city of Trieste itself. No change took place until the spring of 1948.

Then, in the midst of a violent election campaign in Italy, with the Russians backing the return of the Italian colonies in Africa, and the Italian Communists screaming anti-American slogans, and holding over the electorate the threat of force, came a western propaganda counterthrust. At Turin on March 20, 1948, the French Foreign Minister, Bidault, declared that the United States, Great Britain, and France were all prepared to restore to Italy Trieste and the lands originally designated as part of the free territory — which meant the Yugoslav-occupied Zone B as well as Zone A. How far this promise of Trieste contributed to the success of the Italian Christian Democrats at that time we cannot speculate here. What we should note is that the official promise committed all three western powers to an Italian solution: they favored ousting the Yugoslavs from Zone B, which their forces had occupied ever since June, 1945, and which they had been treating, quite illegally, as part of their own dominions. So matters stood, when the quarrel between the Soviet Union and Tito's Yugoslavia broke out into the open in June, and altered the entire diplomatic picture.

Yugoslavia also had a claim against Austria for cession of Slovene-inhabited territory in Carinthia. As early as February 1946, the State Department began its efforts to get the Russians to agree on a Treaty with Austria. Since Austria was not a former enemy state, the treaty would have formally recognized Austrian independence and frontiers. When the powers discussed the question in December 1946, the Russians demanded that a commission be

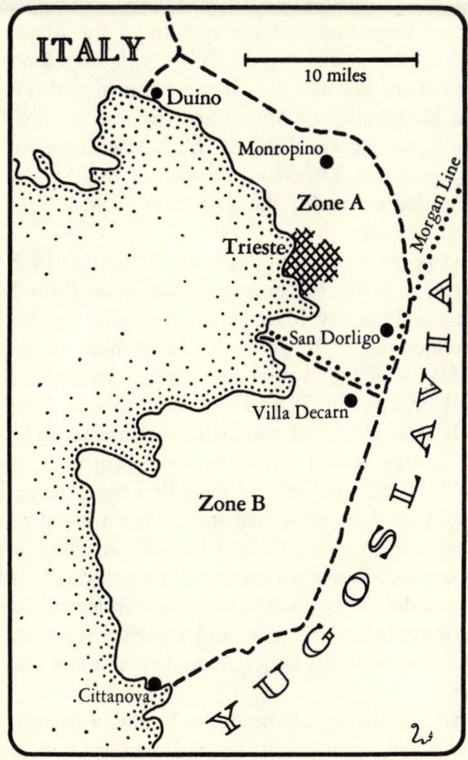

Free Territory of Trieste

appointed to study the Yugoslav territorial claims. Since the free plebiscite in the area held in 1920 had gone against Yugoslavia, the western allies were unwilling to reopen the question. They did not feel in any case that a new Austria would be viable without the territory in question. So the question remained in abeyance. In the months and years that followed down to 1955, it appeared that the Russians really did not wish to make any treaty with Austria at all, partly because they wanted to keep their troops in their zone and in Vienna, partly because so long as they had troops in Austria they were formally authorized by the peace treaties to keep them also in Rumania and Hungary. Thus, in spring 1948, renewed negotiations on Austria again broke down, and the Russians supported the Yugoslav territorial claims once more, perhaps because it cost them nothing, even though by then they had begun their quarrel with Tito.

MACEDONIA

Deprived of their full territorial claims against Italy, Tito and his supporters simultaneously pursued Yugoslav ambitions elsewhere in the Balkans. As the champion of federation and the sponsor of the Macedonian Federal Republic within Yugoslavia, Tito by the fall of 1944 hoped not only to solve the Macedonian problem but also to increase his own and Yugoslav prestige by annexing Pirin Macedonia and arranging a federation with Bulgaria. This would automatically pose a grave threat to Greek Macedonia across the frontier to the south. The powerful Yugoslav influence in the Albanian Communist Party gave promise that eventually the Yugoslavs could transform Albania as well into a Federal Republic.

The Yugoslavs began negotiating with the Bulgarians in November 1944, when Kardelj went to Sofia. He proposed that, after Pirin Macedonia had been united with the Yugoslav Macedonian Republic, representatives of the six Yugoslav republics and of Bulgaria should establish in Belgrade a Commission of South Slav Union, and work out a statute by which Bulgaria would become the seventh republic in Tito's Federal Yugoslavia. Even Communists, as we have already seen, cherished nationalist sentiments, and the Bulgarians, fearful that the Yugoslavs would simply swallow them up, urged instead that Bulgaria join the federation not as one republic among seven but as a joint partner with all of Yugoslavia in a dual state. They wanted to set up in Belgrade a "temporary council of South Slav Union" on which their representatives would negotiate on a parity with those of Yugoslavia. This the Yugoslavs flatly refused to consider. They maintained that Serbia and Montenegro had been independent states before Bulgaria, and argued that the Bulgarians could play a role in the new state no larger than that of these two "Federal Republics."

In January 1945, Mosha Piyade headed a Yugoslav delegation to Moscow and Anton Yugov a Bulgarian one to get Stalin to arbitrate the dispute. According to the Yugoslavs, he heard both sides, and decided for the Yugoslav point of view. Then, Dedijer says, he showed no enthusiasm for the whole project, and the Russian representatives at once said that there were "other difficulties." But Dedijer wrote after the Yugoslav rapprochement with the west, and was doubtless being purposely vague. Piyade himself, who did not, frankly declared that it was objections from the British, who had got wind of the federation plan, which stopped it. Churchill does not mention this, but it would be consistent with his wish to maintain the percentages agreement. The British, it appeared, opposed a Yugoslav-Bulgarian federation, but would consider one which also included Albania, Greece, and Turkey. For this the Russians had no stomach. In the end, even the treaty of mutual coöperation between Yugoslavia and Bulgaria, which the Russians had wanted as the first step to a federation between the two, went by the board. The spate of rhetoric which in late 1944 and early 1945 had been pouring from Sofia and Belgrade, referring to the eternal brotherhood between the two countries, and pleading with the western powers to show an understanding of their wish for solidarity, now petered out.

Apparently Tito now temporarily dropped the question of federation with Bulgaria, and even the lesser matter of Pirin Macedonia. Inside his own Macedonian Republic he faced, as might have been expected, a movement for complete Macedonian independence. We do not know how strong the movement was, or whether any of the politicians, Communist or otherwise, in Sofia lent it aid and comfort. A leading Macedonian Partisan, Antonov-Chento, head of the Macedonian Anti-Fascist Liberation Council (AVNOM), seems to have been at the head of it. In the summer of 1946 he resigned from the government of the republic, and was arrested while allegedly on his way to Greece in an effort to come to Paris and put before the Peace Conference there his plan for an independent Macedonia. The Yugoslavs declared that he was a former IMRO man, which is not at all unlikely. At any rate, in November 1946, the Yugoslavs tried him and sentenced him to eleven years' hard labor. It is understandable that the Tito government suspended negotiations for union with Bulgaria during a period in which they may have felt that Macedonian nationalism posed a threat to Yugoslav internal security in Macedonia. Under the circumstances, to add more Macedonians and Bulgarians might have been to court disruption.

But as early as August 1946, in Skoplye, Kolishevsky, in a speech to the Macedonian People's Front, had expressed the hope that the Bulgarian Fatherland Front government

> would make it possible for our people in Pirin Macedonia to have those conditions for free national development which the Bulgarian minority enjoys in Federal Yugoslavia. We hope that the Fatherland Front Government will introduce the teaching of the Macedonian language and literature, and that it will prevent the placing of obstacles in the way of the free development of a Macedonian national anti-fascist democratic organization within the framework of the Fatherland Front.

Since both Yugoslavia and Bulgaria had Communist governments, he said, they could reach agreement without outside interference. But "to raise the question of the union of Macedonia outside the borders of Yugoslavia means common provocation, and is against the independence and interests of the Macedonian people." This left the Bulgarians little room for argument, and summoned them in effect to honor their earlier promise to grant not only cultural but administrative autonomy to Pirin Macedonia. At the Tenth Plenum of the Bulgarian Communist Party, the Bulgarians knuckled under: they passed a resolution providing that union was to be achieved by joining Pirin Macedonia to the Macedonian People's Republic within Yugoslavia, on the basis of a Treaty of Alliance between Yugoslavia and Bulgaria. Before union could be achieved, a systematic effort at a cultural rapprochement between the Macedonians in the two countries must be made. But the Bulgarian party also resolved to allow the population of Pirin to opt for Bulgarian citizenship, and to remove all customs barriers between Bulgaria and Macedonia, and said nothing about giving administrative autonomy to Pirin Macedonia. Moreover, they did not publish the resolution. It was clearly intended as a sop to the Yugoslavs, but the Bulgarians could not bring themselves to act upon it, and thus lay themselves open to the reproaches from their own people which would surely follow.

Nothing seems to have been done in the matter for a full year. In the interim, according to Dedijer, Stalin was busy trying to stir up trouble between the leaders of the Yugoslav and Bulgarian parties. In Moscow, in late May 1946, Stalin allegedly kept needling and humiliating Dimitrov in Tito's presence. He referred to some Bulgarian wine as "Yugoslav wine the Bulgarians stole from Yugoslavia during the war," and summoned Tito, but nobody else, to stand with the Soviet Politburo at the funeral of Kalinin. Beria also openly insulted the aging Bulgarian number two Communist, Kolarov, in the presence of the Yugoslavs.

Dedijer would have his readers believe that all this was part of a concerted effort to sow distrust between the two parties, but he may possibly be reading too much into what may have been just another exhibition of Stalin's usual boorish horseplay. On the other hand, if it is true, as Dedijer maintains, that Stalin in Dimitrov's presence actually offered to Tito the leadership of the new international Communist organization which he was planning to found, and which was to become the Cominform, this was surely a calculated insult to Dimitrov, the former boss of the Comintern. In any case, Tito declined the honor, and suggested that the French Communist Party initiate the new body. In the end, of course, the Russians did it themselves more than a year later. Whatever Stalin's intentions, the Yugoslav and Bulgarian leaders remained on good terms.

During 1946, the Balkan picture was further complicated by a new outbreak of Communist-led civil war in Greece. Apparently the Russians now regarded the percentages agreement as dead, since the British had so often protested against Communist excesses in Rumania and Bulgaria. In any case, they used the situation in Greece, where British troops remained, as a club with which to beat the British in every international meeting, repeatedly accusing them of fostering fascism and the like. In Greece itself, where elections were held in March 1946, the Russians refused to send observers, the EAM abstained, and the right won a victory. In September, a plebiscite voted for the restoration of the monarchy, and the King returned. In general, the Greek governments of this period treated very harshly those they suspected of belonging to the EAM. The Communists began their new outbreaks in the fall of 1946.

This time, however, their activity was centered not in Athens but in Greek Macedonia. While the Russians charged that the British and American-supported "monarcho-fascist" Greek government had nefarious designs on its peaceful neighbors to the north, these Communist-dominated neighbors, Yugoslavia, Albania, and Bulgaria, actually were giving aid and comfort to the Russian-sponsored Communist rebels against the government of Greece. When pressed by Greek government troops, Communist rebel detachments could retire across the frontier of Greece into any one of the three northern states beyond the pursuit of their opponents, and receive shelter, assistance, and time to rest, regroup, and prepare themselves to slip back across the frontier again for a new attack in a different sector. It was an early instance of what we later learned in Korea to call "privileged sanctuary."

A UN inquiry commission was set up early in 1947, which in turn established a subcommission at Saloniki to observe the frontier. Though the Russians participated in the first commission, they refused to approve the subcommission of observation; and Yugoslavia, Bulgaria, and Albania refused to permit its members to work inside their borders. The commission had plenty of opportunity, however, to observe and report the assistance given the rebels by the three Communist-governed states. In March 1947, President Truman proclaimed that the United States would aid the Greek government. The "Truman doctrine" would keep communism out of Greece.

For Bulgaria and Yugoslavia, the Greek uprising represented opportunity. During the war, the Bulgarians had occupied, as we know, in addition to Macedonia, all of Greek Thrace, including the islands of Thasos and Samothrace. After the war, the Greeks tried to obtain from the powers a small strip of Bulgarian territory, roughly 900 square kilometers with perhaps 150,000 inhabitants, largely for strategic reasons. But the powers at Paris refused to alter the prewar frontier. The Bulgarians none the less kept a "Thracian society" active in Sofia, with a "scientific" section of its own which published propaganda urging Bulgarain claims to Thrace. Thus both Thrace and Greek Macedonia whetted the appetite of the Bulgarians, in addition to whatever Communist solidarity their leaders might feel for the Greek rebels.

As for Tito, during the war, as we have seen, his man Vukmanovich-

Tempo, who had successfully organized the partisan movement in Yugoslav Macedonia, had also visited Greek Macedonia, and prevailed on the Greek Communists to allow a separate Slavic Macedonian partisan movement to develop on Greek soil. This movement, called, like everything else in Greece, by its initials, SNOF, had close relations with the Greek EAM and the Bulgarian partisans, but seems to have owed its main allegiance to the Yugoslav partisans, much to the natural distaste of the Greek Communists. Toward the end of the war, the Yugoslav-oriented SNOF was even on occasion fighting the EAM's ELAS. But after the Germans had left, Tito called off SNOF, summoned its leaders into Yugoslavia, and disbanded its units. He gave the Greek Communists a clear field to win all of Greece without the handicap of having lost Macedonia to the Slavs. His sponsorship of SNOF had made the Greek Communists as angry at him, however, as his infiltration of Pirin made the Bulgarians. When the British defeated the first Greek Communist uprising in January 1945, more Slavic Macedonians from Greek Macedonia fled to the Yugoslav Macedonian Republic, where the press regularly denounced the Greek government for persecuting its Macedonian Slavic minority. For a while longer Tito was still apparently willing to postpone his claim to Greek Macedonia until the Communists should have won all Greece. As late as May 1946, the Greek party line supported Greek territorial integrity.

But when the Greek Communists began their second uprising, in Macedonia, in the fall of 1946, under the command of a Moscow-trained Greek with Macedonian experience, Markos Vafiades, they needed the support of the Macedonian Slavic minority. Tito revived SNOF, now called NOF (National Liberation Front, instead of Slavic National Liberation Front), and sent many of the former Yugoslav political and military advisers to the wartime guerrillas in Greek Macedonia right back into the same territory. Though NOF operated nominally under Markos Vafiades, Titoite influence was from the first strong in the new guerrilla movement. Thus Yugoslavia took the lead in Greece as well as in Bulgaria.

In August 1947, Dimitrov visited Tito at Bled in Slovenia. There they announced the conclusion of an agreement between the two countries, putting an end to frontier travel-barriers and arranging for a later customs union. Though the Yugoslavs once more pressed for an immediate cession of Pirin Macedonia, the Bulgarians said this must wait until after federation. But they did consent to grant the Pirin Macedonians "all rights for free cultural development, . . . and that they should be spiritually united with their brothers in Vardar [Yugoslav] Macedonia." In practice, what "free cultural development" and "spiritual union" meant was a flood of propagandists from Yugoslavia pouring over what had hitherto been the Bulgarian frontier, but had now been virtually dissolved.

Ninety-three Titoite Yugoslav Macedonian teachers came to "assist in the correct teaching of the Macedonian literary language," as the Yugoslavs put it. They also lectured on Macedonian history, and on the glories of life in the

Macedonian Federal Republic. A Macedonian theater, a Macedonian publishing house which issued quantities of propaganda literature, a special Pirin Macedonian newspaper, scholarships for Pirin Macedonians to study in Yugoslav Macedonia, invitations to Pirin youth brigades to labor "voluntarily" in Yugoslav Macedonia: here was the latest, Communist, version of the propaganda struggle between Serb and Bulgar for Macedonian loyalty, a struggle some three-quarters of a century old. The Titoite efforts in Pirin in 1947–48 came as the immediate historic response to the Bulgarian efforts in Yugoslav Macedonia during the war.

For the moment, the Bulgarians had to swallow the pill. Later, after the Cominform break with the Yugoslavs, they could reveal how miserably unhappy they had always felt during this period of Yugoslav penetration of Pirin Macedonia. Then they would accuse their former brothers of waging an anti-Bulgarian campaign, tearing down posters with portraits of Bulgarian revolutionaries, and substituting Yugoslav heroes, requiring oaths of loyalty to Tito, changing the family names of Macedonians from Bulgarian to Serbian forms, popularizing an "invented" Macedonian language instead of the perfectly good "Bulgarian" spoken in the Pirin region already, and a variety of other nationalist crimes. At the time, however, the Yugoslav program seems to have won a good deal of support among the Pirin Macedonians, even the local Communists, some of whom later admitted their "errors" in having assisted it. But as early as April 1948, three months before the Cominform split became known, a Bulgarian-minded Macedonian Communist, Vladimir Poptomov, denounced the whole infiltration of teachers into Pirin Macedonia, the circulation there of the Yugoslav Macedonian newspapers, and the visits of Pirin delegations to Yugoslavia. Poptomov later became Foreign Minister of Bulgaria; it was not a coincidence.

While the Yugoslav Macedonian teachers were doing their work in Bulgaria, Tito visited Sofia in November 1947, and signed the Treaty of Friendship with Bulgaria. "We shall establish coöperation so general and so close," he said in Sofia, "that federation will be a mere formality." Indeed, Tito was now embarked on what amounted to a triumphal tour of the east-European capitals, in which Sofia had followed Prague and Warsaw, and Budapest and Bucharest followed Sofia. Enormous crowds welcomed him, especially in Sofia, Budapest, and Bucharest, whether from enthusiasm, "spontaneity," or mere curiosity is not very important. According to Dedijer, Tito consulted Moscow about each visit, except the one to Rumania. About this he "had not the time to inform the Russians." In Rumania, Dedijer maintains, Bodnaraș, serving as NKVD agent, reported to Moscow the warm regard which the Rumanian comrades had for Tito. He sent word that the other top Rumanian Communists regarded the experience of the Yugoslav army as a better model to study than that of the Soviet armies.

Late in January 1948 the opportunity arose for the Russians to deal a shrewd blow to whatever Balkan plans Tito and Dimitrov might have been hatching. On a visit to Rumania, Dimitrov said, in answer to a question at a press conference, that the question of a Balkan federation was as yet premature, but that it would arise, and when it arose the peoples of the southeastern and eastern European countries would themselves make the decisions:

"It is they who will decide whether it will be a federation or confederation, and when or how it will be formed. I can say that what our peoples are already doing greatly facilitates the solution of this question in the future." He also stressed heavily the point that in his opinion Greece would be one of the countries of "people's democracy" that would make the decision. Indeed, only a couple of weeks earlier, on December 24, 1947, Markos Vafiades had proclaimed the formation of a "Provisional Democratic Government" of Greece in the Macedonian mountains, with its "Free Greece" Radio Station. So Dimitrov's reference to Greece was tantamount to a prediction of a Markos victory.

In Moscow, *Pravda* published this. A day later, on January 29, 1948, in three brief paragraphs, it explained that it could not have avoided publishing the Dimitrov statement, "which had already been published in the press of other countries, where, of course, *Pravda* could make no alterations." The "editors of *Pravda*," however, disagreed with Dimitrov, and did not believe that these countries needed any "problematic and artificial federation or confederation or customs union; what they require is the consolidation and defense of their independence and sovereignty by mobilizing their people's democratic forces. . . ." According to Dedijer, Stalin now summoned the top Bulgarian and Yugoslav Communists to Moscow, although a Yugoslav delegation was there already. Tito himself stayed away, but sent Kardelj and others.

At a Kremlin conference, on February 10, 1948, Molotov scolded the Yugoslavs and Bulgarians for concluding an alliance contrary to the advice of the Soviet Union, which had urged the two countries to wait until Bulgaria was no longer limited by the peace treaty. The Russians were furious with Dimitrov for his statement on federation, and he admitted that the press conference had gone to his head. But Stalin seemed even angrier at the idea that Dimitrov was secretly planning a customs union between Bulgaria and Rumania: when it came right down to it, Stalin said, he did not object to a federation between Bulgaria and Yugoslavia, but there must be no customs union between Bulgaria and Rumania. The Bulgarians protested that they had sent Moscow a draft of the proposed customs union with Rumania, and the Yugoslavs that they had sent a draft of the treaty with Bulgaria; it became clear that the Soviet Foreign Office had been asleep at the switch, and had not called Stalin's attention to these documents.

There was a further source of Stalin's annoyance with the Yugoslavs, however, according to Dedijer. In January, the Albanian government, fearing that Greek government troops would occupy Albanian territory, had appealed to Tito, asking for two Yugoslav divisions to be sent to southern Albania as protection against any Greek advance. There was also a Yugoslav air-force "regiment" on Albanian soil. Stalin berated the Yugoslavs for reaching these military arrangements without consulting Moscow. Kardelj replied that the Yugoslav government had not yet decided whether to send the two divisions. Stalin angrily refused to be mollified, and went on to denounce the Bulgarian-Rumanian customs union once more, and even to deny that the Netherlands formed part of the Benelux customs union.

In the end, he put forward what purported to be his own ideas for eastern European federations: Rumania and Hungary should unite, and Bulgaria and Yugoslavia, after which they should annex Albania. Indeed, he now declared that Bulgaria and Yugoslavia should unite immediately. To Kardelj's soothing remark that Yugoslav views on foreign policy coincided with those of the USSR, Stalin now replied with a denial, and still another instance where he differed with Yugoslav policy: "we do not agree with Yugoslav [*sic*] comrades that they should help further the Greek Partisans. . . . Yugoslav comrades should stop helping them. That struggle has no prospect whatever."

This comment is of particular interest. None of the satellite states ever recognized Markos' government. Markos was obviously suspect in Moscow as one of Tito's men.

After the session, the Yugoslav representatives agreed among themselves that Stalin meant them no good by his pressing for an early federation with Bulgaria. He wanted, they thought, to break up the unity of their country, and they now all felt that they should postpone the federation. Dimitrov too was anxious, and the Yugoslavs thought that he might have detected an intention on Stalin's part to incorporate Yugoslavia and Bulgaria in the USSR. The next day, February 11, 1948, Kardelj was virtually commanded to sign an agreement that Yugoslavia would consult the Soviet Union in future on all questions of foreign policy. Though humiliated by the agreement, and by the harshness with which he was ordered to sign it, he decided to do so.

If we accept at face value Dedijer's account of this extraordinary Kremlin session of February 10, 1948, we can conclude only that Stalin had become seriously displeased with Tito's independent behavior. Although he seems not to have objected in principle to Yugoslav-Bulgarian or even to Yugoslav-Bulgarian-Albanian union, he was apparently determined to have the deciding voice as to the timing and details of all such arrangements. What apparently irritated him was the willingness of Tito to move without informing him: the visit to Bucharest, the question of sending Yugoslav troops to Albania were daily details about which Stalin considered himself entitled to be informed. The alleged failure of Molotov to call to his attention the drafts which had been sent to the Soviet foreign office of the Yugoslav-Bulgarian treaty and the proposed Bulgarian-Rumanian treaty exacerbated his anger: of course he may well have been informed and have decided to forget about it conveniently in order to awe the Yugoslav and Bulgarian Communists with his rage. Further, he clearly suspected Tito's aims in Greece.

Finally, he seems also to have been seriously annoyed at Dimitrov, perhaps not so much at the ill-advised press-conference statement on Balkan federation as for acting in close collaboration with Tito despite earlier efforts to drive them apart, and for interfering with Stalin's plans for Rumania by pressing for a Bulgarian-Rumanian customs union. Such a union, if effected between Rumania and a Bulgaria which was already about to become in effect a seventh Yugoslav republic, would have brought Rumania into the most intimate connection with a Yugoslavia which had acquired Bulgaria, would surely acquire Albania, and already had a foothold in Greece. Stalin suspected that he was witnessing the inception of a great Balkan confederation of forty-odd million population, under the domination of Tito. It seems quite likely that Stalin was right.

THE CORFU CHANNEL CASE

By way of coda to this summary of the main theme of Balkan foreign politics in these years, we may say a word here about Albanian relations with the west. The United States, prepared to recognize Hoxha toward the end of 1945, found that he would not accept as valid the treaties which prewar Albanian governments had concluded with Washington. The Albanian regime adopted a most unfriendly attitude to the United States political mission in the country, even accusing the Americans of sabotaging the Lake Maliq drainage operations, and restricting the movements of the mission's personnel. Our government withdrew it in November 1946. Great Britain, similarly treated, responded in similar fashion, but found itself the victim of even greater provocation when, on October 22, 1946, two British destroyers, sailing through the Corfu channel, struck mines in Albanian waters, and were damaged with the loss of lives. Three weeks later, British mine sweepers cleared the channel of mines.

The British maintained that the mines could not have been laid in these waters without Albanian knowledge, and that the Albanian authorities had not warned foreign shipping that the mines were there. They therefore demanded an apology and compensation. The Albanians refused, declaring that Britain had twice violated Albanian sovereignty by sailing through these waters, both when the destroyers were mined and when the mines were swept. When the United Nations Security Council could not reach agreement on the matter (the Soviet Union vetoed the opinion of the majority that the Albanians must have known about the mines), the International Court of Justice got the case: its first.

Masses of data were submitted to the court, which reached a decision only in April 1949, partly because Albania refused to recognize its jurisdiction. The court decided by a vote of twelve to two that the British were correct in their claim that the Albanians must have known of the existence of the mines. It decided by a vote of fourteen to none that the Albanians were correct in their claim that the British had violated their sovereignty when the mines were swept, but found that there were extenuating circumstances. On December 15, 1949, the court declared that the Albanian government must pay in full for the incident, the sum amounting to 830,000 pounds. The British could recover this sum from Italian gold on deposit in London and destined as reparations for Albania. The whole episode, like the affair of the American planes shot down by the Yugoslavs, demonstrated that the western powers would resort to international machinery to settle their disputes with the satellite states. Like the withdrawal of the American mission to Tirana, and the hostility aroused in the west by Albanian assistance to the Greek guerrillas, it may also serve as an illustration of the increasing isolation of the smallest Balkan state from its former friends in the western world.

Chapter 10

THE COMMUNISTS TAKE OVER: THE ECONOMY OF THE BALKAN COUNTRIES FROM THE FALL OF 1944 TO JUNE 1948

1. Yugoslavia

WAR DAMAGE AND UNRRA ASSISTANCE

OF OUR FOUR COUNTRIES, Yugoslávia suffered most during the war. It is true that an agricultural economy can recover from war-damage more readily than an industrial economy whose industries have been smashed, but the Yugoslavs none the less lost heavily in certain items very hard to replace, such as housing and livestock. Official estimates put the housing loss at one-sixth of all prewar housing, and the livestock losses at 60 per cent of the horses, more than 50 per cent of the cattle, and similar figures with respect to sheep, goats, hogs, and poultry, which are of course more easily replaced. Damage to industry amounted to one-third the prewar value; more than half the coal mines were rendered at least temporarily useless by explosions and flooding. One textile plant in five was destroyed. Transport was in a still more parlous state, with half the railroad track torn up, three-quarters of the bridges out, and more than half of the rolling stock either removed or useless.

Between the end of the war and June 1947, UNRRA undertook the task of providing the supplies necessary to permit the survival of the Yugoslav people. Yugoslavia received more than 14 per cent of UNRRA's entire budget, a total of almost $425,000,000. The UNRRA authorities spent $136,338,000 for food, and $37,188,000 for agricultural rehabilitation. They supplied 30,000 head of livestock, 3,500 tractors, and nearly 700,000 tons of bread-grains. For months on end, UNRRA supplied all the food for between three and five million

Yugoslavs; millions more received part of their daily rations. UNRRA was the only source of civilian clothing and of medical supplies. Providing the needed goods was only the first step. Distributing them throughout the countryside by truck over inadequate and badly damaged roads required heroic effort. Although UNRRA's total expenditure amounted to about one-fifth of the total annual income of Yugoslavia before 1939, and considerably more than the annual tax revenue of the prewar government, it could not make good the wartime losses. For example, it replaced only about 8 per cent of the livestock losses. Nor were its efforts ever intended to transform or even to alter significantly the basic features of the Yugoslav economy. It did prevent the death of millions of Yugoslavs from starvation and disease, and assisted the country to recover. The basic problems of peasant poverty remained and were exacerbated by war.

CURRENCY REFORM

In the various parts of fragmented Yugoslavia, German, Hungarian, Bulgarian, and Albanian currencies were in circulation. In addition, Pavelich Croatia and Nedich Serbia had both had their own currencies. In 1945 the new government therefore passed a currency law, which was effective first in Serbia and Montenegro in April, and soon afterwards elsewhere as well. New dinars were issued at a rate of one to twenty of the prewar dinar. The law permitted individuals to exchange only 100,000 old dinars for the new ones, but required them to declare all their holdings. It blocked bank accounts. It confiscated 70 per cent of all individual holdings above five million dinars, and smaller percentages of smaller fortunes. In 1946 a new law fixed the gold content of the dinar at 17.773 milligrams of fine gold, and the foreign exchange rate at fifty dinars to the dollar, about the same as the prewar rate. The effect of these measures was drastically to reduce the number of dinars in circulation: from 250 billion in mid-1945 to about eighteen billion at the end of the year and about twenty-one billion at the end of 1946. The laws certainly averted the threat of a serious inflation. At the same time they served a political purpose, virtually confiscating the fortunes of the rich, both those who had had money since before the war and those who had made it during the war.

"LAND REFORM" AND COLLECTIVIZATION

Before economic recovery had progressed very far, the Yugoslav regime enacted a new law for "land reform." Passed on August 23, 1945, the enactment expropriated without compensation all "large" estates over forty-five hectares in total area, or with more than twenty-five to thirty hectares of arable land, if worked by tenant farmers or hired labor. In cases of need, the law provided that the owner could retain five hectares for himself. The state also seized land belonging to banks or industrial enterprises, church and monastery estates over 100 hectares, land left without owners as a result of the war, and all land belonging to the *Volksdeutsch* minority, who had been expelled from the country.

From all these sources the government secured 1,600,000 hectares. Most of it lay in the Voyvodina (636,847 hectares alone were former *Volksdeutsch* property), or in the other portions of the former Habsburg dominions. The state then distributed about half of the land (roughly 800,000 hectares) to 316,415 individual peasants, with priority given to Partisan veterans and landless peasants. It kept virtually all the rest (more than 700,000 hectares) as state lands, for state farms (*sovkhoz*), forest-preserves (all forests were nationalized), state-owned industry, and other purposes. The new land reform brought in more than twice as much acreage as the first such act undertaken after the First World War, but benefited only about 40,000 more peasant families.

The Yugoslav regime took advantage of the lands obtained from the *Volksdeutsch* to resettle immigrants from Montenegro and other infertile portions of Yugoslavia, who were far from accustomed to the rich black earth of the Voyvodina. Here too the government founded its first collective farms, as early as 1945. The number of collectives rose from thirty-one in 1945, to 454 in 1946, to 779 in 1947, to 1,318 in 1948. By that year more than 60,000 peasant families were living on collectives, which embraced well over 300,000 hectares. Although forced mass collectivization still lay ahead, Tito had actually moved faster to collectivize agriculture than any other Balkan satellite ruler. The Cominform accusations against him in 1948 included the charge that he had departed "in the countryside" from Marxist-Leninist principles. The charge was an absurdity.

In these early years, it is true, the Yugoslavs scrupulously avoided using the name "collective" for their enterprises, and called them instead "labor coöperative farms." As a usual thing, the government did not employ coercion to force the peasants to join. Moreover, most farms were not of the full-fledged Soviet type, where the peasant surrendered title to all but his own homestead. Instead the Yugoslavs in most places were using intermediate forms, in which the peasant received a percentage of the farm's profits based on the amount of land he had contributed, and from which he might withdraw after a period of trial, taking his land out with him.

THE FIVE YEAR PLAN AND AGRICULTURE

Before all the other Balkan Communists, the Yugoslavs also introduced the first Five Year Plan in 1947, to be completed by 1951. Where all the other countries began with preliminary short-term plans involving recovery to prewar levels, the Yugoslavs alone began with a full-scale Five Year Plan involving both recovery and development. It set extraordinarily, even absurdly, high goals. Subordinating agriculture to industry, the planners maintained that no transition from extensive to intensive agriculture was possible without prior industrialization. In introducing the Plan, Tito denied that it marked a step toward the abolition of private ownership of land. He thus tried to set at rest the fears of those peasants who expected early forced collectivization. But agricultural planning, Tito said, was necessary with regard to the distribution of seed, increased use of farm machinery, and overall sowing. The "state must think of food supplies for the whole population, and it cannot therefore be a matter of indifference how much and how and where the peasant will sow."

The Plan paid special attention to the backward republics: Bosnia-Hertsegovina, Macedonia, and Montenegro. Separate Plans for each elaborated the details of planned activities. The government announced that it would "assist existing peasant coöperatives," and that it would encourage the "voluntary initiative which is becoming ever more manifest among small and middle peasants in the founding of coöperatives for the joint cultivation of land and the rearing of livestock," introducing measures "enabling the peasant coöperatives to develop into model farm estates."

The text of the Five Year Plan repeatedly emphasized that the development of agriculture and of industry must go hand in hand: this was probably designed partly as an answer to those who felt that agriculture was being neglected and industry overemphasized (members of former peasant parties, and convinced anti-Communists of all sorts), and partly as a warning to those who took exactly the opposite view and felt that agriculture was receiving too much emphasis (Communist enthusiasts who believed it possible to build up industry at the expense of agriculture). In April 1948, a year after the adoption of the Five Year Plan, Edvard Kardelj, Tito's right-hand man, reproved both those who persistently underestimated the necessity of agricultural reconstruction and those who felt that all agricultural problems could be solved by mere technical improvements.

Although by the end of 1947, he said, there were nearly 2,200,000 members of consumers' and credit coöperative organizations serving more than 10,000,000 consumers,[1] and although 4,000 coöperative centers were under construction in villages all over Yugoslavia, the state planners, especially those on the finance and planning commissions, persisted in their view that investment in "coöperatives" was not "investment in the socialist sector." This error was all part, he said, of the "greatly mistaken and harmful underestimation of the role of agriculture in our economic development." Kardelj here clearly revealed a disagreement within the ranks of the Yugoslav Communist Party itself between the proponents of the Tito-Kardelj policy of "strengthening" agriculture through the new "coöperative state farms," but without an immediate forced general collectivization, and those who preferred to concentrate planning upon industry, and presumably wanted to collectivize agriculture at once, incurring the risk of disorders and economic disaster which would be sure to accompany such a move, and dismissing anything less as "not socialist."

[1] These are to be distinguished from the producers' coöperatives or collectives.

Kardelj now went further than Tito had gone before. Admitting the importance of "agrotechnical measures," he none the less stressed the need for "modifying the socio-economic structure." Individual small-holdings, he maintained, set a limit of their own to the amount of mechanization it would be possible to introduce; any attempt to go beyond this would penalize the small holder and give unfair advantage to "the village rich," as had happened in "certain western countries with an advanced capitalist agriculture." What Yugoslavia must do, he continued, was to develop coöperatives to assist the small-holder; and this called for state leadership and assistance on all levels. Chiding those of his fellow-Communists who believed that purchase-sale coöperatives were enough, Kardelj put new stress upon "socialism" in agriculture, and upon the need for rapidly equipping "state-coöperatives" (i.e., producers' coöperatives — *collectives*), with machinery of all kinds.

He predicted that this would take time, and that it would meet opposition, and added that it would inevitably entail "a process of liquidation of the capitalist remnants in the villages which do not want to reconcile themselves to the fact that the days of exploitation of man by man in our country are numbered." This remark of Kardelj's was of course strongly reminiscent of the orthodox Stalinist's attitude toward the "kulak." The type of coöperative he envisioned was the *kolkhoz* itself. Kardelj went on to tell a story, which is worth quoting here:

> I know of the example of one village which recently finished the construction of its coöperative center. The village was, as they say, inclined toward reaction. Actually, a few wealthy owners succeeded in exerting influence on the mass of the peasants with small and medium-sized holdings. When initiative for the building of a coöperative center came from the People's Front (Communist Party front organization), strong organized resistance was offered.
>
> *The well-known rumors about common kitchens and common beds began to fly.* [Italics mine: note the admission by a leading Communist of the general peasant hostility to collectives.]
>
> One part of the peasants with small and medium-sized holdings, however, set to work, and when the first results were seen, a turn-about took place in the village. The whole village set to work, and near the end, under pressure from the village, even the wealthy owners, who had been the main organizers of the resistance at the beginning, appeared at the construction site.
>
> When the peasants gathered for the first time in the assembly hall of the newly built center, when they saw the pictures of their shock-workers on the walls and saw the first film in their village, in the center which they themselves had built, then many things became clear to them which had not been clear when the first shovel had struck the earth at the beginning of the construction of the center. Today that village not only has a coöperative center with store-rooms and space for cultural activities and trading but the village itself has changed. *The influence of the remnants of capitalism has been uprooted.* [Italics mine.] And how will that village look tomorrow when co-

operative agricultural machines and the first coöperative tractors help the working peasants to cultivate their land? [2]

This is a highly edifying story, in more ways than Kardelj intended. Its truth is entirely irrelevant. What is important is that he told it, and the implications with regard to policy which may be drawn from it. In this anecdote, the reluctance of the villagers, spearheaded by the rich, to build the center, is overcome by their mere observance of the activities of those who began to work. The example is so powerful that even the rich ringleaders of the "strong organized resistance" finally capitulate and help in the building. And by this very act alone the remnants of capitalism disappear! Certainly this fable would not meet with the approval of orthodox Marxists, *except as a tactic* to calm the apprehensions of the audience. In the story nobody is liquidated; no force is even applied to anyone; nothing is confiscated from anybody; the "wealthy owners" are just as wealthy at the end as they were at the beginning; actually "capitalism" has not been touched in any way except by emotion and sentimentality. And yet Kardelj maintained that these gentle and unorthodox methods had destroyed it. Capitalism, as Kardelj well knew, was a hardier plant than that.

This anecdote was more important than Kardelj's earlier bluster about the "liquidation of the capitalist remnants." Up to 1948, the Tito regime was unwilling to strike a fundamental blow at the foundations of the old agricultural structure. It exhorted; it made the Marxist-Leninist-Stalinist-Titoist vocabulary familiar to the peasants by endless reiteration. It tried to cast discredit on kulaks and put pressure on the richer peasants in order to shame them into coöperation. It encouraged "coöperative farms," which adopted as many features of the kolkhoz as were safe, in the hope that these collectives could prove so efficient that there would be a spontaneous move on the part of the peasants to form others voluntarily. But it would not yet collectivize forcibly, although it would not abandon collectivization as an ultimate aim to be achieved sometime in the future.

COMPULSORY DELIVERIES

In the early years of the Tito regime, however, it is probable that the peasants noticed collectivization less and minded it less than the system of compulsory deliveries. Not only did the government require that the peasant sell his surplus to the state at prices far below what he could have got in the market, but it sent its agents around to the villages to determine for themselves just what constituted surplus. Here was a means of exerting fearful economic and social pressure: many a prosperous peasant lost his whole crop because the government had ruled that all of it was surplus. He could not feed his family.

Sometimes the government demanded more than he had produced, and

[2] *Speech delivered by Edvard Kardelj in the National Assembly, April 25, 1948,* mimeographed English text.

in this case he had to sell a domestic animal, or somehow raise cash to buy from some other source enough produce to make up the deficit. This he would have to buy on the open market at the high prices then prevailing. Since the government took "surplus" of virtually every conceivable farm product, nobody and nothing was exempt. And the local Communists could use the system as a means to bring pressure on the more prosperous peasant, thus softening up the kulak for the future blows the regime would deal him. Indeed, the local agents of the regime could and often did impose arbitrary additional property taxes, which they might even make retroactive, if they found themselves dealing with an "enemy" of the regime. Although collectivization had not yet been launched at full speed ahead, the Yugoslav peasant by the middle of 1948 had suffered severely at the hands of his government.

NATIONALIZATION

If the Tito regime moved with a certain deliberation in the field of agriculture, affecting as it did so large a majority of the population, its policies in the industrial field were clearly impatient to the point of rashness. The Yugoslav Communists were burning to remake their society on the Soviet model, despite their lack of trained personnel at every level. They now claim that they had already nationalized 54 per cent of Yugoslav industry during the war itself. Once the war was over, they accelerated the process. It was made easier by the fact that the Germans had already expropriated the chief mines and other installations which had been foreign-owned (Bor copper, Trepcha zinc, and the like); so the state could now take over all of them as former German-owned enterprises. A series of further laws in 1946, 1947, and finally in May 1948, nationalized virtually everything but land. Without previous warning, the planners pushed the last decree, applying to hotels, garages, and small shops, through the Assembly. Next morning, government agents appeared on the premises which were to be nationalized, to prevent the former owners from removing even the cash in the till. By way of compensation, the owners got nothing approaching the value of the goods they surrendered. Thus the "state sector" of the economy had swollen to include all industry, wholesale and retail trade, banking, and transportation.

INDUSTRIALIZATION AND INVESTMENT

As to industrialization, the Yugoslav government embraced the idea all too enthusiastically, not only for its economic but for its social implications. Recognizing that overpopulation has been the curse of the Balkan peasant countries, but refusing to accept emigration as a palliative, and sounding a strongly nationalist note, Tito remarked before the adoption of the Five Year Plan, that

> The industrialization of our country will make it possible for hundreds and thousands of destitute citizens and landless peasants to find work, and the poorer section of our population will not be obliged to leave their own country

> and wander through foreign lands in search of a job. The industrialization of our country accordingly represents a very important factor in the solving of this difficult social problem.

Specifically, the Five Year Plan called for the transfer of 170,000 workers from agriculture to industry, which would have doubled the Yugoslav industrial labor force. In addition, the Plan envisioned the training of 60,000 additional highly skilled workers and of 20,000 university-educated technicians. If we assume that each of these 250,000 men had a family of four, the transfer over five years of 1,000,000 persons from the farms would have balanced exactly the rise in population to be expected from the natural rate of increase: 200,000 a year. Rural overpopulation would be unaffected.

With 1939 as its year of comparison, the Plan called for 93 per cent increase in the national income by 1951 (from 132 billion to 255 billion dinars). Twenty-seven per cent of the national income was to be invested each year, and almost half the investment was earmarked for industry. Industrial production was to increase in value by 223 per cent (52.7 billion dinars in 1939 to 170 billion in 1951), while agricultural production would increase only by 52 per cent (63.8 billion dinars in 1939 to 96.7 billion in 1951).

RAW MATERIAL OUTPUT: GOALS AND ACHIEVEMENTS

Within industry the plan put particular emphasis on heavy industry. The theory behind this decision was revealed by Tito, who maintained that the reconstruction and development of Yugoslavia could not be achieved by purchases and imports from abroad. It would be too expensive; and then too it would render Yugoslavia "dependent" upon the "capitalist countries." In those days, Tito inveighed heavily against past Yugoslav regimes which had allowed foreigners to invest their capital in Yugoslav resources, and thus to "exploit" Yugoslavia. He frequently pointed to the Bor mines in particular: the French had extracted Bor copper ore and had then, he maintained, sold the Yugoslavs at high prices finished copper products made in France of their own copper. In fact, Tito was, whether deliberately or not, in error: the very "corrupt" rulers whom he was attacking had seen to it that the French provided equipment for smelting Yugoslav copper inside Yugoslavia. At any rate, the Yugoslav leadership was now, in doctrinaire Communist fashion, determined to produce the means of production, exploit native raw materials rationally and completely, and develop heavy industry.

The percentage of total industrial production to be devoted to this branch of activity was to rise from 43 per cent in 1939 to 57 per cent in 1951. For the first time Yugoslavia was to produce heavy and medium machine tools, electrical equipment, locomotives and railroad cars, boilers, turbines, trucks, tractors, agricultural machinery, and heavy construction machinery. New plants to make machine tools would rise in Zagreb, Sarayevo, and Belgrade. The Plan set high goals for individual items, such as bicycles, tractors, trucks, and typewriters.

To support these new industries the plan called for greatly increased output of raw materials in 1951 over the 1939 totals: coal from six to sixteen and a half million tons, iron ore from 600,000 to 1,500,000 tons, pig iron from 100,000 to 550,000 tons, steel from 250,000 to 760,000 tons, with comparable rises in the very important nonferrous metals. Petroleum, which Yugoslavia had hardly produced before the war (1,000 tons in 1939), had been developed during the war by the Germans in Croatia to a point where they were producing 150,000 tons annually. The plan called for this figure to be tripled, to an annual output of 450,000 tons.

Though the coal mines had been very seriously damaged by the Germans in withdrawing from Yugoslavia, and production in 1945 had been down as low as 15 per cent of the prewar figure, it rose through 1946, in spite of primitive tools and methods, and in 1947 official figures showed a rise to 153 per cent of 1939, which would give a total of 9,000,000 tons. In July 1949 the government announced that the industry had fulfilled 46 per cent of the Five Year Plan, a rate of 10,000,000 tons annually. The Plan called for cutting the consumption of coal by increasing the use of electric power, and erecting processing plants to increase the efficient use of lignite.

As to the iron mines, the government estimated the damage done by the war as 70 per cent: only one blast furnace of eight was still in working order, and eight of the fifteen Siemens-Martin furnaces were destroyed. Yet official figures as of September 1946 showed pig-iron production up to 145 per cent of the prewar output, and raw steel at 102 per cent. The announcement boasted that Yugoslavia was now for the first time producing high-grade steels and turning out pneumatic drills and various other kinds of mining machinery. The Plan called for systematic research on manganese, found with some of the Yugoslav iron, the modernization of existing plants, and the building of new works in the Bosna valley. The industry was to cut down on its use of coke, and step up its use of electricity. Again, according to official reports, the iron and steel portion of the plan was on schedule in mid-1948.

In the nonferrous metals, the Germans had reportedly raised copper production at Bor (which they "purchased" from the French and put under the control of the Goering Works) from the prewar level of 43,000 tons to 50,000 tons. On their departure they smashed the machinery and flooded the mines. The Plan set a goal of 40,000 tons a year, somewhat under the prewar output, beginning with the second half of 1948. The government boasted of the repairs made at Bor, and claimed in 1946 that a smashed turbo-generator of a type never produced in Yugoslavia, had been repaired and put into working order with parts made entirely in the country. Like Bor, the Trepcha lead and zinc mines fell into German hands, like Bor they were crippled, and like Bor they were nationalized. The Plan called for lead to rise to 65,000 tons (previous high: 33,000 in 1940) and zinc to rise to 20,000 tons (previous high: 6,300 tons in 1940). It made no specific reference to the output of bauxite, but set a goal of 13,000 tons of aluminum metal, a more than sevenfold increase over 1939, but less than five times the 1940 output. The government planned to enlarge the existing works at Lozovats, to build a new electrolytic smelter at Strnishche and a new rolling mill, to exploit the Mostar region, and to prospect aluminum deposits in Montenegro. The Plan mentioned no specific targets for the production of chrome, manganese, antimony, magnesium, molybdenum or mercury, but it was sufficiently clear that the regime intended to use much of the production at home for the domestic manufacture of finished goods: rolled and compressed products of nonferrous metallurgy were to be increased in 1951 to 26,000 tons. In this field too, the government claimed in 1948 that the Plan was on schedule.

POWER, CHEMICALS, TRANSPORT, PUBLIC WORKS

In their heavy industry program, the Yugoslavs put electrification and the chemical industry side by side with metallurgy. The Germans knocked out many of the Yugoslav power stations, but the Plan called for a fourfold increase in output over 1939: from about a billion kilowatt-hours to more than four and one-third billion. Some of the new power-stations were to be thermal, making use of coal waste, but most were to be hydroelectric. The Plan also envisaged the creation of a native electrical equipment industry: insulators, cables, radios, bulbs, and film-projectors. Though electrification allegedly proceeded according to plan, the production of equipment lagged considerably. The Plan also called for a ninefold increase in the chemical industries (from a value of 900,000,000 dinars in 1939 to a value of 8,130,000,000 dinars in 1951), and for an eightfold increase in the building materials industry (from a value of 800,000,000 dinars in 1939 to a value of 6,500,000,000 dinars in 1951). It scheduled 1,800 kilometers of new railroad construction, and a substantial addition to the highway network, as well as a shipbuilding program designed to raise the tonnage of the merchant fleet to 600,000 gross tons.

The Plan also called for a variety of expensive public works, such as irrigation projects in Croatia, the draining of Lake Scutari (Skadar, Shkodra) to obtain more arable land, and flood control measures in the chief river valleys. Its fulfillment would have transformed Bosnia and Hertsegovina into great ferrous and nonferrous metallurgical centers, and greatly raised the level of industrial production everywhere, fastest of all in Macedonia, the least advanced of the federal republics.

In addition to these projects, which were at least economically desirable, the regime sponsored a number of ostentatious and uneconomic projects, of which the most notorious was the building of "new Belgrade" across the river from the old, where endless quantities of building material and machinery were tied up in a difficult and unrewarding construction job. It is true that such projects cost the Yugoslav government less than they would have cost any non-authoritarian regime, because of the high proportion of "voluntary," that is to say unpaid, labor employed. Considered economically, the continued large expenses for armament and defense also immobilized useful manpower and used up money in unproductive effort, although from a political point of view the expense proved to be necessary.

CONSUMER GOODS FOR EXPORT

Even to approach the fulfillment of this ambitious expansion of industry, Yugoslavia had to import large amounts of equipment. The exports to pay for this had to be mostly timber and foodstuffs as well as minerals and metals. The Plan called for great increases (from 150 to 700 per cent) in the output of processed meats, sugar, lard, edible oils, pastes, and canned fish; while the production of textiles was to double, and shoes to be multiplied by two and a half. On the whole, the increases in consumers' goods were comparatively modest, while it was clear that much of the agricultural produce would have to be exported to secure capital equipment and capital for investment in industry. Thus the very adoption of the Plan implied that the standard of living would remain low. Rations were so short that the population suffered, while fruit and vegetables, cereals and fats left the country for foreign markets, a situation made even more acute by the repeated droughts.

SOURCES OF CAPITAL: THE CITIZEN, REPARATIONS, FOREIGN TRADE

The total cost of the grandiose plan was to amount to roughly five billion dollars. For domestic savings the state could draw upon the nationalized and expropriated property of its citizens; its price and tax policies further made available to it for investment a substantial part of the national income. Further amounts came in from reparations: before the break with the Cominform Hungary was paying at the rate of $8,000,000 a year; but the Yugoslavs renounced $25,000,000 owing them from Bulgaria as a "brotherly" gesture. Italian payments on the total of $125,000,000 began only in 1948, and were to be completed in seven annual installments. As the greatest offender, Germany owed the most: the Yugoslavs were to receive almost 10 per cent of all German capital equipment removed from Germany and over 6 per cent of German assets abroad.

Yugoslavia now oriented its foreign trade chiefly toward the eastern bloc. The Ministry of Trade in 1945 set up an Administration of Foreign Trade, which became an independent Ministry in 1946. Under the Ministry special export-import organizations were set up for machinery, chemicals, lumber, metals, and other products, each with its own name: *Tehnopromet, Hempro, Jugodrvo, Jugometal,* and the like. Beginning with 1947, the government resumed the prewar practice of holding an annual trade fair in Zagreb. Table 1 showed the figures for the first four years, in millions of dinars.[3]

[3] G. J. Conrad, *Die Wirtschaft Jugoslaviens*, Deutsches Institut für Wirtschaftsforschung (Institut für Konjunkturforschung), Sonderhefte, Neue Folge, nr. 17, Reihe A: Forschung (Berlin, n.d. but 1952), p. 92, table 80 (hereafter Conrad, DWJ).

TABLE 1

	Exports	Imports	Balance of Trade
1945	461	1,079	−619
1946	2,789	1,744	+1045
1947	8,642	8,272	+370
1948	15,112	15,783	−670

Table 2 showed the percentages of various items exported and imported in 1947.

TABLE 2

Exports		Imports	
Food	34%	Raw Materials	57.8%
Minerals & Metals	26.6%	Capital construction equipment	19.4%
Timber	21.6%	Industrial equipment	14.9%
Livestock	5.9%	Manufactured goods	7.9%
Industrial products	11.5%		

Table 3 showed the quantities of important products exported, with figures in thousands of tons (in the case of wine, thousands of liters; animals, thousands of head; timber, thousands of cubic meters).[4]

TABLE 3

	1946	1947	1948
Corn	28.8	48.3	432.1
Wheat		29.0	303.8
Tobacco	2.8	6.0	17.8
Wine	61.0	188.0	175.0
Cattle		.1	.3
Pigs		7.1	.6
Meat products		.2	7.9
Timber			2234.9

Figures for ores and other metals for these years are not available, but the figures for 1950 (338,391 tons of iron ore, 16,000 tons of raw copper, 53,000 tons of refined lead, 153,000 tons of bauxite) show how many hundreds of thousands of tons were available for export in that year, and somewhat smaller figures may be safely postulated for 1946, 1947, and 1948. The countries of the Soviet eastern European bloc received amounts varying from 57 per cent of Yugoslav exports (zinc concentrate) to 100 per cent (iron ore). Of the foodstuffs, on the other hand, only Czechoslovakia of the eastern bloc took significant amounts (25 per cent of the corn in 1948), and the rest went to Egypt and

[4] These tables were compiled from figures in Conrad, DWJ, pp. 99 ff.

western Europe; while of the timber Hungary took about a third in 1948, and the remainder went outside the Soviet bloc.

During these years, Yugoslavia imported from the USSR and the eastern bloc heavy industrial equipment, trucks and tractors, coal and coke, oil, cotton, and fertilizers, among other important items. About 55 per cent of Yugoslav foreign trade was with the other Communist countries. But Yugoslavia also concluded a long-term agreement with Sweden (April 1947, about $15,000,000) by which the Swedes were to deliver two complete power stations and other industrial equipment in exchange for foodstuffs, nonferrous metals, and other items, and other agreements with Italy ($50,000,000); Western Germany ($40,000,000), Holland, Belgium, Switzerland, Great Britain, Austria, India, and Argentina.

When dealing with the eastern bloc, before the break in mid-1948, the Yugoslavs found that deliveries were slow, prices high, and trading methods "capitalist." The Yugoslavs found it harsh that the Russians insisted on getting world-market prices for their goods, and the Communist theorists among them chafed at the thought that the "more highly developed country" (the USSR) was profiting at the expense of the "less highly developed." Moreover, they resented having to sell to the USSR so much of their output of strategic raw materials, such as the metallic ores, which they could so easily have sold on the world market. Though such metals formed only 25 per cent of Yugoslavia's exports in 1948, they formed almost half of their exports to the USSR.

"JOINT COMPANIES"

But one of the sorest points of all arose over the formation in Yugoslavia of joint Yugoslav-Soviet companies. The Russians had raised the project in 1945, and discussed it again in the spring of 1946, when Tito visited Stalin. Both leaders agreed that such companies should be set up in the branches of the economy where they would most help the growing Yugoslav industrialization. In August 1946 negotiations began. According to Dedijer, the Yugoslavs found that the Russians wanted to obtain monopolies in the production of raw materials, but were not interested in the industrialization program. "What do you need heavy industry for?" he quotes the Russian representative as saying, "In the Urals we have everything you need."[5]

The negotiators first considered petroleum. The Russian stipulated that the Yugoslav oil fields themselves could not be regarded as the Yugoslav contribution to such a company. When the Yugoslavs pointed out that in Iran and Hungary, the USSR had regarded the oil fields as representing capital contributions, the Russian went on to demand all the oil which the Yugoslavs might export for a period of five years. He further demanded that internal prices meet all production costs plus profits; so that Yugoslavs at home would have had to pay higher prices for their own oil-products than would the Russians. Thus they seemed to want to establish a Soviet monopoly in the Yugo-

[5] Dedijer, *Tito*, p. 278.

slav oil industry. The joint company was to control all distribution and sales of oil-products in Yugoslavia and all prospecting for further deposits. As Dedijer put it: "this proposal to a socialist country contained conditions far more difficult than the Soviet Union had proposed to a semifeudal country such as Persia."[6] In addition to the monopoly, the Russians demanded that the company be exempt from Yugoslav laws, insisting, for example, that it not pay social insurance to the workers according to the Yugoslav laws, but only "insofar as the company was able to do so," and on the basis of a "world average." They advanced similar conditions for the other proposed companies, such as mining and metallurgy.

And their demands reached a peak in the case of the proposed Soviet-Yugoslav Bank, which would have handled the credit, clearing, and cash business for all the joint companies, all trade transactions between the USSR and Yugoslavia, and other banking business as well. Since the joint companies were proposed for the more important branches of the Yugoslav economy, the establishment of the bank would have meant Russian overall control, and the loss of Yugoslav economic sovereignty. The Yugoslavs flatly rejected the proposal for the bank, thus arousing a great deal of hostility in Moscow. It was most instructive to read the story of these negotiations, and to detect the surprise and horror of the Yugoslavs when they found themselves not the recipients of special favors from the socialist big brother but the targets of ruthless Soviet economic imperialism.

Finally, in February 1947 two companies were established: "Justa" for air-transport and "Juspad" for river shipping. "Justa" took over all international air transport and many lines inside the country, much to the detriment of the native *Jugoslovenski Aerotransport*. Though control was nominally vested in a mixed policy board, this met only once a year, and actual policy was determined by the director. He was a Russian, who proved extremely self-assertive, taking over all airport facilities, and even ceasing to let the local Yugoslav authorities know of the arrival of foreign planes. The Russians contributed the planes and technical installations, the Yugoslavs the airports and local means of communication, and both partners put up five million dinars in cash.

According to the Yugoslavs, the Russians estimated the value of their contributions at 1946 and 1947 world prices but estimated the Yugoslav contributions at 1938 prices, which were of course far lower. In their estimate of the value of airports, they would include only the land on which the airport was built, and not the labor or improvement which had gone into the construction of the airport itself. Thus they were able to skim the cream off the profits, when it came to dividing them up. Similarly "Juspad" took over the best Yugoslav ships on the Danube, while the Russians failed to contribute the ships and shipyards they had promised. The Russian director allegedly fixed the shipping freight tariffs in such a way as greatly to discriminate

[6] Dedijer, p. 279.

against Yugoslavia. Yugoslavs were paying more than twice as much as the Russians and half again as much as other Soviet-bloc nationals to ship their own goods on their own ships.

The Yugoslavs did not agree to the formation of any further companies, and in March 1947, Stalin, according to Dedijer, said flatly:

> Of course it is not a good form of coöperation to found joint-stock companies in an allied and friendly country like Yugoslavia. There would always be misunderstandings and differences; in a way the very independence of the country would suffer and friendly relations would be spoiled. Such companies are suitable for satellite countries.[7]

He proceeded to offer the Yugoslavs a credit of $135,000,000 worth of capital goods, to include a steel plant and coking plant, oil, zinc, chemical installations, and rolling mills for copper and aluminum. In the end the Yugoslavs got only $800,000 worth of goods before the Russians renounced the agreement after the break. The story of these two companies is well worth study, and has been told here in such detail as is available because it sheds so much light on Soviet techniques of economic exploitation, and because we shall encounter them again when we come to consider Russian activities in Rumania. Most interesting of all is Stalin's alleged comment, which would indicate that the Russians were quite conscious of the ends to which they intended to put the companies.

WAGES AND PRICES

Finally, we must say a word about wages and prices in Yugoslavia during these years. As in other Communist states, the Yugoslav government determined wages, and the function of trade unions was not to bargain for higher pay for their members but to support management, prevent absenteeism, and assist in whipping up political enthusiasm. But it was not until the end of 1948 that the government introduced into the factories the Soviet practice of payment according to "norm." Wages did not keep pace with the rapidly mounting prices: we have no Yugoslav statistics for these, but a Rumanian journal has published some figures which may be accepted, although with some skepticism. Thus a kilogram of flour cost ten dinars in 1945, fifteen in 1946, forty in 1947, and seventy in 1948; a kilogram of butter rose comparably from forty to 100 to 280 to 400 dinars; eggs from two to five to nine to twenty dinars apiece, and other foodstuffs correspondingly. But these were free market prices, and the government-owned shops sold food on ration cards at much lower rates. Moreover, beginning in April 1948 the government paid the peasant for his "surplus" with coupons in addition to cash; and the coupons entitled him to further discounts in state stores. But it was only the peasant who had this advantage, and the workers, for the period that this lasted, were jealous indeed. At later times, the regime was, as we shall see, to try other

[7] Dedijer, p. 287.

experiments with price-fixing, but on the whole, the period was one of insufficient wages, high prices, and material hardship for all classes.

2. *Albania*

WAR DAMAGE AND UNRRA ASSISTANCE

Even proportionally to their smaller numbers, the Albanians suffered far less than the Yugoslavs during the war. The enemy destroyed an estimated 60,000 houses, but did not have the opportunity to wreak such havoc among Albanian livestock. The guerrilla operations against the Italians and Germans qualified Hoxha's government to receive UNRRA aid. The UNRRA program in Albania amounted to a little over $27,000,000, of which about one-quarter went for food, and one-eighth for agricultural rehabilitation. UNRRA assisted a drainage project on Lake Maliq, designed to reclaim 4,500 hectares of land. It supplied 150 tractors, as well as other farm machinery and seeds. It imported the necessary grain, and fed more than one-third of the population of the country. As in Yugoslavia, UNRRA saved many lives, but neither sought to nor was able to eliminate the basic economic problems of the country. In both countries the alleviation of misery left conditions far better than they had been at the end of military operations in 1944, but far worse than they had been at the beginning of the war in 1939.

"LAND REFORM"

In August 1945, the Hoxha government put through the first land reform in Albanian history. Some hundred large landowners, chiefly in the southern and central part of the country, owned about one-third of the fertile land of the country. Here tenant-farmers worked the lands in holdings ranging from two and a half to forty hectares in size, and the landowners had been able to defeat all proposals for reform before the Second World War. Now the Hoxha regime expropriated all holdings of more than twenty hectares, unless the owners were using "advanced methods" of cultivation, in which case they might keep forty hectares. Church and former state lands were also taken over for redistribution. Tenant farmers settled on the land had first claim to it, followed by families of Partisans killed in the war. Ordinarily the claimant received an allotment of five hectares.

By November 1948, 60,000 peasant families had received a total of 320,000 hectares. Thus the large private estate disappeared from Albania as it had from every other country of southeast Europe. As everywhere else, the uneconomical dwarf holding took its place. And in Albania the lack of any tradition of scientific agriculture and the lack of equipment made the situation worse. The Hoxha regime founded an agricultural school on a former Italian model farm, and UNRRA too assisted the peasants by providing supplies, technical aid, and instruction in the maintenance of the newly imported equipment. By the summer of 1946, the area under cultivation was larger than it had ever been, as were the yields per hectare of wheat and corn. But severe floods brought famine in their wake.

YUGOSLAV ASSISTANCE AND "MIXED COMPANIES"

In these years Yugoslavia took over the role formerly played by Italy in Albania. Poor, unable to produce enough food to feed the population, Albania had always needed a richer patron. We now know something about the pattern which Yugoslav assistance took only because the Yugoslavs have published a good deal about it. In reading their publications, a student must be careful to remember that they told only one side of the story, and were at pains to reveal their benevolence and conceal their ambitions to dominate Albania.

On July 9, 1946 at Tirana, the two countries signed a Treaty of Friendship and Mutual Assistance, which envisioned the formation of Yugoslav-Albanian "joint companies." The Yugoslavs afterwards maintained that they did not favor this "form of coöperation," which they admitted was adopted "on the pattern of the Soviet joint companies," but that Albanian backwardness required it. The Yugoslavs were sensitive to the charge which the observer might level against them that they were trying to assume vis-à-vis Albania the same position that the USSR was trying to assume vis-à-vis themselves. Despite their protestations to the contrary, and their emphasis upon their own disinterestedness as contrasted with the self-seeking of the USSR, the student of the period will not err very far if he thinks of Albania as a satellite's satellite.

A second treaty of November 27, 1946 concluded, like the first for a period of thirty years, was called "Treaty on the Coördination of Economic Plans, the Customs Union and Equalization of Currencies." Its title well described its purposes. It was this treaty which actually founded the mixed companies, including one for the exploitation of petroleum and prospecting for new sources, one for metallic ores, one for railroad construction, one for electrification, one for import-export trade, and an Albanian-Yugoslav Bank. The agreements required equal investments by both partners, but the Yugoslavs later declared that annexes to the agreements provided for unilateral Yugoslav commitments: the Yugoslavs alone would furnish installations, machinery, experts, and skilled labor. To enable the Albanians to buy and become sole owners of the equipment contributed by the Yugoslavs, Yugoslavia advanced to Albania a two billion dinar credit in 1947 and a three billion dinar credit in 1948. The first amounted to 56 and the second to 48 per cent of the annual revenue of the Albanian state in those years.

In the case of the oil company, Albania was to receive outright 50 per cent of the net profit, while the partners were to share the other half according to the value of their investments. In 1947, the Albanian investment took the form of land, buildings, and capital goods, plus the Yugoslav material, which was given to Albania and considered part of the Albanian investment.

The Albanians got 88 per cent of the profits, the Yugoslavs 12. In the case of the railroad company, the Yugoslavs contributed all the machinery, and rolling stock, but the Albanians' share of the profits amounted to 65 per cent. The achievement to which the Yugoslavs point with the most pride is the forty-three kilometer-long railroad line from Peqinj to Durazzo, the first railroad except for narrow-gauge spurs in Albania. This the Yugoslavs financed, and for it they supplied all technical advice, the Albanians contributing only the labor. The Yugoslavs also built a hydroelectric power plant, which they called Velika Selita, to supply the area of Tirana and Durazzo with power.

The oil prospecting yielded new sources in Patos, and increased the output in the Kuchovo region, already under exploitation. Copper and chrome mines, a sugar refinery in Korcha, a marmalade factory in Elbasan, a hemp factory at Rogozin, a fish cannery at Valona, and a printing press and telephone exchange in Tirana: these are some of the contributions to the Albanian economy by the Yugoslavs. They also delivered wheat and oats as gifts, and paid the high Albanian prices (three times world prices) for copper and other materials. Indeed, the Yugoslavs created a special price-equalization fund, which enabled them to pay Albanian prices for Albanian goods.

The Yugoslavs later quoted a number of glowing tributes to their assistance uttered by Hoxha and other leading Albanian Communists, who stressed the disinterest and "brotherliness" of Yugoslav assistance. There seemed little reason to doubt that the Yugoslavs gave the Albanians far better terms than the Soviet Union was willing to give its own satellites; but it seems certain also that the Yugoslavs regarded their investments in Albania as investments in one of their own provinces. In January 1948, according to Dedijer, the following revealing dialogue took place in Moscow:

> Without many preliminaries Stalin began to speak about the Albanian problem. "The government of the USSR has no pretensions whatsoever concerning Albania. Yugoslavia is free to swallow Albania any time it wishes to do so." At the word "swallow" Stalin gestured: he licked the fingers of his right hand.
>
> Djilas was astonished by this remark and retorted, "But, Comrade Stalin, there is no question of swallowing Albania, but of friendly and allied relations between two countries."
>
> "Well, that's one and the same thing," Molotov replied.[8]

However much the Yugoslavs may now demur, and however correct may be their claim to have treated Albania with generosity, there can be little doubt that Stalin's licking of his fingers represented an economic fact. Nor can we doubt that the Albanian economy would have benefited from such an arrangement. The Yugoslav food surpluses would have relieved the perennial Albanian shortages, and permitted the Albanians to produce industrial raw materials which the Yugoslavs could then have processed. But the Albanians clearly resented the arrangement as keenly as Yugoslavia resented the economic

[8] Dedijer, p. 311.

imperialism of the USSR. The moment Titoism against Stalin manifested itself, the appearance of Hoxhaism against Tito was not long delayed.

3. Bulgaria

ADVANTAGES OVER THE OTHER BALKAN STATES

Unlike the other three Balkan countries, Bulgaria suffered little physical damage during the war. It neither needed nor was entitled to receive UNRRA assistance. Moreover, though nominally a member of the Axis, Bulgaria had sent no troops against the USSR, and the Russians did not regard the country with the enmity which they cherished toward Rumania, although they required the Bulgarians to pay the expenses of Soviet occupying troops until the end of 1947. The only reparations which the country owed were $75,000,000 to Greece and Yugoslavia, and the Yugoslavs remitted their $25,000,000. Thus, while Yugoslavia and Albania experienced economic disaster during the war, and Rumania, as we shall see, experienced it at the hands of the USSR after the war, Bulgaria, comparatively speaking, did not experience it at all. Though seriously plagued by the severe droughts of 1945, 1946, and 1947, the Bulgarian economy did not have to face the grave problems of recovery faced by the other southeast European economies, and the Communist planners went early to work to change the system over into that of a full-fledged Soviet state.

COLLECTIVIZATION AND AGRICULTURAL PLANNING

They were able to issue a preliminary Two Year Plan in 1947; but even before that date, official reports gave sufficient hints as to the direction of the change. When the Plan was published, there were already in existence 465 "labor coöperative farms," occupying 150,000 hectares and with 40,000 members. Most of these were founded in 1945 and 1946, although a few had existed in Bulgaria even under the wartime government. As in Yugoslavia, the authorities avoided the use of the word "collective," and emphasized that peasants would join "coöperatives" voluntarily, and would receive a form of rent for the land they contributed, as in one form of Yugoslav "labor coöperative farm." The Plan hailed them as a "major innovation," promised full support to those already in existence, and undertook to increase their number to 560 in 1947 and 800 in 1948. But progress in the direction of collectivization was slower than this. In September 1947, an official report spoke of "more than 500" such farms, and in February 1948 Premier Dimitrov gave the figure of 579, occupying 189,000 hectares and with 50,000 members, a very small rise indeed over the figure given by the planners at the beginning of the Plan. Dimitrov, apparently whistling in the dark, said of these farms in that month that "Farmers already begin to view them as the best path to the development of our rural economy and to the welfare of our people." But if this were the case, it was curious that the government had not been able to persuade more farmers to join.

So too, the Machine Tractor Stations (MTS) lagged: there were twenty in 1946, but only eight had begun to function by the spring of 1947; the Plan called for an increase to thirty in 1947 and fifty in 1948. Without giving figures in his February speech, Dimitrov declared that there would be seventy by the end of that year. The foundation of such MTS in Bulgaria depended upon the ability and desire of the USSR to furnish the necessary tractors. The Two Year Plan called for an increase of agricultural production one-third above 1939, and promised to increase the amount of arable land by draining marshes, particularly along the shores of the Danube. It further undertook to increase the sowing of industrial crops, especially of cotton. Thus, with regard to agriculture, the Bulgarian Communists, up to mid-1948, had hesitated to embark on enforced mass collectivization, preferring to back pilot projects, in the apparent hope that they might make them attractive to the peasantry. According to official figures, agricultural output in 1948 reached only 86 per cent of the plan, but was 102 per cent of 1938 and 138 per cent above 1947, a year of bad harvests.

THE TWO YEAR PLAN AND INDUSTRIALIZATION

It was, however, upon electrification and the development of industry, especially heavy industry, that the Bulgarian planners concentrated even in the Two Year Preliminary Plan. In two years, they wanted to reduce the importance of agriculture in the whole economy from 80 to 70 per cent and to increase industry proportionately from 20 to 30 per cent. Lacking industrial resources, Bulgaria faced difficult if not insurmountable problems in planning massive expansion. Yet the planners called for a 67 per cent rise in overall industrial output over 1939, with emphasis on agricultural machinery, textiles, processed foodstuffs, shoes, and chemicals, especially artificial fertilizers. Of a total investment over the two years of fifty-five billion leva, 45 per cent was earmarked for industry and mining, 15 per cent for transport and communications, 28 per cent for building and public services, and 6 per cent for agriculture. The money was to come two-thirds from the budget and one-third from bank audits. The Plan envisaged whole new or almost new industries: electrical equipment production was to be multiplied almost nine times over 1946, machine tools three times, rubber almost three times, and the like. Coal output was to rise 125 per cent over 1939 and metal ores by 820 per cent. The Plan paid its respects to the shortage of trained personnel: 600 mining technicians were needed, it declared, and Bulgaria in 1947 had only 220. This small figure in itself gave a vivid picture of the small-scale of Bulgarian industrial enterprise, even for a country of fewer than 7,000,000 people.

Because of the shortages of fuel, the hydroelectric plan assumed a particularly important part in the overall thinking of the planners. The Tundja valley was to be the site of a great new dam near Kazanlik, and many others were planned. A whole industrial city, named, of course, Dimitrovgrad, with a big cement plant and chemical factory, was to rise southeast of Plovdiv in the Maritsa valley. Bulgaria ordered the necessary turbines and generators from Czechoslovakia and the USSR. Iron shortages held up the whole industrial program during its first year, but the Soviet Union donated a plant for chemical fertilizers. By February 1948 the regime announced that the first furnace of the "Vulkan" cement plant at Dimitrovgrad had begun to operate; other installations completed or under way included a nitrogen fertilizer plant and a coal distillery.

NATIONALIZATION AND PLAN-FULFILLMENT

In December 1947, during the first year of the Plan, the state nationalized all private industrial and mining enterprises, raising the "state sector" of industry from 30 to 80 per cent by February 1948, and to 93 per cent by December 1948. A group of seventeen State Industrial Trusts for the different fields of industry then combined small and uneconomic enterprises, and reduced their number by one-half. As to the fulfillment of the Plan, students had no data except the official figures reported in the usual Soviet percentage form. These claimed that the Two Year Plan was fulfilled by 106 per cent, but acknowledged that production of electricity reached only 98 per cent and the extraction of ores 89 per cent. Other figures were: machine building 106 per cent, rubber 110 per cent, electrical industry 110 per cent, paper industry 120 per cent, and the like. In addition to shortages of raw materials, and lack of technicians, Bulgaria suffered from a general dearth of skilled labor. The use of "voluntary" labor for road-building and other projects was wasteful and inefficient.

FOREIGN TRADE

Like the other satellites, Bulgaria after the war oriented its foreign trade chiefly toward the USSR. Table 4 gave the figures for the period to the middle

TABLE 4

	Exports			
	1945	1946	1947	1948 Jan.–May
USSR	95.2%	66%	51.9%	41.5%
E. Europe	2.3	17	33.7	34.2
Britain		.5	.1	.3
United States		5.2	6.0	.2
Total (leva)	12,397,000	14,942,000	24,532,740	12,127,909
	Imports			
	1945	1946	1947	1948 Jan.–May
USSR	79.6%	81.9%	60.6%	58.9%
E. Europe	6.8	8.8	26.9	26.2
Britain			.7	1.0
United States		3.5	1.3	1.1
Total (leva)	5,820,000	17,514,000	21,415,418	16,968,786

of 1948.[9] Though the Soviet share fell off during these years, that of the other satellites rose almost proportionally. The drought made it impossible to export foodstuffs, as had been the Bulgarian practice; indeed, some food had to be imported. In 1947, tobacco accounted for 80.5 per cent of the total exports; the chief imports were metal products (20.9 per cent), textiles (15.9 per cent), machines and equipment (14.1 per cent).

In trading with the USSR, the Bulgarians experienced the usual rough treatment: the Russians bought Bulgarian rose oil at less than a third of world market prices, and sold 5,000 kilograms in 1945 at a profit of almost half a million dollars over what they had paid the Bulgarians, a large sum in hard currency for Bulgaria to lose. To Bulgaria the Russians supplied a loan of cereals during the drought year, raw cotton for processing in Bulgarian mills and re-export to the USSR, metals and metal products, textiles, chemicals, railway cars, trucks, automobiles, machinery, oil, fertilizer. In addition, the Bulgarians bought almost 6,000 additional railroad cars and 127 locomotives, and the Russians supplied a $5,000,000 credit for the purchase of a coking plant, a power station, and other installations, and help in setting them up.

4. Rumania

SOVIET DRAINING OF THE ECONOMY

For Rumania too the war did not bring comparable economic losses to those suffered by Yugoslavia and Albania, despite the drain on the economy caused by the demands of the Germans, and the damage inflicted by allied air-raids and by the fighting in Moldavia and Transylvania. Moreover, though the Germans did not pay for much of what they received from Rumania, they did assist industry, so that productive capacity was actually raised during the war. Of course Rumania was not entitled to UNRRA assistance.

Soviet occupation, however, did bring Rumania economic misery. The armistice required Rumania to pay $300,000,000 in reparations to the USSR, a figure which was far less than the value of the damage caused in Russia by the Rumanian troops. But the Russians arbitrarily valued the goods paid as reparations at the extremely low level of 1938 world prices. This enabled the Soviet Union to extract between twice and three times as much as it would have obtained using 1944 prices. Moreover, the USSR demanded from Rumania the return of everything which had been taken since 1941 by the Rumanian armies in Bessarabia and northern Bukovina. It was the Russians alone who identified such property, and they took full advantage of the opportunity to help themselves to Rumanian trucks, cars, barges, and the like. Then too, the Rumanians were required to supply the Russian armies passing through or stationed in the country, an obligation which the Russians also used as an excuse for stripping the country of foodstuffs and other valuables.

[9] M. Dewar, *Soviet Trade with Eastern Europe, 1945–1949* (London and New York, 1951), p. 48.

The Russians also claimed all German assets, but of course paid no heed to German liabilities. This meant that Rumania forfeited the sums which Germany had owed to her, but had to pay the Russians the amounts she had owed to Germany. Finally, especially in the early months of the occupation, the Russians took anything else they wanted, big or small, from individuals or corporations, and called it "war booty." Total loot may have reached two billion dollars.

THE OIL INDUSTRY AND THE "SOV-ROMS"

The Rumanian oil industry affords a particularly striking case of Russian methods. Immediately after the occupation, the Russians seized, mostly as booty, about 50,000 tons of pipe and drilling equipment, most of the available tank cars, and other items of essential machinery. They also took the entire current production of oil, some of it as "reparations"; so that the Rumanians had none to sell abroad, and were therefore unable to replace the confiscated equipment. In these early months it seemed as if the Russians were deliberately ruining the industry. In January 1945, however, they signed a commercial treaty with Rumania, reserving all the oil output for themselves, building a pipe line from Ploești direct to Odessa and using in the process material from a former German pipe line which had run between Ploești and Giurgiu on the Danube. They took over as German assets eleven French and Belgian firms which had previously been seized by the Germans, with a total value of almost two billion lei, representing about one-quarter of the entire industry. These measures signified a change of policy: the installations were not to be ruined but were to be exploited at full blast for the USSR.

In mid-July 1945, the Russians then proceeded to put up their eleven confiscated "German" firms as their share of the assets in a new "joint" Soviet Rumanian company, for the extraction, refinement, and sale of petroleum products, called Sov-Rom-Petrol. The Rumanians had to put up as their share some twenty-five firms of their own, amounting to about a quarter of the industry. Now the Communist-dominated Rumanian government proceeded to exempt Sov-Rom-Petrol from the taxes which the firms outside the new combine (British, American, and Dutch, half the industry) had to pay. It turned over to Sov-Rom-Petrol all the moneys which came in from these taxes, and all the royalties in the form of crude oil paid in to the state by other firms.

Sov-Rom-Petrol alone obtained the right to conduct further prospecting, and even got back some of the equipment which had initially been confiscated. The government forced the American, British, and Dutch companies to raise their wages and lower their prices; it often forced out well-qualified personnel and arrested them. It prevented these companies from obtaining new equipment. It allowed them to sell on the free market only 3 per cent of their output, which kept them too short of cash to buy the equipment they needed. After months of increasing discrimination accompanied by terror, the Rumanian government put administrators into the two biggest firms, accused them of sabotaging the oil industry, and finally nationalized them in December 1947. The rest followed in June 1948. Sov-Rom-Petrol, needless to say, was the only firm in the entire country not nationalized. The United States vainly protested that the discriminatory legislation ran counter to the Peace Treaty. But the nationalized sector of the oil industry also worked for the USSR. Total production was 4,640,000 tons in 1945, 4,193,000 tons in 1946, 3,930,000 tons in 1947, 4,310,000 tons in 1948, as against a previous high of 8,703,497 in 1936.

It will be seen that the USSR, without investing any of its own resources — the French and Belgian firms taken by the Germans and then by the Russians can only be described as booty — managed to obtain control of the richest single industry in southeast Europe. They used the profitable Sov-Rom device of "joint" firms elsewhere in the Rumanian economy as well. By 1948 Sov-Rom Transport was in control of all Rumanian harbors, port installations, shipyards, and the entire Danube River and Black Sea merchant fleets, as well as a few privately owned craft confiscated by the state. The Russian contribution to this firm was a few ships which they had previously seized from Rumania. The assets of Sov-Rom Transport had virtually all been owned by the Rumanian state to begin with; so that in this case the Russians transformed a Rumanian public enterprise into a Russian private one.

Sov-Rom-Lemn· took over the state-owned Rumanian forests, about 30 per cent of all timber in Rumania, the Russians contributing some machinery. TARS controlled all civil aviation. The Russians contributed the airplanes — their imitation of the American C-47, minus seat-belts and stabilizing equipment — ; the Rumanians contributed all the airports and ground installations. TARS flew 3,200 flights in 1947, carrying 40,000 passengers 1,600,000 kilometers. Sov-Rom Bank controlled all banking activities, the Russian contribution having come exclusively from German assets. Other Sov-Roms controlled transportation on the public highways, tractor production, and the production and sale of natural gas. And more were to follow. So the Russians first pillaged and then penetrated and took over the Rumanian economy. What the Yugoslavs feared, the Rumanians actually experienced.

THE TATARESCU MEMORANDUM, NATIONALIZATION, AND PLANNING

At the end of May 1947, Tatarescu submitted his memorandum criticizing production, pointing out that the 1946 level was below that of 1945, and that the 1946 figures were less than half those of 1939. He recommended a large foreign loan. Instead of following his policies, the government gave the Minister of National Economy the power to dictate all details of industrial production. In June 1948 a sweeping decree completed nationalization of all remaining enterprises. They included not only the foreign-owned oil companies, as we saw, but also metallurgical establishments, mines, banks, and insurance companies. State bonds were issued to some of the owners by way of indemnification.

The government set up the first State planning Commission, and announced that Rumania was gradually becoming an industrial country, exporting finished or half-finished articles, "instead of a colonial country exporting raw materials." From now on Rumanian wheat and oil would remain at home to raise the standard of living of the peasant. The luxurious way of life characteristic of the Rumanian bourgeoisie would disappear. Yet, as the government announced this momentous first step on the road to a Communist planned society, its leaders were living in the Bucharest palaces and villas of the former upper classes, and driving about the streets in their Hispano-Suizas. A different élite had taken over the luxurious way of life, but it had not disappeared.

PRODUCTION (RECOVERY)

Table 5 gives some figures for the Rumanian production of significant raw materials and of tractors during these years.[10] The figures show that recovery

TABLE 5

	1945	1946	1947	1948	(1938)
Natural Gas (million cu. ft.)	1304	1332	1176	1260	2130
Coal (thousands of tons, mostly lignite)		2012	2268	2400	2396
Iron ore (thousands of tons)	141	112	121	209	139
Pig iron (thousands of tons)	54	66	90	191	133
Steel (thousands of tons)	118	148	183	341	277
Tractors			340	1000	

had set in by 1948, but that the levels reached were in most cases not significantly above those of 1938.

INFLATION AND CURRENCY REFORM

And as for the people's standard of living, it had declined disastrously. The Russian policy of stripping Rumania of goods, while simultaneously rendering foreign goods inaccessible, had spurred on the inflation which had already got under way during the war. The bad harvests of 1945, 1946, and 1947 only added to the anguish. By summer 1947 the leu was at 450,188 to the dollar; the price index had risen astronomically: taking 100 as the level of 1939, the 1947 level was 483,248. In 1938 there had been 49 billion lei in circulation; by 1947 there were 40,247 billion. On August 15, 1947, the govern-

[10] Figures are taken from tables in G. J. Conrad, *Die Wirtschaft Rumäniens von 1945 bis 1952*, Deutsches Institut für Wirtschaftsforschung (Instut für Konjunkturforschung), Sonderhefts, Neue Folge, nr. 23, Reihe A: Forschung (Berlin, n.d. but 1953), *passim* (hereafter Conrad, DWR).

ment passed a currency reform law. This required, under penalty of life imprisonment, that all gold and all foreign currency be turned in to the government, which would pay for it in new lei. The leu was stabilized at the rate of 150 to the dollar. The public had to turn in their old lei at the rate of 20,000 for one new one, but the law set a maximum amount which might be exchanged even at this rate. Thus a peasant might exchange 5,000,000 old lei, a worker 3,000,000, and others 1,500,000. A peasant would recover a total of about $1.67, a worker $1.00, and all others fifty cents. All of the old currency beyond this amount was absolutely worthless, but had to be exchanged for a receipt.

This action wiped out savings, and, since the shortage of consumer goods continued, created grave hardship for all classes. The regime used force to compel the peasants to sell their produce at fixed low rates, although the prices of the goods which the peasants needed to buy were permitted to rise. The effort at compulsion was not always successful; when it was not, famine threatened the towns, and the peasants had to be allowed to charge more. The Rumanian Communists declared that they were favoring the interests of the urban worker. It was true that workers paid low rents and low taxes, that they might buy at state stores, and benefit by special prices. But the government closed the state stores after the devaluation law, and the workers suffered with the rest. The regime created special squads of "economic police" to ferret out violators of the currency decree, whom it then jailed or shot.

"LAND REFORM"

Meanwhile, the peasantry, after the war, had been offered the "bait" of "land reform." The left-wing bloc began to push its demands for division of the estates almost as soon as the Russians had marched into the country. The new program called for the confiscation of all estates over fifty hectares in size, and the division among the peasants of the land thus obtained. In advancing it, the Rumanian Communists clearly hoped to win the support of the strongly anti-Communist peasantry, as the Bolsheviks had done in Russia in 1917. Indeed, left-wing agencies, particularly local branches of the Ploughmen's Front, frequently encouraged the peasants to seize the land of the large landlord without waiting for a law. But the Rumanian peasants, though often ready enough to take over a local estate whose owner might have fled to Hungary or to Germany, did not respond to revolutionary appeals. According to my own observations in Transylvania, confirmed by those of others elsewhere in the country, there was no passion in the countryside, only a keen sense of traditional injustice and a yearning to have the war over with. And there was little sympathy with the Communists, who were associated in the minds of the peasantry both with the Russians, who were requisitioning everything in sight and whom the peasants hated and feared, and with the specter of collectivism, which was to them a great nightmare. Such land seizures as took place were staged to support the FND demand for land reform.

A little over two weeks after coming to power, the Groza government passed, on March 22, 1945, a decree putting the land-reform into effect. The state confiscated without compensation the lands of all Germans, Rumanians of German origin who had collaborated with Hitler Germany, war criminals, those who had fled to Axis countries, and those who had fled to any country after August 23, 1944, absentees (except those absent by necessity and those who held less than ten hectares), and all holdings over fifty hectares. Farm machinery on expropriated land passed into the possession of the state. Church, crown, coöperative, and certain other lands were exempted. The state proposed to distribute the confiscated lands in order of priority to war-veterans of the war against Germany, widows and orphans and invalids of that war, widows, orphans, and invalids of any war, landless peasants, farm laborers on the expropriated lands, and peasants with less than five hectares. Indeed, nobody owning more than five hectares, even if he fell into one of the high priority categories, would receive land. In each commune, the mayor was to call an assembly of all peasants with lands amounting to less than five hectares, and the assembly in turn would elect a committee of seven to fifteen members. These committees were to draw up the list of land to be expropriated and of peasants who were to receive it. District committees would coördinate the recommendations, and pass them on to the Ministry of Agriculture. The law also provided for the payment over ten or twenty years of a price equal to the average annual value of the harvest of one hectare. If an estate between 50 and 150 hectares in size seemed suitable for transformation into a state farm, it could be kept together as a unit and not redivided.

Inaccurate and rigged statistics prevent us from doing more than estimate the actual impact of the new law, especially since the peasants had seized many estates before it was ever passed. Official figures report that 143,219 proprietors lost 1,448,911 hectares, of which the state kept 387,565 hectares and distributed the remaining 1,057,674 hectares to 796,129 peasants, 72 per cent of those who had claims. The average amount seized was 10 hectares, the average amount received by the new peasant owner 1.3 hectares. It is interesting that more than nine-tenths of the expropriations affecting about 50 per cent of the land involved took place in Transylvania. Here the German communities were now paying special penalties for their years of special privileges.

Like previous land reforms, only to an even greater extent, the new reform multiplied the number of uneconomical small holdings. In 1948, the percentage of holdings below five hectares had risen to 76 per cent of the total number of holdings (as against 63 per cent in 1941), although the very smallest category of all, the holdings under one-half hectare, had fallen off from 12 to 7.3 per cent. The Communists knew perfectly well that this would be the effect of the "reform." They knew that it would not touch the fundamental economic problems of the peasantry. The landless peasantry continued to exist, and would surely increase in number. The reform had created relatively few new owners. In the rich Transylvanian Saxon area, some of the most productive farms had been turned over to landless gypsies. Inexperienced and incompetent peasants, rewarded by the Communists for political loyalty, helped to bring down the crop yields. The famine in Moldavia in 1947 was of course due in large part to drought, but the unnecessary and undesirable "reform" had contributed to agricultural decline. The aim of the Russians, who planned the law, was to lay the groundwork for eventual collectivization, and a recombination of the small holdings into new and larger great estates which should be managed by the state.

This aim, however, neither they nor their Rumanian agents would openly avow, either at the time of the 1945 reform or for a long time thereafter. They limited themselves to promising the peasants a native tractor and farm-machine industry, and to publicizing agricultural machine stations operated by the state for the benefit of the individual peasant. The government collected grain through its so-called "INCOOP," which nominally "assisted" agriculture, but in practice assured the government of deliveries. In November 1946 "REAZIM" appeared, a state-controlled organization for development and improvement of agriculture. By 1948, it had set up 350 state farms, on 153,000 hectares of land, and 130 machine tractor stations. After the famines of 1946 and 1947, the government prevented the poor peasants from selling their lands to those with larger holdings; this showed that it had no intention of allowing a kulak class to grow. Instead of diversifying the crops and helping to consolidate the holdings, the government emphasized extensive mechanized cultivation of cereals: this foreshadowed its interest in collectivization rather than in helping the peasant farmer.

But all through the bad years of 1946 and 1947 and on into 1948, while the Sov-Roms were being formed, and industrial enterprises increasingly nationalized, the government said no word about collectivization. Only those who knew what had been happening in the other countries of the Russian orbit in southeast Europe could suspect that collectivization lay ahead. And even there, the process had so far moved slowly, as we have seen. As late as March 1948, the Rumanian government was officially issuing denials of rumors that the peasants would lose their land. It even allowed peasants with more land than they could till with their families to hire laborers to till it. This was the last ray of light before the storm broke in the summer of 1948.

FOREIGN TRADE

In February 1948, the Rumanian government established so-called State Shareholder Companies for foreign trade; *Romanoexport* (agricultural products), *Romcereal* (grain), *Exportlemn* (timber), *Petrolexport* (oil), and others. Two months later, the state took over the control of all foreign trade, although private traders might still in theory engage in it. In May a new decree created a Ministry of Trade, including directorates for planning foreign trade. The Ministry might set up further companies at its discretion, supplying the necessary capital, and appointing their management. Profits went to the

Ministry of Finance. In October 1948 there appeared a separate Ministry of Foreign Trade.

Table 6 shows the value of Rumanian imports and exports in the years which concern us in this chapter.[11] These figures illustrate the phenomenon

TABLE 6

	Values in Millions of Dollars		
	Exports	Imports	Trade Balance
1946	18	20	−2
1947	34	61	−27
1948	123	117	+6
(1938)	(153)	(133)	+20

we have noted in other fields: recovery in 1948 to near the prewar level after a disastrous slump. Of the exports in 1947, published figures show 26 per cent to have been oil and oil products, 24½ per cent timber, and the remainder, vegetables, chemical products, and miscellaneous. Of the imports in that year, grain amounted to almost 38 per cent, iron and steel to more than 15, cotton to more than 14, and machines and fuel to significant smaller percentages. Because of the disastrously bad harvests of 1947, Rumania had to import $23,000,000 worth of grain instead of exporting valuable quantities.[12]

As in the case of the other Balkan countries, Rumania traded chiefly with the eastern bloc: the estimate for the year 1947 is that more than 86 per cent of the exports went to the eastern bloc (51 per cent of the total to the USSR alone), and more than 60 per cent of her imports came from the eastern bloc (42 per cent from the USSR alone). The estimated figures for 1948 are as shown in Table 7.[13]

TABLE 7

	Exports	Imports
USSR	18.7%	34.8%
E. Europe	47.5%	38.3%
Britain	15%	3.5%
United States		8.1%

In addition to trade, Rumania received from the USSR in 1945 a reduction in reparations payments for that year and a loan of 300,000 tons of cereals, and the Russians agreed to repair Rumanian rolling stock and return ships taken at the time of the armistice (these were soon transferred to Sov-Rom-Transport). In 1946 the Russians advanced a further 144,000 tons of cereals. In 1947, the

[11] Conrad, DWR, p. 80.

[12] Conrad, DWR, pp. 82–83.

[13] Dewar, *Soviet Trade with Eastern Europe*, p. 77.

Russians agreed to deliver to Rumania significant quantities of coke, pig iron, coal, and iron ore, as well as trucks, motors, cotton, and wool; and in 1948 further quantities of raw materials for heavy industry and semi-finished steels were to be forthcoming. Rumania was to furnish manufactured goods. The Russians cut their reparations claims by 50 per cent in June 1948.

As for trade with non-eastern European states, total exports for 1948 were $40,500,000, total imports $33,000,000. The most significant countries were Great Britain (Rumanian exports $13,100,000, imports $3,800,000), Netherlands (Rumanian exports $4,200,000, imports $800,000), Sweden (Rumanian exports $4,900,000, imports $800,000), the United States (Rumanian exports $400,000, imports $7,500,000), and lesser amounts with Switzerland, Italy, Egypt, Turkey, and others.[14]

Thus, in 1947 the Soviet Union began to interest itself in the restoration of economic order in Rumania. With the exception of oil, it showed itself interested chiefly in importing Rumanian manufactured goods. It seemed likely that the food surpluses which Rumania produced in normal years would, when they reappeared, be available once more for trade with western Europe.

Between the end of hostilities and the Cominform expulsion of Yugoslavia in June 1948, the economies of the four Balkan countries thus moved along doctrinaire Soviet-inspired lines. In agriculture, "land reforms" multiplying dwarf holdings served as preludes to future collectivization. Though the approach was gradual, the ultimate goal was not in doubt. In industry, ambitious plans to transform the economy dominated all of the states except Rumania, where almost to the end of the period the Russians were busy milking the country. Foreign trade was strongly oriented toward the eastern bloc. To the observer, Yugoslavia seemed the most orthodox Communist state of all. Tito alone had a sub-satellite of his own. Yet the upheaval of June 1948 would prove how mistaken this analysis had been, would reveal much about the inner workings of the Soviet system of dominating the satellites, and would usher in a new chapter in Balkan history.

Chapter II

THE SOVIET-YUGOSLAV DISPUTE

1. The Background of the Break

IN THE COURSE OF THE LAST THREE CHAPTERS, we have frequently had occasion to observe strain in the relations between Stalin and Tito. During the war, as we know, the Russians gave the Partisan movement no material help and very little ideological support. They tried to play down

[14] Conrad, DWR, pp. 94–95.

the Communist character of the Yugoslav leadership, and to delay if not prevent the organization of political institutions. After the war, we have seen, they felt that Tito was acting too independently in furthering his own political ambitions in the Balkans. Stalin's comment to Churchill at Potsdam that he often did not know what Tito was going to do was revealing. Moreover, the Russians had encountered effectual Yugoslav resistance to the establishment of a whole series of "joint" companies for the exploitation of Yugoslav resources, and the experience of "Juspad" and "Justa" demonstrated that in Yugoslavia the establishment of Soviet economic control faced obstacles of a kind which no other southeastern European state could erect. The Yugoslavs, for their part, resented and sometimes complained about the bad behavior of Russian troops in Yugoslavia in late 1944 and 1945, and felt cheated when Molotov did not tell them in advance that he could not get them Trieste.

SOVIET PENETRATION OF YUGOSLAV AGENCIES

In addition to these sources of friction, however, the Russians were making a systematic attempt to plant intelligence agents in the Yugoslav Army, in the Communist Party, in the secret police, and in the economy — in all the most sensitive organs of the system. It seems altogether possible that the Yugoslavs would freely have given much of the information the Russians sought, had the Russians simply asked for it. But instead they recruited Yugoslavs to serve them as agents. Most of the details of this effort are still kept secret. We know, however, that the Russians began such recruitment among the soldiers of the Yugoslav units formed in the USSR during the war, that they asked Yugoslav officers who agreed to work for them questions about the political attitudes of the top army leadership, and that they had enlisted in their own service the dour Montenegrin, Arso Yovanovich, who had served as chief of staff of the Partisan Army, and had the same role in the Yugoslav Army after the war.

The Yugoslav Government has published a few statements and "confessions" by officers whom Soviet Intelligence allegedly approached in the USSR while they were attending Soviet military academies. According to two major-generals who did not take the bait, the Russians asked them to correspond directly with Moscow after leaving the USSR. One reported that the Russians suspected high-ranking Yugoslav army officers who wanted to utilize English and American as well as Soviet military experience. Others, who accepted the Soviet bid in 1946, found themselves, according to their "confessions," first turning in reports on the Yugoslav National Militia, and then ordered to form teams of three ("troikas") to spread Cominform propaganda and defend the USSR everywhere in conversations with other officers. Others were to report lists of officers dismissed for their pro-Soviet stand after the break.

Elsewhere, the story was much the same. A code clerk in the Security Division of the Interior Ministry reported that the Russian who tried to recruit her services reminded her how often treason had in the past been discovered in high places in the USSR, and said that, although Tito was for the moment not suspect, other top Yugoslav leaders were. The Russians showed a deep interest in the large colonies of "White" Russian refugees who had lived in Yugoslavia since the Russian Revolution of 1917, and recruited many of them for intelligence work. Russian army engineers helping to rebuild the shattered river bridges at Belgrade enlisted Yugoslav engineers and workmen, and established a particularly powerful network in the Yugoslav railroad services. Inside the Yugoslav Communist Party, the Russians allegedly had agents at the very top: Andriya Hebrang and Sreten Zhuyovich-Tsrni.

Andriya Hebrang, a Partisan leader and Secretary of the Communist Party in Croatia during the war, had fallen into the hands of the Ustashe, who exchanged him and thirty-one other Communists, for two Ustasha officials whom the Partisans had captured. After the war, Hebrang became Chairman of the Economic Planning Commission, but was demoted in January 1948, presumably under suspicion as a Soviet agent. Tito later accused him of maintaining an "incorrect attitude" toward the Serbs in Croatia, and even of serving as an Ustasha and Gestapo agent: accusations probably concocted simply to blacken his name. Zhuyovich-Tsrni, a Serb Communist veteran of the Spanish Civil War, was personally much closer to Tito than Hebrang during the Partisan wartime fighting. Like many other Yugoslav Communists, Zhuyovich seems to have expected that some day Yugoslavia would simply join the USSR, but, though appointed Minister of Finance, he apparently also had personal grudges which made him willing to report to the Russian Embassy accounts of the secret discussions in the Yugoslav Central Committee.

SOVIET DOMINEERING

Doubtless, this matter of penetration and subversion was decisive. But, as we have had occasion to observe, Communists have human emotions. Yugoslav Communists have Yugoslav emotions, prominent among them the national pride for which Yugoslavs are celebrated. The Yugoslav Communists felt immensely proud of their struggle during the war, of the hardships they had endured, and of their successes. They were bursting with exuberant self-confidence. And the Russians treated them haughtily, belittled their military achievement, assumed they had never read Marx, Engels, and Lenin, and generally acted as if they were awkward country cousins. As early as November 1944, Stalin disparaged to Kardelj the size and strength and successes of the Partisan movement, and praised the Bulgarian army, until so recently an ally of the Axis, as a "regular army with officer cadres." The insult was doubtless one of Stalin's typical bits of needling, uttered to test the victim's reaction and to see him squirm, but it was not well-calculated to keep the Yugoslavs responsive.

The Russians assumed their superior attitude, although Belgrade remembered with a shiver the looting and mass raping in which the Soviet officers and troops had indulged during their brief passage through "brotherly" Yugoslavia. The Russian high command had denied that these things were happening even while they were going on. And on one occasion the fiery Montenegrin, Djilas, had pointed out to the Russian General Korneyev that the Belgrade bourgeoisie were comparing these Russian atrocities unfavorably with the correct behavior of the British officers attached to Yugoslav headquarters. The Russians rebuked the Yugoslavs for Djilas' remark, but, though he later explained it to Stalin himself, he was never forgiven.

When Zhdanov, Stalin's right-hand man and founder of the Cominform, asked Djilas whether there was any opera in Yugoslavia, it was hard to respond quietly that the country had twelve opera houses and had produced its own composers for more than a century. The Russians tried to get the Yugoslavs to play over the Yugoslav Radio twice or three times as many Russian songs as Yugoslav songs. They tried to force Russian plays on the Yugoslav theater, and Russian films (at ten times the cost of the best British or American films) on the Yugoslav cinema. The Russian press representative appeared weekly in Belgrade newspaper offices with several hundred articles about Russia and Russians which he wanted to jam into the Yugoslav press. But the Russians would not print Yugoslav articles, or would cut and reshape them beyond recognition even when they had been written by Tito himself. As for books, Dedijer reports: "We published 1,850 Soviet books; they published two of ours."

We must remember that, had everything else gone well, the Yugoslavs would surely have swallowed all this, although they would not have enjoyed it. But, when taken in conjunction with economic penetration, attempts at espionage and subversion, and the thwarting of Tito's drive to expand into the rest of the Balkan peninsula, Russian haughtiness rankled bitterly. Once the break between Stalin and Tito had occurred, the Yugoslav public was quick to respond to stories of the way in which the USSR had disparaged Yugoslav achievements. So the Yugoslav propagandists naturally gave a heavy emphasis to this aspect of the affair.

PRELIMINARY INCIDENTS

The Kremlin conference of February 10, 1948, where Stalin showed himself so angry with the Yugoslavs, apparently marked the end of passive Soviet disapproval and the beginning of an active anti-Tito campaign. Two days later, the *Figaro* of Paris published a Bucharest rumor that the Rumanian anthorities were removing all Tito's portraits from public display. The Soviet *chargé* in Tirana responded to a toast proposed to Tito: "I drink to Tito, provided Tito is for unity in the democratic bloc." These incidents passed unnoticed in the non-Communist world. More serious was the Soviet delay in concluding a new trade treaty with Yugoslavia. Though the Yugoslav delegation had been waiting in Moscow for two months, negotiations had not taken place, and now at the end of February the Russians told the Yugoslavs that they would not conclude the treaty. Two billion dinars' worth of vital goods including oil and cotton would now not be available during the second year of the Five Year Plan.

Dedijer reports a meeting of the Yugoslav Communist Party's Central Committee on March 1, which discussed the economic and military differences with the USSR. Tito declared himself unwilling to proceed with the Bulgarian federation which Stalin was now pushing: it would be hard to assimilate the Bulgarian Communist Party; Bulgaria would add economic burdens, including the need to pay reparations of $45,000,000 to Greece; Yugoslavia should not let the Russians push her around, but should wait before leaping into federation. The Central Committee, says Dedijer, except for the Russian agent, Zhuyovich, agreed to resist Russian pressure. Dedijer makes no mention in this connection of Hebrang, but it was at this meeting that he was expelled from the Central Committee. As for Zhuyovich himself, he reported the whole affair to the Russian Ambassador, or so his later confession declared.

Then, on March 18, the chief of the Russian military mission told the Yugoslavs that Marshal Bulganin, Soviet Defense Minister, had telegraphed him to withdraw all Soviet military advisers and instructors because of the "hostility" with which they were surrounded in Yugoslavia. The Russian *chargé d'affaires* then followed with notification that the USSR had also ordered the recall of civilian experts. Here was a double blow.

THE CORRESPONDENCE OF MARCH-MAY 1948

In his reply, written to Molotov on March 20, Tito pointed out that none of the Soviet representatives had ever complained of inhospitable treatment. He admitted that the assistant to the chief of the Yugoslav State Planning Commission had referred the Russian commercial representative higher up for information; this was a normal precaution against allowing "economic secrets" to fall "into the hands of our common enemies." But "Your people were told long ago that the official representatives of the Soviet Government could obtain all important and necessary information direct from the leaders of our country." [1]

To this Molotov and Stalin replied on March 27 that the Yugoslavs had themselves originally requested far more military advisers than the USSR had sent, but that General Kocha Popovich had later expressed the belief that the number could be reduced by 60 per cent. The Yugoslavs had said the Russian advisers were too expensive and had expressed doubts as to the value of their advice. In view of all this, the Russians said, they could understand the "well-known insulting statement made by Djilas . . . that the Soviet officers were, from a moral standpoint, inferior to the officers of the British army." [2] That Djilas had since repeatedly apologized the Russians did not mention. They

[1] *The Soviet-Yugoslav Dispute: Text of the Published Correspondence* (London and New York: Royal Institute of International Affairs, 1948), p. 10 (hereafter *SYD*).

[2] *SYD*, p. 13.

denied that high Yugoslav officials gave them economic information, and accused Yugoslav security agencies of spying on Soviet officials and on the Russian representative in the Cominform. They accused the Yugoslav Communists of criticizing the Soviet Communist Party underhandedly, and called Djilas, Vukmanovich-Tempo, Kidrich (chief of the Planning Commission), and Rankovich "questionable Marxists." "We think," they added, "that the political career of Trotsky is quite instructive."

They criticized the Yugoslav Communist Party as undemocratic and under the supervision of the Ministry of State Security, instead of the other way around; it was not a Marxist-Leninist, Bolshevik organization:

> The spirit of the policy of class struggle is not felt in the CPY. The increase of capitalist elements in the villages and cities is in full swing. . . . The party is being hoodwinked by the degenerate and opportunist theory of the peaceful absorption of capitalist elements by a socialist system, borrowed from Bernstein, Vollmar, and Bukharin.[3]

In Yugoslavia, the People's Front, not the Party, the Russians charged, was the "chief leading force," and declared that this was Menshevik opportunism. Finally, they called Vladimir Velebit, a Partisan colonel who had performed many diplomatic missions for Tito with the British during the war, an English spy, and said they could not understand why he remained as Assistant Minister of Foreign Affairs. The Yugoslavs knew the Russians considered Velebit a spy, and the USSR could not correspond with the Yugoslav Foreign Ministry so long as Velebit remained at his post to censor the correspondence. Perhaps the Yugoslavs had deliberately put an English spy in high office, a bourgeois and imperialist practice.

Nothing could have been more wounding to the Yugoslavs than these ominous charges of Trotskyism, Menshevism, revisionism, and imperialism, accompanied by personal attacks on four trusted members of the Politburo and on Velebit. When the Russians later published the letter, they headed it as coming from the Central Committee of the CPSU (B), and removed the signatures, but when the Yugoslavs received it, it bore the signatures of Stalin and Molotov. Dedijer reports that when the Yugoslav leaders (presumably the Politburo) met to consider this blast, the four men singled out for attack by the Russians offered to resign, but that Tito refused to accept their resignations: "They want to wreck our Central Committee. What the devil should I do if you went?"[4] At the Plenum of the Central Committee on April 12, Tito portrayed the situation in all its dreadful gravity, and all the members except Zhuyovich supported Tito's draft of a reply, which a session next day revised before sending it on. This was the session at which Zhuyovich was expelled.

On April 13, Tito and Kardelj sent Stalin and Molotov the twelve-page response. They blamed the Russian attack on inaccurate information furnished

[3] *SYD*, p. 16.

[4] Dedijer, *Tito*, p. 334.

by Zhuyovich and Hebrang. They expressed their surprise that the Russians had said nothing about their dissatisfaction to the Yugoslav delegation in Moscow in February. They pointed out that as early as 1946 Tito had explained that Yugoslavia could not afford to pay the Soviet military experts, who were drawing salaries amounting to four times the salaries of their Yugoslav opposite numbers of all ranks, and three times the salaries of Yugoslav Cabinet Ministers: a thing which naturally led to discontent among the Yugoslavs. They repeated their former explanations of Djilas' remark about Soviet military behavior. They referred again to the Soviet breaking-off of discussions for the 1948 trade treaty. They denied that they kept Soviet or Cominform representatives under surveillance, and repudiated the suggestion that their proven leaders had made derogatory statements about the USSR. They maintained that the Yugoslav Communists had inculcated "love of the USSR" into the Yugoslav masses, and that pro-Russian sentiment in Yugoslavia was not merely a heritage of Tsarist days. They defended the "democracy" of their party, entered into details with regard to their method of electing members of the Central Committee, and reported their plans for a party congress.

Where, they asked, had the Russians learned that the Yugoslav Party was undemocratic? If from the Soviet Ambassador, Lavrentiev, the Yugoslavs considered "that he, as an ambassador, has no right to ask anyone for information about the work of our Party. That is not his business. This information can be obtained by the Central Committee of the CPSU from the Central Committee of the CPY."[5] They denied that the Ministry of State Security controlled the Party. As to "capitalist elements in the villages and cities being strengthened, . . . since the October Revolution nowhere in the world have there been such firm consistent social changes as in Yugoslavia." They defended the People's Front policy, because the CPY was its nucleus, thus repudiating the charges of Menshevism. They pointed to Bulgaria and Poland as two countries in which the party did not even use its own name, and yet had Soviet approval. They declared that they were studying the Soviet system and applying its lessons, but were also taking into consideration the special conditions prevalent in Yugoslavia. They asked for proof of the charges against Velebit, and expressed their resentment of the way in which the Russians had couched them.

Then they moved to the attack, and declared that they had many reasons for dissatisfaction with Soviet policy: "First, we regard it as improper for the agents of the Soviet Intelligence Service, to recruit in our country, which is going toward socialism, our citizens for their intelligence service. . . . We cannot allow the Soviet Intelligence Service to spread its net in our country."[6]

They further expressed their belief that they had a right to Soviet economic assistance, "because we feel it is to the interest of the USSR for the new Yugoslavia to be stronger, since it is face to face with the capitalist world,

[5] *SYD*, p. 25.
[6] *SYD*, pp. 28–29.

which is endangering not only its peaceful development but the development of other countries of people's democracy and even the development of the USSR."[7] They invited the Russians to send one or more members of their Central Committee to study the Yugoslav situation. So the Yugoslavs stood firm, though obviously deeply shaken. One more passage, coming early in the letter, deserves quotation, since it reveals the crux of the entire quarrel:

"No matter how much each of us loves the land of Socialism, the USSR, he can, in no case, love his country less, which also is developing socialism — in this case the Federal People's Republic of Yugoslavia, for which so many thousands of its most progressive people fell."[8]

In the Yugoslav Communist leadership the Russians were not dealing with a collection of hothouse Moscow-grown subservient Communists like the leaders of the Rumanian party and most of the leaders of the Bulgarian party, but with a group conscious of their own achievements, loyal to their own leaders, not surrounded by Russian troops, and still in tune with the honorable foolhardy Yugoslav tradition of defying threats from outside, the more formidable the better. The wonder is that Stalin, with all his sources of intelligence, did not appreciate this in time. Dedijer remarks that Molotov was highly nervous when the Yugoslav ambassador presented the response to him. The Soviet Foreign Office had indeed made an incredible miscalculation.

The Russians had circulated to all the members of the Cominform their letter of accusations against the Yugoslavs, and asked for comments. When those of Matyas Rakosi, the Hungarian Communist leader, supporting Stalin in every particular, came in to the Russian boss of the Cominform, Zhdanov, he sent them on to Tito, who received them on April 16 from the Cominform representative in Belgrade. According to Dedijer, Rakosi had in the past often complained of the Russians to Tito, charging that they were plundering Hungary and had anti-Semitic tendencies (Rakosi himself, like most of the Hungarian Communist leadership, was Jewish). Tito now replied angrily to Rakosi, and also complained to the Russians at their having circulated the attack without waiting for the Yugoslav reply.

No Bulgarian comment had yet been received, when, on April 19, a Bulgarian Communist delegation passed through Belgrade on its way to Prague, and Djilas went to pay his respects to Dimitrov in his railroad car at the station. Djilas reports that Dimitrov privately urged the Yugoslavs to be firm. When the Bulgarian comments on the Russian attack arrived a little later, however, they proved to be vituperatively anti-Yugoslav. Their author was Dimitrov's brother-in-law, Vulko Chervenkov, a new arrival in Bulgaria after long years in Moscow, and destined to play an important role there, though as yet he was only Chairman of the Committee on Science, Art, and Culture. All talk of Yugoslav-Bulgarian federation naturally came to an end. It was clear that the other Communist Parties were lining up with the Russians. Any other

[7] *SYD*, p. 30.
[8] *SYD*, p. 19.

result would have been extraordinary indeed. On April 24, the Russians accused the Yugoslavs of violating the agreement to consult on foreign policy, which Kardelj had been bludgeoned into signing in February. They used as a pretext the Yugoslav response to the western proposal on Trieste, and declined to tell the Yugoslavs what their attitude would be toward Yugoslav claims in Austria.

Early in May came the second Russian letter, in rebuttal to the Yugoslav reply. Dated May 4, 1948, it runs to twenty-two printed pages in English translation. Its theme was that the Yugoslavs were not accepting criticism "in a Marxist manner, but in a bourgeois manner," and that their reply was "exaggeratedly ambitious" in tone. The Russians now added the name of the Yugoslav Ambassador in London, Leontich, as an English spy, and found it "hard to understand why the United States ambassador in Belgrade behaves as if he owns the place, and why his intelligence agents, whose number is increasing, move about freely, or why the friends and relations of the executioner of the Yugoslav people, Nedich, so easily obtain positions in the State and Party apparatus in Yugoslavia." [9]

With regard to their own ambassador, the Russians answered with asperity Tito's remark that investigating the Yugoslav Communist Party was not his business:

> We feel that this statement . . . is essentially incorrect and anti-Soviet. They (Tito and Kardelj) identify the Soviet Ambassador, a responsible communist who represents the Communist Government of the USSR, with an ordinary, bourgeois ambassador. . . . It is difficult to understand how Tito and Kardelj could sink so low. Do these comrades understand that such an attitude toward the Soviet Ambassador means the negation of all friendly relations between the USSR and Yugoslavia? Do these comrades understand that the Soviet Ambassador, a responsible communist, who represents a friendly power which liberated Yugoslavia from the German occupation, not only has the right but is obliged, from time to time, to discuss with the communists in Yugoslavia all questions which interest them? [10]

In this remarkable and revealing passage on the duties of a Soviet Ambassador, the Russians inserted an extra dig: the statement that it was the USSR which had liberated Yugoslavia. Nothing was more likely to annoy the Partisans, who of course claimed to have liberated Yugoslavia by their own efforts alone.

Now the Russians broadened the attack. They accused the Yugoslav leadership of failing to distinguish between Soviet policy and Anglo-American imperialism, and they quoted from a speech of Tito's made in Ljubljana in May 1945, in which he had said "We demand that every one shall be master in his own house; . . . we do not want to be used as a bribe in international bargaining; we do not want to get involved in any policies of spheres of interest."

[9] *SYD*, p. 34.
[10] *SYD*, pp. 34–35.

As the Russians indicated, the speech was intended as a demand for Trieste. They went on to say that they could not have obtained Trieste for Tito without going to war against the British and Americans for it; and "after such a hard war, the USSR could not enter another." They scolded Tito now for not realizing this, and for confusing Soviet policy with that of Britain and the United States.

But they failed, and naturally, to notice an important point. Tito's mention of spheres of interest in all probability actually referred to the percentages agreement, by which Churchill and Stalin had divided Yugoslavia "50–50." Though this was still an official secret in May 1945, word of it had leaked out, and had been printed in substantially accurate form, for example, in the *New York Times*. In the percentages agreement, the Russians had in fact set down with the British and created spheres of interest. Even the most devout Stalinist would be hard put to it to find any distinction between British and Soviet policies in this episode. We know that Mosha Piyade himself had been invited to a reception for Churchill in Moscow during the very conference in October 1944 which resulted in the percentages agreement. Molotov had congratulated him on the excellent progress of Yugoslav affairs. "But," says Piyade in an article published in 1950, "he did not say that the excellence consisted in chopping our skin in half." [11] The Yugoslavs in all probability early got wind of the agreement, and Tito at Ljubljana, bitter about Trieste, could not resist letting the Russians know he knew.

At the time, the Russian letter continued, they had instructed their ambassador to reprove Tito for the speech, as an attack on the USSR, and the ambassador had communicated the criticism to Kardelj, who had accepted it. Then, the Russians declared, Kardelj had criticized the loose way in which the Yugoslav Communist Party was organized, and had asked the Russian Ambassador to regard Yugoslavia as a future constituent republic of the USSR. This suggestion the Russian had allegedly repudiated. This particular passage in the Russian letter was designed to arouse suspicion of Kardelj in Tito's mind, and thus to drive a wedge between the two top Yugoslav Communists. On the subject of party organization, the Russians returned to the fray with a further attack on the People's Front, into which "a variety of classes are admitted: kulaks, merchants, small manufacturers, bourgeois intelligentsia, various political groups, including some bourgeois parties." The Russians charged the Yugoslavs with lack of democracy in the party: had they not expelled Zhuyovich for criticizing the reply to the USSR? Stalin was conveniently forgetting his own past: the CPSU(B) under his direction could scarcely be regarded as democratic.

But again, the principal issue which emerged from the new Russian letter, as from the rest of the correspondence, proved to be Yugoslav pride in their achievements. And the Russians now strove again to cut the Yugoslavs down to size:

[11] *Borba*, March 22, 1950.

> No one can deny the services and successes of the CPY. . . . However, we must also say that the services of the Communist Parties of Poland, Czechoslovakia, Hungary, Rumania, Bulgaria, and Albania are not less than those of the CPY. However, the leaders of these Parties behave modestly and do not boast about their successes, as do the Yugoslav leaders. . . . It is also necessary to emphasize that the services of the French and Italian CPs to the revolution were not less but greater than those of Yugoslavia. Even though the French and Italian CPs have so far achieved less success than the CPY, this is . . . mainly because, after the destruction of the Yugoslav Partisan headquarters by German paratroopers, at a moment when the people's liberation movement in Yugoslavia was passing through a serious crisis, the Soviet army came to the aid of the Yugoslav people, crushed the German invader, liberated Belgrade, and in this way created the conditions which were necessary for the CPY to achieve power. Unfortunately the Soviet army did not and could not render such assistance to the French and Italian CPs.[12]

In this passage, aside from the interesting but perhaps not surprising revelation that the Russians would have helped the French and Italian Communists to power had they been in a position to do so, we find once more words calculated to infuriate the Yugoslavs. Not only were they told again that they owed their liberation to the USSR, but their "services" were declared to be no greater than those of the other eastern European parties, most of which in fact had done little or nothing during the war. Even the Albanian Party, which the Yugoslavs had brought to birth, nourished, and disciplined as their own offspring, was now hailed as their equal. Stalin certainly knew how to stick the knife in where it would hurt the most. And, by way of twisting it, he ended his letter with a supercilious reminder that the Yugoslavs had not invented partisan warfare but only copied it from the Bolsheviks, who had copied it from Kutuzov, who had got it from the Spaniards' fight against Napoleon. Finally, Stalin refused to send a representative of the CPSU (B) Central Committee to investigate the situation in Yugoslavia. Instead he proposed that the next session of the Cominform discuss the matter.

To this the Yugoslavs replied briefly on May 17 that they could not agree to have the Cominform discuss the case, since all of its members had already taken a stand on the Russian charges. The Yugoslav Central Committee now expelled Zhuyovich and Hebrang from the Central Committee and the Party, and ordered them arrested, despite an alleged Soviet attempt to kidnap Zhuyovich by plane. The Russians now urgently "invited" the Yugoslavs to attend the meeting of the Cominform, and, after much discussion, the Yugoslav Central Committee decided on May 20 to decline. These exchanges have not been published.

According to Dedijer, the Yugoslavs feared that, if Tito should go to such a meeting, he might well not come out alive. They remembered the fate of the

[12] *SYD*, p. 51.

entire Ukrainian Politburo, summoned in 1937 for a meeting to Moscow, and then ordered by Stalin to be arrested and shot. The Russians, in a letter of May 22, now declared that the unwillingness of the Yugoslavs to appear before their "fraternal" Communist Parties amounted to a tacit admission of guilt. The Cominform would discuss the question whether the Yugoslavs came or not, but their refusal "means that the CPY has taken the path of cutting itself off from the united socialist people's front of people's democracies headed by the Soviet Union, and that it is now preparing the Yugoslav party and people for a betrayal of the united front of people's democracies and the USSR. Since the Informbureau is a Party foundation of the united front, such a policy leads to the betrayal of the work done for international solidarity of the workers and to the adoption of an attitude of nationalism which is hostile to the cause of the working class."[13] Behind the jargon the threat lay ill-concealed: excommunication.

2. *The Break Itself*

The Cominform meeting was set for the second half of June. In the interim, the Poles unsuccessfully tried to get the Yugoslavs to reconsider their decision. Dimitrov alone of the eastern European bosses sent "brotherly" greetings to Tito on his birthday, May 25. The Yugoslavs for their part publicly set the date for their Party Congress for July 21, thus putting the Russians on notice that Tito would appeal to the rank and file for support. To the Party Congress would come one delegate for every two hundred party members. Dedijer declares that, at the meetings of the party organizations convened to choose these delegates, the letters between the Russians and the Yugoslavs were given open readings. As June wore on, more and more Yugoslav Communists learned of the parlous quarrel in which their leaders were embroiled.

THE COMINFORM RESOLUTION

On June 20, the Yugoslavs sent a final refusal to attend the Cominform meeting. They could not, they said, accept the agenda. The first letter of the Russians had not been "composed in a spirit of comradely criticism" but was "a rude and unjust accusation," based on "the information of anti-Party elements."[14] The Cominform members had already condemned the CPY in writing. In Bucharest, the Cominform met. The Russian delegates, Dedijer declares, had trouble in persuading the delegates to sign the resolution in the form which the Russians wanted. But Zhdanov said that the Russians knew Tito to be an imperialist spy. On June 28, the Cominform resolution was published, and the world at large heard with astonishment for the first time of

[13] *SYD*, p. 56.
[14] *SYD*, p. 58.

the cleavage which had so long been opening behind the apparently smoot façade of the Communist bloc. Of course, the choice of June 28, St. Vitus' Day the anniversary of the Battle of Kossovo and of the assassination of the Archduke, completed the clumsiness of the Russian operation. No Serb, no matte how anti-Communist, could fail to respond with just a little extra thrill o pleasure to the arrival on that day of the news that his new rulers, whom h loathed, were none the less showing themselves true Yugoslavs in their refusa to knuckle under to an overwhelmingly stronger bully. From the Cominforn point of view, it would have been wiser to rush into print a few days earlie or to delay a few days longer.

The actual text of the Cominform's communiqué approved the previou action of the Central Committee of the CPSU (B) in "exposing the incorrec policy" of the Central Committee of the CPY, and named Tito, Kardelj Djilas, and Rankovich. It reiterated all the charges; indeed the arrest o Zhuyovich and Hebrang was now branded as the sign of a "purely Turkis terrorist regime," and the Cominform declared that Yugoslavia's "nationalis line" could lead only to the degeneration of the country "into an ordinar bourgeois republic . . . and a colony of the imperialist countries." Their communiqué ended with a summons to the "healthy elements" inside the CPY t "compel their leaders to recognize their mistakes openly," or else "to replac them and to advance a new internationalist leadership of the Party." Here wa a direct appeal for internal upheaval against Tito. On the day after its publication, the CPY issued its final statement, summarizing the previous correspondence, rehearsing its own past refutations of the charges, and explaining it course. The excommunication had been launched. The remarkable thing wa that the victim still resisted the thunderbolt.

The comparison with an excommunication is no mere frivolous or sacrilegious figure of speech. To a devout and loyal Communist — and Tito an his followers were devout and loyal — the Soviet Union was the image of thei faith. They had launched their resistance during the war in large measure t assist the Soviet cause. They had sedulously followed the lessons of the sacre writings and had made their revolution. They could hardly credit their eye when they read in the successive letters from Stalin and Molotov that all the had done was incorrect, and that their services to the cause of communisn were rejected, so long as they would not accept Soviet domination in ever aspect of Yugoslav life. Up to the very end they would probably have accepte any compromise which did not involve abject submission and the almost certain loss of position and power to a new leadership which would be subservien to Moscow. But Stalin did not deal in compromises unless he thought it necessary. He did not properly estimate the situation in Yugoslavia, and thought h could oust Tito and substitute his own people. The consequences of his incorrect estimate were to be momentous. But they did not unfold themselve immediately.

THE YUGOSLAV FIFTH PARTY CONGRESS

Inside Yugoslavia, a visitor in that summer of 1948 could sense the general public bewilderment and alarm. In Belgrade, the windows of the various "information centers" of the Communist states blossomed out with exhibitions whose menace was plain to even the least politically sensitive in the throngs of spectators who crowded the sidewalks. Photographs of Albanian army maneuvers showed the arrival in Tirana of the Bulgarian, Rumanian, Hungarian, Czechoslovak, and especially Soviet military observers, and rows of great Soviet tanks thundering down the main street, while the be-medaled Soviet generals looked on. There was no Yugoslav observer. It was not easy to miss the point.

But the Tito regime went ahead with its plans. Instead of concealing from the public the letters from the Russians and the Yugoslav replies, it published the texts of the correspondence, and gave them the widest possible circulation. The Fifth Party Congress met as scheduled in Belgrade on July 21. More than 2,300 delegates, no doubt carefully selected, heard Tito deliver an address which took almost nine hours, and whose English translation runs to 136 pages of print. In it, he reviewed the history of the Yugoslav Communist Party, gave a detailed account of the wartime Partisan movement and of what he conceived to be the achievements of the "new Yugoslavia," and, at the end, turned to the Cominform attack. He recalled the economic aid given Albania, the cancellation of the $25,000,000 of reparations due from "brotherly" Bulgaria, and Yugoslav gifts of grain to Rumania, Poland, and Czechoslovakia, denouncing the Informbureau attack as un-Marxist and untrue. For six days, at the Congress, one speaker succeeded another, all supporting the position taken by the leaders of the CPY, and, at the end, re-electing to the Central Committee all the special targets of Soviet wrath. No Yugoslav spoke a harsh word about Stalin or the Soviet Union. The party cheered them to the echo as usual. But the cry of "Tito-party" spoke volumes to those who knew Yugoslavia.

THE YOVANOVICH CASE

Inside the Yugoslav party, many must have been deeply worried. But the extent of actual defection seems to have been remarkably small, no doubt in considerable part owing to the vigilance of Rankovich's secret police. Arso Yovanovich, Partisan Chief of Staff during the war, and now Chief of Staff of the Yugoslav Army, had studied in the Soviet Military Academy in 1946, and had apparently been enlisted by the Soviet secret police. As a professional military man, he probably felt that the Red Army could and would overwhelm Yugoslavia. On the night of August 12, Yovanovich and two other army officers left Belgrade by automobile, for a "hunting trip" near the Rumanian border, with the real intention of fleeing into Rumania, perhaps to become the leader of a "free Yugoslav" movement in exile. At the border, they were challenged by a patrol, and Yovanovich was shot. One of the other two was captured; the other escaped, but was caught three weeks later trying to cross into Hungary, and later sentenced to twenty years' imprisonment.

The patrol may have been looking for horse-thieves, as the official Yugoslav account declares, but the fact remains that a frontier which the Chief of Staff of the Army cannot cross without getting shot is a well-guarded frontier. Otherwise, the defectors included a few diplomats in iron curtain countries and Major General Pero Popivoda, another army officer. The Soviet direct appeal to the Yugoslav Communist Party to overthrow its leaders met with no response that anyone could see; the Yugoslav security organs took care of whatever response there was. Westerners are unlikely to learn much more about it than the little they know now.

THE DANUBE CONFERENCE

Less than a week after the close of the Party Congress, there opened in Belgrade an international conference on the problems of the Danube. Three western powers, the United States, Britain, and France, sent delegates, as did the Soviet Union, the Ukraine (a riparian state by virtue of the annexation of Bessarabia), and the five Communist-dominated Danubian states: Czechoslovakia, Hungary, Rumania, Bulgaria, and Yugoslavia, with Austria present as an "observer" only. The conference had been scheduled for some time before the break between Tito and the Cominform took place. Indeed, one of the few clues available to the west before June 28 which hinted at future trouble between the Russians and Yugoslavia was Russian reluctance to keep Belgrade as the scene of the conference, and a suggestion that it be transferred to Bucharest. On the basis of this and other indications, the American Embassy in Belgrade actually reported the likelihood of a rift a good ten days before the Cominform published its communiqué; but Washington did not believe the prediction. The Yugoslavs insisted that Belgrade be kept as the site of the Conference, and many observers expected that there might be dramatic fireworks between the Russians and the Yugoslavs, or that the Yugoslavs might vote with the west on some issues.

Nothing of the sort happened. The Balkan peace treaties had guaranteed freedom of navigation on the Danube; and the Russians had undertaken to hold a conference on a new statute for the great river artery within six months after the treaties came into force (September 15, 1947). The west insisted on holding the conference, but the Russians had the majority, and bulled through the Soviet draft convention which gave them complete control over navigation on the river for its entire course below Linz in Austria. The future Danube commission was now to consist of riparian states only, including of course the USSR, while Britain, France, and the United States were excluded. The Soviet draft voted by the conference nullified all previous treaties governing the river, which had protected the interests of non-riparian states. Though the

United States, Britain, and France protested every step of the way, the Russians and their ventriloquists' dummies from the satellites[15] ran roughshod over the objections.

In the end, the British and French simply refused to vote on the new convention, on the ground that the procedure had been illegal, while the United States delegate abstained from voting on each individual article, and voted No on the document considered as a whole. All the way, the Yugoslavs supported every Russian act, speaking and voting as though nothing whatever had happened to cool their relations with the Cominform. It would be some time before the Yugoslavs would begin to work their passage away from the Soviet bloc. As yet, they may not even have realized that they were alone in the world and naked to a terrifying blast.

3. Pressures on Yugoslavia and Yugoslav Counterpressures

ALBANIA DENOUNCES THE ECONOMIC AGREEMENTS

The winds began to blow almost at once. Though the Bulgarian government on June 29, the day after the Cominform resolution had been published, sent a note of reassurance saying that the Cominform declaration of the day before "in no way alters the existing friendly relations between" Bulgaria and Yugoslavia,[16] and promised not to interfere in Yugoslav internal affairs, this was the only "brotherly" country which did not proceed at once to threats. On July 1, the Albanians denounced all their economic agreements with Yugoslavia, because "the Yugoslav Government had reprehensible objectives . . . and it established and put these relations on a capitalistic, exploitive, and anti-Albanian basis."[17] But the Treaty of Friendship "remains in force . . . to serve as a basis for the correct development of relations between our two friendly and brotherly peoples in the future." Thus Hoxha leaped to free himself from the burden of Yugoslav economic penetration, which he no doubt had felt to be as onerous as the Yugoslavs had found the similar efforts of the USSR in Yugoslavia. Yugoslavia, the Albanian note charged, had "endeavored to take over the management of our country's economy, which resulted in the taking over of political administration, in other words in the loss of the independence and sovereignty of the People's Republic of Albania."[18]

Not a member of the Cominform, and quite possibly acting on his own, Hoxha threw off Tito's tutelage and bet on Stalin before the Cominform blast

[15] I was present in the gallery at one session of the conference, and saw Vyshinsky scribble notes on pieces of paper which he then sent around the table to one or another of the satellite delegations. Their representatives would then rise and make speeches, reading from the actual notes openly supplied them by the Russians. It was a deliberate and shameless exhibition of cracking the Russian whip.

[16] *White Book on Aggressive Activities by the Governments of the USSR, Poland, Czechoslovakia, Hungary, Rumania, Bulgaria and Albania towards Yugoslavia* (Beograd: Ministry of Foreign Affairs of the Fed. People's Republic of Yugoslavia, 1951), p. 78 (hereafter WB).

[17] WB, p. 304.

[18] WB, p. 305.

had been in print more than seventy-two hours. In response, the Yugoslavs violently condemned the unilateral and "illegal" breach of these economic agreements, which they regarded as an automatic breach of the Treaty of Friendship as well. "Our military specialists," said their answer to Hoxha, "are being evicted in a hostile manner from Albania and our Army and its leaders insulted in the crudest way." [19] Yugoslavia asked that a joint commission settle the question of Albanian debts to Yugoslavia, which it reckoned as almost two and a half billion dinars, of which 131 million was for capital shares in the six mixed companies. As late as June 1949, the Albanians were still maintaining that they owed Yugoslavia nothing.

THE FORMS OF PRESSURE TAKE SHAPE

By August 25, 1948, less than two months after the publication of the Cominform communiqué, the Yugoslavs had accumulated an impressive list of Rumanian offenses against which to protest. Ana Pauker, writing in *Scânteia,* and in the Cominform paper, now appearing in Bucharest, had called on the CPY to liquidate its leadership. Other Rumanian propaganda organs had accused the Yugoslavs of concluding a financial agreement with the United States. Rumanian writers had, however, ignored the proper Yugoslav behavior at the Danube conference and in the trials of alleged Ustasha agents, which "gave abundant material for the unmasking of the imperialist powers." [20] The Rumanians had shut down a Yugoslav bookstore in Timișoara (Banat center of the Serb minority of Rumania); they had closed the Rumanian-Yugoslav Friendship Society. Indeed, they had been persecuting the Yugoslav minority. The Minister of the Interior, Teohari Georgescu, had arrested the leaders of the Union of Slav Cultural Democratic Associations in Rumania, a Communist front organization of the Yugoslav minority and tried to intimidate them into signing anti-Tito resolutions.

Down had come Tito's pictures in the Serb-inhabited villages of the Banat; out had gone the editors of the pro-Tito Slavic newspaper; Radonya Golubovich, until recently Tito's ambassador in Bucharest, had defected to the Cominform, and the Rumanians were giving him radio time to denounce his former masters in Serbo-Croatian to the people of Yugoslavia. The tone of the Yugoslav protest was more sorrowful than angry, however; hope was still alive. The Rumanians simply rejected the protest. By October 14, 1948, they were expelling the Yugoslav teachers sent in to the country earlier to instruct the Serbian and Croatian minorities.

Despite their earlier assurances, the Bulgarian leaders of the Bulgarian-Yugoslav Society headed by Vulko Chervenkov called upon the membership in August to "adapt" their activities in the spirit of the Cominform resolution, and notably to denounce Yugoslav activities in Pirin Macedonia. By October 1948, the Yugoslavs were protesting against Czech government sponsorship of

[19] WB, p. 311.
[20] WB, p. 83.

a pro-Cominform Serbo-Croatian newspaper, which regularly denounced Tito, and the Czechs were replying blandly that freedom of the press existed in their country, and that moreover they considered the newspaper in question a "democratic anti-fascist periodical which is fighting for the realization of the principle of people's democracy." [21]

Before the end of 1948, the satellite states had expelled members of the staffs of the Yugoslav Legations, including the "instructor of the General Political Administration of the Yugoslav Army attached to the Political Administration of the Albanian Army." [22] Frontier incidents began: shootings, crossings of the border, and "violations of airspace." All the Cominform countries enormously increased the length and number of their Serbo-Croatian language broadcasts to Yugoslavia. Though the pressures had by no means reached their height by the end of 1948, the various forms which pressure would take had emerged: "political warfare," economic warfare, and the actual use of force.

POLITICAL WARFARE

By early 1949, all methods were being drastically stepped up. Yugoslav exile groups under Cominform sponsorship appeared in every Cominform capital. Each had its own Serbo-Croatian newspaper. When the Yugoslavs protested against the Soviet sponsorship of the group in Moscow, the Russians replied on May 31, 1949 by drawing a distinction between Yugoslav government and Yugoslav people. The Yugoslav government, they maintained, had "pursued a hostile policy towards the Soviet Union, . . . fell so low as to join the camp of enemies of the Soviet Union," and "transformed the Yugoslav press into a loudspeaker for the furious anti-Soviet propaganda being disseminated by the fascist agents of imperialism. . . ." [23] Therefore, the Soviet Government had decided "to receive and give shelter to the Yugoslav patriot-exiles . . . true socialists and democrats, faithful sons of Yugoslavia. . . ." [24] The Bulgarians used precisely the same language about their group of Yugoslav anti-Titoites. When the Tito government charged that the anti-Tito Yugoslavs being sheltered in Albania had made a foray across the frontier, the Albanians rejected the note of protest with a countercharge that the Yugoslavs were violating the Albanian frontier.

The Poles invited the dissident Yugoslav group in Warsaw to participate in the "Congress of Fighters for Freedom and Democracy" in the summer of 1949, and excluded representatives of the Yugoslav Partisan veterans organization. The Czechs invited the dissident Yugoslavs to attend their "Peace Conference" in Prague in April 1949, and excluded the Tito delegates. The Bulgarians invited their dissident Yugoslavs to represent Yugoslavia at the

[21] WB, p. 110.
[22] WB, p. 471.
[23] WB, p. 108.
[24] WB, pp. 108–109.

great state funeral for Georgi Dimitrov, who died in Moscow on July 2, 1949, and was buried in Sofia some three weeks later. The Hungarians repeatedly refused to give up to the Yugoslavs the Counselor of the Yugoslav Embassy in Budapest, Lazar Brankov, who went over to the Cominform in October 1948, and whom the Yugoslavs accused of having taken state property from the Legation. He later served the Hungarian regime well, as we shall see.

During the first months of 1949, the Russians repeatedly intervened on behalf of a group of former White Russian émigrés, to whom the Soviet authorities had granted Soviet citizenship, and some of whom, the Yugoslavs alleged, they had enlisted as spies in Yugoslavia. The Tito government had arrested a large number of these Russians, and had expelled twelve of them from the country. It maintained that they had been Ustasha or Gestapo or IMRO agents during the war, and had committed a variety of overt and covert acts against Yugoslavia and, indeed, against the USSR itself. It vehemently rejected the Soviet efforts to assist these White Russians. In one of its notes on this subject, dated August 18, 1949, the Soviet Union officially said that the "Yugoslav Government . . . deserted from the camp of democracy to the camp of international fascism and is trying to do as much mischief as possible to the Soviet Union,"[25] and referred to it as a fascist government, like that of Spain and Greece.

The Yugoslav government answered that, while they would permit no interference in their internal affairs, they would hand over the accused White Russians to the government of the USSR, and give all other Soviet citizens all facilities to leave Yugoslav territory at once. No answer to this proposal was ever received from the Russians, which would seem to indicate that they cared less for the persons of the accused White Russians than for the issue. In December 1949, eleven White Russians were tried in Sarayevo for collaborating with the Germans during the war, and committing espionage for the Russians after it. One committed suicide in prison; the others received prison sentences varying from three to twenty years. Meanwhile, the Russians were neglecting to reply to repeated Yugoslav requests that some Yugoslav children (number not specified), who had been sent to the Soviet Union for education in Soviet military schools, should be returned to Yugoslavia.

In the Cominform capitals, the local authorities allegedly continued to harass Yugoslav representatives: in Tirana, the Albanian security forces watched the Yugoslav Legation from special observation posts, kept barbers, tailors, and restaurant-proprietors from serving the Yugoslavs, broke into the apartment of one Yugoslav official, and expelled three more Yugoslavs in early 1949. In Warsaw, the Poles seized Yugoslav Embassy mail, put pressure on Yugoslav apprentices and officers studying in Poland, put a guard on diplomatic apartments, and threw bricks through the windows. In Sofia, the Bulgarians shadowed Yugoslavs who came to set up a Yugoslav pavilion at the Plovdiv fair, and did not allow the pavilion to open; they followed Yugoslav diplomats

[25] WB, p. 124.

everywhere, sometimes insulting them and shaking their fists at them. They blockaded the Yugoslav Embassy on the Bulgarian national holiday. In Bucharest, the Yugoslav Ambassador reported a series of rather clumsy attempts to compromise his staff.

All the time, the name-calling moved ahead *crescendo.* "Criminal Tito clique," "Judas Tito and his abettors," "despicable traitors and imperialist hirelings," "bankrupt group of sharks," "traitors to proletarian internationalism," "sinister heralds of the camp of war and death, treacherous warmongers, and worthy heirs of Hitler," "gang of spies, provocateurs, and murderers," "dogs tied to American leashes, gnawing imperialist bones, and barking for American capital," "new Tsar of the Pan-Serbs and of the entire Yugoslav bourgeoisie": these are mere samplings of the ordinary verbiage which was endlessly reiterated every day in speeches, newspaper articles, and radio broadcasts.

The political warfare extended also into the international sphere, where the USSR had, as we know, supported Yugoslav territorial claims against Italy and Austria. In June 1949, at the meeting of the four Foreign Ministers in Paris, the Russians accepted the western argument, hitherto advanced in vain since the end of the war, that Austria should lose no territory. Though as things turned out, this brought an Austrian peace settlement no closer, it did represent the international jettisoning of Yugoslavia by the Soviet Union. Rubbing salt in the wound, Vyshinsky accused the Yugoslavs of privately negotiating with the British on their Austrian claims.

ECONOMIC PRESSURES

On the economic front, the Russians on December 31, 1948 printed a notice in *Pravda,* declaring that their trade with Yugoslavia in 1949 would be only one-eighth of what it had been in 1949, "owing to the hostile policy of the Yugoslav Government toward the Soviet Union, in consequence of which it is impossible to maintain large scale economic exchange between the Soviet Union and Yugoslavia."[26] In January 1949 Moscow proceeded to establish a "Council for Mutual Economic Assistance," known ordinarily as "Comecon." All the east-European members of the Cominform were invited to join, but Yugoslavia and Albania were not. On February 1, the Yugoslav Government sent a note to Moscow and all the other capitals saying that it was surprised

> that Yugoslavia was neither informed of, nor invited to participate in, the Conference . . . at which it was decided to establish a Council for Mutual Economic Assistance, although all the countries, without exception, which participated in that conference have treaties on political, cultural, and economic cooperation and mutual assistance with the FPRY.[27]

The Yugoslavs felt that they had suffered unfair discrimination, they wrote, and asked to be allowed to join, provided that the other countries fulfilled

[26] WB, p. 293.
[27] WB, p. 283.

their treaty obligations to Yugoslavia and stopped the anti-Yugoslav campaign.

They must have known what the reply would be. Moscow declared that only Yugoslavia had violated existing treaties, and denied that a campaign was being waged against Yugoslavia:

> it is only the hostile policy of the Yugoslav Government towards the USSR and the countries of people's democracy that is being criticized. The Council for Mutual Economic Assistance has not been set up for purposes of ordinary economic coöperation of the type that exists between the USSR and Belgium and Holland in the field of commerce. . . . This Council was set up for purposes of extensive economic coöperation among countries which are mutually pursuing an honest and friendly policy.[28]

All the other replies were identical: Yugoslavia's participation was desirable, they added, but only if it abandoned its present "hostility." As if to lend point to the Yugoslav exclusion, the Comecon, ten days later, on February 21, 1949, admitted Albania, in response to a request from Tirana dated February 1.

The eastern countries also applied direct economic pressure. The Administration for Soviet Property in Austria had agreed in 1947 and 1948 to supply Yugoslavia with six hydraulic turbines for power plants, totaling almost $1,400,000 in value. Though the Yugoslavs had paid in full, the Russians now simply failed to deliver the turbines. Beginning in August 1948, the Rumanians stopped deliveries of oil to which they had been committed. Their officials refused to load the tank cars and river tankers brought for the purpose, citing orders from the Ministry of Trade. Steel plate and tin plate were also withheld, despite the terms of the trade treaty, and despite the fact that Yugoslavia had a favorable balance of a quarter of a million dollars in Rumania. Moreover, Yugoslav tobacco, scheduled for export into Rumania, was kept waiting at the point of shipment for Rumanian inspectors who never came. The Rumanians would not hold discussions for a 1949 trade agreement. They would not pay their bill for transport of the Yugoslav corn sent them in the famine year 1946.

The Czechs delivered only about 60 per cent of the automobiles for which the Yugoslavs had paid, and carefully left out parts, so that assembly proved impossible. The Czechs had undertaken obligations to Yugoslavia to the tune of more than a billion and a quarter dinars' worth of capital goods to be delivered by June 1, 1949. They actually delivered about 40 per cent of what they owed. The Poles owed Yugoslavia a factory (type not specified) for which the Yugoslavs had paid in advance more than $1,200,000. The Poles did not deliver it, and greatly slowed up their delivery of shipments of pig iron, ingots, cables, and other goods. So did the Hungarians: in the first quarter of 1949, they owed capital goods worth two and three-quarters million dollars which they had not delivered.

As for the Russians, the capital goods agreement with the USSR, con-

[28] WB, p. 285.

cluded in July 1947, had provided for Russian deliveries of $135,000,000 worth of goods. The Yugoslav Ministry of Finance and the Soviet Gosbank were to establish the method for balancing the account, and work out the way in which the Yugoslavs were to pay the bill. By the beginning of 1949, the Russians had delivered a little more than three-quarters of a million dollars' worth of goods, or less than one-half of 1 per cent of the contract. They now asked for payment, refusing to abide by the original agreement for settling the debt. Worse, they stopped deliveries, because as their Minister of Trade, Mikoyan, remarked, "conditions have changed."[29] The Russians admitted that the agreement was "in existence" but that it had "lost its validity." It does not appear that the Yugoslavs ever paid the USSR for the small fraction of the goods due to them which they actually received, although they have "acknowledged their obligation" to do so.

In May 1949, the Czech Government suspended shipments to Yugoslavia, at a moment when the Yugoslavs owed the Czechs 180,000,000 Czech crowns, a little more than half of a credit which the Czechs had established for the Yugoslavs. They asked for payment, and suspended the discussions for a new trade treaty, accusing the Yugoslavs of breach of contract, of sending to Czechoslovakia only "unimportant" goods, not accepting goods contracted for, and rejecting Czech proposals for Yugoslav counter-deliveries. The Yugoslavs maintained that all this was pure pretext, and that the Czech authorities at the last minute insisted on a completely new list of products to be delivered by Yugoslavia, although they had earlier reached agreement on a list of such counter-deliveries. The new list included greatly increased amounts of metals. Thus, relations were suspended in June 1949.

Yugoslav-Hungarian trade relations provide a slightly different story with a similar ending. On June 18, 1949, the Hungarian Government declared null and void its five-year economic agreement with Yugoslavia concluded on July 24, 1947. It maintained that the Yugoslav Government was

> not capable of pursuing a policy of planned economy or does not desire to pursue it, and . . . has a hostile stand toward the states which are proceeding along the road of socialism. . . . The Hungarian Government cannot tolerate the constant violation of the Five Year Agreement by Yugoslavia, and have it fettering and retarding the development of the Hungarian economy.[30]

The Yugoslav reply was sharp: "the Government of the FPRY was inspired . . . by a sincere desire . . . to strengthen the still weak democratic forces in Hungary, regardless of the fact that the peoples of Yugoslavia had sustained heavy losses in lives and material inflicted by the Hungarian invaders."[31]

Yugoslavia had agreed to export to Hungary 50 per cent of the total

[29] WB, p. 294, n. 3.
[30] WB, p. 315.
[31] WB, p. 316.

Hungarian requirements in wood and iron, and had fulfilled its obligations, and on top of that granted the Hungarians a credit of $6,000,000 despite the fact that Hungarian war damage in Yugoslavia amounted to more than a billion and a quarter dollars. At the moment when the Hungarians broke the treaty they owed Yugoslavia almost $25,000,000 in goods, for which they had received advance payment. Even those goods delivered had arrived late. The Yugoslavs angrily called Hungarian industry "technically backward," severely criticized the quality of the goods delivered, and accused the Hungarians of illegality. Their note received no answer. The Hungarian authorities also refused to permit Yugoslav engineers to cross the frontier to work on water-power installations on the Drava, thus violating another special agreement.

As for Poland, in the fall of 1948, the Poles suspended sessions of the Polish-Yugoslav permanent commission for economic coöperation set up by the treaty of May 24, 1947. Early in July 1949, they announced that they were suspending shipments to Yugoslavia, because the Tito regime had "sabotaged" their trade agreements with Poland. To this the Yugoslavs replied with a full-dress review of their trade relations with Poland, in which they alleged that they had fulfilled their agreement for 1947, and 80 per cent of the agreement for 1948, while Poland had lagged behind in both years, especially after the Cominform resolution. Moreover, the Polish failure to deliver almost 90 per cent of the ingots contracted for in 1948 had been a particularly "flagrant" instance of "sabotage."[32] Now the Poles for political reasons were violating existing treaties arbitrarily, and unilaterally putting an end to trade relations between the two countries.

Albania had broken economic relations immediately after the Cominform resolution, as we saw. In January 1949, the Yugoslavs proposed that the two countries conclude an agreement on the draining of Lake Scutari, and the reclamation of more than 31,000 hectares for Albania and more than 13,000 for Yugoslavia, as envisioned in earlier understandings between the two countries. The Albanians refused the invitation. Rumania simply did not answer the Yugoslav invitation in the fall of 1948 to conclude a new agreement for 1949. Bulgaria accepted the invitation, but postponed the date at which negotiations were to begin, and in the end did not send its delegation to Belgrade for discussions. Together with the earlier actions of the USSR, Czechoslovakia, Hungary, and Poland, this completed by the summer of 1949 the economic isolation of Yugoslavia from its former chief trade partners. What this meant for the Yugoslav economy in general and the Five Year Plan in particular can easily be imagined.

As to the two mixed Soviet-Yugoslav companies, "Justa" and "Juspad," the Yugoslavs took the initiative in March 1949, and, declaring that the companies were not fulfilling the tasks assigned to them, proposed that they be liquidated. Denying the charges, the Russians, however, agreed. Amid mutual recriminations, a joint commission met in June 1949. The Yugoslavs

[32] WB, p. 300, n. 7.

wanted to draw up a final balance sheet and liquidate the partnership by dividing the profits or losses according to the shares put up by each partner. The Russians refused; and the Yugoslavs, anxious to get the matter settled, agreed to pay the freight on all Soviet property to the USSR, to compensate the USSR for property which had worn out in the service of the companies, to refund Soviet cash, to take over all but certain specified liabilities, and to bear the expenses of liquidation. Thus terminated the only two mixed companies which the Russians had succeeded in establishing in Yugoslavia.

MILITARY PRESSURES

As for acts of overt hostility, these took a variety of forms. Soviet and satellite representatives in Yugoslavia allegedly engaged in espionage, smuggled Yugoslav citizens out of the country, and engaged in efforts to subvert the Hungarian and Albanian minorities. An Albanian "terrorist" allegedly crossed the frontier into Kossovo-Metohiya and killed seven and wounded three Yugoslav officials on orders from Albanian authorities. According to one of the gang, arrested and tried in Yugoslavia, the object of the murders was to stir up revolution against the Tito regime, to disrupt the machinery of government, and to produce a flight of the citizens (mostly ethnic Albanians) into Albania. A Bulgarian captured crossing the Yugoslav frontier in March 1949 allegedly confessed that he had been hired to preach discontent among the population and to sabotage machinery in the factories. Others were to engage in propaganda for the USSR and against Tito. According to official Yugoslav figures, frontier incidents on the Albanian frontier during the first six months of 1949 totaled forty-three, on the Bulgarian frontier seventy-four, on the Rumanian frontier sixteen, and on the Hungarian frontier forty-four.

THE YUGOSLAV COUNTERMEASURES

This recital of the grave damage done to Yugoslavia by the USSR and its eastern European satellites, however, should not be allowed to create the impression that Yugoslavia was the only sufferer. The economies of the satellites suffered considerably as the result of the end of Yugoslav deliveries, which had been worth $100,000,000 annually. The quarrel also made trouble for the Communists in Greece, whose dependence on Tito doubtless went a long way to explain Stalin's lack of enthusiasm for the Greek uprising. Perhaps because he was a kind of prisoner of the Yugoslavs, Markos was relieved of his command at the end of January 1949; the Greek Communists now proceeded to try to turn the NOF from a pro-Yugoslav into a pro-Cominform organization. The new NOF line called in March 1949 for a united autonomous Macedonia. This meant both the subtraction from Yugoslavia of Tito's Federal Republic, and the subtraction from Greece of Greek Macedonia, hardly a proposal calculated to win the Communists the support of many Greeks. Indeed, both the Greek government and the Yugoslavs propagandized the NOF shift of line as a pro-Bulgarian move. So NOF and the Greek Communists quickly retreated from the new position. There were strong hints that the Communists of Aegean (Greek) Macedonia might now organize a party of their own. But the "Government" of the Greek Communists now took in as "Ministers" a couple of the leaders of NOF, which meant that coöperation between NOF and the Greek Communists had not come to an end. The Bulgarians denied any interest in the proposed "autonomous" Macedonia, and the Yugoslavs responded that they did not believe the Bulgarian disclaimer.

But the confused situation in Greek Macedonia and the fate of the Greek Communist uprising both were settled at once in July 1949, when Tito closed the Yugoslav frontier. For some months, Yugoslav assistance to the Greek guerrillas had declined in volume; now Tito deprived them of their largest privileged sanctuary. The rebels knew of his decision a few days before he announced it publicly. They denounced him and his agents in Greek Macedonia. Tito and Yugoslavia had tried to subvert the Greek struggle since 1944, they now maintained, and had always fought to create a greater Yugoslavia. The Greek manifesto called on all Macedonians to sever their relations with the Yugoslavs.

Tito's Federal Macedonian Republic quickly produced counter-resolutions, and the Yugoslavs gave and publicized their hospitality to refugees from Greek Macedonia. Tito in person denounced the Greek Communist Party, and its (Soviet) backers for their anti-Yugoslav attitude in general and for their mistreatment of Greek Macedonia in particular: they did not give Macedonians (i.e., Slavs) high rank in their armies; they were expelling them from NOF; and they were not founding Macedonian- (i.e., Slavic-) language schools in the "liberated territory" they held. Kolishevsky soon made a speech summoning all Macedonians to think of the Yugoslav Federal Republic as their spiritual home.

The new Yugoslav policy was effective both as political warfare and as a military gesture. It threatened hostile Bulgaria and both the Greek Communists and the Greek government simultaneously. The Bulgarians promptly (August 6, 1949) appointed Vladimir Poptomov Foreign Minister. He was an old IMRO man, and long-time Communist, who had fled to the USSR after 1923, become a Soviet citizen, and worked under Dimiter Vlahov as chief of the press section in the Macedonian department of the Comintern. While Vlahov had become a convinced Titoite, and had received high office in the Yugoslav Federal Republic of Macedonia, Poptomov had come back to Bulgaria after the "liberation," and had become editor of the chief Communist newspaper, *Rabotnichesko Delo,* Secretary-General of the Fatherland Front, and a member of the Bulgarian Politburo. He was as strongly opposed to Tito as his old chief Vlahov was committed to him, and now, as a Macedonian specialist, came to the Bulgarian Foreign Office at a moment when Yugoslavia was threatening Pirin Macedonia once again.

Perhaps still more important, the Yugoslav closure of the frontier dealt the final military blow to the Greek uprising. The well-equipped and well-drilled Greek army, with the help of American advisers, now proved able in the summer of 1949 to destroy the Communist armies, and terminate a rebellion which for almost three years had threatened to overturn the percentages agreement and with it the Mediterranean balance of power, and which had cost first Britain and then the United States much worry and vast sums of money. The Greeks themselves had suffered great hardship, as 10 per cent (some 600,000) of the population of the entire country had fled from the north, and had arrived as penniless and hungry refugees in southern Greece, while the rebels had kidnaped thousands of Greek children and taken them off to the Communist countries to the north. The Greek civil war was a running sore infecting the entire economic and military structure of the country and jeopardizing the success of western European recovery and European defense against the USSR. Tito, for his own selfish purpose of course, now played an important part in defeating it, doing Moscow a disservice perhaps more substantial than any which it had yet done him.

In the Trieste question too, the Yugoslavs moved to try to strengthen their position. In July 1948 they had complained to the Security Council of the UN that the United States and Britain had violated the Italian peace treaty by concluding a number of financial agreements which bound "Zone A" to Italy. Tito's representative charged that the western allies were preparing to annex Zone A to Italy, as they had indicated during the Italian elections that they would like to do. The United States and Britain countered by reminding the Security Council that the treaty permitted the conclusion of such temporary financial arrangements, and that the Yugoslavs themselves had gone a long way toward outright annexation of Zone B. The USSR and the Ukraine alone supported the Yugoslavs. Now, in 1949, when relations with the Soviet bloc had deteriorated to the point where the Russians were even willing to drop their support of the Yugoslav claims to Austria, the Yugoslav government introduced its own currency into Zone B. The United States and Britain protested in July 1949, but to no avail. The aggressiveness of the Yugoslavs had not been blunted but actually whetted by their quarrel with the Soviet bloc.

4. *"Titoism" in the Satellites*

GENERAL REMARKS

One of the most important consequences of the Soviet-Yugoslav dispute is to be sought in the political life of the other Communist parties of eastern Europe. Naturally, every Communist party included men who, because they loved their country or because they loved personal power, or both, resented the ever-increasing domination of their actions by the Soviet Union, and who were injudicious enough to speak their minds. In the sense that "Titoism" means nationalist or anti-Soviet communism, there were Titoites everywhere, even before Tito's own excommunication. Lucretiu Patrașcanu, the Rumanian Minister of Justice, whose downfall some months before the Cominform communiqué we have already chronicled, seems to have been such a man: a Titoite before Tito. From the Soviet point of view, such men needed to be purged instantly, to prevent the corruption of the servile Communist parties from within. Nowhere else could one find the combination of factors which had alone made possible the success of Yugoslav resistance to Stalin: absence of Soviet troops, distance from the Soviet border, existence of a strong loyalty to a national Communist leadership with a record of positive achievement, *through whom* there passed whatever loyalty to Moscow may have existed, and a national tradition of resistance to outside pressure. Thus the real threat of "Titoist" uprisings elsewhere in eastern Europe was very small.

On the other hand, the emergence of "Titoism" in Yugoslavia offered the Russians and those leaders of the native Communist parties who were most subservient to them an extraordinary opportunity to publicize the dangers of opposition to Moscow, and at the same time to get rid of anybody in their party whom they disliked or feared, by trying and condemning him as a "Titoite." As in the model purges held in Moscow in the thirties, the truth of the charges was not important. What was important now was to educate Communists as to the perils of the new heresy, and terrify them into complete conformity with the views of their leaders.

During the summer of 1948, just after the Cominform communiqué had been published, I had an interview with Sava Ganovsky, then Under-Secretary at the Bulgarian Ministry of Foreign Affairs. With deliberate naïveté, I asked him how he explained the simultaneous charges against Tito that he was a Trotskyite, a Menshevik, a Bukharinite, and a tool of the capitalist and imperialist powers. How, I asked, could one man be all these contradictory things at once? Ganovsky replied instantly: "Why, all those ideas are against Stalin, are they not?" The ordinary meaning of words matters little; it is the impressions they can be made to convey that count. The important thing in the purge of "Titoites" which followed was not that all its victims should be *bona fide* Titoites, but only that they should be men whom those in power feared as rivals and wanted to destroy. Some of them of course had real "nationalist" leanings, but none of them was in a position to act upon them.

GOMULKA

In Poland, Wladislaw Gomulka, who had become Secretary General of the Communist Party in November 1943, was the first to go. He did strive to mark out a specifically Polish path for the Polish Communist Party; he had favored mild treatment for the Yugoslavs; he was disciplined all during the summer of 1948, and gradually eased out of his various posts over a period which lasted to the end of 1949. Gomulka was punished for what he was, a Polish Titoite. We cannot examine his case in detail here, since this would take us away from the Balkans and into Polish affairs, but a most interesting analysis is available in Adam B. Ulam's *Titoism and the Cominform* published by the Harvard University Press in 1952.

XOXE

In Albania, on the other hand, the chief local victim of the purge was the Minister of the Interior, Kochi Xoxe, the tinsmith from Korcha, whom we have come to know as the leader of the "workers" faction in the Albanian party, and the enemy of Hoxha and the "intellectuals," the man whom the Yugoslavs trusted more than Hoxha, despite his "inexperience." We do not know the details of the struggle which now went on between Xoxe and Hoxha. After the Cominform communiqué, and Hoxha's instant rush to quit his Yugoslav big brother in favor of the biggest brother of all, Xoxe was clearly vulnerable, as a man who had been loyal to the Yugoslav founders of the Albanian Communist Party. There is no evidence, however, that Xoxe was a Titoite in the sense of favoring "national communism." Instead, he was a Titoite in the rare literal sense of being a follower of Tito. In Albania, it was Hoxha himself, ironically enough, who was guilty of the sin of Titoism—against Tito, since what he apparently wanted was to liberate his country from foreign penetration.

During the summer of 1948, Xoxe apparently tried hard to avoid the coming storm. He himself hunted out and purged "Titoites" in Albania. But in September 1948, Hoxha secured the support of the Albanian Party's Central Committee, and ousted Xoxe as Minister of the Interior. He became Minister of Industry, a steppingstone on the way down. With him, there fell two other members of the Politbureau: Pandi Christo, another old worker from the "Korcha Group," later President of the Control Commission, and Nasti Kerendxhi, a wartime leader of the Albanian Communist youth movement, who had been active in conveying to Albanian youth the lessons he learned on the island of Vis about the organization of youth groups in Yugoslavia, and who after the war had become President of the State Planning Commission. Xoxe's successor as Minister of the Interior, and number two man in the Albanian state was Mehmet Shehu, the ruthless former commander of the first Albanian Partisan Brigade or Division, and author of a book *On the Threshold of Albanian Liberation,* who had been an unsuccessful candidate for the Central Committee in 1947, but who now triumphed.

In April 1949, Hoxha went to Moscow, where he presumably got permission to go ahead with the purge of Xoxe and his friends. The trial opened on May 11, 1949. It was held in secret. The Albanian government later announced that Xoxe had admitted to numerous conversations with Vukmanovich-Tempo about transforming Albania into the seventh republic of Federal Yugoslavia, and unifying the Albanian Army with the Yugoslav under a single General Staff. Nothing could be more probable; but it is equally probable that Hoxha too had had many similar conversations. The charge that Xoxe had attempted to seize power in Albania on instructions from Tito is somewhat but not much less plausible, while the other charges of attempting to isolate Albania from the USSR and espionage followed naturally from the rest.

On June 8, Xoxe was sentenced to be shot; Pandi Christo received a sentence of twenty years' hard labor, and lesser sentences were meted out to four other defendants. By skillful use of the charge of Titoism, Hoxha had rid himself of a dangerous rival, and had temporarily cleared himself, for after all he owed his own elevation to Tito.

RAJK

In Hungary, Laszlo Rajk, of German origin when most of the leading Hungarian Communists were Jews, had spent the years of the Second World War in Hungary in internment and not in Moscow like most of his colleagues. Minister of the Interior from 1946 on, he was a veteran of the Spanish Civil War, and to all appearances a powerful and loyal Communist. He was dismissed as Minister of the Interior in August 1948, within a couple of months of the Cominform communiqué, and, like Xoxe, demoted, but to the Foreign Ministry. On June 15, 1949, four days after Xoxe was shot, Rajk was arrested and jailed. The government announced that he was a Titoist and a Trotskyite.

Three months later, on September 16, 1949, there began his extraordinary trial, a version of which is available in English.[33] Rarely if ever can a trumped-up case have been trumped up with so little skill and verisimilitude. It is almost easier to believe that the Russian General Staff in the thirties conspired with the Germans and the Japanese, that Nazi officials met Trotsky at a nonexistent hotel at a time when he was somewhere else, that the two distinguished Polish Jewish Socialists, Erlich and Alter, whom Stalin murdered, were agents of Hitler, and that Marius van der Lubbe, the Dutch half-wit, burned down the Reichstag building all by himself—all myths which Stalin or Hitler seem to have expected the world to credit—than the farrago of nonsense presented at the Rajk trial.

Rajk "confessed" that he had been a police informer for the Horthy regime since 1931, had gone to Spain to sabotage the anti-fascist efforts of his communist colleagues, had become involved with the Yugoslav intelligence service in France, had worked for the American intelligence services, who had also enlisted Tito, and so on. The testimony is full of internal contradictions: how could Rajk have been expelled from the Communist Party for Trotskyism in 1938, as he says he was, without the knowledge of the party itself, as he says a few pages farther on? Somewhat more credible was the testimony of the Yugoslav ex-diplomat, Lazar Brankov, who asserted that he was privy to Tito's efforts with Rajk to detach Hungary from the Soviet orbit and attach it to that of Yugoslavia, and who told the story of a meeting between Rajk and Rankovich even after the publication of the Cominform communiqué. While it is altogether probable that Tito hoped to some extent to dominate Hungary as he did the rest of his neighbors, it seems improbable that the person he was using in Budapest was Rajk.

[33] *Laszlo Rajk and His Accomplices Before the People's Court* (Budapest: Budapest Printing Press, 1949).

Tito himself told the American scholar, Hamilton Fish Armstrong, that "Rajk was the very one we had least to do with. Most of our contacts were with Rakosi, Farkas, and the others, while Rajk was always silent as the grave."[34] The official Yugoslav communiqué, issued on September 17, 1949, before the Rajk trial was far under way, made the same point: "On the part of Hungary, Matyas Rakosi and Mihaly Farkas were the initiators of the closest coöperation along all lines with the new Yugoslavia."[35] Together with Dedijer's testimony that Rakosi had complained to Tito about the anti-Semitism of the Russians, and had asked for Yugoslav assistance against Russian claims, this suggests that Rakosi may have tried Rajk because he himself felt he was open to a charge of "Titoism," and therefore needed to show himself especially savage in pursuing a fellow-Communist on that charge. Yet this is what the Yugoslavs obviously intended their hints to suggest; so there is no particular reason to accept their word.

Indeed, in the very communiqué that contained the hint against Rakosi and Farkas, the Yugoslavs credited their own ex-diplomat, Brankov, with a past as black and as incredible as the one supplied for Rajk by the Hungarians. Brankov, the Yugoslavs assert, was an old-time fascist and Gestapo spy, who forged papers showing falsely that he had been a Communist since 1941. Brankov was believed because "most of the comrades who knew him were killed during the war."[36] He "managed to get to Budapest" because of the "lack of vigilance of certain comrades." Surely the Yugoslav intelligence services were not as inefficient as that. At any rate, the assertions of the Yugoslav Communists were no more credible than those of the Hungarians. It seemed probable that Rajk was not a Titoist in either of the senses of the term, but someone whom the bosses of Hungary wanted out of the way. Their reasons for this remain a subject for speculation, but still a mystery.

THE COMINFORM STATES DENOUNCE THEIR TREATIES OF ALLIANCE

The Rajk trial served to provide the Cominform states with an excuse to break their treaties of alliance with Yugoslavia. Declaring that the trial had revealed that the Yugoslav Government had been hostile to the USSR and had carried on espionage against it, under foreign imperialist instruction, the Russians on September 28, 1949, four days after the end of the trial, went on to charge that the Yugoslavs had become mere instruments of imperialist aggression and had thus "torn to shreds the Treaty of Friendship, Mutual Assistance and Post-War Coöperation between the USSR and Yugoslavia concluded on April 15, 1945."[37] They announced that they therefore considered themselves no longer bound by the treaty. Within the next few days, almost identical notes arrived in Belgrade from Hungary (September 30), Poland

[34] H. F. Armstrong, *Tito and Goliath* (New York, 1951), p. 253.
[35] WB, p. 129.
[36] WB, p. 135.
[37] WB, p. 140.

(September 30), Bulgaria (October 1), Rumania (October 1), and Czechoslovakia (October 4). Thus economic isolation was followed by diplomatic isolation, which had already been a fact but now received a sort of legality. Only Albania was silent, and the old treaty of 1946 between the two countries remained in effect; but, as we shall see, this in itself was part of a subtle plot against Yugoslavia.

The Yugoslavs replied to the Soviet note, calling it blackmail, and describing the evidence at the Rajk trial as "fabrications." They rehearsed their own grievances against the USSR, citing against Stalin his own wartime promises that the Soviet Union would not interfere in the internal affairs of other states. Bitterness and anger mingled as the Yugoslav regime told Moscow that it had been "surprised at the breach of this Treaty. . . . A number of earlier acts by the Government of the Union of Soviet Socialist Republics actually violated the Treaty and transformed it into a dead letter."[38] The Yugoslavs sent to each of the governments breaking its treaties similar long notes reviewing the relations between Yugoslavia and the country in question. That to the Bulgarians contained a summary of the Macedonian question from the official Yugoslav point of view, and ended with a reproach that the Bulgarians had broken faith with Georgi Dimitrov, their embalmed and canonized leader.

Soviet enmity to Yugoslavia was also vividly illustrated in the efforts of Vyshinsky to keep the Yugoslavs off the United Nations Security Council, and to seat Czechoslovakia instead as the eastern European representative, and in his denunciation of the final election of Yugoslavia as illegal. A few days later (October 25, 1949) the Russians asked for the recall of the Yugoslav ambassador as a spy, incriminated during the Rajk trial. The ambassador, Karlo Mrazovich, was the newly elected President of the Croatian Republic's Presidium, an old Communist, veteran of the Bela Kun rebellion in Hungary and the Spanish war, and of seven years as a member of the CPSU (B) in the USSR. The Russians not only ignored the Yugoslav protests but asked that the Yugoslav *chargé* also be withdrawn. On the basis of the "evidence" at the Rajk trial also, the Cominform, meeting in the last half of November, issued a second blast at Yugoslavia even more violent than anything which had gone before. The German "Democratic Republic" of East Germany expelled the Yugoslav military mission in Berlin, after mistreating and humiliating its members. The mission moved into the British sector of the city. On the Danube Commission, which met for the first time in November 1949, the Yugoslavs objected in vain to the powers which the other (Cominform) states gave to the Soviet secretary.

The reason why the Albanians had not denounced their treaty with Yugoslavia was that, like the other treaties, it bound Yugoslavia to come to the assistance of Albania if that state should be attacked by a third power. Now, with the Greek civil war at an end, and the victorious forces of the Greek

[38] WB, pp. 144–145.

government poised at the Albanian frontier, there was a very real possibility that the Greeks might be tempted to take advantage of the situation to invade Albania and attempt to seize "northern Epirus." The undeniable fact that the Albanian Communist government of Hoxha had long assisted the Communist rebels against the Greek government gave the Greeks a welcome excuse to attack.

If they attacked, the treaty would oblige Tito to come to the aid of his old friend and present enemy Hoxha. If Tito should honor the treaty and send troops into Albania from the north, the Cominform states could accuse him of violating the sovereignty of a friendly state and plotting to divide Albania with the Greek "monarcho-fascists." If he should ignore the Greek move, and not send troops, the Cominform states could accuse him of violating his treaty with Albania. In short, it was clear that whatever Tito's response might be to a Greek attack on Albania, it would give the Cominform states a pretext to attack him and precipitate a Balkan war, with all its incalculable consequences.

The situation was dangerous indeed. As early as August 1949, the Albanians were complaining of Greek violations of their southern frontier. The Yugoslavs called the attention of the British and American Ambassadors in Belgrade to the dangers of these Greek moves. Both Washington and London let the Greek government know that they vigorously opposed any invasion of Albania, and the Greek government launched no invasion. On November 2, 1949, the Yugoslav government invited the Albanians to resume truly friendly relations as implied by the treaty, and rehearsed all its grievances against the Hoxha regime.[39] The Yugoslavs clearly expected and hoped that the Albanians would not respond favorably to this note, and that the treaty could then be broken, with the onus of breaking it resting on Albania.

The Yugoslavs did not publish the Albanian response, but on November 12, declaring it unsatisfactory, they notified Albania that they no longer considered themselves bound by the treaty. They reviewed at length their relations with Albania, emphasizing economic and cultural aid: it now appeared, for instance, that more than 1,500 Albanian students had studied in Yugoslav agricultural and technical schools, and that Yugoslavia had sent to Albania thirty teachers for elementary and secondary schools. The Yugoslavs also summarized Albanian hostile acts against Yugoslavia following the Cominform resolution, and accused them of reviving the old "fascist" slogan of "ethnic Albania," and thus reopening the ancient Kossovo dispute. The danger inherent in the Albanian treaty was thus averted by its abrogation. But the last even nominally friendly tie binding Yugoslavia to its neighbors had been

[39] There were a good many new ones: for instance, the Yugoslavs alleged that a number of Yugoslav "sportsmen" who were also soldiers, had been running relay-races around Lake Scutari, and that the Albanians had seized them on the Albanian shore of the lake, and had remained silent as to their fate. It must be said that a lake with a portion of its shores in another and unfriendly country is a singular place to choose for running army relay-races; one is at liberty to wonder what the Yugoslav frontier guards would have said to a group of the Albanian military who had tried to run a relay-race around the same lake.

broken. Essentially it had been the Rajk trial which served as a pretext for all this diplomatic activity.

KOSTOV

Closer to the special concerns of this book and in some ways more revealing than the Rajk case is the story of Traicho Kostov, the Bulgarian scapegoat in the purge of Titoites. His case was the main feature of Bulgarian politics in 1949. Traicho Kostov, like Rajk, was not a "Muscovite." An old-time true-blue Communist devotee, he had been in the Politburo since 1935 and Secretary to the Central Committee since 1940. He had been repeatedly arrested in the 1920's and 1930's, and had frequently suffered torture from those experts, the Bulgarian police. On one occasion Kostov had thrown himself out of a window in the Sofia jail in the hope that he might kill himself rather than answer questions under torture. He landed on some telephone wires, which saved his life but left him crippled. During the war he had played a leading role in the resistance. He had also been jailed, and released, which was to prove highly important. After the war, he emerged as Vice-Premier and boss of the national economy, and as one of the two or three most important non-Muscovite leaders of the party, the other two being Anton Yugov, the Minister of the Interior, and Dobri Terpeshev, the chief of the planning commission. The two Muscovites, Dimitrov and Kolarov, were getting on in years, and neither of them was very well. Premier Dimitrov would need a successor shortly, while Kolarov held the ornamental post of President of the Presidium of the National Assembly, and was, like Kalinin in the USSR or Ribar in Yugoslavia, largely useful as a relic. Kostov, in his early fifties, was surely a strong competitor for Dimitrov's mantle. To Kostov, on his birthday in 1947, the party sent one of its typical telegrams of greeting:

> Great are your achievements, Comrade Kostov, as builder of the Party, as teacher and instructor of party-members. Under your leadership and inspired by your heroic example, thousands of party members have been educated into absolute loyalty to the party. Your deep Marxist-Leninist theoretical knowledge, your great culture, your famous industry and steadfastness, your modesty, your iron will, your unquestionable loyalty toward the party are those Bolshevik characteristics which beautify your whole fighting life. A loyal colleague of comrade Dimitrov . . . you are today one of the most loved and respected leaders of the Party, a great statesman and builder of the new Bulgaria.[40]

It was signed by Vulko Chervenkov, among others.

Dimitrov's brother-in-law, Vulko Chervenkov, had the dubious distinction of being physically the ugliest of all the eastern European Communist leaders. In Moscow his role had been limited to that of bodyguard for his exalted relative, though some said he spied on Dimitrov for Beria. In any case, Chervenkov had ambitions of his own. It is doubtful whether anybody had ever thought of Chervenkov as a man of brains or ability. His first post in Bulgaria,

[40] M. Padev, "Deviationism in Bulgaria," *The World Today,* VI (1950), 159–160.

to which he did not return until 1946, was the comparatively unimportant chairmanship of the Committee on Science, Art, and Culture. But his influence with the Russians, whose loyal man he was, seemed to be on the rise. When the Yugoslav Politburo met to consider its plight on March 1, 1948, Rankovich, the security policeman, allegedly had this to say as an argument against the immediate federation with Bulgaria which Stalin was by then pushing:

> The Bulgarian Central Committee [i.e., Politburo] is split by factions. In the first are Traicho Kostov and Yugov, in the second Chervenkov and Tsankov [Georgi Tsankov, not to be confused with the right-wing Alexander Tsankov], in the third Dimitrov alone, swimming between those two. The latest reorganization of the Bulgarian Central Committee [Politburo] indicates that men who were trained in Bulgaria are going under. In Bulgaria, the Russians have a finger in everything. The Ministry of the Interior is completely in their hands.[41]

As for Kostov, we find him visiting Moscow with Dimitrov and Kolarov on state occasions in the years immediately after the war. At the fateful Kremlin meeting of February 10, 1948, at which Stalin berated Dimitrov and the Yugoslavs for proceeding too fast on Balkan federation plans, Kostov, according to Dedijer, was present with the two senior Bulgarians. He too had something on his mind that night, but it might have been better for him had he not brought it up. There seems nothing inherently improbable in Dedijer's account:

> Kostov's turn came to speak. He began with an explanation of Bulgaria's economic situation. He had hardly uttered the words, "It is hard to be a small undeveloped country. I should like to raise some economic questions," when Stalin interrupted. "You have definite ministries for that matter," he said. "We called this meeting to discuss the differences in the foreign policy between the Soviet Union on one side, and Bulgaria and Yugoslavia on the other." Kostov fell silent.

But later on in the evening, Kostov "reopened the discussion on economic questions. He stated the Soviet government had concluded a technical assistance agreement with Bulgaria unfavorable to his country. Stalin told Kostov to make a note of it, and Molotov would see what it was about."[42]

It seems quite likely that Kostov had patriotic instincts left: as overall planner in Bulgaria, he doubtless took pride in his job, and worried about Soviet sharp practice. Resistance to Soviet economic penetration, discontent with Soviet economic policies — this was Titoism, practiced, as in the case of Tito, by a man who otherwise was as devout a Communist as Stalin himself.

[41] Dedijer, *Tito*, p. 328. Dedijer has a way of calling the Politburo the "Central Committee," perhaps out of consideration for the tender sensibilities of the western readers to whom his book is primarily addressed. Politburo is a frightening Moscow term which reminds the reader that the Yugoslavs are Communists too. "Central Committee," on the other hand, is relatively innocuous.

[42] Dedijer, pp. 318–319.

With Chervenkov, Kostov was one of the Bulgarian delegates to the Cominform meeting of June 1948 which denounced Tito. When the Bulgarian Party decided to call itself the "Communist" instead of the "Workers'" Party in December 1948, Kostov received confirmation in his Politburo post.

On March 26 and 27, 1949, the Bulgarian Central Committee met. Kolarov now attacked Kostov as nationalist and anti-Soviet. Kostov was dropped from the Politburo, and deprived of his posts as Vice-Premier and Chairman of the Economic and Financial Commission. He had allegedly denied economic data to a Soviet trade mission: entirely plausible. The official communiqué denied that he had been arrested. On April 14, he became Director of the National Library, a ludicrously, mockingly unimportant post; the Bulgarians always do everything more violently than anybody else. At least Rajk had become Foreign Minister on his way down, and Xoxe Minister of Industry. By April 22, an "inner Cabinet" was dealing with all current questions in Bulgaria. It included Dimitrov, Kolarov, Chervenkov, and Yugov, whose position was thus still apparently unshaken. But Dimitrov was away in the USSR, on "sick leave"; Chervenkov had become Secretary of the Party, and Kolarov Premier. Kostov participated in the May-Day celebrations.

By then, the first suggestion that Kostov was a traitor had been made, oddly enough, by Tito. The Yugoslav leaders had been closer to Dimitrov personally than to any other Bulgarian leader. Dimitrov had not signed the Cominform communiqué condemning them, which Kostov had. Tito now asked why Kostov had been released from prison by Boris' government during the war. Was not the answer that, like Hebrang in Yugoslovia, he had been recruited by the Gestapo, and the intelligence services of "certain capitalist states"? Here the Yugoslav Premier was virtually suggesting to Kostov's Bulgarian rivals the line which their eventual case against him would take.

Elections held in May to choose 45,000 members of "people's councils" (local soviets) and "people's jurors" apparently took the Sofia regime's attention away from the Kostov case briefly. The population thoroughly loathed the Communists by now, and the press announced that ballots would be counted as valid even if disagreeable remarks or anti-government slogans were found written on them. With so broad-minded a policy, the Fatherland Front (OF) lists prepared by the National Assembly, the Central Committee of the Communist Party, and the National Council of the OF, naturally scored a victory ranging anywhere from 75 to 98 per cent of the vote cast.

By May 27, the furor over the elections had died down, and Kolarov now amplified the charges against Kostov. The wretched man had wanted to extend the "state secrets act"—which provided heavy penalties for telling a foreigner anything at all about Bulgaria—to include the USSR. He had systematically withheld from the Soviet trade representative the prices at which Bulgaria was selling her goods to the capitalist countries. He had ignored the fact, which should have been obvious to him, that "secrets and commercialism do not exist in our dealings with the Soviet Union. . . . Every manifestation of anti-Sovietism is the most heinous form of national deviationism."[43] This would tend to confirm the guess that the rose-oil and tobacco deals had distressed Kostov, and that he may have tried to avert their repetition.

Early in June, Chervenkov went to Moscow, apparently to discuss the future of Bulgaria in the light of the probability that Dimitrov would not recover. To the Bulgarian Central Committee meeting on June 11 and 12, Kolarov revealed still more about Kostov's iniquities: he had been a left-deviationist before the war, had disagreed with the Dimitrov-Kolarov leadership, had charged Dimitrov with undemocratic leadership of the party, and had admitted error but had not confessed all the harm which he had done.

> The following question has been raised almost everywhere: "Have Traicho Kostov's errors no kinship with Titoism?" There can be no doubt about the kinship. Many Party comrades ask: "Will not Traicho Kostov's anti-Soviet conduct reflect badly on the attitude of the CPSU (B) towards our Party?" There is no doubt that it might have had a most fatal influence, had it not met with resolute resistance in the leadership of the Party and among the members. . . . The measures adopted against Traicho Kostov by the Central Committee . . . have dispelled the last suspicions in the CPSU (B) with regard to our Party and its leadership.[44]

One can hardly accuse Kolarov of obscuring his motives. So on June 14 Kostov was expelled from the party, and on June 17 from the National Assembly, for anti-Stalin and anti-Dimitrov activities.

On July 2, Dimitrov died in the USSR, and the Kostov affair was again interrupted by the obsequies for the old hero. In a supremely generous gesture, the Russians lent the Bulgarians the official embalmer who had preserved the corpse of Lenin. This gentleman, whose name was Sbarsky, and Marshal Voroshilov escorted the remains of Dimitrov back to Bulgaria, stopping off in Bucharest to receive the tributes of the faithful. In Sofia the government decreed that an enormous mausoleum be erected at top speed in the main square; town names were changed, stamps ordered printed, and a variety of ceremonies indulged in before Sbarsky had done his work and the state funeral could be held on July 21.

Soon thereafter, Kolarov became Premier, replacing Dimitrov, and Chervenkov took over as Vice-Premier. The government announced that it would try Kostov. Early in August, Poptomov entered the Cabinet as Foreign Minister, and at the same time Yugov relinquished the Ministry of the Interior to his deputy, Khristosov. The process of easing out Yugov, friend and ally of Kostov and rival of Chervenkov, had now begun. There were now three Vice-Premiers, Yugov, Terpeshev, and Chervenkov, none of whom any longer held ministerial responsibility. But the appearance of equality among them was misleading. Chervenkov's star was rising rapidly. He became a member of the Politburo late in August. Subordinates of Chervenkov in his Committee on

[43] *Rabotnichesko Delo*, May 19, 1949; *East Europe*, V, 234 (June 2, 1949), p. 6.
[44] Hugo Dewar, *The Modern Inquisition* (London, 1953), p. 184.

Science, Art, and Culture, moved into Cabinet and party posts. With that extraordinary skill in discovering posthumous documents which has always distinguished the Bulgarian Communist leadership, *Rabotnichesko Delo* published on August 20 a "letter" of Chervenkov's late beatified brother-in-law, Dimitrov, which sang Chervenkov's praises.

Against an intensifying background of economic crisis, which we shall consider in detail in Chapter 14 below, the party purge moved gradually ahead during the latter months of 1949 toward the denouement. On October 7, the Ministers of Finance and Transport and the Deputy Foreign Minister were dismissed, and a whole group of prominent Communists arrested.[45]

On December 8 began the trial of Kostov. The indictment was somewhat more carefully prepared than that of Rajk, and the testimony contained fewer manifest absurdities. But it was absurd enough: Kostov had been a Trotskyite and friend of the Trotskyites Bela Kun[46] and Tito. He had opposed Dimitrov. He had agreed to work for the police during the Second World War. He had worked for British intelligence beginning in 1944. Kostov's fellow-defendants included ex-Finance Minister Ivan Stefanov, who was the son of a rich landowner, had a western European education, and was related to the prominent Bulgarian Communist Rakovsky, purged in Moscow in 1937. The other defendants included a Yugoslav ex-diplomat, a Macedonian who rejoiced in the name of Blagoi Hadjipanzov, who was to play the role in Sofia which Lazar Brankov had played in Budapest, and several other Macedonians accused of having favored the policy of Yugoslav penetration of Pirin, which the Bulgarian government had itself sponsored.

The testimony weirdly pictured Kostov and Tito plotting to murder Dimitrov with American approval, and planning to keep the new Bulgarian-Yugoslav federation secret from the USSR. The American Minister in Sofia, Donald Reed Heath, had allegedly assured Kostov in a secret meeting that the Yugoslavs would transmit American orders to the Bulgarians. The State Department officially declared that Mr. Heath had never had an interview with Kostov at any time, and added: "This single fact affords ample basis for judging the veracity of the indictment."[47]

Kostov pleaded guilty to a "nationalist deviation in relation to the Soviet Union, which deserves a most severe punishment."[48] He pleaded guilty to opposing Dimitrov. But, though he had been "softened up" for months, Traicho Kostov was still the toughest Communist victim the Communist purgers had encountered. On the witness stand in the courtroom, before all the reporters, he repudiated his preliminary deposition. "I do not plead guilty," he

[45] In the army, the Chief of Staff, General Kirov and the "Political Director," General Bulgaranov, gave way to new appointees. The new Chief of Staff, General Asen Grekov, had been a lieutenant-colonel in the Red Army itself.

[46] The Hungarian Communist leader of the short-lived Bolshevik government in Hungary at the end of the First World War, thereafter a refugee in Moscow.

[47] Dewar, *The Modern Inquisition,* p. 196.

[48] *The Trial of Traicho Kostov and His Group* (Sofia, 1949), p. 67.

said, "to having capitulated before the fascist police, nor to having been recruited for service in the British Intelligence, nor to conspirative [*sic*] activities with Tito and his clique."[49]

As soon as possible, the court shut him off, and read aloud his deposition instead. But he had effectively spoiled the trial. On the other hand, the prosecutor was unable to obtain from him any explanation of his release during the war at the direct intercession of King Boris. The court sentenced him to death and his fellow-defendants to lesser sentences. And, with its usual ingenuity, but a striking lack of care for verisimilitude, the Bulgarian government now came up with a repudiation by Kostov of his repudiation of his deposition. It was dated December 14, 1949; Kostov was executed on the sixteenth, and the new confession was published posthumously, on the seventeenth, with a photostatic copy to prove its genuineness. Even experienced students of Communist techniques could not avoid a shiver when they found the Soviet and the Bulgarian press mocking at Kostov's hunched back, a deformity acquired in resisting the police for the benefit of the very men who would eventually destroy him. In a telegram to Stalin after the case had been concluded, the Bulgarian Communist Party seems accidentally to have hit upon the truth: "Only your deeply penetrating eye," said the telegram, "could see in time the criminal spy gang of Kostov."

With Kostov out of the way, Chervenkov turned on Yugov and Terpeshev. On January 16, 1950, he openly accused both of them of wickedness almost equal to that of Kostov. As head of the Planning Commission, Terpeshev had known of Kostov's anti-Soviet actions, but had not spoken up. As Minister of the Interior, Yugov should surely have discovered Kostov's treachery. Moreover, how was it that Yugov had not located the foreign spies in the state security police? But Yugov remained in the Cabinet as Minister of Industry, Terpeshev moved downward from his chairmanship of the Planning Commission to the far less important post of Minister of Labor and Social Welfare, and a few days later, on January 20, 1950, he was dropped from the Politburo. But these two, though down, were not out. Indeed, Yugov was still in the Politburo. Perhaps Moscow wanted to keep Chervenkov from becoming overconfident. In Bulgaria, as in Hungary, "Titoism" had served as a pretext for a party purge. But Kostov, unlike Rajk, had at least been something of a Titoite, in the sense that he had tried to fight complete subservience to Moscow.

FINAL REMARKS

Thus 1949 saw the Communists in neighboring states seize on "Titoism" as a major heresy, and use it as a pretext for their own party purges, and to serve as a horrible example to those Communists who might be tempted to allow their national loyalties to get in the way of their loyalty to Moscow. While the Xoxe and the Kostov trials affected particularly the course of inter-

[49] *Trial*, p. 68.

nal politics in Albania and Bulgaria, the Rajk trial gave the USSR and its satellites (except, as we saw, for Albania) an excuse to break their treaties with Yugoslavia and thus to complete its diplomatic isolation. The Soviet expulsion of two Yugoslav diplomats in the fall of 1949 was roughly contemporaneous with the Czech expulsion of thirty-three Yugoslav officials of various sorts, the Polish expulsion of fourteen, the Hungarian expulsion of ten, the Rumanian expulsion of four, and the Albanian expulsion of two. Frontier incidents continued into 1950 on all four frontiers with the Cominform states.

Early in that year, the Albanian authorities flatly refused to receive visits from the Yugoslav representative in Tirana; they repeatedly stopped the Yugoslav *chargé* and others on the streets, demanding their papers, cut off telephonic communication with Yugoslavia, confiscated the car of the Yugoslav Legation, and restricted the movements of its personnel. In May 1950, the Yugoslav government "temporarily suspended"[50] the work of the Legation in Tirana, and forced the Albanian Legation in Belgrade to close. The Bulgarians continued to render it impossible for Yugoslav citizens whose properties lay in the frontier zone to use any portion of their land on Bulgarian soil. The Rumanians broke their agreement with Yugoslavia governing railway traffic between the two countries, and in mid-January 1950 stopped all trains and postal service to and from Yugoslavia, on the ground that the Yugoslavs were infiltrating spies into Rumania. Incidents involving Yugoslav shipping repeatedly took place on the Danube. In Czechoslovakia, in December 1949, the authorities closed down the pro-Tito Yugoslav organization, and arrested its President, Dimitriye Dimitriyevich, who soon afterwards "died" in jail. The Yugoslavs maintained that he had been tortured and done to death by the Czechs.

Unresolved, the quarrel between Yugoslavia and its former allies of the Soviet bloc created dangerous tension in the sensitive Balkan area, and produced a major upheaval in world communism. In this way it provided a splendid opportunity for the western allies, whose own relations with the Soviet bloc had in these years degenerated into bitter hostility.

[50] WB, p. 191.

Chapter 12

YUGOSLAVIA SINCE THE BREAK WITH THE COMINFORM

1. Internal Politics

IDEOLOGICAL SOUL-SEARCHING AND INSTITUTIONAL CHANGE

IN REVIEWING THE EVENTS WHICH FOLLOWED so thick and fast upon the Soviet excommunication of Yugoslavia, one must always remember the nature and extent of the shock which the Yugoslav Communist leaders experienced on discovering themselves cast into outer darkness. Their entire training had taught them to accept without question the dogmas of Moscow. They had fought their own revolution with the "great October" revolution always in mind. In all their planning, in all their policies, they sedulously aped the models prepared for them by the Russians. When charged with all the heresies, they cried out that they were innocent, hardly able to credit what was obvious to the non-Marxist world, that the truth of the charges was irrelevant.

As time passed, however, the Yugoslavs pulled themselves together, and surveyed not only their political and economic position but also their ideological position. Liberated from the tutelage of Stalin, they now were no longer obliged to apply the lessons of the Soviet experience with absolute literalness. As Communists, they now had both the opportunity and the obligation to explain to the Yugoslav people and the world in general how it was that the old dogmas had failed, and what it was that must be substituted. It was necessary to show where the USSR had gone wrong, and to hammer out some sort of a "Yugoslav" Marxist ideology on which future political and economic action could be based. The year 1949, full of alarms at home and abroad, full of struggle to resist the ever-mounting political, economic, and military pressure from the USSR and its satellites, also seems to have been the year in which Tito and his immediate circle, of whom Kardelj, Djilas, and Piyade were the most important, grappled in private with this task. For the Yugoslavs it was comparatively easy to answer the savagely rude Soviet and satellite behavior in kind. It was much harder to look at Stalinism with a critical eye, and evolve a Marxist theory of its errors.

What the thinkers came up with was hardly a surprise to anybody educated outside the Marxist-Leninist strait jacket, but none the less represented a serious intellectual effort. The Yugoslavs were trying to rid themselves of their preconceptions while keeping their pride intact. They concluded that Stalin had deviated from true Marxism-Leninism, and that they themselves were the only true Communists. As Secretary of the CPSU (B), Stalin had built up a bureaucracy which since his rise to supreme power had become a monster. Far from "withering away," the state had swollen to enormous size. It was hollow mockery to pretend that the Soviet "proletariat" was exercising the dictatorship, which in fact ruled it with utter ruthlessness. The Yugoslavs saw no excuse for this, now that the "capitalist encirclement" of which the Soviet leaders had formerly complained was a thing of the past. Though the Russians had nationalized their economy, the party bureaucracy had moved into the position formerly held by the landlords and the capitalists. What Stalin had created in Moscow was not communism at all but state capitalism. It was not Marxist or socialist; it was a kind of recrudescence of Tsarism at its worst. It was growing worse all the time, and would continue to do so. Tito and his theoreticians elaborated the theme in many long speeches and articles.

Yugoslavia, of course, must now profit by the lessons to be learned from the Soviet failures. But the destructive criticism of the USSR did not mean that Yugoslavia might now fall back into the hands of "capitalist exploiters" or imitate the western democracies in their multiparty system. Instead, it must imitate neither Soviet nor western practices, but cleave to true Marxism-Leninism, and strike out in the direction from which Stalin and the USSR departed. It must avoid the bureaucratization which Stalin had imposed on the USSR by making the state begin to wither at once.

The Yugoslavs began in the factories the process which they hoped, or said they hoped, would lead to the withering away. In January 1950, it was announced that "workers' councils" would be established in all state enterprises. Such councils, the announcement proudly proclaimed, were unknown in the USSR or in any of the "people's democracies." They would serve to consolidate socialism in Yugoslavia. Specifically, they would repair the deficiencies in the organization of production, control the distribution of the labor force and of technicians, and govern the award of benefits and bonuses to the workers. The director of each enterprise would still perform his functions, and the labor union would still initiate all "socialist competition." The law itself was not actually passed until July 1950.

It prescribed that in each factory all the workers would elect by universal suffrage and secret ballot a workers' council, ranging in size from fifteen to 120 members, and, in plants employing fewer than thirty workers, consisting of the entire labor force. The Council would then choose a management board made up of workers, in number from three to seventeen, including the manager of the factory. This board would be the executive committee of the council, which would ratify its decisions. But the board apparently was not to be, like the Presidium of the National Assembly, the true organ of power while the larger parent body remained a rubber stamp. The workers' council could dismiss the board or any of its members, and must ratify all major decisions. The council, through the board, would also plan the production for the plant, and supervise its books. In the same way it would have control of the funds left the factory from its profits after taxes, the setting aside of sums for investment, and all other expenses. Thus the council, through its board, would fix wages and the amounts to be paid into the fund for workers' benefits. It would issue monthly plans, fix hours and conditions of work, and labor discipline. In short, the council, through the board, and in consultation with the manager, would run the factory. The law provided that at least 75 per cent of the membership of all boards of management must be workers actively engaged in the production process. Within a plant, the manager would be responsible to the board, but all workers would also be responsible to him.

Within each industry, the workers in all the factories would collectively be regarded as a "Higher Economic Association." They would elect an industry-wide workers' council, which in turn would appoint its own board of management, or administrative committee (five to fifteen members). This organ, representing workers in all the plants of the industry, would hire the managers of the individual plants, and would act on any proposal to remove managers submitted by the factory boards. If the managing board of a given factory should recommend a decision of which the manager should disapprove, he might appeal to the industry-wide administrative committee. Each "Higher Economic Association" would have its own manager appointed by the federal republic, or by the central government if the industry operated within the boundaries of more than one republic.

With the enactment of this law, the Ministries of the FPRY which controlled individual industries (electrification, mining, agriculture, forestry, light industry, heavy industry, public works, supply) were abolished and replaced by coördinating councils with representatives from the republics concerned. Thus, the government continued to control industries at the very top, through these coördinating councils, but relinquished direct control at the lower levels to industry-wide, and then to factory-wide, boards chosen by workers' councils, chosen in turn by the workers themselves. The individual federal republics inherited the administrative functions of the former central government ministries. The coördinating councils inherited the job of planning overall economic policy: production goals, investment allocations, and the like. But industry-wide and individual factory production fell to the lot of the new management boards.

Ideologically, the Yugoslav measure was an effort to return to Lenin's old principle of turning the factories over to the workers. In the USSR, the Yugoslavs argued, Lenin's wish had been frustrated by the Communist Party, which had reached out and swallowed the individual soviets. In Yugoslavia, the party would instead nourish the factory soviets by giving them real powers. Administratively, the reform seemed extremely complicated. The old Ministry of Heavy Industry dissolved, for instance, into three sections. A Council for Machine Construction (coördinating council) consisted of a Cabinet Minister, the director-general of the machine-construction industry, the director-general of ferrous metallurgy, the machine-construction ministers of the federal republics, and representatives from the Ministry of Defense. This coördinating council directed the management of machine construction and ferrous metallurgy, and coördinated the republican operations in the field. Below it were two subordinate coördinating boards, one for machines and one for ferrous metallurgy, with similar membership. Below them came the managing boards of the industries, and below them the managing boards of the plants, themselves the organs of the workers' councils.

The state fixed minimum wages and the prices of raw materials, but the industry and factory councils fixed the prices of finished goods, and thus, by making a profit, earned the portion of the workers' wages above the minimum wage-scale. The councils also fixed the amount to be invested in each industry and each plant, within the overall framework supplied by the state. Its apparent unwieldiness aside, the whole effort was an interesting attempt to de-centralize and de-bureaucratize. The Yugoslavs claimed that local initiative and incentive were on the rise, as the tedious need to get authority for everything from Belgrade disappeared. Yet the experiment also entailed economic problems. For example, workers' councils, when given discretion in a country where raw materials and consumers' goods were always short, tended to cut the labor force in an effort to keep profits up. Thus unemployment, allegedly the curse only of capitalist societies, reappeared in Yugoslavia. Moreover, the individual workers who formed the management boards, except in rare cases, could hardly have the wide administrative or technical knowledge necessary to make sound decisions. This would be true even in a country where the economy and the level of education were ahead of that in Yugoslavia. The government thus faced the dilemma whether to accept ill-advised decisions, and promote further economic inefficiency, or to ignore them and belie its own democratic pretensions by undermining the very institutions it was trying to foster.

The boards' terms were limited to one year; only one-third of the last year's membership was eligible to be re-elected; nobody could serve more than two consecutive terms. At least initially, there was every reason to think that the Yugoslav Communist Party representatives in the factories saw to it that the workers' councils and therefore the management boards were packed with loyal party members. Indeed, this was suggested by an amendment to the original procedure, prescribed in 1952, according to which individual candidates and several lists of possible choices were to be presented to the workers voting for their workers' councils, instead of the standard Communist single list. That the state was not wholly satisfied with the way in which decentralization was working was also suggested by a measure adopted in the summer of 1953, providing for inspection committees to oversee the financial activities of individual enterprises, and to recommend sanctions to the local people's councils in cases of bad management.

The effort to make the workers' councils an effective part of the economic machinery was followed by steps to incorporate them into the political structure of the country. In April 1952, a law transformed all the district and town "people's councils" into bicameral bodies, by the addition of "producers' councils" at each level. The new councils of producers were thereafter elected by workers and employees actively "producing material goods," whether privately or in nationalized enterprises. The decree set up three categories of producers: those engaged in agriculture, including only members of collectives or coöperatives; those engaged in industry, transport, or trade; and those engaged in handicrafts. Each category was to be represenetd in the producers' councils. The local people's councils and the local producers' councils together would vote the local social plan and the local budget, but the producers' councils would have no voice in matters of local education, health, administration, and culture. The decree abolished the executive committees of the people's councils, which had shown a tendency to concentrate all authority in their own hands, but permitted the people's councils to establish *ad hoc* committees to deal with the different branches of their own local concerns.

The regime then proceeded to introduce producers' councils into the governments of the federal republics, and finally into the federal government itself. The whole process of constitutional change culminated in the adoption of a new constitution on January 13, 1953, which greatly modified the 1946 constitution, so closely modeled on the Soviet original. The National Assembly would continue to be bicameral, but a chamber of producers would replace the chamber of nationalities as the second chamber. The chamber of nationalities would indeed almost disappear into the first (federal) chamber. This first chamber would now consist not only of the deputies elected by the whole country, on the basis of population, but also of the deputies from each republic elected by the republican assemblies. On all questions except constitutional ones affecting the status of the federal republics, the two kinds of deputies would sit together. On constitutional questions, the deputies chosen by the republican legislatures would sit separately *as* a chamber of nationalities. Thus the two chambers of the 1946 constitution would now be almost merged, and the old chamber of nationalities, as such, would have very restricted duties.

The new second chamber, the chamber of producers, was to be two-thirds the size of the federal chamber, and would have one deputy for every 70,000 producers. It was to be elected by workers proportionately to the contribution to national production made by each of the three categories of "producers." It would have equal rights with the other chamber, and a special voice in economic affairs. For certain special purposes it would sit with the other chamber, but ordinarily the two would sit separately. It was interesting to note that members of the federal chamber would receive regular salaries, while members of the chamber of producers would receive only compensation for earnings lost while carrying on their duties, plus expenses. The assembly could, if it chose, refer to the entire population for a referendum any piece of legislation, before or after it had been voted upon by the assembly. This too was an innovation.

On September 9, 1953, after months of delay (elections had initially been scheduled for March), the regime finally produced its "Law on the rights and duties, the election and recall of the Federal People's Representatives," which described in detail how the new constitutional provisions would be carried out in practice. The delegates to the federal chamber, on the basis of one to each 60,000 inhabitants, would total 282.[1] In addition, there would be a total of seventy sent by the assemblies of the individual republics,[2] to sit when necessary as a chamber of nationalities, or a grand total of 352.

For the Chamber of Producers, the electoral law reduced the number of categories of producers envisioned by the early decree from three to two, amalgamating artisans and craftsmen with the industrial producers. There would be one representative for every 70,000 producers.[3] The proportion between industry and agriculture in no sense reflected the distribution of the population: indeed, there was perhaps one representative for every 30,000 workers as against one for about every 150,000 peasants. The chamber of producers was not representative in any sense understood in the west.

In each electoral district, any group of 200 voters could nominate by petition a candidate for the federal chamber. In addition, within thirty days after the announcement of an election, the president of each people's council was to summon voters' meetings. One-tenth of the number of voters of the district would constitute a quorum, provided that fifty were present. In each electoral district this meeting would choose a seven-to-fifteen-man nominating committee—selected as a unit—and submit to it the names of candidates for the federal chamber who were backed by at least ten voters. The nominating committee would then pass on the candidates. If it were to reject all of them, a new nominating committee would be chosen. Otherwise any candidate whom it approved, who then received the approval of one-third the number of voters assembled in the voters' meeting, as signified

[1] One hundred and seventeen from Serbia, including twenty-nine from the Voyvodina and fourteen from Kossovo-Metohiya, sixty-five from Croatia, twenty-four from Slovenia, forty-seven from Bosnia-Hertsegovina, twenty-two from Macedonia, and seven from Montenegro.

[2] Ten from each plus six from the Voyvodina and four from Kossovo-Metohiya.

[3] The following table (*Sluzhbeni List* [Belgrade] 36 [September 1953]) shows the details.

	Industry	*Agriculture*	*Total*
Serbia (incl. Voyvodina and Kos-Met)	44	30	74
Croatia	35	14	49
Slovenia	18	4	22
Bosnia-Hertsegovina	25	12	37
Macedonia	10	5	15
Montenegro	3	2	5
Total	135	67	202

by a show of hands, became a candidate. The only difference in the method of selecting candidates for the chamber of producers was that the approval of one-fourth the number present was enough to nominate. Nominees for either chamber would receive the approval of district electoral commissions.

On election day, the voter received a list of all candidates for his district with their names numbered. In the voting-booth he would check in private the number beside the name of the man he wished to elect. This entire procedure differed widely from the single-list system in use in the Soviet bloc. In Yugoslavia, the citizen was still hedged about by Communist Party safeguards: it was obvious that the Communists could pack a voters' meeting or reject the name of an "unsuitable" candidate either in the nominating committee or in the electoral commission. None the less, the citizen was given an opportunity first to join in the selection of candidates, and later to choose among a group of individuals the one for whom he would vote, rejecting the others.

Further regulations decreed that elections would be held every four years, that there would be by-elections if a representative should die, that no member of either house might hold government office, that officials or judges who might be elected to either house would lose their other posts, that no candidate might run in more than one district, and that a successful candidate automatically became a member of the district people's council or district producers' council. He was to report to his constituents, and one-third of the voters could demand an accounting of him, while a majority of those in a voters' meeting, similar to the nominating meetings, could effect a recall. On November 22, 1953, the elections under the new constitution and electoral law took place. There were 527 candidates, or only a few more than the 484 seats to be filled by voting.

The new constitution further provided that together the two chambers would choose the Federal Executive Council, and elect the President of the Republic. Thus the "Presidium of the National Assembly" and its President, both copied from the Soviet model, disappeared from the Yugoslav constitution, and the new President would no longer be solely ornamental. He would be chairman of the executive council, commander in chief of the armed forces, and in charge of foreign affairs. He would have veto-power over decisions of the executive council, but would be obliged to refer such questions to the assembly, to which he was responsible. In view of the real importance of the new office, it was hardly a surprise when the Assembly, with one dissenting vote, elected Tito himself to the post. Indeed, it had been designed by Tito for Tito.

The new Federal Executive Council combined the functions of the old Presidium of the national assembly and those of the Council of Ministers, or cabinet, which also disappeared. It was to range in number between thirty and forty-five members, and the first one chosen actually had thirty-seven. It had most of the powers of both the bodies from which it was descended, the Presidium and the Council of Ministers. It was to put into effect the laws passed by the assembly, and also to recommend new legislation to that body. It had wide emergency powers in wartime.

The new constitution distinguished between what it called the "political" and the "administrative" aspects of government. The new President and the new Federal Executive Council together handled the "political" side. The "administrative" side the constitution entrusted to a variety of organs, of which the most important were five secretariats, like ministries, except that their secretaries did not necessarily have what we would call "cabinet rank." These were foreign affairs, national defense, internal affairs, the national economy, and the budget. The Federal Executive Council appointed and dismissed all the secretaries and under-secretaries in these secretariats, as well as the public prosecutor, and the governor of the national bank. It could create enterprises and agencies at will, but only new legislation could transform any of these into a full-fledged secretariat.

These were the most important constitutional changes made by the Yugoslav leaders in their effort to get away from the Soviet model, and to create their own system of socialism. It was difficult (and too early) to pass judgment on their innovations. One could see, however, in the lowering of the prestige ordinarily attributed to cabinet ministries, and the reduction of such posts to "administrative" secretariats depending on a "political" executive council and president, an effort, if a rather pathetic one, to begin the process of withering away. The whole constitutional revision somehow smacked of the struggles of incurable bureaucrats to stop being bureaucratic. To a western observer the new machinery seemed at least as cumbersome as the old, and the highly touted "decentralization" an illusion, since everything in the end returned to the dictatorship of Tito and the party. Yet the Yugoslav leadership also saw this, and made an effort to modify it.

REFORM OF THE PARTY AND THE PEOPLE'S FRONT; HERESY

Before the reforms, the Yugoslav system, as we saw, had faithfully copied the Soviet practice of making the party structure and the structure of the government virtually identical by putting key party members into key governmental posts, and less important party members into less important government posts. It was precisely this system which, the Yugoslavs now claimed they had discovered, had led to the USSR's deviation from the true course and into the Stalinist dictatorship. Thus the Yugoslavs could hardly retain it themselves while at the same time striving to reverse the course of "bureaucratization." As early as the fall of 1950, they deprived party leaders of many of the special privileges that had made them a caste apart: special ration cards, special housing privileges, and the like. In advance of the Sixth Party Congress, held in Zagreb early in November 1952, Rankovich announced that the congress would harmonize the Party's work with the changes which have occurred in connection with the establishment of the workers' councils and the practical realization of the program of decentralization and democratization . . . the Congress is expected to adopt decisions which will suppress dangers of bureaucracy in the Party and set the Party's course towards its becoming primarily a political and ideological factor — namely, ***membership in the party does not mean any special rights or privileges in government and society.***[4] (Italics mine.)

The party leadership pointed especially to the draft statute which the congress would (of course) pass, which would greatly enhance the importance of the Communist Parties of the individual republics. Contrasting its provisions with the Soviet rules governing the competence of a party congress in an individual republic (in Russia the republican congresses could only "examine" important questions), the Yugoslavs proudly emphasized that their own republican party congresses would hereafter not be limited to determining "the *tactical* line of the republican party within the framework of the general political line of the national party," but would now "determine the *political* line of the republican party within the framework of the general political line of the national party." To show that the change in wording really had the significance which they attributed to it, the regime's propagandists gave the following example of the new situation which it created: whereas in the past, it would have been the national party which would have fixed the number of collective farms to be created in Croatia within a given time, and the function of the Croatian Party would have been limited to implementing the decree, now it would be the Croatian Party which would determine how many collectives should be created and at what pace.

Moreover, whereas in the USSR (and in Yugoslavia up to now), no local party organization could expel any member without getting the approval of two higher party committees, or make any effort to expel any member who was also the member of any central committee at any level, the new Yugoslav statute permitted any local party organization to expel any member. The local organization need ask no permission of higher party authorities, although it was still required to inform them of its action. Other provisions in the new statute called for increased mass participation in party decision-making and in control over the party organizations. "As a rule," moreover, all party meetings were to be public, and workers who were not members should attend them. "The activity of the basic Party organizations should unfold itself as much as possible under the control of and with the participation of the masses."[5]

In giving his report to the actual session of the Sixth Congress, Tito recurred to the duties of the party in the future, and made two striking additional "suggestions": that the name of the party be changed from Com-

[4] *Yugoslav Review,* I, 10 (December 1952), p. 3.
[5] *Yugoslav Review,* I, 10, p. 15.

munist Party of Yugoslavia to "League of Communists of Yugoslavia," and that the name of the People's Front be changed to "Socialist League of the Working People of Yugoslavia," while its structure should be reorganized to enable it to play a more effective role. In his speech, Piyade pointed out that the change in name would serve to distinguish the Yugoslav Party from the "so-called" Communist parties of other countries, and especially to emphasize the contrast between the Yugoslavs and the "Great-Russian bureaucratic caste" of the USSR.

The actual resolution of the Congress gave a further explanation:

> The Congress considers that the development of social relations in the direction of an ever-greater management by workers and the ever-more democratic forms of authority should be established as the basic task and role of communists: political and ideological work in the education of the masses.
>
> In connection with this, the Congress has decided to change the name of the Communist Party of Yugoslavia to the League of Communists of Yugoslavia.
>
> The League of Communists is not and cannot be . . . the direct operative leader and giver of orders either in economic life or in the life of state and society. Its role is to carry on political and ideological activities chiefly by persuasion in all organizations, agencies, and institutions, which it induces to accept its line. . . .
>
> The League of Communists is the most conscious, organized part of the working class.
>
> The qualities and role of a communist, a member of the League of Communists, are expressed in his social consciousness and social activities, unselfishness, self-sacrifice, loyalty to his objectives, personal morality, and modesty.[6]

The last section suggested the transformation of the Communist Party of Yugoslavia into something like the Boy Scouts. Even though the rest of the resolution was less moralistic, it must have been difficult indeed for old party members to swallow. They were to give no more orders, and carry on their work "chiefly" by persuasion and setting the proper example. If the resolution were to be taken seriously, it required an extraordinary effort on the part of the individual Yugoslav Communist. In line with Tito's other "suggestion," that the People's Front also change its name, the Sixth Party Congress also passed an appropriate resolution, but action was deferred until the Fourth Congress of the Front itself, held in Belgrade on February 22, 1953.

Twenty-two hundred delegates of the Front (the regime claimed that more than 80 per cent of the voters were members) heard Tito admonish them to "adopt an organizational form . . . sufficiently elastic to enable all the working people of our country to rally to it . . ." and at the same time to "acquire the most Socialist ideological tenor possible . . . because our socialist reality has reached such a high state of development. The decentralization and

[6] *Yugoslav Review,* I, 10, p. 16, translation modified for the sake of idiom.

democratization of government in our country imperatively require a developed socialist consciousness on the part of our citizens." The "struggle of opinions" was "to be cultivated and freely developed"; but an "indispensable prerequisite is the tenacious and patient re-education of the people." As was his wont, Tito attacked both the Cominform and the "sinister reactionary circles in the West," and hailed the future role of the front in the international field, as a "collaborator with the socialist movements." Indeed, the Front heard a good deal about Yugoslav foreign policy, presumably in part to prepare the rank and file for the news of the pact with Greece and Turkey, whose announcement lay less than a week in the future.

But the delegates also listened to much windy talk on the effort which their leaders were pursuing to effect the withering away of the state, and to ensure political, economic, and social self-government. Only through democratic forms could socialist substance be reached. But democratic forms did not in Yugoslavia mean a multiparty system, which, Kardelj told his hearers, only had meaning as reflecting class-interests where class-antagonisms existed. Yet socialist democracy meant full attention to the free and full development of the individual.

The League of Communists did not claim a monopoly in determining "the political line of struggle for the construction of socialist relationships in our country." This would be "the result of the conscious and active coöperation of the working masses organized in the Socialist Alliance" (the new name for the Front). The League of Communists had "rid itself of the outside forms of a political party and of political monopolism," and had become "the ideological champion and inspirer of socialist practice and of the socialist political action of the broadest working masses." From now on, it would be judging its members by their successes in their work among the masses. Inspiration, education, this was the job of the League, in contrast to the role of the Stalinist parties. Indeed, said Kardelj, taking the offensive, the Yugoslav reform would "awaken certain positive forces within the Cominformist parties to shake off the chains with which they are bound today by Stalin's 'theory' on the party."

Now, as part and parcel of the change, the front must move away from the past, to which it was bound by tradition, on toward new methods of political and social activity. It must become a mass public forum in which ideas would be freely exchanged "upon a general socialist platform." It would supervise the various self-governing organs of state and society. It would be broad enough to admit all citizens who did their social duty, and accepted the general aims of socialism. It should "function as an all-national parliament which is constantly in session."

Thus the changes in name represented real changes in function. No longer would the *Communist Party* organizations decide "all political and social questions, and then simply forward these decisions to the *People's Front* organizations for approval." Now the *League of Communists* would work on problems of ideology and education, while the *Socialist Alliance* would settle "directly concrete political and other social questions," would supervise the social organizations, and would coöperate with international labor and socialist movements. Amid the drumming of inspirational oratory, the Front changed its name and its functions accordingly.

Nobody acquainted with standard Communist practice could fail to see what a narrow tight-rope the new doctrine gave the party members to walk. On the one hand, it required them to abandon their habits of command and of bureaucratic behavior: the "subjectivity of the economic bureaucrat" must give way to the "free play of objective economic laws." The arbitrary local official and party boss who had got his way and the state's way by intimidation and bullying not only had to vanish, but had to transform himself into an educator and missionary. From now on, he would hold the system together by persuasion, making mass assemblies popular, and preventing their acting as mere rubber stamps for an arbitrary élite, but still "directing the working class," and "raising the mass intelligence" to the level of his own. It was little wonder that many of the party functionaries found themselves baffled, and, unable to adapt themselves to the new ways, sank into a bewildered passivity.

The Yugoslav people, for their part, clearly thought that they were now free to admire the west, which was, on the whole, the natural attitude for many of them to take. So serious did this become that in June 1953 the League of Communists instructed its local sections to fight against "the vicious Western influences upon the cultural and political life of Yugoslavia," and conducted a campaign against the United States Information Service, and the British Council. Many citizens were intimidated into staying away from the reading-rooms of the western powers in Belgrade or into canceling their subscriptions to the daily press releases which the information services issued. The Yugoslav leadership, apparently frightened at the relief with which the population greeted what looked like a relaxation, was trying the familiar Soviet device of counterirritant.

These were not the only difficulties involved in the preaching of the new doctrines. If pushed to their logical conclusion, they led straight to new heresy. Milovan Djilas, still under forty, the Montenegrin intellectual, veteran member of the Partisan inner circle, fell into it only a few months after the February 1953 meeting of the Front. As early as August he was known to have spotted the weaknesses in the system: the human beings involved either became apathetic, and thought they had nothing to do, or reverted helplessly to their old bureaucratic ways. Beginning on October 11, 1953, Djilas began to write a series of weekly articles for the Communist newspaper, *Borba,* which by November and December 1953 were criticizing the new system very sharply. On December 20, it was announced that henceforth the articles would appear three times a week, and the tone grew still sharper. In the absence of replies from other leading members of the

"League," the public naturally assumed that Djilas' writings represented official doctrine, as they had often done before. Kardelj remonstrated with Djilas, but to no avail. Yet, if the party leadership should order the series stopped, when it had been announced that there would be eighteen or twenty more installments, the public would learn that its leadership was divided.

With his colleagues in this embarrassing situation, Djilas just went on writing. On December 27, 1953, he suggested that the "League of Communists" should really become what the new doctrines suggested it must eventually become: "a loose association of ideologically kindred spirits which would have its own aim and line but would not be ossified into an organization which would divide itself from the masses." He wanted the League to stop being a political party in fact as well as in name. The new reorganization he proposed would in fact have reorganized the old Communist Party out of existence. On the publication of this startling suggestion — which none the less was fully implicit for the long run in all the efforts at "democratization" carried on since 1950 — the press began an inquiry among "League" members. This disclosed that most of those polled (whether or not because they thought they were agreeing with their masters as they had always been accustomed to doing) strongly favored the disbanding of the "League" in the way which Djilas was advocating. It happened that Tito himself was out of town at the time the December 27 article appeared, and the editor of *Borba* was unable to obtain any authoritative guidance. A few days later, Tito read the article for the first time, and expressed his disapproval to Djilas, but did not order the series suspended. Indeed, five more articles were published down to January 7, 1954.

At this moment there appeared another article by Djilas in the January issue of his magazine *Nova Misao* (*New Thought*). In this piece, Djilas severely criticized the private lives of the top party comrades. He not only accused them of continuing to be the bureaucrats they had always been, but charged their wives with having snubbed the new wife of the Chief of Staff, General Dapchevich. The party ladies, Djilas declared, had not accepted this girl because she had not been an active partisan fighter during the war, and because she was an actress. He pointed out that she had been a child during the war years, and added that the moral behavior of the party ladies themselves could hardly stand close inspection. This wide-open personal attack seems to have been the last straw. The *Borba* series was stopped. It was the *Nova Misao* article, with its sensational personal charges, that was chiefly noticed in the west, but it seems safe to say that it was the ideological content of the *Borba* series which truly embarrassed the party leadership, rather than the personal content of the *Nova Misao* article, which Tito himself called an "obscure feuilleton." Djilas proclaimed himself a democrat, and castigated his associates as bureaucrats. Djilas' thought was close to what his fellow-Titoites pretended to believe, but he carried their "self-criticism" one step further:

> No class or political movement can claim the exclusive right to represent society as a whole or to proclaim their ideas as objective truth. What the elect proclaim as truth may be true at the moment it is proclaimed. But the truth becomes ossified in dogma, and in the meantime reality has flowed on, generating new ideas and new forces which come into conflict with the ruling group. And if the ruling group resists, as inevitably it will, then there is a danger that it will degenerate into the priest and gendarme of socialism.

Nobody could deny that the top leadership grasped the nettle firmly. On January 16 and 17, 1954, the Central Committee of the League of Communists held a special session in Belgrade. The entire discussion was broadcast, and reported verbatim in the press; so that the general public had the fullest access to the material of the dispute. Members of the Central Committee denounced Djilas' suggestion that local Communist organizations meet less often; this was unacceptable "at present" because it would lead the public to believe that the League was beginning to dissolve. Once the public believed this, the dissolution itself would soon take place. The League would become nothing but a group of clubs for intellectuals. Despite Djilas' suggestions, the "class enemy" was still present, and the Communists had to continue their job of arousing the "socialist consciousness of the masses." Djilas' ideas smacked of anarchist individualism. Could the party cease altogether to govern, and become a mere proselytizing agent?

The logical conclusion to which Djilas' arguments led would certainly have been the emergence of at least a "socialist" opposition, and perhaps the growth of a full-fledged system of political parties. This the Yugoslav leadership was not ready to tolerate. Tito himself called the Djilas articles "reactionary deviations," and "revisionism of the worst type." The Central Committee expelled Djilas, as did the Yugoslav Politburo, and he resigned his Vice-Premiership and his Presidency of the National Assembly, as well as his seat in that body. With him there fell from office Vladimir Dedijer, Tito's close friend and official biographer, whom we have so often quoted in these pages, and who was the only member of the Central Committee to support Djilas fully. But this was no Soviet-style purge. Djilas defended himself for three hours with vigor, and went to his defeat without "confessing" or apparently being expected to confess. He then quietly retired into private life, as did Dedijer. Both moved freely about the country, and continued to reside in Belgrade, where in the summer of 1954 Djilas was reported working on a translation and appreciation of Plekhanov, the founding father of Russian Marxism.

In criticizing Djilas, Tito declared that he himself was still a believer in the withering away of the League, but repeated that this could not take place within a year or two: it would have to be a long-range process. Before it could take place, the last "class enemy" must have been "put out of action" and "socialist consciousness" must have "penetrated the minds of the broadest ranks of our citizens." Yet Tito also declared that he would not have felt it necessary to summon the special disciplinary session of the Central Committee had he not seen how the press of the western countries was hailing the Djilas articles and interpreting them to mean that Yugoslavia was moving closer to the adoption of western democratic forms.

Here was one of the crucial points for Tito: in turning away from Soviet communism, he was absolutely determined not to allow Yugoslavia to go back to anything remotely resembling the prewar political system. Navigating away from the shoals of Soviet bureaucracy, he could not wreck his craft with its "socialist" crew upon what he and they regarded as the reefs of capitalist democracy. Most of his followers retained their contempt for the old system, and had listened without conviction when Clement Attlee and other western socialists urged the restoration of political parties. Not until all vestiges of "petty-bourgeois" thought had disappeared, when there would be no former shopkeepers and craftsmen hoping for the restoration of their former enterprises, when the opposition too could be trusted to be entirely "socialist," could Tito, in his own view, allow an opposition to come into being:

> I do not, of course, entertain any doubts about the integrity and social consciousness of the enormous majority of communists, but there are still thousands upon thousands who would strengthen the ranks of the waverers and various kinds of adventurers, and who could do immense harm. Our country would not only suffer a loss in its prestige, but it would have to win back again what it had already won once.

Tito also criticized Djilas for publishing the articles without informing the Central Committee of the tone he intended to give them.

> We have never, and especially never during the last few years since we have broken away from the Soviet Union, prevented the free expression of opinion, but these opinions must be aired in the proper place, they must be the fruit of common discussions, they must be progressive and forward-looking opinions capable of advancing our reality.

This definition of free expression of opinion would hardly receive the approval of anybody outside the Communist world. Tito had modified the system, but he had not abandoned it. As a theoretician and not a day-to-day worker, he further maintained, Djilas had no right to criticize as "bureaucrats" those who did the "socialist work, . . . the real work." Indeed, apart from the question of the abused party hierarchs, Djilas had forgotten the working class, now being given its opportunity actually to govern through the new arrangements in the factories.

Instead of workers, Djilas would create a new "elite of the class which champions our socialist consciousness, which champions the development of our socialist construction, of our socialist reality." Djilas' élite, said Tito, aiming directly at Djilas himself, would be "various coffee-shop debaters, political obscurantists, people who float around various editorial offices, some writers, and others from the . . . ranks of the small bourgeoisie. . . ." One member of the Central Committee asserted that Zagreb had already become the center for such a movement of dissident intellectuals, which he called an "underground of geniuses." He associated Dedijer with them, and accused them of wishing to relegate the "League of Communists" to a museum as an antique.

Yet despite the sharpness of the criticism, there was a paternal tone in Tito's reproofs. He finished by admonishing the Central Committee that

> it would be absolutely wrong, . . . useless . . . harmful if we . . . were . . . to act now as we were obliged to act during the days of the sharp revolutionary struggle . . . . we are today so strong that we can afford to conduct the struggle against such attempts in an entirely different and new way — in our own way. We do not have to seek to ruin and annihilate people who make mistakes, even the greatest mistakes, but can afford to make it possible for them to see their errors and to do . . . whatever lies in their power to repair . . . the damage they have done.

The opportunity which Djilas had received to publish his articles even after Tito and Kardelj had both remonstrated with him, the full publicity given to the Central Committee's handling of the case, and the mildness of the punishment inflicted, compared with that which was standard in Cominform countries, all served to substantiate the view that the Yugoslav system was different from that which obtained under Stalin in the USSR and its satellites. That it was nothing like western democracy was also abundantly clear. The leadership was having its difficulties, on the one hand with fanatical Communists, some of whom no doubt loved the Soviet Union, but most of whom in any case could not bear to relinquish their perquisites or change their ways, and on the other hand with theoreticians like Djilas who wanted to realize immediately Tito's promises of freedom, and then move on towards western democratic forms. But it seemed in 1954 to have kept both groups under control, and to be moving steadily, if painfully, toward a system neither Soviet nor western but Yugoslav.[7]

Far from withering away, the Yugoslav League of Communists, according to Rankovich, had 700,030 members on March 29, 1954, as against 629,108 for the CPY in March 1951. Of these, 191,655 were workers, 189,392 peasants, 189,231 officials, and 129,752 others. There were 121,159 women. During 1953, 25,096 new members had been admitted, but 72,467 had been expelled, — a total reduction of 47,371 for the year. Rankovich lamented the small proportion of workers. Thus, despite the change in name and a 7 per cent reduction in membership during 1953, the League much resembled the old CPY, and

[7] The reported suicide of an alleged follower of Djilas, Shprlyan, member of the Central Committee of the Croatian Communist Party, and the reported flight to Austria of other sympathizers with Djilas were somber notes indeed, but hardly decisive indications of a return to full-scale Stalinite tyranny.

the contradictions between its old habits and its new duties remained unresolved.

THE COURTS

Accompanying the reforms in local and national government, and in the organization and purpose of the Communist Party and the People's Front, went a reform in judicial procedure. This was forecast as early as 1951, when Rankovich issued a sensational report to the Central Committee, in which he openly admitted the atrocities which his police had been committing. Forty-seven per cent of the arrests made by the notorious UDBa in 1949 had been, he declared, unjustified arrests. The courts had refused to examine evidence indicating the falsity of indictments. They had inflicted illegal punishments. Local Communist organs had provided police agents with court decisions signed by judges and imposing sentences to forced labor camps, with the name of the victim left blank, so that the police could in effect use the blank sentence for anybody they chose. People had been punished for wartime collaboration with the enemy, when in fact they had suffered in the enemy's own concentration camps.

There was, of course, no habeas corpus, and citizens arrested arbitrarily often languished in jail for months or years before being brought to trial or even being informed of the charges against them. Many instances of individual anguish as a result of this outrageous mockery of justice may be found in Professor Alex N. Dragnich's book entitled *Tito's Promised Land*.[8] This kind of thing is well known to all students of Communist judicial practice. The difference between Tito's Yugoslavia and the USSR and its satellites was that the Yugoslavs in 1951 admitted their past shameful record, and announced their intention of instituting judicial reform. Rankovich added, however, that the new courts would not be any less severe in dealing with the "enemies of socialism," but would continue to be "most merciless" towards them.

Some piecemeal reforms were made soon after Rankovich's report. A decree forbade arbitrary arrest and detention. The police and the party were deprived of their right to sentence people without trial — so-called "administrative punishment." Yet mention of such sentences continued to crop up. In June 1952, Rankovich announced that the UDBa had been demilitarized, and transformed into a regular branch of the civil service. It was not until 1953, the year of the new constitution and the new party and front statute, that the new code of criminal procedure was adopted. Official apologists for the new code declared that United Nations documents on human rights, drafted since 1948, had served as part of the inspiration for the change. In any event, legality of procedure, legal indictment as against administrative procedure, liberalized rules of evidence, public proceedings, a guaranteed defense, and

[8] New Brunwick, N. J.: Rutgers University Press, 1954.

habeas corpus now received formal recognition. Torture was forbidden, as were cruel and inhuman forms of punishment, and legal remedy was guaranteed for "all acts which violate the fundamental constitutional rights of man."

The new code, its proponents pointed out, limited the term of imprisonment during investigation, forbade the extraction of confessions by the use of any form of pressure, accepted confessions as evidence only when there was independent evidence supporting them, and provided for compensation to anyone arrested or sentenced in error. In line with decentralization in other fields, the new code deprived the Public Prosecutor of the function of conducting the preliminary inquiry and investigation, and left him only the function of asking that such inquiry be initiated. The actual inquiry was the responsibility of the local authorities. They alone could order arrests. Custody was limited to a period of three to eighteen days, and imprisonment during investigation to a maximum of ten months, but any period over four months required republican court approval, and any over seven that of the Federal Supreme Court.

Thus the Public Prosecutor lost his former right to order imprisonment during investigation. Prison reform was built into the code, including the proviso that all persons in custody were entitled to eight hours' uninterrupted rest during each twenty-four hours, a grim reminder of the Communist practice of extorting confessions by depriving the accused of sleep. At the same time, it was announced that the police force had been steadily reduced in number.[9]

Of course the mere existence of the new code was no guarantee that it would be observed. It would be a notably difficult task to change the habits of the police. It was too early to say whether the new safeguards would actually work to protect the citizen against the agents of his government. It was appropriate to maintain an attitude of entire skepticism. Yet it was also undeniable that, in admitting its past atrocious behavior, in whittling down the powers of the Public Prosecutor, and in adopting and publicizing a code containing many of the provisions observed in the western democratic states, the Yugoslav regime had acted differently from that of any other Communist state.

Administration, from the lowest level to the highest, had been given a new appearance by the introduction of the "producers' councils," themselves a reflection of the new managerial system of workers' councils in the factories. The process of curbing the party and strengthening its "mass organization" apparently reflected a wish to experiment with "democracy" as well as with "decentralization." And the new code of criminal procedure suggested that justice might become more just. By the early months of 1954, the Yugoslav leaders had gone a long way toward meeting on paper the challenge they

[9] In 1950, 41,247; 1951, 35,760; 1952, 31,700; 1953, 28,076, *Yugoslav Review*, III, 1–2 (January-February 1954), p. 12.

had set themselves: to create a political system which should be neither "soviet" nor "western."

Except for Djilas, whose case was rather a special one, they ran the country without purges of top Communist personnel. The Politburo was presumably unchanged in membership, except for the dropping of Djilas. In the new constitutional system, the same faces appeared at the top. Tito, of course, was President both of the Republic and of the Federal Executive Council (FEC). Kardelj, Rankovich, Vukmanovich-Tempo, and Radolyub Cholakovich (successor to Djilas) were Vice-Presidents of the FEC. Piyade was President of the Assembly. Familiar second-rank names still held the positions at the next lowest level of the government. Kidrich, the chief economic planner, died early in 1954.

On November 25, 1950, Sreten Zhuyovich-Tsrni, one of the two alleged Cominform agents in the top Yugoslav party hierarchy, was released from prison. He wrote a recantation, admitting his contacts with the Soviet embassy, and confessing to having played the role which he had been accused of playing. He also denied Polish press reports that he had died in jail. Criminal proceedings against him were dropped, and he returned to private life. The other chief Yugoslav Cominform agent, Hebrang, died in jail without recanting. Lesser Cominformists also began to emerge from jail. In June 1951, Rankovich reported that 8,403 citizens had been arrested for pro-Cominform activity, of whom 3,718 had already been released. The rest were doing "socially useful work" and were being treated "severely but humanely," adverbs which had to be interpreted in the light of Rankovich's record. But the government was still arresting, trying, and sentencing people for pro-Cominform activities in January 1952, when a former Deputy President of the Economic Council and six others received jail sentences.

Indeed, as in the other Balkan countries, trials of enemies of the state were a regular feature of life in Yugoslavia during these years. Alleged Cominform spies, both of Yugoslav origin, and from the neighboring countries, were constantly before the courts. Others were accused of acting as Ustasha agents, of "disturbing Serbo-Croat relations" by "chauvinist outbursts," of being royalists carrying out "espionage and diversion on behalf of King Peter," of belonging to an "underground royal army" (Serbian), or a "Croat People's Committee," of working for Bulgarian intelligence, of being Chetniks, of spying for the "Chetnik intelligence service" in Trieste, of conspiring for Croat independence, spying for the Vatican, and the like.

In January 1954, Tito asked rhetorically: "Has there ever been any other revolution whose leaders have liquidated so courageously the conditions which they have themselves promoted and which they have now found to be obsolete and erroneous, so that they might bring into being conditions which are new and better?" [10] It was perhaps less of a rhetorical question than he intended. The

[10] *Yugoslav Review*, III, 1–2 (January-February 1954), p. 19.

Yugoslav Communists were experimenting, but their preconceptions remained the same. Within the limits allowed them by Marxist dogma they could move, but the limits were narrow indeed.

2. *Foreign Relations*

WITH THE WEST

Western Aid. In foreign policy, the expulsion from the Cominform gave the Yugoslavs an opportunity to form new and friendlier relationships with the west. Indeed, objectively viewed, their isolated situation seemed to require that they lose no time in reaching with the western powers an understanding that would at least offer them some protection against attack and annihilation, if not against economic collapse. However, the Yugoslav Communists were at first no more objective than the Serbs who had made the coup of March 1941: they virtually invited attack and annihilation, and were not prepared to accept western aid or guarantees if there were any strings attached. They seemed to prefer to suffer economic hardship, and to run the risk of destruction. Moreover, the Yugoslav leadership, in the months immediately following the break with the Soviet bloc, seemed to feel that it could not afford to lose the support of the rank and file of the Yugoslav Communist Party by accepting western aid, and thus lending substance to the charges, already beginning to be hurled against them by the Cominform, that they were deserters from socialism and renegades to the capitalist and imperialist camp led by the United States.

The American government in 1948 and 1949 fully appreciated the difficulties of Tito's position. To Washington the unprecedented quarrel among Communists offered an obvious opportunity. The wider the rift between Stalin and Tito, and the more sympathizers "Titoism" might gain (in its sense of nationalist anti-Stalinist communism), the better for the west. Yet to leap too fast to embrace Tito might be to destroy him and the western opportunity together. The situation called for patience. The United States must quietly hold open for Tito a door through which he might pass when he should choose to do so. It was one of the successes of American foreign policy in this period that it was able to pursue this delicate course.

Within three weeks of the publication of the Cominform communiqué, on July 19, 1948, the United States reached agreement with Yugoslavia on matters which had hitherto hung fire. The Yugoslavs undertook to compensate the United States for losses incurred when American property in Yugoslavia had been nationalized, and to meet American claims for lend-lease debts and for civilian relief before the creation of UNRRA. The United States unblocked Yugoslav assets in this country, which included $47,000,000 worth of gold, for which the Tito government had long been pressing. The Yugoslavs also began to look to the west for trade, although their failure to keep lines open during the period when their country had been in the Soviet bloc had depleted their reserves of hard currency, and thus created an additional obstacle to the realignment of trade relationships. In December 1948, however, Britain concluded a one-year trade agreement with Yugoslavia to the amount of 30,000,000 pounds, the first intimation of the new alignment with the west which Yugoslavia would gradually reach in the months and years to follow.

By mid-1949, with the Communist bloc tightening its economic blockade, Tito declared that he intended to strengthen Yugoslav trade ties with the west. But he was still most suspicious and truculent, emphasizing that he would make no political concessions. Yugoslavia had also asked for a loan from the International Bank for Reconstruction and Development, but here too Tito blusteringly proclaimed his willingness to get along without the money if any concessions were asked of him. Most of the bluster seemed designed for domestic Communist consumption. At least, Washington so interpreted the matter.

American exports to Yugoslavia, which had amounted only to a little over $8,000,000 in 1948 rose to almost $21,000,000 in 1949, and imports from Yugoslavia increased in value from a little over $5,000,000 to almost $15,000,000. In contrast with American policy toward the Cominform bloc, which forbade the export of "war potential" items, the United States on August 17, 1949 agreed to export to Yugoslavia within a year a steel-finishing mill valued at $3,000,000. A little over three weeks later, while the World Bank was still considering the Yugoslav application for a loan, the Export-Import Bank, an American institution, agreed to advance Yugoslavia $20,000,000, of which the Yugoslavs were to use $12,000,000 to buy mining equipment in the United States. In agreeing to the loan, the Bank announced that the development of Yugoslav nonferrous metal resources was a matter of interest to the western powers. Thus by the fall of 1949, at a moment in time which coincided with a high pitch of the Soviet effort against Yugoslavia — the Rajk trial and the breaking of the treaties of friendship — the United States was stretching out an effective helping hand.

In the United Nations, Yugoslavia, abandoned elsewhere, now turned away from its former allies. Its representatives criticized the Soviet bloc freely and vigorously, and adopted a policy of voting with Moscow only when Yugoslav interests were actually felt to demand it. The United States supported the Yugoslavs for membership on the Security Council, against the United Nations precedent whereby the eastern European members could successfully nominate their own choice for the post. Despite violent Soviet opposition, and although the British supported the precedent, and thus opposed the Yugoslav candidacy, the Yugoslavs were successful on October 20, 1949.

American support for Tito went further than this. The Yugoslavs were now permitted to buy civil aircraft, equipment, and aviation gasoline. On December 24, 1949, the two countries concluded a significant civil aviation agreement, which permitted an American airline to operate regularly over

Yugoslav territory and to use Yugoslav airfields, and gave the Yugoslav airline the same privileges in the American zones of Germany and Austria. It was only a little more than three years since the Tito regime had shot down unarmed American aircraft, but much had happened in the interim. Washington also encouraged the conclusion of other important trade agreements between Yugoslavia and the west: a one-year treaty with Western Germany (December 1949: $60,000,000), and a five-year treaty with Great Britain for 220,000,000 pounds, including an 8,000,000-pound credit. Switzerland and Italy also extended credits.

To support Yugoslavia effectively, however, involved not only efforts to prevent the Yugoslav economy from collapsing; it required also that the Cominform states entirely understand that the United States would be unlikely to allow an attack on Yugoslavia to go unpunished. In December 1949, this notification too was forthcoming, as the newly appointed American Ambassador to Yugoslavia, George V. Allen, quoted President Truman's views in a press interview just before leaving for Yugoslavia: "As regards Yugoslavia, we are just opposed to aggression against that country as against any other [*sic*], and just as favorable to the retention of Yugoslavia's sovereignty."[11] It was clear that Washington had extended economic and political aid not out of any affection for a Communist dictator, whose policies at home were in 1949 still as ruthless as those of his old teachers, but out of a clear-eyed sense of American interests, which required the preservation of the first successful Communist rebel against Moscow. Moreover, the Americans had not asked for any political concessions. At home in Belgrade, no sign of "reforms" had yet materialized. And in the UN, the Yugoslavs continued on into 1950 to take the side of the Chinese Communists, and to stay neutral on the question of Korea.

As so often in the history of the Balkans, it was the weather which presented the Yugoslav regime with arguments stronger than any which human beings could have advanced. The drought of the summer of 1950 made further help urgently necessary. Moreover, the period of Yugoslav ideological contemplation was drawing to an end, and the conclusions the leaders had reached, which we have already reviewed, gave them a new theoretical basis on which they felt they could build genuine collaboration with a western bloc which continued to make no demands on them. In a tentative way, the Yugoslavs tested their new hypotheses, by resuming diplomatic relations with "monarcho-fascist" Greece, and concluding a reparations and financial agreement with Italy, their rival for Trieste.

In the fall, the full bad news about the harvest having come in, Yugoslavia asked for $55,000,000, but later estimates put the need at $75,000,000. The United States at once made available cash and foodstuffs to the tune of $31,400,000. The Export-Import Bank and the Economic Coöperation Administration were the American agencies involved. The Mutual Defense Assistance

[11] *N. Y. Times*, December 23, 1949.

Act, moreover, empowered the administration to assist any European nation which appeared to be threatened, and which was regarded as strategically important to western defense. Under this provision, the American government advanced the Yugoslavs a further $16,000,000 for army rations. The sum of $38,000,000 more was provided by Congress before the end of the year by special legislation called the Yugoslav Emergency Relief Act.

Yugoslavia agreed to use the assistance "to prevent the weakening of the defenses of the Federal People's Republic of Yugoslavia," not to transfer the assistance to any other government without the prior consent of the United States, to supply the United States with "reciprocal assistance" in the form of "raw or semi-processed materials required by the United States," and to make dinars available to the United States to cover the administrative expenses involved. Moreover, the Yugoslavs would allow American officials and newspapermen to observe the distribution, would report on the use of the assistance, and would give full publicity among the Yugoslav people to the fact that it was the United States which was feeding them. The agreement formalizing these arrangements was signed in Belgrade on January 6, 1951. Relief shipments of food, clearly marked as coming from the United States, helped build American popularity in the country. Britain too provided smaller amounts of assistance.

Within the next few months, the situation along the Yugoslav frontiers grew more menacing than ever, and the possibility of a Soviet or satellite attack loomed very large. Tito himself announced that Yugoslavia would resist aggression anywhere in Europe, if Yugoslav independence were threatened. He thus put the Soviet bloc on notice that they could not count on the neutrality of some thirty Yugoslav divisions if they attempted aggression anywhere. The United States, on April 17, 1951, gave Yugoslavia additional Military Defense Assistance funds to the amount of $29,000,000 on the same basis as before, but with new arrangements for making dinars available to the United States. This advance was followed by a joint American-British-French agreement reached in June 1951, by which the three western powers jointly undertook to meet the expected Yugoslav foreign trade deficit during the next year (total perhaps $150,000,000), of which the United States alone would pay 65 per cent, Britain 23, and France 12 per cent. In October 1951, the International Bank for Reconstruction and Development advanced a loan of $28,000,000 in seven European currencies to enable Yugoslavia to finance the state investment program.

In early November 1951, President Truman notified the Senate and House Chairmen of the Foreign Affairs and Armed Services Committees that

> Particularly during the past year, steps have been taken by the Soviet Union to augment the size and effectiveness of the armed forces of the Soviet satellites bordering on Yugoslavia. To meet this situation there is an urgent need to strengthen the Yugoslav armed forces, which . . . constitute a significant obstacle to aggression in Southeastern Europe . . . . the security interests

of the United States and also of the free world now require that we undertake to provide military assistance to Yugoslavia.[12]

Economic assistance would also be continued. Thus the United States took an additional step forward in undertaking to give the Yugoslavs outright military assistance. Acceptance of American military aid was a significant milestone along the road which the Yugoslavs were tracing away from isolation between the two great groupings of powers in the world and toward a closer alignment with the west.

Indeed, economic assistance to Yugoslavia now became a regularized and continuing part of the obligations assumed by the United States and the other western powers. The fiscal year July 1951–June 1952 saw a total of $120,000,000 provided: $78,000,000 by the United States, $27,600,000 by Great Britain, and $14,400,000 by France. A new agreement was signed in Belgrade in January 1952, and in February President Truman notified Congress that Mutual Security funds for Yugoslavia were being transferred from military to economic assistance.

In October 1952, the western powers and the Yugoslavs agreed on the continuation of the program for the twelve months of the fiscal year July 1952–June 1953. The new sum was to be $99,000,000, with the United States contributing $78,000,000, Great Britain $12,600,000, and France $8,400,000. To help offset the new and severe drought of 1952, $30,000,000 was made available at once. In January, in April, and in June 1953, the Mutual Security Agency advanced $46,000,000 more for the same purpose, making the year's total $145,000,000.

The western governments asked the Yugoslavs to follow a system of priority criteria in planning their investment program, and urged them in future to look to the International Bank for Reconstruction and Development as the source for loans. But they affirmed their belief in the importance both of industrial development and of increased agricultural production in Yugoslavia. Only these twin advances would enable the country to emancipate itself from the need for continued aid. They also undertook to provide technical assistance for the Yugoslavs.

Promptly, on February 12, 1953, the International Bank announced a second loan of $30,000,000 to Yugoslavia, to be made available in the currencies of ten European countries. The money was to pay for the importation by Yugoslavia of equipment needed for twenty-seven projects in seven "sectors" of the economy: electric power, coal-mining, nonferrous metals, iron and steel production, manufacturing, forestry, and transportation. It was expected that all the projects, in which the Yugoslavs themselves had already made large investments, would be in operation by 1956. Indeed, the total cost of the projects would be $465,000,000, of which $343,000,000 was in domestic currency. The new loan came as the result of recommendations made by representatives

[12] Department of State, *Bulletin*, XXV (647), November 19, 1951, p. 826.

of the Bank and consultants from the British steel industry and the American aluminum industry. The loan was for a term of twenty-five years, and bore an interest of 4⅞ per cent, repayment to begin in August 1956 and continue until the loan should be retired by 1978. It was expected that the projects to be financed under the loan would improve the Yugoslav balance-of-payments position by the equivalent of $50,000,000 annually, by making possible increased exports of metals and metal goods and decreased imports of these and other products.

The Foreign Operations Administration during the first half of 1954 allotted a total of $25,000,000 to Yugoslavia to purchase American surplus wheat. In accordance with the Mutual Security Act of 1953, the United States was to use the dinars with which the Yugoslavs were to buy the wheat to purchase military equipment and supplies produced in Yugoslavia. Thus Yugoslavia, by early 1954, had received outright economic and military aid, loans, and "offshore procurement" orders from the United States. The Eisenhower administration elected in November 1952 had made no fundamental change in the Truman-Acheson polity toward Tito, but was continuing to view him as a useful potential ally.

The Balkan Pact. Indeed, as the intimacy developed, the western powers more and more strove, without attaching to their aid "conditions" of the sort which might make Tito balk, to bring about the integration of Yugoslavia in their developing plans for European defense. The chief problems here were, first, to encourage the growth of closer relations between Yugoslavia on the one hand and Greece and Turkey on the other, and, second, to bring about a settlement of the long-standing Trieste quarrel, which alienated Yugoslavia from Italy, and thus prevented the arrangement of a satisfactory defense of the Lyublyana gap against possible Soviet or satellite attack. By October 1954, both efforts had at last met with extraordinary success.

In September 1950 the Greek and Turkish governments were invited to "associate themselves" with NATO's military planning for the defense of the Mediterranean, and a year later both countries were asked to join the organization. They were separated from their western European allies not only by the Soviet bloc but by Yugoslavia. It was greatly to the interest of all concerned that a rapprochement take place. During the summer of 1952, efforts in this direction, which had been proceeding for some time, received their first publicity. "Good-will tours" of the three countries by parliamentary and other delegations produced a bumper crop of optimistic and friendly statements. Premier Plastiras of Greece, calling Tito a great man, and saying that he would "make any agreement with Yugoslavia because Tito is at its head," praised the Marshal for his initiative in moving towards closer collaboration with Greece. Piyade and Tempo in Athens discussed collaboration and trade, but Piyade was still declaring that Yugoslavia's policy was not to conclude any written agreements. In a cordial interview with Turkish newspapermen, however, Tito explained that it was only "paper agreements that have no real basis" which he fundamentally opposed, although it had so far been Yugoslav policy not to sign any pacts at all for fear of "irritating our eastern neighbors, who are already fond of provocations."

Despite these faintly chilling notes, harmony prevailed, and the exchanges of visits between the countries became more numerous, while the visitors' rank mounted each time. In January 1953, the foreign minister of each country visited the other two. Toasting Foreign Minister Köprülü of Turkey, Tito declared that

> coöperation in the Balkans between three threatened countries will be correctly understood among all the peace-loving nations . . . because peace and stability in the Balkans . . . lessen the chance for an aggressor to venture on some sort of an aggressive adventure in this part of Europe. We do not have the same internal system, but we have the same aspirations — to preserve our freedom and peaceful development, our independence and integrity.[13]

But again, he soft-pedaled the possibility of a written agreement, declaring that such formal instruments merely confirmed existing understandings. None the less, on February 28, 1953 at Ankara, Yugoslavia, Greece, and Turkey signed a five-year "Treaty of Friendship and Coöperation."

Reaffirming their loyalty to the UN, the three governments agreed to consult each other on all problems of mutual interest, to hold at least annual conferences of Foreign Ministers, to consider their problems of security in concert, to continue coöperation among the three general staffs, to coöperate in the economic, technical, and cultural fields, to solve peacefully problems which might arise among themselves, to stay out of any other alliance or any action which might be aimed at any one of their number, and not to conclude any agreement which might run counter to this one. An article specified that the Greek and Turkish obligations to NATO were in no way affected. The text also contained a very important article, inviting "any other state whose coöperation all parties to the treaty shall consider useful" to join the treaty under the same conditions as the three signatory powers.

The Balkan pact represented a success for American foreign policy. It was the first formal undertaking into which Yugoslavia had entered since the Cominform communiqué. In itself, the linking of Yugoslavia and Greece represented the renewal of an old tradition, going back to the old days of Serbian-Greek friendship, but it was none the less remarkable that mutual confidence could have grown so rapidly and developed so far between Tito and the "monarcho-fascists" he had worked so hard to overthrow until the summer of 1949. It was true also that the economies of the three were rather competitive than complementary, although Greece would surely need to import grain from the other two.

From a military point of view, the pact brought together for consultation the general staffs of three countries with a total force conservatively put at

[13] *Yugoslav Review,* II, 2 (February 1953), p. 6.

seventy 10,000-man divisions, thirty Yugoslav, thirty Turkish, and ten Greek. The forces lacked much modern equipment, but the west was working on this problem. Among them, the three states had splendid potential naval and air-bases, and collectively their entire resources were far stronger than they would have been separately. The invitation to other states to join the pact was a shrewd piece of political warfare, since it was sure to create feelings of unrest and uncertainty, especially in Bulgaria and Albania. The conclusion of the pact was followed in March 1953 by a state visit of Tito to London, when Queen Elizabeth, Prime Minister Churchill, and all of British officialdom tendered him a splendid welcome. The official communiqué spoke only in the vaguest generalities about the course of the discussions, although it hailed the new Balkan Pact.

Yet it remained to complete the Balkan Pact by a military alliance. This important step was delayed for more than eighteen months, despite the conclusion of further agreements on trade and navigation, air traffic, and various questions of payments and financing, and the creation of a permanent secretariat early in 1954. The delay was due, in large part at least, to the hope, long kept alive during protracted negotiations, that the Yugoslavs and the Italians might first reach an agreement on Trieste, and that Italy too might then adhere to the Balkan Pact, thus solidifying the defense of the whole eastern and central Mediterranean basin. But the hope, as often before, proved illusory, and in the end the other three countries went ahead with their military alliance, despite Italian unhappiness.

Signed on August 9, 1954 at Bled, the military alliance scrupulously recognized the obligations of all its members to the UN, and of Greece and Turkey to NATO. But its signatories also agreed to regard an act of aggression against any of them as an act of aggression against all of them. Individually or collectively, they would help the party attacked with all means at their disposal, including armed assistance. None of them would make a separate peace with an aggressor without prior agreement. For measures beyond this, the three would consult. Indeed, they now set up a permanent council, consisting of the three foreign ministers and such other officials as might be thought desirable, which would meet at least twice a year, its functions to be carried on in the intervals by the permanent secretariat. Special consultation among the three powers would take place if the international situation should deteriorate gravely, or if another power with whom any of the three had an alliance should be attacked. This last clause was obviously included in order not to oblige the Yugoslavs automatically to help any NATO power, which the Greeks and the Turks, or NATO members, were bound to do. Collaboration among the general staffs would continue.

Trieste. Although the pact marked a further significant advance, it did not bind Yugoslavia to NATO. Yet it went some distance toward that "association" of the Yugoslavs with NATO for which Admiral Carney, American commander of the area, had expressed a hope in June 1953. Trieste remained the great stumbling block and the major continuing liability for western policy toward Yugoslavia, and the completion of a Mediterranean defense system. Until the autumn of 1954, American and British handling of this problem seemed inept by comparison with the other aspects of their policy toward Yugoslavia.

Washington and London were still bound by the declaration of March 20, 1948, by which they had expressed themselves in favor of returning all of the free territory, Zone B as well as Zone A, to Italy. But this declaration had been issued at a time when the western powers could not know that the Cominform was about to expel the Yugoslavs. Though not abandoning the declaration formally, the western powers could hardly be expected to support it any longer, in view of its conflict with their aim of not alienating Tito. Yet they could not give it up either, without losing the support of Italian public opinion and strengthening the hands of the Italian Communists, now free to clamor for Trieste.

On March 1, 1952, Tito proposed that Italy and Yugoslavia take turns in naming a Governor of the whole Free Territory, each governor to serve for three years, with a Vice-Governor of the other nationality and a Director of Security to be appointed by a third power. But the Italians had no conceivable reasons for accepting such a system. There was much rioting in Italy in March. On May 9, 1952, after negotiations in London, the American, British, and Italian governments reached an agreement with regard to "arranging for a closer coöperation in Zone A." "Without prejudice to a final solution of the problem of the future of the Free Territory as a whole," the communiqué declared, "this understanding is designed to give greater practical recognition to the predominantly Italian character of the Zone." [14] The three governments agreed that the Italian government would appoint an Italian political adviser to the zone commander to represent Italy in all matters affecting Italy there. He would have a status similar to that enjoyed by the American and British political advisers. Moreover, the Italian government was to propose, and the Zone commander to appoint, a "senior director of administration," responsible to the Zone commander, who would have under his direction a "Directorate of Interior" and a "Directorate for Finance and Economy," staffed by Italians. The new arrangements clearly indicated that the United States and Britain were preparing the way for full Italian civil administration of Zone A. They were announced two weeks before the Italian provincial and municipal elections.

The Yugoslavs, who claimed that they had not been told in advance of the proposed discussions, erupted before they were held, and announced that they would not be bound by any agreements which might be reached. Tito freely compared the Italian government to that of Mussolini, and loudly boasted that Yugoslavia would contribute more in the event of war than Italy. He warned that Trieste was just the beginning of Italian claims, and that

[14] Department of State, *Bulletin,* XXVI (673), May 19, 1952, p. 779.

they would soon be demanding all of Istria, Zara, Dalmatia, and Montenegro. He accused the Russians of stirring up the trouble in Italy, and the Italians of taking advantage of Yugoslavia's difficult international position. The tone of his speech reflected the sudden blow which the United States and Britain had struck their own prestige in Yugoslavia.

By inviting the Italians to confer without consulting or inviting the Yugoslavs, the western powers had revived the old Yugoslav suspicions, never very far below the surface, that the United States and Britain were just as ready as the Soviet Union to impose unilateral decisions on small countries, and to engage in international bargaining with Balkan territory in old-fashioned "imperialist" style. Four days after the London agreement was published, Yugoslavia delivered notes in Washington and London protesting against the decisions as violations of the peace treaty and declaring that the recognition of the "Italian character" of Zone A "opened the road to still greater deprivation of rights of the Slovene inhabitants of the Zone." The USSR also protested, and its protest was rejected. The Commander of the British-United States Zone (A), Sir John Winterton, proceeded to put the agreement into effect.

The next major decision by the western allies with regard to Trieste was announced on October 8, 1953. The United States and Britain, declaring that they were distressed at the deteriorating relations between Italy and Yugoslavia over Trieste, and that solution by conciliation had proved impossible, announced that they were

> no longer prepared to maintain responsibility for the administration of Zone A. They have therefore decided to terminate the Allied Military Government, to withdraw their troops, and having in mind the predominantly Italian character of Zone A, to relinquish the administration of that Zone to the Italian Government. . . . It is the firm belief of the two Governments that this step will contribute to stabilization of a situation which has disturbed Italo-Yugoslav relations during recent years. They trust that it will provide the basis for friendly and fruitful coöperation between Italy and Yugoslavia, which is as important to the security of Western Europe as it is to the interests of the two countries concerned.[15]

If the two powers really believed that this measure would contribute to the lessening of tension, they were sadly mistaken. The Yugoslav reaction this time was even more violent than it had been in May 1952, when the United States and Britain had announced their intention of bringing Italian administrators into Zone A. The Yugoslavs noted that, while turning Zone A over to Italy, the powers said nothing about Zone B. Washington and London probably expected that the Yugoslavs would annex it outright, since Tito had long been moving in this direction. Indeed, Tito had several times indicated that he would accept a compromise giving Zone A to Italy and Zone B to Yugo-

[15] Department of State *Bulletin,* XXIX (747), October 19, 1953, p. 529.

slavia, while it had been the Italians who had continued to press for all or at least part of Zone B, in line with the allied declaration of March 1948. It was, therefore, not the actual boundary which the great powers now drew which infuriated the Yugoslavs, but the fact that it was the great powers alone who were drawing it, and that the decision had once again been announced without previous consultation or even warning.

The Americans and the British ought by now to have been familiar with the extraordinary Yugoslav sensitivity on questions of prestige. Tito still thought of his countrymen as the victorious heroes of the war, and of the Italians as defeated fascists. In a speech at Leskovats in the fall of 1953, he remarked "Nobody has the right to place us and Italy on the same level." He was not sufficiently realistic to note that the Italians had worked their passage back, were members of NATO, EDC, the European Coal and Steel Community, and the Strasbourg Assembly of Europe, while Yugoslavia was none of these, partly through his wish. The English and Americans had, so to speak, forgotten the Italian role in the war, but many of them still remembered Tito's hostility in the years immediately after the war. This true appraisal he never made.

To Tito, as a Yugoslav and a Communist, the allied aid, and perhaps even more the magnificence of his reception on the official visit to London were clear signs that the west desperately needed Yugoslavia. To the west the economic and military aid was a limited if important commitment, part of a gamble, and the London visit a courtesy. Tito had no alternative, as the United States and Britain saw it, but to continue his alignment with the west. He could not go back to the Soviet bloc. He could not survive alone. The United States and Britain had no alternative, as Tito saw it, but to consult him every time they made a decision affecting Yugoslavia. His own estimate of his importance was a high as ever, if not higher. He was still the same man who had thought he ought to have been informed when Roosevelt and Churchill met.

The Italians rubbed salt in these wounds by declaring that they had not relinquished their claims to Zone B. The Yugoslavs accused them of having massed troops on the borders of the Free Territory as early as August, 1953, in preparation for a take-over. As Tito and other Yugoslav officials protested against the new decision, savage anti-American and anti-British demonstrations broke out in Belgrade. Such demonstrations can take place in a Communist country only when the government wants them to take place. The rioters in Belgrade attacked the United States Information Office, and severely beat its director, William King: the choice of the Information Office was no accident. For most Yugoslavs in Belgrade it was the source of those "vicious western ideas" which the Yugoslav people somehow still found so attractive. The public indignation with the new decision on Trieste must be made to serve domestic ideological purposes as well as those of Yugoslav foreign policy. Despite Tito's denunciation of the rioters' excesses as a very great "mistake," the entire episode gave great comfort to those Yugoslav Communists who still hankered after Moscow, to Cominformists outside Yugoslavia, and therefore to Moscow itself.

On the specific issue of Trieste, moreover, the Russian proposal that the old terms of the Italian peace treaty now be followed to the letter, and that, after the long lapse of time, a civil governor be appointed for the Free Territory, now suited the Yugoslavs. It was more important to them to have the Italians lose Zone A than to retain Zone B for Yugoslavia, especially if the decision were one in which they had not participated. Thus, for the first time since Moscow had cast them out, the Yugoslavs and the Russians were in fact in agreement on policy, despite the Yugoslav denunciation of the Soviet gesture as "hypocritical." Moreover, by the fall of 1953, Stalin's successors were in office, and the possibility could not be overlooked that they would seek a rapprochement with Tito, and try to throw the blame for the initial break upon Stalin alone.

So the whole Trieste issue grew from a liability into a positive menace to allied planning, largely as a result of American and British ineptitude. If it were really true, as the Yugoslavs claimed, that the State Department, on the very eve of the announcement on Trieste, had officially told the Yugoslav Ambassador that there was no truth in the newspaper stories which were predicting it, then the Americans had compounded their ineptitude by prevarication. Press stories, which the Yugoslavs considered inspired, to the effect that during his London visit Tito had secretly agreed to the decision, and was now protesting just for the record met with an angry denial in Belgrade. Tito simply threatened to send troops into Zone A if the Italians should begin to occupy it. He did make it clear that he would not send his forces against American or British troops, but added that if the Italians should enter under allied military protection, the reaction in Yugoslavia would be "catastrophic." Faced with the threat of open war between two countries both of which were deemed essential to western defense, the allies backed down. They accepted the loss of face which they incurred by their failure to stick to their announced policies and withdraw their troops from Zone A. Leaving the troops where they were, the Americans and British returned wearily to the less spectacular, but possibly the only reliable, policy of negotiation, serving as intermediaries between Belgrade and Rome through the long months of argument ahead. The Trieste issue, which had been certified by Yugoslavia to the Security Council of the UN, was repeatedly taken off the agenda for discussion, as both Italy and Yugoslavia withdrew troops from the borders, and settled down for the long pull toward the very same obvious goal which the allies had tried to attain in a single leap.

The tempest stirred over the attempted Trieste decision of October 1953 died down, and by the time the Yugoslav Federal Executive Council issued its report on Yugoslav foreign relations in January 1954, relations with the United States were already back on an even keel. The report gave full credit to the United States for the economic and military aid extended to Yugoslavia, acknowledged its importance, and repeated that there had been no strings attached. Of the Trieste affair the report said:

> Precisely on account of these friendly relations and of our interest to develop them further, it should be stressed that the support lent by the western powers, including the U.S.A., to the unjustified Italian claims to the Yugoslav areas of the Free Territory of Trieste have dealt a considerable blow to the present development of friendly relations between the U.S.A. and Yugoslavia. The Government of the FPRY has reason to believe that the Government of the U.S.A. . . . is ready to strengthen its coöperation with the Government of the FPRY in the efforts to reach an agreed solution of the problem.[16]

The tone of the section in the report dealing with Yugoslav-British relations was similar.

All during the first nine months of 1954, it was clear that eventually a solution on Trieste would be reached which in principle would award Zone A to Italy and Zone B to Yugoslavia. A glance at the map will show what an extraordinarily large gain in territory and population the Yugoslav state had made in the region of the Julian March as compared with the frontiers before the Second World War. The final solution would be more generous to Yugoslavia than even the French proposals of 1946, which had been the most generous of those made by any of the western powers. When Yugoslavia should have acquired Zone B, which it had increasingly treated as part of its territory, it would have obtained more territory than any power but the USSR and Yugoslavia itself had claimed.

Though a solution along these lines was expected, and was apparently almost reached during the summer of 1954, the details of the settlement continued to block the final conclusion of an accord. The American press in September reported that the Yugoslavs were claiming a small part (100,000 square yards) of Zone A, called Lazaretto, which included a military hospital, and were raising questions concerning the linguistic privileges to be enjoyed by the Slovenes left in Italy. The Under-Secretary of State, Robert Murphy, visited both Belgrade and Rome. The expected announcement finally came on October 6, 1954.

The settlement was embodied in a memorandum of understanding between the governments of Italy, Yugoslavia, the United States, and Britain. This called for Zone A to go to Italy and Zone B to Yugoslavia, with boundary adjustments assigning a portion of Lazaretto and Crevitani to Yugoslavia. Italy and Yugoslavia undertook not to prosecute any resident of the area for past political activities, to work out together agreements controlling border traffic, and for the period of one year to allow any former resident to return to the jurisdiction of either country, and any resident who wanted to leave to take his property with him. A special annex guaranteed full equality

[16] *Yugoslav Review,* III, 4 (April 1954), p. 4.

to the Slovenes who would now be in Italy and the Italians who would now be in Yugoslavia, and set up machinery to enforce it.

Both governments had given up their most extreme demands, and the solution met with only a lukewarm reception in both countries. But elsewhere in the west, observers hailed it as a great triumph, since it removed the most dangerous cause of tension still remaining between Yugoslavia and the west. The western powers were careful to call it a *de facto* solution only, in order to answer the expected Soviet protest in the UN. But in its new effort to heal the breach with Yugoslavia, the USSR announced that the Trieste settlement was a move toward peace, which it would not oppose. The way now lay open for Italian adherence to the Balkan pact, or Yugoslav adherence to NATO. A dangerous gap in western defenses had been plugged. The passage westward had been stormy but had been virtually completed.

WITH THE SOVIET BLOC

With the eastern European countries, Yugoslav foreign relations continued to be extremely bad until after the death of Stalin in March 1953. The USSR continued to build up the satellite armies far beyond treaty strength. The million or so men disposed for attack in the satellites conducted military maneuvers along the Yugoslav frontiers in 1951 and 1952. The Yugoslavs officially recorded a total of 937 "frontier incidents" in 1950, 1,517 in 1951, and 2,390 in 1952. In the period between the break of June 1948 and the *détente* of 1953, the Yugoslavs gave the figure of "about one hundred" soldiers and civilians killed on the borders. The Cominform governments expelled more Yugoslav diplomats; the Bucharest embassy was shut down for eight months in 1950, and the Tirana embassy was not reopened after being shut in May 1950. We have already noticed the constant trials of alleged espionage agents for the Cominform bloc.

The Hungarians signed in August 1949 an agreement to participate in mixed border commissions to investigate incidents, but abrogated the agreement in October, less than three months later. They rejected two later efforts of the Yugoslavs to re-establish such commissions. Similarly, the Bulgarians did not abide by their agreement of the same sort, reached in 1950. The Rumanians would not permit the delivery of mail or parcels from Yugoslavia, after interrupting all rail traffic between the two countries in January 1950. As late as March 1953, the Albanians kept demanding that the Yugoslavs return a Lake Scutari tugboat and its crew, which had been wrecked in a storm, and ignored the kind offer of the Yugoslavs to hand over the wreckage of the boat and the corpse of the skipper. The Yugoslav White Book of 1951, detailing most of the incidents down to that time, was debated in the UN General Assembly, which recommended that the governments concerned conduct their relations in accordance with the UN Charter, conform to ordinary diplomatic usages, and settle frontier disputes by mixed commissions or other peaceful means. All of this the Yugoslavs alone were ready to perform, and the Cominform bloc alone voted against the resolution.

Certain new issues arose between the Soviet bloc and Yugoslavia in these years, and certain old ones reappeared in all their old trappings. Belgrade, for example, early in 1950 charged that the USSR was mistreating the Lusatian "Sorbs" or Wends in Eastern Germany because they sympathized with Yugoslavia in the Cominform dispute. The Communists in Eastern Germany had therefore, according to the Yugoslav Radio, cut down the representation of the Sorbs in the diets of Saxony and Brandenburg, expelled them from the "Social Unity Party," and broken up their youth group to integrate it with the German youth group.

With Bulgaria, political warfare was constant, Radio Sofia having begun anti-Yugoslav broadcasts in Macedonian in January 1949. The Yugoslavs laid down at least as steady and effective a propaganda barrage on Macedonian matters as did the Bulgarians. Early in 1950, for example, Belgrade changed the name of the Yugoslav Macedonian town of Tsaribrod, very close to the Bulgarian frontier, to Dimitrovgrad, after the late lamented Bulgarian Communist leader, whose friendship they continued to claim. At the same time they expressed a pious hope that the frontier between the two portions of Macedonia would disappear. This of course outraged the Bulgarians, who shrieked blasphemy at the top of their editorial voices, doubtless much to the enjoyment of Belgrade. Later in the spring of 1950, Tito in a press interview declared that he believed the internal situation in Bulgaria and Albania was too threatening to permit either country to attack Yugoslavia. He added blandly that he could not comment on the affairs of the other satellite states, because Yugoslavia maintained no intelligence services behind their frontiers. The implication, of course, was that in Bulgaria and Albania, Yugoslav agents were busy night and day sending in reports. No doubt this was true, but the admission was hardly calculated to reassure the neighbors.

The Bulgarian press meanwhile adopted the practice of referring to the Yugoslav Federal People's Republic of Macedonia as the "western Bulgarian regions," to which Belgrade replied that the Sofia Cominformists had turned all Bulgaria into a mere Danubian province of the USSR, strongly implying that they had assassinated Dimitrov and Kolarov to make way for tools of Moscow. The Bulgarians passed a "nationality law" conferring (the Yugoslav government said "imposing") Bulgarian citizenship on Yugoslav citizens residing in Bulgaria, and eliciting protests from Belgrade. Djilas and others made regular reference to Pirin Macedonia in their speeches, declaring that the unfortunate inhabitants had the right to achieve a peaceful union with the Macedonians in Yugoslavia. The Macedonian Cultural Organization in Bulgaria passed resolutions declaring that only the inhabitants of Pirin Macedonia were free, the Yugoslav Macedonian republic being the "negation of independence," and urging the elimination of Titoism, which they equated with the IMRO. Though such information was a secret, there were surely

Macedonians on each side of the frontier who sympathized with the power on the other side. Thus the Yugoslavs dismissed three of their Macedonian Republic officials in March 1949.

Similarly, the Yugoslavs maintained pressure on Albania. In Kossovo-Metohiya, the Albanian minority was perpetually holding meetings and pronouncing routine condemnations of the Hoxha regime. Belgrade gave much publicity to the enthusiasm for Tito allegedly felt by his Albanian subjects. Two hundred and twenty-seven thousand Albanians were members of the People's Front in 1949. There were 70,000 Albanian "anti-fascist women." Of the 2,646 members of the Kos-Met soviets in March 1950, 1,652 were Albanians. In June 1953, it was announced that 170,000 illiterate Albanians in Kos-Met had learned to read and write their own language. A committee of Albanians, set up to oppose Hoxha and to spread propaganda for an Albania linked to Yugoslavia, included our old acquaintance Dushan Mugosha, one of the Yugoslav founders of the Albanian Communist Party in 1941. There was also an Association of Albanian Political Refugees in Yugoslavia, which held a meeting in Skoplye to draft a program in October 1952. But here again, there were defections both ways. A. Lleshi, an Albanian member of the Yugoslav national assembly, fled to Albania in 1950, and reported that life in his home district of Debar (Dibra) was grim indeed, and that the Minister of the Interior of the Macedonian People's Republic, Marko, had put constant pressure on him to recruit spies to perform espionage in Albania.

Similarly, on the Danube commission, the Cominform countries, which could not exclude the Yugoslavs because they controlled a vital stretch of the river, gave them as little scope as possible. Their authorities delayed Yugoslav vessels and molested their crews. They closed Yugoslav shipping agencies and evicted the personnel connected with them. In 1952, the Yugoslavs tried but failed to replace the secretary of the commission, who was (of course) a Russian, and who ran everything his own way, by a director who should be responsible to all eleven members. The Cominform states refused to pay their dues for ships passing through the Iron Gates, although the Yugoslavs warned that this practice represented a "threat to navigation."

It was, however, along the Danube waterway, vital to the economic life of all the riparian states, that there appeared the first signs of reconciliation, at least in practical matters, between the Yugoslavs and the Cominform. After a whole series of incidents, a joint Yugoslav-Rumanian commission, appointed at the suggestion of Yugoslavia, began to meet in April 1953, holding its sessions at the Iron Gates, alternatively at Orșova on the Rumanian shore and at Tekiya on the Yugoslav shore. In May, the commission reached an agreement that the two countries would have the same number of employees in the group that controlled shipping through the Iron Gates, and that the land-based locomotive-powered tugging service on the Yugoslav shore would be made available for Rumanian ships. At the ninth session of the Danube commission, meeting in Galați in December 1953, the Yugoslavs were reconcilled with the other members of the commission. A Yugoslav was elected Secretary, thus obtaining the post whose existence in Russian hands Belgrade had so long opposed. The commission chose a Hungarian president and a Bulgarian vice-president, and moved its headquarters to Budapest. Whether or not all this represented Soviet delegation to the satellites of immediate control over the Danube, it was clearly an advance toward the normalizing of relations and the lessening of tension between Yugoslavia and the Soviet bloc.

In the summer of 1953 also, the USSR proposed to Yugoslavia that the two countries once again exchange ambassadors. The Yugoslavs consented, but commented officially that the step only proved that Soviet policy since 1948 had been a failure, and did not indicate that the Russians were any better disposed toward Yugoslavia than they had been. Soon afterwards Moscow removed the restrictions which it had imposed on the movements of Yugoslav diplomats within the Soviet Union, leaving frontier regions only closed, and Belgrade reciprocated. Rumors began to circulate to the effect that Yugoslavia was returning to her old allegiance, or that a secret agreement between the USSR and Yugoslavia had been concluded, and Tito took many occasions to deny that he had any such intentions or commitments.

Quietly, Yugoslav-Bulgarian and Yugoslav-Hungarian commissions were set up to deal with border incidents, and to regulate traffic across frontiers. In January 1954, Tito expressed again his willingness to negotiate all pending questions with his neighbors. He was gratified at the re-establishment of full diplomatic relations, and pleased with the agreements so far concluded, but he pointed to a number of serious matters remaining unsolved: the return of Yugoslav prisoners held by the Cominform countries, and the fate of the Serb and Croatian minorities in Rumania, where they had been subject to brutal deportations.[17] Moreover, even railway communications had not yet been truly "normalized," since the Orient Express was not yet crossing Bulgaria, but followed the route Belgrade-Saloniki-Istanbul. The process of normalization continued during 1954, Belgrade reaching frontier agreements with Bulgaria and Hungary in April, signing a barter agreement with Hungary to the amount of $2,500,000 in May, accepting a Rumanian Ambassador in June, agreeing on the reopening of rail communications with Rumania in July, and signing a barter agreement to the amount of $3,500,000 of goods each way with Czechoslovakia in August, to run until the end of 1954. A trade agreement with the USSR was concluded in the autumn of 1954; but when some voices in the west expressed their alarm lest this presage a return of Yugoslavia to the Soviet bloc, Yugoslav officials pointed out that they had denied the USSR the strategic materials which the Russians sought, and had themselves been denied Soviet wheat. In October 1954, on the occasion of the tenth anniversary of the liberation of Belgrade, Yugoslav and Soviet officials together participated in a ceremony honoring the war-dead, while the Soviet press for the first time since mid-1948 spoke warmly of the Yugoslav war

[17] See below, Chapter 13.

effort. It was clear that Malenkov and his colleagues were making strenuous efforts to erase the incredible blunders of Stalin. They were wooing Tito assiduously, as their decision not to protest the Trieste settlement also showed.

The easing of tension and the gradual resumption of economic relations surely came in part at least as a result of the improved power-position of Yugoslavia since the conclusion of the Balkan Pact, which had thus already performed one valuable service. The change was also to be viewed as part of a general Soviet policy of limited relaxation following the death of Stalin, the installation of collective leadership, and the elimination of Beria. Could it be interpreted as a sign that Yugoslavia was retreating from the association with the west, which alone had preserved its existence during the years of Cominform hostility and menace? In the late summer of 1954, when France rejected the European Defense Community, Tito issued an official pronouncement favoring the acceptance of western Germany by the North Atlantic Treaty powers. He took occasion also to remark that relations between Yugoslavia and the Soviet bloc could never again be as warm as in the years after the war. Soon afterward, however, he began to talk of "coexistence."

Since 1948 he had successfully performed an extraordinary balancing act, in crossing the gulf of hostility between the Soviet bloc and the western bloc. The west had helped him by advancing aid without strings. But had the west attached strings, there is little doubt that he would have refused the aid, whatever the consequences. He did not like to trust the west fully; his whole education, his Communist beliefs, his native Yugoslav suspicion and lack of perspective with regard to the position of Yugoslavia in the world combined to prevent it. But would he ever fully trust the east again, having learned more thoroughly than any other man the nature of the strings which Moscow attached to Soviet aid, and having witnessed the disintegration overnight of "brotherly" relations with his neighbors when Moscow spoke the word? At the time this book was written, it seemed likely that Tito would use his bargaining power to the best possible advantage.

WITH THE SOCIALISTS AND NEUTRALISTS

But for ideological companionship, so to speak, the Yugoslav leadership looked neither to the west nor to the Soviet bloc. Denouncing both impartially, it looked toward anti-Stalinist leftists, "socialists" and "neutralists" everywhere in the world, but especially in Asia. (The state visit of Haile Selassie to Tito in 1954 was piquant, but not likely to prove important, and was clearly intended to dramatize to Italy the solidarity of two old "anti-fascists.") A good many well-known individuals in the western countries emerged as "Titoites" in the years following the break. Konni Zilliacus, Finnish-born maverick left-wing member of the British Labor Party, paid repeated visits to Yugoslavia, wrote favorably about Tito, and enjoyed a personal friendship with the Yugoslav leaders. Jean Cassou, former intellectual leader of the French Communist Party, praised Tito in print. O. John Rogge, once Assistant Attorney-General of the United States, and leading figure in the 1948 Communist-manipulated campaign of Henry Wallace for the presidency, took service with Tito as an official propagandist for Yugoslavia in the United States. Wallace himself, recovering from his rough experiences at the hands of the Stalinists, and sadder if not wiser, endorsed Tito. Fritz Sternberg, veteran anti-Stalinist "socialist," wrote for Yugoslav official propaganda organs. Relations with the leaders of the British Labor Party were also close, both with the Attlee group and the Bevanite insurgents. Jules Moch, stanchly anti-Communist French Socialist, wrote a detailed and thoroughly uncritical book describing and praising the new Yugoslavia.[18]

It was, however, in Asia that Yugoslavia looked for entire countries which might devolop along "Titoite" lines. Djilas and Deputy Foreign Minister Alesh Bebler attended the Asian Socialist Conference in Rangoon, Burma, in January 1953. Djilas lectured the Burmese, visited India and Pakistan, and on his return to Belgrade declared:

> in Asia, particularly in India, Burma, and Indonesia, there exist very strong fighting forces which are capable of fighting not only against the old colonialism but also against Cominformism and Soviet hegemony. These forces are manifesting a high political consciousness on internal questions, particularly in the detecting of the importance of the peasant question, and on external questions . . . in their struggle for independence and equal relations. . . .[19]

He praised the Asian Socialists for creating their own organization, and for their willingness at the same time to coöperate with the Second International, provided that that body should take a more decisive stand against "colonialism." He hailed their "strong sympathies" with Yugoslavia, and saluted them for understanding how "anti-socialist" the USSR really was, and for "taking from the hands of Stalinism the banner of socialism and anti-colonialism." At about the same time, a Yugoslav good-will mission including the Macedonian Premier Kolishevsky visited India on the invitation of the Indian government, which received them cordially. The Indian Minister of Finance compared the two countries' struggle for independence, their efforts to raise their standards of living, and their policies toward a multilingual population. In June 1954, Madame Pandit, Chairman of the UN Assembly and Nehru's sister, visited Yugoslavia.

In the United Nations, Yugoslav policy pursued a policy of support for these distant Asian nations, with whom it was linked chiefly by a fellow-feeling for people who did not want to "belong" either to the western or the eastern power-bloc. In April 1953, it warmly supported the Burmese in the question of Chinese nationalist forces active on Burmese soil. Indeed, it was thoroughly hostile to the Chinese Nationalist Government on Formosa, without supporting the Chinese Communist regime in Peking. It followed the

[18] *Yougoslavie, terre d'expérience* (Monaco: Editions du Rocher, 1953).
[19] *Yugoslav Review*, II, 2 (February 1953), p. 9.

Indian position on Korea, supporting neither the Communists nor Syngman Rhee. Remote though Yugoslavia was in tradition, in language, and in space from Burma, India, and Indonesia, it was in these Asian countries that the Yugoslavs recognized peoples whose economic conditions they understood, and whose ideology they shared. If the west were to succeed in Asia in its policy of supporting strong independent native movements which were stanchly anti-Soviet, it might well find Yugoslav policy and sentiment a considerable asset, not because Yugoslav power or prestige could reach out into the Indian Ocean, but because recent Yugoslav history provided a reassuring example of a country which the west had helped but had not tried to dominate.

3. The Economy

AGRICULTURE

It was, of course, not only in the sphere of domestic and foreign politics that the Yugoslav liberation from Soviet dictation offered opportunities for the development of fresh policies. The Yugoslav economy too now provided a field for experiment and a new approach. Indeed, the institution of the workers' councils in the factories, as we saw, though based on a revised ideology, and leading directly to political and constitutional change, was in its inception just as much an economic as a political move, since it initiated the entire concept of decentralization and removed the planning function at least in detail, from the hands of the central government. So too, in foreign affairs, coöperation with the west began with economic aid, and continued to depend upon its continuation, while the tempo and nature of the aid itself affected the development of the economy and the plans of the Yugoslav leadership for the future development of agriculture and industry.

The "decentralization" of planning left to the Federal Economic Council the function of fixing the general production targets in both industry and agriculture, on the basis of information furnished it by the competent authorities in the individual republics. This information in turn was ideally to be prepared on the basis of data passed up from smaller administrative units, which should have obtained them from the individual enterprises. The Five Year Plan of 1947–1951 was at first "extended" by two years in 1951, but thereafter single-year plans were adopted for 1952 and subsequent years. Unlike the satellite regimes, the Yugoslav government published statistics in absolute figures. How reliable they were it was not possible to say with certainty.

In agricultural policy, change was long in coming. Committed before the break with Moscow to a policy of collectivization, and in June 1948 further advanced along the road to collectivization than any other satellite, Yugoslavia did not slow down the program automatically after the break, but stepped it up considerably, almost as if the leadership believed the Cominform charge that it had been too lax in the villages. The year 1949 was the year of greatest pressure to collectivize, and, though the pace slackened in 1950, the process continued. The accompanying figures told the story, so full of anguish for the peasantry.[20]

TABLE 1

Year	Number of Collectives	Households	Hectarage
1948	1,318	60,158	323,984
1949 (1st quarter)	3,046	166,287	868,798
1949 (2nd quarter)	4,535	226,087	1,241,065
1949 (3rd quarter)	5,246	255,733	1,400,000
1949 (4th quarter)	6,625	340,739	1,839,978
1950	6,968	418,659	2,226,166

In 1949 alone, the number of collectives, the number of households, and the hectarage of the collective sector more than quintupled.[21] The slow-down of the pace in 1950 was explained officially on the grounds that the "coöperative organizations consider that on the present level of agricultural development there are sufficient peasant working coöperatives (i.e., collectives)." By the fall of 1950, there was one in every major village in the country, and it was considered more important to "strengthen" those which already existed than to create new ones. This was shown by the fact that in 1949 the average number of homesteads belonging to each new collective had been only fifty, while in 1950 it was 200.

Yugoslav collectives belonged to four classes. In the first, the peasant contributed his land to the partnership without losing his title to it. He received a share of the income proportional to the amount of land he had brought with him: a form of rent. In the second, the peasant retained title, and received the rent in accordance with the worth of the land, not its size. In the third, he retained title, but relinquished all rent, and received recompense according to his labor. In theory, a peasant could withdraw from any of these three forms of collective after a three-year trial. The fourth was the true Soviet kolkhoz: the peasant lost title to his land, retaining only his homestead and a garden plot, with a few implements and domestic animals. According to official figures, the percentages of the total number of collectives belonging to each type in the summer of 1950 were: type one 8.4 per cent; type two 26.3 per cent; type three 53.7 per cent; and type four, 11.6 per cent. It was the regime's policy to push existing collectives as fast as possible toward type four, a "higher" type. By the summer of 1951, type four was reported to include 15 per cent of the total number.

Behind the statistics lay a story of coercion, intimidation, economic dis-

[20] Conrad, DWJ, p. 33.

[21] Together with the Voyvodina, Macedonia, with 58 per cent of the arable land collectivized, with more than 44 per cent of the number of homesteads, led the provinces in collectivization by January 1950. Even here, however, the independent farmer delivered 60 per cent of the production.

crimination, and violence. Recalcitrant peasants found their delivery-quotas suddenly and outrageously increased, their supplies of seed and fertilizer cut off, and themselves haled off to prison or forced labor camps. Sometimes they lost their land. Sometimes they were taken away from it at critical times to participate in "voluntary" labor projects. Again, it was the drought of 1950, perhaps together with the ideological shifts, that led to the first changes from the Soviet pattern.

The first intimation of change came in September with the news that the Machine Tractor Stations (MTS), those characteristic features of Soviet-type agriculture, were being "decentralized." From the "people's authorities," they were being transferred to the "specially elected bodies of the coöperatives," i.e., the workers' councils of the individual collective. In effect, this meant the dissolution of the MTS, one of the chief means by which party and government exercise political control in the countryside of an ordinary Communist state. Figures and claims soon began to appear: 1,350 tractors in the Voyvodina (one of the heavily collectivized areas, and one of the few where tractor farming could be really profitable) had been turned over to the collectives. All the MTS in Bosnia-Hertsegovina had been abolished, and their machinery distributed.

But the measure did not contribute to the popularity of the collective farm. Pressure to form new collectives ceased, except in Macedonia. The figure for the end of June 1951 was 6,994 collectives, 429,784 households, and 2,595,000 hectares. Though this was a peak, the regime now faced a full-fledged crisis, as the peasants in collectives of types one, two, and three reached the end of their three-year "trial" period, and in droves petitioned to get out. By the sheer use of terror, the state stopped what would surely have been a mass flight from the collectives. Both the peasants and the lawyers who drew their petitions suffered arrest and violence. In his recent book, Professor Dragnich reports an interview in 1952 with a Yugoslav official who admitted that in 1951 the state had used "administrative measures" to prevent the peasant from taking advantage of his legal right to withdraw from the collectives. Even at the time, official pronouncements gave the outside world a clue to what was happening. Speaking at Skoplye, capital of a province about 60 per cent collectivized, Boris Kidrich for example on July 16, 1951 denounced those "enemies" who were trying to undermine the "coöperative movement." It was a mistake to believe that the government would tolerate a return to capitalist agriculture. Collectives were an economic necessity. In the future their members would enjoy enormous economic advantages, because they would be issued special vouchers with which to buy consumers' goods. So far, this had not proved possible because of the shortcomings in the Five Year Plan, for which the Soviet Union and its satellites were largely blamed. This was supposed to have been completed by the end of 1951, but now received a two-year extension.

Toward the end of 1951 came a series of decrees and announcements which proved the regime's stubborn intention to continue but to modify its policy of collectivization. On November 2, a decree provided that a collective could acquire adjacent private lands and incorporate them, compensating the owner. This was an effort to enable the collectives to mass scattered holdings, and round out their properties. Supposedly, seizures would take place only where necessary for rational agriculture. All care was to be taken not to "disturb" the owner unduly; but it is hard to imagine what could disturb him more than the loss of his farm. It was further announced that collectives would be formed only in appropriate regions, "where conditions warrant," a reference to the excess of zeal which had led to the creation of collectives in the limestone regions of Dalmatia and elsewhere where the terrain was not suited to large-scale farming. All members were to obtain remuneration in cash as well as a share of the profits, a distinct modification of types three and four.

Indeed, the collectives already formed in the karst areas were dissolved. Elsewhere, the regime tried to induce the members of collectives to stay where they were, and to make it attractive for the private peasant to join, by exempting collective farmers from income-tax payments, limiting their obligations to a 3 per cent levy on the harvest, extending free health service to them but not to private farmers, and similar measures. Perhaps most important, the hated system of compulsory deliveries was now abolished late in October 1951, both for collectives and for private farmers.

This measure was accompanied by a series of other economic enactments: rationing was abandoned, and was replaced by a system of issuing coupons to those performing "socially useful" work, who were allowed to buy some consumers' goods at one-fifth free market prices. The cost of transport and of other public services was to rise sharply, while the prices of agricultural and industrial goods were to fall. The policy of deflation included a cut in investment, an effort to withdraw money from circulation, and shifts in the system of distribution, with a view to marketing goods at lowered prices, in an effort to raise the purchasing power of the population.

Thus the regime now abandoned its system of price controls, and decided to let prices seek their own level, promising to intervene only if the standard of living should be threatened. The decision was connected not only with the agricultural crisis but also with the general wish to decentralize and to encourage competition in the reorganized industries. Soon afterward, the dinar was devalued, a measure long overdue. The new rate was 300 to the dollar, instead of 50; the gold content was also one-sixth of the former figure: 2.96223 milligrams of fine gold as against 17.7734. Though the ratio to the dollar was still artificially high, the move was a step toward realism. The decentralization of the Ministry of Foreign Trade, and the division of its work between the Federal Economic Council (made up of representatives from the republican ministries), and the Ministries of Finance and of Foreign Affairs, also reflected the new philosophy.

Free market prices, which had been about sixteen times the prewar level, now began to fall, and some forms of private shops were reported opening in Belgrade. New wage decrees, setting the figure at twenty to thirty dinars per hour for workers and 3,800–6,000 per month for employees did not come into effect until April 1952. The peasant still sold his produce largely to the state-run coöperative for purchasing and marketing, and he still was vulnerable to the whim of the local Communist bureaucrat who happened to be fixing his taxes. Collectives were encouraged to open their own food-shops in the nearest town. By January 1952, their number had fallen to 6,908 with 2,580,000 hectares, a decline of 86 collectives and 15,000 hectares since the year before.

The drought of 1952 was worse than the drought of 1950, and the regime was forced to admit that its agricultural policies had failed. The five-year average of grain production was below the prewar level. But for the first time alarming news was released about the livestock position. The value of livestock production in 1951 was fifteen billion dinars less than the average prewar level. And here was the crux: though the yields both of grain and of industrial crops save for sugar beet were substantially higher on the collective farms than on private farms,

> agricultural experts assert that the process of formation of coöperatives during the last two years has had certain negative consequences especially on the development of stock-raising. They say, for instance, that in Serbia almost one-fourth of the total number of livestock, which the peasant did not put into the coöperative and could not feed, was destroyed.[22]

Here the regime itself, in one of its own propaganda organs, was found admitting that the Yugoslav peasant of the late 1940's and early 1950's had done just what the Russian peasant had done in the late 1920's and early 1930's. On a smaller scale, the Yugoslav crisis reflected the earlier crisis in the USSR. Though in other publications the regime tried to blame the decline in the number of livestock on the failure of the peasant to sow enough acreage to fodder crops — which essentially was the fault of the regime itself — the true cause for this disaster was the bitter unpopularity of the policy of collectivization, and the peasant's determined passive resistance to it.

The regime responded to the new crisis — or rather the enhancement of the continual crisis — in a variety of ways. The 1952 drought, it was estimated, had cost 100 billion dinars, some 15 per cent of the whole national income. Prices, which had fallen in 1951, began to rise sharply once again. The Federal Economic Council decided to shift investments for 1953 from heavy industry into agriculture and housing, limiting capital investments to essential hydro-electric plants and transportation.

In line with decentralization, the regime tried to "democratize" the management of the individual collective. As with the individual factory, the individual collective farm was now to "reach its own decisions," and "even the Plenum of the Coöperative Federation, the highest organization of the

[22] *Yugoslav Review,* I, 8 (October 1952), p. 6.

association of coöperatives" was not allowed to intervene except by recommendation. The government limited its own role, in theory, to the granting of credits, and the sending of experts. The presidency of each collective, which had been a paid post, was now made an honorary one, and the president was to work in the fields alongside the other members. The members were to elect the management in a general assembly, and the manager would be an employee responsible to the president and the members. He might be dismissed at any time. Thus the regime strove to apply in the collectives the principles of the "workers' councils" long since established in the factories.

But it was clear that the modification of Soviet practice had not progressed far enough to overcome the crisis or to satisfy the peasantry. The private peasant still tilled more than two-thirds of the arable land in Yugoslavia. He was necessary to the regime, but the regime had been persecuting him. The peasants in the collectives wanted to leave, but the regime had not been allowing them to do so, except in the special case of collectives formed in regions where they were uneconomic. The 1952 drought and peasant resistance had led to famine conditions, and dependence on American aid. The American taxpayer surely sympathized with the Yugoslavs, who would have starved without assistance; many if not most Americans could understand the policy of assisting Tito to hold out against the USSR and its satellites. But it was unlikely that many Americans realized that much of the assistance on its way to Yugoslavia at their expense might not have been necessary, even if the droughts had taken place, had it not been for the regime's doctrinaire insistence on aping Soviet models in the countryside.

The decree of March 30, 1953 represented another major retreat. This law allowed any peasant to leave the collective who wished to do so, taking his land, livestock, and implements with him. But he could not claim as his own any land, livestock, or implements that had been "attained by collective effort." Nor could any farm buildings so "attained" be assigned to individual peasants leaving the collectives. Moreover, he could not claim as his own any land he might have obtained through the "land reform" of 1946. This would be public property. Since this land had been distributed initially to proprietors of dwarf holdings to make their holdings larger, they were now left, if they chose to withdraw from the collective, with their pre-reform dwarf holding once again. Any peasant who might withdraw would have to reimburse the collective for any improvements which might have been made on the property he had contributed and was now removing. He also found himself saddled with a percentage of the collective's debt corresponding to the percentage of the collective's total holdings represented by his property. Since no peasant would have the cash to pay off such obligations, he was obliged to take a mortgage on his own land.

The regime thus strove to take away with one hand the opportunity it was offering with the other, and the press abounded with declarations that the new decree represented not the abandonment but the strengthening of

"Socialist agriculture." Yet the peasantry thronged to get out of the collectives, despite the new obligations they would assume, and the disadvantage of returning to private farming in a weaker position than the one they had enjoyed at the moment when they abandoned it. The regime said that it expected a good many "coöperatives" to shut down: "Artificial shoring up of uneconomic coöperatives by government subsidies and special assistance has been found to be opposed to sound and realistic agricultural policy," a thing which any American undergraduate student of agriculture could have told the Communist planners from the beginning. By May 1953, the number of collectives had sunk to 4,821, fewer than at any time since mid-1949, and the hectarage was given in percentage figures as 19.6 per cent of the arable, as against claims of 22 per cent in February 1952. The press declared that in the Voyvodina (44 per cent of the households collectivized) some peasants had left the collectives, but farming continued normal. In Serbia proper, many farmers had "misunderstood" the decree, and had left the collectives. In Croatia, the decree was "well-received," but most of the peasants had left the collectives the previous year. The same was true of Bosnia-Hertsegovina. In Macedonia, the peasants were "trying to discover where their best interests lie."

The double-talk did not conceal the exodus. By 1954, the regime declared that more than 2,000,000 hectares of land out of the 2,600,000 which had once been collectivized, were back in private hands. Of the 9,782,000 hectares of arable land in Yugoslavia, only 600,000 were still collectivized; about 430,000 were state property, the rest was privately owned.

The regime had not abandoned collectivization and mechanization as its goals. On May 27, 1953, it passed a second decree, which went a considerable distance toward nullifying its pretense at a reform of collectivization practices. The new law set an upper limit of ten hectares, about twenty-five acres, on the land which an individual peasant household might own. All land above ten hectares held by individual peasants was to be confiscated by the state and to become part of the community and state "reserves." This measure simultaneously did away with any substantial private holdings which might have survived the regime's previous enactments, and aimed to level the size of peasant's holdings down to the point where individual peasants would one day have to join a collective out of sheer need.

The language in which the decree was couched clearly revealed that the Communists had not fundamentally altered their long-range intentions. The law aimed "to realize the principle of the Constitution that the land belongs to him who tills it, to protect the working peasant from exploitation, to assure the development of agriculture in accordance with the socialist social order, and to ensure the property rights of the working peasant to the soil which he works himself."[23] It would "create socialist relationships in the villages," and prevent the growth of "capitalist tendencies in agricul-

[23] *Sluzhbeni List* (Belgrade), 22 (May 27, 1953).

ture." A household might continue to use its surplus of land over ten hectares until it had actually been confiscated. The district people's councils could permit very large families, who could not survive if their surplus over ten hectares were removed, to keep this surplus. In regions where the soil was bad, or in *zadrugas* of several families, the republican assemblies could raise the limit to fifteen hectares or even beyond. The decree did not apply to vineyards.

The land to be confiscated would in each district be controlled by the people's council, from whose decisions appeals might be taken to the republican executive councils. In each district, the people's council was to choose a five-man commission, whose chairman would be one of the judges of the district court; while in each republic there would be a republican commission of the land reserves, with a president, who must be a member of the republic's executive council, a vice-president, and the necessary members chosen by the executive council. All this new machinery — in a land which was allegedly striving to cut down on bureaucracy — would hand out the confiscated lands to villages, communities, agricultural coöperatives, and other agricultural institutions. The decree seemed to empower these bodies to turn over the land confiscated from private peasants to collectives already in existence. If the institution which had obtained the land should cease to exist, the land would revert to the reserves. Otherwise, it was inalienable, could not be exchanged or sold, except for the purpose of acquiring another piece of land, and then only with the approval of the district people's court.

No land could be confiscated between the dates of October 1 and December 31, so that the owner might bring in the harvest for the last time. Owners would receive compensation varying in amounts between 30,000 and 100,000 dinars, which would be paid them over twenty years, the installments not being taxable. The decree provided machinery for complaints and appeals. Table 2 presents the figures and percentages on the size of Yugoslav private landholdings as of spring 1953 and permits further conclusions to be drawn with regard to the decree.[24]

TABLE 2

Size of Farm in Hectares	Percentage of All Farms	Percentage of Total Area of Yugoslavia	Percentage of Yugoslav Arable	Average Size of Farms Total Area	Average Size of Farms Arable
Under 5	65%	34%	28.2%	2.5	1.9
5–10	21%	31.3%	33.1%	6.9	5.0
10–15	5.6%	14.6%	13.7%	12.3	7.9
Over 15	4.0%	19.4%	14.1%	—	—

The decree thus affected 9.6 per cent of all Yugoslav farms, covering 34 per cent of the total area of the country, and 28 per cent of the arable land. The

[24] *Wissenschaftlicher Dienst Südosteuropa* II, 7/8 (July 31, 1953), p. 150.

average size of the farms over ten hectares was reported to be 16.9 hectares total land and 9.5 hectares arable land. Many of the larger farms were even worked by hired labor.

There were about 90,000 farms in Yugoslavia worked with some hired labor; and it was of course these, whose owners were automatically kulaks in the Communist dictionary, at whom the decree was mainly aimed. The Belgrade district, the district of Banya Luka, and the Voyvodina were the regions with the largest percentages of such large private farms. Experts reckoned that the government could confiscate 200,000 hectares in all from these owners. Though the total land thus acquired was not a large amount, the farms affected were the most productive and advanced of all Yugoslav farms. Nor would the decree help the small holder or the hired farm laborer, since the confiscated land would in no case be given to him.

The decree was clearly just the latest in a series of approaches to collectivization which the regime had tried. Its goals remained unchanged, and the probability seemed high that agricultural crisis would continue, and that the American taxpayer would have to foot the bills. It was all very well to avoid interference in the domestic affairs of a sovereign state, if the sovereign state did not ask you to pay for its follies. Yet, if any American representative had suggested that further aid to Belgrade should depend upon the abandonment of ruinous farm policies, the Yugoslav leaders would have been sure to shriek "imperialism," and moan that the United States had "abandoned" its "temporary" policy of not attaching strings to economic aid, and had thus "unmasked" its wicked intention to dominate the poor small Balkan countries.

In a speech on September 27, 1953, Tito declared that collectivization had been introduced too fast; it had become clear that one could not change people in a few years. But nobody should interpret the decree permitting departure to mean that collectivization had been abandoned. Of 6,000 collectives (the actual figure had been much nearer 7,000), there were only 2,000 left. These would be supported. There were 9,000 tractors in Yugoslavia, but 45,000 were necessary, as were many other sorts of farm machinery. The population of the country was rising at the rate of 300,000 a year, so that in ten years the total would be 20,000,000. Thus agricultural development must now receive priority, and the level of production must rise.

It was of major interest that this declaration of Tito's should have come within a few weeks after the adoption of a "new course" had been announced in the USSR, Hungary, Rumania, and Bulgaria. In the next two chapters we shall consider in detail what this policy meant in the Balkan satellites. Here it is enough to point out that the Communist leaders in all the countries were putting a new emphasis on agricultural development and on consumers' goods. One way or another, all were admitting the failure of past agricultural policies. Tito was doing the same thing.

In the spring of 1954, a propagandist for the regime claimed that the industrial sector of the economy had been so increased that the percentage of those employed in agriculture had dropped from 76.3 per cent of the population in 1939 to 61.7 per cent in 1953. He further indicated by percentage figures certain changes in postwar planting practices, which were translatable into roughly accurate absolute figures. The area of plough-land was the same as before the war (7,552,000 hectares in 1938) but the area planted to fruit trees had increased by about 25 per cent (667,000 hectares in 1938, or about 833,000 in 1954); and pasture-land had increased about 4 per cent (4,379,000 hectares in 1938, or about 4,554,000 hectares in 1954). Cereal crops covered only 89 per cent of their prewar area (6,186,000 hectares in 1938, or about 5,405,540 in 1954, but only 5,115,000 in 1949, 5,177,000 in 1950, and 5,710,000 planned for 1951, showing that the decrease was not voluntary). The area sown to industrial crops had doubled (184,000 hectares in 1938, or about 368,000 in 1954—although other figures gave 447,000 for 1950 and 500,000 for the 1951 plan): the area sown to vegetables by 9 per cent (428,000 hectares in 1938, 466,520 in 1954, 650,000 planned for 1951); and the area sown to fodder crops by 85 per cent (356,000 hectares in 1938, 658,600 in 1954, 840,000 planned for 1951). Intensification had thus clearly begun, along lines recognized to be desirable by all students of Balkan agriculture. But the 1954 figures, even if accurate, showed that the country was still lagging far behind the 1947 Five Year Plan's goals for the year 1951.

The same writer claimed that wheat yields had risen 6.5 per cent (10.8 quintals per hectare in the 1933–1937 period, 11.45 in 1954), potato yields by 20.3 per cent (60.9 quintals per hectare in the 1933–1937 period, about 73 in 1954), sugar beet by 9.5 per cent (178.2 quintals per hectare in 1933–1937, about 195 in 1954). Corn, however, had fallen by 4.8 per cent. All these figures indicated that progress had been painfully and unnecessarily slow, even taking into consideration the disastrous droughts. The investment figures for agricultural development were 5,120,000,000 dinars in 1952, 6,400,000,000 in 1953, and the figure for 1954 was to be 13,056,000,000, or 140 per cent of 1953.

Collectives continued to enjoy special privileges: favorable terms for settling of debts and interest payments on loans, tax rebates, short-term credits to enable the purchase of equipment and fertilizers in the spring, and cash advances to the value of 20 per cent of the crop. But now in 1954 for the first time the private farmer could also obtain credits, from a special fund of 2,300,000,000 dinars set aside for the purpose. Two billion dinars would go for irrigation in Macedonia and in the Voyvodina, where a canal was to be built between the Danube and the Theiss (Tisza). Six billion dinars would go for additional purchases of agricultural machinery.

The "social investment" portion of the budget also set aside 6,600,000,000 dinars for food industry projects, such as silos and mills. The republican budgets were being written with the same shift in emphasis. The regime abandoned as a failure its efforts to tax the real, annual earnings of the individual peasant. Instead, the average earnings of proprietors of farms of given size would be computed for an entire area; and taxes would be levied on the average incomes for their area, their crops, and their size farm. This, the regime hoped, would act as an incentive to higher production and harder work, since, no matter how much a farmer might raise his income, his taxes would not rise until such time as average incomes might be recomputed. Tax yields were expected to be larger by five billion dinars in 1954 than in 1953 (31,500,000,000 as against 26,500,000,000), because of the great amount of land which had been returned to individual private farmers. Finally, a new regulation provided that all economic organizations which used public land were to pay a ground-rent amounting to 6 per cent of the yield. This was apparently designed to influence those who needed to build new buildings to choose as sites the most infertile land available, and to keep the fertile lands under cultivation. One of the major reasons for the entire "new course" in agriculture was the regime's belated recognition that Yugoslavia must continue to export agricultural produce to pay for its imports from the western countries and to reduce the national debt.

INDUSTRY

The repeated agricultural crises, and the eventual modification, though not abandonment, of the policy of collectivization found their counterpart in the failure to achieve the goals of the original Five Year Plan in industry. Much of this was blamed by the regime on the break with the Cominform countries, although aid from the west eventually more than canceled out these losses. Overambitious planning and inefficient execution provided a far sounder explanation. The key electrification plan, for example, saw only eight of the thirty-one hydroelectric power stations in the Five Year Plan completed by 1950. Their annual output of current was 225,000,000 kilowatt hours, but even when this considerable output was added to the new current provided by the building of some new thermal stations, and the enlargement and standardization of old ones, output in 1953 fell far short of the four billion and more kilowatt hours planned for 1951. The figures were: 1949, 2,214 million kilowatt hours; 1950, 2,408 million; 1951, 2,550 million; 1952, 2,700 millon; and 1953, 2,982 million (1,500 million of it hydroelectric). Despite the fact that the electrification plan was lagging far behind an unrealistic goal, the output was going up strikingly. When many of the major installations, such as the often delayed complex at Yablanitsa on the Neretva, should have been completed, the original goal (168 megawatts) of the Five Year Plan would not be out of sight.

Table 3 told the story of production goals and achievements with regard to key industrial raw materials and certain related semifinished items.[25]

[25] Savezni Zavod za Statistiku i Evidenciju, *Indeks*, III, 7 (July 1, 1954), for all figures except plan for 1951; these are from *Five Year Plan* (Belgrade, 1947).

TABLE 3

Thousand Tons	1939	1951 (Plan)	1951 (Actual)	1952	1953	Peak, If Not Shown
Coal	7,032	16,500	12,042	12,092	11,246	12,819 (1950)
Oil	1	450	148	152	172	
Iron ore	667	1,500	582	676	794	878 (1948)
Copper ore	984		1,173	1,264	1,343	
Bauxite	719		484	577	462	
Lead-zinc ore	775		1,189	1,203	1,432	
Pig iron	101	550	248	273	270	
Steel	235	760	434	442	515	
Rolled products	151	570	301	293	320	
Blister copper	42	30	32	32	31	40 (1950)
Electrolytic copper	12	12	14	21	28	
Refined lead	11	65	60	67	71	
Zinc	5	20	13	14	15	
Aluminum (tons)	1,795	13,000	2,828	2,563	2,792	
Cement (thousand tons)	894	2,200	1,159	1,313	1,281	

The figures showed absolute gains over 1939 in every case except bauxite and blister copper. They showed a failure to reach the 1951 plan by 1953 in every case except blister copper, electrolytic copper, and refined lead. Moreover, the key coal industry was not advancing towards the goal. Production had reached twelve million tons in 1949, and had remained roughly the same until 1953, when it declined markedly. Pig iron, rolled steel products, cement, and others also showed signs of leveling off.

In heavy industrial items for which the plan had either not specified goals or whose categories had been altered since 1947, there could be no doubt that considerable advance had been scored. This is shown by Table 4.[26]

TABLE 4

	1939	1950	1953	1951 Plan
Iron castings (tons)	27,833	69,247	66,854	
Steel castings (tons)	1,827	8,238	10,666	
Nails (tons)	13,062	15,970	16,967	
Structural iron plates	6,703	20,279	39,442	
Trucks		826	1,329	6,000
Bicycles		10,895	20,660	50,000

The electrical industry, virtually new since the end of the Second World War, produced in 1953 more than 3,000 tons of transformers, 37,000 radios, and a variety of other types of equipment. The chemical industry considerably surpassed the 1939 level in sulphuric acid, caustic soda, and other key items. The building materials industry reached the peak of its output

[26] Figures from same sources as those in last table.

in 1949, and lagged thereafter in most cases. So did the production of timber.

In textiles, among the light industries, the figures in Table 5 represented the output of important items. These figures showed a failure in every field

TABLE 5

	1939	1951 (Plan)	1951 (Actual)	1952	1953	Peak
Cotton yarn (tons)	18,947	47,400	26,894	25,909	27,720	29,936 (1950)
Cotton fabrics (million square meters)	111	250	122	112	129	161 (1948)
Woolen fabrics (million square meters)	12	24.2	23.3	19.9	17.3	28.7 (1948)
Ready-made outer clothing (million square meters)	1.4		8.5	5.7	5.3	9.2 (1950)
Stockings (thousand pairs)	23,401	20,500	21,141	22,635	18,635	25,916 (1948)
Leather shoes (thousand pairs)	4,208	6,500	6,863	5,375	4,781	9,141 (1949)
Rubber boots	5,154		7,736	7,875	6,464	

to reach the 1951 goals. Moreover, in every case except for rubber boots, the 1953 figure was well below peak production. Not only had the high goals for the plan not been met, but the industries did not seem to be moving toward these goals. Textile shortages plagued the population, and provided one of the major sources of domestic discontent. Selected figures in the food industry were shown by the figures in Table 6.[27] They showed the same general pattern as the figures in textiles and leather.

TABLE 6

	1939	1951 (Plan)	1951 (Actual)	1952	1953	Peak
Sugar (tons)	107,599	230,000	201,050	57,560	172,200	
Vegetable oils (tons)	21,285	75,000	20,127	19,158	26,390	41,053 (1948)
Canned meat (tons)	1,328		3,251	1,845	2,140	
Dry paste	11,147	80,000	24,268	23,857	28,843	
Starches	10,782		9,336	9,410	4,994	
Starch products	3,797		5,894	4,459	4,010	6,393 (1948)

Both light and heavy industry in Yugoslavia in 1953 lagged far behind the goals set in 1947 for 1951. The outlook was that the 1951 targets would not be reached for some years to come. In most cases, they probably could be reached, and in some, no doubt, surpassed. This was not to deny that the regime had certain accomplishments to its credit. The Belgrade-Zagreb highway, 392 kilometers long, was opened for traffic on July 29, 1950. It provided the first link between the Serbian and Croatian capitals, and thus served as a political symbol as well as a key artery. Better communications

[27] Tables 5 and 6 come from the same sources as those above.

between the interior and the coast were still woefully needed. But the extension and improvement of highways, and railways, and the building of power plants was going forward.

The regime suppressed or soft-pedaled the news of its worst failures. Thus it seemed doubtful whether a highly expensive plant designed to make coke from lignite would ever function as expected; the vast sums sunk in the river sands to create the at least temporarily abandoned New Belgrade were not mentioned; and many of the products (tractors, radio tubes, electrical equipment) of the new heavy industry cost much more to produce than it would have cost to buy the better products of the western countries. Professor Dragnich's book contains a large number of specific examples of waste, inefficiency, corruption, and overproduction of low-quality items.

To approach and overtake the original goals for 1951, the regime would need to complete work on the key projects. In electricity these included not only Yablanitsa, but Mavrovo (Macedonia), Zvornik (Serbia), and others. In coal they included the increase of production at the Kreka lignite mine in Bosnia and the Kolubara mine in Serbia, which together would account for more than a quarter of Yugoslav production. Bosnia and Hertsegovina were to become a far more important center for coal-iron, and steel than previously. Though petroleum was being produced only in Croatia and Slovenia, exploration was going forward in Montenegro and Serbia as well; existing refinery capacity was being enlarged. Zenitsa and Yasenitse remained the key iron and steel centers, but were undergoing major expansion. Both the Bor and Maydanpek copper mines were to increase in capacity; and new rolling mills (Sevoyno, Serbia), and aluminum plants (Kidrichevo, Slovenia) were to be opened. The regime had not abandoned its uneconomic plan to produce machinery; indeed a new truck plant and enlarged railway car shops were further planned, as well as new railway lines, and a new port for Bar (Antivari) in Montenegro.

FINANCE: THE BUDGET

Table 7 contains the official Yugoslav budget figures in millions of dinars.[28] In 1952 and after, the dinars are the new devalued dinars with a nominal value of one-sixth of the old ones. The figures for 1950, 1951, and 1952 are planned figures rather than actual figures. Moreover, the 1952 figure

TABLE 7

	1950	1951	1952	1953
Income	172,600	172,662	259,512	878,838
Expenditure	167,600	172,662	259,512	949,337
	5,000	0	0	−50,675

[28] Conrad, DWJ; *East Europe,* January 8, 1953; *Yugoslav Review,* I, 4 (April 1952).

included only the federal budget, omitting republican and local budgets, under which, beginning with the decentralization of that year, vastly larger sums were spent. Nor does the 1952 figure include the amount called for by the year's economic plan for investment in capital construction. The 1952 figure, including republican and local budgets, would total 909,732 million dinars, and we should also add an additional special fund of 156,421 million dinars, for capital construction to be managed by the "economic enterprises together with the state." Thus a total figure for 1952 would properly be 1,066,153 million of the new dinars, or only a little more than the 1951 budget in old dinars nominally worth six times as much. The drought, and, no doubt, over-expenditure on capital construction led to an actual reported 1952 deficit of 9,500 million dinars. The 1953 budget figures show a planned deficit, and include both republican and local budgets as well as the federal budget and the funds for capital construction.

The sources of the federal income for 1952, according to the regime, were as follows: "from the economy" 200,985 million dinars, from the activities of government agencies and institutions 1,317 million dinars, from other sources 415 million, and from foreign loans and aid 56,794 million. The largest item, the income "from the economy," was largely derived from the so-called "rate of accumulation." For each branch of the economy, and often for individual enterprises, the state determined a ratio between the salaries to be paid the workers and a sum to be paid into the treasury. To say, for example, that the "rate of accumulation" in mining was 582 per cent, was to say that for every dinar paid to a worker in the mining industry the state expected a revenue of 5.82 dinars for itself. In 1952, this rate of 582 actually did obtain in mining; that in forestry was 146 per cent (1.46 dinars to the state for every dinar in salaries to forest-workers); that in the textile industry was 200 per cent (two dinars to the state for every one paid to textile workers).

Before 1952, the rate of accumulation varied from plant to plant within a given industry. In that year, it was made uniform for all plants within a given industry, but still varied widely from industry to industry. Much was said by government spokesmen about using the money thus obtained for social purposes, but in fact it was used to meet any expenses which might arise. In June 1953, the regime announced that this was no longer regarded as a proper form of taxation, and that it would be abolished, perhaps as of early 1954. The loss in revenue would be made up by levying interest on fixed and circulating capital, taxing rent (charging state economic enterprises a proportion of the annual worth of the mine or other installation which they worked), and taxing profits and sales: all ordinary capitalist methods. A small portion of the revenues of the regime before the "reforms" came from state loans, to which the population was virtually forced to subscribe. The Yugoslav government in this way raised three billion dinars in 1949 and five in 1950.

As for expenditures, the 1952 federal budget showed the accompanying

TABLE 8

	Millions of Dinars
Defense	200,000
State reserve	21,038
Social security	12,705
Donations to economic branches	9,532
Education and culture	1,705
Public health	1,000
Administration and judiciary	4,797
Donations to underdeveloped republics	8,735
	259,512

figures. Thus almost 80 per cent of the federal budget went for defense. But the budgets of the individual republics were not charged with any portion of this large item. One therefore obtained a more revealing percentage figure of less than 20 per cent if one compared the defense outlay against the *total* budgets of federal government, republics, and localities, plus the special fund for capital investment: 1,066,183 million dinars. The propagandists for the regime called the attention of the public to the relatively small expense for administration which appeared in the federal budget, and hailed this as a sign that the war against "bureaucratization" was being won. They also emphasized the donations from the federal government to the underdeveloped republics, explained the small size of the social security figure by pointing out that the individual republics now largely controlled this item, and indicated that all local bodies from the local people's councils on up to the republican governments were now in charge of their own revenue and expenditures. The 1953 budget showed a substantial drop in the defense item: from 200,000 to 180,000 million dinars. The fund for capital construction had risen from 156,421 million to 167,341 million.

WAGES AND PRICES

In the course of discussing the political and economic developments of the years since 1950, we have had to touch on wage and price policies. By 1953, wages were in theory fixed by the workers' councils in each enterprise, but in fact its schedule of rates had to be approved by the union. The State Federation of Labor Unions had established a scale for most sorts of work, and would not allow substantial deviations from it. It would be rare that the local workers' council would find a job for which a wage scale had not already been fixed. Some workers received hourly pay, some weekly (a forty-eight hour week, plus overtime), some monthly (a 208-hour month), and some were on piece-rates. In addition, those enterprises which succeeded in making profits could distribute them to the workers as extra wages. As soon as the extra pay exceeded the national average by 10 per cent, the enterprise had to pay taxes on its profits, which cut the amount to be distributed.

The national average in mid-1952 was 9,000 dinars a month, or $30.00, at the still substantially unrealistic official rate of exchange. During the first half of 1953, according to the regime's propagandists, a special survey of 800 workers' families in Serbia, with an average number of two children, showed an average monthly income of 17,187 dinars, of which 5,606 dinars represented allowances for the children. The figure for a "white-collar" family was 17,422 dinars, of which 5,434 was allowances for these children. These figures were surely very high "averages" indeed.

Table 9 represents the official prices in dinars of important items, in June 1954.[29] Private advices indicated that the levels were actually much

TABLE 9

	Dinars
Rent (2 rooms and bath) per month	906
1 kilogram bread	29.4
1 kilogram lard	224
1 kilogram pork	239
1 kilogram butter	452
1 kilogram sugar	145
1 liter milk	31.8
1 egg	11.9
1 pair shoes	2,534
1 ready-made suit	9,900 (1952)
1 man's shirt (cotton)	1,102
1 pair socks	119
1 kilogram soap (washing)	158

higher. These prices, which had leveled downward during the second half of 1953, after reaching even higher levels as a result of the drought of 1952, showed that for a city-dweller rent was low (but accommodations were extremely scarce). Food-prices, though high, were in most cases not out of reach for a regularly employed worker or employee, and the peasants did not need to go hungry. But the children's allowances were cut in mid-1953, which sharply reduced the workers' and employees' incomes. And textile prices were exorbitant, putting even absolute necessities beyond the reach of the workers, and especially of the peasants, whose cash reserves were, as always, extremely limited. Only American aid and the importation of foodstuffs had averted a still worse crisis. Yet, even these measures only met an emergency and did nothing to meet the basic problems of the economy. It seemed clear that the standard of living of the individual Yugoslav was in 1954 lower than it had been before the outbreak of World War II.

[29] All figures except the suit from *Indeks,* III, 7 (July 1954), pp. 38–39. Suit cost as of 1952 from Dragnich, p. 255.

FOREIGN TRADE

Table 10 shows the value of Yugoslav foreign trade in 1949 and the years since in millions of dinars, with all data for 1951 and subsequent years computed in new dinars (six to one of the old).[30] The unfavorable balance in each year was substantial, in 1951 and 1953 amounting to more than the entire value of Yugoslav exports.

TABLE 10

	1949	1950	1951	1952	1953	1954 (1st five months)
Exports	10,193	7,930	53,618	73,958	55,794	25,285
Imports	15,136	11,790	114,860	111,925	118,591	40,328
	−4,943	−3,860	−61,242	−37,967	−62,797	−15,043

Table 11 shows the value in millions of dinars of Yugoslav foreign trade by countries in 1953, and the first five months of 1954.[31] (See opposite page.)

The figures for imports in this table included the amounts of aid received from the United States, Great Britain, and France. They showed that Yugoslavia had a generally unfavorable balance of trade not only with the industrialized states of the west, but also with such less industrialized countries as Iraq, Malaya, and Brazil, from which cotton, rubber, and coffee were imported. Only with Trieste, the Balkan partners, Greece and Turkey, and the African countries was the balance favorable. It was interesting also that, despite the ideological sympathies we have noted for India, Burma, and Indonesia, trade with these countries was as yet relatively insignificant, and the regime's statisticians lumped them and others together as "other Asian states." There were as yet no official figures showing the values of the renewed trade with the Cominform bloc, but we have observed that the initial barter agreements were for small amounts.

Table 12 showed the value of exports and imports in 1952 and 1953 by commodities in millions of dinars, according to the international and Yugoslav classifications.[32] (See page 448.)

The drought was clearly reflected in the rise of food imports and the fall of exports in 1953 over 1952. A study of the table showed how far from self-sufficient Yugoslavia still was in coal, oil, and ferrous metallurgy. It was the nonferrous metals and the timber, in addition to the food surpluses which might be expected in good years (with rational farming), on which the country would for many years need to depend for exports. But that the trade balance might be improved within a few years by the development of native heavy industry and the consequent lowering of import needs was also clear.

[31] *Indeks,* III, 2 (February 1954), p. 30, and III, 7 (July 1954), p. 32.
[32] *Indeks,* III, 2 (February 1954), p. 31.

TABLE 11

Foreign Trade in 1953 (Millions of Dinars)

	1953		1954 (1st 5 months)	
	Exports	Imports	Exports	Imports
Netherlands	1,504	4,036	882	1,021
Austria	3,511	6,261	1,936	2,633
Belgium	646	3,725	263	1,063
Great Britain	6,421	7,406	2,745	3,787
Italy	7,261	8,291	2,942	2,715
West Germany	9,279	20,714	4,751	7,167
Denmark	241	361	103	690
France	1,900	8,930	1,226	2,683
Switzerland	1,957	1,728	880	1,008
Sweden	492	1,847	182	342
Trieste	1,384	187	533	149
Greece	1,767	673	1,315	285
Turkey	6,734	3,756	3,045	3,615
Other Europ. countries	282	468	274	170
Israel	514	54	194	143
Iraq	87	2,376	3	973
Malaya	2	491	1	229
Syria	348	. . .	160	61
Other Asian states	478	365	277	160
Algiers	295	74	70	36
Egypt	1,069	914	186	256
South Africa	48	266	1	125
Other African states	332	77	245	152
Canada	17	2,760	22	5
U.S.A.	7,874	40,748	2,557	9,948
Argentina	106	161	316	337
Brazil	488	1,025	599	213
Paraguay	140	. . .	44	. . .
Other American states	122	144	39	203
Australia	3	434	2	152
N. Zealand			6	7
Totals	55,392	118,272	25,285	40,328

[30] Savezni Zavod za Statistiku i Evidenciju, *Indeks,* III, 7 (July 1954), p. 32.

The whole picture of the Yugoslav economy in these years was what one might have expected from the peculiar political experiences which the leadership had undergone. From strict Stalinism, the government moved uncertainly into a period of experiment and tinkering with the machinery. The Communists showed themselves far less flexible, far less able to rid themselves of belief in their old dogmas in economics than they had in the fields of internal politics and international relations. Though the mechanization of agriculture by collectivization was in most regions uneconomic and in all unpopular, they clung to it as a long-range goal even after they had been forced to abandon it as an immediate policy. As a result, crisis on the farm was a perpetual feature of the economy, greatly exacerbated by the two bad droughts. Though forced-draft industrialization was extremely expensive, and though the emphasis upon heavy industry damaged the economy in the short

TABLE 12

	Exports		Imports	
	1952	1953	1952	1953
Food	28,225	10,677	24,437	32,226
Beverages and Tobacco	2,937	2,180	....	36
Raw Materials	19,386	20,944	15,528	15,006
Fuels and Lubricants	1,167	680	8,731	9,270
Vegetable and animal fats	....	4	1,391	1,507
Chemical products	2,944	2,954	5,196	5,126
Finished goods	18,062	15,946	19,802	14,968
Tools, electr. equipment, vehicles, and parts	35	888	35,137	37,735
Miscellaneous final products	461	877	1,703	1,398
Other	741	242	....	....
Total	73,958	55,392	111,925	118,272

	Exports		Imports	
	1952	1953	1952	1953
Coal, coke and products	583	507	5,493	4,401
Petroleum and derivatives	598	214	3,505	4,879
Ferrous metallurgy	884	124	8,365	6,694
Nonferrous metallurgy	17,409	12,444	1,337	1,093
Non-metals metallurgy	1,930	1,734	2,542	2,327
Metal finished goods	237	1,430	30,962	33,122
Electrical equipment	25	160	8,006	7,523
Chemicals	2,079	1,976	5,189	5,694
Building materials	17	59	4	4
Timber	10,838	14,937	148	91
Cellulose, paper, pulp	770	753	1,304	836
Textiles	1,118	3,419	14,657	12,679
Leather	491	829	1,291	1,092
Rubber	3	34	2,616	1,917
Food products	3,828	2,942	7,326	7,846
Tobacco	2,566	1,766	....	36
Foodstuffs	18,385	2,967	15,560	27,604
Fruit	700	722	136	96
Livestock	7,216	5,167	3,269	109
Fishery products	408	209	1	1

run at least, they clung to this as well. A history of their price and wage policies would be a jumble of bewildering regulations and counter-regulations, some of them repealed or contradicted almost before they had come into effect. The large annual budget deficits and the grossly unfavorable trade balances were redeemed only by the flow of aid from the west, whose political and economic system the Yugoslavs still affected to despise, and whose assistance they doubtless interpreted as a sign of weakness.

Chapter 13

POLITICAL LIFE IN THE BALKAN SATELLITES SINCE 1948

POLITICAL LIFE IN A SATELLITE STATE "which is going toward socialism" is carried on only among the Communists and whatever other groups they may for tactical reasons be tolerating at any given moment. The population participates only in single-list elections and in demonstrating spontaneously whenever the need arises. The regime apes the Soviet policies of rigid control over all citizens. Administrative changes may well take place frequently, as officials strive in vain for efficiency. The party occasionally purges itself, and some of those who have been most powerful and ruthless disappear into limbo as a warning to others not to grow too confident of Moscow's affections. The constitution itself may be changed or replaced. The role of the Communist Party, no longer concealed, is vividly manifested in the practice of issuing "joint" party and government decrees on all major issues. An almost constant series of trials of alleged agents of the western powers, spies, saboteurs, or recalcitrant relics of former bourgeois regimes edifies the public. And all of this goes on to the monotonous but deafening accompaniment of a steady shrill barrage of propaganda, all day every day, about the surpassing virtues of the camp of peace and the incredible villainy of the imperialist warmongers.

1. Rumania

Rumanian politics after 1948 bore out these generalizations. Yet full consolidation of Communist strength took longer in Rumania than elsewhere in southeast Europe. The Communists could count on no genuine mass support, and economic recovery was long delayed, in large measure as a result of Soviet policies. None the less, the Russians had a stronger natural strategic interest in Rumania than in any other Balkan state.

INSTITUTIONAL CHANGE

Institutions which sprang up naturally or with a little encouragement in Yugoslavia or Bulgaria had to be created by *fiat* in Rumania, and decrees were constantly shifting responsibilities, and establishing new agencies of control long after the machinery elsewhere in the Balkans was running with relative smoothness.

So it was that on January 12, 1949 the national assembly passed a bill setting up "people's councils," those soviet-like organs of state power in the villages, towns, districts, and counties of the country. The people's councils would "realize the socialist order in local life," help achieve the economic plan, care for public health, invalids, and the aged, and fight sabotage. The Yugoslavs had established their parallel organs during the war itself, and afterwards had brought them under state control. Later, as we saw, they tried to give them more authority and added "producers' " councils to them. To a lesser extent, "people's councils" had appeared in Albania and Bulgaria during and after the war. But in Rumania they were artificially called into existence by decree.

Initially, in April 1949, the regime itself appointed the members of these "people's councils" in all localities, presumably since it could not ensure in any other way the choice of reliable Communists. The "people's councils" took office in July. In the spring of 1949, however, the government did proceed to the election of "people's jurors," to man the local courts. The jurors were chosen by acclamation, after biographical sketches of the candidates chosen by local party organs had been read aloud to the electorate assembled in factories and other centers. By June 29, 1949, the official report declared that almost 41,000 "jurors" had been elected in this way. The categories given were "working peasants," "workers," women, and intellectuals, and the total numbers were respectively 23,878, 12,193, 7,469, and 2,116.

In September 1950 came a new law prescribing the methods by which the "people's councils" were to be elected. This new enactment was closely related to a sweeping reorganization of the administration of the whole country. It replaced the fifty-eight *județe* (counties), into which Rumania had been divided under the prewar regimes, by twenty-eight regions. It singled out eight industrial cities and put them directly under the central government. It further subdivided the twenty-eight new regions into 177 districts, and put forty smaller towns under regional administration. Finally, it subdivided the 177 districts into 4,052 communes.

This large scale redistricting was what Americans call a gerrymander. It abolished, so far as practicable, purely agricultural units, and joined them to the nearest urban center, for ideological regions. The rural Szekler counties, for example, were lumped with the industrial town of Brașov, where the Communists commanded support among the workers. The decree, it was announced, would "consolidate the dictatorship of the proletariat." The union of the Szekler area to Brașov would "drag it out of backwardness." Accompanying the gerrymander went an electoral decree providing that candidates for the new people's councils would be put up by the "mass organizations from among those who were loyal to the workers," and excluding from candidacy and from the polls all mentally deficient persons, former industrialists, bankers, merchants, kulaks (called "chiaburs" in Rumania), and enemies of the people.

But the Communists were clearly not yet confident, even with all these measures, perhaps because there were about 110,000 people's councils to be chosen. In October 1950, they revived the old "front" organization for the elections. The "Workers" Party (Communist), the Trade Unions, the Ploughmen's Front (of which little had been heard for some time), the Hungarian People's Alliance (Madosz), the Union of Working Youth, the Union of Democratic Women, and a variety of other "mass organizations" announced that they had united in a Central Council of the People's Democratic Front to support the candidates for the people's councils, who would be nominated by the constituent bodies, on the basis of their records. Groza became chairman and Teohari Georgescu vice-chairman of the new body. The newly resuscitated front organization issued manifestoes to the population, set up its own councils in every locality, and soon announced that a candidate could be eligible to run in more than one district, thus making truly trusted Communists doubly or triply "available." Yet on November 19, the Front declared to voters that despite all precautions, hostile elements including kulaks had managed to get their names on the lists.

Voting was of course on the single-list principle, but in towns citizens voted for town, district, and regional councilors on three separate cards distinguished by different colored stripes. On December 3, 1950, the people went to the polls, and elected 109,311 members of the soviets. A little less than four weeks later, on December 30, 1950, a new decree requiring all persons to register their personal documents with their local people's council revealed that the councils were to function as local organs of control. Their term of office was to be for four years.

But the election system and much else in Rumania was changed, when the regime published a new constitution in draft form on July 18, 1952. The "forward march of our working people" had now "far outstripped" the former constitution. Comrade Stalin's teachings had guided the preparation of the new constitution, which the government declared to be suitable for the stage Rumania had now reached. The implication clearly remained that when "socialism" reached a further stage, still another constitution would be required. The preamble declared that the RPR was a state of the workers of town and country which owed its origins to the glorious victory of the Soviet armies over German fascism. The USSR as friend and ally guaranteed the independence, sovereignty, development, and prosperity of the RPR, whose policies were those of friendship and alliance with the USSR and the countries of people's democracy. Thus the Soviet Union made its appearance as a sponsor in the actual text of the new constitution of Rumania.

Divided into nine major chapters and containing 105 articles, the 1952 constitution provided that the Grand National Assembly as sole legislative organ was to be elected every four years, with one deputy to every 40,000 inhabitants. It would elect its own Presidium, form the government, modify the constitution, declare war and make peace, establish the national economic plan, approve the budget, establish the number of ministries and any changes in their number or functions, decree major administrative territorial reorganizations, and grant amnesties. The President of the Presidium could decree partial or total mobilization and ratify treaties with foreign states. Twenty-seven ministers formed the Council of Ministers or Cabinet, the highest executive organ of the state, responsible to the Assembly. Local government and the judicial system remained unchanged; the Public Prosecutor, as in all Communist states, wielded enormous powers, enforcing the laws on behalf of the government. The Assembly appointed him for five years. The Communists gave sanction to their leading role by an article which declared that "the most active citizens and those with the greatest conscience, are united in the Rumanian Workers Party, the vanguard of the working class in the fight for development of the regime of people's democracy and the building of the socialist society."[1] The voting age was to be eighteen, and the minimum age for candidates twenty-three. Members of the armed forces might vote and run for office. All voting was direct and by secret ballot. But candidates might be named only by the Communists (Workers Party), labor unions, coöperatives, youth organizations, and other "mass organizations," including cultural organizations. Deputies had parliamentary immunity, which might be withdrawn at any time in accordance with the laws. The RPR received a new national coat of arms: "wooded mountains from behind which the sun is rising; to the left an oil well. The crest is framed by wheat-sheaves. Above, a five-pointed star."[2] The national flag retained the red-yellow-blue tricolor, but added the new device in the center.

The most important innovations, however, appeared in Chapter 2, which described the organization of the state. This consolidated the twenty-eight regions provided by the decree of September 1950 into eighteen: Arad, Bacau, Baia Mare, Barlad, Bucharest, Cluj, Constanța, Craiova, Galați, Hunedoara, Iași, Oradea Mare, Pitești, Ploești, Stalin (Brașov), Suceava, Timișoara, *and* the "autonomous Magyar region." The regrouping around major cities was thus carried a step further, since each of the new regions had an industrial center as a nucleus. Even more striking, however, was the creation by constitutional *fiat* of the "autonomous Magyar region." The next articles (19, 20, 21) defined the new region as follows:

> The Magyar autonomous region of the RPR is formed from territory inhabited by the compact Magyar Szekler population. . . . It includes the regions of Ciuc, Gheorgheni, Odorhei, Reghin, Sangergiu de Padure, Sfântu Gheorghe, Targu Mureş, Targu Secuiesc, Toplița. The administrative center of the autonomous Magyar region is Targu Mureș.
>
> The laws of the RPR and the decisions and decrees of the central organs of the state are obligatory for the Magyar autonomous region.
>
> The government (*regulamentul*) of the Magyar autonomous region is determined by the people's council of the autonomous region, and is subject to the later approval of the Grand National Assembly of the RPR.[3]

[1] *Cronica Româneasca,* III, 11 (November 1952), p. 40.
[2] *Cronica Româneasca,* III, 11, p. 49.
[3] *Cronica Româneasca,* III, 9 (Sept. 1952), pp. 35 ff.

This new autonomous region created by the Rumanian Communists ended the brief linkage of the Szekler counties with Brașov (Stalin). It was modeled on the Soviet autonomous regions within the individual Soviet Republics, such as, for example, the Ossetian Autonomous Region within the Georgian SSR. Though subject to the laws of the Republic of which it formed a part, its own administrative organs took responsibility for public order, the enforcement of the laws, local economic and cultural activities, and the approval of a regional budget and economic plan. The 1952 constitution of Rumania apparently envisaged a similar position for the new Magyar autonomous region, though it specified only that the people's council of the region would be responsible for its *regulament* or local constitution, not yet worked out or not regarded as having a place in the constitution of the RPR.

The new creation obviously represented a Russian-sponsored Rumanian Communist attempt to deal with a long-standing Rumanian problem, and to remove one of the ancient sources of friction in Rumania: Szekler discontent with rule from Bucharest. At the same time, it held out to the non-Szekler Magyar population living in the other parts of Transylvania, where their numbers are far less "compact," the hope that perhaps they too might some day be given "autonomy" in its Soviet form. Simultaneously, it served as a warning to the Rumanians of those areas of Transylvania that, if they were not thoroughly subservient, they might some day find themselves part of a "Magyar" region. It must also have awakened nationalist stirrings in the hearts of Hungarian Communists at home in Hungary proper: if such a further "autonomous Magyar region" were ever erected *outside* the Szekler area, would it not be natural to put its administration under Budapest in Soviet Hungary? And when that happened, would it not also be appropriate to transfer the administration over the Szekler autonomous region from Bucharest to Budapest? The decision to organize the Szekler region in this way put the Russians in a position to balance the old Transylvania question between Rumania and Hungary much as Hitler had done during the war.

At the same time, the effort marked the first Soviet attempt in their still loyal satellites (we must leave the Yugoslav federal arrangement out of consideration here as Stalinist in conception but Titoist in execution) to introduce their own concept of "cultural autonomy." Communists from Bucharest, Moscow, and Budapest allegedly poured into the autonomous Magyar region in an effort to make it a kind of show-piece of Communist achievement. An interesting report from the fall of 1952 gave the name of the chief Agitprop instructor as Eldessi.[4] Under his direction some twenty special schools were set up in the region to teach Marxist-Leninist theory. A Russian, whose name was given as Kowalchev, and who was said to be a close friend of Yudin, Soviet editor of the Cominform paper in Bucharest,

[4] *East Europe and Soviet Russia,* VIII, 394 (September 25, 1952), pp. 5 ff.

directed the chief school in Targu Mureş, giving six-week courses to youn Magyars destined to serve as the cadres for future party organizations. Loc party youth groups nominated those eligible to attend; they wore speci uniforms, and lived at their school. Patrols allegedly moved about the stree at night asking everybody they met why they were not attending a part meeting. To the Targu Mureş textile plant came twelve women Stakhanovit from Hungary, to expound to the Szekler girls employed there the beauties socialist competition.

The area, always rather backward and predominantly rural, received general face-lifting, as Communist squads repaired and improved roads, pu up new sign-posts, and refurbished shabby public buildings. With the chang came heightened terror; the party leaders investigated the political past every individual farmer, discharged and deported the high-school teache left over from the old regime, and began to arrest members of the clerg whom they regarded as recalcitrant. Significantly enough, it was reporte that Eldessi regularly visited both Bucharest and Budapest. The Budape symphony orchestra played at Targu Mureş in September 1952. In the sprin of 1953, the name of the Party secretary of the region was announced a Ludovic Csupor. Except for the usual slick-paper propaganda printed i Rumanian government publications destined for consumption abroad, littl more has emerged about the autonomous Magyar region. It seems altogethe probable, however, that the Szeklers have added, in their agglutinative wa a word to their language which literally translated would mean "a-stinke from-Bucharest-from-Budapest-from-Moscow."

After the new constitution had been approved by the National Assembl it was presented to the public for debate. The People's Democratic Fron swung into action again, setting up propaganda centers all over Rumani with thousands of "agitation points." In Timișoara alone, for example, ther were almost 500 such "agitation points," and squads of "agitators" went fron house to house to make sure that the individual citizens were reading th draft of the constitution and "debating" it. The government turned out mor than 2,000,000 copies of the document in Rumanian, and smaller number in the minority languages, and almost half a million pamphlets providin answers to questions which the public might be likely to ask, as well a numerous other pamphlets on different aspects of the subject. Agitators wer

> to emphasize the superiority of the great socialist-soviet and people's demo cratic order to rotten hypocritical western democracy which always violates it own constitutions and makes them mere words on paper. Agitators must un mask the fascist character of capitalist countries, and especially that of th United States by giving concrete examples.[5]

[5] *News from Behind the Iron Curtain,* I, 11 (November 1952), p. 13.

This agreeable task accomplished, and the public presumably thoroughly enlightened, the constitution went back to the Assembly for a final two-day debate. Gheorghiu-Dej alone spoke for half a day. He said that 10,000,000 citizens had debated the new constitution, and had suggested no fewer than 18,836 amendments. Some thirty of these, mostly technical, the government had accepted. Of the remaining 18,806 which it had rejected, Gheorghiu-Dej mentioned specifically only eight, of which one would have denied freedom of conscience to "hostile clergy." This, said Gheorghiu-Dej piously, would not have been democratic. Presumably, as we shall see, he felt it to be more democratic simply to kill them off. On September 24, 1952, the new constitution was finally enacted.

On November 30, 1952, elections were held for the National Assembly. The government issued the usual figures, showing that almost 98 per cent of the electorate had voted (about ten and a half million people), and almost 99 per cent of the voters had voted for the candidates of the Front. Observers abroad noted with interest that only 93 members of the assembly elected in 1946 were renominated in 1952. Even of the Communists, only twenty-four of the seventy were renominated, while only five of the Ploughmen's Front ran again, including of course Groza himself.

As for the "organs of local government," the people's councils, elections were held on December 20, 1953, after the group chosen in 1950 had served for three years. Although the first postwar constitution had provided for a four-year term, the new constitution of 1952 reduced this to two years, and provided that the new elections be held one year after its adoption. In 1950, as we saw, 109,311 councilors had been elected. In 1953 the number rose to 135,220, as a result of new electoral provisions and the redistricting introduced by the new constitution. Regulations governing the presentation of candidates remained unchanged, but the law now gave smaller regions proportionally more representatives in the eighteen regional soviets.[6] Fifty days before the voting, the government fixed the limits of the electoral districts at the village level. Thereafter, the sole preoccupation of the press was the extremely complicated election procedure, with the different colored cards for each level of council to which each voter was entitled to elect representatives. The candidates toured their constituencies, and allegedly discussed local problems with the people. Finally the voters chose the 135,220 members of the eighteen regional soviets, 183 district (raion) soviets, 161 city soviets, and 4,088 village soviets. Again, the government announced that it had got out the vote: 95 to 98 per cent of the electorate voted, and more than 98 per cent of the voters voted for the government lists, only 1 to 1½ per cent

[6] Thus a region with fewer than 600,000 population was to have one representative for every 7,000 inhabitants; one with 600,000–800,000 would have one for every 8,000; one with 800,000–1,000,000 would have one for every 9,000; and one with over 1,000,000 would have one for every 10,000. At the village community level, the voters chose one representative for every hundred inhabitants.

voting against them. Of the councilors almost a quarter were women, abou 43 per cent were Communist Party members, the remainder belonging to n party. Thirteen per cent belonged to the national minorities.

The election figures, incidentally, can be used to show that in Rumani the city population had risen from about 20 per cent of the whole in 193 to about 30 per cent at the time of this election at the end of 1953.

MINORITY POLICIES

Though the autonomous Magyar region was the most striking effort o the Rumanian Communists to introduce Soviet nationality policies int Rumania, it was by no means the only move in this direction. Being the onl "compact" group, the Szeklers obtained the only, or at least the first, "autonomous" region. But the existence of the "Madosz" still gave the remaining Magyars a chance to vote Communist in their own language. Early in 1950, a Hungarian-Rumanian convention was announced, which provided that anybody whose father had been born in Transylvania was required to register his citizenship by March 15. Though little publicity was given to this, it may have been intended to allow those Magyars who chose to do so to opt for Hungarian citizenship, and perhaps eventually to move to Hungary.

Hungarian cultural activities, all of course within the Communist framework, received wide opportunity and full publicity. Besides the 318 elementary schools, fourteen "middle-grade" technical schools, five "middle-grade theoretical schools," and six vocational schools, the autonomous Magyar region alone boasted, in September 1952, a medical-pharmaceutical institute in Targu Mureş with more than 900 students, and two Magyar-language theaters. Outside the autonomous region, Cluj had a separate Magyar University, and institutes of pedagogy and the drama, while the other educational institutions in the city offered instruction in both Magyar and Rumanian. Timişoara was another center of Magyar-language education.

The German minority in Rumania, though considerably depleted by the departure of those who had withdrawn with the German armies and those who had been forcibly deported to the USSR by the Russians, also received appropriate opportunities. Early in February 1949, *Scânteia* proclaimed that the old Hitlerite superiority complex must be rooted out, that the Germans must abandon their old ideas about sharing a common destiny with Germany, and that they would need their own intensive Marxist-Leninist training. Sure enough, in March 1949, a German "anti-fascist" committee produced a German-language newspaper, appropriately entitled *Neuer Weg* (The New Road, a favorite Communist periodical title).

By the end of 1950, there were some 361 German-language elementary schools, and twelve middle and technical schools; in mid-1951, the number had risen to 380 elementary schools and twenty-six middle and technical schools; by early 1952, the figure was broken down as follows: 116 kindergartens, 242 four-class elementary schools, twenty-seven middle schools, ten trade schools. In September 1953, a German workers' evening lyceum was founded in Arad. The German-language press gave publicity to members of the minority whose achievements the Communist regime was rewarding. In the people's councils the Germans had 1,200 representatives. Others held important posts in the large factories, where several hundred had become Stakhanovites and had won the "labor medal," or had won prizes for making suggestions or innovations which increased industrial productivity. One collective farm in the Banat, appropriately named "Karl Liebknecht," after the celebrated German Communist, sent its president to a "Congress of Master-Peasants" in Bucharest in 1953, and he and other Germans were elected to the presidium of the congress.

The German-language publishing program included not only school-books, but an anthology of German literature, translations of Rumanian classics, and original works by members of the German minority. In 1952, 115 titles were printed. A "Swabian" poet, Franz Liebhart of Timișoara, got out a collection of his own lyrics called *Schwäbische Chronik,* which purported to portray the errors of the Germans in Rumania in the days of Hitler, and to point out to them the new way of socialism. The *Neuer Weg* was joined by the *Kultureller Wegweiser* (*Cultural Guide*) and the *Banater Schrifttum* (*Banat Writings*) of Timișoara, which also boasted a German theater with Liebhart as its literary secretary. Saxon and Swabian song and dance groups gave performances all over Rumania. In Sibiu, the Brukenthal Museum, traditionally a center of "Saxon" culture, with a fine collection of paintings, reopened, nationalized and equipped with new historical and pharmaceutical sections. Forty-five thousand workers were said to have visited it in 1952. The management even discovered there the previously unknown manuscript of a new symphony by Haydn, the Hermannstadt (Sibiu) symphony, which the Bucharest Symphony Orchestra played and broadcast.

The government also gave much publicity to its Tartar, Ukrainian and Armenian policies, since these nationalities had so many representatives in the Soviet Union. In November 1949, an announcement claimed that sixty-eight Tartar schools and three Tartar kindergartens were operating in the Dobrudja, and publicized a message of thanks from the Tartar teachers to the Rumanian government, which had obtained the necessary Tartar textbooks from the USSR. In February 1951, in the Constanța region alone, the government claimed that there were sixty-five schools instructing 3,000 Tartar pupils. In September 1951, the press declared that the Tartar minority was the most active of all the minorities in "socialist construction," providing front-rank workers for the factories near Constanța and for the building of the Danube-Black Sea Canal. In addition to the schools, the new announcement referred to thirty-two "Houses of Tartar Culture," and a society for the dissemination of Tartar cultural and scientific knowledge. The Rumanian Workers Party founded in February 1950 a "Democratic Committee of the Russian and

Ukrainian People in Rumania," and announced that it would have its own periodical. The center for Ukrainians was of course southern Bukovina. In Siret, by early 1953, there was a Ukrainian section in the local normal school, and in Suceava fifty-seven Ukrainian-language elementary schools, with 4,000 pupils. In May 1950, an Armenian Committee came into existence in the same way. In December 1949, the Armenian minority in both Rumania and Bulgaria celebrated with much fanfare the twenty-ninth anniversary of the founding of the Armenian SSR. Official statements appeared accusing Turkey of having "annexed Armenian territory." Indeed, by early 1953, there were fourteen such committees, including one each for the very small Greek, Bulgarian, and Turkish minorities, and one for the Gypsies.

This warm attention paid by the regime to even the smallest of the minorities led some exiled Rumanians to conjecture that the Communists were trying to destroy the national consciousness of the Rumanians themselves while emphasizing that of the minority groups. There is indeed further evidence pointing toward such a conclusion. The government gave a good deal of publicity to the totally fallacious theory that Moldavians and Wallachians are separate peoples. Since the Soviet Union has a Moldavian SSR including much of Bessarabia, immediately across the frontier from the Moldavian province of Rumania, a Communist-sponsored publicity campaign to create a specifically "Moldavian" national consciousness could serve as a preliminary to the annexation of Moldavia to the Moldavian SSR.

In the summer of 1953, for example, the regime set aside a special ten-day period for the glorification of Soviet Moldavia. Teams of "Moldavian" peasants and workers, artists and scientists, crossed the frontier from the USSR into the RPR, and toured Rumania, making speeches about the achievement of socialism in Soviet Moldavia, and bringing the "good wishes of the Moldavian people." The word for people, used self-consciously, was not the usual Rumanian word of Latin origin—*popor*—but the Slavonic *norod*. The Moldavian SSR's state choir adopted the name of *Doina,* a native Rumanian popular lyric chant. Some of the beauties of life in Soviet Moldavia might perhaps prove less attractive to the Rumanian public than the Soviet propagandists hoped; for example, the boast that "In Soviet Moldavia there is no village without its radio. The entire region can listen to Moscow's beloved voice"; but the entire tour was clearly intended as part of a deliberate effort to sponsor "Moldavian" rather than Rumanian national consciousness. If the Soviet Union indeed expected at some future date to annex Rumanian Moldavia, this would serve as a further reason for creating the Magyar autonomous region. For there can be little doubt that an overwhelming majority of Rumanians would bitterly resent the separation of their two historic provinces, and the Russians might well need all the Magyar loyalty they could command.

The Communists accompanied the effort to emphasize Moldavian nationality by a concerted propaganda designed to Slavonize both branches of the Rumanians. Part of this was little more than the forcible introduction of

Russian language instruction, a regular feature of life in all the satellite states. The University of Bucharest had its own "Maxim Gorky Institute" for Russian studies, and there were a good many other such centers, while Russian was regularly taught in the schools. More conclusive was the effort of Rumanian linguists, after their professional society had been reorganized in the summer of 1951, to "reform" the orthography of the language in such a way as to minimize its Latin origins and emphasize its ties with Slavic. Such works as Seidel's *Slavic Forms of Expression in the Rumanian Language,* and a comparative grammar of Russian and Rumanian were designed to spread these ideas among teachers in contemporary Rumania, who would then pass them on to their students.

Similarly, archaeologists and students of early history strove to demonstrate the Slavic origins of the Dacians and the intimate connection between the early Slavs and Rumania, while denying the importance of the Roman occupation. Attractively arranged public exhibitions of archaeological discoveries stressed the same ideas for the thousands of workers and other Rumanians who were more or less required to visit them. Students of later history wrote particularly on Russian influences in Rumania. As we shall see, when we come to examine Rumanian education in these years, Soviet influence dominated the new curriculum.

Only two minorities experienced a treatment different from that of the rest. These were the Yugoslavs and the Jews. The relatively large Serbian and Croatian groups had fallen on very evil days after the break between Stalin and Tito. Full-scale persecution of the Yugoslav minority began in May and June 1951, when the government ordered large-scale transfers of population from the Banat, especially along the Danube border with Yugoslavia, between Turnu Severin and Timișoara, and inland to a depth of some fifty kilometers.

The measure was clearly primarily military, as a good many Germans and Rumanians seem to have been affected also (perhaps 20 per cent of the population of the Banat); but Professor Boris Popovici, Chairman of the Union of Slavic Cultural Associations, and Professor of Mineralogy at the University of Timișoara, writing in *Scânteia* for October 5, 1951, provided the political excuse for the action: Tito and his followers had been trying since 1944 to "fan Yugoslav chauvinism" among the Serbian and Croatian minorities in Rumania. The deportees were literally dumped into the desolate Baragan steppe region in eastern Wallachia, where shelter and food were totally inadequate. The Rumanians issued no figures on the numbers of those deported, but there seemed no reason to doubt the Yugoslav figure of 10,000–15,000. Conditions among them, as among their wretched Rumanian fellow-sufferers, were miserable indeed.

The Jewish problem, as always in Rumania, had many more aspects than the purely religious. Virtually all the Jews remaining alive after the war longed to go to Israel, but the Communists were determined to fight Zionism among the Jews as a disruptive movement in the state. In November 1948, the state dissolved the Rumanian Jewish Union, which had looked after the interests of the Jews and had sponsored emigration, and replaced it by a "Jewish Democratic Committee," under the leadership of the Jewish Communist deputy, Berku Feldman. He set up special classes for Jews in Marxism-Leninism, and began a violent propaganda attack on Zionism and on Israel. Denouncing "Jewish nationalism," the Rumanian government propaganda organs, including the Yiddish-language press, declared that Jews must be integrated into Rumanian life and put to doing productive work at home. Zionism was called "permanent anti-Semitism." The whole issue put Ana Pauker personally in a delicate position: her father and her brother were in Israel, where Prime Minister Ben-Gurion denounced her in the fall of 1949, and set up a radio station to reply to the Rumanian charges against his country, but in Rumania itself she naturally was open to the charge of favoring the Zionists.

By 1950, the Rumanian radio was giving much time to broadcasting alleged letters from Jews in Israel reporting on the great discomforts of conditions there, and also railing against individual Jews in the "bourgeois" world. Soon, the anti-Israeli attacks were mingled with pro-Arab broadcasts: the Mufti of Iraq had signed the Communist-sponsored "peace appeal." In Rumania, the government arrested leading Zionists, sent Jews to forced labor camps, took children away from their parents, and sent them to "study in Moscow." By the end of 1950, the Rumanian authorities were calling Ben-Gurion a Hitler and a Tito, comparing him with Sir Oswald Mosley and the South African Premier Malan, and accusing him of ingratitude toward the USSR, which had made Israel's existence possible. The Motor Vessel *Transylvania* with a capacity of 1,800 had been making weekly trips to Israel, but with many fewer passengers than it could hold, and it was estimated that 100,000 Jews were on the list to leave Rumania.

Early in 1951, the regime began to give much publicity to Jews who had allegedly returned disappointed from Israel, some of whom appeared to be persons who had actually been sent there for the specific purpose of returning and denouncing conditions. Special teams of Communist activists visited those Jews who had put their names on lists of those wishing to emigrate, and put pressure on them to take their names off. Since the Jews had not received exit-permits, they feared they might lose their work and food-cards if they insisted on leaving their names on the lists, and many withdrew them, as the waves of arrests increased, especially in Moldavia. Leading Zionists, including Marcus Benveniste and Jacques Kummer, were arrested. About 20,000 Rumanian Jews arrived in Israel during the first five months of 1951, but the 350,000 left in the country were experiencing persecution comparable to what they had suffered under Antonescu.

Early in 1952, some 30,000 Jews in Israel, immigrants from Rumania, were reported to have signed a petition asking for the release of the Zionist leaders arrested in Rumania, and to have handed in a copy at the Soviet Legation in Tel Aviv. The Rumanian government stopped issuing exit-permits, and the *Transylvania* no longer called at Haifa. Though Jews in Rumania were not persecuted for their faith alone, they were required to abandon hope of leaving the country where they had suffered much, and where there now ruled a doctrine to which most of them could not subscribe.[7]

THE INSTRUMENTS OF CONTROL

The entire population experienced during these years an ever-growing subjection to state instruments of control, much like those which have become notorious in the USSR. A bill passed in early 1949 provided the death penalty for crimes endangering the security of the state or the development of the national economy. Soon thereafter, on January 23, the state created a new militia, with its own general directorate, under the Ministry of the Interior. At the same time, the decree abolished all other police and gendarmerie. The new police force's duties included the maintenance of public order, the issuance of passports, the regulation of the movement of the population, and keeping a record of all foreigners. Its commander was Lieutenant General Pavel Christescu. It also had the right of issuing permits to reside in Bucharest, a duty whose sinister aspect did not at once manifest itself, although there had been some deportations from the capital as early as 1947.

In 1952, however, there began mass deportations not only from Bucharest but also from all the other major cities of Wallachia and Transylvania. A decree of February 16, 1952 required the progressive removal from the capital of three categories of persons. The families of war-ciminals, deportees, persons condemned to jail or serving jail sentences, and persons who had fled abroad were to receive notice twelve to twenty-four hours before being deported, and were allowed to take with them fifty kilograms of luggage. Soldiers purged from the army, former judges, lawyers, industrialists, and merchants, and those who owned more than ten hectares of land were also to be removed, but might take all their property with them. Chances were, however, that they would have none left to take. Finally, "saboteurs," "relapsed criminals," and retired persons under the age of seventy all had to leave. House and street-wardens would assist the militia in locating and removing these unfortunates.

One reason for the brutal measure was the tremendous overcrowding of Rumanian cities as a result of the forced-draft industrialization which was an essential part of the regime's economic plan. As we have seen, urban population had risen rapidly. On February 2, 1949, a law decreed that all city housing space exceeding the needs of its present occupants was automatically available

[7] The total number of schools for the minorities in early 1954 was reported as follows: 1,597 Hungarian, 329 German, 137 Russian and Ukrainian, 56 Tartar, 48 Serbian, 28 Slovak, 16 Turkish, 8 Croatian, 8 Czech, 4 Polish, and smaller numbers of Greek, Armenian, and Yiddish. *Wissenschaftlicher Dienst Südosteuropa,* III, 3/4 (April 15, 1954), p. 94.

for allocation. A husband and wife were entitled to one room, and to an additional room for three children up to the age of eleven. More space was available for state employees, workers who had won the medal of Lenin, high officials, scientists, artists, and writers. A further decree of April 17, 1952 provided that, as of the next July 1, each ordinary city-dweller would be entitled to a maximum of eight square meters of space.

That same summer of 1952, the militia began to arrest children between nine and seventeen years of age, presumably those of "unreliable" parents. The police would search the dwellings of the parents, and then remove the children. By August 1952, a figure of 300 such arrests was current for Bucharest alone, although the regime did its best to conceal the whole operation from the outside world, militiamen warning the parents not to reveal what had happened. President Truman took official cognizance of these actions which had taken place elsewhere in Soviet-dominated territory, but not in the Balkans. On May 28, 1952, he referred to them as "one of the most outrageous things . . . in the history of the world," but unfortunately the protest, like earlier ones, had no effect. A children's concentration camp was reported at Hațeg in Transylvania.

The adult refugees from the deportations were herded into the dreadful camps on the Baragan steppe, guarded by the militia. Reports from the area declared that the camps were located near towns, and were named after them, but that the militia permitted no communication between town and camp. Starvation, cold, and disease were reported causing great ravages among the internees, although some of the able-bodied were taken off to do forced labor on the Danube-Black Sea Canal and other projects of the state. By the end of 1952, no resident of a Rumanian city might change his residence within the city without special permission from an "Office of Rental Accommodations." The militia controlled all movement from town to town. They permitted such moves only upon presentation of evidence that the applicant's health required it or that he was moving in line of duty. Any person staying in any place more than twelve hours had to register with the militia: this included all guests at hotels, people staying with relatives, and the like. A foreigner required a permit for any trip whatever.

Like its Soviet counterpart, the MVD, the militia became known as "troops of the Ministry of the Interior" (MAI). In mid-1952, it was said to include 120,000 men, of whom perhaps one-quarter were stationed along the frontiers as special guard units. It had its own training schools, and five "directorates" or branches, including, in addition to the militia proper, a staff directorate, a political directorate, a penal directorate, and a directorate for national security. It had apparently taken over the work of "Paza," a paramilitary organization with a reported 60,000 members in 1951, which had been established especially to defend against sabotage vital installations, such as bridges, factories, and prisons.

The regime had at least two other bodies to assist it in maintaining its network of controls. One of these was the Union of Working Youth, parallel to the Komsomol in the USSR, with a central committee in Bucharest and local organizations all over the country. It maintained five subdivisions: the pioneers, for children under fourteen, and others for teen-agers, university students, young workers, and young soldiers. The Youth organization had its own para-military body founded in 1949, and called "Ready for Defense and Work," which popularized such sports as target-shooting, obstacle races under arms, skiing with weapons, and the like. In June 1952, the Secretary of the Youth organization was dismissed "for moral and political disintegration"; the Communists apparently had the same kind of difficulty with their youth leaders as the Nazis.

Completing the national security picture was of course the army. Though limited by the peace treaty to a force of 120,000, Rumania had perhaps 500,000 men under arms. In the RPR, military age ran from fifteen to forty-seven, a total of more than 3,500,000 men or some 15 per cent of the population. Roughly 114,000 reached military age every year. Perhaps 20 per cent were rejected as unfit, 10 per cent mobilized on their regular jobs, and 10 per cent considered "unadaptable," and sent to do forced labor. With roughly 70,000 a year thus entering the service for a period of three years, the army forces alone probably totaled well over 200,000, with twice as many more in training, and the 120,000 militiamen in addition.

From the old Tudor Vladimirescu division grew seven new infantry divisions, one cavalry, one armored, one motorized, one artillery. Rumania also had a naval division and an air corps. In addition there were anywhere up to 100,000 Russian troops in the country. General Bodnaraş presided over the Armed Forces Ministry, with sixteen directorates under him, including the usual service branches, a "Superior Political Directorate," and a directorate for military justice. The four army commands, at Bucharest, Craiova, Iaşi, and Cluj, controlled the most important regions of the country.

The Rumanian army also had a war college, which accepted promising officers over thirty-five after a year's "political re-education" at a special school at Breaza. The system of promotions and retirements was copied directly from that of the Red Army, as indeed was much else. Each soldier, upon enlistment took oath as follows:

> I, ——— a citizen of the RPR, upon entering the ranks of the army, swear devotion to the working people, to my fatherland, and to the government of the RPR. I swear to hate from the bottom of my heart the enemies of the fatherland and of the working people. May the heavy penalties of the RPR law strike me and may I incur the hatred and contempt of the workers if I violate this oath.[8]

[8] *Information Bulletin,* Rumanian National Committee, no. 37 (April 1952), p. 13.

In each unit of the army the Rumanian "political responsible" received his instructions from a Soviet officer attached to every unit from the battalion up. The "political responsible" in turn directed the work of the "soldiers' council" in each unit.

Whereas in the pre-Communist Rumanian army, regimental and corps courts could impose death sentences only for treason or desertion in wartime, the RPR army courts could do so in times of peace and for "crimes of intention" as well as crimes actually committed. Indeed, the military code of Rumania received no fewer than five revisions between May 1948 and the end of 1950, each change bringing the system into closer conformity with that of the USSR. Military courts had jurisdiction over nonmilitary as well as military crimes committed by soldiers; preventive arrest might last indefinitely; and a party "special commissar" was attached to every military court.

The future élite of the Communist Party received its training at the Zhdanov School for Social Sciences in Bucharest. With an enrollment limited to 250, and a student body selected from students of proletarian origin and not educated under former regimes, the student body spent two years in study of Marxist philosophy and history, the Russian language, economics, contemporary politics, and other useful subjects. On vacations all students practiced agitation and other Party work. The schedule was vigorous indeed, leaving no time for relaxation or contemplation, and involving careful indoctrination of all students in the practice of criticizing each other. Mutual distrust replaced ordinary friendships, loyalty to the USSR ordinary patriotism. Most of the well-drilled products of the school moved directly into the middle and high echelons of government and Party.

It would hardly be fruitful to list here all the various trials which the RPR publicized during these years. The defendants included alleged "terrorists," of whom groups were apparently operating in the Banat in 1949. Sometimes they were "kulaks" or "chiaburs," that is to say, peasants actively opposed to the regime, accused of terrorism and murdering local Communists or of spreading rumors or concealing sacks of grain. At the end of 1953, it was estimated that 8,000 of these kulak trials had been held in the last few months of the year alone. Sometimes the defendants were persons who had had ties with the West, such as four former staff members of the American and British Information Offices.

The government arrested Dinu Bratianu and a group of other former Liberal politicians in May 1950. It tried King Michael's former pilot for espionage in a group of six, including the chauffeur of the Apostolic Nuncio, two of whom received death sentences (July 1950). It tried twenty-four engineers, technicians, and former members of the management of the oil companies of the pre-Communist era, charging them with efforts to sabotage the oil industry at a time when most of them were in jail. The judge was the former director of prisons in Rumania under Antonescu, and the defendants received sentences running from five years to life imprisonment (February

1953). Some of the victims in this case were former employees of the Romano-Americana Company, and the courtroom proceedings offered much opportunity for violent attack on the United States. The State Department vigorously protested against the "slanderous statements" made, and took the opportunity to inform the Rumanian Government that "all of the so-called espionage information of the type involved in the Ploeşti trial is, insofar as the American petroleum industry is concerned, freely available in published form in the United States, and can thus be openly obtained by the Rumanian Legation in Washington."[9] At the time of the alleged espionage, the Rumanian "state secrets" act was not in force. As to the decline of production in the industry, the American official memorandum put the blame for that where it belonged: on the USSR and its postwar depredations.

INTERNAL SHIFTS AND REORGANIZATIONS

During these years, ministries were created, merged with other ministries, abolished, enlarged, contracted, multiplied and divided, as the Communists strove for efficiency and for Moscow's favor, and struggled to eliminate their rivals before their rivals could eliminate them. Much of the explanation for the specific changes remains, as always, mysterious. Much is surely to be sought in the need to sacrifice some important figures because of the desperate unpopularity of the regime's social and economic policies, the details of which must wait until the next chapter. Here we may cursorily review the main developments in governmental organization and the chief personal gains and losses among the Rumanian Communists.

Early in 1949, the Ministry of Finance, held by Vasile Luca, was reorganized to include four deputy ministers and two councilors, and its competence was expanded to include supervision over the State Bank, the Bank for Credit, and all insurance and savings banks. Soon afterward a similar reorganization took place in the Ministries of Communications, and Trade and Food, and a new ministry took over direction of the Sov-Rom companies, which by now numbered eight. The Ministry of Arts and Information extended its authority over all broadcasting, graphic arts, the Folklore Institute, and other cultural institutions, and received its first Communist incumbent (G. Mezincescu). On April 16, 1949, Ana Pauker and Vasile Luca, Foreign Minister and Finance Minister respectively, became vice-premiers, replacing two non-Communist holdovers from the days when the FND had been important. A week later, Miron Constantinescu, a rising young Communist, took over the State Planning Commission, and Communists for the first time appeared as Ministers of Mines and Petrol (G. Vasilichi) and Education (N. Popescu-Doreanu). All this may be regarded as a further process of consolidation of specific Communist controls. Josif Chişinevschi, a Bessarabian Jew, became Secretary of the Central Committee of the Communist Party. His star was on the rise, and his wife, Lyuba, also came to occupy increasingly important jobs. The Secretary-

[9] *Department of State Bulletin*, XXVIII (714), March 2, 1953, p. 334.

General of the party was Alexander Moghioroș, a Hungarian. Moghioroș had reportedly been in jail with Gheorghiu-Dej, and had been part of the conspiracy against Foris, as had Chivu Stoica. Soon afterwards, Tatarescu, out of office since 1947, was arrested, together with other former Liberals of his own dissident wing of the party, and charged with a variety of crooked financial deals.

In the fall and winter of 1949 came further shifts in the Cabinet. The Minister of Construction lost his post, perhaps because of difficulties encountered in digging the Danube-Black Sea Canal. The Minister of Justice, Avram Bunaciu, who had succeeded Patrașcanu in February 1948, now became Chairman of the State Control Commission, and his former Ministry received a reorganization with deputies and councilors. In December, the Ministry of Industry was divided into a Ministry of Engineering and Chemical Industries (Chivu Stoica) and a Ministry of Light Industry (A. Sencovici); the Ministry of Trade and Food into a Ministry of Domestic Trade (V. Malinschi) and a Food Ministry (J. Vinti); the Ministry of Forestry acquired new functions and became the Ministry of Forestry and the Timber Industry (C. Prisnea). This decentralization of function in some of the important economic ministries was probably intended to increase efficiency in places where it had been notably lagging. All the appointees seem to have been Communist Party members. Just after the reorganization, *Scânteia* in commenting on the Kostov trial then in progress in Bulgaria, was sounding an ominous note. The "bourgeois nationalist, Patrașcanu," it declared, had been caught in time, but not all nationalist tendencies had yet been liquidated. Rumania had arrested its lone "Titoite" even before the Tito-Cominform break. Would it now follow Albania, Hungary, and Bulgaria and have a Titoite purge? The question must have kept some prominent Communists awake at night.

In January 1950, the fifth plenum of the Communist (Workers) Party met, and engaged in a good bit of self-criticism. The party was showing "bourgeois anarchist tendencies." Its discipline was slack. Its social composition was "unjust." District party secretaries had been receiving appointment without the approval of the Central Committee. The party therefore created an Orgburo (Organizational Bureau) to combat these tendencies. Its members included Pauker, Luca, Gheorghiu-Dej, Teohari Georgescu, Moghioroș, Chișinevschi, Chivu Stoica, Miron Constantinescu, and eight others. Orgburo decisions, like those of the Politburo and the Party General Secretariat, would have the validity of Central Committee decisions. The Central Committee also determined to set up a control commission of its own to deal with the administrative and financial problems of the party. Inside the government there were to be now three new "political directorates"; one for railways, one for the Ministry of Agriculture, State Farms, and Machine Tractor Stations, and one for the Construction Ministry. Here were clearly some of the sensitive places in the state.

After the fifth plenum, Teohari Georgescu, Chivu Stoica, and Josif Chișinevschi all became vice-premiers, joining Pauker and Luca. It is interesting that Chișinevschi, although a vice-premier, held no ministry in the government. In March 1950, a further shake-up hit two further important ministries: the Ministry of Construction, responsible in part for the Canal, was turned over to the army generals, Borila and Popescu, from the Ministry of Defense; while their replacements in the Defense Ministry were the former responsible authorities in the Ministry of Construction (L. Salajan, C. Doncea). It was not possible to explain this exchange of officials between the defense and construction ministries on the basis of information available, unless the switch represented a further effort to bring some efficiency into the construction of the canal.

Writing in the Cominform paper in June 1950, Gheorghiu-Dej reported that at the end of 1949, membership in the Rumanian Communist Party had been 750,000, only 40 per cent of whom were workers. About 20 per cent, or 192,000, had therefore been purged, amid considerable violence: "activists" engaged in the purging had been killed in Iași and Cluj. Though the membership had again risen to 720,000, 60 per cent were new workers, a gain, but not yet a satisfactory percentage. But soon afterwards, *Scânteia* gave different figures: despite the purges, only 42 per cent of party members was made up of workers; but in "leading party organs" the percentage was 64. It later added that in the government itself party membership among officials had risen from 24 per cent to 70 per cent. It had been the unification with the Social Democarts, *Scânteia* remarked, ominously for them, that had introduced "petty-bourgeois" elements and spoiled the social composition of the party.

In October 1950, Bunaciu moved from the State Control Commission into the Foreign Office as Ana Pauker's deputy. Two others were appointed at the same time; so the Foreign Ministry was now receiving its long overdue reorganization. Vidrascu took over Bunaciu's post at the Control Commission. Shifts continued in the Construction Ministry, as the General Manager of the Canal, G. Hosu, took it over in March 1951; General Borila moved to the State Planning Commission. The Minister of Mines was ousted in late March. On April 5, more economic ministries decentralized their functions: the Ministry of Communications was subdivided into a Ministry of Transport (A. Alexa), and a Ministry of Posts and Telegraphs (V. Roman); the Ministry of Forestry and Timber Industry was subdivided into a Ministry of Forestry (P. Stefan) and a Ministry of Timber, Paper, and Cellulose (C. Prisnea). A State Supply Commission was set up under Dumitru Petrescu, with cabinet rank. On May 19, 1951, a General Directorate of Manpower Reserves was set up, attached to the Cabinet. It was to recruit and direct the country's skilled and unskilled labor reserves in city and country. Pressure for economic efficiency would seem to explain these changes.

None of this proliferation of posts and shifts in office-holders could begin to compare in importance to the sensational developments which began in March 1952. On the ninth of that month Vasile Luca was removed from office as Minister of Finance, and replaced by the Chairman of the State Supply Commission, Dumitru Petrescu. Luca's Ministry had just been responsible for putting through another "currency reform," which we shall describe in detail in the next chapter, but which was naturally tremendously unpopular. He continued in office as Vice-Premier, but the press soon began to accuse him of having harmed the interests of the state and the peasants and workers by violating the provisions of the currency reform bill. Luca's three Deputy Finance Ministers were all dropped with him. The "reform" had actually been prepared by Soviet "experts"; so that Luca's dismissal seemed to be only a pretext.

But what was in the wind was not merely the dismissal of a single important Rumanian Communist; it was a real purge of the top leadership. At the end of May, Luca was dropped as Vice-Premier and member of the Central Committee of the Party. Teohari Georgescu was ousted as Minister of the Interior for "lack of combativeness in the struggle against the enemies of the working class." Major-General Alexandru Draghici succeeded him. And, most surprising of all, Ana Pauker was dropped from the Politburo, although remaining as Foreign Minister. Lotar Radaceanu, a former Social Democrat, also lost his seat on the Politburo. In the days that followed, the customary Communist double-talk concealed rather than revealed what had really happened. It was reported that Moghioroș, Luca's close friend, had been required to write the denunciation of his work. Luca had admitted hostile elements into the Finance Ministry and the Banks. He had discriminated in favor of kulaks and exploiters, and had helped them evade segregation. He was responsible for the failure of the agricultural produce collection program. He had held back funds destined for socialist enterprises, drawn up faulty accounts, spread rumors, created panic, and upset the state economic plan. These, one may suppose, were the standard charges to be leveled against any official connected with the economy and slated for disgrace. Pauker too was guilty of these "rightist deviations": she "lived on the slope of aristocracy and tore herself from the masses."

The bill of particulars against Luca continued: he had lost contact with the working-class, and drifted from the party; he had become the exponent of an anti-Marxist doctrine; he had opposed the extension of class warfare, and believed in a well-to-do peasantry rather than in industrialization. He and Pauker and Georgescu had *indulged in separate discussions among themselves with the aim of establishing a policy of their own* (italics mine). Now these charges suggest that the deposed trio had opposed the speed with which "socialism" had been introduced to Rumania. It is certainly true that the rapid economic changes had produced more dangerous unrest than can have been comfortable. It is not implausible that the three veteran Communists should have advised caution. But it is probable that their separate consultation together was their real crime. The Soviet advisers and Gheorghiu-Dej could hardly allow such a threat to pass unnoticed or unpunished.

None of the other explanations seemed particularly plausible: it was suggested that the dropping of Pauker was a sop for Rumanian anti-Semites, and in line with Soviet anti-Semitism as shown at this period in the USSR itself and in Czechoslovakia. But Pauker's fall led to the further rise of Chişinevschi, and other Jews; while Luca, who also fell, was known to be personally anti-Semitic. Nor could the observer discern any "Titoism" in these three: so far as we know, they had always been subservient to Moscow. Some observers recalled the trial in Switzerland in June 1949, of a Rumanian named Viteanu or Witzman, who had been blackmailing Rumanians with funds abroad, committing espionage, and extorting money from those who wanted to flee Rumania; and suggested that Pauker was being punished for her close connection with him. But it was not clear that Rumanian Communists regarded Viteanu's actions as reprehensible nor could one explain why such punishment should be delayed three years. Pauker, Luca, and Georgescu probably fell because they failed to bring off a plot to make themselves supreme. The Politburo now consisted of Gheorghiu-Dej, Moghioroş, Chişinevschi, Miron Constantinescu, Bodnaraş, Chivu Stoica, and three new members replacing Luca, Pauker, and Georgescu: Gheorghe Apostol, Petre Borila, editor of *Viaţa Sindicala,* the trade union paper, and Constantine Parvulescu.

For a time, Pauker remained Foreign Minister, Vice-Premier, and member of the Orgburo. But on June 2, 1952, Gheorghiu-Dej, victorious over all his rivals, became Premier. Groza, who had served his Communist masters well for more than seven years, was kicked upstairs to become President of the Grand National Assembly. Chivu Stoica continued as Vice-Premier, as did Chişinevschi, and they were joined now by Gheorghe Apostol, old railway workers' union comrade of Gheorghiu-Dej, and leader of the trade unions. On July 5, Pauker was replaced in the Foreign Ministry by Simon Bughici, who had up to that time been Ambassador to Moscow. Other officials, including the Public Prosecutor, perhaps a friend of Pauker's, also lost their posts. But the purge now tapered off. In late August, Pauker's deputy in the Foreign Office, Avram Bunaciu, was dismissed for "unsuitability and serious errors," and the Minister of Health, Vasile Marza, for "grave negligence." The number of ministries continued to multiply, as a new Ministry of State Farms was created on July 13, and in August the Ministry of Coal and Oil was divided into two separate ministries, one for each fuel. Miron Constantinescu became Secretary of the Central Committee of the Communist Party. But the major shifts had ended. The government which took office early in 1953 was substantially unchanged, except that Gheorghe Vidrascu now appeared as a fourth Vice-Premier. There were by now no fewer than forty-two ministries and other posts of Cabinet rank.

Compared with 1952, 1953 was a quiet year politically in Rumania. No new constitution, no new purge, ruffled the surface of the national life. Early in the year, the Minister of Foreign Trade, Barladescu, and six lesser officials were dismissed for "provocations" and "anti-Marxist activities." Four of th seven were Jews. In the USSR, of course, Stalin died and Beria was purged The only apparent reflection of this in Rumania was the removal of the nev Vice-Premier, Gheorghe Vidrascu, in September 1953. Commentators instantl labeled Vidrascu a "Beria man," but, while plausible, this was not demonstra ble. It was of great interest that no trial was held for Pauker, Luca, an Georgescu, one or more of whom might yet stage a comeback. Indeed, rumor were current that Ana Pauker had been seen quietly sitting in the audienc at this or that political meeting. At a press conference given during the sum mer "Youth Festival" in August, Gheorghiu-Dej, faced with the unaccustome embarrassment of questions from foreign newspapermen, declared that An Pauker was still in Bucharest. And at the celebration of "liberation day" o August 23, observers noted two former socialists, Voitec and Radaceanu, th latter of whom had been purged from the Politburo with Pauker, Luca, an Georgescu, sitting on the platform with the leaders of the government an the party. It was at least possible that a reconciliation among former to Communists might be in the making.

In late 1953 and early 1954, ministerial changes and reorganizations con tinued to take place, but the trend was now reversed: instead of multiplying ministries and dividing functions, the government now began to recombin ministries and thus to increase the power and responsibility of the holders. A new Ministry of Food took over all the separate ministries concerned with food-production and distribution. A new Ministry of Education combined not only the former Ministries of Public Education and Higher Education but also the General Directorate of Labor Reserves, surely a rather sinister combination, suggesting that students were expendable. All the cultural bureaus, and there had been dozens of them, combined into a Ministry of Culture, including radio, press, books, cinema, and other mass media.

A new Ministry of Agriculture included the former Ministries of Agriculture, Forestry, and State Farms. The Ministry of the Interior seems to have taken over the Ministry of State Security. In keeping with the enhanced importance of the posts, high Communists took them over. Thus General Borila became Minister of Food, Ilie Murgulescu of Education, Constanța Craciun, leading woman Communist, of Culture, and Gheorghe Apostol, the trade unionist, of Agriculture. Chivu Stoica became Minister of Metallurgy, a combination of several former ministries, and a Ukrainian named Gavriliuk Chief of the State Control Commission. Alexandru Draghici remained Minister of the Interior, but received two new deputies, one of whom was reported to be from the autonomous Magyar region. The Minister of Domestic Trade, Malinschi, was replaced in February 1954 by Mircea Oprișan, while in April 1954 Constantine Popescu took over Apostol's post in the Ministry of Agriculture.

April 1954 saw further important party shifts. Apparently imitating the 'collegiate" government which the USSR claimed to have been practicing since the death of Stalin, the Rumanian Communists abolished the post of Secretary-General of the Party, which Gheorghiu-Dej had held, and also the short-lived Orgburo. They announced that the Politburo would itself hereafter deal with organizational work, while operational and control work would be performed, under the guidance of the Politburo, by the four-man secretariat to the Central Committee. None of these would hold government office. The four were to be Apostol, in the new post of first secretary, and Niculae Ceaușescu, Mihail Delea, and Janos Fazekas as fellow-secretaries. Ceaușescu had long experience in charge of political work in the army; Fazekas was clearly a Magyar. Ceaușescu and the Minister of the Interior, Draghici, became candidate members of the Politburo. Moghioroș moved into Apostol's vacant Vice-Premiership.

These changes took the place of a Party Congress which had been scheduled for March 1954, and which was now promised for October, and postponed again. At the April session, Gheorghiu-Dej, as was customary, mingled praise for the party's achievements with bitter criticism of its faults. He lashed the "majority of regional and city party committees" for failure to do their work properly. He demanded that party members stop intimidating the workers. He followed the Soviet post-Stalin line about "liquidating . . . all manifestations of the personality cult." He explained the new changes as essential to relieve the busy men who had been active simultaneously in the Politburo and the Cabinet. It was clear that another major step in the development of the Rumanian Communist Party had been taken along lines laid down in Moscow.

Also in April 1954 came the long-delayed trial of Patrașcanu, under arrest for more than six years, and ten codefendants, on charges of opposition to the regime in the period between 1945 and 1947. The regime announced that Patrașcanu and one other victim had been condemned to death and instantly executed. It imposed three life-sentences, and six lesser prison terms. Rumors circulated that Patrașcanu had become insane in prison, and even that the victim of the trial was not the same Patrașcanu as the former Minister of Justice, but these could not be verified. The Rumanian government charged that Patrașcanu had been in touch with the chief of the Iron Guard's security department as early as 1940, and further alleged that he had been involved with the "American agents," Hall and Hamilton, for conspiring with whom Maniu had been sentenced.

Among those tried with Patrașcanu was Ion Stârcea-Mocsonyi, the former Marshal of the Royal Palace, who had played so important a role in the arrest of Antonescu in 1944. Stârcea, who had already been sentenced to five years in the Maniu trial, now received an additional fifteen years at hard labor. It was obvious that the regime was determined not to let him out of prison, as his first sentence had expired. It was a sad symbol of the distance traversed by the Rumanian regime since 1944 that ten years later this brilliant young man who had prevailed upon the King to surrender to the Russians, should have been a criminal in the country he had helped to "liberate."

In the summer of 1954, the Party issued the draft statutes scheduled to be adopted at the Congress in October. These imitated recent Soviet changes, emphasizing the need to strengthen party discipline, referring openly to the party control of trade unions and the army, and establishing severer qualifications for new members. All industrial workers with more than five years' experience could be received into the party if sponsored by two party members of three years' standing. Other workers, members of kolkhozes, technicians, and engineers needed three sponsors, and working peasants and clerks needed four. Anyone who had belonged to a former political party would need five sponsors of eight years' standing, two of whom had membership dating back to 1944. The August 23 celebrations put heavy emphasis on the army, and it was instructive to note that Bodnaraş, Borila, and Miron Constantinescu, the first two generals and the latter chief of the planning commission, all became Vice-Premiers. They remained somewhat less prominent than the other three: Chişinevschi, Moghioroş, and Chivu Soica, who became "first" Vice-Premiers. Following the Soviet example, the regime granted an amnesty to persons under five-year jail sentences and less, with the exception of those guilty of "offenses against state security."

FOREIGN RELATIONS

Rumanian foreign relations during the years since 1948 developed along the normal satellite lines: intimacy with the USSR and its satellites, including those in Asia, hostility and rudeness toward the west. During 1950, East Germany and Rumania concluded the usual series of agreements on cultural and technical collaboration and on trade, and it was announced that an economic treaty would be signed later. There was endless coming and going of cultural and other delegations between Rumania and the other satellites, and for the first time Rumanians became aware of Korea and Koreans, as they had to contribute to clothing and other drives for the "democrats" there. The presence of so many Asians in Bucharest and the other Balkan capitals reminded the student sharply of the Axis days, when the Japanese had solemnly sent representatives to Zagreb and Bratislava.

Repeatedly in 1949, the United States and Britain protested that the Rumanian government was violating the Peace Treaty, but the notes either went unanswered or were rejected, and the summons to call a conference of the signatories to the treaty went unheeded. In April 1950, the government declared that the United States Information Office was an appendage of the American Legation, and "incompatible with normal diplomatic relations." When the American government closed it soon afterwards, the Rumanians proceeded to a new demand: that the United States cut the size of its Legation staff in Bucharest. It numbered nineteen, as against three Rumanians on the staff in Washington. The Rumanians asked that there be ten in both capitals. In May 1950, the United States, in reprisal for a similar regulation in Rumania, announced that the personnel of the Rumanian Legation in Washington would not be permitted to travel more than thirty-five miles from the capital without special permission. The next month, the Rumanian press gave wide currency to a tale that the American military attaché's office in Rumania had dumped cases of arms into a lake not far from Bucharest for the use of the "Zionist fascist bands" of the Irgun.

The Mutual Security Act of 1951 contained a provision which most of the Communist governments of the world used as a pretext for making protests. This was the appropriation of funds for the support of groups or activities within such states hostile to the Communist regime. In December 1951, the Rumanian government protested against this, and demanded that it be rescinded. Great publicity was given to the Communist charges that the United States had employed "germ warfare" in Korea, and in the early months of 1952 subservient Rumanian ecclesiastics joined in the "protests" against this. The charges against many of the victims of the regime who were brought to trial included espionage for the United States or serving American imperialist masters. In the fall of 1953, the government announced that thirteen spies had been parachuted into Rumania by the American intelligence services, and had all been apprehended, tried, and executed. Like the rest of the Communist press the world over, the Rumanian press wept buckets of tears at the fate of Mr. and Mrs. Rosenberg, executed in the United States for treason, and printed numerous articles sympathizing with their unfortunate children.

A striking contrast to the solicitude for the two young Rosenbergs was shown in the episode of Rumanian-American relations which drew most public attention in the United States during these years: the affair of the two Georgescu boys. The boys, sons of Mr. and Mrs. V. C. Georgescu, had been caught in Rumania by the advent of the Communist regime, and separated from their parents, who were on a visit to the west and could not return. Mr. Georgescu, who became an American citizen after the war, had repeatedly sought in vain to obtain the release of his children. On May 26, 1953, the Department of State revealed that Christache Zambeti, the first Secretary of the Rumanian Legation, had tried to use the Georgescu boys as a means of blackmailing their father. He had promised their release if Mr. Georgescu, an official of the Standard Oil Company, would "collaborate" with the regime of the RPR. Realizing what the consequences to his children might be, Mr. Georgescu none the less refused, and told the State Department about the matter. Zambeti was expelled as *persona non grata*. The Turks in 1948 had similarly asked for his recall from Istanbul, where he was Consul-General.

The Voice of America publicized the whole affair in its Rumanian broadcasts, putting the children in the "trust" of the Rumanian people. Eventually, almost a year later, the RPR set the boys free, and on April 13, 1954 they rejoined their parents in the United States. The second State Department announcement declared that the release was the "result of a long series of approaches by the Department, in which President Eisenhower and Secretary Dulles took a personal interest."[10]

2. *Bulgaria*

In Bulgaria, as we know, the Communists had moved with greater speed than in Rumania. The years after 1948 brought no new constitution, no elaborate political sovietization beyond the advanced level already reached. Early in the period, the United States broke relations with Bulgaria. Minority problems were limited to those of the Turks, but these led to grave difficulties and friction with Turkey. The political jockeying of individual Communists for power continued. Often the chief reasons for an individual's political failure lay in the country's economic program, in which much of the interest of these years is concentrated. But following the ups and downs of the personal fortunes of the chief Communists gave occasional valuable clues.

THE RECORD OF THE 1946 SOBRANIE; ELECTIONS

In the course of our discussion of the Kostov case, we reviewed the most important political developments in Bulgaria during the year 1949, and found Chervenkov in the saddle as a result of the death of Dimitrov and the purge of Kostov. The last two political parties which had maintained even the fiction of a separate party organization and funds, Zveno and the small Radical Party, both dissolved early in February 1949. The Obbovite Agrarians announced in July that they had given up their old ideology, which favored an agrarian government, and that they would henceforth use all their energy to strengthen the cause of the OF. On September 17, the Grand National Sobranie was dissolved, and it was announced that elections would be held within three months. This was the same assembly that had been elected in October 1946, for one year. It had twice extended its term of office, "owing to exceptional circumstances," as provided in the Constitution. In those 1946 elections the opposition had polled almost 30 per cent of the total vote, despite all the pressure that the Communists could bring. But now the opposition deputies had long since been expelled, and Petkov's party, which had commanded most of the opposition support, had been liquidated in 1947.

The assembly had adopted the constitution and the first (two-year) economic plan; it had ratified all the treaties which bound Bulgaria to the states of the eastern bloc. In the 1949 session, it had passed bills providing for compulsory military service and for the election of local "people's courts," like the "people's jurors" or "assessors" in Rumania. It had also redistricted Bulgaria into fifteen regions: Sofia, Vratsa, Vidin, Pleven, Gorna Orekhovitsa, Ruschuk, Varna, Shumen, Burgas, Yambol, Stara Zagora, Khaskovo, Plovdiv, and Gorna Dzhumaya. These fifteen regions were now to have their own

[10] *Information Bulletin*, Rumanian National Committee, no. 57 (March-April 1954), p. 26.

"people's councils," which would serve as a link between the central government and the people's councils of the districts into which each of the regions was divided. There were ninety-five such districts in all. The elections for the regional people's councils were to take place simultaneously with those for the delegates to the National Sobranie. Both sets of elections were held on December 18, 1949, two days after the execution of Kostov, and the government obtained the usual majority. In the new assembly, which was half the size of the old one, since it was not a "Grand" National Sobranie with a constitution-making role, there were 239 deputies, all Communists and their collaborators.

Thereafter considerable complaint arose about the functioning of these people's councils, the State Control Commission, for example, reporting in August 1951, that in two cities and twenty villages they had discovered that the councils had left complaints uninvestigated and unanswered, and had even lost them. The next elections for the councils were held in December 1952. Almost 60,000 members were chosen, all, of course, candidates of the OF. As for the National Assembly, when its four-year term was nearing its end, new elections were held in December 1953. The percentage of the electorate which voted was 99.48 per cent and 99.8 per cent cast their votes for the OF candidates.

THE BREAK WITH THE UNITED STATES

On January 21, 1950, three days after the opening of the new Assembly, the aged Kolarov, Premier since Dimitrov's death the summer before, died. On February 1, Chervenkov succeeded him. The most striking event of these days was the interchange of messages with the United States. The Bulgarian Government was demanding the recall of the American Minister, Donald R. Heath, whom it had "implicated" in the Kostov case. The United States replied that the demand must be withdrawn or relations would be severed. On February 20, the United States broke diplomatic relations with Bulgaria. As of the present writing (1955) they had not been renewed. The Bulgarian government had just before announced that it had arrested for espionage and sabotage five Bulgarians, two of whom had been employees of the American Legation, which, the Bulgarians alleged, had provided them with false documents. One of those indicted was Michael Shipkov.

Shipkov had been arrested by the Bulgarian police on an earlier occasion. They had interrogated him, and broken him down by forcing him to stand for hours leaning against a wall, while supporting his weight on two fingers only. He had signed a confession stating that he had worked against Bulgaria for the Americans, and agreeing to serve the Bulgarian government as informer. The police had then released Shipkov, who told Mr. Heath about his experiences and put them into an affidavit in which he also denied that the Americans ever told him to commit espionage or sabotage. This affidavit the American Minister kept secret. He did, however, try very hard to obtain for Shipkov and his wife exit visas from Bulgaria. In October 1949, the Bulgarian Foreign

Minister, Poptomov, led Mr. Heath to believe that he had personally recommended that the Shipkovs be granted visas, and told him that the mistreatment which Shipkov had experienced was contrary to Bulgarian policy.

Shipkov had received asylum in the American Legation, but tried to leave Bulgaria, and was arrested. Though he was about to stand trial, the American authorities did not yet publish the Shipkov affidavit, presumably because they hoped that Shipkov might still receive permission to leave the country. On March 4, 1950, two days after his trial opened, the State Department published his affidavit under the title *Forced Confession*. It made a mournful contribution to the growing knowledge of Communist techniques, and served as an eloquent testimony to Shipkov's own personal courage. Eventually he received a sentence of fifteen years.[11]

In breaking relations with Bulgaria, the United States froze Bulgarian assets in this country, and at the same time brought the real blame for the affair home to the guilty party, the Soviet Union, which, as the State Department said, was striving to deprive Bulgaria of all contact with the outside world, and to keep its people at the mercy of their present rulers.

THE TURKS

In 1950 also, Bulgarian policy toward the Turkish minority brought relations with Turkey, strained ever since the Communist assumption of power in Bulgaria, to a very dangerous degree of tension. In September 1949, the Bulgarian consulate in Istanbul was allegedly attacked and the Turkish consulate in Plovdiv bombed. There were mutual protests. Within a few days the Bulgarian government was giving publicity to "messages of loyalty" sent by the deputies of the Turkish minority in the Sobranie to the Central Committee of the Communist Party, the OF Council, and other government bodies. In October 1949, Radio Sofia accused "reactionary Turkish circles" of trying to persuade members of the Turkish minority to emigrate from Bulgaria. By March 1950, the Bulgarians were assuring Turkey that they had arrested and punished the perpetrators of the Plovdiv bomb outrage, but were now accusing the Turks of treating much too leniently the criminals who had attacked the Bulgarian consulate in Istanbul.

Further tension arose during the spring and summer of 1950.[12] The real question at issue was that of the Turkish minority, and all the other matters were trumped up by the Bulgarian government to justify a tone of wrath in its diplomatic dealings with the Turks. The truth of the matter

[11] He had not been the only Bulgarian employee of the American Legation to suffer: Joseph Dimitrov and Dragan Peev had been arrested, held incommunicado for months, and tried secretly for espionage. The Legation had not been permitted to send an observer to the trial. The accused received death-sentences. Ivan Seculov, a translator who had worked in the Legation, was tortured to death in a Bulgarian prison.

[12] The issue was an automobile which the Bulgarians alleged had violated their frontier at Svilengrad, and which the Turks maintained had simply belonged to a Turkish journalist who had lost his way in the dark. The Bulgarians also declared that the Turks were threatening to confiscate the property of the Bulgarian Exarchate in Istanbul.

was that the Bulgarians had determined to expel a large number of Turks from Bulgaria.

As we know, the Turkish minority was the only one of any size in Bulgaria. When the Bulgarians got southern Dobrudja by the Treaty of Craiova with Rumania in 1940, they acquired an additional 150,000 Turkish subjects; so that the total in 1950 must have been about three-quarters of a million, or well over 10 per cent of the population of Bulgaria, virtually all of them peasants. They had always been an extremely docile group. In 1925, the Bulgarian and Turkish governments had concluded a treaty at Ankara which obligated each country to allow nationals of the other to emigrate freely and take with them all movable property, including livestock and agricultural implements. Those who wanted to emigrate could not be drafted into the army or into government labor forces, and were to enjoy full legal protection, even receiving legal aid if necessary. On the basis of this Ankara treaty of 1925, there had emigrated from Bulgaria to Turkey every year until the outbreak of the war a number of Turks — ranging from 11,000–12,000 in 1928, down to 680 in 1933, and up again to 16,000 in 1939. The size of the emigration, which totaled nearly 100,000 between 1925 and 1939, was apparently determined in any given year by the amount of freedom allowed inside Bulgaria. In the years when the Bulgarian government followed relatively democratic policies (1930–1934), Turkish emigration was very low, and vice versa.

After the Second World War, the Bulgarian Communists initially strongly discouraged Turkish emigration. They began to apply the kind of measures which the Soviet authorities had long since employed toward their own Muslim population: nationalization of the mosques and schools, and collectivization of land. The number of exit visas given dwindled to a trickle, only ninety-six in 1948. As late as October 1949, as we saw above, the Bulgarian authorities were attributing the very idea of emigration to reactionary Turkish circles. But during 1950, the Bulgarian government completely reversed its policy, quite probably because it wanted to confiscate the lands of the Turkish peasants in the Dobrudja, where a large-scale new experiment in reclamation and collectivization was going on, as we shall see, and which was of great strategic interest to the USSR.

Early in 1950, the Bulgarians announced that emigration could be resumed, and the numbers rose from 860 in January to over 7,000 in August. On August 10, the Bulgarians sent a note to Turkey, declaring that the convention of 1925 had provided for free emigration, that more than 250,000 Turks in Bulgaria had applied to leave, and that the Bulgarians had given more than 54,000 exit visas, but that the Turks had given only 15,836 entry visas. The Bulgarians sharply accused the Turks of inquiring into the political views of the applicants, and of trying to elicit information from them. The note demanded that the Ankara government grant entry visas for the whole quarter of a million Bulgarian Turks within three months:

by November 10, 1950. This the Turkish authorities were reluctant to do for a number of reasons: they needed time to check on Communist agents planted among the immigrants, and their economy could hardly adjust rapidly to the support of so many new arrivals, whom, they correctly suspected, the Bulgarians would not allow to take their property with them in accordance with the Ankara Treaty.

Intending themselves to break the treaty, the Bulgarians now proceeded to accuse the Turkish government of having broken it. Early in September, Ankara replied that it must have the right to refuse admission to undesirables, and a few days later closed the frontier with Bulgaria. The Bulgarians proceeded to try to drive across the border groups of Turks whom they had uprooted from their homes in the Dobrudja. When the Turkish authorities would not admit these refugees, they drifted into Greek territory at the point where the three countries come together. The Greek government promptly protested, and stopped the Simplon-Orient express. By early October, the Bulgarian officials were calling the Turks "racists" (because they did not want to admit Gypsies) and corrupt (because they "gave visas only to the rich," as usual, a very flexible word).

To protests against the closing of the frontier the Turkish authorities replied that it would stay closed until the question of the emigrants should be settled by negotiation. The Bulgarians threatened to close the Turkish consulates in Bulgaria. They said the Turks were keeping 131 railway carriages (actually, the miserable refugees were living in them); they accused the Turks of sending back 100 refugees, exhausted and depressed, to receive food and shelter from the "kind" Bulgarian frontier guards. By the end of October, the Bulgarians were claiming that almost 5,000 of these Turks were now waiting with the necessary documents on the frontier. The Grand Mufti of Bulgaria visited the frontier and sent a telegram to the Turkish Legation in Sofia, protesting against the closing of the frontier. In November, the Bulgarians became a little more amiable, declaring that if the Turkish authorities could prove that any of the emigrants were really Bulgarian Gypsies, the Bulgarian authorities would take them back.

And then, suddenly, on December 2, 1950, the Bulgarians signed an agreement accepting most of the Turkish requests. They agreed not to issue exit permits until the Turkish consulates in Bulgaria had first issued entry permits. This would prevent the pile-up of refugees. The Turks could thus, to some extent at least, guard against the infiltration of Communist agents. The Bulgarians also agreed to take back seventy-one Gypsy families whom they had expelled without waiting until they had Turkish entry permits. Most important, the Bulgarians promised in the future to respect the Ankara agreement so far as property was concerned. They had so far been stripping the poor Turkish deportees of all their property, including ox-carts, and driving them out in the Balkan winter to wait hopelessly without shelter on a closed frontier.

It seems certain that the reason for the sudden Bulgarian willingness to meet the Turkish stipulations on the refugees was that the Turkish government had threatened to bring the whole matter before the United Nations. The USSR, we may reasonably conjecture, wanted no evidence presented before the world that its satellite had violated the most elementary considerations of humanity as well as standard Soviet nationality policies. The expulsion of 250,000 Turks had been decreed to enable the Russians to achieve their ends in the Dobrudja, and the less attention their projects there received from international bodies the better suited they were. As it was, the Turks found themselves forced to accept, over a short period, hordes of homeless refugees, who presented them with a grave problem in their own country.

The Turkish question in Bulgaria was not dropped after the reaching of the December 2, 1950 agreement with Turkey. Doubtless the whole Turkish world, all the way out to central Asia, had heard of the brutality of Bulgarian behavior. So now, the Bulgarians and their Russian bosses began a propaganda drive to reassure Turks abroad about the happiness of the life led in Bulgaria by the remaining Turkish minority. In February 1951, a delegation of thirteen representatives from the Azerbaidjan SSR toured the portions of the country inhabited by Turks. In May, the press declared that some Turks were returning clandestinely from Turkey, and that the Bulgarian authorities were caring for them. In November, the Turkish government closed the frontier again, charging that the Bulgarians had tried to smuggle into Turkey 1,500 Gypsies. The Bulgarians protested in January 1952 that American and British agents were using Turkey as a base of operations against Bulgaria. A few weeks later, they protested the Turkish adherence to NATO, and the close Turkish military ties with the western powers, which they declared to be a threat to Bulgarian security. On March 25, 1952, the Bulgarian government sent a note to Turkey saying that the responsibility for reopening the frontier rested with Turkey alone. Turkish estimates set the total number of deportees before the second closing of the frontier at 220,000.

While relations with Turkey remained most unfriendly, the Bulgarian authorities, having partially cleared the Dobrudja of Turks, adopted for the remainder of their Turkish population the "cultural autonomy" nationality policy invented in the Soviet Union, and applied in Rumania to the minorities there. In the fall of 1952, the press gave much attention to the "ever more prominent role" played by Turkish youth in Bulgarian life. Turkish theatrical companies were giving performances in Sofia. At the University of Sofia the authorities opened a special section in which lectures were given in Turkish on history, philosophy, and literature. In 1953, there were 1,805 students.

The educational section of the report on the Five Year Plan, published in 1953, maintained that, whereas in 1939 less than 15 per cent of the children belonging to the Turkish minority went to school, the percentage in 1948 was over 80 and in 1952 over 97. In 1952, the Turkish minority had 1,020 elementary schools and three teachers' training schools. Illiterate Turks who had learned to read and write numbered 130,000; 83,400 children were attending school. In Ruse alone, there were 2,000 Turkish children at the various schools, which trained girls as well as boys. The government claimed also to have taken a great number of measures designed to improve the health of the Turks and increase the medical facilities available to them. In spite of the expulsions, it was clear from the report that the Dobrudja was still the center of the minority.

THE PARTY AND THE GOVERNMENT

Within the Bulgarian Communist Party and the government, the real currents of power could be judged as usual only by their surface manifestations. Even before the Kostov trial in December 1949, it had become clear that, as an institution, the OF had lost its importance for the Communists except at election time; Chervenkov resigned as its Secretary-General in February 1949, allegedly to devote himself fully to his work in the party, that is, preparation for the purge of Kostov. His first successor was Foreign Minister Poptomov, but he too left this increasingly insignificant post in October 1949, and was replaced by Dobri Terpeshev, whose star, as we saw, was sinking fast. After the Kostov trial, Terpeshev, still losing ground, gave way in March 1950 to Ferdinand Kozovsky, a former Comintern employee, not in the top rank of Bulgarian Communists but clearly a trusted Chervenkov man. The Bulgarian Communist political control machinery outside the party, the OF, the government, and the soviets, had nothing particularly remarkable about it. The "Dimitrov People's Youth Union" for example, had well over a million members in May 1954, including almost 600,000 children enrolled in the "Dimitrov Organization of Pioneers — Little Septembrists." There were the usual collection of party, police, civil defense, and paramilitary organizations, and the army, restricted by the treaty to 85,000 men, was built up to a force two to three times as great.

The months following the trial of Kostov were marked by further purging. All party organizations were commanded to get rid of "Kostovites," and to choose new officers. On April 11, 1950, the ex-Minister of the Interior, Yugov, who had slipped to the Ministry of Industry with the disgrace of Kostov, engaged in self-criticism, agreeing with the new boss Chervenkov as to his own shortcomings, and saying, "My inadmissible blindness and confidence in respect to the enemy was rightly criticized." He abjectly admitted his errors again at a party conference in June 1950, as did Terpeshev, now Minister of Labor, and others. On the way up, Ruben Levy, who had succeeded his old boss Chervenkov as Chairman of the Committee on Science, Art, and Culture, and was now also head of the propaganda department of the Central Committee of the Communist Party, vigorously criticized the

Minister of Education, Dramaliev, whose self-criticism Levy found unsatisfactory. It was clear that Levy was out to take the press and propaganda division of the Ministry of Education away from Dramaliev and add it if possible to his own empire. Indeed, Dramaliev was ousted soon afterward.

In his speech to the June 1950 party conference, Chervenkov declared that the party had 428,848 members and 13,307 candidates. During 1949, 92,500 members had been purged. Forty-four per cent of the members were peasants, 25 per cent workers, 18 per cent civil servants, and 13 per cent artisans. Levy added that 30,000 party members were illiterate, and gave the figures of those studying at special party schools as 336 at the central party school and 1,802 at the various departmental schools, while 130,000 were in local schools.

Pursuing Terpeshev inexorably, the party leadership accused him of issuing a decree as Minister of Labor which reduced working hours from eight hours a day to seven or six. When he defended himself against the charge, he was dropped from the Central Committee. The others criticized were all ministers in charge of various aspects of the economy, in which crisis reigned. Meanwhile, in late May, Poptomov, though retaining his post as Vice-Premier, had been replaced as Foreign Minister by Mincho Neichev, a Chervenkov man. General Georgi Damyanov moved from the Defense Ministry to the Presidency of the National Assembly, and General Peter Panchevsky, who held the rank of colonel in the Soviet army, became Minister of Defense. The summer of 1950 also saw the secret trial and imprisonment for life of seven "Kostovite" Communists, all of whom had been arrested the year before. One of them, Petko Kunin, former Finance Minister, was reported to have committed suicide in his cell. The published materials about this trial threw the blame for foreign espionage upon Great Britain, perhaps because the United States no longer had any diplomatic representation in Sofia.

The purge then died down, and the Communist leadership at the very end of 1950 began to subdivide ministries, a process which we have observed taking place in Rumania at a somewhat later date. The Ministry of Domestic Trade lost many of its functions to a new Ministry of Supplies and Food. The Ministry of Labor and Social Welfare was abolished, and its duties divided between the General Labor Union and the Ministry of Public Health, which took over the Social Welfare functions. At the same time, a system of deputy ministers began to be introduced into the ministries, as was also to happen in Rumania. The Minister of the Interior, Khristozov, moved into the new Ministry of Supplies and Food, with three deputies; he was succeeded in the Interior Ministry by G. Tsankov-Veselinov, who also had three deputies. It was reported that the new Interior Minister had been in Moscow between 1924 and 1944, and that he had moved up in Bulgaria after the war from Chief of the Sofia Police to Chief of the Trade Unions before obtaining his new post. Early in April 1951, Terpeshev appeared as the new Bulgarian Ambassador in Bucharest. He had escaped the worst. Yugov too hung on: his Ministry of Industry was divided into a ministry for heavy industry and a ministry for light industry, but he managed to keep the former.

On June 23, 1951, the government dismissed the Minister of Agriculture, Titko Chernokolev. Though the main reasons were of course connected with the crisis in the economic policies of the regime, and will be examined in the next chapter, the action was none the less noteworthy from a purely political point of view. Chernokolev, a peasant by origin, had spent twenty years in the USSR as an agricultural economist. His position might have been thought strong. But it was not possible to collectivize and simultaneously to deliver the quantities of food which the Russians were demanding. So Chernokolev was ousted from his ministerial post and from the Politburo. Even the Cominform journal was by the summer of 1951 maintaining that the situation in Bulgaria had grown intolerable, with the different cliques of comrades circling around each other waiting to close in for the kill.

More and more, the Russians themselves were running Bulgaria unconcealed. Special legislation passed during the early months of 1951 waived all educational requirements for Soviet citizens holding office in Bulgaria, and all obstacles to naturalization in Bulgaria. The severe restrictions on travel, on registering, size of domicile, and staying in one's job which applied to all Bulgarians were specifically declared not to apply to Russians in Bulgaria. From the Bulgarian treasury they received salaries said to average about four times as much as those paid to Bulgarians doing the same work. As early as the fall of 1950, a special school was opened in Sofia for their children. Colonial administrators, the Russians lorded it over the "native" Bulgarian population.

In the spring of 1952, much began to be heard of a "Voluntary Organization for Collaboration with the Defense Forces," abbreviated as DOSO, a paramilitary outfit. Widespread publicity was given to the need for civil defense, and a set of courses was introduced to educate the public. Back from Rumania came Terpeshev to become the President of the Central Council of DOSO in May 1952, a post without apparent political importance, but one for which his career as a Partisan general presumably fitted him. Vice-Premier Poptomov, long since relieved of his duties as Foreign Minister, died on May 1.

Towards the end of the summer, Yugov re-emerged in the limelight, and resumed his post as Vice-Premier. Thus Chervenkov apparently lacked the power to rid himself of his old enemies, or else perhaps the Russians were protecting them and therefore threatening him. Rumors that Chervenkov was scheduled for imminent disgrace made their way into the press outside Bulgaria. One story maintained that the Bulgarian Politburo had come to blows in a meeting during July 1952, and that since that painful occasion Chervenkov had not attended to his duties. But all that happened was a further series of ministerial disgraces: the Minister of Foreign Trade, the Minister of Agriculture, both in September, and the Minister of Roads and

Construction in October. Georgi Tsankov, whom some foreign commentators had regarded as a likely successor to Chervenkov, moved into the Chairmanship of the State Planning Commission instead, a strategic but also a dangerous spot. Chervenkov stayed in office. So far as overt developments were concerned, 1953 was a quiet year for the party, perhaps because the death of Stalin put the leadership in a quandary. It is true that Chervenkov had begun a campaign against General Georgi Damyanov, President of the National Assembly and Politburo member, accusing Damyanov's wife, a writer, of right-wing deviations, but it stopped late in the year, perhaps on orders from the new bosses in Moscow.

Before Stalin died in March, the Bulgarian assembly had passed a law of unparalleled harshness dealing with those who left the country without permission. Such persons were now automatically declared to be traitors punishable by death. Moreover, any relative who had known of the intention to commit this crime but had not informed the government was punishable by a five-year prison term and a fine of 10,000 leva. The remaining members of the family would lose their civil rights, might have all or part of their property confiscated, and were subject to sentences to forced labor or to deportation from their homes. The savagery of this statute aroused protest in the British House of Commons, and in various international bodies. The first form of the law provided that, if the guilty party returned to Bulgaria within six months, he might receive a suspended sentence; in October 1953, this period was lengthened to twelve. On November 4, 1953, the law was repealed; the guilty party might now receive no more than a sentence of five years' imprisonment, and his relatives were not to be punished. The modification and repeal of this particular law may well reflect the somewhat gentler policies adopted by Moscow after the death of Stalin. Disorders broke out in Plovdiv in the summer of 1953, when tobacco workers rioted, allegedly in anger against new methods of tobacco-curing introduced by the regime. Yugov, himself a former tobacco-worker, was sent to the scene, and promised to try to get the decree repealed.

When the "new course" was announced by Chervenkov in September, its content was almost wholly economic. But politically, the new policies expressed themselves, as in Rumania, by the consolidation of ministries: the Directorate of the Food Industry, which had been part of the Ministry of Supply, was now combined with the Ministry of Light Industry into a new Ministry of Light and Food Industry. What was left of the Ministry of Supply was combined with the State Reserves section of the Ministry of Light Industry into a new Ministry of Supply and State Reserves. After the elections of December 1953, the government automatically resigned, and all its members were reappointed to the same posts except for Karlo Lukanov, one of the six Deputy Prime Ministers, who dropped out of sight. He was regarded abroad as a close follower of the late Vasil Kolarov, and his star had probably set with the disappearance of his chief.

From February 28 to March 5, 1954, the Bulgarian Communist Party held its Sixth Congress, the first since December 1948. Chervenkov reported that the party had 368,142 full members and 87,109 candidate-members, or a total of 455,251. About 34 per cent were now workers. The party was maintaining some 24,000 cells, political schools with 400,000 students, and a quarter of a million "agitators." He declared that, though the elimination of Kostov had represented a great triumph, the enemies of the party were still active. Yet, he warned against identifying all non-Communists as enemies. Former army officers, in particular, he declared, members of the army reserve forces, should not be punished automatically. Party members were no longer to rely completely on "black lists" of persons who had once been hostile. Some former enemeis who had been released from prison might now render useful services to the OF. Such people had rights as citizens and must be given a right to re-educate themselves. These pleas for gentle action threw a lurid light on the party's past practices. Chervenkov's whole performance indeed had a curiously defensive note about it, and, after the denunciation of bureaucratism, officialdom, negligence, sycophantism, careerism, formalism, egoism, liberalism, greed, theft and waste — all vices rampant in the party — he concluded with a plea for collective work and collective leadership.

This last point, following the pattern established by the Soviet Politburo after Stalin's death and the killing of Beria, had now become dogma in Bulgaria too. Observers had already noticed that the Bulgarian Politburo had begun to sign its telegrams with the names of the signers arranged in alphabetical order, and not in the order of their political importance. But the line which the party would take in the future was laid down at the congress in a speech by Todor Zhivkov. Zhivkov demanded that the Bulgarian Communist Party follow the example set it by the CPSU (B), and "eliminate the cult of personality as a foreign element in Marxism," while establishing a "collective leadership."

Data on Zhivkov's career was not easy to find. He had apparently served in 1949 as Chairman of the Sofia Regional Soviet, from which he had resigned in November. The post he held between then and late 1950 is not known to me, but in November 1950 he became a candidate-member of the Politburo, and in January 1951, Secretary of the Central Committee. He had apparently not held a ministerial post, but was clearly a "coming" man. The party adopted the new party statute which he recommended. Like the Rumanian statute, this abolished the post of Secretary-General of the Party, and replaced it with a Secretariat of the Central Committee. There were three secretaries in Bulgaria as against four in Rumania.

Zhivkov now took office as the "first" of these three secretaries in a role which corresponded to that of Apostol in Rumania. Zhivkov was now also a full member of the Politburo. His fellow secretaries were Dimiter Ganev, and Boris Taskov. Abandoning his "General Secretaryship" like

Malenkov before him and Gheorghiu-Dej soon after him, Chervenkov retained the Premiership and his membership in the Politburo. Encho Staikov, propaganda boss of the party, became a Politburo member, as did Vice-Premier General Ivan Mihailov. General Peter Panchevsky became a candidate-member.

That Chervenkov had experienced a setback was also revealed by the re-emergence of Yugov as a member of the Politburo. We have traced his career from the Ministry of the Interior to the edge of the abyss and back to a position of power. Was it likely that he would forget the violent criticism that Chervenkov had hurled at him after the death of Kostov, or the humiliating self-criticism he had twice been forced to perform? Would the Order of Georgi Dimitrov (whom he had once been accused of betraying), awarded him on his fiftieth birthday in the summer of 1954, mollify him? The new Central Committee elected at the Sixth Congress had some familiar faces, including that of Dobri Terpeshev, who had now also successfully retraced the road back from disgrace. In May, Terpeshev was relieved as head of DOSO, but received the Order of Dimitrov on his seventieth birthday. Another surprise on the new Central Committee was Slavko Trunsky, who had been a commander of Partisans in northwest Bulgaria during the war, and had been in close contact with the Yugoslavs. His squads of ex-Partisans had played an important role in the strenuous but unsuccessful Soviet and Bulgarian Communist effort to intimidate the Congress of the Agrarians in 1945, when the left had wanted to get rid of "Gemeto." After the break with Tito, Trunsky seems to have disappeared, and was rumored to be in the USSR. Now in 1954, he was elected to the Central Committee. Was it possible that the Russians, relieved of Stalin's presence, wanted the Bulgarians to make an approach to the Yugoslavs? At any rate, the two "people's generals," Terpeshev and Trunsky, had emerged from limbo.

Terpeshev and Yugov were certainly "Kostovites." The new Central Committee apparently included some others as well: General Boyan Bulganov, formerly chief of the political department of the army, purged in 1949; and Kiril Dramaliev, the former Minister of Education, whom Chervenkov's man Levy had so violently attacked at the last party conference. Moreover, Chervenkov's ally, Mincho Neichev, seemed to be in disgrace, and others who had allegedly been close to him were also apparently on the downgrade. It was too early to say what the future would be, especially since all conjectures as to the relationships between individual Bulgarian Communists and individual Soviet Communists seemed to be pure guesswork. But one thing was clear: whatever happened to the Bulgarian Communist Party and the Bulgarian government would be determined in Moscow and not in Sofia.

The Communists in the Bulgarian regime did not confine themselves to arresting and trying each other. There was seldom a moment when some sensational trial was not in progress. Many of these were trials of priests or ministers, and these we shall examine below. But the State Secrets Act o October 22, 1948 made it illegal to give out any information whatever o military affairs, and even to hint at the location of a factory, or to tell wha it produced or how many workers it employed. Under the circumstance victims were easy to find, and fulfilled a political purpose, serving as dread ful warnings to other citizens. Alleged Titoite agents, some of whom wer also identified as IMRO men, succeeded each other in the dock. In July 195 a new law held responsible the family of anybody who fled to Yugoslavi Six "American spies" allegedly infiltrated from Greece were executed i September 1951. Ten more, allegedly infiltrated from Turkey, were tried i January 1953, and the leader shot. These instances merely serve as example

FOREIGN RELATIONS

We have already examined many of the important aspects of Bulgaria foreign relations during these years. We need only note the intimacy wit the Soviet Union and its other satellites, European (now including Easter Germany) and Asian (North Korean students appeared at the Universit of Sofia in the early fifties). But relations with Greece deserve special atten tion. After the defeat of Markos' rebellion in the summer of 1949, the Bul garians continued on the worst possible terms with Greece. In Sofia, Greek-language Communist daily newspaper was printed for the refugee from across the border. In the summer of 1952, a serious incident took plac on the frontier.

Here the Bulgarians put troops ashore on two small reedy islands i the Maritsa River (Evros) which serves as the boundary between the tw countries in eastern Thrace. The islands were known as "alpha" and "gamma," being too insignificant to have acquired names. The Greek governmen warned the Bulgarians that, if their soldiers were not withdrawn by Augus 6, it would resort to force. The United Nations advised Athens not to mov against the Bulgarians until a UN committee could make observations o the spot, and hand in recommendations. But immediate danger was averte when the Bulgarians did withdraw their forces within the time set by th Greeks. The Sofia government protested to the UN, and the Bulgarian pres published a map purporting to show that the two islands in question wer Bulgarian.

The conclusion of the Greek-Yugoslav-Turkish accord, on February 28 1953, brought together in alliance three neighbors to which Bulgaria wa hostile. The clause in the treaty which threw open the new accord to any power wishing to participate on an equal footing with the three original partners served as an effective piece of political warfare against Communis Bulgaria. Many Bulgarians must rather wistfully have longed for a real end to the perpetual fear, artificial and real, which they felt for all their neighbors except Rumania. No doubt, the Bulgarian public, if free to express itself would have welcomed the opportunity of easing tension in the Balkans by joining the pact. But it was manifestly impossible for a Soviet satellite regime, though warmly invited to do so, to collaborate in an arrangement between three powers who were "tools of the imperialists." At the same time, the policy of violent propaganda attacks on all three neighbors had clearly grown more dangerous now that all three were allied, and were contemplating even closer military ties. Unless the Soviet Union wanted to take responsibility for the increase of Balkan tension, it had better decrease it.

By September 1953, Chervenkov was holding out his hand, especially to Greece, while displaying the usual venom against the United States. The tone of such pronouncements can be conveyed only by direct quotation:

> a certain reanimation . . . has become apparent among the hostile elements in our country, which had lain low for some time. Birds of a feather flock together (*laughter*). . . . the organizers of wrecking and subversive activity in the People's Democracies, generously supplied with dollars from sums specially voted by the American Senate for brigand actions in the socialist and democratic countries, have of late been feverishly sending bandits entrusted with subversive tasks to our territory, whom our security organs are successfully laying by the heels and sending to secure places. (*Prolonged applause. Animation and laughter.*)
>
> The People's Government desires to see all disputed and unsolved issues with its neighboring countries, Turkey, Greece, and Yugoslavia, settled. We have no aggressive intentions toward any one of them. We do not want to impose our social system on anybody. We want to live on good terms with them, and are ready to negotiate with them on the principles of mutual respect. . . .
>
> Nothing justifies the continuation of the present state of affairs in our relations with Greece. Negotiations for the settlement of certain disputed questions concerning our frontiers show that when there is good will and mutual understanding all questions can be discussed and solved. At the same time they show the necessity of a speedier resumption of diplomatic relations between Bulgaria and Greece in the interest of peace in the Balkans.[13]

Despite the anti-American tone of the speech, Chervenkov added that he "found no justification" for the suspension of diplomatic relations between the countries. If he expected that Washington would greet this overture with joy, he was disappointed. All that the State Department did was to "note with interest" the statement he had made, and to "reaffirm the sentiments of deep and abiding friendship which the American people and government have toward the people of Bulgaria."[14]

Chervenkov added nothing about the issues between Bulgaria and Turkey or Bulgaria and Yugoslavia. At the same time, Bulgarian propaganda broad-

[13] "Report of Vulko Chervenkov . . . to the . . . meeting of September 9, 1953 . . . ," *Bulgaria Today,* no. 18, supplement (September 20, 1953), pp. 27 ff.

[14] Department of State *Bulletin,* XXIX (743), September 21, 1953, p. 375.

casts in Serbo-Croatian, Macedonian, Turkish, and Greek strove to emphasize the ethnic and past political differences among the new allies, and to create as much mutual distrust as possible.

Chervenkov's mention of the settlement of frontier disputes with Greece referred to the labors of a Greek-Bulgarian commission, which had been meeting to settle the question of the Maritsa islands and to restore the signposts along the frontier. Speaking on December 20, 1953, Chervenkov returned to the subject, and declared that the Greeks had acknowledged that the behavior of the Bulgarian delegates to the commission showed how peaceful Bulgarian intentions really were. He announced that his government hoped to revive the frontier commission with Yugoslavia, and repeated his wish for friendly relations with all three neighbors. Indeed, the Bulgarian and Greek governments were about to negotiate for the reopening of diplomatic relations, on the strength of an invitation to the Greeks sent them through the UN by the Bulgarians on October 29. The Bulgarian press none the less bitterly denounced the Greek-American agreement of October 12, 1953, which permitted the United States to use Greek bases and keep American troops in Greece.

On December 5, 1953, the Bulgarian and Greek governments signed a trade agreement involving $1,800,000 worth of goods for 1954. On December 30, 1953, at Saloniki, the frontier settlement was signed by representatives of the two states. The Bulgarian press remarked that "the frontier along the Maritsa is now permanent and independent of any deviation in the river's course."[15] All destroyed signposts had been restored. Finally in May 1954, after months of negotiations carried on largely in France by the ambassadors of the two powers, Greece and Bulgaria reached an agreement to reopen diplomatic relations. Bulgaria agreed to recognize the obligations imposed by the Peace Treaty, and to give the Greek government a list of Greek citizens, not political refugees, who might wish to return to Greece, and to facilitate their repatriation to Greece. A three-member committee, including representatives of the International Red Cross, and the Greek and Bulgarian Red Cross, would scrutinize the list. Thus the Bulgarians apparently gave in, at least in principle, on the outstanding issues remaining between the countries; the Treaty obligated them to pay $45,000,000 in reparations to Greece, and the "Greek citizens" to be listed and repatriated were the children kidnaped from Greek Macedonia during the Greek civil war and brought to Bulgaria by the Communists. During the summer of 1954, the Greeks suspended talks on the reparations question, and turned down the first Bulgarian suggested as Ambassador: Kiril Dramaliev, a strong Moscow man, and former Minister of Education. In August, the Bulgarian regime was negotiating for the resumption of the talks. Thus the Greek-Turkish-Yugoslav pact, bolstered by the new firm military alliance, had served as an extremely effective instrument of pressure on Bulgaria.

[15] *Bulgaria Today,* no. 25 (January 20, 1954).

3. *Albania*

The pattern of political sovietization in Albania was the one familiar to us, modified only by the primitive conditions prevailing in the country, and the further delays and strains incident to Albania's transfer from Yugoslav to direct Russian domination.

ELECTIONS

In March 1949, came the redistricting of the country which was the necessary preliminary to the choice of the new "people's councils." There were twenty-five new regions, subdivided into 186 districts and 2,579 villages, each unit to have its own people's council. The government fixed the average size of each district at 6,000, which put the population at roughly 1,116,000. On June 12, elections were held: 95 per cent of the electorate voted; 98 per cent of them voted for the Democratic Front candidates. Not including the twenty-five regional people's councils, there were 18,350 members of the others, including, according to figures published in 1952, 15,708 peasants, 248 workers, and 1,600 employees, teachers, and scientific workers. New elections, with a similar vote, were held on March 7, 1954.

Early in 1950, the National Assembly passed a decree enfranchizing all citizens of eighteen, and permitting the army to vote. Only the politically "unreliable" were excluded. The decree also provided that the new National Assembly would be twice as large as the old: it would have one representative for every 10,000 inhabitants instead of one for every 20,000. The assembly adjourned toward the end of March, and the government announced that elections for the new one would be held in May. It had passed 345 new laws, and all its work, as its President, Gogo Nushi, declared, had been modeled on the glorious precedent set by the USSR. On May 28, the elections took place: 99.43 per cent of the electorate voted; 99.18 of their ballots were cast for the front candidate. There were of course no others. The new assembly had 121 deputies, including, interestingly enough, only fifteen peasants and twenty-six workers, one ecclesiastic and seventy-nine employees. Here was a fine excuse for a later charge of "bureaucratism" if this were to be thought appropriate. The next elections were held in the spring of 1954. There were 137 constituencies of 10,000 inhabitants each, which indicated the population rise since 1950.

By early 1951, it was clear that something had gone wrong within the people's councils. It was announced that permanent committees were to be chosen within the councils to "strengthen them in their tasks." Probably few of the thousands of members could be made to understand or assist the government's program, and surely the Communists needed to establish their own people firmly in control. But details were not available, although the general conclusion was amply supported by the announcement in April that all membership cards in the Democratic Front had to be submitted for renewal. New village and town front committees were to be chosen in May. A purge on the local level seemed to be under way.

PARTY AND GOVERNMENT

Within the Communist Party and the government, the Xoxe purge continued during 1949 and 1950, and changes in personnel were frequent. Ramadan Citaku was expelled from the Presidium of the National Assembly in March 1949, before Xoxe was tried. In October, the party's third plenum heard reports from Mehmet Shehu, and from Spiro Koleka of the Politburo. Shehu in particular leveled especially violent denunciations against Albanians abroad. They had formed a Free Albania Committee in Paris, headed by Midhat Frasheri, the former leader of the Balli Kombetar, who had escaped in 1944, and including Abas Kupi and Said Kryeziu. Others against whom Albanians must guard were the Anglo-Saxons, the Greeks, and especially the Yugoslavs, whom Shehu charged with 540 "provocations" since early 1949. Not only had they sent gangs across the frontier and "violated Albanian air-space" but they had entered the Albanian Legation in Belgrade and kidnaped an Albanian citizen. Moreover, Yugoslav "Trotskyites" had tried to rescue Xoxe, but had been foiled in time.

The choice of Koleka to deliver the report to the plenum suggested that he was on the rise. By November 1949, he was Chairman of the Planning Commission and Deputy Premier. At the same time, Gogo Nushi gave way as Minister of Industry to Abediu Shehu. Soon afterward, Major-General Haxhi Lleshi was relieved as "acting" Chairman of the Control Commission, and was replaced by Manush Myftiu. Lleshi remained as Minister without Portfolio. Premier Hoxha promoted himself from Colonel-General to Army General. But early in 1950, Abediu Shehu was not only dropped as Minister of Industry but expelled from the Central Committee. Tuk Jakova of the Politburo replaced him in his ministry. Niazi Islami, Deputy Minister of Communications was also dismissed, apparently because he had criticized the USSR for late delivery of trucks; the charge, however, was "Trotskyism." The powerful Koleka took over the Ministry of Public Works, as a temporary post. It was clear that there was not enough personnel to go around, and that economic and political crisis was endemic. When the "Workers" Party held its second national conference in April 1950, Mehmet Shehu found it necessary to deny the truth of the report that there were 15,000 guerrillas operating against the regime in the mountains. The "Abediu Shehu group" and the other hostile forces led by certain army officers were to be liquidated. One of these was A. Vinxhani, an old Partisan and a graduate of the Voroshilov Academy in Moscow.

Prominent Communists continued to interest themselves in the "Democratic Front," which still played a more important role than was any longer necessary, for example, for the Bulgarian OF. Hoxha himself remained

President of the General Council of the Front, and Tuk Jakova, Gogo Nushi, Medar Shtylla, Myslim Peza were all Vice-Presidents, while Hysni Kapo was Secretary General. In July 1950, Hoxha formed a new government. Mehmet Shehu was Minister of Foreign Affairs and Defense; Tuk Jakova was Vice-Premier and Minister of the Interior. Hysni Kapo, Spiro Koleka, and Spiro Pano were all Vice-Premiers. Manol Konomi held the Ministry of Justice; Rita Marko, Industry; Zenel Hamiti, Mining; J. Reka, Agriculture; Gogo Tashko, Forestry; Abdyl Kellezi, Finance; Shefqet Peci, Communications; R. Dervici, Construction; K. Ndjela, Trade; Kahroman Ylli, Education; V. Kati, Foreign Trade; Leften Goga, Deliveries; Medar Shtylla, Health; Manush Myftiu, Control Commission; and Kocho Theodosi, Planning Commission. Twenty-one ministries was a good many for a small country with few trained bureaucrats. The multiplication of ministries and the division of their functions had obviously begun.

In March 1951, a new wave of party and government changes took place. Spiro Pano and Rita Marko were relieved as Vice-Premier and Minister of Industry respectively, the new Minister of Industry being A. Tchartchani. Manush Myftiu resigned as head of the Control Commission, and Mehmet Shehu took his place without resigning any of his other posts. Shehu was now Minister of the Interior, although it is not absolutely clear when he had succeeded Tuk Jakova, who was severely disciplined at this time for showing "too great leniency toward the Roman Catholic clergy." Jakova may have been dropped from the Politburo temporarily, but this is not certain.

From the Control Commission Manush Myftiu moved into a Vice-Premiership and the Ministry of Justice, where he replaced Manol Konomi. Konomi was also ousted from the Central Committee for weakness. The "cadres" director of the Central Committee, Theodore Heba, was dropped, and the party secretaries at Tirana, Elbasan, and Valona lost their jobs. Party and government decreed martial law, called for the surrender of rifles, and announced that all terrorist activity against the government must be liquidated. The Albanian regime was clearly very much frightened. The press admitted that guerrillas were crossing the frontier from Yugoslavia, and Belgrade published full accounts of the activities of various anti-Hoxha Albanian groups in Kossovo. Moreover, in February, a bomb had gone off in the Soviet Legation in Tirana, after which it was reported that at least forty Albanians were executed. The political purges may well have been ordered by the Russians as a result.

Speaking on November 8, 1951, the tenth anniversary of the founding of the Albanian "Workers" Party, Hoxha reported that, as of June 1951, there had been 48,087 members, and that the party had 2,579 organizations in Albanian villages and towns. The Central Committee, as a tenth anniversary decision, had decreed that all workers who had "laid the foundations for socialism" would be taken into the party. While between 1944 and 1948 only 4,684 Albanian Communists had formally studied Communist theory, now there were 12,264 at work on it. One hundred comrades a year wer taking the one-year course; 283 the two-year correspondence course; 1,21 three-month courses. Forty-two per cent of the party membership had attende such schools. Fifty-five thousand copies of the *History of the CPSU* (B) an 41,000 of the life of Stalin had been printed in Albanian. In every village party libraries and reading-rooms were established.

In September 1951, Vice-Premier Hysni Kapo took over the Agricultur Ministry, the former Minister, Reka, remaining as his deputy. Gogo Nushi be came a Vice-Premier. Mehmet Shehu relinquished the Control Commission t Josif Pashko, but retained his other posts. Bilbil Klosi became acting Ministe of Justice, replacing Manush Myftiu. In December 1951, Communication Minister Shefqet Peci succeeded Zenel Hamiti as Minister of Mines, and Mil Klosko became Minister of Communications. In March 1952, it was reporte that Bilbil Klosi was now Minister of Justice. He had been succeeded a Public Prosecutor by Sotir Kyriaki. This announcement suggests that Klosi who had been acting Minister of Justice for some months, had held the pos simultaneously with that of Public Prosecutor, a remarkable combination The Ministers of Agriculture and Education were relieved in April 1952 fo neglect and incompetence.

On September 1, 1952, a new and rigorous penal code came into effect It imposed the death penalty on anybody twelve years old or older fo conspiracy against the state, damaging state property, and economic sabotage For other offenses in the "people's democracy" the death penalty might no be inflicted on anybody under the age of fourteen. All those who migh criticize the Soviet Union were to be jailed. Indeed all offenses against th Soviet Union were offenses against the Albanian state. The Minister of Justice Bilbil Klosi, said of the new code:

> we were inspired by the Soviet penal code. But taking into consideration th repeated attempts at revolution in our country, which are supported an directed by alien elements, we found ourselves constrained to include mor severe measures and penalties than those sanctioned by the Soviet penal code.[16]

In early August 1953, the party, the government, and the Presidium o the People's Assembly were said to have chosen a new government. Hoxh was still Premier, and Mehmet Shehu Minister of the Interior and Deput Premier. Hysni Kapo was Deputy Premier and Minister of Agriculture an Agricultural Collection. The remaining ministers were: Foreign Affairs, Beha Shtylla, an old Korcha associate of Hoxha; Defense, Bequir Balluku, traine in Moscow; Industry and Construction, Spiro Koleka; Trade and Communi cations, Gogo Nushi; Education and Culture, Bedri Spahiu; Finance, Tul Jakova; Justice, Bilbil Klosi; Health, Medar Shtylla; State Planning Com mission, Kocho Theodosi; and State Control Commission, Shefqet Peci From twenty-one ministries in July 1950, the number had shrunk to ten

[16] International Peasants' Union, *Bulletin*, III, 11–12 (November-December 1952), p. 5.

Much combining of function had taken place. Dr. Omer Nishani, who had been President of the Presidium of the National Assembly, asked to be relieved of this post, and Haxhi Lleshi was appointed to it. On the same occasion, Mehmet Shehu was relieved of his post as Secretary-General of the Party. The announcement of the change gave no further details, but Hoxha apparently replaced him. It seemed that no new party statute had yet been adopted.

All through these years, Hoxha had managed to hold on to his power. Rumors of conflict with Shehu, however, were practically constant, and émigré Albanian circles were wont every few weeks to predict that Shehu would surely turn Hoxha out before long. The report seemed reasonable enough: by the end of 1953, there was nobody left of the original Albanian Central Committee except Hoxha himself, Tuk Jakova, and Bedri Spahiu. New men were coming to the top, and Shehu had the ruthlessness and perhaps the strength to oust Hoxha himself. But it was unsafe to generalize too freely about the powers of Communist Ministers of the Interior: Beria himself could not in the end use his tremendous influence effectively. Georgescu and Yugov had been ousted. Only Rankovich remained firmly in office; he did so by virtue of loyalty to Tito. Nobody had suggested that he wanted to supplant his boss.

It was not until the summer of 1954 that news finally came of a major shift in the Albanian party and government. On July 12, at the meeting of the Central Committee, came the expected new party statute. The post of Secretary-General, apparently held by Hoxha, was abolished, and he became instead first Secretary of the Central Committee. Gogo Nushi (also President of the National Assembly) and Liri Belishova were the other two, while Manush Myftiu and Josip Pashko moved out of the party secretariat. On July 20, Hoxha resigned as Premier, and, for the first time, was not immediately reappointed. His successor was Mehmet Shehu, who formed a new government. The two first Vice-Premiers were Hysni Kapo, Minister of Agriculture, and Lieutenant-General Beqir Balluku, Minister of National Defense. Manush Myftiu and Tuk Jakova were also Vice-Premiers; Pashko was Minister of Construction, Spiro Koleka head of the State Planning Office, and Shefqet Peci head of the State Control Commission. Hoxha, it was announced, would devote all his time to party work. It was far too early to count him out.

The Albanian party and government struggled to imitate the standard instruments of Communist influence and control. In addition to the party itself and the Democratic Front, there was of course an Albanian-Soviet Friendship Society with 1,128 branches and 50,000 members in August 1950, and 114,000 members only three months later, in November. It had thirty-seven branches and 2,000 clubs, and Tuk Jakova as its President. By late June 1951, there were 145,000 members, and Bedri Spahiu was President. A year later, there were 154,000 members. Equally of course, the Albanian Anti-Fascist Women flourished, with 246,000 members in October 1950, and Hoxha's wife, Madame Nexhmije Hoxha, as Chairman of its presidium. At that time, the Albanians boasted that 20 per cent of the workers of the country were women (a total of 21,000 in August 1952), that there were seventeen woman deputies in the Assembly, and 575 in the people's councils. Then there was the Union of Working Youth, whose Secretary, Pipi Mitrodjordji, said in July 1952 that it had 81,000 members, and was modeled directly after the Komsomol. By early 1954, the number was reported well over 100,000. The Trades Union membership rose from 25,000 workers in 374 organizations in 1945 to 82,500 in 970 organizations by January 1954. Tirana had 1,225 Stakhanovites and 7,200 shock-workers, 60 per cent of the town's industrial force having attained these honors.

The Russians themselves were much in evidence. In the fall of 1950, their numbers were estimated at 3,000, and there were also said to be more than 300 Polish "specialists" helping Albanian infant industry. But another report of 1952 put the number of Russians as under 1,000. Those who escaped from Albania often commented on the luxuries which the Russian advisers enjoyed, with a block of flats built especially for them in the part of town called "new" Tirana, automobiles, servants, and more and better food than the native population. Russian salaries were reported to be 30,000 leks a month as against an average of 2,500–5,000 for Albanians. The Chairman of the Presidium of the National Assembly was kept busy decorating especially prominent Russians in token of Albanian gratitude to them for their help. On the eighth anniversary of "liberation," November 25, 1952, a large Soviet delegation made its appearance, together with delegations from all the satellite states, including Outer Mongolia and North Korea.

They heard the Albanian army commander, General Petrit Dume, tell his troops that the Albanian army was an integral part of the Soviet army. Plainer speaking they could hardly have demanded. Indeed, the Russians dominated the militia as well as the army, though reports of Russian submarine pens at Saseno appeared to be in error. Albania celebrated Red Army Day, and the Soviet Red Cross and Red Crescent allegedly sent 400,000 rubles' worth of supplies and drugs to the Albanian victims of the severe snowfall of the winter of 1953–54. Twelve hundred Albanians were reported attending schools in the USSR and the other people's democracies in the summer of 1952. Every official speech or pronouncement of any kind expressed fulsome thanks to the USSR.

Trials were a continuous feature of the Albanian scene. In May 1950, the United States was accused of dropping three members of BK in parachutes from planes flying from Italy. Their death sentences were commuted because they had helped Albanian security organs. Early in 1951, the government announced that it had captured five more parachutists from Italy and killed four of them. The total number of agents infiltrated and captured in

1950 was said to be twenty-nine, and they had also come from Greece and Yugoslavia, of course on orders from Washington and London. The same charge continued to be repeated during 1951. In four days during November of that year alone, the Albanians complained, they had picked up sixty-seven spies. This time, the Albanian Deputy Minister of Foreign Affairs, Mihal Prifti, sent a note to the UN, accusing the United States, Britain, Italy, Yugoslavia, and Greece of large-scale hostile action against Albania. He also accused Yugoslavia of oppressing the Albanian minority in Kossovo, of interfering with postal communications between the two countries, and of suspending air travel. Albania, like the rest of the satellites, also protested against the Mutual Security Act, and professed to believe that this meant the United States would support espionage and subversion in Albania.

Frontier incidents and protests continued in 1952 and 1953; the regime showing some nervousness with regard to Zog's move from Egypt to the United States in 1952, and in 1953 returning vigorously to the attack on the BK, which they called a tool of the United States, Abas Kupi's Legality, which they called a tool of Britain, and other Albanian émigré groups in Italy and Greece. In April 1954, the Albanians were still indefatigably trying and condemning alleged Albanian parachutists from Greece. Six were shot, one hanged, and one sentenced to ten years' imprisonment as American agents.

FOREIGN RELATIONS

This nervousness on the part of the Albanian regime reflected the true power picture in the Mediterranean. Cut off from its fellow-satellites, Albania bordered only on hostile Greece and Yugoslavia, and faced Italy, also a member of the western bloc of nations. The Russians could reach Albania only by ship. They had many obligations and commitments in the rest of the world, and Albania was expensive to maintain in relation to the profit to be had from it. There seemed little doubt that, if the western powers had wished to do so, they could have used Albanian forces from Yugoslavia, together with a small trans-Adriatic landing-force, and at small cost liberated the country from its native Communist masters and the distant Russians. Albania indeed was the only satellite which might have been thus cheaply freed, perhaps without the danger of precipitating a major war, and there was no doubt whatever that any invasion force would have been rapturously greeted by the miserable population.

Yet there were numerous deterrents to this adventure, attractive though it might be to set the Albanians free. In the first place, one could not be absolutely positive that the Russians would not fight. In the second, if the effort should succeed, the economic liability of Albania would simply be transferred from the Russians to the west, especially the United States. In the third, until 1953, there was some likelihood that the Yugoslavs and the Greeks would simply partition Albania between themselves if it should be freed, and plunge themselves and the western allies into a morass of Balkan territorial disputes, while leaving the Albanians little better off. So the experiment, if it was ever contemplated, was never tried. There was, however, good reason for Hoxha to worry when he contemplated the possibilities.

A few months after the conclusion of the Greek-Turkish-Yugoslav pact in February 1953, the Greek, Turkish, and Yugoslav Foreign Ministers issued on July 13 a statement to the effect that an independent Albania was desirable for the peace and stability of the Balkan area. Though at first glance this might seem to have disposed of the possibility that at some future date Albania would be partitioned between Greece and Yugoslavia, and might therefore be supposed to allay Albania alarm, at second glance it may be realized that it did nothing of the sort. The statement was vague, and its very vagueness rather underlined than removed Greek ambitions to annex southern Albania (northern Epirus). If this were done, what was left of Albania would hardly prove a viable state, and the Yugoslavs would probably be irresistibly tempted to annex it. Moreover, Tito had once almost swallowed all of Albania in his Federated Yugoslavia as an additional republic, and the Yugoslavs might well not yield even the southern portion to Greece with any satisfaction. The Albanian problem thus remained a potential source of discord in the new Balkan alliance, and one which the great-power sponsors of that alliance might therefore well prefer to leave alone for the moment, in spite of the possible temptation to overthrow the Albanian Communists and win an easy victory over the eastern bloc. Even this small step toward achieving the American Republican Party's professed foreign policy goal — liberating the oppressed peoples under Soviet domination — seemed too expensive, and the United States continued to recede from it.

Twice in 1953, the State Department expressed official American friendship for the Albanian people, and sympathy with them in their plight. In a letter of August 27, to Hassan Dosti, Chairman of the Executive Committee of the National Committee for a Free Albania, Secretary Dulles said:

> This government shall continue its efforts to support the Albanian people in their endeavors for the establishment of a free and representative government . . . recent declarations by Albania's neighbors (i.e., Greece and Yugoslavia) of their peaceful purpose toward Albania . . . constitute significant refutation of Communist charges that Albania's neighbors are bent upon partition of Albania." [17]

On November 28, in a press release, the Department officially noted Albanian independence day, made graceful reference to Skanderbeg (by now the hero of a Soviet-made film), and assured the Albanians of American support in their struggle against Communist tyranny.

[17] Department of State, *Bulletin*, XXIX (747), October 19, 1953, p. 530.

Chapter 14

THE BALKAN SATELLITE ECONOMIES SINCE 1948

IN THE YEARS AFTER 1948, the Communists continued to apply oviet methods to the economies of the Balkan satellites, at different speeds nd with varying success. Economic plans on the Russian model were dopted everywhere, with the same emphasis on industrialization and espe-ally on heavy industry. Each satellite regime had its own "big projects," arallel to the building of major canals and power installations in the USSR. ll of the governments commanded collectivization of agriculture, in the face f the determined hostility of the peasants, who also groaned under the system f forced deliveries. State loans and currency "reforms" brought the regimes a art of the enormous amounts of capital they needed for their overambitious vestment programs, and helped push down the already dangerously de-ressed standard of living.

Through the devices of the "joint" companies in Rumania, domination of l foreign trade, and the rendering of "assistance," the USSR tightened its lready firm grip on the economies of all three countries. In the summer of 953, following the "new course" adopted by the Soviet Union after the death f Stalin, the satellite regimes slowed down the pace, set aside or modified ome of the most costly investment schemes, and paid a mild obeisance to the eed of supplying more consumers' goods and improving the lot of the popu-ation. But they had not abandoned their goals or thought of new methods for eaching them.

1. *Rumania*

In Rumania, as we saw, adoption of a plan was long delayed by the slow ecovery from the economic chaos produced after the war by the various forms f Soviet plunder and by the droughts. The year 1948 brought nationalization, he centralization of industrial controls, and the establishment of the first tate Planning Commission. For 1949 and 1950 the regime adopted one-year lans, and in 1951 the first Five Year Plan, launching it to the tune of a slogan hat it must be completed in four years, or by the end of 1954.

Every three months, the government reported the degree of plan-fulfill-nent so far achieved. These published quarterly reports presented the analyst vith difficulties familiar to all who have tried to work with their Soviet coun-erparts: the achievements of the plan were reported in percentage figures of goal whose absolute figure was often not known. Similarly, percentages of improvement were given when the original figure was unknown. The reports often included internal inconsistencies: branches of industrial production mentioned in one report were omitted from the next, while branches previously omitted suddenly made a first appearance. Yet the texts of the plan-laws themselves, and prewar statistical publications sometimes gave the absolute figures to which the percentages allegedly referred, and the most important Communists in the government occasionally made speeches containing important economic data. The Rumanian professional economic journal, *Probleme Economice,* sometimes added to available knowledge. Even when one had extracted from these sources all that was in them, the further question as to their reliability arose to plague one. There could be little doubt that they were often falsified for propaganda purposes, to encourage the public and to inure them to the necessary hardships. The doctored figures, however, were all the student had, and he was therefore compelled to use them. The picture which emerged before him was of a country whose entire structure was undergoing fundamental change.

AGRICULTURE

In 1948, the population of the urban industrial centers in Rumania was 3,800,000. In May 1953, Gheorghiu-Dej put the figure at 5,500,000, and predicted that it would be 7,000,000 by 1960. The ratio between city and countryside would then be 40:60. One-sixth of the population of Rumania would have moved to town. To feed them, the countryside would need to be mechanized, and it must first be collectivized. The Five Year Plan called for increasing the area under cultivation to 10,000,000 hectares from 9,300,000, and for the reduction of the area under corn from 2,500,000 hectares to 1,750,000, while quadrupling the area devoted to industrial crops from 250,000 to 1,000,000 hectares, and doubling the area under fodder crops to 1,200,000 hectares. All this was to be accompanied by the driving of the peasants into collectives.

The drive to collectivize in Rumania got under way slowly in the second half of 1948. Members of the government gave speeches favoring the "socialist forms of agriculture." In these early days, however, the term seems to have meant only a form of producers' coöperative, or peasants' partnership formed for a season to bring in a given crop, and dissolved again after the job had been completed. The early machine tractor stations (MTS) formed in this period assisted these partnerships to perform their tasks. There were eighty MTS at the end of 1948. In January 1949 the Minister of Agriculture announced that many more would be founded during the year, and declared that the government was about to embark on "a long and patient campaign of enlightenment to convince the peasantry that they can escape misery and exploitation by turning their small holdings into collectives."[1] In March, the government announced that the local branches of the Ploughmen's Front would assist the peasants to form "working associations," to which the state

[1] *East Europe,* V, 216 (January 27, 1949), p. 7.

would then give assistance and the use of tractors. On March 15, 1949, the Central Committee of the "Workers" Party decided that wherever conditions were favorable, collectives should be introduced.

Just before this announcement, the regime had taken on March 2 a necessary preliminary step. This was a further "land reform," the latest in the postwar series in the Balkans, and the second and last for Rumania. The state confiscated overnight all estates of fifty hectares or more, including those which had hitherto been preserved as "model" farms. The alleged purpose of the decree was to prevent "sabotage of the sowing plan," and to ensure the development of Rumanian agriculture. The expulsion of the owners began before the decree had been published. The police drove them from their homes into the nearest town, leaving them with a bare minimum of personal belongings. The amount of land obtained was not announced, but it may have run to half a million hectares. The state did not distribute it, but used it, together with some 200,000 hectares of former crown lands, as the nucleus for a series of state farms.

In July 1949, the regime produced an agricultural tax bill, levying graduated taxes rising from about 7 per cent on an income of 12,000–15,000 lei to 37 per cent on 400,000 lei. In addition to these taxes, the people's councils might, in their discretion, levy a further tax ranging from 20 to 50 per cent on "chiaburs." A chiabur, or Rumanian kulak, was any peasant owing more than ten hectares or employing hired labor on his land. The government forbade the chiabur to discharge any hired employee, and set the salaries of farm laborers at 3,300–7,000 lei a month. The Ploughmen's Front began to give courses for "agitators" against the chiabur. The "class war in the countryside" was on. As Gheorghiu-Dej said in the spring of 1950:

> The class struggle in the countryside is developing under conditions in which the large peasants are being curbed and the first collective farms formed. The curbing of the large peasantry is achieved by following a class policy in taxation and levies and by the development and strengthening of the associations (i.e., collectives).[2]

Luca, the Finance Minister, had earlier given the number of chiaburs as 195,-000 families, or 6 per cent of Rumanian peasant households. The regime now embarked on an effort to tax them out of existence, and to arouse the hatred of their neighbors against them.

In September 1949, there were forty-one collectives; by the end of 1949 there were fifty-six, embracing 4,058 households and over 15,000 hectares of arable land. There were eighty MTS with 2,289 tractors. The year 1950 saw an intense effort to increase collectivization. In February, Moghioroș took over as head of a special commission to ensure the compulsory deliveries of farm products. The figures as they were announced from time to time told their own story: at the end of the first quarter of the year, 184 collectives; at the end

[2] Conrad, DWR, p. 30.

of the second quarter, 547; on July 18, 623; on July 30, 724; on August 17, 848; on September 5, 972; at the end of the third quarter, 1,006; at the end of the year, 1,027, with 67,719 peasant households, and about a quarter of a million hectares of arable land. But in the fall there were signs that the campaign was slackening, as announcements declared that the main task now was to consolidate the existing farms: i.e., to add to their size and membership, rather than to form new ones. The drive would now continue, said the government, on a "voluntary" basis. There were now 138 MTS with 6,153 tractors, or a gain of 1,530 tractors over 1949.

It was pointed out, however, by students of Rumanian agriculture, that in 1944 there had been 8,200 tractors in Rumania, and that the position had therefore not yet reached the level of that wartime year. Moreover, the cost of producing each tractor in the highly touted plant at Brașov was approximately three times what it was in the USSR. News of peasant opposition to the collectivization leaked out; there were reports of a great fire set by the members in a collective in Oltenia, and the arrest of the president of the farm for negligence. The report on the Plan for 1950, however, boasted that the output of bread grains was up 160 per cent over 1949, and rice 340 per cent.

Early in 1951, the compulsory delivery system was extended to milk, and used as a further weapon against the chiabur. Any peasant holding more than twenty hectares must deliver 1,500 liters of milk whether or not he owned cows. Those who did not have cows would have to buy the milk for cash in order to turn it over to the state. But they might not sell their crop surpluses until they had a certificate from the State Milk Central Coöperative declaring that they had fulfilled their obligations. At the end of 1951, there were only sixty more collectives than there had been at the end of 1950, and only a few more than 7,000 new families had joined. The totals as of December 1951 were 1,089 collectives, 75,065 families; no figure was released on the number of hectares of arable land. But the tractor output increased steadily, and the existing farms presumably were far more mechanized than before. There were now 188 MTS, with 8,500 tractors.

On September 10, 1951, the Central Committee of the "Workers" Party reviewed the accomplishments of the two-and-a-half-year period since March 1949, when the government had initiated the collectivization drive, and issued a new decree. Declaring the drive a great success, the report maintained that the collectives were bringing in a grain yield anywhere from 25 to 50 per cent above the yields produced on private farms. But there had been serious departures from the party line: members of the collectives had violated the statute; organization had been poor; members of collectives had been spending too much time on their own plots; in their haste to form additional collectives, regional and district party committees had failed to educate the members of the new farms.

The decree also criticized severely the failures of the producers' coöperatives or partnerships, which were not collectives (since they involved no surrender of land or cattle), but were mere associations for limited times and limited purposes. The decree reaffirmed the new policy of consolidating existing collectives rather than founding new ones, and laid especial emphasis on the proviso that nobody must be coerced to join. Persuasion yes, pressure no. The stress here clearly indicated that such pressure had been commonly employed to get the peasants to join collectives.

Most important, the new party decree provided for the establishment of a new type of collective in Rumania, the form which the Russians called a TOZ. The TOZ was a voluntary productive association, in which each participant kept and did not surrender his property rights in his land and cattle. The members removed the barriers between their fields and worked in common for a mutual profit: in short, this was a genuine producers' coöperative. The peasants had a general assembly, and elected a managing committee each year. In the USSR, this form of peasant association had been much more popular in the late twenties than the *artel* or full-fledged collective. In 1930, when Stalin had imposed full-scale collectivization, the TOZ had decreased in number until in 1932 only 4,300 remained of the more than 42,000 which had existed in 1929. The Sixteenth Party Congress of the CPSU (B) in 1930 had decreed that in certain areas the TOZ might be allowed to continue to exist as a step toward the formation of the artel. In some of the other satellite states, after the Second World War, the TOZ-form of association had been allowed until the break with Tito, but the Rumanians had not permitted it, and Luca himself, in the Cominform paper for August 1, 1949, had said that the TOZ was an "inferior" form of agricultural production coöperative.

Now, however, the Rumanian Communists found themselves compelled to retreat, and to decree that the TOZ form would hereafter be encouraged and assisted. It seems probable that the party had several main purposes in modifying its policy. In the first place, it could now label as TOZ-type associations many of the *ad hoc* partnerships which already existed. This would help the statistics in each year's annual report, and indeed it might induce some peasants to look with favor on coöperative production. It would also be more efficient, since the partnerships would now not dissolve after each harvest, but would be regularized as TOZ-type coöperatives. Then, when the time came, they could be collectivized, and the "transitional" role of the TOZ would have been fulfilled. Moreover, the fanfare for the transitional TOZ-form helped to obscure the undoubted fact that the Rumanian peasant loathed the collective, and could be driven into it only under severe pressure. The 1951 figure for the partnership arrangements was given in October as 354,000 peasant heads of household, entering into more than 4,000 contracts for the joint cultivation of 428,000 hectares.

Thus 1952 apparently opened under a new dispensation. Bucharest Radio said in March that the peasants were coming to realize that they might retain their land in the new type of association, and were flocking to apply to join. The currency "reform" of January had created a great crisis, as we shall see, in all branches of the economy; one of its purposes may well have been to bring so much financial pressure to bear on the peasantry that their opposition to collectivization would be weakened. The collective farms were exempt for two years from the heavy compulsory deliveries of fats and meat announced in January. The chiabur's quotas alone were increased by 30 per cent. In the summer, peasants who informed against chiaburs for hoarding grain were promised 25 per cent of any grain the government might recover. Thus the pressures mounted. And the pace quickened once more; the new dispensation was more apparent than real.

Speaking at the August 23, 1952 anniversary of the 1944 "liberation," Gheorghiu-Dej declared that there were now 1,420 collectives with 120,000 families, and 860 TOZ-type associations with 36,000 families. As a result of the purge of right-wing deviationists from the party, he said, referring to the disgrace of Luca, Pauker, and Teohari Georgescu, 40,000 peasants had applied to form 1,200 more TOZ-type associations, and others, whose number he did not mention, were asking to be allowed to form new collectives. Thus the unquestioned boss of Rumania linked the previous failures and slowdowns in collectivization with his former colleagues, whom the regime now accused, as we know, of having been too gentle with the peasants. The drive to collectivize was being stepped up once more.

From 1,420 collectives and 860 TOZ in August, the respective numbers mounted to 1,478 and 1,380 in late October. Miron Constantinescu, Chairman of the State Planning Commission, announced in November that 16 per cent of the arable land in Rumania had already been collectivized. By the end of 1952, there were 1,795 collectives, with 165,411 families. More than 700 had been created during the year, as against sixty in 1951. The total number of families had more than doubled during the year. The 1951 slowdown had been only temporary. There were now 218 MTS with a total of 9,680 tractors. The 1952 constitution itself seemed to point the way to more stringent rules for members of collectives. Where the draft version had provided that "Peasants who are members of collective farms *have a personal right to* some land around the house," the version which was actually adopted showed an amended text, which had apparently not been debated, and which read: "Peasants who are members of collective farms *may use* the land around their houses." This might be the entering wedge for enactments even more severe than those in force in the USSR.

The 1952 report on the fulfillment of the plan for food production showed great lags: sugar and canned vegetables were deficient, while the production for the Ministry of Meat, Fish, and Milk reached only 71 per cent of the plan. So bad was the vegetable and fruit situation that a joint decree issued by the party and the government on December 17, 1952 ordered the creation of vegetable-producing zones around the larger towns and cities to increase the supplies. The shortage, of course, was the fault of "right-wing deviationists," but the Ministry of Agriculture had also failed to "give guidance to the people's councils." Transylvania was the hardest hit: the industrial centers of Brașov, Hunedoara, and Reshița had had to import vegetables from Bucharest; many had arrived spoiled, and the cost had been very high. Early in 1953, the government announced that its own Committee for the Collection of Produce and the executive committees of the local people's councils would appoint delegates to visit all threshing outfits, and ensure the deliveries of quotas to the state.

In April 1953, the regime produced a draft statute for collective farms. Open to small and middle peasants by their free consent, the collective, the statute declared, simultaneously served the public interests of the state and of the farm and the private interests of the members. Each entrant contributed his land, cattle, inventory, seeds, and fodder. He retained his homestead and a plot of one-fifth to one-third of a hectare. He also kept such implements as were necessary to work this plot, and one cow, two heifers, a brood sow and her young up to the number of three, ten sheep or goats, twenty beehives, and any number of poultry and rabbits, as well as the farm buildings necessary to shelter these. All work was to be performed by labor brigades. Profits would be reckoned and distributed according to the "labor days" contributed by each member. Profits would be calculated after all deductions from the yields had been taken for compulsory deliveries, taxes, and contributions to the fund for crèches and kindergartens. But compulsory deliveries would not be required during the first two years of a collective's existence. The general assembly of peasants of each farm would elect the management board annually.

All peasants who had sold their cattle or other productive animals within a period of two years prior to their admission to a collective farm would have to pay the farm back the equivalent value of the animals in four equal annual installments during the four first years of their membership. This provision is especially instructive, since it shows that the peasants had been selling their cattle in the hope of realizing money on them before entering the collective farms and having to give them up. In the USSR, it will be remembered, the Russian peasants had slaughtered their beasts. Every fit member of each peasant family must work at least 120 days a year on the collective farm. A "Congress of Leading Farm Workers" would discuss this draft in May 1953.

Figures given revealed that the state farms (*sovkhoz*), about whose development no separate statistics had yet been published, amounted now to 670,000 hectares. The Rumanian term for them was *Gospodarii Agricole de Stat* (GAS). The ordinary collective (kolkhoz), *Gospodarii Agricole Colective* (GAC), had 375,000 hectares, the TOZ-type of associations 90,000, and the seasonal partnerships 469,000. In view of the fact that Rumania had about 10,000,000 hectares of arable land, it seemed that 8,420,000 hectares were still unaffected by any coöperative arrangement and were farmed privately.

At the Congress of Leading Farmers on May 21, 1953, Minister of Agriculture Constantine Prisnea and Prime Minister Gheorghiu-Dej gave speeches using slightly different figures. Prisnea said there were now 1,977 collectives with 177,792 families, and 1,980 "peasants' associations" (TOZ) with 105,104 families. Gheorghiu-Dej, on the other hand, said there were 1,966 collectives and "nearly 2,000" peasants' associations, and gave the total number of families in both types as 268,000. Looking ahead, Gheorghiu-Dej predicted that by 1960 the population of Rumania would be 18,000,000 to 18,500,000. Of this number more than 7,000,000 would be workers. Therefore, food production must rise, and the yields per hectare must increase, especially in the "socialist sector" of agriculture, the collective farms. Prisnea also admitted errors. "In some places," he said, "the party and the state activists have disregarded the party ruling that no methods of coercion should be used in bringing the peasants into the collective farms." Moreover, some of the state farms had not begun to exploit their opportunity to become the living examples of socialist agriculture. The Ministry of Agriculture itself was to blame if some of the MTS in the past had not honored their contractual obligations. There were by now 9,650 tractors in the MTS. By 1954 the figure was 12,500 in 250 MTS.

On August 23, 1953, the ninth anniversary of "liberation," Gheorghiu-Dej brought Rumania into line with the Soviet Union's "new course," which had already been announced in Hungary by Premier Rakosi. The "new course," reduced to its simplest essentials, slowed the tempo of industrialization and collectivization and transferred to agriculture and consumers'-goods-production substantial funds originally earmarked for investment in industry. Commentators often compared this to the "New Economic Policy" (NEP) of the USSR in the period between 1921 and 1928. But while the NEP had at the time aroused speculation that socialization in the USSR would not be resumed, the "new course" was almost surely designed as a temporary period of relaxation and consolidation. It did not imply the abandonment of any major policies. It did mean a temporary halt to collectivization. On July 24, 1954, figures were 2,000 kolkhozes and 2,300 TOZ-type associations, with 300,000 families and 457,000 hectares of arable land. By 1954, then, collectivization in Rumania, if one included state farms and seasonal partnerships as well as the other two forms, had extended to only a little more than 15 per cent of the arable. It was the private farmer who still bore the main burden of feeding Rumania. As Gheorghiu-Dej said in his speech, the government had failed to take into account the fact that the private farmer still supplied the state with 75 per cent of its salable cereals. It had failed to extend him sufficient credit for the purchase of tools and seeds. He would now be encouraged for a while.

The regime now granted the peasants a 25 per cent cut in water and sewerage rates and in the rates for garbage collection. It canceled any part of the compulsory delivery quotas for 1952 which might be overdue and had not yet been delivered. It reduced taxes on both individual farmers and on those collectives which were more than two years old and therefore had to pay them. It reduced the previously exorbitant insurance rate on rural buildings, and promised free veterinary service and free fire-fighting facilities. It cut the very heavy charges for electricity an average of 35 per cent, and lowered school, day-nursery, hospital, and court charges. Moreover, it now transferred title to 448,000 hectares of land which had been held as "state reserves," and which it described as consisting chiefly of small and isolated plots. These lands were now turned over to collectives, to the executive committees of the local people's councils, and also, in some cases, to individual "working peasants."

The official report for plan-fulfillment in the third quarter of 1953, published in December, showed that the harvest had been a good one. It praised individual collective farms for achieving high rates of yield, but made no mention of the rates achieved by the individual private peasant. But bread-output was up 28 per cent, sugar 7, cotton cloth 24, and other consumers' goods comparably, over the corresponding quarter of the previous year. It was, however, significant that the report made no mention of meat, fat, or eggs.

In September 1953, the government published its decree covering planting, harvest, and autumn deep-ploughing plan for 1953–54, using absolute figures instead of percentages. This enabled the student for the first time to make reasonably certain comparisons between prewar and postwar Rumania with respect to the areas planted to certain crops. Rumania, in 1938 however, had included Bessarabia, Northern Bukovina, and Southern Dobrudja, while 1953 Rumania had lost all these areas. The 1938 figures had been compiled for Bessarabia separately; so it was possible to subtract these, but figures had not been compiled for the northern and southern *parts* of Bukovina and Dobrudja. The 1938 figures in Table 1 therefore excluded Bessarabia and all of Bukovina, and included all of Dobrudja, as the best possible, though still only approximate, method to arrive at a reasonable basis of comparison with the 1953 figures.[3]

TABLE 1

Crop	Area Planted 1953–54 Hectares	(Hectares) Area Planted 1938 (Excluding Bessarabia and All Bukovina, Including All Dobrudja)
Grain	6,963,000	8,537,000
Potatoes and vegetables	460,000	245,000
Legumes	200,000	108,000
Industrial crops	979,000	254,000
Fodder crops	900,000	636,000
	9,502,000	9,780,000

The table showed that the new regime was making a serious effort to cut back acreage devoted to grain and to increase that devoted to industrial crops and fodder crops. This was part of the general push for self-sufficiency noticeable in all the satellite states, a step likely in the end to lead to the improvement of conditions. But, although the acreage planted to cereal crops had been

[3] *Wissenschaftlicher Dienst Südesteuropa* III, 1 (January 15, 1954), p. 16.

notably decreased, the necessary corresponding increase in grain yields had not been achieved. This was partly due to bad harvests, which continued to plague southeast Europe, only the years 1948 and 1951 approaching prewar normalcy. Shrinkage of the grain acreage, together with this bad weather and peasant uncertainty due to the collectivization policies, reduced the total grain harvest from an average of roughly 8,000,000 tons within Rumania's prewar borders to somewhere between 6,000,000 and 7,000,000 tons. The Plan called for a 10,000,000-ton yield by 1955, but success seemed highly doubtful. Food shortages would continue until this problem could be met. Gheorghiu-Dej called also for a 1960 crop of 3,200,000 tons of potatoes (about one-third above 1938).

Gheorghiu-Dej put much emphasis on livestock: he called for 5,500,000 head of breeding cattle by 1960 (as against 3,477,000 in 1938, 4,273,000 in 1950, 4,930,000 as target in 1956); 15,000,000–16,000,000 sheep (as against 10,087,000 in 1938, 10,960,000 in 1950, and 13,800,000 as target in 1956); and comparable increases in horses, swine, and poultry. The yield of wool per sheep was to rise. The area sown to fodder crops would be increased from 760,000 hectares in 1952 to 1,300,000 hectares in 1960.

Of the industrial crops, the regime gave special attention to cotton, sugar beets, oil-seeds, hemp, flax, rice, and citrus fruits. All of these had been grown in small amounts and largely for experimental purposes in prewar Rumania. In 1935, 919 hectares had been planted to cotton, and the yield had been 430 tons. It was this tiny figure in terms of which the Communist regime chose to give its percentages of increase, probably because they could be made to look very impressive. In 1938, 3,188 hectares had been planted to cotton, and 1,410 tons produced. The new Rumanian government planted 125,000 hectares in 1951, 200,000 in 1952, and planned 300,000 by the end of the Five Year Plan, most of it in the Danube plain and in the Dobrudja, and much of it on land rendered fertile by irrigation planned or under construction. According to the regime, the yields had far exceeded those of 1938 (460 kilograms per hectare), and peak yields were 1,782 kilograms per hectare. The plan sought to make 1,100–1,200 the average goal, and in the end to produce a surplus for export. By 1953, Rumania was producing 36 per cent of its own needs for its own textile industry. Some figures on the other cash crops are shown in Table 2.[4]

TABLE 2

	1938	1952	1955 Plan
Sugar beets	46,800 ha	100,000	130,000
Oil-seed	200,000		380,000
Hemp	40,000	80,000	
Flax	14,000	35,000	
Rice			30,000

[4] *Wissenschaftlicher Dienst Südosteuropa* II, 9 (September 15, 1953), pp. 190 f.

Since much of the prewar beet and oil-seed planting had been in the lost provinces of Bessarabia and northern Bukovina, the rise in acreage was much more marked than the table shows. The government also claimed that yields were up. The sugar-beet yield was 18,000–20,000 kilograms per hectare in 1952 as against 15,380 in 1938. The 1952 crop was 2,500,000 tons of beet yielding 300,000 kilograms of sugar. One way of encouraging the planting of the cash crops, adopted by the regime early in 1954, was the exemption of farmers who would grow them from compulsory vegetable deliveries on the area sown with the new crops. Bonuses and free seed were given to peasants who fulfilled their quotas; taxes on income from the crops reduced up to 30 per cent; free sowing machinery offered; and special privileges extended to the producer to buy consumers' goods at the state stores at low prices. As with other privileges, the bonuses were set at four levels: collectives got half again as much as independent peasants, TOZ-associations 20 per cent more, and partnerships 10 per cent more. Similar inducements were held out to vegetable and fruit-producers.

In the summer of 1954, the regime announced further new measures designed to increase agricultural production. Compulsory grain delivery quotes would be levied by the hectare, irrespective of the number of hectares held by the private farmer. This was a break for the chiabur, the first for many years, since he would no longer be subjected to the former sharply rising assessment for his few extra hectares. Collective farmers would receive bonuses for overfulfillment of the plan; a new agricultural bank would offer credits; the state would continue to increase its investments in the agricultural sector. Indeed, the regime issued a kind of new three-year plan for agriculture, while the Five Year Plan was still theoretically in effect.

Irrigation was important to all of the cash crops. It was estimated that, if all Rumanian water resources were utilized, an area of 1,200,000 hectares could be irrigated. The Five Year Plan called for an increase to almost half a million hectares. The major reclamation and irrigation project of the regime was carried on in the Dobrudja. Here, the government tried to reclaim sparsely inhabited or uninhabited steppe land, partly treeless, windswept, and subject to droughts, by planting shelter-belts of trees, a practice which the Russians had employed with success in the USSR. Beginning in 1949, the Rumanian authorities set up in Constanța special headquarters for this enterprise. Between 1949 and 1953, they planted some 50,000 hectares of seedlings, dividing the steppe into parcels surrounded by belts of woods. They maintained that they had set out twenty million seedlings, which had by 1953 reached heights between twelve and eighteen feet, and included mulberry-trees for a future silkworm industry, acacias, and others useful for bee-culture. Official reports claimed that the improved harvests in the Dobrudja had in one year repaid the cost of all the trees. This project was carried out with the help of special MTS with mechanical tree-planters. The plan was overfulfilled every year, and in the first half of 1953 the overfulfillment reached 160 per cent. During th winter months special courses were given the workers on the projects wh lived in housing specially built for them.

The machinery, the technical assistance, and the inspiration for thi project were obviously Russian. It was interesting to note that across th frontier in the Bulgarian southern Dobrudja a similar project was also goin on. In both countries, the governments proudly pointed to the irrigation, elec trification, building of new villages, and similar achievements in the Dobrudja As we shall see, it was also the area in Bulgaria most nearly completely col lectivized, and the one from which so many of the Turks had been expelled all of which bespoke a special Soviet interest in its strategic position. Else where in Rumania, the regime gave attention to the forests, devoting 314,00 hectares to new planting in the years 1948–1951, and setting a goal of 670,00 by 1955. The total forest area was 6,500,000 hectares in 1951.

INDUSTRY

The Rumanian economic plans gave major weight to industry. In the two single-year plans for 1949 and 1950, the percentages of investment ear marked for industry were 47.2 and 55.4 respectively, while of the entire in vestment 36.8 per cent was to go to heavy industry in 1949 and 44.8 per cen in 1950. The Five Year Plan adopted in 1951 for the years 1951–1955 set the investment percentage at 51.4 for all industry and 42.2 for heavy industry. Table 3 gives the Five Year Plan investment figures in billions of lei.[5]

TABLE 3

	Billions of Lei
Total Investment	1,330
All Industry	683
Heavy Industry	559
Electrification	146
Oil and Natural Gas	129
Iron	86
Machine and metal-products	86
Chemicals	31
Timber	23
Coal	26
Building Materials	32
Light Industry	124
Textiles	59
Foodstuffs	32
Paper	11
Leather and Shoes	10
Others	12

The actual investments, however, were impossible to calculate accurately because of the various intervening currency reforms. All achievements were

[5] Conrad, DWR, p. 47.

announced in terms of 1948 production as 100. The year 1949 reached 140; 1950, 192.2; 1951, 247.4; 1952, 304.3. The plan for 1955 called for 469.

Considerable light was thrown on the general problems of industrial production in southeast Europe by the Hungarian Premier Rakosi in a statement made in 1952. He remarked that "The common difficulty of our industry is still that it cannot produce rhythmically. In the first ten days of a month we experience a great set-back, which we then have to try to overcome in the latter part of the month by over-time, rushed work, and the like."[6] The same was true of any given quarter-year or year. His comment held even truer for Rumania, which lagged behind Hungary in industrial experience and industrialization. Failure to complete one or another single installation might delay an entire industry. The entire process was not a natural one, but forced. The strain was presumably greater in these earlier years than it would be as time wore on. In the USSR, annual industrial increments of 10 per cent had by the 1950's become normal, but the Russian experience was longer and their training of "cadres" far more advanced. Thus, everywhere in the Balkans, not least in Rumania, where the regime and its program were the objects of general loathing and execration, the urge to fulfill the plans created immense strain. Achievement of an initial goal was hailed each time with shouts of "more" and "faster," "five years in four," and the like, until not only the government but virtually every citizen must have been caught up in the tension and sense of desperate urgency.

In Rumania, in 1952, according to the published percentage figures, coal, iron ore, cement, and sulphuric acid lagged behind the plan, but the other heavy industrial branches met or somewhat overfulfilled their targets. The total plan fulfillment was declared to be 101.7 per cent, and the rise over 1951 was 23 per cent. The first quarter of 1953 showed a 101 per cent fulfillment and a further 23 per cent rise over the corresponding quarter of 1952. For the first time, the coal industry reached its target, and the other laggards of 1952 were also reported over the 100 per cent mark; but now oil was lagging at 95.4 per cent of the plan. By the second quarter of 1953, foreign experts had reached the conclusion that the regime now could calculate maximum production in advance very closely, and that large overfulfillments were increasingly improbable. The rise over the second quarter of 1952 was 19.1 per cent especially marked in the mining industry. But coal was behind once more. In the third quarter of the year, the "new course" began.

When Gheorghiu-Dej announced the "new course" on August 23, 1953, he was, as we saw, following Malenkov and Rakosi. Rakosi had declared that excess of zeal in Hungary had led to mistakes, especially in the neglect of the standard of living of the population. These errors would be corrected, but there was no admission that there was anything the matter with the original conceptions of the economic plan. Gheorghiu-Dej took the same line. The investment in industry, especially in heavy industry, had been far too high,

[6] *Wissenschaftlicher Dienst Südosteuropa* II, 3–4 (March 31, 1953), p. 61.

he said. The regime would no longer urge completion of the Five Year Plan in four years. It would transfer five billion lei which had been earmarked for heavy industry into investment in agriculture and consumers' goods production. In 1955, the investment in these areas of the economy would be double what it had been in 1953. For 1954 and 1955 the "accumulation-fund" for investment in new industry would go down to 27.8 per cent of the national income, and 72.2 per cent would go into the "consumption-fund" for immediate expenditure on the needs of the workers. He talked of 50,000 workers' houses, and of expanded social security benefits.

The report on plan-fulfillment in 1953, published early in 1954, rang the same notes: consumers' goods production had been slow, limited in variety, and unsatisfactory in quality. The bread, meat, and vegetables were low-grade; shortages of fuel, shoes, cotton cloth, fish, and sugar persisted. There was a great need for simple agricultural implements: picks, scythes, rakes, shovels, seed-drills, and ploughs. It became impossible to draw conclusions about production goals and achievements, since percentages were now given in terms of a "modified plan," but nobody had ever published figures specifying what the modifications were to be. Rumania had completed 100 per cent of the plan, but coal (94.8 per cent) and food (90.2 per cent) lagged behind. The "Central Union of Artisans Coöperatives" had overfulfilled by 113.3 per cent, but this was a state-controlled institution making and marketing embroidered blouses and other items of peasant art, and had little economic significance. More important was the fact that the "Central Union of Supply and Marketing Coöperatives" had met only 87.5 per cent of its requirements. These data showed both that the new course was long overdue, and that the regime's goals were unchanged.

By early 1954, if one could accept the official figures or anything like them, considerable progress toward the Five Year Plan had been achieved. At the heart of the plan for industrialization lay electrification. The Central Committee of the "Workers'" Party produced an electrification plan in the fall of 1950, which ran for ten years. It divided the country into seven regions: Muntenia, Oltenia, Northern Moldavia, Southern Moldavia and the Dobrudja, and Central, Northwest, and Southwest Transylvania, each of which would have an independent power system. The major new power plants were to rise at Stejaru near Bicaz, where the plan called for damming the Bistrița River, at Filipești de Padure and Doicești in Muntenia, and at Petroșani in Transylvania. Along the Danube, near the Iron Gates, the river was to be harnessed. The 1950 power capacity of the Rumanian stations was 740,000 kilowatts. In 1955 it was to be 1,700,000 (after the "new course" of 1953, this was reduced to 1,380,000); in 1960, 2,600,000. Current production would rise from 2,100 million kilowatt hours in 1950 to 4,700 million in 1955 and 7,000 million in 1960. The percentage of hydroelectric power as against thermal would rise from 8 to 17.5 to 29.4, and the power available per inhabitant would be quadrupled. Though presented as absolutely new, the plan bore, as the Rumanian National

Committee in the United States pointed out, a close resemblance to one worked out in 1921 by a Rumanian engineer named Leonid.

By 1953, Doicești, called after Gheorghiu-Dej, was completed, so far the biggest power station in the country, burning lignite, and providing about 400 million kilowatt hours of current to Bucharest, Ploești, and Brașov (Stalin), the major industrial centers of the country. Another had been opened in the Dobrudja. The production of current is shown in the accompanying table.[7]

TABLE 4

Millions of Kilowatt-Hours				
1938	1,148		1950	2,100
1946	700		1951	2,457
1948	1,511		1952	2,890
1949	1,858	Plan	1960	7,000

It was clear that the plan had a long way to go. The "Lenin" hydroelectric station at Bicaz was one of the Rumanian "big projects," which alone would have a capacity of 210,000 kilowatts and produce 430 million kilowatt hours of current annually. But it had not yet reached completion, despite the use of forced labor under circumstances which were reported to be appalling.

The other "big project" was even bigger, and served as a graveyard for thousands of political prisoners. This was the Danube-Black Sea Canal, undertaken in 1949. This project had been discussed as early as 1837, and about a century later British engineers had worked out a plan. Construction had actually begun under King Carol in 1938, but the great expense involved and the advent of the war prevented much progress. The scheme called for cutting a canal across the Dobrudja from Cernavoda, where the Danube turns north, direct to the Black Sea, at Constanța, a crow's-flight distance of about fifty kilometers. As planned, the canal was to end in Lake Tasaul, north of Constanța. It would have shortened the distance to the Black Sea by about 280 kilometers. More important, perhaps, by giving the river in effect a new mouth, it would obviate the necessity of dredging the channels at the delta, which had become increasingly expensive, as the silt piled up at a rate of 82,000,000 tons a year. On the other hand, it would probably ruin the river ports of Braila and Galați. The engineering problems included crossing a watershed and a marsh in the so-called Carasu valley. This lengthened the proposed canal to a total of seventy kilometers.

Work began in the summer of 1949 under the direction of a special directorate headed by G. Hosu (or Hoszu) with headquarters at Constanța. The administration of the canal, the Trade-Union Commission, and the Communist Party of the canal workers published their own weekly newspapers. From the first, the canal used forced labor, and experienced grave difficulties.

[7] Conrad, DWR, pp. 53–54.

In the spring of 1950 the Minister of Construction, the Canal Directorate, and the "SovRom" Construction Company held a meeting, and decided to lower building costs by at least 18 per cent, which suggested that the government was feeling the pinch. Propaganda on the canal, however, continued to flood all organs of the regime: the tempo of construction, the gaping world was told in May 1952, was four times as fast as that which had prevailed at Suez and six times that at Panama.

But on July 31, Tass, the Soviet news agency, announced that the Rumanian Security Police had uncovered a band of diversionists and saboteurs in the Canal Administration. Indeed, it claimed that the chief of the Planning Department, the Engineer Niculae Frangopol, and five other engineers in key positions had all the time been undermining the entire operation. On September 1, a military court sentenced five of the accused to death, and five others to life or twenty-five years' imprisonment. Under orders from their American and British masters, they had sabotaged, disorganized, slowed-down, agitated, falsified, and menaced the peace. This was only the most dramatic and sensational of a number of such trials.

In the summer of 1953, rumors began to circulate that work had been stopped. On August 10, 1953, the Deputy Foreign Minister, Preotoasa, was asked at a press conference, during the international youth conference at Bucharest, whether these rumors were true. He replied with a masterpiece of double-talk, which none the less was comprehensible:

> The . . . material and moral forces of the people should be concentrated on those works that most rapidly raise their living standards. The continuation or discontinuation of work on the canal is not important. What is important is that the government see to it that living standards are raised.[8]

His hearers interpreted this to mean that work on the canal had indeed stopped or at least been greatly slowed. His remarks were a prelude to Gheorghiu-Dej's "new course" speech delivered less than two weeks later. But the declaration that the canal was not important by a representative of a government which had killed thousands of people in an effort to build it convinced nobody of anything except Communist cynicism and inefficiency.

Before work stopped, much had changed in the Dobrudja as a result of the canal enterprise. Two new power stations, Ovidiu I and II, supplied electricity to the villages of the area and the new workers' settlements built along the shore, and aided in the mechanization of some of the soil removal and digging. Cernavoda, at the Danube head of the canal, acquired a new harbor. On the canal itself, Megidia, formerly the center of the Rumanian Tartar minority, changed from a small provincial village into a substantial town, while Poarta Alba, at the point where the railroad turned away from the course of the canal, was a wholly new settlement. New railroad spurs, many new roads, swamp-drainage, and the planting of the shelter-belts which we

[8] *Information Bulletin,* Rumanian National Committee 53 (August-September 1953), p. 3.

ave already considered altered the landscape and the character of the country. The boom probably slowed down markedly with the summer of 1953. Since vork began at several places at once, and the regime never published any letails, it was impossible to say how much was actually accomplished on the anal itself, but one reasonable estimate put the figure at twenty kilometers of he planned sixty or seventy, which would mean that, at the rate of progress ndicated, the completion of the project would have taken fifteen more years.

Beyond electrification and the "big projects," the oil industry naturally ontinued to play its central role in the Rumanian economy. SovRomPetrol lominated all production and exploration. Its organization was both regional nd functional: seven local trusts at the various local centers each had seven ections dealing with "norms," salaries, extraction, erection and drilling, rospecting, liquid and gas products, and administration of common property: vorkers' housing, canteens, and the like. The investment plan shows what mportance the Russians and the Rumanian Communist rulers attributed to he petroleum industry. According to the official reports, production rose rom 4,300,000 tons in 1948 to 4,700,000 in 1949, 5,300,000 in 1950, 6,500,000 in 951, 8,300,000 in 1952 and 9,300,000 in 1953. The 1936 record figure of ,700,000 tons was therefore allegedly surpassed, and the plan called for 0,000,000 tons in 1954.

Many western authorities on the oil industry expressed strong doubts hat these figures could be accurate. They pointed to the destruction or bsolescence of much of the equipment, to the poor quality of Russian and Rumanian equipment, and to the ousting of the real experts in the industry. They also suspected that the known resources were nearing exhaustion, and loubted whether the new finds reported in Moldavia and elsewhere could nake up the losses. Their estimate was that output could hardly have gone ar above 4,000,000 tons in any year, despite the official claims. Oil products vere severely rationed in Rumania; kerosene served as a kind of illegal urrency, and city-dwellers were limited to two liters a month at exorbitant rices, while farmers stood in line for it by the hour. This might either eflect the truth of these western experts' skepticism of official production reorts or simply indicate that the Soviet Union was taking virtually the entire utput of the Rumanian wells and refineries. The same doubts applied to he regime's figures on the output of natural gas, which in millions of ubic meters were as follows:[9] 1936, 2,130; 1949, 1,575; 1950, 1,956; 1951, 2,566; lanned 1955, 3,900; reduced plan after new course 1955, 3,800.

That the regime itself and the Russians were in fact experiencing difficulty with equipment for the oil industry may have been indicated by the ounding in August 1952 of a new Sov-Rom, called "Utilaj-petrolifer," to leal both with equipment and prospecting. One hundred and seven thousand neters was the figure for new borings in 1952, and five new refineries were eported built on the Black Sea coast, while new pipelines were unofficially

[9] Conrad, DWR, p. 58.

reported running both to Odessa and to Turnu Severin. Late in 1953 the regime announced the discovery of an entirely new oil-field south of the Carpathians near Pitești, fifty kilometers west of the main deposits. Here housing was reported in progress for the new workers. There were 1,000 more technicians than in 1952, and 10,500 workers were reported taking courses in special technical training institutes. On the whole, it seemed unsafe to accept with too much complacency the western view that all official Rumanian data on the oil industry were hopelessly padded.

Rumanian coal production represented one of the serious bottlenecks to the industrialization program. In the summer of 1949, Sov-Rom Carbune was formed to run most of the mines, distribute most of the output, and absorb most of the investment: 310,600,000 lei out of the 357,400,000 earmarked for coal in 1952. Production figures in thousands of tons were as shown in Table 5.[10]

TABLE 5

	1949	1950	1951	1952	1953	Plan 1955
Hard coal	170	220	300	320		
Lignite	2,700	2,920	3,550	4,000		
Total	2,920	3,220	3,850	4,320	6,000	8,535

As we have observed, production fell behind the plan in almost every year. In 1953, for example, production was announced as only 87.3 per cent of the plan, an extremely bad record. Reports, which could not be confirmed, but which seemed entirely plausible, spoke of unrest in the great Jiu valley coal center in Transylvania. At the end of 1953 an official report described a special coal-mining institute at Petroșani, called after Gheorghiu-Dej, and boasting its own building, sports facilities for the students, a mineralogical museum, nine laboratories, and a library of 16,000 books, mostly Russian.

It was of course the iron and steel industry which depended most heavily on the coal production. Sov-Rom Metal, founded at the same time in the summer of 1949 as Sov-Rom Carbune, controlled not only the important Reshița iron works but 90 per cent of the coking of Rumanian coal. Coke-production figures were 120,000 tons in 1950, and 700,000 planned for 1955, much of it to be derived from coal that would be saved when some of the thermal power stations were replaced by hydroelectric power. Still, coke-shortages and the lack of good coking-coal required the Rumanians to make uneconomic efforts to coke their lignite. The increases in iron and steel-production called for by the plan required an increase in the number of Rumanian blast-furnaces, and the expansion of existing facilities.

Hunedoara in Transylvania became an increasingly important center.

[10] Conrad, DWR, p. 59; 1953 figure from *News from Behind the Iron Curtain*, 3, 7 (July 1954), p. 4.

Its "Kombinat" included the five prewar furnaces, of which four were modern Siemens-Martin installations imported from Germany just before the war, and, in 1952, the large new Gheorghiu-Dej blast-furnace, opened amid a good deal of fanfare. The regime boasted that it had been made in Rumania of Rumanian materials, and that its capacity would be 300,000 tons a year. The figure 42,000 tons a year was given by a Rumanian publication prepared in the United States, and there seemed no way of reconciling the discrepancy. Reshiţa and Bucharest itself were the other major iron-producing centers. Available production figures in thousands of tons were shown in Table 6.[11]

TABLE 6

	Iron Ore	Iron	Steel
1949	324	133	277
1950	395	935	556
1951	477		643
1952	653		694
1953			750
1955	700	800	1,250
Plan 1955 reviewed after new course		800	1,000

It was plain that the Rumanian iron and steel industry would continue to depend in some measure on imports of coal, coke, and ore. The country began again in 1949 to produce small amounts of chrome, manganese (65,000 tons), and other metals.

In addition to the former plants making trucks, planes, building machinery, locomotives and the like, which were rehabilitated, renamed, and put into production by the regime, it built new plants in Bucharest and elsewhere to produce electric motors and similar products. Planned production figures for 1955 were:[12]

TABLE 7

Freight-cars	5,200
Machine tools	1,540
Combustion motors	98,000
Electric motors	433,000 kilowatts
Transformers	215,500 "
Radios	100,000
Tractors	5,000
Tractor-drawn plows	6,520
Seamless pipe	190,000 tons
Threshers	420
Cable	3,300 tons

[11] Conrad, DWR, p. 61; *News from Behind the Iron Curtain,* 3, 7 (July 1954), p. 4.
[12] Conrad, DWR, p. 66.

The quality of all this category of goods was very poor by western standards.

Other significant Rumanian industrial enterprises included timber and paper. Matches, furniture, window-frames, prefabricated houses were manufactured, and lumber of various grades produced. The paper output was 92,000 tons in 1951 and was to reach 180,000 in 1955 according to the plan. In chemicals, sulphuric acid, caustic soda, artificial fertilizers, and natural-gas chemistry were all important. Sov-Rom Gas attended to the last and Sov-Rom Chim to the others. There was even a joint Hungarian-Rumanian methane gas production company: Romagchim, and in 1952 a joint Rumanian-East German enterprise to produce chemicals, including dyes and plastics, under German technical direction in Rumanian plants. Table 8 gives some figures in thousands of tons.[13]

TABLE 8

	Fertilizers	Sulphuric Acid	Caustic Soda
1949	3.75	37	14.4
1950	4.83	51	15.3
1951	9.20		19.5
1952	18.14	143	21.9
Plan 1955	69.00		52.00

Textiles, though a light industry, none the less received much attention from the planners, and obtained more funds for development than metals, for example. The plan was clearly aiming at Rumanian self-sufficiency in this field: we have already observed the attention given to cotton, flax, hemp, and wool. The prewar textile-production figures in Rumania were expressed in tons; the postwar regime used square meters; so that comparison was not possible, but the goal for 1955 was estimated to be double the 1938 output. Table 9 gives figures in thousands of square meters.[14]

TABLE 9

	1949	1950	1951	1952	Plan 1955
Cotton cloth	100.5	145	170.7	197.5	266.5
Woolen cloth	16.3	20.6	25.3		39.4
Silk cloth	11.4	12.7	13.8		41.8

As to transport, the railroad system in Rumania suffered from a severe shortage of rolling stock, which even fulfillment of the plan would not raise to the prewar level, itself inadequate. The condition of the motor roads seemed to have deteriorated after the war and not to have taken any notable upturn, nor was there any notable addition to the network. The number of

[13] Conrad, DWR, p. 68.

[14] Conrad, DWR, p. 70.

trucks in 1950 was only a little above that in 1938, but there were less than half as many private automobiles in 1950, and only 1,942 buses as against 2,880 in 1938. Almost all of the investment earmarked for the transportation section of the economy was set aside for the Danube-Black Sea Canal.

The years after 1949 saw an ever-deepening extension of Soviet influence over the Rumanian economy, which by 1954 had become more intimately tied to Russia than that of any other satellite. The SovRom companies were extended not only to the fields of oil production and oil equipment, natural gas, transport, aviation, timber, chemicals, metals, coal, and tractor production, but in the summer of 1949 to all construction (SovRom Constructie) and to insurance (SovRom Asigurare). The former was reported in 1953 to have nine functional branches, including one for roads, one for bridges, one for the canal, and two for the oil-fields. In Bacau, Moldavia, for example, the local sub-unit of the Moldavian SovRom Constructie office in Iași was working on a ball-bearing plant and a military school. Sov Rum Asigurare complemented the SovRom Bank, which acted as banker for all the other SovRoms. In August 1952, SovRom Naval was founded to control all river and sea-going vessels. Since these were already under the control of SovRom Transport, it seemed probable that the new SovRom was simply an offshoot of the old. The last to appear was SovRom Quartz for uranium exploitation, where operations were, of course, secret.

FINANCE

Before we can understand the fiscal policies and budget figures of the regime, we must examine the second major postwar currency "reform" of January 27, 1952, which ruined the political fortunes of Vasile Luca, and the economic fortunes of most Rumanians who still possessed any. This decree arose from the inflationary tendencies produced by the continued absence of consumers' goods from the market, and consequent excess purchasing power. Soviet military requirements added to the pressure. The decree called in all "old" lei (that is, those which had been in circulation since the first "reform" of August 15, 1947), and required that they be exchanged for new.

State enterprises, including SovRoms and collectives, workers, and foreign legations received one new leu in exchange for twenty old ones; savings deposits up to 1,000 lei were exchangeable at a rate of one to fifty, the next 2,000 lei at a rate of one to 100, and all amounts over 3,000 lei at a rate of one to 200. Cash sums could be exchanged at a rate of one to 100 for the first thousand, one to 200 for the second, and all over that one to 400. All exchangers were to present their identity cards, and state where they had obtained the money they were exchanging. All money had to be exchanged within four days, after which the old notes became worthless.

The new leu was given a nominal gold content of 0.0793476 grams of fine gold, and was pegged to the ruble at a rate of 2.8 lei to the ruble. Current accounts of state institutions and the others privileged to exchange at twenty to one were evalued at the same rate, while for everybody else the rate was 200 to one. Debts were evalued at twenty to one, and wages and prices were divided by twenty.

Rumors of the coming "reform" had circulated before the decree itself was published. Reports leaked out of the country describing a fantastic buying spree, on which the population embarked in order to get something for its money before the state took it all away. At astronomical prices Rumanians, especially peasants, would buy electric appliances for which there was no current available in their villages, such remnants of the vanished bourgeois world as automobile spotlights, furs, antiques, musical instruments, umbrellas, and toothpicks. The decree cut the purchasing power of the Rumanian public by more than two-thirds. Though prices were also scheduled to be cut, the fact was that at the official new prices there was very little for sale. But the USSR, by binding the leu to the ruble, itself overvalued, enabled its agencies to sell to the Rumanians dear and to buy from them cheap. This was the second major purpose of the reform.

The fact that consumers' goods did not appear, and that the purchasing power of the new leu was therefore perhaps only half what it was supposed to be, meant that inflation, though checked, was not wiped out. The Rumanian State Bank itself could not pay salaries in the new lei, because it did not have enough of the new currency. The pinch on the worker continued, and the peasant stopped deliveries. The amounts of food on the market fell, and prices continued to rise. It was Soviet experts who had prepared the reform, but it was Luca who had to take the blame for it and for its faulty application.

Just about two years later came a third currency reform, which, however, seemed not to have domestic inflation as its target. On February 1, 1954, it was decreed that the leu would now have a fine gold content of .148112 instead of .079346. It was now pegged to the ruble at a new rate of one ruble to one and a half lei instead of one to 2.8. It was conjectured that the revaluation might mean that the USSR was intending to withdraw some of its capital from Rumania, and was planning to increase the amount it could claim by virtually doubling the gold content of the leu. Moreover, the USSR had in the past required Rumania to pay some of its foreign debts, notably to Finland, and now owed Rumania some 400,000,000 rubles. By raising the value of the leu the Russians cut their debt in half.

Rumanian budget figures on total income and expenditure are given in Table 10 in billions of lei for the years 1949–1954[15] In the years through 1951, the figures are in old lei; thereafter they are in new. (See opposite page.)

The annual surpluses derived in part from the two currency reforms which had robbed the population of its cash. Moreover, continued inflation

[15] Conrad, DWR, p. 17; *Information Bulletin*, Rumanian National Committee 57 (March-April 1954), p. 3.

TABLE 10

	1949	1950	1951	1952	1953	1954
Income	272.3	399	490.9	33	38.7	40.8
Expenses	233.4	381.3	434.2	28	35.4	39.3

enabled the state to drain off large sums through indirect taxation. A sales tax, comparable to the Soviet "turnover tax," and levied on virtually all transactions, brought in between 40 and 50 per cent of the revenue. Individuals paid as soon as they offered their goods for sale, state enterprises only after the goods had been sold. A profits tax, very heavy on individuals and state enterprises alike at the beginning, but relaxed for the latter to permit re-investment in 1951, brought in roughly 15 per cent. An income tax brought in considerably less, and provided ever-decreasing percentages of the budget. We have already examined the way in which this tax was manipulated in the countryside to render collectivization attractive and the life of the "chiabur" totally wretched.

The range, according to a law of January 1949, was from 5 to 25 per cent on incomes earned by state employees, from 20 to 40 per cent for those earned by independent professional men, from 25 to 43 per cent for independent artisans and others who did not employ hired help, from 40 to 60 per cent for those employing one worker, and additional amounts for those employing more, ranging to 70 per cent. The remaining national income — up to 35 per cent — came from taxes on services, pleasures, and tolls, fines, stamp-duties, revenue from the MTS, and social insurance. Further details as to the precise sources were lacking. Income taxes were reduced, as part of the new course, in December 1953.[16]

TABLE 11

Monthly salary	500		750	1,000	2,000	2,500
Old tax	...		10.7%	14%	20%	35%
New tax	...		7.6%	9.5%	12.5%	16%
Pay increase (percentage)	2%		3.1%	4.3%	7.5%	10%
Pay increase (currency)	10.25	lei	22.25	43.25	148.25	475

The sums collected were reported spent on "financing the people's economy," social and cultural purposes, administration, defense, internal obligations, and miscellaneous. The first item took roughly from 40 to 60 per cent in any given year. The second fell as the first rose, but ranged between 15 and 25 per cent. Administration costs declined from about 12 per cent of the budget in 1949 to about 4 per cent in 1953. Defense costs mounted from 8 to 18 per cent over the same period. Observers suspected, however, that the regime spent

[16] *News from Behind the Iron Curtain*, 3, 7 (July 1954), p. 10.

much less on social and cultural purposes than it claimed, and far more on defense than it admitted.

One clue to this was the sudden publicity given in June 1952 to "autoimpunirea," the self-taxation or self-assessment law. Working-peasants, the press caroled, were welcoming it with great joy. Previously not allowed to build anything, they might now meet and assess themselves by offering "voluntary" contributions of money and labor. All over Rumania, cultural homes, elementary schools, kindergartens, now began to rise by the hundreds because of the peasants' joyful self-assessment. Money collected had to be deposited immediately in the RPR state bank, and spent as soon as possible. Working-peasants were to exercise their revolutionary vigilance, and see to it that the chiabur paid up the amount he had been assessed. It is interesting to note that the chiabur did not assess himself; he was assessed. Thus, the cultural items which appeared in the budget, and for which the state was allegedly spending between 15 and 25 per cent of its revenue, were in part at least not built by the state's money but by the peasant's further contributions, whether in the form of unpaid labor or additional cash. The state surely used for the army the money it saved in this way.

On prices and the standard of living the regime published no regular data after 1947. It was certain, however, that the direction of the Rumanian standard of living was steadily downward, at least until the "new course" of summer 1953, and that even thereafter very little improvement can have been registered. Estimates of the level in 1951 ranged from 55 to 80 per cent of that prevalent in 1937. The government fixed wages and salaries in the Soviet fashion: according to a norm, calculated on the basis of the average accomplishment of workers engaged in the same tasks. Those who surpassed the norm received proportionately higher pay; those who failed to meet it, proportionately lower. Socialist competition, and the creation of Stakhanovites, "heroes of labor," and the like resulted in the constant raising of the norm; overfulfillment of the new norm meant the establishment of a newer and higher one. In addition to higher wages, workers who overfulfilled their norms obtained special privileges: free holidays, state assistance in building a house, scholarships for their children's education, and such lagniappe as free theater tickets. Before the second currency "reform" of 1952, workers received monthly salaries of from 4,000 to 6,000 lei, Stakhanovites up to 85,000, and employees and officials from 4,500 to 10,000. After the reform, workers received from 200 to 300 of the new lei, Stakhanovites up to 2,000, and employees and minor officials from 225 to 500. Managers of state enterprises received up to 5,500 lei a month. With the new course came wage increases and a bonus system for overfulfillment in many industries, as well as reduced taxes.

After the first currency reform of 1947, the regime stopped regular publications of price-figures. We know, however, that many goods were in theory available at lower prices for those with ration cards, while those without them had to buy on the "free" market. Former employers, landowners, and merchants were not entitled to ration cards; the unemployed received cards entitling them to buy very small quantities of goods at the low prices. In addition to the former categories of persons who were denied cards, no food card would be issued to anybody owning a hectare of land. The cards came in seven colors: purple for workers engaged in exceptionally heavy labor, brown for those whose work was very hard, pink for those whose work was hard, blue for salaried employees, green for wives, parents, and grandparents of workers and employees, orange for children under fourteen and for expectant mothers in the last four months of pregnancy. The bureaucratic complications were almost unbelievable: a telephone operator's ration card, for example, depended upon the number of people serviced by her exchange.

Food shortages were endemic: meats, fats, vegetables, fruit, milk, and eggs, and manufactured goods of all sorts were also in short supply. Though after the second currency reform in 1952,. prices were allegedly divided by twenty to adjust to the new lei, actually the price level in the state stores ran from 5 to 20 per cent above this. As soon as the first shortage of the new currency was overcome, the prices on the free market began to rise. Some price figures for early 1952 before the currency shortage was overcome are shown in Table 12 in lei.[17]

TABLE 12

	Ration-Card	Free Market
1 kg. black bread	.7	2.
1 kg. wheat flour	1.	4.
1 kg. corn meal	.5	2.74
1 kg. sugar	2.8	9.
Pair of shoes	82.85	150.75
Ready-made suit	227.5	500–1,500

Table 13 shows the rise on the free market between early and late 1952 of certain important foods.[18]

TABLE 13

	Ration-Card	Free Market Early 1952	Late 1952
1 liter edible oil	3.	11.	25–30
1 kg. pork	4.8	7.56	12–20
1 egg	0.65	1.	

Incomplete though these figures were, it was possible to conclude that Rumanians, except for the Communist élite, to whom none of the rules applied, were living at a miserably low level.

[17] Conrad, DWR, p. 27.
[18] Conrad, DWR, p. 27.

As part of the "new course" came a series of efforts in November and December 1953 to improve conditions. Not only were compulsory deliveries cut, but prices of shoes and clothing were lowered for the peasants; workers' wages were raised, and the taxes on them lowered; credits at an annual interest rate of 0.1 per cent were advanced for the building of private houses, with priorities to Stakhanovites and recipients of awards for speeding production, and the new homes were to be free of taxes for ten years in villages and fifteen in towns. Liberalized rules for old-age pensions, rent reductions for workers, new bonus schemes were all to make life easier. But rents, low all along, had been limited to a maximum of 10 per cent of a worker's wages in any case.

Available figures on Rumanian foreign trade for the period were as shown in Table 14 (figures in millions of dollars).[19]

TABLE 14

	Exports	Imports	Balance
1949	159	181	−22
1950	174	229	−55
1951	211	252	−41

Trade was conducted by state corporations, of which the names of fourteen were available in mid-1953. They were: *Agroexport* (seeds, fodder, grain), *Fructexport* (fruit), *Petrolexport, Prodexport* (export of meat and animal products, alcohol, import of coffee, tea), *Romanoexport* (export of building materials, electrical equipment, metalware, leather, handicrafts, pottery, railroad supplies, import of cotton, wool, silk, hides), *Centrul de librarii si difuzare a cartii* (books, periodicals), *Exportlemn* (timber and wood-products, including paper), *Chimexport* and *Chimimport* (chemicals), *Energoimport* (radio and electrical equipment, transformers), *Industrialimport* (ores, coke, motors, compressors, pumps, shipbuilding and oil industrial equipment, export of pipe, bulbs), *Mașinimport* (other industrial machinery), *Technoimport* (tractors, printing-presses, office equipment, cork, asbestos, ball-bearings). The names and products involved gave a qualitative picture of Rumanian foreign trade.

The percentage of Rumanian foreign trade with the USSR and the other states of the eastern bloc was as follows:[20] 1949, 82; 1950, 83; 1951, 79. The Soviet Union had 51 per cent in 1951, and the other states 28 per cent. According to Soviet propagandists, the long-term trade agreements between the lands of the "democratic camp" enabled each of the states to count on the resources of the others to develop their economic plans, and each could therefore concentrate on its own specialities. Despite the Russian propaganda, the south-

[19] Conrad, DWR, p. 80.
[20] Conrad, DWR, pp. 85 ff.

eastern European states were all apparently striving to become self-sufficient in everything, while the benevolent assistance of the USSR was extremely profitable to Moscow and extremely expensive for the satellites. Gheorghiu-Dej wrote in 1953 that the long-term credits and loans from the USSR had been extended to Rumania on terms so favorable as to constitute a new form of economic aid, but the truer picture of what was happening to Rumania with all branches of the economy in the hands of the SovRoms might be obtained from the far less thoroughgoing brief Yugoslav experience with Justa and Juspad. As a Yugoslav authority on the subject pointed out, even in Marxist terms the joint companies were a "classical example of plunder."

To their Rumanian dependency, virtually part of the USSR despite all the repeated asseverations about sovereignty, the Russians did deliver large amounts of heavy industrial equipment, raw materials, and technicians; they got petroleum, meat, fat, timber, and the products of the new Rumanian industry all at prices far below the world level. Second to the USSR, Czechoslovakia provided Rumania with capital equipment in exchange for Rumanian food and raw materials. The Doicești power station, described above, was built by Czech technicians with Czech materials. The two countries did $75,000,000 worth of business in 1949. East Germany rose rapidly to third place, from $1,500,000 in 1949 to $50,000,000 in 1952. Hungary and Poland followed in that order. Less developed industrially than any of these countries, Rumania exported mostly raw materials and imported mostly finished goods and capital equipment. The relationship between Rumania, and Bulgaria, Albania, and China was the reverse. In exchange for Bulgarian iron ore, tobacco, seeds, and hides, Albanian iron and chrome ore, copper, wool, hides, and citrus fruits, and Chinese tea, antimony, and edible oils, Rumania sent them petroleum products, glass, paper, chemicals, and finished industrial goods. The Bulgarians also got electric current.

The remaining 20 per cent of Rumanian foreign trade was carried on with the rest of the world. Of these the leading exporters to Rumania in 1952 were Belgium and Luxemburg ($12,200,000), West Germany ($9,700,000), Great Britain ($7,000,000), Switzerland, and Austria ($5,900,000 each). Rumania's most important customers outside the Soviet bloc were Finland ($9,200,000), Austria ($4,000,000), West Germany ($3,000,000), Italy ($3,100,000), and Egypt ($2,600,000).

2. *Bulgaria*

In December 1948, the preliminary Two Year Plan completed, the Bulgarian government adopted the first Five Year Plan, covering the years 1949–1953. It declared that the objectives of the Two Year Plan had been "in the main" achieved, and put the 1948 industrial output at 171 per cent of 1939. The ratio between the value of industrial and agricultural production was now 30:70. By the end of 1953, it was to be 45:55. The ratio between the value of heavy and light industry, which had been 24:76 in 1939, and had becon 30:70 in 1948, was to reach 45:55 in 1953. Vast new advances were schedule for electrification and mining. The plan called for a total investment in indu try alone of 425 billion leva of which 62 per cent were to be spent on constru tion and installation, and 38 per cent for industrial equipment. In agricultur 60 per cent of the production was to come from the collectives by 1953.

In May 1953, after months of pressure, the government announced th the Five Year Plan had been completed in four, and that a new plan w already under way. But, perhaps as part of the new course, the second pla actually was not published until the Sixth Party Congress in March 1954. covered the years 1953–1957; so it had presumably already been in effect f more than a year. In accordance with the pattern in other satellites, but to lesser degree, the plan put increased emphasis on consumers' goods an especially on agriculture. Investment in agriculture would be more than twi as much as during the first Five Year Plan (three billion new leva, or sevent five billion pre-1952 leva). The big task in agriculture would be to make up th lag in livestock breeding, largely a result of the excessive speed at which th government had collectivized, the peasants often slaughtering their anima Credits for light industry and food industries would be raised by 2.4 times ov the amounts made available in the first Five Year Plan. There would be, i 1957, 250 per cent more sugar, 97 per cent more canned vegetables, 86 per ce more meat, 62 per cent more fish, 55 per cent more vegetable oils, 52 per ce more woolen cloth, 34 per cent more cotton cloth, 39 per cent more shoes. Th percentage increase of pie in the sky was not specified.

In the second plan, industrial growth was not neglected. Indeed, inves ment in industry would also be doubled. An average 10 per cent rise a ye was indicated, according to the pattern which had proven possible in th USSR. Power output would be doubled; coal and nonferrous metallurg received special attention.

It was of course too early to comment on the degree of success which th Bulgarian government had scored in the second Five Year Plan. But the fir had been completed, and though, as usual, reliable statistics were ofte lacking, observers agreed that, despite a perpetual state of crisis and a incalculable amount of human misery, the regime had probably accomplishe much of what it had set out to do. The "socialist" transformation of th country on the pattern made familiar by the USSR had proceeded furthe than that of any other satellite. Of the social changes the most important fo an agricultural country was, of course, collectivization.

AGRICULTURE

On May 30, 1949 the state ordered a new land survey, to register a fields, vineyards, rose-gardens, orchards, pastures, forests, and non-arable lan The Vice-Minister of Agriculture, Chernokolev, later to become Ministe declared that the new survey was needed because the "mass formation c labor coöperative farms" was now under way. They would be established in every village. There had been no new register, he said, since 1936, and thus kulaks and others now were in a position to conceal their true holdings from the state. It would be to the interest of private owners not to hide anything from the government, he warned, because all undeclared land would be awarded to the collectives.

A few days later, Chervenkov went to Moscow, and returned apparently prepared to go easy on collectivization for a time. The press reported his indignation at illegal confiscations of land from private owners, and at the use of coercion by party members when "persuading" peasants to join collectives. The peasants would be allowed to keep more surplus (i.e., compulsory deliveries would be cut). Moreover, they would get more money for their surplus produce, because the state would deprive the Union of Coöperatives of its sole right to buy, and would allow the peasants to sell privately by free negotiation. It would also assist private farmers. This looked like a large measure of appeasement and the adoption of a soft policy on collectivization. In line with this pronouncement, grain prices were raised 30 per cent, while workers received a 2 per cent increase in wages to help them meet the new higher price of bread, which now went back on the ration.

The government soon afterward announced that the local people's councils would investigate every single collective, and would inquire into its needs and the errors of the management. Small collectives with less than 200 hectares and too many members would be raised in size to a minimum of 250 hectares, although there was no indication of where the land would come from. All collectives must now exclude "unsuitable" members, and every effort must be bent to admit no new member who did not fully understand his rights and duties. Massive indoctrination sessions throughout the countryside were clearly envisioned. The halt in collectivization was probably largely due to the bad harvest, which necessitated deliveries of grain from the USSR. In August 1949, the Russians promised to deliver 160,000 tons of wheat, 100,000 of them before the end of the year. With food in such short supply, it was obviously courting complete disaster to push the collectivization program any harder.

The figure for collectives as of October 1949 was 1,605 with 147,191 families, embracing 548,016 hectares. The number had more than doubled over October 1948 (714); the number of families had almost tripled (49,000), but the amount of land had just doubled (270,000 hectares). This suggested that overcrowding on the individual collective might prove a problem: the peasant families were available, but Communist legerdemain could not cure land-shortage. In addition there were ninety-one state farms (Sovkhoz) with 85,000 hectares (as against fifty-four with 14,000 hectares in 1948), and eighty-six MTS with 5,000 tractors. It was also clear that the "commassation" of collectivized plots was causing difficulty. In one village in the Karnobat district, for example, 340 hectares had been collectivized. Two hundred and sixty had been consolidated into forty-five parcels, but the remaining eighty were scattered in 140 parcels of various sizes. Here was the dwarf holding rising to plague the new masters of Bulgaria.

Moreover, on individual collectives, the brigade leaders and the management boards were chosen for their political reliability, which often led them into conflict with those who knew something about farming, and made for the dissipation of funds, bad utilization of land, and the improper functioning of credit and sales arrangements. Indeed, on October 31, 1949, the Secretary of the Central Union of Coöperatives attacked his own functionaries as petty bourgeois. They had allowed the coöperatives to degenerate into mere mechanisms for collecting forced deliveries from the peasantry. As a result, free market deliveries in 1949 were to more than triple the amounts so delivered in 1948 (2,390 million levas as against 715 million). Quota deliveries would therefore decrease by about the same proportion. Worse, the coöperatives had not set up proper machinery for locating surpluses (and this is where the shoe pinched); so there were arrests, and the Central Committee of the Communist Party put its own chairman in as head of a new executive committee for the coöperative union.

The virtual cessation of collectivization continued on through the first months of 1950. As of January 1, there were 1,606 collectives, only one more than October 1949. They now had 161,000 families, and 566,000 hectares. There were, however, increasing signs that the drive would soon be resumed. Late in January, a special institution called *Zemustroi* was established inside the Ministry of Agriculture to supervise all collectives and state farms. The people's councils were instructed to give the private farmers their sowing instructions for the spring. Soviet agricultural specialists were reported in large supply.

During March and April, Chervenkov engaged in public correspondence with Bulgarian citizens. A certain comrade Kanev of Kazanlik criticized the boss (which he certainly could not have done unless permitted), and declared that the slowdown in collectivization was an error, because it made the peasants believe the regime was abandoning collectivization as a goal. Chervenkov's answer was long and heated, but its gist was that he never had intended to abandon the policy; he had only sponsored a shift in tactics. Soon afterward, the chief of the Marxist-Leninist training center in Pleven, one L. Radev, inquired of Chervenkov how many social classes there were in Bulgaria, and whether the peasantry ought to be regarded as a class or as a guild. Chervenkov replied that there were two classes in Bulgaria: the workers and the working-peasants (that is to say the poor and middle peasants), united under the leadership of the workers. Collectivization was an absolute necessity to destroy the acquisitive instincts of small producers. In the towns, the capitalist class had been destroyed, but in the countryside it remained in the form of the kulak. The struggle of the poor and medium peasant against the kulak was the class struggle. As for the intellectuals, they were not a class but a "social complement."

The exchange with Kanev revealed the discontent of the party activists with the slowdown in collectivization. It provided them with their chief's rationalization of the policy, and reassured them as to his ultimate purposes. The exchange with Radev prepared them and the public for the eventual resumption of the drive. On March 7, 1950, the Ministry of agriculture issued a decree establishing the number of collectives to be created by a given date in each district, and the number of peasants to be enrolled in them. But on May 5, the government and party jointly revoked this decree because it had violated the instructions about voluntary enrollment of the peasants by fixing the number to be enrolled. It was thus "harmful and incorrect." The party and government advised the people's councils that they would severely punish anybody who should apply coercion in recruiting the peasants for the collectives. The party and government forbade the Minister of Agriculture to instruct the people's councils in future without authorization from party and government. Chernokolov, now the Minister, received a reprimand, and the Director of the *Zemustroi,* Minkov, was dismissed. This rather extraordinary incident seemed to reveal that the zealots in the Ministry of Agriculture had actually tried to steal a march on the government in issuing the decree of March 7, specifying for every district the number of collectives and the number of peasant members for each. On the other hand, of course, the repeal of the decree may have been intended for publicity purposes only, and the Ministry may have been lulled into issuing the decree just so that its chiefs might get a public reprimand.

In any case, the very next day after its repeal (May 6, 1950), the government issued its collective farm statute, providing that entrants might keep their homestead and one-fifth hectare in regions of intensive cultivation, or one-half hectare in regions where cereals were grown, as well as the usual cow or buffalo, other livestock, and the necessary implements. All the rest was to be pooled. This was the signal for the drive to re-commence. Between May and September 1, the number of collectives rose from 1,615 to 2,053, the number of families from 161,000 to 362,000, and the number of hectares from 550,800 to 1,433,300. In the single month between September 1 and October 1, the number rose from 2,053 to 2,479, the number of families from 362,000 to 474,800, and the number of hectares to 1,883,080. In the next two weeks, the number rose to 2,566, the families to 570,000, the hectares to 1,994,600. The party activists need not have worried. No other satellite had collectivized so much or so fast. From about 11 per cent of the arable land in Bulgaria in mid-May, the Communists had collectivized 41 per cent in mid-October. From 14 per cent of the peasant population they had dragooned 46.5 per cent onto collectives in the same short five months.

Chervenkov faced the plenary session of the party Central Committee on October 7 and 8, and reported that for the first time the grain deliveries had been a success. Stocks were in hand for an entire year. Medals were awarded to party members for their work in collecting the grain. High-ranking party-members and cabinet ministers had gone in person into the districts where deliveries had lagged. Peasants' homes were searched for concealed grain. This had "impressed" them, and deliveries were stepped up. Chervenkov had personally fired anybody who had said the goal could not be reached. But, he admitted, there had been only 418 collection-points in all Bulgaria, and many peasants had had to travel thirty to forty kilometers to turn in their grain to the government. Then they had had to wait two or three days for the privilege of handing it over, and two or three days more to be paid; and when they were paid, the Prime Minister reported, they were usually cheated. But the grain was in. As for the drought, there was no use waiting for rain for the fall plantings: if the earth was too hard, it must be broken with pickaxes. It was not often that the living actualities behind triumphant announcements were so blatantly revealed, or that the reader could so vividly gauge the measure of human suffering imposed by the new regime.

The drive continued. In October 1950 a new decree commanded the people's councils all over the country to lead the peasants into the collectives. All kulaks were of course to be rigorously excluded. Twenty-two new MTS would be set up. A series of courses was to be offered to collective farm chairmen and accounts. The National Bank would grant the new farms both short and long-term loans. In every region special inspection offices of the Ministry of Agriculture would supervise the whole procedure. Indeed, the Ministry would take on 10 per cent more employees. An ominous decree of November 23 commanded that the peasants must not slaughter their livestock before entering collectives: a clear sign that the Communists had learned nothing from the Soviet experience, and that the Bulgarian peasant was responding in 1950 as the Russian peasant had in 1930. Compulsory deliveries for 1951, it was announced, would be on the same scale as those for 1950. There were ninety-five MTS, only nine more than in 1949 before the great drive had started. More crisis clearly lay ahead.

By April 1951, Chervenkov, in a speech to party agitators, was reporting grave weaknesses in the collectivization campaign. Not only were rumors of war circulating among the population, and reports that Agrarian guerrilla bands were in the mountains under the command of Stamboliisky's son, but the peasants were actually leaving the collective farms. Although the land contributed by the peasants joining the Bulgarian farms had not been nationalized, and although most of them were receiving rent for their contributions, Chervenkov now declared that they might not take their lands, animals, or implements with them when they withdrew. The withdrawal of peasants had in fact been stimulated by the government's own insistence on maintaining the farcical pretense that the whole collectivization drive was "voluntary," nd continuing to pass resolutions condemning the use of force. Some easants apparently believed it had all somehow been a mistake, and took the overnment's pronouncements at face value.

On June 3, 1951, a new decree established a political administration inside he Ministry of Agriculture, and introduced political representatives into the dministration of the MTS and the state farms, in order to bring the governnent and party into close association with the direction of these institutions. The Ministry henceforth undertook to direct "political work" on each collecve farm. On each, a political director would see to it that the brigade system vas properly set up. Each of the four- to seven-man brigades would work in he fields under a responsible controller to see to it that the daily quota would e fulfilled. Every ten controllers would report to a super-controller, who vould have charge of re-educating them "in the spirit of respect to the Soviet Jnion and the great Stalin."

Though no absolute figures were published, the press complained of saboage, and asserted that, despite the fact that 50 per cent of Bulgarian peasant amilies were now collectivized, the collectives had only 18 per cent of the attle, 23 per cent of the sheep, and 5 per cent of the pigs of the country. Reports came through of revolts in the Kula and Teteven districts, and of esapes into Yugoslavia. The press reported that the army and frontier guards, nd representatives from youth organizations, the civil service, and the uniersity, as well as authors, artists, and intellectuals had been sent to the villages s "volunteers" to "help" the peasants. It was in the midst of this crisis that Chernokolev, Minister of Agriculture, was dismissed in late June, taking the ap for the government's own "dizziness with success." Examples of waste and nefficiency, about which the regime constantly complained, included the loss f 25,000,000 leva on the State cattle-breeding farms as a result of paying excesive wages, the withering of saplings and the loss of 50 per cent of the investnent in re-forestation, the carelessness which had allowed much valuable nachinery from the USSR to deteriorate. Indeed, the press declared, one could bserve that "anti-mechanization sentiment" was widespread among the peole.

In addition to machinery, the peasants also bitterly disliked another of the egime's prescriptions: deep ploughing. It put a strain on their farm animals, nd required a tractor to be done properly. Although there were nowhere near nough tractors to go around, the new Minister of Agriculture, Apostolov, imself decreed that shallow ploughing was reactionary, harmful, and antievolutionary, an act favoring capitalist exploitation, and a blow to mechanizaion. Even agricultural specialists, he declared, did not fully realize the antitate character of shallow ploughing. Deep ploughing, on the other hand, was ocialist. Appropriate orders had been issued to the MTS.

In November 1951, at the third annual conference of leading farmers, the Minister of Agriculture gave the first figures in some time on the progress of ollectivization. There were now 2,649 collectives, including 575,947 private farms. The average size of a collective, he said, was 845 hectares, which gave a total figure of 2,238,405 hectares. The rise in the year since the fall of 1950 had been much slower: fewer than a hundred new collectives, fewer than 6,000 new private farms, fewer than a quarter of a million hectares. It was interesting to note that the government had obtained comparatively large amounts of land as against the number of new collectives reported. It might also be significant that the figure of 575,947 was given as former private farms, instead of peasant families or households resident on collectives. This may have reflected the government's unwillingness to divulge how many peasant families had left the collectives. The USSR had sent tractors to Bulgaria but the figure given (7,314) was calculated artificially in terms of fifteen-horsepower units, which made it impossible to determine the actual number of machines.

On August 19, 1952, the government and party issued a joint decree establishing a Council for the Development and Consolidation of Collective Farms. Its duty was to enforce the observation of the statute governing the collectives. Soon afterwards new figures revealed that there were 2,738 collectives, including 52 per cent of the rural households. They disposed of more than 12,000 fifteen-horsepower units of Soviet tractors, a gain of more than 4,500 in ten months, and more than 1,000 combine harvesters. A further small rise took place in the number of collectives: by December 1, 1952, they numbered 2,745, with 575,531 households. Thereafter, the process continued to be gradual. By the end of 1953, the regime claimed 2,512,500 hectares, but the number of collectives had risen only to 2,800 and the number of households was now given as only 553,000. Some specialists doubted that the percentage of arable land in collectives was as high (60.1 per cent) as the government claimed, since they put the figure for total arable land at approximately 4,900,000 hectares.

Sixty-three per cent of the grain, and 70 per cent of the industrial crops (75 per cent of the cotton, 68 per cent of the oilseeds, 86 per cent of the sugar beets) were declared to be in the "socialist sector." But it was notable that the collectives owned only 22.3 per cent of the cattle, 28.8 per cent of the sheep and goats, and only 13.3 per cent of the pigs, though collectives and state farms together had 25.2 per cent of the cattle, 29.9 per cent of sheep and goats, and 17.6 per cent of the pigs. In the collectives, many of the cattle were still used for work, and the milk yields were consequently low, the average being 555 liters of milk per cow in 1953. (The American figure was 2,400 liters in 1950, the Danish 3,420.)

The good harvests of 1952 and 1953 went a long way toward easing the agricultural crisis. The Bulgarian version of the "new course" was considerably milder and came a little later than the Rumanian, beginning with Chervenkov's speech on September 9, 1953. On October 3, collectives obtained a complete remission of all overdue income taxes down to the end of 1952. The government also canceled all debts owed to itself and to the MTS down to the end of August 1953, and forgave nonpayment on insurance policies. It cut irrigation and drainage charges and insurance rates. Perhaps the government wiped out much of this indebtedness because it knew that it could not collect. The same day, another decree cut compulsory delivery quotas. Members of collectives received a 20 to 30 per cent cut for milk to be delivered from their private cows. Wool deliveries were cut 6 to 7 per cent for collectives, 10 to 12 per cent for the privately owned sheep of their members, and for the sheep of private peasants with herds of more than fifteen heads. Collectives also benefited hugely by cuts in meat quotas, which now were set at a level 40 to 50 per cent of that still obtaining for private peasants.

On December 25, a further decree reduced the grain quotas for collectives which patronized the MTS and for the private plots of members of the collectives; but increased them for the private peasant. This, together with the previous regulations, made it clear that the "new course" would provide little relief for the private peasant, but would, on the contrary, increase the squeeze on him. Here Bulgarian policy contrasted sharply with Rumanian: Gheorghiu-Dej had to conciliate the private peasant, because collectivization had not progressed nearly as far in Rumania as in Bulgaria; but Chervenkov could now add to the pressure on the private peasant, and continue to force him toward membership in a collective. Indeed, Vice-Premier Chankov, explaining that the party must assist private peasants as well as collectives, referred to all private peasants as future members of kolkhozes.

By the end of 1953, Bulgarian agriculture had apparently met most of the heavy requirements put upon it by the plan. While 10,000 tractor-units had been the figure set for 1953, the number at the end of 1952 was already 12,295, and in March 1954, 15,302, in 150 MTS. Instead of the 100 combines planned for 1953 the country disposed of 363 at the end of 1952. These gains were entirely due to deliveries from the USSR. From 3,400,000 hectares in 1939, the area sown to cereals had dropped to 3,157,000 hectares in 1953, while the area sown to industrial crops had risen from 332,342 hectares to 600,000 hectares. To cotton alone, 187,000 hectares were to be planted in 1953. The yields of cereals were also up. Although absolute figures were often lacking it seemed clear that the food shortages which made the Rumanians' life so much harder were not present in Bulgaria. Though the plan fulfillment was reportedly only 95 per cent in food for 1952, the 1953 reports were better, and in the second quarter of that year, for example, the output of meat, butter, cotton cloth, woolen cloth, and shoes rose over the corresponding period in 1952 by percentages ranging from 11 (shoes) to 35 (butter). The cash crops rose also in the year: cotton by 26.7 per cent, tobacco 18.8 per cent. Indeed, the 1953 harvest was an especially good one, and the reports for the last quarter of the year showed the whole food industry at 32.3 per cent above the last quarter of 1952. Yields per hectare from collective farms were reportedly 20 to 30 per cent higher than those from private farms.

An occasional absolute rather than percentage figure turned up in propaganda about the state farms. There were 108 of these, very highly mechanized, according to the regime. All sowing was done by tractor-drawn seed-drills, and 97 per cent of the ploughing, 84 per cent of the reaping, were done by machine. Yields mentioned were 4,629 pounds of wheat per acre, 3,825 liters of milk per forage cow during lactation, and 26.6 pounds of wool from a single ram.

On October 14, 1953, as part of the "new course," and before the publication of the second Five Year Plan, the regime and party passed a joint decree "for the uplift of the rural economy." This set absolute figures as 1957 goals for livestock-breeding, where the chief emphasis of the new plan lay. By 1957 there should be 2,090,000 head of cattle, including 700,000 cows, 9,700,000 goats and sheep, 2,200,000 pigs, and 18,000,000 poultry. Milk productivity should be 1,050 liters per cow. The Ministry of Agriculture, the people's councils, and the local party committees were to take in hand the task of setting up "fodder bases" on every collective. The area planted to fodder crops in 1954 should rise by 100,000 hectares over 1953, and by 1957 should reach a total of 1,940,000 hectares, including 1,150,000 hectares of grain fodder. Beginning in 1954, the decree ordered the creation of large numbers of artificial insemination stations, as well as stables, sties, and poultry runs. For 1957, yields were to be 1,930 kilograms of wheat per hectare, 1,850 kilograms of corn per hectare, and similar high figures for other crops including the industrial crops. The most important remaining provision called for the building of two well-equipped repair shops in each MTS.

The Bulgarian "big projects" included the counterpart to the Rumanian reclamation project in the Dobrudja. The decree for the "transformation of nature" there, passed early in 1951, involved the planting of 800 square kilometers of shelter-belts, and accompanying projects for irrigation, electrification, and raising the yields of the province. This was the most completely collectivized area in the whole country: 70 per cent in early 1951, and in the Balchik region 95 per cent. Stalin personally was reported interested in the fate of the Dobrudja project, and allegedly ordered the delivery of the necessary machinery. The other big projects were part of the irrigation and electrification programs. In the Danube valley, Soviet engineers were reported working under the direction of a certain Shubladze in 1949 on dams and on irrigation network in several places along the river, including Nikopol and Svishtov. A system of dams was planned for Thrace. The largest, the Stalin dam in the mountains above Sofia, completed in 1953, spanned the Iskar River, and provided power for the capital and the whole valley.

The Studena dam, near Dimitrovo (Pernik), harnessed the Struma, and provided power for the "Lenin" iron and steel works. The regime's propaganda declared that this dam, second in Bulgaria, was built according to the Noetzli hollow wall construction system, as the soil was too weak to support a solid concrete dam. It took three years to build, was 286 yards long, retained thirty-one million cubic yards of water. The adjacent Republica hydroelectric station was the largest in the Balkans. The dam also provided drinking water for Dimitrovo and irrigation for 1,000 hectares of orchards and vegetable gardens. In a speech delivered in December 1953, Chervenkov called for a total irrigated area of 500,000 hectares by 1957.

INDUSTRY

In 1939, Bulgarian electric power had totaled 267,000,000 kilowatt hours. During the Two Year Plan, some thirty-four power stations, fourteen of which were thermal and the rest hydroelectric, were built. The power output had been 560,000,000 kilowatt hours in 1948, and by 1952, as a result of further construction, was about 1,350,000,000 kilowatt hours. The 1,800,000,000 envisioned by the first plan was clearly in sight. The Bulgarians obtained some power also from Rumania. Two thousand villages were electrified for the first time. The electrical equipment industry, previously virtually nonexistent, was now producing Bulgarian needs in transformers and other important items. These gains were not accomplished without the usual crises and charges of sabotage. The Vice-Minister of Electrification was dismissed in November 1949 for opposing the decisions of Soviet experts, and there were other indications of grave trouble in the program. The second Five Year Plan called for the doubling of electric power output by 1957, and multiplication of electrical equipment production by 2.8. Its biggest project was to be the Batak complex, including several dams, reservoirs, and power-stations, with a capacity of 186,000 kilowatts, scheduled for completion in 1958.

By 1952, coal production was up from about 2,370,000 tons in 1939, of which 2,300,000 was lignite, to 7,410,400 tons, of which probably the same percentage was lignite. A further rise of 89 per cent in hard coal and 27 per cent in lignite was called for by the second Five Year Plan ending in 1957. The large Lenin blast furnace was built in Dimitrovo (Pernik) as part of the effort to render Bulgaria self-sufficient in iron and steel production. Late in 1953, the metal works there went into production "experimentally," with an announced capacity of 50,000 metric tons of steel and 40,000 of rolled metals, which were to be further increased "severalfold." The second plan called for an almost threefold increase in iron ore output, a fifteenfold increase in pig iron, and a tenfold increase in rolled goods.

At Dimitrovo, Bulgaria was beginning for the first time to produce its own machinery. Trailer-harvester combines, cotton-sowers, tree-planting machines, concrete-mixers, and railroad equipment were all mentioned in reports, but quantities were not revealed, and were probably still quite small. Figures were given only in percentages: 1951 production of threshers was eleven times that of 1949, but the 1949 figure was unknown. In 1951, one report declared, Bulgaria was already 58 per cent self-sufficient in machine production, but no further claim of this sort seemed to have been made later. Indeed the final report on the Five Year Plan declared that the machine output for 1952 had exceeded the planned output for 1953 by 38.1 per cent. Finished metal-goods, ploughshares, and the like had not yet reached the 1953 goal in 1952. It seemed probable that when the Dimitrovo installations should reach full blast, Bulgaria would achieve self-sufficiency in this field. Until then, much would have to come from the USSR, which had obviously decided, however, that it was correct for Bulgaria to have its own machine industry. There was some production of oil, copper, and light metals, but probably not very significant. The second plan called for a 78 per cent increase in machine-output over 1952. The chemical industry also started from virtually nothing, and began in these years to produce caustic soda, fertilizers, tanning-stuffs, aniline dyes, cellulose, wood-distillates, and matches. The large Stalin chemical Kombinat at Dimitrovgrad was to have a capacity of 70,000 tons of artificial fertilizers annually. The final report on the first Five Year Plan reported that chemical production exceeded the 1953 goal in 1952 by 4 per cent. Plans called for the building of factories for pharmaceuticals and penicillin.

Bulgarian light industry, textiles, and food-processing also progressed. The 1951 production of cotton cloth was reported to be 8,000,000 square meters as against 4,700,000 in 1939. In Gabrovo, the new Balkan cotton plant was the largest in Bulgaria, with 60,000 spindles; the "Ernst Thälmann" plant, opened in 1951 with equipment imported from Eastern Germany, was also a new modern installation. The Maritsa textile combine produced 1,235,000 knitted garments and 16,000,000 pairs of men's and women's hosiery in 1953. The tripling of the sugar output over 1939 enabled very substantial advance in the food-preserving industry, always important in Bulgaria. Porcelain, glass, and leather awaited development in the second plan, which also called for the "construction and partial exploitation" by 1957 of a new cotton textile plant with an annual capacity of 24,000,000 square meters of cloth and 5,000 tons of yarn. New canning plants were called for.

In transport, the new railway line connecting Sofia with Varna and Burgas was opened in September 1952. The regime boasted that it had 219 bridges, and nineteen tunnels including the Koznitsa tunnel, the longest in the Balkans. Soviet specialists received credit and thanks for their assistance. In April 1953, the Railroad Administration was reorganized under the Ministry of Transport, with three major regional suboffices, in Sofia, Plovdiv, and Gorna Orekhovitsa. Efforts were made to add to the rolling stock, and a new "Zhdanov" repair shop established in Dryanovo. The new plan called for a 50 per cent rise over 1952 by 1957.

Civil aviation was under the control of the "joint" Soviet-Bulgarian company: TABSO, which operated all internal airlines, the Bulgarians furnishing the airports and facilities, and the Russians the planes. At Varna and Burgas, KORBSO controlled the shipyards. The two harbors were enlarged, and shipbuilding was booming, much of it apparently for delivery to the Russians. Much of the trade with the USSR plied between these ports and the Soviet Black Sea cities. Other "joint" companies existed for uranium exploitation, for ores (GORUBSO), and for industrial construction (SOV BOLSTROI). But there were many fewer than in Rumania, and they were less important to the economy. Soviet citizens controlled them.

The whole picture was that of an underdeveloped agricultural country proceeding under forced draft towards industrialization. In these years the emphasis lay upon producing the means of production, and the consumer suffered. But it seemed that Russian deliveries to Bulgaria had been more conscientious than those to Rumania, for example. The strategic importance of the country, as anchor to the southeast, the historic ties between the two peoples, the apparent affection of the Russian rulers for their Bulgarian Communist disciples, perhaps the similarity in language which made it so much easier for a Russian technician to make himself understood to a Bulgarian than to a Rumanian or Albanian: these factors may all have played a part, especially after the break with Yugoslavia, in speeding Russian help to Bulgaria.

The surplus manpower for industry was readily available from agriculture. In 1950 alone, 26,300 workers entered industry; in 1951 the industrial labor force was almost 40 per cent above the 1948 level; the total of new workers during the whole Five Year Plan 1949–1953 was 333,043. The old social structure was being warped into a new form. Economically, one could see the result in the figures on national income shown in Table 15.[21] Socially, the

TABLE 15

Percentage of National Income Derived from	1939	1948	1952
Industry	24.3	37.1	47.3
Construction	2.9	5.3	5.8
Agriculture	55.9	52.6	34.3
Transport, trade, etc.	16.9	11.0	12.6

45:55 ratio between manpower employed in industry and manpower engaged in agriculture had been reached by the end of 1952. In 1953, it was 47:53. Within industry the heavy-light ratio was also declared to be 45:55. In the next five years, industry would overtake agriculture, and would employ more than half the Bulgarian labor force.

In his speech of September 9, 1953, in which he announced the "new course," extended to the collective farms the various forms of relief which we have reviewed, and emphasized the need for consumers' goods, Chervenkov said that Bulgaria had been

> freed from the crushing burden of developing all branches of heavy industry in this country . . . since the socialist camp headed by the Soviet Union . . . enables all countries constituting it to plan their industrialization in such a

[21] *Wissenschaftlicher Dienst Südosteuropa* II, 7–8 (July 31, 1953), p. 146.

> way that each one of them can develop those branches of heavy industry for which the most favorable conditions exist within the country.[22]

But he did not specify which branches Bulgaria could safely ignore, nor had he and his fellow-planners so far chosen to ignore any, or to choose those for which Bulgaria might be suited. And even while proclaiming the new emphasis on consumers' goods, and promising housing and much help to agriculture, he added: "during the Second Five Year Plan . . . priority will naturally be given to the growth of production of the means of production. . . ." He made the point almost parenthetically, but there could be no doubt of its impact. For Bulgaria the new course would mean only slight modifications of existing policies.

FINANCE

Like Rumania, but five months later, in May 1952, Bulgaria had a "currency reform," planned by Soviet experts who had favored several satellites with their presence and advice. For a period of four days the people might exchange their cash holdings of all old leva at the rate of one new lev for 100 old ones. After that, the old currency was worthless. Bank account exchange ranged between 1:25 and 1:100, with state enterprises getting the better rates. At the same time, all wages and prices were to be divided by twenty-five. The new lev had a fine gold content of .113067 grams. The reform wiped out three-quarters of the cash in circulation, and one-half to three-quarters of the savings. Not as ruthless as the Rumanian decree, it was still severe enough. But inflation in Bulgaria had never raged so violently nor was the shortage of consumers' goods so stringent. Rationing was abolished, price-cuts of 10 to 50 per cent were announced, and some wages, salaries, and pensions were raised. This took much of the sting out of the reform for those who had only small accumulations of cash, since their revalued savings would buy as much at the new rate as they could have bought at the old, which was not true in Rumania, where prices rose and goods stayed in short supply after the reform. The lev was pegged at 1.7 to the ruble; and the official rate was 6.8 to the dollar.

With the currency reform in mind, we can proceed to examine the figures on the Bulgarian budget in Table 16. The 1950 figures are in old leva; all after that date have been converted to new.

TABLE 16

	Millions of Leva				
	1950	1951	1952	1953	1954
Income	207,752	12,379	13,894	19,021	18,297
Expenditure			11,839	17,923	17,027
State	151,954				
Local	46,054				
Total	198,008				

[22] *Bulgaria Today*, no. 18 (September 1953), supplement, p. 20.

The drop in the budget for 1954 reflected the new course, with its policy of less heavy investment, as was shown even more clearly by the breakdown in Table 17 of expenditure for the two years.[23]

TABLE 17

	1953	1954
National economy	13,982	9,461
Social and cultural	2,139	3,639
Public health and Social Assistance	994	1,144
Defense	2,076	2,933
	19,191	16,177

In the case of 1953, the published figures added up to more than the total announced expenditure; in the case of 1954, they added up to 1,000 million leva less. This puzzle was unexplained; but the direction of the expenditure was clear enough. The national economy item, largely heavy industry, was cut about one-third, while defense was cut slightly, and the two items which eased the lot of the population both received substantial increments. As for the defense budget, it was interesting to note that, after a steady rise every year since 1948, until the figure for 1953 given above was five times that for 1948, it had moved below its peak, at least if one took the figures at their face value and did not search for hidden defense moneys concealed behind the "social and cultural" item. If the slight drop in military expenditures might in fact be posited, it would reflect a similar policy to that followed in the USSR: the moving toward a slight lessening of tension which was observable in the year following the death of Stalin.

As to sources from which the Bulgarian government derived its revenue, the figures it published indicated that the sales tax (turnover tax) had produced 45 per cent of the total in 1951, 50 per cent in 1952, and 51 per cent in 1953, and an estimated 76 per cent in 1954. "Taxes on the population" accounted for small and steadily decreasing percentages (7.5 per cent in 1951, 7.3 in 1952, 6.6 in 1953, and an estimated 6.1 in 1954). In Bulgaria, they included a graduated income tax, passed in May 1950, the incidence of which is shown in Table 18.[24] (See page 538.)

A peasant's cash income was computed according to the following scale: income from one decare (one-tenth hectare) of land sown with grain was 120 leva, a decare sown with tobacco 180 leva, a cow 480 leva, a goat 96 leva, and a pig 60 leva. His tax increased 10 per cent for one hired worker (which made him a kulak), 15 per cent for two, and 30 per cent for three. A peasant member of a collective paid no tax on the "labor-day" cash he received or the payments in kind from the farm. He paid only on income from his own plot, and

[23] *Soviet Orbit*, X, 462 (February 12, 1954), p. 103.

[24] *News from Behind the Iron Curtain*, II, 4 (April 1953).

TABLE 18

Farmers, Private or Collective		Workers		Lawyers		Professionals, Artisans, Income from Rent	
Annual Income	Annual Tax	Monthly Income	Monthly Tax	Monthly Income	Monthly Tax	Annual Income	Annual Tax
2,000	80	200	4				
4,000	180	400	13.6	400	32	4,000	180
12,000	1,600	720	40.8	800	80	8,000	1,020
40,000	10,900			3,200	805	40,000	12,460
		over 720	12%	over 3,200	48%	over 40,000	48%

on rent received from the collective for the land he had contributed to it. In addition, the collectives as such paid a 7 per cent tax on their income plus a tax on their profits ranging from 25 to 50 per cent. These taxes only became effective after a collective had been in existence for two years. It should be remembered that the figures in Table 18 are in pre-currency-reform leva, and that the income taxes were substantially modified for farmers after the new course began in the fall of 1953.

There were no land taxes, and no excise taxes. The local soviets collected a small property tax of one per mil for state holdings and two per mil for private holdings, to finance their own activities, and also collected inheritance taxes, which were graduated from 2 per cent for sums up to 8,000 leva to 50 per cent for anything over 120,000. There was also a military tax of eighty leva per year plus 1 per cent of income after taxes, which fell on all male citizens between the ages of twenty and fifty who had not served in the army or the labor force, and were incapable of serving.

From March 1951 on, by party and government joint decree, the National Bank of Bulgaria was the sole state bank, which regulated the flow of funds, issued banknotes, granted short-term credits to economic organizations, supervised their work, mobilized their spare capital, and safeguarded the realization of the State Budget, both for income and expenditure. In addition to tax-funds, the system of state loan subscriptions served to provide the state with substantial funds and at the same time to drain off excess purchasing power. There apparently were four of these in the postwar years. The first, in 1945, had as its goal 600,000,000 (old) leva, and actually brought in a billion. The second, in 1951, had as its goal 400,000,000 (old) leva, and brought in 600,000,000. The third, in 1953, had as its goal 400,000,000 (new) leva, and brought in 529,000,000; and the fourth, "for the second five-year plan," in early 1954, had as its goal another 400,000,000 leva and brought in 501,000,000. The loan mingled the features of a bond issue and a state lottery. Subscribers bought twenty-year bonds. Twice a year, the state held drawings, and a certain number of the bonds won cash prizes. Those bondholders whose bonds won a prize forfeited their interest for the year; those who failed to win a prize, collected interest. According to the state announcement, one bond in three won a prize at each of the forty drawings. The government claimed that it had awarded almost fourteen million leva in prizes at one such drawing alone. At the end of twenty years, all bonds which had not won prizes were paid out to the holder at their face value. The regime apparently found the scheme profitable enough to warrant its frequent repetition. It cut the workers' purchasing power, for one thing, and helped render the repeated price cuts far less effective than they seemed.

After the currency reform of 1952, as we saw, prices were cut, and this was only the first of four such cuts which were to follow by spring 1954. The second cut, made in September 1952, ranged from 6 per cent to 10 (milk, butter, cheese, eggs) or more (bread, twenty; flour, thirty). The third, on August 1, 1953, averaged 10 per cent on foodstuffs and 20 per cent on industrial goods. Though the regime hailed it with fanfare, the population was apparently greatly disappointed. Chervenkov, very much on the defensive, in his speech of September 9 attributed this belittling of the cut to "enemies":

> They began to hint, before it took place, that it would be no less than fifty per cent for all goods. This was obviously done on purpose . . . this was a rumor spread with a view to afterwards accusing the government (*sic*) that it had given an . . . insufficient reduction. . . . Every more or less economically literate person knows that such miracles do not occur, that a reduction in prices is not an arbitrary phenomenon, but is conditioned by the actual state of the national economy. . . . The reduction of prices of individual goods is determined by the extent of their quantity. A reduction of prices which does not take this into consideration is a paper reduction; it is demagogy, an adventure. The population wants a real reduction, not formal reductions. What would the population say to the People's Government if it were to declare a fifty per cent reduction in the price of an article and several days later this article were to disappear entirely from the market? . . . . an average price reduction of ten per cent on foodstuffs and of fifteen per cent on industrial goods, made only eleven months after there has already been a price-reduction is a serious tangible reduction.

It is notable that this passage seemed not to have elicited any "laughter, animation, and applause" from even the Communist audience. The fourth price reduction, announced March 28, 1954, provided cuts of from 9 to 22 per cent in bread, 15 to 20 in fodder, 5 to 18 in meat, 7 to 40 in textiles, 4 to 22 in shoes, 5 to 25 in ready-made clothing, as well as a long list of other cuts. There were no reports of shortages or inflation after the cuts.

But price cuts were accompanied by measures to reduce the purchasing power of the population by deducting percentages from monthly pay-checks for a system of "voluntary" savings accounts. The accompanying tables represented wage levels and commodity prices current in Bulgaria after the second price cut of September 1952 but before the third one of August 1953.[25]

[25] *News from Behind the Iron Curtain*, II, 7 (July 1953), pp. 28 ff.

TABLE 19

	Wages in Leva (6.8 to the Dollar)
Unskilled worker	13–18 per day
Skilled worker	18–23 per day
With high school education	320–440 per month
With university training	480–800 per month
Top officials	1,000 per month
Army officers	800–1,400 per month
Militia	350–1,400 per month
Party functionaries	2,000
	State Store prices in leva
1 kg. black bread	1.96
1 kg. white bread	4.80

TABLE 20

	State Store Prices in Leva
1 liter sunflower oil	15.00
1 liter skimmed milk	3.80
1 kg. meat	12–32.50
1 egg	.960
1 kg. sugar	9.60–10.00
1 meter woolen cloth	200–300
1 pair shoes	180–280

Propaganda for the regime claimed that "in many" collective farms a farmer made seventeen-eighteen leva per day on farms where cash crops or stock-breeding was the main occupation. On those where grain was the chief staple, the cash yield was lower but the income in kind was substantial. The family of coöperative farmer Anghel Marinov received in 1953, according to this account, 16,400 leva in cash, four and a half metric tons of wheat, 286 pounds of sugar, 330 pounds of rice, 350 liters of wine, vegetable oil, cheese, fodder for his animals, and so forth. Lucky Marinov was billed as an average peasant with a family of three able-bodied children, "with twelve and a half acres of land," presumably a plot of five hectares which he had contributed to the collective, and from which he was receiving rent.

With his savings, a citizen might build up a savings account in the State Savings Bank. The deposits were secret, drew 3 to 4 per cent interest, and might be withdrawn at will. Only if the money could be shown to have been obtained illegally could the state garnishee the account. In 1953, there were 4,660,935 such accounts. The State Insurance Institute would insure his life, or the Bulgarian Investment Bank would give him a housing loan on special terms. Between 1947 and 1952, holders of insurance policies were said to have doubled in number. It was only such propaganda materials as this which gave even the most unnaturally lighted glimpse into the financial life of the individual Bulgarian citizen. What might be said of him, in the light of our knowledge, was that he seemed to be considerably better off than his fellow-sufferers in Rumania.

Bulgarian foreign trade was operated by state enterprises. *Hranexport* handled all agricultural products except fruits, vegetables, and alcoholic drinks, which were under the control of *Bulgarprodexport*. *Bulgartabak* dealt with tobacco export, *Bulgarska Rosa* with rose and other oils. *Rudmetall* handled coal, and metal ores; *Industrialimport* imported raw materials, and manufactured goods, including textiles; *Metalimport* handled machines and electrical equipment, *Rasnoisnos* paper, half-finished goods and handicrafts, and *Balkantourist* the travel business.

As in the case of Rumania, Bulgaria did most of her business in these years with the Soviet bloc: 82 per cent in 1949, 88 per cent in 1950, and 92 per cent in 1951, a steadily mounting figure, in those years for which we had figures, rather than a moderately constant one, as in the case of Rumania. The USSR alone accounted for 58 per cent of Bulgarian trade. In addition, Bulgaria had trade agreements with western Germany, Egypt, India, Austria ($11,000,000), Italy, Greece ($180,000), and Finland, in the order of their conclusion. It was interesting that Bulgarian exports were in every case agricultural products including tobacco, except in the agreement with India, which called for Bulgarian deliveries of threshing-machines, electric motors, pneumatic pumps, and chemicals, in addition to the foodstuffs, in exchange for Indian tea, pepper, wool, cotton, medicines, electric cable, shellac, leather, and bamboo. Part of the new course was a steady propaganda for increased trade with the west, which by 1954 had not materialized to any notable degree. The total volume of trade with the western countries was reported as $8,300,000 in 1951 and $15,400,000 in 1952. If the $8,300,000 were taken as the 8 per cent of the 1951 trade outside the eastern bloc, the dollar figure for the other 92 per cent would be $95,450,000 as the total value of the trade inside the eastern bloc. In 1953, Bulgaria imported $1,300,000 worth of goods from Great Britain, and $4,300,000 from Austria.

3. Albania

For Albanian economic development in the period since the break between the Soviet Union and Yugoslavia we have somewhat less fragmentary materials than for the other satellite countries, because of the Albanian practice of publishing a good many absolute figures. The total pattern was clearly discernible, and entirely familiar. Denouncing Tito for his diabolical effort to merge the two countries and equalize their currencies, and hailing the Soviet Union as the new protector, Albania officially adopted a preliminary Two Year Plan in June 1949, after it had been in effect since the start of the year. The total investment planned was 4,147,000,000 leks, of which 25 per cent was set aside for industry and trade, 25 for transport, 20 for mining, and 14 for agriculture. The break with Yugoslavia necessitated an admitted 20 per cent cut in the investment plan for 1949, and the fulfillment of the Two Year Plan was only 91.4 per cent: "Yugoslav sabotage" was the cause.

The first Five Year Plan came into effect at the beginning of 1951, and was to run until the end of 1955. The total investment was to be 21 billion leks, of which almost nine billion, or about 43 per cent, was for industry and mining. Almost three billion, or about 14 per cent was for agriculture, the same amount for transportation, about 16 per cent for social welfare (3,460,000,000 leks). The proportions of investments, so far as could be told, remained roughly the same in the Five Year Plan as in the two, except in the case of transport. The annual amounts to be invested, however, had more than doubled. Moscow extended substantial credits to make any such program possible. The aim was triple: to expand consumers' goods production, to produce more raw materials for export, and to advance education. The rate of increase of industrial production, 10 per cent a year during the Two Year Plan, was to rise to 30 per cent during the Five Year Plan. But, though the figure given was 47.1 per cent for 1951, it fell below 20 per cent in 1952, and rose only to 22 per cent in 1953; the target for 1954 was lowered to 14.7 per cent. Total plan fulfillment percentages were 105.8 for 1952, 96.5 for the first quarter of 1953, 97.1 for the second quarter of 1953. After that no figures were available. It was clear that Albania was lagging behind an overambitious plan, but that the country was moving speedily in the direction chosen by the planners. The ratio between the values of agricultural and industrial production (82:18 in 1938) had reached 40:60 in 1953. But 70 per cent of the population still worked the land.

AGRICULTURE

Albanian agriculture, especially after the postwar "land reform," was so backward that immediate large-scale collectivization seemed less important to the planners than increasing the area under cultivation, improving the yields, and introducing cash crops. Yet the ideal of a collectivized mechanized agriculture was always held out as the goal, and the movement towards it was considerable. In February 1949, there were twenty-five "coöperative" farms with 2,500 families. In November, the Tirana Radio declared that "coöperatives" on the Soviet model would be introduced into Albania, but that entry would be purely voluntary. The state would assist all peasants who might consent to join. In August 1950, Mehmet Shehu said that collectivization would be of prime importance, but repeated that it must be gradual and voluntary. There were now fifty-nine "coöperative farms." By mid-November, the regime claimed that there were ninety. It divulged no data as to the number of households or the size of the area collectivized, but declared that the farms were 25 per cent mechanized.

In April 1951, the tenth plenum of the party apparently directed a major speed-up in collectivization; in May the Central Committee met, with Hoxha presiding, and denounced the plenum's action. Reviewing the entire question, the Central Committee declared that the decision of the previous month had been incorrect: the present task was not to increase the number of collectives but to "consolidate" the ones which already existed. There must be no haste, no pressure, no mistakes. No figures appear to have been published until August 1952, fifteen months later. There were now "more than 100" collectives, only a few more than there had been in November 1950. The pace was slow indeed, compared to that in Bulgaria or even in Rumania.

In April 1953, Hoxha made a speech bemoaning the lag, and attacking the management of the 115 collectives then in existence. There were five collectives in the Gjinokaster district, Hoxha said, but only nine peasant families had joined in the past year; in the Korcha district, the rate was five a year. Moreover, peasants on the collectives worked as little as sixty days a year, and spent the rest of the time cultivating their own plots. They were reluctant to let their women work. Those who had joined had often sold their cattle first. Hoxha predicted complete collectivization of cattle, and the eventual triumph of the state over the peasant's individualism. But in November 1953, there were still only 128 collectives, and in April 1954, at a conference to improve Albanian economic leadership, it was announced that the "socialist" sector of agriculture accounted for only 12.8 per cent of the output, the private sector 87.2 per cent. One might estimate that collectivization had gone about half as far in Albania as in Rumania, and that the peasants of the smallest and most primitive of the satellites had so far been largely spared to cultivate their own lands.

They were plagued, however, by the onerous burden of compulsory deliveries, which obtained in Albania as elsewhere. In the times of extreme stringency following the break with Yugoslavia, these were apparently set extraordinarily high, and for a while famine conditions prevailed. The rationing system introduced in January 1949, for example, entitled only workers and state employees to receive rations. Early in 1951, the compulsory delivery quotas of cereals and beans were reduced by 25 to 50 per cent for individual peasants, and by 35 per cent to 60 per cent for collective farms, depending upon the quality of the soil.

Albania too had its version of the new course. In late June or early July 1953 it canceled all the peasants' back debts and overdue delivery quotas as far back as 1949. On September 8, 1953, the party and government issued a joint decree abolishing all grain delivery quotas for some lands, and reducing them by one-half for all collectives and coöperatives. Peasants who themselves did not own cattle were excused from delivering meat and wool to the state for a period of three years. Olive deliveries were cut 50 per cent, and the state tripled the prices it would pay for the olives which had been brought in. It was impossible to say whether these concessions represented anything more than the regime's recognition that it had no hope of collecting the back debts.

As for the technical as against the social aims of the Albanian planners in agriculture, their own reports, to be viewed with the usual caution, showed a substantial success. The announced percentage of plan fulfillment for 1949 was 112; for 1950, 128. The sown area had increased in 1950 by 3 per cent; 260 acres had been reforested. In 1953 the sown area was 362,000 hectares, as against 223,000 in 1938; 400,000 was called for in 1955. Irrigated areas amounted to 60,000 hectares, a rise over 35,000 in 1950; and 83,000 were planned for 1955. Cereal areas were 269,000 in 1950, and were to reach 284,700 in 1954. Cotton, sugar beets, oil-seeds, and tobacco were pushed. Of these cash crops there were 27,100 hectares in 1948, and 40,000 hectares in 1950–51 as against 2,900 in 1938. Forty-six thousand were planned for 1955. A major plan to increase olive output over fifteen years was adopted in 1953.

At the time of the publication of the Five Year Plan, the regime gave 1950 wheat yields as 9.7 quintals per hectare; the 1955 target was 11.5 quintals. Corn was to rise from 8.8 quintals per hectare in 1950 to 12.5 in 1955; rice from 17.6 to twenty-five quintals per hectare, cotton from 4.4 to eight, sugar beet from 45.1 to 200, and potatoes from 72.2 to 100. The area planted to oil-seeds was 31,000 hectares in 1950; it would be 46,000 in 1955; rice was 12,000, and was to rise to 15,700; pasture land would increase from 18,000 to 30,500 hectares. The 1953 tobacco crop was four times as big as that of 1952. More than 500 tractors and other farm machines would be imported.

The livestock position of the country was poor. There were 134,000 head of cattle in 1938, and 140,000 in 1946, but only 129,000 in 1950. No figures were available after 1950, and the total fell off still further. A similar picture was presented by the figures for all other livestock except pigs.

INDUSTRY

In industrializing the country, the planners tried to exploit the most important natural resources, the petroleum reserves. A "joint" company, Al Sov Petrol, was set up for exploration and development. A 1948 report declared that the output was already 60 per cent above prewar output; and this and other percentage figures led some authorities to set the figure of 300,000 tons for 1950. But when the Five Year Plan figures were published, the figure for 1950 was given in absolute figures as 131,500 tons, considerably below the prewar peak, and that for 1955 was set at 263,000, obviously simply a mechanical doubling of the 1950 figure. The Cerrik refinery, begun in 1952, scheduled for completion in 1954, was to have a capacity of 150,000 tons a year. Reports also mentioned a pipe line from the fields to Tirana. The plan fulfillment percentages for 1952 reported a 22 per cent rise over 1951.

The other mineral resources as given by the Five Year Plan figures included chrome ore (52,000 tons in 1950, 120,000 planned for 1955), coal (figure for 1950 unknown, 250,000 tons planned for 1955), copper (900 tons in 1950, 2,500 planned for 1955), and bitumen (26,300 tons in 1950, 80,000 planned for 1955). Comparable figures for cement were 15,000 tons in 1950, 58,000 planned for 1955, when a new plant at Valona would be in production. But the total ineral production lagged; the percentage figure for 1953 published in 1954 'as only 85.7 per cent of plan fulfillment for minerals overall.

With plenty of water-power potential, the Albanian planners, like their unterparts elsewhere in the Balkans, focused on electrification. The Yugo-avs had helped with the Selita plant above Tirana, which was now called e Lenin works, and which included an aqueduct supplying Tirana with ater. A dam called "Enver" after Hoxha was scheduled for building across e Mati River. This was to supply the power for a station near Uj, in the urrel district, which would have 20,000 kilowatts capacity, and could provide 0,000,000 kilowatt hours of current annually. This was the "big" project of e Five Year Plan, and a joint party and government decree ordered it com-leted by 1955. The Five Year Plan total figures were 21,000,000 kilowatt hours 1950, and 121,000,000 planned for 1955, the new power all coming from the 'j station.

Albanian industry, consolidated into seventy-nine state enterprises, was ill entirely light industry, and the planners themselves failed to speak of ture steel combines and machine-tool plants. They did claim greatly to have creased the output of the textile and food industries. The 5,000-spindle textile ant in Shkodra was scheduled to be joined by the large "Stalin" textile-ombinat in Tirana with 21,000 spindles, 2,000 workers, and an ultimate annual pacity of 20,000,000 square meters of cotton cloth, enough to take care of lbanian domestic needs. It opened on November 9, 1951, but the 1952 output 'as to be only 8,000,000 square meters, and the plant would not reach capacity ntil 1955. Production before it opened was only about 1,000,000 square meters, resumably from the Shkodra mill; in 1955 it would be 21,000,000. Cotton gin-ing works in Fjeri and Rogozhina would supply the raw material. Shoe out-ut, put at 272,000 pairs in 1950, would be 598,000 in 1955. The Maliq sugar ant, in the course of construction, would raise the annual output of sugar om 610 tons in 1950 to 11,000 in 1955. Olive oil would rise from 1,300 tons 5,150. Plywood for the first time would come at the rate of 40,000 square eters a year from the new woodworking Kombinat at Elbasan. The value f the total food industry would rise from 340,000,000 leks in 1950 to more than vo billion in 1955, while the all-over consumers' goods industries would rise om two and a half billion leks in 1950 to more than eight billion in 1955.

Transport was obviously a major need in Albania. On February 15, 1951, e regime opened a new railway line of thirty-eight kilometers from Peqin Elbasan, continuing the Durazzo-Peqin line of forty-three kilometers which e Yugoslavs had built. A long-planned Durazzo-Tirana line also came into peration, and this was to be extended to connect with Valona. A Shkodra-ukes line was also planned. The total railroad network of Albania had eached 131 kilometers by the end of 1952. The regime also claimed to have uilt 400 kilometers of hard-surfaced roads, much of this apparently improve-ents in already existing roads connecting main centers, but also including a new military road along the Yugoslav frontier from Kukes to Peshkopije. Truck transport, always the chief form of transport in the country, had allegedly multiplied by ten since the war in amounts of freight carried and by fifteen in number of persons.

FINANCE

Table 21 gives the published Albanian budget figures for these years in millions of leks.[26]

TABLE 21

	1949	1950	1951	1952	1953	1954
Income	6,379	7,800	9,500	10,300	10,340	10,800
Expenditure	5,265	7,700	9,100	10,200	9,760	9,900

The items of expenditure were, as usual, the national economy, social and cultural projects, public health, and defense. For 1951, 1952, and 1953, the figures were as shown in Table 22, in million leks.[27] The defense budget remained roughly constant at 11 per cent of the total budget.

TABLE 22

	1951	1952	1953	1954 Plan
National economy	2,988	3,800	5,437	
Social & cultural	1,526	2,150	2,400	2,000
Health	290	547		
Defense	1,112	1,133	1,250	1,128

The defense budget remained roughly constant at 11 per cent of the total budget.

The income derived from the usual sources: "the national economy" (40 per cent in 1951, 53 per cent in 1952, 56 per cent in 1953, and 66 per cent in 1954), a turnover tax, taxes on the population, and revenue from Soviet and satellite aid (perhaps 20 per cent), whose exact size was unknown. But Albania, like Bulgaria, derived some of its revenue from the state loans, which were in fact compulsory. The first, in the summer of 1949, set 250,000,000 leks as its goal, and was oversubscribed by one million. The second, early in 1952, set 300,000,000 as its goal, and was oversubscribed by 35 per cent, the total actually collected amounting to 405,135,800 leks.

The regime did not publish regular figures for wages and prices. According to reports of early 1951, workers were receiving 70 to 90 leks per day for

[26] *East Europe,* VI, 275 (March 30, 1950), p. 6; *East Europe and Soviet Russia,* VII, 336 (June 21, 1951), p. 23; *ibid.,* VIII, 371 (March 20, 1952), p. 23; and *Soviet Orbit,* X, 472 (April 30, 1954), p. 254; *News from Behind the Iron Curtain,* III, 5 (May 1954), p. 16.

[27] Sources as in n. 26.

unskilled labor and 100 to 150 a day for skilled labor. Civil servants' salaries ranged from 2,500 leks per month for a schoolteacher to 15,000 for a Cabinet minister, who had in addition the privilege of buying in six special shops set aside for the party élite. The purchasing power of the lek was extremely low; it was reported at the same period that one kilogram of meat cost 15 leks in state shops, and 130 in the free market, and that one kilogram of sugar cost 35 leks in the state shops and 350 on the free market. For the peasant there were coupons which he would receive in exchange for his surplus entitling him to purchase consumer-goods in state shops. But the payments were too low, the goods in the shops scarce, and the compulsory delivery quotas to which he was subjected so high that he had little surplus to dispose of in any case.

In 1949, 1950, and 1951, 100 per cent of Albanian foreign trade was with the Soviet bloc. The USSR alone accounted for 57 per cent in 1951. In January 1953, the Committee on a Free Europe published in its periodical, *News from Behind the Iron Curtain,* the following data contributed by a former employee of the Albanian Ministry of Foreign Trade, who had escaped to the west. From the Soviet Union, Albania imported agricultural machinery, oil extraction equipment, textiles, wheat, corn, liquid fuels and lubricating oils, automobiles and spare parts, railroad equipment, pharmaceuticals and chemical goods, iron, steel zinc, copper, tin, bronze, and fishing boats. From Czechoslovakia, it imported automobiles and spare parts, industrial machinery, textiles, household utensils, paper, iron, and steel. From Poland, it imported mining and other machinery, petroleum pipe, dynamite and other explosives, railroad cars and spare parts, iron, and fishing boats. From Hungary, it imported machinery, automobiles, including busses, electrical equipment, aluminum, iron and steel, textiles, wheat, corn, pharmaceuticals, and pure-bred horses. From Rumania, it imported small amounts of machinery, wheat, corn, liquid fuels, coal, paper, pure-bred animals, cement, and fishing boats. From East Germany, it imported machinery, spare parts, chemicals, mimeograph machines, and telecommunications equipment. From Bulgaria, it imported machinery, cement, textiles, quality plants (grape vines), paper, and window-glass. Quantities given for some of these commodities in 1953 were as follows: 30,000 tons of wheat, 20,000 tons of corn, 18,000 tons of cement, 200 tons of dynamite, 13,000 tons of paper, 170 kilometers of percussion cable, 60,000 square meters of window glass, 104 trucks, 150,000 percussion caps, and 18,000 blankets.

Albanian exports consisted of agricultural products, livestock, timber, minerals, and petroleum. The informant gave from memory some items and figures for 1951–52: 5,000–7,000 tons of sunflower seeds, cotton seed and cotton, 1,000 tons of olives, olive oil, resin, flax, linseed, tobacco, 340 tons of oranges and lemons, honey. Five hundred and ten tons of cheese, butter, wool, 50,000 goat-skins, ox and sheep-gut, timber, acorns, herbs, 97,000 tons of unrefined oil, copper chrome ore, tar, nuts, fruits, arrack, soap, salt.

Albania was enabled to pay for the goods sent by the other Soviet-bloc states by a long-term credit agreement, to be repaid by Albanian exports. The informant gave the accompanying figures in millions of rubles for Albanian imports as planned through the Five Year Plan.

TABLE 23

	1952–53	1953–54	1954–55	Totals
USSR	22.2	26.7	28.6	77.5
Czechoslovakia	14.2	14.2	9.9	38.3
Poland	8.1	8.6	8.1	24.8
Hungary	4.2	4.3	4.8	13.2
Rumania	11.2	7.0	8.0	26.2
E. Germany	7.4	5.4	5.9	18.7
Bulgaria	5.4	7.3	3.3	16.0
Totals	72.7	73.5	68.6	214.8

The figures illustrated vividly the fact that Albania represented an economic liability to the Soviet bloc, which those states had to carry for reasons of prestige. It would be many years before Albanian exports could begin to pay for such substantial amounts of goods, if indeed that time were ever to arrive. Meanwhile, the Albanian development program would be pursued with little regard to the standard of living of the unfortunate people, who would continue to suffer there, as they suffered everywhere in the Soviet orbit.

Behind the statistics indeed lay a life of which the westerner could catch only an occasional glimpse, from the reports of those who escaped, or those who took the risk of writing freely to the outside world. As details emerged, they greatly resembled what the west knew about the life in the Soviet Union. On a state farm (sovkhoz) in Transylvania in 1951, for example, the mixed Rumanian-Hungarian labor force of peasants had enough to eat in their communal canteen, but could not eat at their own discretion any of the food they raised. Indeed, since all the produce had to be sold to the state at fixed prices, the peasants who planted and harvested could not even buy a single one of their own tomatoes. As a result, they stole regularly whatever they could safely lay their hands on, despite the supposed moral uplift provided by visiting teams of lecturing propagandists for the regime.

The management committee of five, nominally run by the director, who was an agronomist, actually took orders from the assistant director, who kept the books, and was in charge of the political work among the peasantry. The party representative acted as liaison man with the village party organization, working with the mayor and militia, and directing the requisitioning of needed articles for the farm. The managers ate in a separate canteen, where they got better food, and drank wine. They also stole produce for their relatives, juggling the figures in their books to conceal their dishonesty, and squaring their friends in the village administration. Inspectors arrived every week or so, enjoyed a cordial welcome from the management, and contentedly reported the failures to reach production goals as due to acts of God. They too got their share of the graft.

In a factory in Bucharest, running two eight-hour shifts, the workers arrived fifteen minutes early to listen to the compulsory reading of *Scânteia,* attended two political meetings a week, and were subject to call to attend other meetings at any time. Everybody had to attend on his own time a two-hour weekly discussion of politics. Struggling to meet advancing production quotas, faced with wage cuts or charges of sabotage for failure to do so, able to procure sick-leave only with a doctor's certificate, and then receiving only three-quarters pay for time off while sick, the workers made at best a bare living wage. Without a doctor's certificate, absence was punishable as absenteeism. Every week, in addition, each worker had to perform two half days of "voluntary" labor for the regime, sometimes traveling to the country to try to persuade the peasants of the beauties of the system, or circulating peace petitions, collecting gifts for North Korea, and the like.

The factory canteen every day at 3 P.M., when the shift changed, served a bad expensive meal; eating on the job was forbidden. In the canteen, the spoons had one sharpened edge to serve as knives; there was one drinking-glass for every three workers; and napkins had been abolished as "bourgeois formalism." The medical care was woefully insufficient; of 1,650 workers in this particular plant, 680 were said to have lung lesions. To see a doctor they had to stand in line for many hours; he had insufficient drugs. Everybody's salary was docked for compulsory subscriptions to official newspapers, union dues, dues to the Society of Friendship with the Soviet Union (ARLUS), and other contributions. The factory had a small stuffy club room, and a library of 200 "progressive" books.

The differences between this picture and equivalent ones for the other satellites were differences of degree and not of kind. Bitter resentment smoldered in the countryside and in the cities, without finding an outlet, even in the drunkenness that was the Soviet Russian's own answer to oppression. All that could be said was that the peasant usually got enough to eat. The worker could count on no more than the bare minimum necessary for survival. The program of the regime used up all his energy, health, and time, and the party representatives did what they could to prevent his having leisure enough to contemplate his troubles or energy enough to resist his masters.

Chapter 15

THE SOUL AND THE MIND

1. Religion

AS IN THE SOVIET UNION, the Communists in the Balkan countries were personally hostile to religion of any denomination, and did not themselves belong to a church. Yet, as in the Soviet Union also, they found themselves governing populations to whom religion had traditionally meant not only spiritual solace but national identity. Unable to close the churches and forbid divine worship, which they would have liked to do, the Communist regimes sought to dominate and control religion. Their methods and their timing varied from country to country, and from faith to faith within each country, but their aims remained the same: to make sure that the churches and the clergy could in no way encourage popular opposition to communism, enter on any undertaking independently of the state, or maintain any links with the western world, and especially to strip the churches of their schools, and their traditional role in education. Beyond this they sought by propaganda to denigrate religion, especially among children, and by cutting down on electricity for churches, scheduling important party functions for Sunday mornings, and other indirect methods, to undermine the religious habits of the population. The constitutions all guaranteed freedom of religion, and proclaimed the separation of church and state.

In general, the Orthodox Church, which traditionally reflected the views and policies of whatever government might be in power, put up relatively little opposition. Although many individual Orthodox clerics bitterly detested the new regimes, the state quite easily found others whom it could manipulate as it pleased. The same was true of the Muslim clergy as a whole. Much was made of the "brotherhood" between Balkan Orthodox and Muslims and those in the USSR. The Roman Catholic and the Uniate clergy, on the other hand, for a time resisted pressure, and served as centers of opposition to the new governments. These in turn regarded the Catholic and the Uniate clergy as agents of the Vatican, which they denounced with increasing bitterness as an agency of American imperialism. Severe persecution accompanied the efforts of the Communist regimes to create a body of Catholic clergy which would be loyal to them, and independent of Rome, an effort which, to a considerable extent at least, had succeeded by 1954. As for the Protestant groups, always small in number, the regimes could afford to persecute them outright, especially those which had direct connections with the west. The minor sects presented no particular problem. The Jews, as we know, continued to exist in significant numbers only in Rumania, where they suffered persecution for political rather than for religious reasons.

THE ORTHODOX CHURCHES

In Yugoslavia, the Orthodox faith was intimately connected with the historic past of the Serb people. Serbia was the center of all loyalty to the monarchy and to the memory of Mihailovich and the purely Serb resistance. The church stood for Serbian nationalism. It also owned much property. In all these capacities, it incurred the enmity of the Communists. The postwar "land reform" bill, as we saw, stripped the church of most of its real estate. Those priests who were best known as supporters of the Chetniks or of Nedich fled the country or suffered persecution. A good many churches were shut down, and some were destroyed. The Patriarch, Gavrilo, who had been deported to Germany during the war, returned to his post at the head of the church. Soon after he died, in the spring of 1950, his successor, Vikentiye, declared that coöperation between church and state would be possible, and exchanged visits with Tito.

One of the regime's devices for securing the loyalty and support of the clergy was the formation of "priests' associations," government-sponsored groups whose members received special favors, such as social security and free medical care, not available to those who refused to join. These associations could be used by the government as sounding boards for its own programs, and as agencies of pressure to recruit more and more members of the clergy. Beginning in 1952, the government stepped up its efforts to force priests to join. The Holy Synod of the Serbian Orthodox Church stoutly refused to recognize the associations, and the press abused the synod freely, accusing the bishops of wanting to dissolve the associations, a charge the synod officially denied. By December 1952, there were reportedly five Orthodox associations with a total of 2,000 priests as members. The numbers grew, and members of the Orthodox hierarchy would sadly admit in private that an overwhelming proportion of the priests had joined.

In May 1953, the regime produced and the National Assembly passed a "religious communities" bill. This proclaimed itself to be supplementary to the constitutional provisions guaranteeing the freedom of religion. Its text read as if it had been the product of amicable discussions between the government and the churches; and in fact the churches had been consulted, but only the Orthodox and Muslim clergy had actually helped draft the measure. The bill produced no startling changes, but simply regularized already existing practices.

According to its provisions, a Yugoslav could belong to any faith or to none, a change from the prewar law, which had required that all citizens belong to some church. The bill forbade any effort to force membership in any faith or to prevent the abandonment of any, or to require church-members to participate or not to participate in any rite. This in effect forbade parents to send to church any child who did not want to go, and prevented clerics from enforcing obedience to ecclesiastical precepts. Violations were punishable by two weeks' prison sentences or fines. A new religious community might be founded at any time, and would automatically enjoy the same status as all others; all were juridical persons, without special privileges. Membership in none excused the member from performance of any required duty to the state, military service, for example. Rites might be performed only in churches or in their grounds, such as cemeteries. Families might celebrate weddings and have funeral services in their homes, but any other religious celebration outside the cult's buildings must be specifically authorized by the local people's council. Hospitals and homes for the aged were permitted to receive priests to visit any inmate who wished it. The state reserved the right to use church bells to sound warnings in times of danger.

The state required that births be registered before baptism, and that civil marriage precede any religious ceremony. One parent at least must consent to baptism, and if the child were over ten, his own consent might be accepted by both parties, but had no legal weight in the eyes of the government. No religious schools might exist, but religious instruction might be given in the cult's buildings outside of school hours. The child himself, as well as both his parents, had to agree to attendance. Any church was at liberty to found its own middle and high schools for the education of its own priests, and select their faculties and design their curriculum, but the state reserved the right to supervise their conduct. Nobody was to attend who had not completed the required schooling in the state schools. Churches might issue their own newspapers and periodicals within the general framework of the law on the press. These publications were forbidden to serve a political purpose, to incite hatred, or to stir up religious conflict.

Nobody might be compelled to give or prevented from giving money to the churches. Collections were legal inside church buildings. They might not take place elsewhere without specific approval from the local people's council. Priests were free to accept money or payment in any other form for holding divine service. In each republic, the republican executive council could vote support to the churches; so could the federal executive council. The churches might freely use funds given to them, unless there was some restriction on the gift. In that case, a report on the use of the funds might be required.

Though many of the provisions of this bill seemed not unreasonable when considered against the background of religious hatred which had existed in Yugoslavia, and which had played a role in the Ustasha efforts to force Orthodox conversions and in their massacres of the Orthodox, everything depended upon the way the state interpreted its own law. In practice, there was a steady barrage of anti-religious propaganda, designed to keep people, especially children, away from the churches, and to bring shame and disrepute on those who went. Much standard atheist propaganda was circulated with the approval of the government.

From abroad, the Pan-Serb former Premier Slobodan Yovanovich urged the Orthodox clergy not to yield to the state. Some difficulties continued, as the press gave publicity to statements by its own pet groups of priests: for example, the Orthodox clergy of Kossovo-Metohiya in September 1953, "condemned" the attitude of the Synod toward the Orthodox Priests' Association, and "demanded" that the Synod recognize it. The Commissioner for Religious Questions, Radosavlyevich, "met" with the Synod, and the press declared that 80 per cent of the Orthodox priests belonged to the association. The Synod apparently held out; but its resistance seemed unlikely to affect the long-run picture: the regime had almost complete control over the Orthodox clergy. The trial and sentence to eleven years' hard labor of Arseniye Bradvarevich, Orthodox Metropolitan of Montenegro, in the summer of 1954, on charges of "conspiracy to overthrow the government," were perhaps designed to emphasize this fact.

Observers in Yugoslavia reported that in many Orthodox families the women alone continued to be faithful adherents to the church, and that it was chiefly the grandmothers and other members of the oldest generation who still strove to expose the children to religion. Orthodoxy as a religious system had always contained a far larger element of Serbian nationalism than of religious piety. It seemed possible that the regime's disapproval of the nationalism had deprived the church of whatever support it had in the past commanded among the Serbian menfolk. Yet there were surely some who still went to church just *because* any other expression of their Serbian patriotism was forbidden. However, it was doubtful if the clerical members of the government-dominated priests' association would give such patriots the spiritual meat they sought.

In Rumania, the regime had much less difficulty with the Orthodox Church, which was not so closely identified with so anti-Communist a sentiment as Serbian nationalism. The first Minister of Cults in the Groza regime, the former Iron Guardist Burducea, himself founded a "Union of Democratic Priests," to serve as a nucleus for those willing to collaborate with the Communists. In 1947, the state passed two laws, one enabling the Ministry to pension such priests as it might choose to retire, and the other permitting the redistribution of sees. These two enactments enabled the regime to get rid of those clerics who were most hostile to it. It was estimated that 30 per cent of the parish priests were dropped. At the same time, faithful adherents of the Communists received their reward. In November 1947, three "people's hierarchs" became Metropolitan Archbishops, and in May 1948, Justinian Marina, handpicked instrument of the Communists, became Patriarch after the death of Nicodim. From then on, the direction of Orthodox Church affairs was in the hands of a man as subservient to Moscow as any of the political leaders in Rumania. Justinian signed any "peace appeal" that might be handed to him.

He gave currency and the authority of the church to all Communist propaganda claims, even the one accusing the United States of germ warfare in Korea.

A statute of May 1949 empowered him to oust clerics who disapproved of his extreme pro-Soviet views. He helped the regime reorganize the church administration, so that the eparchies corresponded to the new administrative divisions. The bishoprics of Suceava and Moldavia were united early in 1950 into an "exarchate," with headquarters at Iași, and the bishoprics of Constanța and Galați were united into an "Exarchate of the Lower Danube." Justinian assisted the regime in its savage campaign against the Uniates. He presided over regular meetings of other collaborationist clerics, Protestant, Muslim, and Jewish. Early in December 1950, he presided over the consecration of the Reverend Andreiu Moldovan of Akron, Ohio, as new Bishop of the Rumanian Orthodox Church in the United States. Moldovan's predecessor, Polycarp, having refused to return to Rumania on orders from Justinian, Moldovan came to the United States, although the episcopate of the church in the United States had decided to recognize nobody appointed by Justinian. Justinian also assisted the forced retirement of Bishop Nicolae Popovici of Oradea Mare, who had begun as a supporter of the regime, but had not been able to stomach some of the excesses. As Popovici's successor, the former Iron Guardist priest Valeriu Zaharia, took office in November 1951.

There was no doubt that Justinian had fully earned the Star of the Republic, first class, which the Communist regime bestowed on him in 1953 for "patriotic activity and services to the cause of peace." Sebastian, Metropolitan of Moldavia and Suceava, received the same decoration second class, as did Nicolae Balan, Metropolitan of Transylvania, while Zaharia had to content himself with a third class award. It was Zaharia, writing in *Universul* for September 28, 1951, who gave an account of the position of the Orthodox Church in Rumania. Bucharest, Sibiu, and Cluj all had their theological schools, which enjoyed University rank. In addition, there was a seminary for monks at Neamța, two for nuns at Plumbuița and Agapia, and nine schools for cantors scattered throughout the country. The machinery of the Orthodox Church in Rumania continued to operate under the new management, and entirely subservient to it.

The general pattern was similar in Bulgaria. Beginning at the end of 1947, when they had attained full political control, the Communists began to eliminate their opponents among the higher clergy of the Orthodox Church. In September 1948, the Exarch Stefan, who had so far seemed persona grata to the regime, and who had accepted his title from the ecumenical Patriarch at Constantinople with Moscow's consent, resigned under duress, and was interned in a monastery. One strongly anti-Communist Archbishop, Boris, was simply murdered at the door of his church. The regime confiscated church property, took over church schools, closed down all the theological schools except for one in Plovdiv, in order to limit the number of priests who would be graduated, and began to censor all religious publications. All printed messages, instructions to communicants, pastoral letters, and other publications had to be submitted to the government's own department for religious confessions. The Ministry of Health took over all church-managed welfare organizations.

Exarch Stefan was succeeded by a government appointee, Mihail. All the government's activities received the support of its own "Union" of Orthodox priests, which held a congress in October 1948, and proclaimed its loyalty to the regime. Its chairman, Ivan Bogdanov, was put in charge of propaganda among the Orthodox clergy, and it issued a newspaper of its own. The governing body of the church, the Synod, had twelve members, only three of whom were pro-Communist, but two of these held the offices of President and Secretary, and thus managed the affairs of the body, including the editing of its newspaper. A decree of March 1949 put the control over all religious buildings and personnel under the state, forbade the clergy to maintain any connections abroad, and set prison sentences for any cleric who criticized the government. This law was called, doubtless without intentional irony, the "Law on the Freedom of Religion." Like his Rumanian counterpart, the Bishop in charge of the Bulgarian Orthodox Church in the United States (and Australia), Andrei, was dismissed for refusing to obey a summons to return to Sofia. For propaganda purposes, the "Red Dean" of Canterbury was useful to both Rumanian and Bulgarian regimes; he visited both countries, and gave pro-Communist and anti-American interviews, at meetings with the regimes' clerical appointees.

Having thus far followed standard procedure, the Bulgarian regime in May 1953 took a startling step. A National Congress of the Bulgarian Orthodox Church, a form of assembly which had met only a few times since the institution of the exarchate in 1870, convened, and elected Metropolitan Cyril of Sofia to be the first Bulgarian Patriarch since the death of Patriarch Euthymius in 1395, during the Turkish conquest of the country. This dramatic move had several obvious propaganda advantages for the regime.

In the first place, it enabled Chervenkov to pose as the friend of the Orthodox Church. In the second, it enabled him to pose as an apostle of peace, because the Bulgarian church had always before taken the position that there could be no Patriarch until "all Bulgarians" were safely inside the borders of Bulgaria. This had special reference, of course, to Macedonia. Thus the creation of a Bulgarian Patriarch in itself was a kind of renunciation of Macedonian territorial claims. It would not be binding if the opportunity for aggression against Yugoslavia and Greece ever seemed to be propitious, but it would attract the attention of the Greek and Yugoslav regimes. Since these had only a few months earlier concluded the Balkan pact, and "invited" Bulgaria to join, the election of a Patriarch was a kind of counter-propaganda move, which needed no explanation in the Balkans.

Though many western observers assumed at once that the new Patriarch must be a completely subservient instrument of the Communists, those who were best-informed on Bulgaria pointed out that he had been educated in Zagreb, Vienna, Berlin, and Paris, that he had in the past shown himself pro-western and anti-Communist, and that, as Bishop of Plovdiv, he had produced a series of able and popular historical writings in which he had made his views known. It was said that the Communists had interned him in a monastery between 1944 and 1946, and had not allowed him to exercise his functions. But it was also true that in recent years he had signed the Communist peace appeals, and had reached some sort of modus vivendi with them. He had attended the Communist-sponsored "World Peace Congress" in Vienna in December 1952, as the Bulgarian delegate. Yet his speeches and articles were said not to be pro-Communist in tone. It seemed surprising that he had been admitted to candidacy for the post of Patriarch. But it was perhaps rash to see in his elevation a triumph of the church over the party. It was almost certain that the new Patriarch would collaborate properly with the regime.

In Albania, though the Orthodox church commanded the allegiance of only 20 per cent of the population, as against its dominant position in the other Balkan countries, the Communists applied the same measures to secure their domination over its clergy. The head of the church, Archbishop Christopher Kissi, was interned or arrested late in 1948, and in the summer of 1949 was deposed, allegedly for working with the Italians during the fascist occupation, and for "wanting to throw our church into the bosom of the Vatican," not a very credible charge to make against an Orthodox prelate. Others deposed were the deputy Metropolitan Ireneo of Korcha, and Bishop Agathangeli of Berat. The synod of the church, by then under Communist domination, chose the Bishop of Korcha, Paissi, as the new Archbishop. Paissi dutifully opened his term of office by issuing a blast against the Vatican, and sending a telegram to Moscow. Early in 1950, a Church Congress officially announced that the Albanian Orthodox Church was now a member of the "camp of peace," and invited the daughter church in the United States to adhere to it. The faction headed by Bishop Fan Noli in Boston accepted the invitation and the jurisdiction of Tirana. His opponents of course did not reply. When the Constantinople Patriarch sent a new Bishop, Marko Lipa, to organize a new Albanian episcopate in the United States, the pro-regime Noli rejected him, while the Tirana press of course referred to Lipa as a "monarcho-fascist," agent of the American intelligence service, and a "renegade Athenian dog." Paissi visited Moscow in 1950, and in 1951 a Russian delegation paid him a return visit. He joined in all the propaganda moves required by the regime. A "people's executive council" meanwhile administered the four chief monasteries of the Orthodox, and the opposition was entirely crushed.

THE ROMAN CATHOLIC AND UNIATE CHURCHES

To the Communists, all the Orthodox Churches were potential instruments of Moscow. The Roman Catholic Churches, on the other hand, were subjects of Rome, of their most vigorous enemy, the Vatican. In Yugoslavia, the regime saw them also as former supporters of the Ustasha, agents of fascism, and links with the western capitalist world. Yet the faith of millions of Croats and Slovenes could not be uprooted. After the war, the Yugoslav government resumed diplomatic relations with the Vatican, although Kardelj later called this "an anachronism, reflecting the one-time privileges of the Catholic Church, and as such alien to contemporary inter-state relations."[1] But the regime also moved to punish individual clerics whom it accused of collaborationism and war-crimes.

There was no doubt that some clerics, including members of the hierarchy, had collaborated with the Ustasha regime, and had approved and assisted in its anti-Orthodox and anti-Jewish atrocities. Many of these were tried and found guilty. But the Tito government tried to link with them the Catholic Primate of Yugoslavia, Msgr. Aloysiye Stepinats. As we know, Stepinats' duties had required him during the war to deal with the Germans and Ustasha, and to appear with the "independent" Croatian authorities on public occasions. It was thus possible to produce photographs of the Archbishop in company with these murderers. Moreover, a number of official ecclesiastical publications which appeared in Stepinats' see during the war contained both violent anti-Orthodox and anti-Jewish diatribes, and boasts that their authors had worked secretly for the Ustasha organization in the years before the war. But even a study of the regime's own case against Stepinats failed to produce any clear evidence that he himself had endorsed the Ustasha excesses. He had never denounced the Ustasha regime, and had done nothing to stop forced conversions, but he is known to have protected prospective victims when he could. His condemnation was of major importance to the Communist regime. He was tried in October 1946, and sentenced to sixteen years' imprisonment.

At the time, and later, public opinion in the United States was strongly aroused at the sentence. After the Cominform communiqué, the Tito regime found the presence of the Archbishop in confinement a source of embarrassment in its developing relations with the west. Journalists were admitted to interview Stepinats, and reported that he was not suffering physical mistreatment, and that he was allowed to worship in his own private chapel. But he became ill in prison. The regime would have liked to set him free if he would leave Yugoslavia, but he firmly rejected any such conditions. The possibility that he might die in prison and thus attain martyrdom, however, was probably the decisive factor which led to his release in December 1951, after more than five years of imprisonment. He was, however, not permitted to resume his post as Archbishop of Zagreb, and was required not to leave his native village.

[1] *Yugoslav Review,* II, 1 (January 1953), p. 3.

The Vatican pointed out, after Stepinats' release, that the Bishop of Mostar and more than 200 priests and monks were still in prison, that the Yugoslav government had taken steps to dissolve some religious orders and to confiscate monastic property, and that official anti-religious propaganda, especially anti-Catholic propaganda, was still strong. Both the Slovenian and Croatian republics, however, continued to give large sums annually for the maintenance of the Catholic church, permitted the clergy to receive aid from abroad without duty, and extended their own social security acts to cover the clergy. So long as the clergy would be subservient to the regime, and as dependent as possible, they might be tolerated.

The struggle between the Yugoslav government and the Catholic Church continued to be severe after the release of Stepinats as before. In March 1952, thirty students were expelled from the Maribor (Slovenia) Teacher's College on a charge of being under the influence of Catholic priests. The government denounced all the clergy of all faiths in Bosnia-Hertsegovina as spreaders of hostile propaganda. In September 1952, fifteen people received jail sentences of varying lengths in Lyublyana for acting as spies for the Vatican. When the Vatican announced that Stepinats had been made a Cardinal late in November 1952, the Yugoslav regime reacted violently. Tito and others identified the Vatican as an agent of Italian foreign policy, helping in a new effort to split Yugoslavia up into its component parts. It was on these alleged grounds that the government severed diplomatic relations with the Vatican on December 16, 1952. In an effort to answer the move at home, the regime sponsored a film called "The Cardinal," purporting to show scenes from the career of Stepinats which revealed him as a "fascist." Though popular in Serbia, the film was quietly withdrawn after a few showings in Zagreb.

Beginning in 1952, the regime strove to create its own "associations" of Catholic priests. In Slovenia, the "Cyril and Methodius Organization" was successfully founded, and an association was also started in Bosnia-Hertsegovina, but in Croatia the bishops, allegedly on orders from the Vatican, held out against the establishment of a similar body. In November 1952, at a meeting in Sarayevo, the existing "organizations" of the three major faiths decided to set up a national inter-faith body linking all of them. At the time, there were three Catholic associations with 800 members (as against 2,000 Orthodox in five associations). The Croatian association had been founded despite the opposition of the bishops. Indeed, by April 1953, the Croatian association had its own periodical, *Vijesti*. In the spring of 1953, a fourth association for the Catholic clergy was formed in Serbia.

At the same time, during the preliminary discussions for the religious communities bill, the government complained that the Catholic clergy were demanding their own schools, and compulsory religious marriages. Conversations between the government and the Catholic clergy on the bill were broken off. The Bishops of Banya Luka and Mostar became particular targets for the anger of the press. The bill, when passed, made, as we saw, no concessions to the point of view allegedly advanced by the Catholic representatives. Perhaps as a result of Catholic opposition to the bill, anti-Catholic propaganda was stepped up very markedly in the summer of 1953. "Popular opinion," said the press, "was indignant at the Bishop of Shibenik (Dalmatia) because he had decided to excommunicate those who joined the government's priests' associations." The incidents ranged from accusations that the Vatican and its minions were engaged in a plot to "spoil" the sixtieth anniversary of the Slovene mountaineering association by holding a religious ceremony at the foot of Mount Triglav, to serious molestations and beatings inflicted by Communist thugs on Catholic priests. A number of these outrages were witnessed by American tourists.

Hostility between the regime and the Catholic Church would certainly continue. Under the pressure which the regime would bring, it seemed probable that the clergy would unwillingly bow to the political provisions of the religious communities bill, and would join the associations, membership in which would entitle them to financial and social benefits. The Yugoslav Communists, however, had to consider public opinion in the western countries, especially the United States, and thus were not so free to persecute the churches as were their fellow-Communists in the satellites. For the consumption of the Communists and the Orthodox, they would doubtless continue to denounce the Vatican. But the churches would stay open; the people would worship in them; monasteries and convents would flourish (indeed in the section of Istria annexed by the Yugoslavs, monasteries deserted by monks who had fled to Italy reopened with Yugoslav inmates); in time, people would forget the association of some of the Catholic clergy with the Ustasha terror. In all probability, a compromise would eventually be reached, whereby the Catholic Church, by bowing to the dictates of the state and accepting the separation of church and state and secular education, would continue to command the loyalty of one-third of the population of Yugoslavia, and would maintain its ties with Rome.

Elsewhere in the Balkans, the numbers of Roman Catholics were much smaller than in Yugoslavia. But in Rumania, with 1,600,000 Uniates (almost all ethnic Rumanians) and 1,050,000 Roman Catholics (almost all Magyars or Banat "Swabians") in 1948, 17 per cent of the population owed its religious allegiance to Rome. The Communists adopted different policies toward the two groups. In line with their practice in other regions where the Uniates had been strong (former eastern Poland, Ruthenia), they determined to suppress this church altogether by persecuting its clergy and requiring its faithful to "return to the Orthodox faith of its ancestors." Soon after the election of Justinian as Orthodox Patriarch in June 1948, the campaign of propaganda and intimidation began. The regime found some priests who would "revert" to orthodoxy. These it convened at a "Congress" in Cluj in October 1948. Though two delegates were supposedly chosen by the clergy of each district in Transylvania, the police actually forced the local Uniate clergy to sign blank ballots, so that the names of those who had deserted to orthodoxy might later be inserted.

The Congress of thirty-eight delegates met. Unanimously "and with great enthusiasm," according to *Universul* for October 15, 1948, it accepted "the re-entry into the bosom of the Rumanian Orthodox Church and the definitive severance of the ties with papal Rome." Before the Congress, severe measures had been employed against recalcitrant Uniate priests. After it, came violent persecution. To the objections of the papal nuncio, the police arrested many members of the clergy. The Ministry of Cults announced that no salary would be paid to any Uniate priest who refused to enter the Orthodox Church. Uniate churches were shut, and handed over to members of the Orthodox clergy. Finally, in December 1948, the Presidium of the Grand National Assembly passed a law declaring the legal existence of the Uniate church at an end.

One of the Uniate Bishops who had broken with Rome, Horinceanu, received the Orthodox Bishopric of Roman and Husi. Others, who refused, were hauled off to forced labor camps or the prisons, and some were tortured to death or executed. Individual Uniates, who tried somehow to retain their faith, might not mill their grain, or hold down jobs as employees. No will made by a Uniate had legal validity. While it was a historic fact that the Uniate church owed its birth in 1699 and its later existence to Catholic discrimination against the Orthodox, no such argument could justify the twentieth-century persecution of its adherents by the Communists and their Orthodox puppets.

The Catholics, belonging as they did to ethnic minorities as well as to a religious minority, could not simply be absorbed into the Rumanian Orthodox Church. The regime determined that they should be cut off from all contact with the west, and transformed into a sect as subservient as the others. The propaganda campaign began in 1947. The regime dismissed priests, closed down Catholic schools and other institutions, such as hospitals and orphanages, confiscated property, suppressed publications, and arrested and tried members of the clergy. In July 1948, the former Concordat between Rumania and the Vatican was unilaterally revoked by the regime, which declared that Vatican intervention in Rumanian internal affairs must now be eliminated. All but two of the Bishops were removed in 1948. New laws sanctioned the depredations which had already taken place: in July 1948, a statute deprived the church of all its schools, and in November another nationalized all hospitals.

In the summer of 1949, the persecution was resumed. The two remaining Bishops, Aron Marton of Alba Iulia, and Anton Durcovici of Iași, were arrested in Bucharest, where they had gone to confer with the Ministry of Cults. Accused of ties with the Hungarian prelate, Cardinal Mindszenty, they were deprived of their stipends, and disappeared into jail. At the same time

137 Catholic priests were arrested, making a total of perhaps 600 of the 800 active in the country before the persecution. Bishop Marton in particular was a hero to his people because he had assisted all Magyars, Protestant as well as Catholic, and Jews also, during the excesses of the Antonescu regime in southern Transylvania after the Vienna Award of 1940.

As if to underline the efforts against the Catholics and their solution, the Patriarch Justinian called a meeting of nine clergymen representing nine faiths, all of whom expressed their complete satisfaction with religious conditions in Rumania, and pointedly noted that only one sect was complaining. Those represented, in addition to the Orthodox, included the Magyar Reformed Church (Calvinist, 730,000 adherents), the Evangelical Church (Lutheran, about 250,000 German adherents), the Jews (about 372,000), the Baptists (120,000 Rumanians), the Unitarians (about 75,000 Magyars), the Armenians (a few thousand), the Lipovans (Russian "old believers," about 30,000), and the Muslims (10,000 Turks and Tartars). Of course, the clergymen by no means represented the views of their flocks, any more than Justinian was representative of the ordinary Rumanian Orthodox citizen. These were the regime's puppet clerics.

In April 1950, began the regime's effort to launch a "national" Catholic church. At Targu Mureș, later to be the capital of the new autonomous Magyar region, a packed conference of Catholics formed a "Catholic Action Committee," whose purpose was to appeal to the Catholic clergy, what was left of it, to "join the forces for peace and condemn the warmongers." The head of the new organization was the priest Andreas Agota, who was soon excommunicated by the Vatican. Arrests of Catholic priests continued, including the assistant Bishop of Iași, Max Glaser, who had ordered the clergy of his diocese publicly to condemn the Targu Mureș "Catholic Action Committee" as nothing but a Communist front organization. Moldavia, however, was not the center of Catholic population, and it is doubtful whether the courageous gesture had much effect. Glaser soon afterward died in prison.

On July 4, 1950, the regime passed a new statute for the Catholic Church. To the papacy it left authority on questions of dogma and morals. The state assumed the jurisdiction over all other departments of Catholic life: the creation and modification of sees, the nomination of bishops, the organization of new congregations, the establishment of seminaries, and the management of church property. Bishops might communicate with the Vatican only through the Ministry of Cults and the Ministry of Foreign Affairs. Three days after the passage of the new law, the Papal Nuncio, Msgr. O'Hara, left Bucharest with his staff at the request of the government, which had "implicated" him in one of its numerous trials for espionage. The Communists had smashed one of the few remaining links between Rumania and the west.

Early in September 1950, at Gheorgheni, the Agota "Catholic Action Committee" held a rally of "peace-loving" Catholic priests and laymen. Agota and his adjutant, a priest named Pozsony, announced that new relations between the state and the Catholic church must be established. Since the leaders of the church had refused to accept the draft statute which had been offered to them, it was now necessary to call a general congress of Roman Catholic representatives to establish an "autonomous" church, free from outside interference by "warmongers." Needless to add, this church would have no connections with the Vatican. In December 1950, Patriarch Justinian held another of his "inter-faith" meetings for propaganda purposes. In addition to those who attended the first session, there were now also included representatives of the Seventh Day Adventists (60,000 Rumanians), and the even smaller Pentecostal and "Gospel Christian" groups. They issued one of the standard Communist propaganda handouts, and a week later the Catholic Action Committee enthusiastically endorsed it, which was clearly one of the chief reasons why it had been issued.

Early in 1951, the government took the next step, a most ingenious one from the legal and constitutional point of view, in its effort to create a new sort of Catholic Church in Rumania. It announced that it had extended the "Status Catholicus" of Transylvania to the whole of Rumania. The "Status Catholicus" was a kind of parliament of Catholic priests and laymen, which had managed the affairs of the church in Transylvania in the seventeenth century when there were no bishops in the province. The Habsburgs had recognized it; the Vatican had never approved it; but after 1918, when Transylvania became Rumanian, the Vatican also recognized it. It consisted of an administrative council and a general assembly; some members belonged ex officio; others were elected. It met once a year, and the Bishop presided. In the period between the two World Wars, it had been a source of disagreement between the Vatican and the Rumanian state; but by the Concordat of 1932 both parties recognized it as the "Council of the Latin Rite of Alba Iulia." At that time, the Rumanian government was strongly suspicious of, and inclined to use financial discrimination against, this essentially Magyar Church, some of whose clerics refused to take the oath of allegiance to Rumania.

Now the Communists were prepared to use the old "Council" as an instrument to alter the condition of the Roman Catholic Church in Rumania. Having infiltrated it with its puppet priests and collaborationist laymen, the Rumanian government allowed a session to meet in Cluj in February 1951, which called an extraordinary meeting for March to vote the acceptance of the new regulations prepared by the Catholic Action Committee, to adopt a schedule of pensions for teachers, and to plan for the renovation of the Cathedrals of Cluj and Alba Iulia. The Roman Catholic laymen of Transylvania saw nothing unusual about this agenda, since it was the sort which had traditionally lain within the competence of a "Status Catholicus." Thus the government put forward its program under the cloak of legality. The Ministry of Cults advanced the funds necessary for the repairs of the buildings.

On March 15, 1951, at Cluj, the general assembly met, with 221 delegates from all over Rumania, as befitted the newly enlarged "Status." It formally extended the "Status" to include the whole country, called for good relations with the government, offered state salaries to clerics who would adhere, and announced that arrangements would soon be completed for the appointment of a bishop. The announcement that four "disloyal" priests had been arrested was the only indication that reached the outside world of what must surely have been bitter opposition to the foundation of a schismatic national Catholic church in Rumania. Soon afterwards the Vatican Radio announced that the Rumanian choice of a canon to hold the post of Capitular Vicar of Bucharest was illegal.

In September 1951, the government, having fairly well disrupted the Magyar Catholics, turned on the Banat Swabians. The Bishop of Timişoara, Msgr. Augustin Pacha, and Joseph Schubert, a Canon, were tried for plotting against the state, and being in the pay of the Vatican and the Italian intelligence service. Other western legations were also implicated. Pacha was seventy-six years of age. He was sentenced to eighteen years' hard labor, after "confessing" that he had been pro-Hitler, had been hired by the Vatican in 1923, and had carried out the instructions which the Nuncio, Msgr. O'Hara, had communicated to him. Bishop Pacha was later reported to have been sent to forced labor on the Danube–Black Sea Canal, where he "met with an accident." He was released in August 1954, for "reasons of health." The Swiss newspaper, *Tribune de Genève,* in its issue of February 19, 1952, gave a list of the missing Uniate and Roman Catholic prelates, indicating their fates so far as they were known. Some were dead in prison; others were at work in Soviet coal mines and steel plants. The Vatican Radio later confirmed the account given. Thus, to the accompaniment of savage atrocity, the Rumanian Communists strove to dominate the Catholic Church in their country.

In Albania, where the Catholic population amounted perhaps to 140,000 living mostly in the north, the regime's policies were entirely similar. There were ninety-three priests, and ninety-four Jesuits and Franciscans at the end of the war. As early as December 1944, the regime took over the schools and kindergartens, and confiscated Catholic publications. The press abused the church regularly, maintaining a column in its newspaper with the hortatory title: "Fascists in clerical clothes should be shot in the head." One of its favorite targets was the Franciscan Father Anton Harapi, Catholic member of the former German-sponsored regency. Persecution of the clergy cut down their ranks. The Metropolitan Archbishop of Durres (Durazzo), Monsignor Premushi, a notable poet, was arrested and jailed without trial in January 1948. He died in prison. The Bishop of Lesh (Alessio), imprisoned in 1946, was released in 1947, arrested again and shot in March 1948. The Archbishop of Shkodra died in 1946, and was not replaced. The eighty-year-old Bishop Bernardin Shillaku of Pulati was kept under house arrest in the northern mountains.

By the end of 1950, of the ninety-three priests seventeen were executed, thirty-nine imprisoned or in forced labor camps, and eleven drafted into the army. Ten died, three escaped from the country, and only thirteen survived at liberty. Of the ninety-four Jesuits and Franciscans, sixteen were shot, thirty-one exiled, thirty-five imprisoned or sent to forced labor. Six died and thirteen were reported in hiding. All members of religious orders who were of Italian origin were deported. Thus, by the summer of 1951, the regime had made virtually a clean sweep of the religious leadership of the church.

On June 26, the government presented to a handful of priests at Shkodra, the draft of a new statute, and obtained the signatures they demanded. A few days later, the People's Assembly issued a decree establishing a "national" Catholic Church. It would have no political or economic or jurisdictional relations with the Vatican. The task of the clergy would be "to develop feelings of devotion to the people's will." It would submit to the laws of the Republic. Canon Law would apply only when it did not conflict with these laws. The government would permit seminaries for the clergy to exist, but only in conformity with its own regulations. Priests might celebrate mass, bless their flocks, and perform religious rites. The government would subsidize the church in accordance with its needs and the state's resources. The Metropolitan Archbishop, or in his absence the Bishop who might be his deputy, might communicate with religious communities abroad. But this would involve no political, economic, or jurisdictional dependence. Such messages might deal with religious questions only, and must pass through officials of the Albanian government.

That the measures were regarded as extreme even by some Communists was indicated by the attack made by Hoxha on the veteran Communist, Tuk Jakova, in March 1952. According to Hoxha, Jakova had not "properly acted against the Catholic clergy," appreciated the danger they posed, or "hated them enough." Jakova duly repented. That the measures had produced the effect the regime desired was shown by the appearance in the summer of 1952 of Msgr. Bernardin Shillaku, the interned aged Bishop of Pulati, as "head" of the Albanian church, joining with a new "head" of the Franciscans, and the Orthodox, Sunni, and Bektashi leaders in a standard Communist denunciation of the United States, the Vatican, and the Orthodox Patriarch of Constantinople.

In Bulgaria, the number of Catholics was only about 60,000, well under 1 per cent of the population. It was not worth the while of the regime to undertake to found a "national" church. But it was necessary to discredit the church publicly. The regime waited until the autumn of 1952, when it brought to trial Bishop Eugene Bossilkov, and twenty-seven priests and twelve laymen on charges of espionage and conspiracy against the republic. The Bishop and three priests received death-sentences, and the others jail-terms ranging from two to twenty years. The twenty-eight priests were one-quarter of the entire Bulgarian Catholic hierarchy. All proceedings were given the utmost publicity, the trial being broadcast verbatim over the Sofia Radio. The government closed down the Catholic college in Plovdiv and the two schools in Sofia. To serve as further warning to the population, the regime had the other churches, under their puppet leaders, join in condemning the Roman Catholic Church. The Vatican accurately described the whole affair as "premeditated murder."

PROTESTANT CHURCHES

Among other Christian sects in the Balkan countries, we need give special notice here to the Bulgarian Protestants: Congregational, Methodist, Baptist, and Pentecostal. These numbered only about 20,000 in all, but traditionally maintained the warmest and most friendly relations with American missionaries in the country, and with English Protestant centers. The regime therefore arrested some twenty of their pastors in mid-1948, and in February 1949 brought fifteen of them to trial on charges ranging from black-market activities to espionage and advocating that Bulgaria be occupied by the three major allies in concert. In keeping with Communist practices, the accused had been kept incommunicado in prison during many months, and the police had extracted "confessions" from them.

Amid the usual tornado of "resolutions" from factory committees and the like, howling for their blood, the Protestant pastors, neatly dressed and well-groomed by the regime for their appearance in court, admitted to having worked for the Gestapo, to having spent half their time in sorting and transmitting secret intelligence, and to plotting with each other, though in fact relations between them, especially between the Methodists and Congregationalists, had long been strained. The "confessions" were as full of internal contradictions as those in the trials of Petkov or Kostov. The four leading pastors of the four sects received life-sentences; the others terms ranging from five to fifteen years.

In Rumania, where the 1,250,000 Protestants had no such intimate ties with the United States, their leadership seems in the main to have coöperated with the regime, and there was at least no headline instance of mass-persecution to compare with the trial of the pastors in Bulgaria. Vasarhely, Bishop of the Magyar Reformed Church (Calvinist), the largest denomination with about 750,000 members, in 1952 hailed the formation of the autonomous Magyar region, and the "cultural freedom" which his people enjoyed. According to propagandists for the regime, the Protestant Theological Institute at Cluj had a "Reformed" section for training Magyar Calvinist ministers, a Unitarian section for ministers of that Magyar faith, and a "Protestant" section for Rumanian Baptists, German Evangelicals, Adventists, and Pentecostals. Each of these sects had its own periodical, and the last four had formed a federation among themselves. Representatives of the Protestant churches regularly attended Patriarch Justinian's inter-faith propaganda meetings, and before election joined in appeals for all the faithful to vote the FND ticket.

MUSLIMS

We have already examined the fate of the Muslim minority in Bulgaria. The 10,000 Turks and Tartars in the Rumanian Dobrudja seem not to have created any problem for the regime. Their Mufti had his headquarters at Constantinople, and they maintained a theological seminary in Megidia. It remains then to examine briefly the fate of the Yugoslav and Albanian Muslims under Communism.

In Yugoslavia, with well over 2,000,000 adherents chiefly in Bosnia-Hertsegovina, Macedonia, the Kos-Met autonomous region, and other parts of Serbia, they were the third most numerous sect after the Orthodox and the Roman Catholics. But they coöperated with the Communist regime, as they had with all earlier regimes of whatever political complexion. Indeed, their leaders regularly joined other religious representatives in hailing the Tito government for its tolerance. They also served as propagandists for Tito abroad. In the fall of 1949, the Grand Mufti of Yugoslavia, Sheikh Ibrahim Felyich, made a pilgrimage to Mecca, and toured the Middle Eastern countries, assuring those who interviewed him that the Muslim faith was flourishing at home. In Ankara, he reported that Yugoslav Muslims, especially those of Macedonia, listened freely to the Turkish Radio, that he would like to encourage the importation of Turkish books, and that he looked forward to a strengthening of relations between Yugoslavia and Turkey. In 1951, he denounced a statement made at the World Muslim Conference in Karachi, which referred to the sufferings of Muslims in Yugoslavia.

But the regime did intervene to alter what it regarded as the "reactionary" custom of the veil or yashmak for women. In the summer of 1950, the Sarayevo workers formally "requested" the Bosnian-Hertsegovinan Republican Assembly to ban the veil, and soon afterwards the Mufti declared that, although the request had created a great furor, it was not contrary to the tenets of the Muslim faith. He endorsed the workers' petition. The workers had surely not thought of the idea themselves; the regime had taken pains to see that the move seemed to come from below. The furor was natural enough: the Muslims clung to their ancient ways with true conservative zeal. Promptly in September 1950, the Bosnian Assembly passed the anti-yashmak bill. Immediately afterwards, the workers of Novipazar begged that the Serbian Assembly would do the same. Thus one of the most picturesque features of the Muslim regions of Yugoslavia vanished, although visitors would still see many women quickly draw a kerchief across their faces on meeting a man. The reform doubtless caused some shock but little suffering; it was parallel to what Kemal had long since decreed in Turkey.

The Muslim faith, like the others, was required to establish a government-dominated and sponsored "priests' association," which in December 1952 had some 600 members. There were no reports of resistance to this or to any other innovation imposed by the regime. In November 1952, for example, the

Supreme Muslim Vakuf (Church Property) Assembly, meeting at Sarayevo, voted to abolish its religious schools for very young children (mektebes) and its monasteries (tekiya), a move which the government must have required of them. At times the government would lump Muslim clergy with Orthodox and Catholics in a general denunciation of all religious leaders as enemies of the state or as formerly linked with the Chetniks or Ustasha groups.[2]

In Albania, the situation was more complicated because of the division among the Muslims between Bektashi and Sunni. Initially, the two Bektashi Abbots, who had played a part in the resistance, Baba (Abbot) Faya of Martanesh and Baba Feza of Malakastre, were elected to the national assembly. But in 1947 they were both murdered. It was not clear whether the murders were instigated by the Bektashi leadership to punish the two clerics for their loyalty to the regime, or whether the Communists themselves had grown tired of their erstwhile comrades. In any case, many Bektashi leaders were arrested and later executed. It was not until the spring of 1950 that the Bektashi sect adopted a statute bringing it into line with the government. By that time their anti-Communist world-primate (Dede, grandfather), Abazi, had committed suicide, and Ahmed Myftar (or Mukhtar) had served as Dede for at least a year. Ahmed Myftar Dede had already represented his sect at inter-faith propaganda sessions, and regularly issued statements urging all the members of his priesthood to "wage an unremitting fight against the American imperialists and their agents." In the fall of 1950, the Khalveti sect of dervishes affiliated itself with the Bektashis, and both proclaimed their great love for the Hoxha regime and the Communist Party.

Anti-Communist Sunni Muslim leaders also suffered considerably in the first years after the war. Reports told of Hafiz Sherif Dibra, chief of the sect, in prison, of the Mufti of Shkodra hanged head downward and flogged in front of a statue of Stalin, and of a split between pro-regime and anti-regime leaders. The chief spirit of the opposition, the Mufti of Valona, was reported murdered on Hoxha's orders in January 1951. This helped make the subservient Hafiz Musa Haxhi Ali secure as leader of the Sunnis.

As the only primarily Muslim satellite, and the center of the Bektashi movement in the world, Albania had to play an important role as a subsidiary center of Communist propaganda to the Middle East. Tirana Radio broadcast that there was no conflict between Marxism and the Koran, claiming, almost surely falsely, that Hoxha was a devout attendant at the mosque, and pointing out that the Albanian Muslims had broken the ties that bound them to the "imperialist" world without sacrificing their religion. In the summer of 1950, Hafiz Musa Haxhi Ali led a Muslim delegation on a visit to Soviet Central

[2] In August 1953, for example, the Vice-Chairman of the Republican Executive Council of Bosnia-Hertsegovina, Davidovich, denounced the Catholic Bishops of Mostar and Banya Luka, the Orthodox Bishop of Sarayevo, and "some priests" of all three faiths, who, he said, were "playing politics." This sort of occasional warning seemed sufficient to keep the docile leaders of Yugoslav Islam thoroughly subservient to the government.

Asia, on the invitation of the Office of Religious Affairs for Central Asia and Kazakhstan. He and the Soviet Muslim leaders uttered the expected assurances that complete religious freedom prevailed in their respective countries. The fact that the British would allegedly not permit Hafiz Musa Haxhi Ali to make his pilgrimage to Mecca, because of epidemic conditions, gave him an additional propaganda note to strike. In May 1951, a Soviet Muslim delegation paid a return visit to Albania, where both Sunni and Bektashi leaders acted as hosts. On August 15, 1951, Ahmed Myftar Dede appealed by radio to all Bektashis in Egypt, Syria, and Turkey to sign the Soviet-sponsored "Peace Appeal." Thus the Communists brought the leadership of both leading Muslim sects under their control, after having ruthlessly dealt with the opposition.

CONCLUSION

In all four Balkan countries, the churches had been effectively destroyed as potential centers of opposition. Ordinary members of the larger faiths could still worship, but their spiritual leaders had been coerced, cowed, or removed and replaced by instruments of the regime. Doubtless there were many among the clergy, as among the faithful, who bitterly deplored and resented the conditions under which they lived and labored. But temporary silence was their only hope for survival. The regimes possessed one weapon which they had not yet used to the full, but which they held always in reserve: the active support of atheism against all religions.

In Rumania, the "Society for the Dissemination of Science and Culture," whose aim was "relentless warfare" on all "mysticism and superstition," remained small, with only 25,000 alleged members. But it was holding an astonishing number of public lectures (13,800,000 people were said to have attended in 1951), and printing books and pamphlets in all the languages of the country. Its target was for the present apparently limited chiefly to those who helped publicize the miraculous apparitions or occult manifestations which always multiplied in Rumania in difficult times. These, the society explained, were only kulaks wrapped in sheets or capitalist charlatans writing on the windows at night to frighten honest proletarians. But at any moment the society could become a full-fledged propaganda institute directed against the churches. If the Communists continued in power indefinitely, the society and its counterparts elsewhere would eventually become far more influential. A cleric or a pious member of any faith could only bide his time and hope that something would free his country from the Communists.

2. *Education*

The Communist regimes in the Balkan states adopted very active policies in the field of education and culture. At the lowest level, they aimed to wipe out illiteracy among adults. They gave the widest possible circulation to the products of their controlled press. They strove to make elementary education available to all children except, in some cases, those of former members of classes now outlawed. They encouraged the use of minority languages in schools and in handbooks for adult education. They modeled the curriculum upon that in the USSR. This contrasted vividly with that common in the west. Instead of a general humanistic training, followed by specialization, a student received a narrow technical education, on a foundation of "Marxist-Leninist" ideological indoctrination. Mass-programs of Russian-language instruction were undertaken everywhere in the satellites.

The authorities purged their school and university faculties of those members who had been known to have anti-Communist opinions. They encouraged research, especially "collective research," but the products of their scholars had not only to conform to basic Communist tenets, but somehow to further the official political program. Those scholars, writers, artists, and musicians who succeeded best in "advancing the cause of socialism" won high salaries, much renown and publicity, and perhaps state prizes of money for their work. Except in the fields of technological advance or improvement and rationalization of production-methods, where the details could often not be judged, their products often seemed puerile, sterile, and, in the case of historical or archaeological or linguistic research, simply wrong. So far as possible, then, the satellites followed the pattern set by the USSR, in which they received instruction direct from Soviet officials and citizens.

Only the Yugoslavs after 1948 were emancipated from paying slavish devotion at the Soviet shrine. But they found themselves in a dilemma: they did not want to encourage devotion to western cultural models either. It was not impossible, as we have seen, to work out an ideology and a political and economic system varying markedly from both western and Soviet models. But to establish a wholly new and fresh culture with an educational system to match was a task for which nothing had prepared the Yugoslav leadership, and which confronted them with virtually insurmountable difficulties. In this field, they seemed undecided and wavering, sometimes reproving a scholar or an artist for addiction to western ways. Devotion to their own brand of "socialism," however, naturally continued to be the test which they tried to apply.

ILLITERACY

The wiping out of illiteracy was a major task, and one which men of all shades of political opinions would agree was necessary. The larger question as to what sort of literature would be made available to the newly literate remained the chief grievance of anti-Communists. In Rumania, in August 1952, for example, the press claimed that of four million illiterate citizens at the time of liberation in 1944, three million could now read and write.

In Albania, the population in 1944 was perhaps 80 per cent illiterate, the highest percentage in all of Europe. By 1952, more than half a million people had been taught to read and write. A law of 1949 required every citizen between the ages of twelve and forty to learn. Several thousand evening classes and instruction groups worked steadily toward the goal of a completely literate nation. There seemed little reason to doubt the figures, or the implications which might be drawn from them: that before too long illiteracy would have virtually disappeared.

THE PRESS AND THE RADIO

What the people might read was typified by the products of "Scânteia House," the huge new press-building, rising in pure Soviet style in the middle of Bucharest, whose capacity was the proud boast of the authorities. With forty-two linotypes, twelve rotary presses (one for newspapers and eleven for books), seven hydraulic presses, and a variety of other up-to-the-minute Soviet equipment generously advanced by Moscow, it could in 1950 turn out 200,000 books and pamphlets a day, and 35,000 pamphlets in four hours. This was a real fountainhead of propaganda.

From it there poured forth *Scânteia* itself, the *Pravda* of Rumania, identical in format and in line, with a daily circulation of "almost 1,000,000" in 1954, five other dailies, nine weeklies, six reviews, and 92 per cent of all Rumanian schoolbooks. In Sofia, *Scânteia*'s (and *Pravda*'s) opposite number was *Rabotnichesko Delo* (The Worker's Deed, or Action, circulation 500,000), in Tirana *Zeri i Popullit* (Voice of the People, circulation 37,000). The names of the editorial staff of these papers were no longer printed by 1953. Any one of them on any given day would contain about the same mixture of official news, praise of the Soviet Union, and attacks on the west. On the front page, the first two columns would contain the lead editorial, and three columns of news of domestic developments, and events in the other "people's democracies." Page two would be filled with articles on the problems and activities of the Communist Party, pages three and four with foreign news, page five with applied Marxist theory, and page six with drama, cinema, and sports news. The other papers in each country (circulation 900,000 in Bulgaria) included the organs of the Trade Unions, the army, the youth organizations (circulation 320,000 in Bulgaria), the "people's front" (circulation 180,000 in Bulgaria), and, in Rumania, two special publications for peasants.

Provincial papers were modeled on those issued in the capital, but contained many articles of local interest, emphasizing the progress or lack of progress in the local fulfillment of the Plan, hailing labor pioneers and innovators, discussing local theatrical performances, and the progress of local hospital-building, clubs, libraries, and sports facilities. Reports indicated that the network of unpaid correspondents for these papers, who were at work in every local factory, collective, or other enterprise, enjoyed enormous unpopularity among their fellows as the source of unfavorable personal publicity. Then there were in Bulgaria and Rumania the specialized weeklies and monthlies, including a political journal which corresponded to the Soviet *Komunist,* a literary journal corresponding to the Soviet *Literaturnaya Gazeta,* an economic journal corresponding to the Soviet *Voprosi Ekonimiki,* and a humorous journal corresponding to the Soviet *Krokodil.* This last received a good deal of latitude in criticizing the mistakes of the bureaucrats and poking fun at the discomforts of daily life.

As in the Soviet Union, journalism was a well-paid profession, and its successful practitioners enjoyed high rewards. And as in the Soviet Union, the regime made every effort to see to it that its publications were not only bought but read. So in factories, on collective farms, in all offices, wherever a man might work, he would have to listen to the compulsory reading aloud of selected passages from the newspapers on regular "press days." Mere illiteracy was no excuse for unfamiliarity with the news and the "line." The ending of illiteracy meant an increased obligation to keep up with both. For everybody, including the illiterate, the electrification program of the regimes brought to the villages the wired receiver, loudspeakers wired to a central radio reception and broadcasting center in which the party functionaries kept the receivers tuned to official programs. The "radiofication," as the officials called it (it was known as "radiofixation" in Rumania), assured the regime of a captive audience in all public places, and limited the private owner of a private loudspeaker to the option of turning it off. Much propaganda endeavored to assure the public that wired radio was better than wireless: it was cheaper, needed no tuning, and could carry no poisonous broadcasts from the west. Even wireless radio sets manufactured in the satellites were limited-reception one-wave sets, on which the listener could not pick up foreign broadcasts.

THE SCHOOLS AND TEXTBOOKS

The Rumanian school law of August 3, 1948 provided for optional day-nurseries and kindergartens, for children from three to seven. Then came the compulsory Soviet-model elementary school, for ages seven to fourteen, with seven years of classes, of which four were required. Above this came the four-year "middle school," for ages fourteen to eighteen, above which came the universities and technical and professional schools. The goals of the new school system might be seen in their purest form in Albania, where education had previously been so badly neglected. The regime claimed that by 1951 it had 2,200 schools and 160,000 pupils (209,300 pupils in 1952), as against 638 schools and 52,000 pupils in 1938. The number was steadily rising. Of the schools, some 700 or one-third — a surprisingly high number — were "middle schools." In the trade middle schools, emphasis was upon narrow technical specialization. At the top of the system were three totally new foundations, a Polytechnic Institute, a Pedagogical Institute, and an Agricultural High School. In 1952, a new Medical Institute was set up with a faculty of eight; and schools of art and music were apparently also in operation. In Albania, the Communists were starting virtually from scratch. Elsewhere, there was already a well-established educational tradition, which they proceeded to modify.

In higher education, for example, the Rumanian government put into the hands of a special ministry the complete reorganization of the prewar system. This had included four universities (Bucharest, Iași, Cluj, and Cernauți), with varying numbers of faculties. Cernauți, of course, was lost to the USSR, and the Cluj faculty had been dispersed to Sibiu and Timișoara during the period of Hungarian government in northern Transylvania, but was now re-established. In addition, there had been one independent law faculty, one theological faculty, two technical, three agricultural, and two trade high schools, one architectural academy, and six special high schools: three for music and the drama, two for the arts, and one for physical education. This structure the new regime proceeded to spread very thin indeed, founding nine new "university" centers, by a process of subdividing existing faculties (after first purging them), and using a fragment of an old faculty as a nucleus for a new one. One hundred and sixty faculties replaced the prewar total of forty-five. General education and training in the humanities almost vanished in favor of "practical" training.

At Bucharest, in addition to the University and Teachers' College, there were now the Maxim Gorky Institute for teaching Russian, with a special section for training translators, the Lenin Institute for economic planning (which had succeeded the technical high school), a new school of journalism giving a five-year course in Marxist-Leninist ideology, languages, and literature, and many special technical institutes. Bucharest was still the center of Rumanian higher education, and grandiose plans burgeoned for a new University City, like the Moscow model. Many of the new centers had only one faculty apiece: thus Arad concentrated on animal husbandry and veterinary training, Constanța on fisheries, Brad on mining, Petroșani on coal, and Câmpulung on forestry. At Stalin (Brașov), there were both forestry and mechanics, at Galați shipbuilding and agriculture, at Craiova machines and electrical equipment and agronomy. In addition to Bucharest, Cluj, Iași, Timișoara, and Targu Mureș all had multiple faculties. We have already remarked upon the sixteen separate Magyar-language faculties at Cluj, Targu Mureș, and Timișoara. The total number of students reported in these higher institutions in 1952, was 62,000, as against a figure of 30,500 for 1939 which had included Cernauți and the high school in Chișinau, both now in the USSR. The Five Year Plan called for a total of 78,000 by 1955. The regime boasted that, whereas in 1944, only fifty-eight students out of a total of 20,472 were of working-class origin, in 1952 the figure was 95 per cent of the 62,000.

The emphasis was clearly on quantity and ideology, not on quality. There was every reason to think that the level of instruction had fallen considerably below that common in prewar years. That the Rumanian regime realized this was indicated by a decree of August 1953, announcing a state-sponsored competition for admittance to a special three-year scientific course to be offered in the universities in an effort to produce people qualified to do scientific research. Any high-school graduate under forty might take the qualifying examination, which consisted of three papers: one on Marxism-Leninism, one on the Russian language, and one on the student's special field. A successful candidate would be given full tuition and an allowance in addition for three years. The regime was interested chiefly in natural sciences and technology, although a certain number of places might be won by students of the social sciences, properly steeped in the orthodox ideology.

The publication of new textbooks at every level became a major industry in these years in all three satellite countries. In 1950, a technical publishing house was set up in Rumania, which produced almost 900 different titles in its first year. Many of these were translations from the Russian. In addition to texts, they included a series of handbooks for skilled workers in various industries, and one on popular science, as well as a large Rumanian technical dictionary in five volumes of 1,000 pages each, prepared by 400 collaborating architects and engineers, a Russian-Rumanian technical dictionary, and smaller versions of these larger works for regular use by workers and technicians, containing 10,000 useful economic and agricultural terms. Most of the less elaborate works were printed in Magyar and German, as well as Rumanian.

Similarly in Bulgaria, as the Ministry of Education remarked,

> public instruction today is a means of instilling in our students progressive knowledge, the dialectic-materialistic outlook, and Communist morality. . . . The assistance of Soviet educators was invaluable in the development of our own instruction and in the unmasking of bourgeois instruction which was deeply rooted among our educators.

Russian language study began for many Bulgarian children in kindergarten, while for those Bulgarians who were so old and unfortunate as to have obtained their education under pre-Communist auspices, great numbers of adult-education courses in Russian were established, running into many thousands by 1953. The University of Sofia was greatly expanded, with two of eight planned new five-story buildings in the "University City" completed, a new institute to train librarians, and the like. As to books in Bulgaria, it was dramatic to compare the figure for translations from the Russian in 1944, which was 3.24 per cent of all titles printed, with that for 1950, which was 90 per cent of all titles. From a value of 574,000 leva in 1945, the sales in Bulgaria of Soviet books still untranslated from the Russian rose to more than 200,000,000 leva in 1951. Bulgarian newspapers denounced Bulgarian architects for using "bourgeois" formulas to determine the strength of concrete installations. Rumanian newspapers denounced a Rumanian physician for prescribing for a patient the American drugs, glutamic acid and aureomycin. He was a "tool of the imperialists, . . . so dazed by cosmopolitan poison that he had lost his honor." His activity was "not compatible with the activity of a doctor in the RPR."

Even in Albania, book publishing was booming. In the four years between 1934 and 1938, a total of 840,000 copies of books had been printed in the country. In 1952 alone, there were 7,500,000 copies of 700 different titles. Especially large were the editions of the "Short History of the CPSU (B)," which ran to 55,000, and the short life of Stalin, which ran to more than 40,000. The number of users of the Tirana Library went up from 10,000 in 1938 to 50,000 in 1951. It had 150,000 volumes in 1952, and 60 per cent of its acquisitions were Soviet works. Eleven new regional libraries were established, 200 village libraries, and 500 motorized libraries, penetrating, with their cargoes of Communist literature, wherever the roads led.

SCHOLARLY RESEARCH

At the level of scholarly research, the Communist regimes showed, of course, a special interest in technological and scientific advance. Outside this field, their favorite areas for investigation were philology and archaeology, both of which had strong implications for ideology and politics. Apparently, the Communists preferred to work in "collective" teams of scholars, perhaps because the blame for ideological error would then have to be shared. Their projects were usually enormous dictionaries or encyclopedias, multi-volume handbooks and works of reference, rather than individual investigations on the frontiers of knowledge. Thus, for example, in Rumania, a "collective" of twelve scholars was at work on a twelve-volume survey of Rumanian plants and their popular as well as scientific names, to contain many color-plates. Other such collaborative works included a three-volume Rumanian grammar, a multi-volume atlas, dictionaries of the Rumanian language, both contemporary and of the seventeenth and eighteenth centuries, as well as studies of Magyar dialects, Rumanian-Magyar, Magyar-Rumanian, and Russian-Rumanian dictionaries, and collections of Rumanian historical documents.

All of this work was under the direction of the completely reorganized Rumanian Academy. Formerly a small group of the most distinguished Rumanian scholars, it had been largely a club, to which election was an honor. Now it obtained laboratories, libraries, research institutes, its own press, branches all over the country, and many new members, who had hundreds of assistants in their labors to advance Rumanian science. It boasted the development of an electromagnetic device for controlling the carbon content in steel-manufacture, new plastics, synthetic rubber, and a project for building small Rumanian airplanes for use in agriculture. Its projects for 1954 included a special study on methods of raising the yields of corn, potatoes, sugar beets, and cotton per hectare, investigations into new fertilizers, and research on cattle-breeding, fruit-growing, and a variety of problems in applied chemistry. Thus one might observe the intimate connection between research and the economic planning of the government.

Titles of papers read at the meeting of 1953 included "The battle of Soviet psychologists for an objective method in psychology," "The building of the new man in the Rumanian People's Republic," "The superiority of the people's democracy over bourgeois democracy," none of them reflecting scholarly objectivity as understood in the west. The archaeological papers ("The unscholarly position of bourgeois scholarship on the Dacians"), like all archaeological research, were designed to demonstrate that the early Dacians were really Slavs, or closely connected with the Slavs. The historical papers ("The influence of Russian revolutionary movements on the beginnings of the workers' movement in Rumania") were designed to show that whatever was good in the Rumanian past at any period came originally from Russia. Much of the linguistic work of the academy (especially the dictionary of seventeenth- and eighteenth-century Rumanian) was undertaken to prove that Rumanian was really a Slavic language. A typical production was the work of a Rumanian professor on "Slavic expressions in the Rumanian language." The Academy indeed maintained a special subsidiary for the sole purpose of translating and disseminating Soviet literature. It regularly published in Rumanian a digest of 180 Soviet scientific periodicals, which it distributed to all scientific institutes in the country. It also provided them with bibliographies of Russian scholarly publications. This subsidiary had its own Russian library with 54,000 scientific and 54,000 literary works.

The Rumanian Academy was the most highly organized and largest in the Balkan satellites. But its Bulgarian counterpart engaged in similar activities. The hero of the Bulgarian Academy was Dr. Methody Popov, an elderly scientist who died in 1954, and whose field was the artificial stimulation of seeds in order to increase yields. He was also a Communist, who had not received much help from previous regimes, but obtained his own research institute from the Chervenkov government. Bulgarian propaganda organs claimed that seeds treated by his methods produced 8 to 18 per cent increases in yields of rice, sugar beets, corn, and tobacco, and pointed with pride to praise of Popov from Soviet scientists. If the claims had any justification, it was somewhat surprising that the Popov methods were not mentioned outside Bulgaria, and that the Rumanian Academy was apparently investigating the same subject without reference to Popov's achievements. He also claimed that his methods of stimulation worked with animal tissue, and cured both ulcers and hemolytic disease in women (child birth disturbance produced by negative Rh factor).

In Bulgaria, in February 1953, Professor Romansky's new dictionary aroused a considerable storm of protest, because many of his definitions were considered ideologically dangerous. The OF newspaper attacked him for defining "theology," for example, as "a philosophical theory of the adequacy of the universe," instead of as "a reactionary idealistic pseudo-science, in contradiction to scientific deductions." Another howler was his definition of "colony," as "a primitive country under the domination of a cultural country." About this, the OF paper remarked bitterly, "The imperialist colonizers can thank Professor Romansky for this definition." The denunciation seems to have been the work of a professional rival of Romansky, who hoped to get the dictionary condemned. Chervenkov himself stepped into the breach, and said that the mistakes were not sufficient to warrant a condemnation of the new dictionary, which would be published.

It seemed possible that Romansky's definition of colony was not so inaccurate after all. In any case, the practices of the Soviet learned world had found their Bulgarian imitators. In Rumania, the linguists were in trouble for their very subservience to the Soviet overlords. They had begun their Communist period, the Rumanian press complained, by praising Professor Marr, the Soviet court linguist, and by trying to follow him slavishly; then they were trapped by Stalin's own blast against Marr, and crawled to apologize. But they had been dismissed for sterility, said the press, and their successors too had had to be dismissed for "lack of combativeness" and for holding "idealistic conceptions." A scholar's life in the RPR was grim indeed. It would be long before Albania produced any sizable crop of native scholars and scientists, but even there archaeology was being zealously pursued. An Illyrian city had been uncovered, and a whole series of archaeological and ethnographical museums opened. It would not be surprising if the Illyrians, like the Dacians, proved to have been Slavs all along.

STATE PRIZES

In Rumania and Bulgaria, the state prize was the highest award to which a scientist, scholar, or artist in any field might aspire. It signified that the regime had judged his work an extraordinary contribution, and brought him the title of "State Prize-Winner," as well as a gold or silver medal and a sum of money, the amount depending on which of three classes of prize work he had won. In Bulgaria the prize was named after Dimitrov, and in both countries the system of awards was patterned on that of the Stalin prize in the USSR. Again, the emphasis was usually practical: the Rumanians awarded a prize under the category of "scholarship" for the discovery of a new deposit of gold and silver ore. One winner was the designer of the new blast furnace at Hunedoara, another had written a mathematical introduction to the theory of fluids. The artistic winners in Bulgaria included the sculptor of a statue called "The Girl of Dimitrovgrad," the new Maritsa valley industrial town, and in Rumania the author of a new symphony entitled "Summer Day on a Collective Farm."

3. Culture

COMMUNIST ART AND LITERATURE

Art, music, and literature indeed concentrated on revolutionary themes, sometimes from the period of the national awakening. In Bulgaria, of course, the Russian war against the Turks in 1877–78, which had led to liberation, proved very popular; in Rumania, the Communists adopted and embraced the nineteenth-century dramatist, Caragiale, as one of their own forerunners. Communist martyrs of the Tsankov persecutions in Bulgaria were immortalized on canvas and in stone; so were the Rumanian peasants of 1907. In style, all the arts aped the Soviet models. This meant that painters and sculptors produced realistic and representational imitations of the "Stalin-by-moonlight" school, looking rather like the *London Illustrated News* of the 1890's, but full of revolutionary fervor. Muscles bulged, brave young proletarians strode forward bearing monkey-wrenches or machine-guns, the Russian brothers greeted the Bulgarian peasantry at the Shipka pass, the defiant revolutionary bared his chest to the capitalist firing-squads, confident of a glorious resurrection. From an aesthetic point of view nothing could have been more deplorable.

In literature, the themes were also hortatory and didactic. A Rumanian novel based on a historic incident of 1949 dealt with a group of anti-Communist guerrillas in the Banat, under the command of an officer of the former Rumanian army. In the novel, they are all vicious kulaks, and their commander a sadist and a tyrant, preying on the good loyal Communist peasantry, listening to radio broadcasts from the warmonger western stations, and committing indiscriminate murders until the government wipes them out. A Bulgarian novel contrasted a splendidly competent Communist political commissar of an army regiment with his commanding officer, who had allowed his position to turn him from a loyal party man into a bourgeois martinet.

THE THEATER

The Communist regimes showed themselves particularly interested in the theater, as a useful vehicle of propaganda to the illiterate or semi-literate. Amateur theatricals became virtually a compulsory part of membership in a trade-union. The performances of these "Artistic Agitation Brigades" were designed to arouse enthusiasm for high production among the workers, a kind of self-indoctrination process. The Ministry of Culture had general supervision over the effort in Bulgaria, while in Rumania two Soviet Russians, neither of whom spoke Rumanian, formed a commission responsible for the drama. The theater-groups were called "collectives," like the teams of scholars at work on collaborative research projects, and had their own plan to fulfill. The need to exhort, to instruct, and to arouse hatred of the enemy rendered the plays as monotonous as the other forms of literature. After Stalin's death, Soviet critics began to comment more openly on this. Even the satellite press showed signs of restlessness with its own theater, and little wonder. A typical Rumanian play dealt with the efforts made by Tito's agents to subvert members of the Serbo-Croatian minority in the Banat, and the stanch efforts of the government and the loyal villagers to destroy the conspiracy.

One way to counteract boredom was to present permissible classics instead of original works. A little judicious editing transformed the Montagues and Capulets into exploiting reactionary capitalists, while Romeo and Juliet themselves stood for the "progressive" younger generation. Molière, Chekhov, and Gorky, as well as Shakespeare, lent themselves to presentation with only a little editing, and in addition allowed those who presented them and those who saw them to feel very "cultured" indeed, one of the few privileges left in Communist countries. But there was a good deal of official demand for a national drama, and the classics were not entirely safe either.

LITERARY CRITICISM

Literary critics were faced with the same horrible dilemma that faced them in Stalin's Russia: how to have a definite and consistent opinion on a piece of literary work without either praising it or blaming it, lest higher party authority disagree. When they voiced a definite opinion in their literary periodical ("Dimov's lovers are not attracted to each other by their social optimism, by the struggle for the victory of the collective. Dimov is a prisoner of the bourgeois, Freudian, idealistic concept of the individual. He is too objective. He is romantic. His new work does not answer the requirements of our times"), they might stir up a hornet's nest in the Party newspaper ("Dimov points out how the bourgeoisie robbed the people, sold them to foreign imperialism, and imposed their anti-national policy and terrible terrorism on the working masses. He realistically describes the strikes, street-riots, guerrilla movement. The novel ends with the people's victorious uprising accomplished with decisive help from the Soviet Army. This novel is a sharp weapon in the struggle for peace. This is the way it should have been criticized. Our critics are suffering from megalomania, do not understand Socialist realism, do not learn from Soviet literature. The guilt of the Union of Bulgarian writers is serious because no steps have been taken against Talmudism, sectarianism, and individual taste in our criticism"). But when they avoided praise or blame and limited themselves to description and summary, they were in trouble too ("Certain reviews are flat and descriptive. Instead of courageously revealing and promoting everything that is advanced in a writer's work so that ideological shortcomings can be combated, they are limited to recording the publication of books by giving perfunctory characterizations of the heroes and summarizing the plot. Lack of political criteria in the appraisal of a work of art leads the authors of such criticism into a morass of bourgeois objectivism and bourgeois formalism"). The critic was damned if he did and damned if he didn't.

FILMS

The regimes made an effort to found movie industries in the satellites. In Rumania, a large film-production center was built in Buftea, north of Bucharest, where a former palace and its outbuildings were turned into film studios. The schedule called for twelve pictures a year, and to meet it the government set up a special school in Bucharest to train "cadres." Grandiose propaganda declared that the center would be the biggest in all Europe. As early as 1952, a film produced by the Rumanians, *Mitrea Cocor,* won a prize in a competition in Czechoslovakia for the greatest contribution to the advancement of socialism. Of course, the success of the project depended entirely on the Russians, who also began a film industry in Albania. The first product, actually shot in the country, but largely a Russian production, was *Skanderbeg,* a historical movie shown in the United States in the summer of 1954.

THE "FRIENDSHIP" SOCIETIES

The satellites, indeed, belonged to a kind of cultural pool, in which the Soviet Union enjoyed an ever more privileged position. In every aspect of cultural life, the Russians acted as dictators and salesmen. One of the agencies that assisted them most was the "Society for Friendship with the USSR," which operated in all the satellite states. By the end of 1953, the Bulgarian society had a membership of 1,800,000, in 5,100 sections; the Rumanian society a membership of 4,900,000 in 20,000 sections. More than a quarter of the total population of each country belonged. Organized in local committees with a directing bureau, maintaining sections in every business concern, office, and school, the societies were directed at the top by Soviet representatives, from the VOKS agency, who did their work behind a façade of native officers elected from among the most prominent Communists in the country. They sponsored the ever-growing number of Russian-language courses, furthered the circulation of Soviet newspapers, periodicals, and books, "helped" the local publishing houses with translating, prepared and disseminated posters, organized special courses for Stakhanovites and agricultural technicians, and issued technical pamphlets, giving the "results of Soviet experience."

The societies also kept up a constant barrage of lectures on life in the Soviet Union. Soviet art exhibitions, films, theatrical performances, ballet, concerts, photography shows, illustrating the best in the USSR, traveled constantly from place to place in the satellites. Sports contests against Soviet teams were frequent, and when the home team won (it happened only rarely), the victory was attributed to successful absorption of Soviet methods. Native delegations of people from all walks of life chosen to visit the USSR came back from their red-carpet tours loaded with inspirational literature and singing for their suppers on a series of lecture tours. Each year these efforts reached their climax in a special "Friendship month," when festivals, ceremonial occasions, receptions, banquets, took place constantly, and propaganda in press and radio attained a pitch of feverishness impossible for a westerner to credit. Only a little less hectic were the activities and pronouncements of the friendship societies which bound the Balkan satellites to each other and to the other countries of the Communist world, including China, Outer Mongolia, and North Korea. The comings and goings of official delegations, and the mutual greetings of brotherly emissaries filled the press and the radio. The members of the "camp of peace," panted with cultural affection for each other.

Although most citizens of the satellite countries had doubtless begun by discounting the barrage, no American interested in appraising the situation accurately could afford to overlook the probability that the effort was proving effective. In the first place, mere repetition tended to dull disbelief or indifference. In the second place, daily life in the satellites was normally so drab that even the monotonous character of these celebrations lent it a little color, a little change, a little excitement. The banquet of the Soviet friendship society might be the one entertaining or amusing experience of the year, and, by contrast, become a memory to be cherished or an event to be longingly anticipated.

4. *The Yugoslav Exception*

In Yugoslavia, after the Soviet cultural stranglehold was broken in 1948, cultural life developed with somewhat greater freedom than in the satellites. The regime combated illiteracy both among Yugoslavs and among the minorities, all of whom could buy journals published in their own languages. Newspapers and periodicals multiplied. In their intolerance of dissent, however, they did not differ markedly from those in the Cominform neighbors. Education was decentralized, but remained under the guidance of the party. Schools and especially universities were overcrowded, and the faculties, though purged, continued to include a substantial number of non-Communists. Tuition was free, but a student's expenses at the university were met partly by direct allowance from the state, and partly by the student's assuming an obligation to work in an "economic enterprise," under what was called a "contract scholarship." In 1954, the press reported that the Yugoslav Students' Association had asked that the allowances be abolished, and that the scholarship system be extended.

The Association, whose views could not have been aired without government approval, maintained that the allowance system was unfair to the children of workers and peasants, and unduly favored the children of white-collar workers. Indeed, only 5 per cent of university students were of worker or peasant origin, and the system also favored residents of university centers. Moreover, the allowances bore no relation to a student's academic successes, since all young people of a certain age were entitled to receive them. On the other hand, as we saw in an earlier chapter, the "children's allowances," which the Association, and perhaps the government, now intended to abolish, formed a critically important part of the wages and salaries of workers and employees. They had already been cut, and to abolish them without a drastic revision of the wage and price scale would bring severe hardship.

When expulsion from the Cominform put an end to the Stalinization of Yugoslavia, the regime usually substituted persuasion and vague threats for the coercion of students and faculties which had characterized its previous behavior and continued to be standard practice in the satellites. Though party doctrinaires at congresses might rail about the persistence of bourgeois elements, the continuing growth of "careerism" in academic life, the "sabotage" of effort to change the old system, and the strength of "idealism" as against "materialism," the fact remained that, where other ideas were even reluctantly permitted, orthodox Communist doctrines had severe competition and often went to the wall. The only way to enforce conformity was by Stalinist methods, and these were now to some degree out of favor. So the regime surveyed its own educational system with some concern and discontent. Dangerous and open heretics among students could be and were promptly expelled, but the man who pretended to conform, while all the time eagerly drinking in western "idealistic" culture, could stay in the university; though the authorities might rail at him, he was hard to catch. Yet cases like that of Dr. Kostich, a distinguished professor forced out of the Belgrade Medical School for political reasons, whose experiences Professor Dragnich relates in some detail, indicated that the doctrinaires were still capable of scoring victories over individuals dangerous to conformity.

All culture in Yugoslavia continued in the same twilight zone between western freedom and Soviet tyranny. Certain books circulated, such as *Gone With the Wind,* the works of Gide, Stendhal, Thomas Mann, and Somerset Maugham, which nobody could have found in the satellite bookshops. The theater produced plays of Ben Jonson, Tennessee Williams, and Sartre. Anti-Stalinist literature sold well, for example, Weissberg-Tsibulsky's *Plot of Silence.* But the most publicized American plays were still those which voiced vigorous social criticism of American institutions: *Deep are the Roots* by Gow and d'Usseau, Miller's *Death of a Salesman,* and the works of Lillian Hellman. Hemingway, Sinclair Lewis, and Theodore Dreiser led American novelists in popularity. *The Old Man and the Sea,* violently attacked in the Soviet world, was widely read in Yugoslavia. In 1954, Remarque's *Arch of Triumph* was the most popular single novel among the students at Belgrade University. Russian literature, chiefly Gorky and Dostoevsky, naturally continued to be strong. The movies showed American, French, British, Italian, and Mexican productions, none of which would have been available in the neighboring countries. Soviet films, on the other hand, ubiquitous elsewhere in the Balkans, were not to be found in Yugoslavia.

Yugoslav classics, such as the sixteenth-century plays of the Dubrovnik playwright Drzich, received production, together with the contemporary party-line plays of Krlezha, who was also the regime's favorite novelist. The stage showed the Shakespearean works so popular elsewhere in the Balkans, but without the ideological editing common outside Yugoslavia. Molière, Lope da Vega, and Ostrovsky varied the menu. Yugoslav opera and ballet flourished. The regime used the theater for its own political purposes, especially in Macedonia, where a whole new dramatic literature glorifying the heroes of the Macedonian past was being written in the language of the republic. No doubt there were many Communist doctrinaires who were made uneasy by the failure of the regime to condemn specific western works. But uncertainty and contradiction characterized official policy. Tito and others would occasionally issue a blast against the capitalist world. But their self-proclaimed efforts to dilute if not to liquidate the bureaucracy prevented them from imposing the old-time Stalinist censorship. Without it, the Yugoslav people enjoyed a good deal of once forbidden fruit.

EPILOGUE

The Immediate Past and the Foreseeable Future

NO BOOK DEALING WITH CURRENT AFFAIRS can ever be up-to-the-minute at the time of publication. The author wrote the final portion of this work in the autumn of 1954. Developments since that date suggest that the era which began with the expulsion of Tito from the Cominform may have come to an end, and a new period begun. The last chapters of this book chronicle and assess the last years of an era dominated by Stalin. Even after his death, his successors could not speedily shake off the influence of his modes of operation. The execution of Beria, the demotion of Malenkov, reflected the difficulties of substituting government by junta for government by dictator. Tensions no doubt continued strong even after these adjustments; probably the competition for supreme power in the Soviet Union had died down only temporarily.

The new Soviet junta, moreover, faced the growing successes of western foreign policy. Though the long-planned European Defense Community failed to materialize in the form for which Washington had pushed, a British suggestion helped produce a satisfactory substitute. German manpower and arms would join American and western European units in defending the rest of the continent against the USSR and its satellites. Stalin's methods of preventing the alignment of western Germany with NATO had failed. But Soviet aims remained the same. The junta would try new methods. So it was that the relaxation of tension, notable to some degree almost from the moment of Stalin's death, became more and more marked during 1954, and took on sensational character in the first six months of 1955. The Balkan countries played their own role in the process.

In the fall of 1954, the USSR announced the "sale" to Rumania of the assets of all the SovRom corporations except SovRomPetrol and SovRom-Quartz (uranium). Keeping their hold on the most important and the most secret industrial operations, the Russians liquidated, at least on paper, the other organizations through which they had come to control the entire Rumanian economy. Perhaps they had come to feel that the Rumanian government was now sufficiently reliable to be allowed to manage the other industries on its own. Perhaps they expected that the gesture would remove one of the most overt symbols of foreign domination, and help them with Rumanian public opinion. Perhaps they were convinced that such devices as the "joint" companies were, as Stalin once said, suitable only for satellite states, and therefore outmoded. Perhaps the whole affair was simply a fiscal device adopted in order to extract more money from the Rumanians, while management of the installations remained under Soviet control. In any case, though one should probably not insist too much upon the significance of the act, Moscow made the gesture.

The Russians, after years of delay, also agreed to a treaty with Austria, despite the fact that its ratification simultaneously deprived them of the pretext for keeping Soviet troops in Rumania and Hungary (to "protect the line of communications" to the Soviet Zone in Austria), and opened up the hitherto sealed portions of the Hungarian and Czechoslovak frontiers with Austria. The integration of the satellite military forces in an "anti-NATO" at Warsaw probably reflected not only the Russian wish to counter western military preparations by a propaganda gesture, and to symbolize a divided Europe which they then could magnanimously offer to reunite, but also the Russian conviction that the satellite armies were now so thoroughly integrated with the Red Army that the formal withdrawal of Soviet troops from Hungary and Rumania, were it to occur, would make no difference to Soviet military control. In the United States, political voices urged that our government put pressure on Moscow to withdraw from the satellites, but the effort of Senator McCarthy to require the President to take this position went down to complete and dramatic defeat in the Senate. In negotiating with the USSR, President Eisenhower had this card to play, but could choose to play it, if at all, in his own time.

Most startling, as usual, were the sudden changes in Yugoslav affairs. After further dramatic efforts to symbolize his alignment with the "dynamically neutral" Indians — he toured India and photographed tigers as the guest of a native prince — Tito found himself in May 1955 the recipient of an extraordinary overture from Moscow. He played host to Premier Bulganin and to N. S. Khrushchev, secretary of the CPSU. In Belgrade, Khrushchev hailed the traditional bonds of friendship between Yugoslavia and the USSR, cemented by their alliance against Hitler. He "sincerely regretted" the destruction of good relations between the two states and the two Communist parties, and blamed Beria, the enemy of the people, as the fabricator of all the false charges against the Yugoslav leaders. He called for the renewal of friendship between the two peoples, and, more significantly, the two parties. The Russians now warmed to Tito with as much cordiality and humility as they had shown arrogance and brutality between 1948 and 1953.

Of course, nobody in Yugoslavia was taken in by the absurd pretense that Beria had been responsible for the excommunication of Tito. Bulganin himself had denounced Tito in unmeasured terms, and everybody remembered that the letters of 1948 had been signed by Stalin and Molotov. Indeed, it was significant that Molotov stayed away from the great reconciliation scene, although of course he still held his post as Soviet Foreign Minister. The Yugoslavs welcomed the "normalization" of diplomatic relations, and pressed their economic claims dating back to the rupture of economic ties in 1949. But Tito apparently resisted Khrushchev's overtures to the Communist League of Yugoslavia. As the most experienced victim of Soviet efforts at penetration of a native party, and the only survivor of a national Communist revolt, he was hardly likely to walk back into the Russian political embrace. How far Khrushchev was disappointed one could not say. The passages in his speech calling for a renewal of the bonds between the parties were perhaps addressed not to the Yugoslav top leaders but to whatever portion of the rank and file regretted the days of Soviet influence. How many such Yugoslavs there were nobody in the west could know. After appropriate tours to Yugoslav scenic resorts, the Russian and Yugoslav officials issued a joint communiqué, in which Tito seemed to endorse the new Soviet neutralization platform for Europe, and specifically urged the cession of Formosa to the Chinese Communists. The USSR had won substantial ideological advantage from the humiliating trip to Belgrade.

The western powers received renewed assurances that Tito did not contemplate a return to the Soviet bloc. But suspicion ran high in the United States, and voices in Congress called for careful scrutiny of further appropriations for aid to Yugoslavia, whose total, in the summer of 1955, amounted to about a billion dollars, about half of which represented military items. Tito, moreover, American military authorities felt, was not living up to the requirement, which in 1951 he had accepted, that he permit American inspection of the use to which his army was putting military aid from the United States. To questions privately put he replied publicly, indicating that he did not intend to submit to such inspection, and would rather forfeit the assistance. One possible explanation for this was partly technical. Washington had always rejected Yugoslav requests for aid in establishing plants that would build jet planes in Yugoslavia, maintaining that the costs would be such that the United States would not care to meet them. No doubt aware of this, Moscow had reportedly offered to finance the building in Yugoslavia of plants to manufacture Soviet MIG jets. In July 1955, the American Ambassador in Belgrade warned the Yugoslavs that acceptance of such an offer would adversely affect the course of American assistance to Yugoslavia.

Soviet-Yugoslav economic negotiations also led to the cancellation of Belgrade's claims for damages against Moscow, which would probably shortly be followed by further cancellations of similar claims against the satellites, chiefly Czechoslovakia and Hungary. In return, Moscow cancelled an outstanding Yugoslav debt of $90,000,000 for economic aid advanced by the USSR before the break in 1948. The debt must have represented military items previously unreported, because official figures showed that the USSR, not Yugoslavia, was the debtor and indicated a level of trade far lower than the $90,000,000 figure. Tito publicly announced this "understanding" act, late in July 1955, in a speech in which he also objected to the high rates of interest Yugoslavia had to pay on western loans, and harshly criticized Western Germany for failure to pay the full Yugoslav reparations claim of $70,000,000. Did all this mean that Yugoslavia was now beginning to sever ties with the west and intended to return to the Soviet bloc?

Certainty on the point was not possible in July 1955. But the evidence so far did not warrant any such conclusion. Tito was understandably anxious to settle outstanding economic disputes with the Soviet bloc. He would surely welcome the chance to use a Soviet offer of MIG-manufacturing facilities as a lever against the United States, in order to reduce, if possible, interest rates on western loans, and to avoid, if possible, permitting western inspection. He had his own Communists to satisfy. But he took particular pains, in the July speech, to praise President Eisenhower as a man of peace, and to single out Eisenhower's Geneva proposal for the interchange of military information between the United States and the USSR as the kind "of idealism which could lead to" realistic results. This proposal Moscow had not accepted, and Tito's endorsement of it could not help but remind his listeners that Yugoslavia was still balancing between east and west, extracting the maximum possible benefits from both sides, and making as few concessions as possible to either. Tito was following the example of Nehru, who, like Premier U Nu of Burma, visited Yugoslavia in this same eventful summer, and who also endorsed the Soviet position on the neutralization of Europe and on Formosa. Though many westerners deplored Nehru's affection for Moscow, few suggested that he planned to transform India into a Soviet satellite. So far as his resources permitted, Tito apparently hoped to become the Nehru of Europe.

The new period had just begun, but already certain repercussions were clear. The leaders of the Balkan satellites had committed themselves to Moscow's policies, and had risen to power over the bodies of Titoites. Now they found, not only that Tito was forgiven, which would have been hard to understand, but that Moscow declared that he had been right all along. If Tito had been right, had not Rajk, Xoxe, Kostov, also been right? Did not their corpses cry out for vengeance? Would not Rakosi, Hoxha, Chervenkov have to go the way of Beria, the "fabricator" of the charges against the Titoites? No doubt to soften the harshness of the blow, Khrushchev and Bulganin stopped in Sofia and Bucharest on their way home from their May trip to Belgrade, but no reassurances could conceal the threat that remained. Whenever Moscow's purposes might require the jettisoning of a Bulgarian, Rumanian, or Albanian leader, he could now justly be charged with participating in the foul plot against Tito. The whole episode served to underline once more, and this time for the Balkan Communist leaders themselves, the complete dependence of their countries and their own position upon Moscow.

Still only faintly foreshadowed in July 1955 was a possible development which might yet produce a still more sensational change in the balance of Europe. All comment on it here is speculation, yet such speculation seemed warranted. Had Moscow perhaps given Tito assurances that, in exchange for a substantial abandonment of his pro-western positions, he might have a free hand in attracting the other southeast European satellites to himself? Had Khrushchev issued Tito the license to build for himself the Balkan empire he so badly wanted, which Stalin had snatched out of his hands? The suggestion might seem fantastic were it not for a few faint signs that it had substance. Tito denounced Premier Rakosi of Hungary in late July 1955, and the speech received publicity in *Pravda*. Certain Bulgarians known for their support of Tito in the past began to receive promotions and emerge from limbo. Moscow was well aware that in the months to come the west would press for the lessening of Soviet controls in the satellites. If the Balkan Stalinite leaders should now be purged in favor of Titoites, if Yugoslav influences should replace Russian, Soviet security would suffer no decrease, but the west might be asked to believe that concessions had been made. To achieve his Yugoslav-dominated Balkan federation Tito would make great sacrifices. If Moscow were in fact dangling this bait before him, it behooved the west to be wary indeed.

Meanwhile, on the other hand, the Greek-Turkish-Yugoslav Balkan pact, so useful a part of the western defenses of the Mediterranean, and so clear a threat to the Balkan satellites, now declined in effectiveness and importance. The Turkish-Greek differences over Cyprus contributed markedly to this. But more important was the effect produced in Ankara and Athens by the rapprochement between Tito and the Russians. Suspicion, always the hardiest of plants in the Balkans, sprang up again, nor was it withered by Tito's reassurances that he clung to the pact, since he minimized its military aspects and emphasized its economic and social importance. At the same time, the hope, strong after the Trieste settlement, that Italy might adhere to the Balkan pact, thus plugging the Lyulbyana gap, and linking Yugoslavia even more firmly to NATO, vanished with Tito's reception of the Soviet leaders. Italian political leaders felt, even more strongly than Greek or Turkish or American, that the Balkan pact had ceased to be a valid instrument.[1]

The Austrian treaty and the rapprochement with Tito the Russian leaders put forth as evidence of their desire for peace. The west had insisted upon concrete acts, they maintained; here they were. Secretary Dulles properly retorted that this was to make virtues of necessities. Yet such had been the tension generated by the cold war period, and so great was the relief at the spectacle presented by a drunken, apparently bumbling, Khrushchev reeling about at Yugoslav banquets, that much of the world, outside the cool realistic atmosphere of the State Department, accepted the virtues as virtues. In the summer of 1955, as these lines were written, thousands of citizens of Iowa were cheering a Soviet agricultural delegation, and joyously allowing high Soviet officials to feed ice cream to the children, while thousands of citizens of Kharkov milled about until dawn outside the hotel in which the corresponding delegation of American farmers was staying, in the hope of cheering them personally. Englishmen of every shade of political opinion rejoiced at the news that the boorish Khrushchev would visit London next year. For their part, the

[1] The horrifying anti-Greek demonstrations in Turkey which took place while this book was in the press contributed greatly to the weakening of the pact. Misguided, the Turkish government made a major contribution to the Soviet cause.

Soviet leaders, facing economic strain, even crisis, showed themselves aware of their own public opinion, and were seemingly bent on convincing the world of their peaceful intentions.

For the United States the initial danger lay in the possibility that we might not have the flexibility to meet the new tactics, and that the western Europeans might allow their wishful thinking to triumph over their experience, and come to believe that the USSR was the friend and America the foe of peace. This danger President Eisenhower at least temporarily obviated by his general demeanor and specific proposals at the "summit" conference. At the time of writing, the outlook was for a period of conferences on all major issues dividing the world.

One such major issue was that of the European satellites, including three of our four Balkan countries. The restoration of their freedom to create their own regimes and control and develop their own economies might, in theory, come about by a war in which the USSR should be defeated. But the nature of the new weapons rendered it more probable that a war would not regain such freedom for the Balkan satellites but would lose it for all mankind. Partly because we realized these dangers, we were striving to postpone such a war indefinitely, and, for the moment, the Russian leadership appeared to share this view. Diplomacy might conceivably offer us, at a future conference, the opportunity to press for the liberation of the Balkan countries. But it was difficult to imagine the west developing diplomatic positions of such strength that we could insist on the complete withdrawal of Russian influence, or even obtain, for example, the holding of elections of the sort whose results we could accept.

In July 1955, the best prospect for a restoration of liberty to the Balkan countries appeared to lie in a possible change within the Soviet empire itself. If, as some argued, the Russian regime were slowly becoming more liberal, presumably its satellites would eventually experience their own version of that liberalization. This offered cold comfort indeed to those who hoped that institutions of a free western type would ultimately take root in the Balkan countries. Moreover, it offered no comfort at all to those who did not share the major premise with regard to the USSR itself, and this author must admit that he cannot see any reliable evidence on which to base such hopes. Whatever might be the chances for peace between the great powers, the chances for a liberalization of tyranny in the Balkan satellites seemed remote indeed. Yet the United States, as one of the powers sharing the responsibility for the imposition of the tyranny, would fulfill its international responsibilities only by seizing any opportunity to demand its removal. Should the Russians withdraw, Washington would then have to play a large part in protecting these countries against the ambitions of Tito. Firmness, vigilance, and policies based on sound knowledge of the past and reliable information about the present would be the least that the future would require of us in the Balkans.

AFTERWORD: THE BALKANS IN 1973

I

REFLECTING ON THE BALKAN COUNTRIES IN THE YEARS since 1955, one realizes that the repeated dips and zooms in Soviet-Yugoslav relations provide a dominant theme. After the great quarrel of 1948–1955 had been settled, the Hungarian uprising of 1956 precipitated a second one. Tito denounced the initial Soviet intervention; but when the revolt in Hungary took on a wholly anti-communist character, he failed to oppose the massive Soviet military operations that crushed it. His strained relations with Khrushchev were eased by a second public reconciliation in the summer of 1957. But by November of that year a third quarrel broke out, as Tito continued to insist upon the rights of individual communist states freely to make their own decisions, and, naturally enough, refused to denounce "revisionism," which would have meant in effect saying "mea culpa." In the 1960s, the whole Soviet-Yugoslav disagreement was gradually swallowed up in the much graver and increasingly heated dispute between China and the USSR.

Always afraid of the reassertion of Yugoslav influence in Albanian affairs, and aware that a genuine reconciliation between Tito and the USSR might once again free Tito's hands for intervention in their own country, the Albanian communist leaders in 1961 switched their allegiance from Moscow to Peking. This gave the Chinese their first and only European satellite — an economic liability, but a strategic asset with much nuisance value. For a time, the USSR disguised its polemic against China by couching it in the form of denunciations of the Albanians, while the Chinese disguised their polemic against the USSR by couching it in the form of denunciations of the Yugoslavs. By late 1962, Khrushchev and Tito were reconciled for the third time. And, no doubt under the stress imposed by the break with Peking, the Soviet leadership in 1963 saluted Yugoslavia as a socialist and fraternal country from whose innovations even the USSR might learn. The Chinese for their part denounced Khrushchev and Tito equally as "revisionist" traitors to Leninism.

As the inventor of communist disobedience to Moscow, Tito could, however, never expect or even desire the restoration of truly "fraternal" relations with the USSR, since this would have restored the subservience he had found intolerable. Moreover, it was only when the Russians were preoccupied with China that they found it expedient to make even tactical concessions to the Yugoslavs by abandoning overt hostility and "normalizing" their relationships. All the reconciliations were merely apparent and temporary: as soon as the USSR found it necessary to resume an active policy in eastern Europe, the fundamental antagonism between the Soviet regime and Tito became manifest once again.

So, when in the summer of 1968 the Brezhnev regime repeated, with variations, in Czechoslovakia the Krushchev intervention of 1956 in Hungary, Tito publicly condemned the action (this time with the support of powerful western communist parties), and the Soviet-Yugoslav rift opened for the fourth time since 1948. Indeed, the Yugoslavs had been encouraging the Dubcek regime in Czechoslovakia in its liberal course. And the Czechs had openly been discussing a revision of those clauses of the Warsaw Pact which authorized the USSR to hold military maneuvers on the territory of any member state. The prolonged Soviet occupation of Czechoslovakia and the increasing repression by which it was accompanied, together with the "Brezhnev doctrine" that justified it, postponed until 1971 a fourth "reconciliation" between Moscow and Belgrade. Tito could never feel that Yugoslavia was secure from the danger of Soviet intervention. To make invasion less attractive, the Yugoslav government instituted a new "all peoples' defense system" in which every inhabitant of the country would play a part.

2

But it was far more difficult to combat Soviet intrigue. Despite the dramatic changes wrought in the Yugoslav social and economic system under Titoism, the traditional Yugoslav "nationality" problem persisted, and rendered the country peculiarly vulnerable to subversive influences from outside. No reader of this book will be surprised to find that — as Yugoslav communism modified its dictatorial ways and relaxed its control over the individual in the late 1950s and the first half of the 1960s — the ancient tension between Croat and Serb began to reassert itself. It was this, together with Tito's aging and the problems of arranging for his succession, that offered the USSR its opportunities for disruptive intrigue.

As might have been foreseen, the first open Croatian demands came in a traditional Balkan way: a dispute over language. In 1967 a group of Croatian intellectuals issued a manifesto repudiating their earlier understanding of 1954 with the Serbs to work toward a common Serbo-Croatian language. They now demanded that Croatian be recognized as a separate tongue. Serbian intellectuals countered by demanding that the Serbs resident in Croatia be permitted to use the Cyrillic alphabet. Although Tito intervened and the authors of the Croatian demands were expelled from the League of Communists, the tension only persisted and grew. Behind it lay issues more concrete, if no less emotional, than those of language and alphabet.

As in prewar Yugoslavia, the Croats felt oppressed and exploited by

Belgrade and the more numerous Serbs, and this despite the new opportunities for self-expression that Titoism had provided. Together with the far smaller Slovenia, Croatia was the most advanced industrially of the republics of Yugoslavia, with 90 per cent of the ship-building, 80 per cent of the oil-refining capacity, and 75 per cent of the tourism: all of which were the major earners of foreign currency. Yet no Yugoslav enterprise was allowed to retain more than 10 per cent of the foreign exchange it earned. In addition, almost 40 per cent of the approximately one million Yugoslav workers abroad (1973) — half of them in West Germany — were Croats, sending or bringing home annually large amounts of needed foreign currency. "Foreign resources to those who earn them" and "End the plunder of Croatia" became popular slogans.

It did no good to point out, for example, that the Croatian income from tourists derived to a great extent from hotels and highways built along the Dalmatian coast with federal money. Croatian nationalists continued to proclaim, and with much justice, that hard-earned Croatian money was being siphoned off to pay for development in the less affluent republics in the south, including Serbia itself. To put it in historical terms, former Habsburg territory was still being heavily assessed to help former Ottoman territory catch up. And the Croatians were convinced that the money was being badly or perhaps even corruptly managed by those people in Belgrade, those Serbs, those traditional economic and political exploiters of Croatia.

In this way, Croatian public opinion, inside and outside the League of Communists of Yugoslavia, had by 1971 come to resemble Croatian opinion in the year 1938. The centralized communist regime was regarded as a recrudescence of Serbian exploitation. The demands swelled for more powers to be granted to the Croatian republic. There was even agitation for a Croatian national state with its own representation in the UN. Ustashi refugees in Germany, in touch with the Croatian workers there, fanned the flames. According to Tito, so did "cominformists": anti-Titoite Croatian communist refugees in the USSR. In April 1971 two Croatians murdered the Yugoslav Ambassador in Sweden; a plane was hijacked in an effort to get the murderers to safety; a Yugoslav plane was mysteriously blown up in flight. Yugoslavia seemed threatened by internal disintegration.

Tito summoned all the leaders of the League of Yugoslav Communists to a conference, won from them a promise of good behavior and cooperation, and proceeded to purge the Croatian communist leadership which, he said, had been guilty of "lack of vigilance, complacency, and rotten liberalism," and had been flirting with "counter-revolutionaries, various nationalists, chauvinists, and the devil knows who else." The offending cultural organizations were closed down. One concession was made, however: all enterprises might now retain 20 per cent of their foreign exchange earnings instead of a mere 10 per cent. And Tito simultaneously moved a long distance toward meeting the malcontents' demands for decentralization.

The Constitution of 1963 was drastically amended to give the individual republics control over capital and over new projects for investment. The Presidency of Yugoslavia was already a fifteen-man body, consisting of Tito himself, and two members from each of the six republics (Serbia, Croatia, Slovenia, Bosnia-Hertsegovina, Montenegro, Macedonia), plus one each from the two autonomous provinces of Kossovo (formerly Kos-Met) and Voyvodina. So all that was necessary to ensure true economic decentralization was to give each republic the right of veto inside the collective presidency. The Yugoslav federal government retained control only over foreign affairs, defense, and overall economic planning. After the crisis had simmered down, Tito himself said that, had it not been for prompt action, a shooting civil war might have begun within six months, and that "somebody else" — meaning the Russians, of course — might have "marched in to restore order." Newly re-elected to the Presidency for a period of five more years, Tito thus publicly referred to the strong possibility of a Soviet invasion. To deal with the obvious danger that the Serbs, who had naturally opposed the decentralization as strongly as the Croats had favored it, might become too disaffected at the loss of their hitherto disproportionate influence, Tito also thoroughly purged the Serbian branch of the League of Communists.

3

The preservation of Titoist Yugoslavia at the end of 1971 may have marked only a temporary lull before the ancient Serb-Croat conflict should break out once again in some other form. But, although Serb-Croat tension surely was the greatest internal menace to the continued existence of Yugoslavia, it was only one of the major sources of strain within the country. Despite strenuous efforts to push ahead with economic development in the less advanced republics, and despite genuine gains (Macedonian per capita income tripled between 1947 and 1966), the more developed regions were advancing still faster, and the gap between the more and the less affluent grew wider. The Albanian minority in Kossovo, in particular, had real cause for grievance. Amidst the continuing poverty, Albanian nationalism manifested itself in the form of anti-Serbian demonstrations and in occasional overt expressions of sympathy with the Hoxha government across the border. After the purge in 1966 of Rankovich, chief of the security services and regarded as a potential heir of Tito, the government acknowledged that his forces had perpetrated horrible massacres against the Albanians of Kossovo, "losing all sense of human behavior." Some Serbs had even joined the service for the express purpose of committing anti-Albanian atrocities. In the years after the admissions, as Albanians migrated northward into Serbia, they experienced frequent displays of fierce racial hatred. Although the days of the worst oppression had apparently ended, the memories remained fresh.

Moreover, the regime's economic policies produced a variety of tensions. The 40 per cent currency devaluation of July 1964 — without adequate preparation or explanation — helped correct the Yugoslav balance-of-payments deficit but caused a serious domestic inflation, as the cost of living rose 50 per cent in a single year. The government had undertaken to liquidate uneconomic enterprises, but now could not fulfill the promise, because of the strains that an increase in the already severe unemployment would put upon the population, and sometimes because of local patriotism. In Montenegro, for example, it was politically impossible to move against the notoriously uneconomic Nikshich steel works, the special pride of the leading Montenegrin communist, Svetozar Vukmanovich-Tempo. This in turn encouraged other politicians with special pet enterprises to protest against their liquidation and to protect and perpetuate them. Yugoslav agriculture lagged, and about $100,000,000 worth of wheat had to be imported annually from the United States. Although 88 per cent of Yugoslav farming was private, the incentives to production had not proved sufficient.

The transition in the mid-sixties to "market socialism," with state intervention drastically reduced, led to further migration of workers abroad. At the other end of the economic scale there now appeared individual millionaires, flaunting the signs of the wealth that the Marxist rule books said could never exist under socialism. A law in 1967 that enabled foreign companies to make direct investments in Yugoslav enterprises, sharing proportionately in the management and in the profits, proved attractive to new capital: Yugoslav labor was cheap and Yugoslav natural resources rich. Annual profits of 15 per cent and higher could be obtained.

The regime limited foreign ownership to 49 per cent of any enterprise; it levied a direct tax of 35 per cent on all profits; it limited to one third the fraction of the profits that could be taken out of Yugoslavia from sales to hard-currency countries; and it required that the first 20 per cent of net income be reinvested inside Yugoslavia. Despite these drawbacks, there were by the early seventies more than 180 joint agreements with foreign firms. An Italo-Yugoslav concern produced refrigerators in Zagreb; a Fiat plant was turning out some 70,000 cars a year, a Volkswagen plant 20,000. Private cars were everywhere: 180,000 new ones appeared during 1970 alone. Yugoslavia was becoming a consumer society, and those who lived well lived better than Yugoslavs had ever lived before.

Financing came in part from the International Financing Corporation or the World Bank, and in December 1970 thirty-nine western and fifteen

Yugoslav banks formed a joint International Investment Corporation for Yugoslavia, with an initial capital of $12,000,000. From Slovenia and Croatia came complaints that the process was still too slow, and that incentives were insufficient. From doctrinaire communists came cries of horror that foreign capital should be admitted on any terms. The regime did make some agreements also with East Germany and with Czechoslovakia. From more than five million foreign tourists a year, Yugoslavia earned approximately $300,000,000 annually in hard currency from tourism. This, added to $250,000,000 worth of hard currency from the Yugoslav workers abroad, helped reduce the balance-of-payments deficit, which still stood at $657,000,000 in 1969. With its varied successes and failures and its concomitant social tensions — increased by a new devaluation in the spring of 1971 — Yugoslavia was in a class by itself as a pioneer in market socialism.

Most formidable of all its problems were the uncertainties posed by Tito's advancing age. Eighty-one in 1973, and not scheduled for retirement until 1976, he was nonetheless surely mortal. The cumbersome fifteen-man Presidency had been designed largely to ensure a geographically representative body to substitute for one-man rule at the moment of his death. Whether it could in fact avert grave troubles over the succession, nobody could be sure.

4

The frictions, tensions, and unresolved problems of Yugoslavia, the dangers that called into question its future survival, too often occupied the center of a western observer's view, and obscured the positive achievements of Tito's regime. The governmental system the Titoists built was properly described as "exuberantly complex." Whereas other communist states, following the Russian pattern, opted for government by ideology, by the party, by the *apparat,* and by administration, the Yugoslavs opted for government by law, by constitutionalism, and by "self-management." They forced their own Communist Party to transform itself from the chief instrument of power into a mere supplier of ideological inspiration. Except for Tito himself, nobody held office in both government and party.

Moreover, the federal government itself no longer dictated detailed production plans or investment schedules. Even the republics, to which so much responsibility was delegated, had to turn for support to the communes (*opshtine*) — the sub-units into which they were divided, the basic building-blocks of the society. In the individual commune resided all powers not specifically allocated to republican or federal authorities. The communes had formal and legal equality with the larger units. They fixed their own revenues, passed their own rules. In addition, many functions ordinarily associated with government — for example, social insurance — had been transferred from the state to non-governmental bodies, usually co-operatives. Decentralization and the stripping of functions from government were essential principles of the Yugoslav system.

Elected assemblies ("Chambers") at both the republic and the federal level actually exercised strong control over the administration; and the bureaucracy tended to attach itself to these chambers rather than to the executive. By the 1963 Constitution, as amended in 1967 and 1968, the Federal Chamber — the Chamber of Nationalities — represented the communes and the republics. Four subsidiary specialized chambers of elected representatives — often non-political experts — shared in its work: one each for the economy, for education and culture, for health and social welfare, and for social self-government. No bill could become law unless jointly enacted by the Federal Chamber and the individual chamber most concerned with the subject-matter. And before a bill could be drafted, it passed through long and careful discussion and debate designed to refine out of it in advance any impractical or unpopular aspect. Once so drafted, it could often be passed enthusiastically, even unanimously.

The elected members of the assemblies received assistance from two civil-service bodies. A Secretariat for Legislation and Organization supplied preliminary expert opinion on a bill from those who might later have to administer its provisions. A Legislative-Legal Commission provided a thorough preliminary legal scrutiny and a comparison with already existing statutes. Even after the Federal Chamber had enacted a law, it was regarded chiefly as a declaration of policy, a framework to be filled in by the republican chambers, which cherished and guarded their right to render federal laws effective. Western observers found these processes successfully underway.

The system assigned a critically important role to constitutional courts: one in each republic, and one for the federation. They reviewed all legislation and all administrative decisions, gave constitutional advice, and acted as a complaints-bureau for individuals and agencies. Theirs was the job of co-ordinating the mass of legislation, of keeping the system consistent, and of protecting the rights of the individual. These functions derived in part from American models and in part from a strong tradition in south Slav administrative law. In addition, the Federal Constitutional Court could initiate its own legislative suggestions to the Federal Chamber.

From the small but epoch-making beginnings of the workers' councils in factories in the early 1950s, the Yugoslavs had been spreading the principle of "self-management" to schools, to hospitals, and to the government itself. For two decades they had been trying to combine in their system the recommendations of some of the most humanistic Marxist thinkers, honored only in the breach or wholly forgotten in other Marxist countries, with some of the most fruitful libertarian constitutional traditions of the West, and with their own basic willingness to try anything, no matter how impractical or clumsy it might seem at first. The result was unlike anything ever seen before. No wonder it was complex. It was interesting; it deserved study; it deserved respect. It was all the more remarkable because it had been constructed in a relatively poor country of only twenty million people, with determined enemies close by, and with a population divided — after centuries of maladministration and human cruelty — into groups at best mutually suspicious and at worst full of hatred, all faced with the problems of engaging in twentieth-century economic development without the necessary resources.

Dissent, however, had its limits, as the case of Mihajlo Mihajlov served to show. A Yugoslav-educated son of Russian parents, Mihajlov in 1965 published an attack on life in the USSR, and thereafter tried to conduct an opposition magazine, *Free Voice,* from his home in Zadar. Mihajlov, who believed in parliamentary democracy, maintained that his actions were in accord with the 1963 Yugoslav Constitution; but in fact that document gave to the League of Communists of Yugoslavia the power to direct "guidance and ideology." Mihajlov was indicted; he could have emigrated but refused; he was allowed to receive foreign visitors while awaiting trial. In 1966 he was sentenced to nine months in prison, to which was added an earlier three-months' suspended sentence. He allowed the *New Leader,* published in New York, to print his defense, and for that was sentenced in April 1967 to an additional four and one half years. Though treated far more gently than he would have been in any other communist country, Mihajlov was the victim of the tyrannical tradition, albeit in a highly weakened phase.

A group of Zagreb philosophers, on the other hand, fought such suppression of dissent. They gathered around the magazine *Praxis.* Striving to update Marxism and even to revolutionize it by using its own terminology and assumptions, they put the individual will first, and proclaimed that socialism was a goal to be sought only by free will. Drawing on Marx's early writings, on Hegel, Feuerbach, and Nietzsche, with little attention to Engels and none to Lenin, they wished to eliminate the last vestiges of Stalinism in Yugoslavia, and complained that true democracy was still lacking. It was not only capitalist exploitation, they argued, that alienated man from his "real human essence" but petty bureaucratism and bossism in the communist countries. They debated with Soviet philosophers, who declined to regard them as Marxists at all, and in 1966 the Yugoslav regime made difficulties for them. For a time publication of *Praxis* was suspended, its state subsidy terminated. When it began to reappear in March 1967, it was an "international" journal, and its board included some foreigners. If such cases indicated that Titoism had still a long way to go before it approached non-communist ideas of freedom, they also indicated once more how far it had come since its early days of Stalinism.

5

The continuation of Yugoslav-Soviet friction was in 1955 both predictable and predicted. But in 1955 nobody would have foreseen that Rumania — closest geographically to the Russians of any Balkan state, and long occupied by Soviet troops — would find within its own Communist Party leaders courageous enough to defy the USSR and skillful enough to do it successfully. The Rumanians began their efforts to detach themselves from Soviet domination when Gheorghiu-Dej protested against the 1958–1959 plan of the Comecon that would have kept the emphasis of Rumanian production focused on raw materials. He insisted upon continuing the force-draft development of Rumanian industry, openly rejecting in 1961 the Soviet dictation of an "international socialist division of labor" as likely to condemn Rumania to a future economy limited to agriculture and oil-production. Not far below the surface of the Soviet economic demands lay a territorial threat: that the lower Danube region might be "integrated" into the overall eastern European economy, and somehow lost to Rumania. In repudiating the idea, the Rumanians even found the courage to protest against their loss of Bessarabia and northern Bukovina to the USSR in 1940, and to hint that these territories should now be restored.

Gheorghiu-Dej died in March 1965, and his successor, Niculae Ceaușescu, energetically strove to carry still further the effort to give Rumania a foreign policy independent of the USSR. He too referred (May 1966) to the loss of "certain territories inhabited by an overwhelming majority of Rumanians," and kept alive the grievances over Bessarabia and northern Bukovina. Becoming head of state (December 1967) he soon down-graded Gheorghiu-Dej's work by "rehabilitating" Patrașcanu (1968). With the West, including the United States and West Germany, he concluded new agreements on trade. At the same time, he pointedly remained neutral as between the USSR and China. By 1968 Rumania, Yugoslavia, and the newly liberalized Czechoslovakia were drawing together in what looked like a curious revival of the old "little entente" of the years between the two World Wars. The brutal Soviet intervention in Czechoslovakia ended such illusions, and forced the Rumanians once again to face the harsh reality that their proximity to the USSR made real independence of Moscow a mirage.

Yet in 1970 and 1971, by exchanging state visits with President Nixon, by renewing his overtures to Peking, and by making a state visit to China, Ceaușescu pursued his independent policy more vigorously than ever. The possibility of a new "pro-Chinese" alignment of Balkan states, including

Yugoslavia as well as Rumania and Albania, surely alarmed the Russians. And late in 1972, following the Yugoslav example, Rumania passed a new law calling for "total" national defense, and specifically forbidding any Rumanian to "accept or recognize" any action of a foreign state designed to "hurt Rumania." The text of the statute itself thus directly referred not only to the Soviet danger but to the possibility of domestic disloyalty by pro-Russians among the Rumanian communists.

Meanwhile, early and late, the Rumanians used every available international forum to press for general agreements on principles that would render their own policies less hazardous, and minimize the danger that the Russians would treat them as they had the Czechs. They wished to see Soviet signatures on documents declaring that all states were independent, sovereign and equal, with full rights to make their own policies at home and to choose their own friends abroad, and that no other state might interfere or threaten the use of force "irrespective of membership in military and political groupings." In the preliminary discussions looking toward the general European security conference so long urged by the USSR, the Rumanians wanted precisely those words included in the statement in the agenda. Although the final text said only "irrespective of their political, economic, and social systems," this in itself represented a major Soviet concession. At the Conference, which opened in early July 1973 in Helsinki, the Rumanians would surely continue to support these principles, so important to them, so acceptable to the West, and so embarrassing for the USSR.

It remained for Chou En-lai to comment in lapidary form with regard to the long-range effectiveness of the Rumanian efforts abroad. "Distant waters do not quench fires," he said to a Yugoslav newspaperman late in August 1971. At the time, the USSR had been conducting military maneuvers in Hungary and Bulgaria, crudely but effectively reminding the Yugoslavs and, even more pointedly, the Rumanians where real power lay in southeast Europe. And Chou was saying that Chinese friendship might be all very well, but that if Ceaușescu were to try Brezhnev's patience too far, there was little that the Chinese could do to help.

As if to underline the point, Brezhnev himself visited Belgrade in September 1971, and for the fourth time ostensibly repaired relations between the USSR and Yugoslavia. The Rumanians, who had been hoping that they might cement a firm alliance with the Yugoslavs, and thus emerge from isolation, while defending their common interest in maintaining independence from Moscow, found themselves frustrated. For Brezhnev now once again conceded Yugoslavia's right to follow her own "road to socialism." At the same time, he pointedly reserved to the USSR the right to re-interpret "in the light of present day conditions" the exact meanings of past agreements between Moscow and Belgrade.

Rumanian efforts to break away from Moscow's tutelage in foreign relations were notably not accompanied — as they had been in Yugoslavia — by modifications of domestic repression or by economic and administrative experiment. Paradoxically, the Ceaușescu regime remained more Stalinist in its attitudes toward freedom of expression than, for example, the Hungarian government, which was wholly loyal to the USSR in foreign policy. Moreover, Rumanian economic policies remained rigid and inefficient.

True, there had been notable achievements: the 1968 gross industrial product was fourteen times that of 1938; national income had multiplied by five, and wages by two and a half. Industrial production was doubling every five years, two to three times as fast as the rate in the major industrial countries. Between 1961 and 1968 the annual Rumanian rate of growth was 13.2 per cent annually, equal to that of Japan, and three times that of West Germany. Rumania produced 4,751,000 tons of steel in 1968; the 1970 planned production was to be 6,300,000, that for 1975 ten to fifteen million. The Galați iron and steel complex was booming; trucks and tractors were produced at Brașov; a Rumanian automobile factory at Pitești, built with French cooperation, turned out Renaults, with 50,000 cars annually scheduled for 1975. The joint Rumanian-Yugoslav hydroelectric plant at the Iron Gates of the Danube produced 11.3 billion kilowatt-hours annually.

But Rumanian production capacity remained under-utilized: an ill-advised investment policy concentrated on providing new capacity instead of using what was already available. Equipment lay idle, while new giant projects were pushed through. Spending 30 per cent of the national income on investment — more than any other government in the Comecon — Rumania concentrated overwhelmingly on heavy industry at the expense of consumer goods and agriculture. The national per capita income was the lowest of any Comecon state, standing in 1968 at 82 per cent of the 1965 figure, as against 150 per cent for the USSR and 83 per cent for Bulgaria. The machine-building industry, turning out equipment that could neither be absorbed at home nor compete with western products in the international market, had to pass on its surplus as "aid" on credit to Algeria, Egypt, and other developing countries. Agricultural output remained the weakest point of all: it had risen only to 1.6 times that of 1938, as against the 14-fold rise in industry. 1969 saw a major crisis, with crops remaining unharvested until too late. The production of grain per hectare lagged behind that in East Germany, Hungary, and Czechoslovakia, where the soil and other conditions were far poorer than in Rumania. Although 53.6 per cent of the Rumanian labor force was still engaged in agriculture, their labor produced only one quarter of the national product.

The 1971–1975 five-year plan and the guidelines published for the period 1976–1980 showed that the same pattern of investment would continue, although at a somewhat slower rate; almost 60 per cent of the total investment figure going to industry, and more than three quarters of that to heavy industry, with a new emphasis on electro-technical, electronic, and automation equipment; while agriculture would receive only 14 per cent of the investment. As Rumanian trade with the Comecon states declined in the 1960s from about two thirds to only a little over 40 per cent of the total, and that with the West rose to almost the same 40 per cent figure, the Rumanian balance of payments suffered, and West Germany in particular became the major Rumanian creditor. The protectionist policies of the European Economic Community were closing western European markets to Rumanian food-stuffs; so the problem was becoming ever more acute, since the Rumanians could not hope to find a market in western Europe for their inferior and overpriced industrial products.

Rumania had accomplished some of the easier tasks: a backward economy had been rapidly expanded, and industry had been developed at the expense of the standard of living of the people. But to increase industrial efficiency, to improve quality, to overhaul management, to institute effective pricing policies — all this was more difficult, and remained largely unattempted. Ceaușescu had repeatedly declared that the present generation of Rumanians would feel the benefits of Rumanian economic planning; but this had not happened, and there were grave fears spreading among the population that it never might.

Rumanian membership in the International Monetary Fund and in the World Bank, however, dated only from 1972, and it was still too early to be sure how far these might prove advantageous. Inefficiency and mismanagement had adversely affected the progress of domestic schemes for development, and the standard of living remained persistently and disappointingly low.

Among the naturally anti-Russian Rumanian people, the bold national foreign policy of the 1960s and early 1970s had long been so popular that the deficiencies of their government in other respects had not mattered so much. But by 1973 the continued domestic dictatorship, accompanied by the chronic unavailability of the good things of life, had begun to produce rumblings of discontent. Unlike the Tito regime, the Ceaușescu regime could not be regarded as responsive to public opinion except in its bold defiance of the Russians, or as sensitive to the public need in any way whatever.

6

Of our four Balkan states, only Bulgaria in 1973 had without visible resentment maintained unchanged the dependency upon the USSR that characterized it in 1955. The Bulgarians did not break away or invent original contributions to Marxist-Leninist theory and practice, like the Yugoslavs; nor did they, like the Rumanians, cling to orthodox theory at home while striving abroad to play an international role independent of the Soviet Union. Instead, they faithfully, sometimes almost comically, followed the patterns of behavior set in Moscow. "Our political watch," said the Bulgarian Premier and Party leader in May 1962, "is set exactly to the second to Moscow time." And so it often seemed.

After Khrushchev purged Molotov, Malenkov, and Kaganovich as "anti-party" elements, the Bulgarians purged three leading communists of their own on similar charges (July 1957). After Khrushchev had pushed through a sweeping administrative and territorial reform, the Bulgarians too abolished their 13 large provinces (*okrugs*) that had been subdivided into 117 counties (*okolyi*), and re-organized the country into 30 new *okrugs,* farming out to the new provincial authorities administrative powers that had formerly been centralized (January 1959). Soviet experiments with voluntary workers' detachments, with new "comrades' courts" in each enterprise, with party control commissions in all sectors of the economy were all duly adopted (early 1960s); and in Bulgaria, as in Khrushchev's Russia, the result was an epidemic of new meddling and a plague of new busybodies. When the Soviets adopted a twenty-year plan for economic development, Bulgaria did the same (1962).

In Bulgarian domestic affairs, the list could be extended indefinitely, while in foreign policy as well the Bulgarians faithfully followed Moscow. After Khrushchev fell in 1964, Todor Zhivkov — by then both First Secretary of the Bulgarian Communist Party and Premier — who owed his success in large part to Khrushchev's support, said not a single word of regret for his old mentor now in disgrace, but instantly cuddled up to Brezhnev and Kosygin. The Bulgarian satirical magazine *Sturshel* itself printed (May 1965) the following verses by way of comment:

The Master of the Dog has died.
Poor orphan dog!
The months pass, he suffers,
Without a boot to lick.
Hangdog, he crawls,
Toadying to his master's enemies.
They greet him: "You dog,
You belonged to the other man.
How come this skillful transformation?
You're a faithful slave again?"
Slobbering, the dog replies:
"I cannot live without a master!"

Within the Bulgarian party and government, Zhivkov, ex-printer and ex-partisan, a "home" communist who had spent his life in Bulgaria making his career largely in the Sofia District Committee, moved with bureaucratic sure-footedness but with much deliberation to eliminate his two rivals, Chervenkov and Yugov. Already out as Party Secretary in 1954 (above, p. 484), Chervenkov slipped another notch at the April Plenum of the party in 1956 when he had to surrender the Premiership to his old rival Yugov, the former Plovdiv tobacco worker, still strongly supported in that region, now making a comeback from the disgrace he had suffered because of his ruthlessness as Minister of the Interior in the 1945–1948 period. This second demotion of Chervenkov came as the result of Khrushchev's denunciation of Stalin and the "cult of personality." Chervenkov, however, remained in the Politburo, and in 1957 and 1958 as Minister of Education and Culture took charge of suppressing any sign of Bulgarian sympathy with the Hungarian and Polish uprisings.

Not until late in 1961, after the Soviet Twenty-Second Party Congress had embarked on a new round of de-Stalinization, could Zhivkov safely proceed to the next step. Chervenkov was now dismissed from his deputy premiership, from the Politburo, and from the Central Committee for "mistakes and vicious methods," for making himself the center of a personality cult, and for underestimating the importance of the Agrarian Union (the puppet former splinter of the old Bulgarian party, much touted by Khrushchev). And it was still another year (Eighth Party Congress, November 1962) before Zhivkov's control over the party secretariat had given him the strength and the confidence to oust Yugov from the Premiership, the Politburo, and the Central Committee, allegedly because he had denied guilt in "violating socialist legality" in the 1945–1948 period, because he had only pretended to be an enemy of the cult of personality, and because he had conspired against the party. Perhaps Yugov had been heard criticizing Khrushchev adversely for yielding to Kennedy over the Cuban missile issue; but surely one of Zhivkov's charges against him was true: he had "wanted to be first man in the country."

Zhivkov now became Premier. At the same time, Chervenkov's ruin was completed by his expulsion from the party. In the USSR itself the premiership and party leadership were separated once again after Khrushchev's fall, but Zhivkov has held on to both posts since 1962. Yugov's fall meant the triumph of the party apparatus over the security forces, and so resembled the fall of Beria in the USSR in 1953, and the later dismissals of Rankovich in Yugoslavia (1966) and Draghici in Rumania (1968).

Though not well-educated, inspiring, or personally magnetic, Zhivkov apparently possessed exactly the right combination of timid willingness to move slowly and bureaucratic skills suitable for the leader of a satellite country. In 1965 he managed to survive some sort of army plot against him, apparently led by a celebrated wartime partisan commander, with strong grass roots support in the Vratsa region, who committed suicide to avoid arrest. Probably the fall of Khrushchev had encouraged the plotters to think that they might succeed in overthrowing Zhivkov in his turn. In the late 1960s there were still traces of opposition to Zhivkov both in the Vratsa region and in the army. A major scandal erupted late in 1969 in the new big combine of the Merchant Fleet Economic group, which included ship-building, transport, and allied undertakings, with the power to negotiate foreign trade deals. The Minister of Transport and all other persons allegedly responsible for "crude violations" and "lack of principles" were dismissed. The strong hint of corruption was a setback to the regime.

And in the early 1970s there were indications of strong dissatisfaction with Zhivkov. He had been in power for almost two decades, and had been unconscionably slow about getting new blood into the party apparatus and government. It was plain to the brethren that Yugoslavia and Rumania and Albania, by following an adventurous course and playing the Chinese and the Americans off against the USSR, had gained advantages that Bulgaria's docility had not provided. Moreover, there was something undignified and degrading about the quality of Zhivkov's subservience. And the constantly recurring bickering with the Yugoslavs about Macedonia surely grated on the nerves. The Central Committee itself demanded to be kept in better touch with the Politburo's and the government's deliberations, and set up special commissions to assist it. In time these might infringe upon the supremacy of Zhivkov's party secretariat.

Bulgaria's massive economic and social change involved the total transformation of a peasant society. And here alone the observer discovered examples of originality and innovation. In October 1958 there began a drastic movement to fulfill in three to four years the rather moderate third Bulgarian five-year plan, then only a few months old. Zhivkov's "new tempos and new scales of production" announced in January 1959 reflected the new Soviet seven-year plan. Bulgaria, however, used the Chinese terminology: a "great leap forward." The 1959 national product was to double that of 1958, and the 1960 to triple it. All Bulgarian farms had now been merged into some 1,000 collectives averaging 4200 hectares apiece. Partly because of Bulgaria's large obligations to supply vegetables and fruit for the other Comecon countries, agriculture was now to receive large new investments. Industry had failed to absorb the large numbers of peasants displaced by collectivization and mechanization.

The goal of creating 400,000 new jobs by 1962 was apparently achieved. But doubling and tripling the national product proved an illusory objective. Late in 1960, when it was announced that the aim of completing the third five-year plan in three years had been achieved, this was made plausible only by using the figures for the rate of growth instead of those for the value of the gross national product. The Chinese overtones of the whole effort caused dismay in the USSR: Chervenkov, as the chief enthusiast, was forced to admit that he had been wrong when he had declared that communism was being achieved: it was, after all, only a "form of socialist construction." For the brief period 1958–1960, the romantic drama of the Chinese experiment had swept the Bulgarian leadership up in an effort that smacked of Maoism, now becoming heresy. Amidst disillusionment and the public Sino-Soviet quarrel, the Bulgarian pace slackened in 1961.

The twenty-year plan announced in 1962 was of purely Soviet inspiration, and called for the "completion of the material-technical basis of socialism and the gradual extended building of the material-technical basis of communism in Bulgaria" by 1980. Until 1976 the emphasis would be on heavy industry. Emphasis would also fall upon improving the housing shortage in the cities, now bursting with new immigrants from the countryside. Industry was to triple by 1970, and to multiply sevenfold by 1980. Electrification, mechanization, and automation were the keys, and by 1980 Bulgaria would produce some five sixths of the electric power it needed, with the remainder coming from the Cominform grid. The new refinery at Burgas signalized the growth of the new Bulgarian oil industry. A Soviet nuclear reactor was scheduled for purchase and completion by 1974. Ferrous metallurgy was concentrated not only in the Lenin plant in Dimitrovo but in a wholly new center at Kremikovtsi near Sofia, begun in 1960 as a major economic show-piece, opened in 1963, and enlarged in 1967. The ore deposits, on which major hopes had been based, proved too low-grade, and ore had to be imported from Algeria, Brazil, and India; coke supplies were also inadequate, and had to be imported from Poland. Soviet technicians and planners were responsible both for the success and for the shortcomings.

With agricultural production still very low and industrial growth-rates disappointing, the Eighth Party Congress of 1962 paid attention to the implications of the celebrated recent article by the Soviet economist, Liberman, about profits and incentives. The Bulgarian leadership even contemplated something like the Yugoslav system of workers' councils in the individual factories. But decentralization moved at a snail's pace, and not until 1965 was decision-making delegated to the individual "industrial association" or trust. Wages were to be tied to results in production. The trusts, as the new centers of economic power, controlled funds for development, for new products, for social-cultural matters, and for wage reserves. Simultaneously three new sets of prices were adopted: prices fixed by the state for the most basic goods; variable prices, with the maximums and minimums fixed by the state, for a second category of products; and free prices for a small category of seasonally produced or locally produced items. The idea closely resembled one that the Czechs had pioneered. But the application of this newest reform went very slowly until mid-1967, and a year later centralized planning was resumed. Caution and conservatism had won out.

On the Bulgarian collectives, as in the USSR, the Machine Tractor

Stations were phased out, as the collectives themselves bought out their machinery. The individual private plots, their size depending inversely upon the intensity of cultivation, remained of major importance not only for the farmer himself but for the Bulgarian livestock position. In 1967, for the first time, new agricultural statutes gave farmers the same benefits that workers had long been entitled to: paid vacations, a health code, maternity benefits, family allowances, and disablement compensation. The introduction of a guaranteed minimum wage made Bulgaria the first communist country to abolish the detested "labor-day" method of reckoning agricultural earnings. Each collective was to distribute surplus income proportionately to the work performed. Self-supporting production brigades, elected by the membership, took over responsibilities for output. A general assembly of members on the collective elected managers by secret ballot, and the elected management handled the three funds: for expansion and technical improvement, for special and cultural matters, and for the remuneration of labor.

Here was pioneering of a sort that the Bulgarian communists had never shown in any other field. They carried the originality and initiative further, when, beginning experimentally in 1969, they introduced the Agro-Industrial Complex, still further enlarging and recombining the collectives. By 1973 the 1,000 or so collectives had been transformed into 170 very large "agros" (shades of Khrushchev's failed "agrogoroda" of the early 1950s, for which he made Malenkov take the blame). The new Bulgarian "AICs" averaged 20,000–30,000 hectares, and the largest reached 50,000. In 1973, the first new "Industrial-Agricultural-Complexes" (IAC) made their appearance. In one of the seven known to exist, a large sugar factory in Ruse combined with two beet-growing AICs to form something like a vertical trust for sugar-production.

There had been occasional indications that in 1969, at the twenty-fifth anniversary of the Fatherland Front victory in 1944, Bulgaria would announce that it had ceased to be a People's Republic, and had become a socialist state, with a new constitution. But the occasion passed without the shift. And yet, with its completely collectivized agriculture, and its subservience to the USSR, perhaps it deserved the title. Only the streams of foreign tourists — perhaps three million a year — provided a jarring note. Tolerated because of the hard currency they brought, but often accused of introducing the innocent natives to nameless western-style wickednesses on the sunny Black Sea beaches, they were perhaps the chief anomalous feature of the otherwise strait-jacketed life of Bulgarian subjects in the 1970s.

7

Stalin's death in 1953, followed in 1955 by Khrushchev's first healing of the Soviet breach with Tito, put Enver Hoxha's Albanian regime in deadly peril. Hoxha could be sure that, no matter what form a restoration of Yugoslav influence in Albania might take, it would surely mean his own ruin. Soviet exports of capital goods fell off ominously, and although a minor long-term loan was arranged with China (late 1954), a temporary improvement in Albanian agriculture was reversed after a vigorous new collectivization drive in 1955. Tuk Jakova was purged as a pro-Yugoslav in 1955, and after the Hungarian uprising in 1956 several other Albanian communists including Liri Gega — allegedly pregnant at the time — were executed. Hoxha maintained his power by ruthlessness and constant aggressive terrorist action against possible enemies. No doubt the national fear of resurgent Yugoslav influence gave him some help.

Chinese subsidies quintupled between 1955 and 1957. But the Russians also increased their aid, and between 1957 and 1959 Albania had almost more income than it could use. The economy surged ahead, oil-production tripling (almost 500,000 tons in 1959, all refined in Albania itself). The drive to abolish illiteracy among adults was completed, a new social security system adopted, and health standards raised. Only agriculture failed to respond to the opportunities presented during these years when the Chinese and Russians were quietly competing for Albanian affections.

Not until mid-1960 did the Chinese make open their quarrel with Moscow. On the first visit to China (June 1960) of two leading Albanian communists, Haxhi Lleshi and Liri Belishova, the Chinese hailed the eternal bond between China and Albania, praised Hoxha's correct anti-Yugoslav line, and promised Chinese support. But the Albanians were still hedging their bets, and Belishova, in particular, made a pro-Soviet speech. It was only a few days later that Khrushchev publicized his sympathy with Greek claims to southern Albania, thus threatening to split Albania. And a few days later still, when the Russians and Chinese violently aired their differences at the Rumanian Party Congress in Bucharest, only the Albanians supported the Chinese. The die was cast. And, in accord with the new view of Yugoslavia as an instrument of Soviet policy, during the summer of 1960 the Albanians described it as "A Hell where the darkest terror reigns, and where a clique of traitors, fed on American imperialist dollars soaked in the blood of the workers, has for the first time in history installed a revisionist Trotskyite regime."

The Russians cut their economic aid; a severe drought was threatening the Albanians with starvation; the Chinese — in the midst of a famine of their own — bought grain in France for hard currency and delivered it to Albania, and the first Chinese specialists arrived. Khrushchev allegedly tried and failed to unseat Hoxha by a coup, led by Belishova, Kocho Tashko, and others, who were arrested. Throughout 1960 the dispute deepened, and by November Hoxha himself had publicly denounced Khrushchev at a meeting of eighty-one communist parties in Moscow.

Between late 1960 and October 1961 the Russians halted work on the Tirana Palace of Culture, withdrew their specialists from Albania, and praised Tito repeatedly in public; the Albanians, meanwhile, ostentatiously celebrated Stalin's birthday, subjected Soviet specialists to severe security checks, and denounced Tito early and often, while exchanging expressions of mutual admiration with the Chinese.

After nine months of such escalation, Khrushchev denounced the Albanians at the Twenty-Second Congress of the CPSU on October 17, 1961, for persecuting friends of the Soviet Union and "undermining Soviet-Albanian friendship." The Chinese objected, and Chou En-lai walked out; Khrushchev returned to the charge; and the Albanians responded with a violence remarkable even for them: Khrushchev was "a real Judas," "a plotter and common putschist," "a base, unfounded, anti-Marxist"; simultaneously they praised Stalin unstintedly. Diplomatic relations were broken after the Albanian embassy in Moscow had distributed documents in the case (November 1961). Henceforth, the Albanian regime followed the Chinese line in the great dispute with the USSR of the early 1960s, putting the struggle for national liberation ahead of the struggle for peace and against atomic war, opposing cooperation with non-communist labor unions, identifying the United States, rather than West Germany, as the leading enemy. Albanian propaganda linked its own traitors with the American Sixth Fleet, the Greeks, and the Titoites, and now harmoniously included Khrushchev in this sinister band of conspirators against Hoxha. The savagery of the polemic faded briefly in mid-1962, but no steps toward a genuine reconciliation have ever been taken, and the Albanians were excluded from Comecon.

In the dozen years since the break with Moscow, Albania's lifeline has extended all the way to Peking. Between 1960 and 1962 Albanian trade with the USSR fell from 3.5 billion leks to 1.3 *million,* a factor of 3,000; while that with China rose from about 450 million to 2.7 *billion,* a factor of 6. Moscow demanded instant repayment of $210,000,000 (not due until 1970). Probably the Albanians ignored the demand. The Chinese moved into the gap with credits; and the Albanian debt to Peking gradually increased, boosted by the continuing unfavorable balance of trade between the new partners. In 1964 alone the Albanians exported to China $38,000,000 less than they imported. A new loan of more than $200,000,000 was floated in 1966: by then the Albanian debt to China was also about $200,000,000, not including amounts owed for military equipment and military advisors, for technical assistance, and for shipping costs. Since the Albanians were giving the Chinese some assistance with social insurance and public health systems and with the building of small hydroelectric power stations in mountain districts, and since the Chinese technicians in Albania worked for low wages, many of them giving advice on rice-growing and the development of by-products from rice, perhaps these costs did not greatly swell the Albanian debt. But the Chinese did buy French, Canadian, and Australian wheat, which was delivered to Albania in vessels belonging to those nations. Wheat and transport charges had to be paid for in hard currency; so these additional costs were high ($6.6 million worth of grain in 1962, $10.1 million in 1964, exclusive of shipping). With the Chinese their partner for 60 per cent of their foreign trade, Albania was once more a satellite.

When Khrushchev had been their foreign overlord, the Stalinist, industry-minded Albanian leaders had hated to hear him call Albania the future "orchard of socialism," but they had perforce to listen to the same message when it came to them from Mao. Agriculture, said the Chinese, must come first, and self-sufficiency in wheat was the prime goal: between 1962 and 1966 the Chinese sent 400 tractors a year and 20,000 tons of chemical fertilizers. In the industrial sector priority went to the export industries, oil and mining, and the import-substitute industries, concrete, metallurgical plants, and power stations. The 1961–1965 plan failed to reach its targets, and the 1966–1970 plan called for the decentralization of planning, set modest goals, and guaranteed a continued austerity (a 35–40 per cent rise in agriculture, a 28–33 per cent rise in investment, an oil output of 1,208,000 tons). Chinese-built plants rose at Elbasan (ferrous metallurgy), Tirana (tractor spare-parts), Berat (textiles), and Shkodra (copper wire, with six hundred Albanian workers and eleven Chinese technicians). The Albanians blamed slow progress on an "imperialist-revisionist blockade." But China was very far away; Chinese and Albanians had to communicate for the most part in Russian, which neither spoke very well; and the Chinese often failed to supply spare parts. By 1970, new nickel mines had been opened up, 200,000 hectares of drained land newly made available for agriculture (an area equal to all of Albanian arable land in 1938), and trade relations had been opened with Italy, France, Rumania, Scandinavia, and other countries.

Khrushchev's fall in 1964, though welcomed by Hoxha, did not change the international realities, and the Albanians soon declared that Brezhnev and Kosygin were just as bad, if not worse. So when the Chinese embarked late in 1965 on their Great Proletarian Cultural Revolution that convulsed its government and society until 1969, the event set up echoes of its own in Albania. But the Albanians were far from imitating the Chinese in all aspects of the upheaval. Though exercised in an almost infinitely smaller theater, Hoxha's power was in fact more absolute than Mao's, and he felt no need to make himself the center of constant hysterical reiterations of loyalty. There was no struggle within the Communist Party in Albania comparable to that in China. Nor did Hoxha need to give new scope to the army, as Mao did. He called the Albanian activities only "revolutionization," a mere continuation of developments already under way.

Well before the Chinese cultural revolution began, Madame Hoxha had denounced Albanian youth for continuing to look at the world "through the prism of the individual" instead of plunging into revolutionary experience. And early in 1966 the leading Albanian communists were sent to the countryside for a period of work in local party organizations: back to the grass roots. In the army all military ranks and insignia were abolished, and political commissars reinstituted after an interval of ten years. To prevent the growth of a bureaucracy like that in Russia the salaries of high and middle-rank officials were cut, and the prevailing "lust for white-collar jobs" denounced. As party-workers were dragooned into production-brigades, the army was put to work opening new land to cultivation, and by late in 1966 were producing enough food for its own consumption and a surplus of milk, grain, fruit, and eggs to sell to the state.

The Chinese precedents gave Hoxha an opportunity to act in accordance with his own predilections; he already distrusted intellectuals and bureaucrats. Tensions between workers and intellectuals, between the capital and the provinces, were, it was announced in 1966, being repaired amidst floods of enthusiasm: forty writers were sent out of the capital; one declared publicly that he was full of joy to find himself away from Tirana, where his fellow-writers "debated about their personalities," and amongst the "simple people who toil all day and all night, and know neither luxury nor leisure." Zhuvani, author of a novel called *The Tunnel,* dealing with the construction of a tunnel needed for the great Bistrice dam (left partly finished by the Russians at their withdrawal), was denounced for emphasizing the sacrifices of the Albanian people instead of the heroism of the workers who had done the job, and for painting the harsh conditions of work, the death-like aspect of the dam-site, and the brutality of the construction-manager.

After the Fifth Party Congress in November 1966, during which Hoxha spoke for nine hours on "negative phenomena" in Albanian society, the revolutionization, in modified Chinese style, was stepped up. The size of the private plots in the collectives was reduced by two thirds, allegedly by the "free and happy vote" of the members. Early in 1967 came an Albanian endorsement of the Chinese Red Guards as the "first swallows of the proletarian revolution," and there were even some Albanian Red Guards, sent to remote mountain areas in the country to disprove "the profoundly conservative and reactionary misconception that it is impossible to work in the mountains in the winter": still a far cry from the violent and uncontrolled activities of their Chinese counterparts.

In a major speech in February 1967, Hoxha singled out the three main targets for a continued Albanian drive: the bureaucracy, religion, and the inequality of women. Bureaucrats had been undemocratically patronizing the masses, and staying for ten or fifteen years in their white-collar jobs. Revolutionary wall posters, Chinese-style, called for their humiliation and correction. Many high officials were forced to admit their errors. Publicity was given to the transformation of a single church into a "house of culture," and to the new design for a popular cigarette package: the familiar camel and mosque were to give way to an industrial installation. Forty-one clerics (no faith mentioned) had announced they were throwing away their robes, abandoning religious services, and turning their buildings over to the people. They quoted Hoxha, "The faith of an Albanian is Albanianism." And by September 1967, with the closing of 2,169 churches, mosques, and monasteries, Albania, it was proudly announced, had become the first atheist state in the world.

Although the state itself recognized that old habits would be a long time dying, and that faith seldom disappears through fiat, the Hoxha regime had been moving as vigorously as possible to stamp out the last vestiges of the traditional Albanian attitudes and ways of life. And of course the custom of arranging marriages, sometimes uncongenial or unsuitable, in exchange for money, kept women in a subservient role; and—this was explicitly recognized—reduced the availability and the efficiency of their work. This would have to go.

Thoroughly Albanian in content though somewhat Chinese in form, the changes were completed by the late 1960s. By the time of the Sixth Party Congress in autumn of 1971, calm had been restored. First Secretary for thirty years now, Hoxha seemed altogether secure, and was apparently working harmoniously with Shehu. For the first time since 1961, the Politburo was expanded by the addition of three new members, only one of whom was replacing a deceased member. The center of a cult of personality of his own, Hoxha was trying to find youthful talent without alienating the old guard. Party membership had risen by 20 per cent to about 87,000 members, and for the first time workers were the largest element (36 per cent, as against 30 per cent peasant and 34 per cent white-collar workers), while the number of women members had more than tripled (from 7 to 22 per cent). There was even a literary revival: Ismail Kadare's novel, *The General of the Dead Army,* dealing with the Italian occupation, was receiving the applause of the regime, and a Franco-Italian company was filming it in Albania.

The excesses of the Chinese cultural revolution had undoubtedly caused some anxiety among the Albanian leaders about the stability of their indispensable partner; but any temptation to relax their dependency was halted instantly by the 1968 Soviet invasion of Czechoslovakia. Although Dubcek was an "ultrarevisionist," the USSR was the great villain.

Albania formally withdrew from the Warsaw Pact, by now a mere formality. And in the wholly new circumstances of international relations that began to take shape in 1971, Albania, while clinging fast to Mao, now on terms with the United States, would also seek nearer home some safeguards for self-preservation. Still a backward society, with life for the individual harsh and austere indeed, Albania needed ties to the Balkan world as well as to distant China.

8

In the late 1960s and early 1970s, despite ideological barriers that one would have imagined to be impenetrable, a new warmth and intimacy began to appear in the relations among the four Balkan states and between each of them and the Greek government of the colonels. Although the USSR, together with the Poles, Czechs, and East Germans, predictably denounced the Greek regime as a puppet of NATO, and while Greece itself staunchly maintained its anti-communist line, a general rapprochement regardless of ideology began between the government at Athens and the four Balkan governments that called themselves communist but that differed so wildly in their individual interpretation of that term. With Maoist Albania the Greek colonels resumed diplomatic relations for the first time since 1939, in pursuit of a policy of "good bilateral" understanding; and a trade agreement promptly followed. With the domestically Stalinoid but internationally independent Rumanians the Greek leaders exchanged friendly state visits: it was Premier Papadopoulos' first official trip abroad. A commission to manage Greek-Rumanian trade was established. And so too the Greek regime reached satisfactory understandings with the Titoist Yugoslavs and the Muscovite Bulgarians, the Bulgarians emphasizing "peaceful co-existence among states of differing social systems" and Balkan cooperation.

As the four "communist" states cemented friendly relations with the "fascist" Greek colonels, Albanian-Yugoslav hostility, so long a fixture in Balkan international politics, also thawed somewhat. The Soviet invasion of Czechoslovakia put the Albanians, as well as the Yugoslavs and Rumanians, on renewed notice that the Russians were prepared to use force. Always suspicious of Albanian ambitions to annex Kossovo, the Yugoslavs at first did not respond with any enthusiasm to an Albanian offer to assist them in case of a Russian attack; and viewed with disapproval — as probably directed against them — the re-opening in 1970 of relations between Albania and Bulgaria. But in 1971 Yugoslav-Albanian relations were also renewed; the Albanian press spoke of the friendship between the two peoples, despite the "unbridgeable" differences between their two systems, and of the Albanian intention to assist Yugoslavia if "various imperialists . . . common enemies" should threaten Yugoslavia

Tito's response was to appoint a prominent Albanian from Kossovo as his first ambassador to Tirana since 1948. Rumanian-Albanian relations — especially in the cultural field — were also friendly, as were those between Rumania and Yugoslavia and even those between Rumania and Bulgaria.

If all the edifying progress thus summarized reminds a reader of Balkan diplomacy in 1912 and 1913, or in the 1930s, the parallel can be carried still further. Just as the other Balkan states joined against Bulgaria in the Second Balkan War in 1913, and just as Bulgaria, as the dissatisfied state of the post-World War I period, was the target of the Balkan Entente formed by the others, so in the early 1970s it was Bulgaria's position that stood in the way of unanimous good feeling among the Balkan states. Not that the Bulgarians themselves did not want it this time. They surely did, and were even prepared to take the lead in organizing a Balkan "summit" conference with a view to general agreement on mutual security and good relations. This, however, the USSR vetoed. Bulgaria was the one reliable Balkan client-state left, and in 1971 Soviet policy apparently required the others — Rumania, Yugoslavia, and Albania — to live in fear that the Russians would use Bulgarian territory as a springboard to launch an attack against them. While it was clearly not forbidden for the Bulgarians to ease their relationships with Greece, Moscow preferred tension among the other four.

The Yugoslavs too remained incurably suspicious of Bulgaria. The ancient Macedonian issue was still exacerbated periodically. Bilateral talks sponsored by the Bulgarians produced no results. Even if the Macedonian quarrel could somehow have been papered over, the Yugoslavs would have remained convinced that the Bulgarian regime was a tool of Moscow. So long as Tito believed that Soviet intrigues were making his own internal Croatian problem more difficult, so long as the Russians continued to use the intimidating device of military maneuvers on neighboring territory, including Bulgaria, it would be impossible for the Titoists, obsessed with their future after Tito's disappearance, to join hands with the Bulgarians and to make a new Balkan entente unanimous.

9

Beginning in 1971, momentous changes shook international relations out of the fixed patterns in which they had for so long remained seemingly frozen. The rapprochement between the United States and China, and that between the United States and the Soviet Union (including the Russo-American agreement on "Basic Principles of Relations"); the American withdrawal from Vietnam: these made possible Brezhnev's visit to the United States in the summer of 1973, and made plausible his proclamation then that the Cold War was over. Within the overall détente, steps toward European understanding were speeded. The initiatives of the Brandt government in West Germany led — in sequence — to treaties between the West Germans and the USSR, between the West Germans and Poland, and finally between the West Germans and the East Germans. The postwar frontiers were painfully accepted by the West Germans, and the treaties painfully ratified. The road toward a reconciliation between the two Germanies had led through Moscow. The Berlin Wall stood, but the tensions that had created it had notably relaxed, and Berlin itself became the subject of a new four-power pact that at last defused a mine which had repeatedly endangered international peace since 1945. The entry of Great Britain into the Common Market made the European Economic Community a genuine economic super-power, despite the continued existence of national sovereignties and the maintenance of national armies.

In this newly emerging international order, what would be the role of the Balkan countries? The European Conference on Security and Cooperation, just getting under way in Helsinki as this was being written early in July 1973, had long been sought by the USSR, primarily as a means of ratifying its domination over eastern and southeastern Europe; and had long been opposed by the West because the Russians seemed likely to be the sole gainers. But Soviet fear of China, and Soviet economic failure, and Soviet need for technological assistance had led to Soviet concessions on the agenda, which now declared, as we have seen, that the USSR would henceforth respect the sovereignty of all states, "irrespective of their political, economic, and social systems," would refrain from the use of force in dealing with them, and would acknowledge their right to fundamental freedoms. Even the Soviet pretext that there had been no intervention in Czechoslovakia because the Czech government had asked for aid could not wholly negate the importance of the phraseology of the Helsinki agenda. If taken seriously, the commitment would prevent a repetition elsewhere of the Soviet actions in Hungary in 1956 and in Czechoslovakia in 1968. Would the Russians take it seriously?

Did the loudly proclaimed end of the Cold War mean that the Rumanians, Yugoslavs, and Albanians could now abandon their vigilance and relax? Had the Balkan area been effectively neutralized at last? Could the Yugoslavs continue without worry their bewildering proliferation of heretical experiments in politics, economics, constitutional practice, administration? Had Tito's succession — however intractable — been reduced to the level of a wholly domestic Yugoslav question, to be tackled without fear of Soviet intrigue or intervention? Might the Rumanians henceforth without fear make their own international arrangements with China, with Latin America, with Africa, with the West? Could Bulgaria heal the breach with Yugoslavia now, and a genuine five-way Balkan Entente with Greece come into being? Would the Balkan region, so long the source of rivalry among great powers, now become a peaceful backwater, in which its gifted and energetic inhabitants might develop their resources and lead their cultural and spiritual lives in peace?

Or did the new developments mean only that the Soviet authorities believed themselves so secure in southeast Europe that they could afford to commit themselves publicly not to resort again to invasion, because they could control the area by less drastic means? Had they matured their plans for taking Yugoslavia back into camp, without fighting, by waiting until the eighty-one year old Tito should die or be incapacitated, and then by moving rapidly to take advantage of Yugoslav weakness: of the hiatus in leadership that would surely open up, of the clumsiness of the fifteen-man Presidency (fourteen without Tito), of the economic "contradictions" and national hatreds of the Yugoslavs? Would they then help divide the country into a group of squabbling non-viable former provinces easy to dominate or annex one by one, or would they swallow it whole once again for Muscovite communism? Did the Russians now believe that it hardly mattered how many independent noises the Rumanians might make, since in any case Rumanian influence could hardly extend beyond the borders of Rumania, with its economic life in disrepair and with Soviet power next door? Did they think of Albania as an unimportant little country and an economic liability, without whose subservience they had got on very well since 1960, and which they were prepared to let wither on its own vine, not worth their trouble?

While in 1973 it was far too early to venture even tentative answers to these major questions, it was plausible to predict that the Yugoslavs and Rumanians would continue to expect the worst, and that no dramatic changes might be expected overnight. But it was also at least possible that in 1973 the Balkan countries stood at the beginning of a new era, that the "Our Time" in which this book was originally conceived, and which extended for at least fifteen years after it was first published, might at last be over.

APPENDIX

Useful Works in Western Languages

WHAT FOLLOWS IS NOT A BIBLIOGRAPHY, still less a list of sources consulted in the preparation of this book. It is a selection of works in western languages to assist readers who wish to examine some aspect of the subject more thoroughly than I have been able to do here. It normally omits works already mentioned in the text or cited directly in the footnotes. It includes an occasional very recent or relatively obscure work, not necessarily because of its value but just because it might otherwise be totally overlooked. For two reasons it is much fuller for the seven chapters in the first portion of this book, dealing with the prewar years, than for the eight dealing with the postwar years. The first seven chapters here are in themselves highly condensed, and may therefore make it necessary for the reader to seek details elsewhere, while the later ones provide a full treatment; moreover, we have a far larger number of reliable works on the earlier period.

The Division of Bibliography of the Library of Congress produced in 1943 five mimeographed bibliographies on the Balkan area: *The Balkans:* I. *General;* II. *Albania;* III. *Bulgaria;* IV. *Rumania;* V. *Yugoslavia,* all of which are useful, listing chiefly works in English and the western European languages. An earlier and more detailed work, with more references to studies in the native Balkan languages, and lists of periodical articles current in any year, is Léon Savadjian, *Bibliographie balcanique* (Paris: Société générale d'imprimerie et d'édition, 1920–1939), eight volumes, the first covering 1920–1930, the second 1931–1932, and each of the remaining six a single year.

Among general works in English which have become standard, Sir Charles Eliot, *Turkey in Europe* (London: Arnold, 1908), is both solid and extremely entertaining. Of books on individual countries, the best is R. W. Seton-Watson, *A History of the Roumanians* (Cambridge: University Press, 1934), covering the entire period from Roman times to the end of the First World War, and containing excellent bibliographical references. Less valuable but still useful is H. V. Temperley, *A History of Serbia* (London: G. Bell and Sons, 1919). *Yugoslavia,* ed. R. J. Kerner (Berkeley and Los Angeles: University of California Press, 1949), is a collaborative work with some weak and some strong contributions. Comparable works on Bulgaria and Albania are lacking. George Finlay, *A History of Greece,* is one of the few studies in English dealing at length with the Turkish period. For the Balkan territories which were once

Hungarian see C. A. Macartney, *Hungary and Her Successors* (London, New York, Toronto: Oxford University Press, 1937).

For centuries, travelers to the Balkans have written accounts of their voyages and impressions, some of which are of extraordinary interest: John Paget, *Hungary and Transylvania,* new edition, 2 vols. (London: John Murray, 1850), is one example among many which could be cited from the nineteenth century. In our own day, the most celebrated work of this sort is Rebecca West's classic *Black Lamb and Grey Falcon* (New York: Viking, 1941), which means Yugoslavia to many Englishmen and Americans. The book is both learned and perceptive, and written with such fire and passion as to hold many readers hypnotized. Yet it has an unmistakably pro-Serbian bias, and should be read for pleasure, not for instruction.

On geography, the classic work is that of the distinguished Serbian scholar, Yovan Cvijic (Tsviyich), *La péninsule balcanique, géographie humaine* (Paris: A. Colin, 1918).

On the Balkan peoples, some of the writings of that indomitable English lady traveler, Mary Edith Durham, are interesting and readable, notably *High Albania* (London: Edward Arnold, 1909), and *Some Tribal Origins, Laws, and Customs of the Balkans* (London: G. Allen and Unwin, 1928), which deals mostly with Albania and Montenegro. A. J. B. Wace and M. S. Thompson, *The Nomads of the Balkans* (London: Methuen, 1914), deal with the Vlachs. Eugene Pittard, *Les peuples des Balkans* (Geneva and Lyon: Georg; Paris: Leroux, 1920), is an anthropological study, concentrating on the Dobrudja. Irwin T. Sanders, *Balkan Village* (Lexington: University of Kentucky Press, 1949), is a sociological study of Dragalevtsy, a Bulgarian village near Sofia. Of its kind it is far and away the best book, sensitive, scholarly, and excellent reading. Olive Lodge, *Peasant Life in Jugoslavia* (London: Seeley, Service, no date but 1941), collects peasant customs and folklore; P. Kemp, *Healing Ritual* (London: Faber and Faber, no date but 1935), discusses south Slav tradition and folk-beliefs in the field of medicine. Louis Adamic, *The Native's Return* (New York: Harper's, 1934), reveals a young Slovene's reaction on revisiting his native village, after years spent in the United States. Ruth Trouton, *Peasant Renaissance in Yugoslavia 1900–1950* (London: Routledge and Kegan Paul, 1952), is a study of Yugoslav educational development, in many respects of great value, but rather uncritically laudatory of the Tito regime.

On the period summarized in Chapter 4, the standard work in English on Byzantium is A. A. Vasiliev, *History of the Byzantine Empire* (Madison: University of Wisconsin Press, 1953); the best one-volume work in any language is G. Ostrogorsky, *Geschichte des byzantinischen Staates,* 2nd ed. (Munich: C. H. Beck, 1952), of which an English translation by J. M. Hussey was promised in 1955 for imminent publication. The work of Stephen Runciman, *A History of the First Bulgarian Empire* (London: G. Bell and Son, 1930), is both authoritative and lively. On the second Bulgarian Empire see R. L. Wolff,

"The 'Second Bulgarian Empire,' its Origin and History to 1204," *Speculum,* XXIV (1949), pp. 167–206. On the mediaeval Serbs, there is nothing reliable in English; the first volume of Konstantin Jireček, *Geschichte der Serben,* 2 vols. (Gotha: Perthes, 1911, 1918), contains the best available summary. Though much has been written since, H. A. Gibbons, *The Foundations of the Ottoman Empire* (New York: The Century Company, 1916), is still highly regarded; Paul Wittek, *The Rise of the Ottoman Empire* (London: The Royal Asiatic Society, 1938), is a brilliant and controversial essay. There is a German monograph on the battle of Kossovo by Maximilian Braun, *Kosovo* (Leipzig: Markert Peters, 1937), and the student will find available a good many English translations of Serbian folk-ballads, as well as scholarly studies of the genre. Pending the appearance of the authoritative work of Professor A. B. Lord of Harvard, one may consult Dragotin Subotic, *Yugoslav Popular Ballads, Their Origin and Development* (Cambridge: University Press, 1932). On Ottoman institutions, the splendid book of A. H. Lybyer, *The Government of the Ottoman Empire under Suleiman the Magnificent* (Cambridge, Massachusetts: Harvard University Press, 1913), may be supplemented by the work, still in process of composition, by H. A. R. Gibb and Harold Bowen, *Islamic Society and the West* (London: Royal Institute of International Affairs, 1950), of which volume I only has so far appeared. On Ottoman decline, the contemporary travelers are among the best sources, and of these none is more shrewd or observant than Sir Paul Rycaut, *The Present State of the Ottoman Empire* (London, 1668). No one work satisfactorily covers the history of the Balkan subject peoples under Ottoman domination; indeed, this is a subject badly needing investigation. Laszlo Hadrovics, *Le peuple serbe et son église sous la domination turque* (Paris: Presses universitaires de France, 1947), and Alois Hajek, *Bulgarien unter der Türkenherrschaft* (Stuttgart: Deutsche Verlagsanstalt, 1925), are two useful monographs. Louis Voinovitch, *Histoire de la Dalmatie,* 2 vols. (Paris: Hachette, 1934), is standard for Dalmatia, including Ragusa.

On the period between the last portion of the eighteenth century and World War I, William Miller, *The Ottoman Empire and Its Successors,* fourth edition (Cambridge: University Press, 1936), is a solid monograph, with useful references to additional literature. Two good books, one in French and the other in German, discuss developments in the Yugoslav lands. They are Emile Haumant, *La formation de la Yougoslavie* (Paris: Bossard, 1930), and Hermann Wendel, *Der Kampf der Südslawen um Freiheit und Einheit* (Frankfort: Frankfurter-Societäts-Druckerei, 1925). C. E. Black, *The Establishment of Constitutional Government in Bulgaria* (Princeton: Princeton University Press, 1943), is more than a monograph on the Tirnovo Constitution of 1879; it includes an excellent introductory section on conditions in nineteenth-century Bulgaria. J. Swire, *Albania, the Rise of a Kingdom* (London: Williams and Norgate, 1929), has chapters on Albania in this period, though it devotes more space to a detailed treatment of the years after 1912. L. S. Stavrianos, *Balkan*

Federation (Northampton, Massachusetts, 1944), Smith College Studies in History XXVII (1–4), October, 1941–July, 1942, is a careful scholarly treatment of movements toward Balkan unity, with much of interest on other matters. The first 195 pages deal with the period before 1914.

The Serbian intellectual movement is discussed by G. R. Noyes in a chapter in *Yugoslavia,* ed. Kerner, cited above. Professor Noyes has also edited and translated *The Life and Adventures of Dimitrije Obradović* (Berkeley and Los Angeles: University of California Press, 1953), University of California Publications in Modern Philology, Volume 39, a work of great interest and importance. The Serbian Revolutions are best studied in Stojan Novaković, *Die Wiedergeburt des serbischen Staates, 1804–1813* (Sarajevo: Bosnisch-Hercegowinische landesdruckerei, 1913), and G. Yakchitch, *L'Europe et la resurrection de la Serbie, 1804–1834* (Paris: Hachette, 1907). T. W. Riker, *The Making of Roumania 1856–1866* (London: Oxford University Press, 1931), is a careful, detailed study both of Rumanian domestic developments and international diplomacy during this crucial decade; W. G. East, *The Union of Moldavia and Wallachia, 1859* (Cambridge: University Press, 1929), is a briefer account of an even shorter period. From the enormous literature on the crisis of 1875–1878 we may single out the treatment in William L. Langer, *European Alliances and Alignments 1870–1890,* second edition (New York: Knopf, 1950); B. H. Sumner, *Russia and the Balkans 1870–1880* (Oxford: Clarendon Press, 1937); and M. D. Stojanović, *The Great Powers and the Balkans, 1875–1878* (Cambridge: University Press, 1939). On Macedonia, almost all the ostensibly scholarly literature is actually biased. Only slightly pro-Bulgarian is H. N. Brailsford, *Macedonia* (London: Methuen, 1906); H. R. Wilkinson, *Maps and Politics* (Liverpool: University Press, 1951), is the work of a professional geographer. On the Albanian awakening see the three interesting recent articles of Stavro Skendi, "Beginnings of Albanian Nationalist and Autonomous Trends: The Albanian League, 1878–1881," *American Slavic and East European Review,* XII (1953), pp. 219–252; "Beginnings of Albanian Nationalist Trends in Culture and Education (1878–1912)," *Journal of Central European Affairs,* XII, 4 (January 1953), pp. 356–367; and "Albanian Political Thought and Revolutionary Activity, 1881–1912," *Südost-Forschungen,* XII (1954), pp. 1–40. Useful works on the early years of the century include W. S. Vucinich, *Serbia Between East and West, the Events of 1903–1908* (Stanford and London: Stanford University Press and Oxford University Press, 1954), Stanford University Publications, University Series, History, Economics and Political Science, IX; M. E. Durham, *The Struggle for Scutari* (London: E. Arnold, 1914), and *Twenty Years of Balkan Tangle* (London: Allen and Unwin, 1920); Colonel Léon Lamouche, *Quinze ans d'histoire balcanique 1904–1918* (Paris: Payot, 1928), by the French delegate for the reorganization of the Macedonian gendarmerie; B. E. Schmitt, *The Annexation of Bosnia 1908–1909* (Cambridge: University Press, 1937).

On the Habsburg lands, convenient accounts in English are to be found in A. J. May, *The Hapsburg Monarchy, 1867–1914* (Cambridge: Harvard University Press, 1951), and R. A. Kann, *The Multinational Empire,* 2 vols. (New York: Columbia University Press, 1950). Professor Sidney B. Fay's work, *Origins of the World War,* 2nd ed. (New York: Macmillan, 1936), is the classic in its field. Aside from the standard general works on the First World War and the Peace Conference, the following may be noted as particularly useful or original: J. C. Adams, *Flight in Winter* (Princeton: Princeton University Press, 1942), dealing with the Serbian campaigns in 1914–15 and the heroic retreat to Corfu; Milosh Boghitchevitch, *Le Procès de Salonique* (Paris: A. Delpeuch, 1927), on the still mysterious trial which dissolved the Black Hand; and G. P. Genov, *Bulgaria and the Treaty of Neuilly* (Sofia: H. G. Danov, 1935), which gives the Bulgarian point of view.

On the period between the wars, the best single general work is Hugh Seton-Watson, *Eastern Europe Between the Wars* (Cambridge: University Press, 1945), which deals not only with the Balkan countries but also with the other lands of eastern Europe. Albania, however, is omitted. The work reflects wartime hopes, widely shared, that the Soviet Union would prove coöperative in the future: hopes since disappointed, as the author recognizes in his later books. P. B. Stoyan [Stoyan Pribichevich], *World Without End* (New York: Reynal and Hitchcock, 1939), is well-written and well-informed. David Mitrany, *The Land and the Peasant in Rumania. The War and Agrarian Reform 1917–1921* (London: H. Milford, 1930), is a classic written against a carefully prepared presentation of the historical background. It is continued and supplemented by H. L. Roberts, *Rumania: Political Problems of an Agrarian State* (New Haven: Yale University Press, 1951), a masterly study both of politics and economics, covering the period through the Second World War and the postwar years down to 1948. Henri Prost, *Destin de la Roumanie* (Paris: Editions Berger-Levrault, 1954), is much more conventional, but comes down to 1954. No comparable books exist on any of the other Balkan countries. On Yugoslavia, C. A. Beard and G. Radin, *The Balkan Pivot: Yugoslavia* (New York: Macmillan, 1929), is a useful constitutional study for the period before Alexander's dictatorship. Stephen Graham, *Alexander of Yugoslavia* (New Haven: Yale University Press, 1939), is a somewhat romanticized biography of the king. Gilbert In der Maur, *Die Jugoslawen einst und jetzt,* vol. III (Berlin: Verlag für Wirtschaft und Kultur, 1938), is the fullest account in a western language of the domestic developments, written with a strong German bias. J. Swire, *Bulgarian Conspiracy* (London: R. Hale, 1939), gives a full account of IMRO personalities and policies; Kosta Todorov, *Balkan Firebrand* (Chicago: Ziff-Davis, 1943), is the autobiography of a left-wing ("Pladne") Agrarian, giving a somewhat romanticized view of Bulgarian politics. N. P. Nikolaev (ed.), *La destinée tragique d'un roi* (Uppsala: Almqvist & Wiksells, 1952), is a collection of essays on Boris III by some wholehearted admirers. For Albania, one must consult the work of Swire, already cited, which covers the ground in great detail down to 1928; Swire's other book, *King Zog's Albania*

(New York: Liveright, 1937), is a more journalistic traveler's account. Vandeleur Robinson, *Albania's Road to Freedom* (London: George Allen and Unwin, 1941), is somewhat flippant and topical. The mimeographed summary by Stavro Skendi, *The Political Evolution of Albania, 1912–1944* (New York: Mid-European Studies Center, Mimeographed Series No. 19, March 8, 1954), is useful.

David Mitrany, *Marx Against the Peasant* (Chapel Hill: University of North Carolina Press, 1951), is an interesting essay on the conflict between Marxism and populism. G. M. Dimitrov (the Agrarian leader, *not* the Communist), "Agrarianism," *European Ideologies,* ed. Feliks Gross (New York: Philosophical Library, 1948), pp. 396–451, presents an authoritative summary of populist doctrine as modified in the twentieth century. One of the few statements by Balkan Communists available in a western language is L. Patraşcanu, *Sous trois dictatures* (Paris: Editions Jean Vitiano, 1946), a Marxist analysis of the 1930's and the first two years of the war, the three dictatorships being those of King Carol, the Iron Guard, and Marshal Antonescu.

Of the various territorial questions, a good many have never received dispassionate treatment, and such works as exist, even in western languages, are often propaganda for one side or the other in the controversy. It is instructive, for example, to examine the volume issued in French by the Academie Roumaine, *La Transylvanie* (Bucharest, 1938), and that issued in German by the Hungarian Historical Society, *Siebenbürgen* (Budapest, 1940). Elisabeth Barker, *Macedonia, Its Place in Balkan Power Politics* (London and New York: Royal Institute of International Affairs, 1950), has a good chapter of fifty-seven pages on the period between the wars. E. P. Stickney, *Southern Albania or Northern Epirus in European International Affairs, 1912–1923* (Stanford University Press, 1926), is a standard monograph on the subject. Perhaps the best single work on Istria is that of A. L. Moodie, *The Italo-Yugoslav Boundary* (London: G. Philip & Son; Liverpool: Philip, son and nephew, 1945), by a professional geographer. R. J. Kerner and H. N. Howard, *The Balkan Conferences and the Balkan Entente, 1930–1935* (Berkeley: University of California Press, 1936), provides a workmanlike discussion of the subject.

On the general problems of the pre-1939 Balkan economy, Doreen Warriner, *The Economics of Peasant Farming,* provides a useful introduction. General works on the interwar period include three prepared by the Royal Institute of International Affairs: *The Balkan States I. Economic* (Oxford University Press, 1936); *South-Eastern Europe, a Political and Economic Survey* (*ibid.,* 1939); and *South-Eastern Europe, a Brief Survey,* Information Department Papers, No. 26 (*ibid.,* 1940). Highly qualified experts contributed to the PEP study (Political and Economic Planning), *Economic Development in S. E. Europe* (London, 1945), but the work looked toward a future which never came. Wilbert E. Moore, *Economic Demography of Eastern and Southern Europe* (Geneva: Economic, Financial, and Transit Department, League of Nations, 1945), spells out the problem of overpopulation. On various aspects of the Yugoslav economy, the mimeographed series edited by Nicholas Mirkovich, entitled *Jugoslav Post-War Reconstruction Papers* and published during the war by the Office of Reconstruction and Economic Affairs of the Government of Jugoslavia, 812 Fifth Avenue, New York, is extraordinarily useful. On Albania, the Italian occupiers produced a number of studies, of which Ferdinando Milone, *L'Albania Economica* (Padua: Cedam, 1941), deserves mention.

All the prewar Balkan governments issued their own statistical publications, which often translate essential rubrics into French.

On the opening of the Second World War in the Balkans, the book of former Rumanian Foreign Minister, Grigore Gafencu, *Prelude to the Russian Campaign* (London: F. Miller, 1951), is illuminating. Leigh White, *The Long Balkan Night* (New York: Scribner, 1944), is the best of the reporter's accounts, covering the early period of the war. Andreas Hillgruber, *Hitler, König Karol, und Marschall Antonescu, die Deutsch-Rumänischen Beziehungen 1938–1944* (Wiesbaden: Franz Steiner Verlag GMBH, 1954), Veröffentlichungen des Instituts für europäische Geschichte, Mainz, Band 5, is a detailed, careful study drawn from the German documents and from interviews with leading German participants. On the Yugoslav resistance, Stephen Clissold, *Whirlwind* (London: Cresset Press, 1949), supplements MacLean; while Jasper Rootham, *Miss-fire* (London: Chatts and Windus, 1946), presents the story of a British officer with a Chetnik band. Strongly pro-Mihailovich are David Martin, *Ally Betrayed* (New York: Prentice-Hall, 1946); R. H. Markham, *Tito's Imperial Communism* (Chapel Hill: University of North Carolina Press, 1947); and Constantine Fotich, *The War We Lost* (New York: Viking, 1948).

On the postwar years, Andrew Gyorgy, *Governments of Danubian Europe* (New York: Rinehart, 1949), deals with the first postwar constitutional changes. Ygael Gluckstein, *Stalin's Satellites in Europe* (London: Allen and Unwin, 1952); François Fejtö, *Histoire des démocraties populaires* (Paris: Editions du Seuil, 1952); and Hugh Seton-Watson, *The East European Revolution* (New York: Praeger, 1951), are useful condensed accounts including treatments of the satellites outside the Balkans as well as of the Balkan states. R. R. Betts, ed., *Central and Southeast Europe 1945–1948* (London and New York: Royal Institute of International Affairs, 1950), contains somewhat uneven chapters on the Balkan countries except Albania. R. H. Markham, *Rumania under the Soviet Yoke* (Boston: Meader, 1949), provides valuable eyewitness testimony to Communist political behavior. Jack Lindsay and Maurice Cornforth, *Rumanian Summer* (London: Lawrence & Wishart, 1953), is pure propaganda for the Communist regime. Doreen Warriner, *Revolution in Eastern Europe* (London: Turnstile Press, 1950), is an effort at an economic study, interesting chiefly as an example of the degree to which a formerly sound economist could be won to an uncritical acceptance of the Stalin line. In addition to the Mihailovich, Rajk, and Kostov trials, that of Petkov is also available in English: *The Trial of Nikola D. Petkov* (Sofia, 1947). On the Tito-Stalin break, see further the interesting essay of Harry Hodgkinson, *West and East of Tito* (London: Gollancz, 1952).

For the most recent period, one must turn chiefly to newspapers and magazines. The National Committee for a Free Europe, Inc., 110 West 57th Street, New York 19, has produced a number of highly useful special studies in the mimeographed series published by its Mid-European Studies Center. In addition to current reports published monthly in Rumanian, Bulgarian, Serbian, Croatian, and Slovenian, it has also published monthly since 1952 the excellent English-language periodical, *News from Behind the Iron Curtain.* The Countess of Listowell and her collaborators have published in London since 1944 a weekly paper called successively *East Europe* (1944–1949), *East Europe and the Soviet Union* (1950–1953), and *Soviet Orbit* (since 1954), including summaries of developments in all the satellites. Unfortunately, these summaries since 1954 have been condensed so greatly as to diminish their value. The *Wissenschaftlicher Dienst Südosteuropa* (12 numbers a year), published by the Südost-Institut in Munich, contains solid information on all aspects of life in the Balkan countries, and is particularly useful for those wishing to keep up with demographic and economic change. Since 1950, the Rumanian National Committee in the United States has been publishing monthly its *Information Bulletin. The World Today, The Journal of Central European Affairs, The American Slavic and East European Review,* and *Osteuropa* all carry occasional important contributions. Other interesting recent articles include T. T. Hammond, *Yugoslavia Between East and West,* Headline Series, Foreign Policy Association, 108 (November-December, 1954), and "The Djilas Affair, and Yugoslav Communism," *Foreign Affairs,* January 1955; and Illyricus, "Tito's Brand of Communism," *South Atlantic Quarterly,* 54:177–184 (April 1955). In addition, the governments of Yugoslavia, Bulgaria, and Rumania themselves issue periodicals in western languages, which must of course be read with due allowance for the fact that they are intended as propaganda. The *Yugoslav Review,* published monthly by the Yugoslav Information Center, 816 Fifth Avenue, New York 21, often contains translations of decrees and official pronouncements. *Free Bulgaria,* now *Bulgaria Today,* published biweekly in Sofia, is far less skillfully edited, but reprints an occasional important official pronouncement in full. The Rumanian regime publishes no comparable journal in English; *La Roumanie Nouvelle* and *Rumänien Heute* are of little interest. The *Bulletin* of the International Peasant Union has in the past published valuable commentaries on current developments by native Balkan opponents of the Communists now in exile in this country.

While this work was in the press, there appeared the following additional books, which will prove highly useful to scholars: *Dix années d'historiographie Yougoslave, 1945–1955* (Beograd: Comité National Yougoslave des sciences historiques, 1955), a volume of bibliographical essays on the Yugoslav contributions to their own history, by period, in the ten years since the war; M. Hasluck, *The Unwritten Law in Albania* (Cambridge: University Press, 1954), whose publishers well describe it as "A record of the customary law of the Albanian tribes, a description of family and village life in the Albanian mountains, and an account of the waging of blood-feuds."

INDEX